AN ENGINEERING APPROACH
TO DIGITAL DESIGN

*"Sound digital systems like great
works of art don't happen by chance.
They are the result of the conscientious
articulation of discipline,
sound principles and imagination."*

AN ENGINEERING APPROACH

TO DIGITAL DESIGN

WILLIAM I. FLETCHER
Utah State University
Logan, Utah

PRENTICE-HALL, INC., *Englewood Cliffs, New Jersey 07632*

Library of Congress Cataloging in Publication Data

FLETCHER, WILLIAM I
    An engineering approach to digital design.

    Includes bibliographies and index.
    1.–Digital electronics. 2.–Logic design.
3.–Machine theory. I.–Title.
TK7868.D5F5   621.3815   78-27177
ISBN 0-13-277699-5

Printed in the United States of America
10 9 8

Editorial/production supervision
   and interior design by *Virginia Huebner*
Page layout by *Gail Cocker*
Cover design by *Edsal Enterprises*
Manufacturing buyer: *Gordon Osbourne*

PRENTICE-HALL INTERNATIONAL, INC., *London*
PRENTICE-HALL OF AUSTRALIA PTY. LIMITED, *Sydney*
PRENTICE-HALL OF CANADA, LTD., *Toronto*
PRENTICE-HALL OF INDIA PRIVATE LIMITED, *New Delhi*
PRENTICE-HALL OF JAPAN, INC., *Tokyo*
PRENTICE-HALL OF SOUTHEAST ASIA PTE. LTD., *Singapore*
WHITEHALL BOOKS LIMITED, *Wellington, New Zealand*

To my students

CONTENTS

PREFACE

DIGITAL DESIGN: PAST, PRESENT AND FUTURE

Since Claude Shannon systematized and adapted George Boole's theoretical work in 1938, there has been unprecedented growth in the application of digital concepts. Other fields that emerged in the late 1930's and early 40's have "peaked" and leveled or declined, while the application of digital concepts is still growing exponentially. Each day digital concepts are being applied to problems that could only be solved by analog methods several years ago. Fast, reliable and modestly priced Analog to Digital and Digital to Analog converters are presently available, facilitating the application of digital concepts for solving complex analog problems using the "microprocessor" and other programmable digital systems. In short, the rapid expansion of discrete practices has served notice to the academic community to restructure curricula to treat discrete mathematics and other discrete sciences. Certainly the "microprocessor" revolution has penetrated all fields of endeavor and will continue to do so for many years.

As a result of the microprocessor revolution it is conjectured that the microprocessor will supplant the presently known logic design efforts with "programmed logic concepts." However, it is felt that this is simply not so. Certainly, microprocessor applications have changed requirements, and consequently, the direction of logic design, but in few ways will they ever replace it. In short, microprocessors and other system level LSI devices have accentuated the "interface design" facet of logic design. In fact, in view of these and other expected advancements, we are forecasting that logic design is largely "interface design," and the logic designer of today and tomorrow should be prepared to *interface anything to anything*. To accommodate this, the approach to logic design certainly must be updated, and developed in such a way that a common thread of direction carries the student uninterruptedly from a fundamental beginning through interface design to programmable sequential machines and on into microprocessors. This markedly diminishes the stark contrast between AND gates and counters today and microprocessors tomorrow. In particular, it is believed that fundamentals should be developed with a strong emphasis on documentation methods and device familiarization, and then these fundamentals should be applied with an interface philosophy to system controllers, small programmable sequential machines centered around bit-slice processors, and the application of microprocessors as a general digital design component. Documentation, one of the major efforts of contemporary logic design, will be stressed throughout this text.

ABOUT THIS BOOK

If you are familiar with other material related to digital design or if you are just beginning your studies of digital design you deserve to know that the presentation of material in this text differs considerably from that of other texts treating the same subject. This is not to say that the material presented here is totally revolutionary but that it is presented in a different way and with different emphasis. For example, the concept of MIXED LOGIC is stressed to make your designs more conceptual and understandable.

This mixed logic idea is the one major break from tradition and will require those familiar with logic design, as well as the new starters, to develop some structural approach to device interconnection. Thus you are asked to "try it" and "apply it" because it is firmly believed you will "like it."

Since the industry is rapidly converting to a mixed-logic symbology, one must be familiar with mixed-logic symbolism to be able to read manufacturers' device data books and modern schematic diagrams.

Another major break is the treatment of multi-input sequential machines and their application for system controllers. Here a method is developed around the "divide-and-conquer" philosophy; that is, a system design is partitioned into conceptual subfunctions and fitted and linked (interfaced) together such that a centered master controller orchestrates the operation of these subsystems, and this becomes the hardware equivalent of the operating system software for a computer system.

1-2-1 PHILOSOPHY

The material presented here is based on the consideration that the present digital device technology is progressing at such a rate that design methods become quickly outmoded. Therefore, design methods must be developed which are (1) based on theory, (2) easily learned, and (3) provide design realizations which are straightforward, reliable, and debuggable in the shortest possible time. Hence the ENGINEERING APPROACH to digital design is aimed at developing first a conceptual understanding through selected theoretical treatment with conceptual examples, and then developing time efficient design methods which lend themselves to the realization of hardware which is well-documented, straightforward, reliable and debuggable.

Further, it is intended that more time be spent in the *definition* and *design phases* of digital system development. In short, if the "conception to completion time" is scaled from 1 to 10 then 1 to 5 or 6 should be dedicated to definition and design. It has been proven many times over that well thought out designs work better, "come up" easier and last longer than those developed with the "design-as-you-go" methods. Designers frequently feel pressure during the design phase because hardware is not being put together; however, bending to this pressure almost certainly spells disaster during debug time. As a case in point, the author once worked with a group on a large system that required $3\frac{1}{2}$ times more engineering time to debug than it did to design, and after it was debugged the complete design was scrapped and started over, costing five times more than it would have cost to do it right the first time. Therefore it is strongly recommended that you think out your designs from start to finish and leave nothing to the chance that it "might work."

1-2-2 CONTENT

First it should be understood that digital design is broken into two major categories:

(1) Combinational
(2) Sequential

Each is broken down into specific areas in a definite manner for specific purposes. However, volumes of material are presently available treating each of these categories, thus it is next to impossible to treat each facet in depth between the covers of a single text. Therefore, only those subject areas commensurate with the criteria set forth by the philosophy stated above are covered in this book, and much of the material related to long and detailed design processes, and those areas dealing with very specific subject matter have been omitted. However, the last four chapters discuss "large-scale" sequential machines in depth because of the related importance of the material.

The following statements summarize what this text *is* and *is not*.

1. This text *is not* a laboratory manual although it does utilize specific examples centered around devices presently used.
2. This text *is not* a "cook book" of digital circuits for special applications. There are some suggested applications but, in general, the author has tried to develop a general design methodology that fits a wide range of varied and diverse applications.

3. This book *is not* strictly devoted to digital computer design although the developments contained would certainly support a course in computer architecture. The author feels that the field of logic design is much too wide to be considered as strictly "computer design."

4. This book *is* a book about interface design. The author feels that logic design as presently practiced is largely *interface design. Interfacing is the connecting of two or more separate and distinct entities in such a manner that predictable and desired behavior is achieved.* For this reason, special efforts are taken in Chapter 2 to develop special names (*mnemonics*) for logic lines and a mixed logic symbology such that even the smallest designs are treated as a "system-type" design. Then, when larger designs are undertaken the documentation will be natural.

5. This book treats digital design as special *language* and therefore a good deal of structure is used in the approaches to the development of design methodology. History points to the fact that most bad habits evolve from the lack of discipline.

6. Recognizing that digital design has matured and times have changed and the emphasis is now much different than it was even five years ago, this book was written to attempt to bridge the gap between the traditional approach to logic design and present technology.

7. This book *is not* strictly about microprocessors and their applications; however, the bit-slice machines are covered. This book provides the control concepts required to underpin a study covering programmable digital machines.

CHAPTER SUMMARY

In Chapter 1 we develop some basic understanding of "systems" in general and digital systems in specific. The concept of a digital language is developed. Contrasts are drawn between the real world and the discrete world of digital applications. A brief introduction to inter-domain converters is given including Analog to Digital and Digital to Analog converters. Number systems are treated briefly in the light of Interdomain conversion. This information is then extended to an introduction to "codes."

Chapter 2 is the "cornerstone" chapter of this text. In Chapter 2 we develop the fundamentals of combinational design and analysis. The concept of "MIXED LOGIC" is developed using "hardware" transfer function analysis. Most importantly *documentation* ideas are introduced and then stressed.

In Chapter 3 we introduce the concept of using various methods of *reducing* Boolean expressions. The Karnaugh map is developed and then extended into what is called a VARIABLE-ENTERED-MAP. Further, we tie the complete combinational design process together with the concepts treated in Chapter 2. Finally an inserted computer-aided reduction approach is introduced, culminating in a computer program to be used for large reduction requirements.

Chapter 4 treats the solution of traditional combinational design problems by the application of standard MSI and LSI devices. Further, a good deal of practical information related to the actual use of integrated circuits is given. Important items such as "loading" and propagation delay are discussed.

Chapter 5 introduces the concept of a *sequential* machine. The true nature of the sequential machine is reinforced by studying it from a control system point of view. The concept of a machine STATE is introduced. The concept of "MEMORY" is treated and then extended to a cellular idea, and then progresses to Flip-Flop analysis, design and conversion. Further, practical information is presented relative to the actual use of integrated circuit Flip-Flops. Timing constraints are discussed including SET-UP and HOLD time requirements.

In Chapter 6 the practical application of traditional sequential machine analysis and design are demonstrated. The concepts related to state diagram design methods are covered and the other eleven steps to design are treated. The concept of a "counter" is introduced and various special purpose counters as well as integrated circuit counters are treated. The "Register" and register design are introduced along with various applications for registers including ring counters, data storage, SAMS, FIFO and RAMS.

Chapter 7 is the other "cornerstone" chapter of this text. In this chapter the contemporary approach to multi-input state machines is introduced. Flow Diagrams and MDS diagrams are used for sequential definition. Along with this a structured philosophy is developed centered around a "system controller" concept. Much practical information is presented and related through some "real life" examples.

In Chapter 8 the methods of utilizing combinational MSI and LSI devices for state machine design are treated. Decoders, multiplexers, ROM's, PROM's and FPLA's are applied to sequential multi-input state machines.

Chapter 9 introduces the concept of a *programmable multi-input system controller*. The concepts developed in this chapter are based on the use of MSI and LSI *sequential devices* for designing sequence controllers. Micro-programmed as well as "fixed" instruction set controllers are treated.

Chapter 10 introduces both the traditional and contemporary approach to the analysis and design of *asynchronous circuits*. Flow chart methods are outlined that allow for multi-input asynchronous machines to be developed and, at the same time, avoid the tabular drudgery normally associated with asynchronous design.

At the end of each chapter a summary and exercise set aids your assimilation of the material presented.

ACKNOWLEDGMENTS

To all who have contributed in any way to this book, I offer my thanks. To all my past students who have suffered through rough drafts and revision after revision, but still call from time to time asking, "Is it finished?"—a special thanks. To Paul Hansen and Richard Ohran from Brigham Young University; Glen Langdon from I.B.M.; Ken Morley, Mark Manwaring and Mike Chiodo; my friends from China Lake; my department heads Kay Baker and Ron Thurgood, who have all suffered with me and for me, offering reviews and technical support,—a most hardy thanks.

To a precious few, Debb Harris who sorted through, trying to bring order to, some sixty pounds of handwritten notes; to Anne Ferguson and Charlotte Middlebrooks who have read and edited the final manuscript, to my personal secretary and technician, Kathy Zollinger, who has stuck it out from start to finish, doing everything from technical illustrations to marketing,—what can I say but, "Thanks, I needed that."

Logan, Utah   William I. Fletcher

CHAPTER 1

INTRODUCTORY DIGITAL
DESIGN CONCEPTS

1-1 INTRODUCTION

Digital design underpins the creation of the myriad of imaginative digital devices that surround us. Such devices as digital computers, hand-held calculators, digital watches, microprocessors, microwave oven controllers, digital voltmeters, and the host of others too numerous to mention are all products of digital design efforts. The very basic digital design can be defined as the science of organizing arrays of simple switches into what is called a *discrete* system that performs transformations on two-level (binary) information in a meaningful and predictable way. Certainly this is true, but digital design as we know it today is much more exciting than this definition portends. Digital design has matured since 1938 when Claude Shannon systemized the earlier theoretical work of George Boole (1854). Since then, design methods and devices have been developed, tried, and proven, leading the way into one of the most fascinating and challenging fields of study. The author notes that seldom will you find a field of study as vast as that of digital design and its related applications, yet seldom will you find a field in which you can become more productive in as short a period of time.

In short, with a limited background in the other basic sciences and a desire to create, you can start designing digital circuits in a limited period of time. However, you are warned at this time and will be warned continually throughout this text that the "ease" with which you can get started in digital design can also be your "undoing" as a designer of sound, reliable, and maintainable hardware. Thus you are asked to strive to grasp both the *concepts* and the *structure* of the design methodologies set forth, for today it is not enough to design a system that is finally "functional," but it must function reliably, and more importantly it must be "definable" (documented) such that others can maintain it should it ever fail.

Digital design is contrasting yet complementary to yet another developmental science we call ANALOG DESIGN, which over the years has produced systems such as radio, linear control systems, analog computers, stereo, and all sorts of other conveniences that we classify as ANALOG or CONTINUOUS systems. However, it is interesting to note that it is becoming increasingly difficult to delineate the two technologies because of the inevitable integration of the two. For example, you can now purchase a DIGITAL STEREO POWER AMPLIFIER capable of delivering some 250 watts per channel. Until recently linear amplifier design has been one of the strongest bastions of the analog world, but now we have this component that incorporates the advantages of the two technologies, resulting in a superior product. This same sort of mix is witnessed each day in all areas of measurement instrument design where we see digital voltmeters, digital oscilloscopes, switching power supplies, and other useful gear.

The next few sections are intended to familiarize you with some of the basics of both sciences so that you can better appreciate the applications of both and how they relate to each other. The rest of the text is devoted to helping you develop an in-depth understanding of digital design and helping you discover that digital design is truly one of the most useful and productive developmental sciences ever conceived and one whose application appears to be unbounded.

With this in mind, we proceed using a rather poignant statement made by Rudyard Kipling as a guide to the rest of our studies:

> I had six honest serving men
>   who taught me all they knew.
> Their names were WHERE, and WHAT, and WHEN
>   and WHY and HOW and WHO.

1-2   WHY AND WHEN DIGITAL?

Before we start our studies of digital design, we must develop some common understanding as to what digital systems are, what sort of signals digital systems function on, and some of the language concepts and ideas related to this field. We do this by classifying and defining what a SYSTEM is considered to be.

As has been mentioned earlier, we classify systems in one of two ways: (1) analog or continuous, and (2) digital or discrete. *A system can be defined mathematically as a unique transformation or operator that maps or transforms a given input condition into a specific output.* A simple analog system that provides an example of a mapping operator is the resistive voltage divider shown in Figure 1-1.

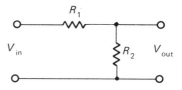

Fig. 1-1. An example analog system.

Here we see that the operation of transforming or mapping the input (V_{in}) to the output (V_{out}) is a function of time-invariant resistance values and is expressed mathematically as

$$V_{\text{out}} = f(V_{\text{in}})$$

or

$$V_{\text{out}} = V_{\text{in}} \frac{R_2}{R_1 + R_2}$$

Discrete data systems also exhibit a transforming property, but they operate on sequences of quantized data rather than continuous input signal. A simple example of a special digital system is shown in Figure 1-2. Here we see what is referred to as a *binary-coded-decimal 7 segment decoder driver.* The transforming property of this system is one of converting a four-wire digital input (d, c, b, a) into a humanly recognizable numeric display. Actually this system could be considered to be an

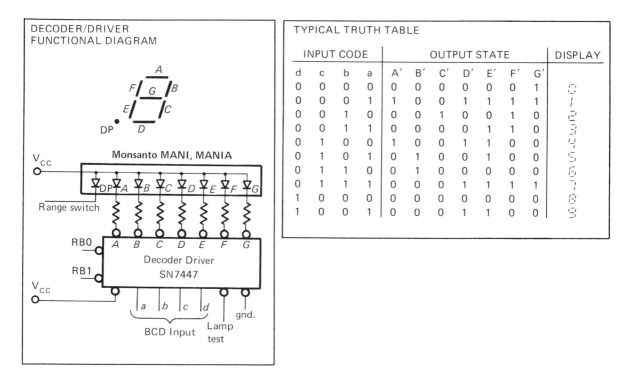

Fig. 1-2. An example of a digital *system.* (Courtesy of Monsanto)

interdomain converter of sorts, but it does exemplify the system-oriented transformation feature defined by the INPUT/OUTPUT table shown. In this table each of the seven outputs are defined uniquely as

$$A' = f_a(d,b,c,a)$$
$$B' = f_b(d,b,c,a)$$
$$\vdots$$
$$G' = f_g(d,b,c,a)$$

with each f defining a different transformation operator on the inputs. The transformation operator is often denoted as

$$y(\text{output}) = T[x(\text{input})]$$

and is usually depicted as

$$x \rightarrow \boxed{T[\ \ ]} \rightarrow y$$

Classes of systems are defined by placing certain constraints on the operator $T[\ ]$. Some of these are:

    (1) linear vs. nonlinear;
    (2) stable vs. unstable;
    (3) time or shift-invariant vs. time or shift-variant;
    (4) causal vs. noncausal.

The class of linear systems is defined by the principle of superposition. If y_1 and y_2 are the responses of the system to inputs x_1 and x_2 individually, then the system is linear if and only if

$$T[ax_1 + bx_2] = aT[x_1] + bT[x_2] = ay_1 + by_2$$

for any arbitrary constants a and b. This might seem to be a little full-blown, and so we can also more simply describe a linear system as one in which the output can *always* be determined by multiplying the input by a nonvarying constant as shown in Figure 1-3(a).

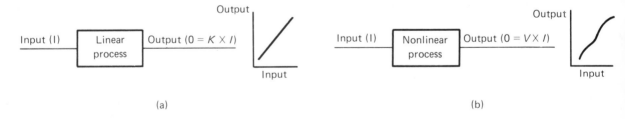

(a)   (b)

Fig. 1-3. (a) A linear system, where K is a nonvarying constant. (b) A nonlinear system, where V is a multi-function variable.

The variable V is considered to be a constant under isolated and static conditions; however, at any point in time, it can be a function of such things as:

(1) The magnitude of I (overdrive or underdrive);
(2) the temperature of the processing system;
(3) deformation of the physical properties of the devices used to develop the process.

It is important to note that we can have both linear or nonlinear continuous or discrete systems and at times it may be difficult to differentiate between the two. A simple example is a room light that is controlled by a switch or a rheostat. The function of the light in the first instance, involving the switch, is an example of a discrete or quantized entity: either the light is burning (the switch is on) or the light is not burning (the switch is off). In the second case, the light still has the two properties of being ON or OFF, but now has the extra dimension of degree—just *how much* is the light ON or OFF. And, in fact, for all practical purposes, this variability is a continuous phenomenon and we can say that the light can be on to any particular degree we choose, from all the way OFF to all the way ON or anything in between, as determined by the continuously variable rheostat. This is a particularly interesting example, for if you study light theory more closely, you will find light to be a discrete phenomenon: one of discrete packets of energy called "photons" delivered from some emanating source. Coupling this discrete nature of light with the continuous nature of a rheostat, which is undoubtedly operated by some extremely nonlinear human, one has an excellent example of a nonlinear-discrete process, which appears to be a nonlinear-continuous process. Therefore, let us define continuous and discrete processes and then further examine some of the difficulties one has in differentiating between the two.

Continuous is defined in many sophisticated ways for a wide variety of reasons and purposes. However, for the purposes here, let us assume that *continuous signals or events are processes which change from one condition to yet another condition in such a manner that no detector can perceive any disjoint or quantized behavior brought about by this change.* For example, the temperature of the air around us changes from time to time, and at times it changes quite rapidly and in a nonlinear fashion, but never does it change so rapidly that some specialized electronic thermometer cannot track its change.

Discrete signals or processes are defined as those processes that change from one condition to yet another condition in a perceived disjoint or quantized manner. Two explanations could be that:

(1) there exists no detector that can trace the quantum transitions in a continuous fashion or, maybe,
(2) it is best described to be discontinuous for specific reasons.

What is implied here is that there are processes that are continuous in every sense of the word; however, their changes are dominated by rapid transitions from one condition to the next. Thus, it makes more sense to define it as a discrete process. For example, consider the three signal waveforms shown in Figure 1-4. In Figure 1-4(a), we have what we call a sinusoidal waveform that is nicely defined by the continuous mathematical expression

$$V(t) = A \sin 2\pi ft$$

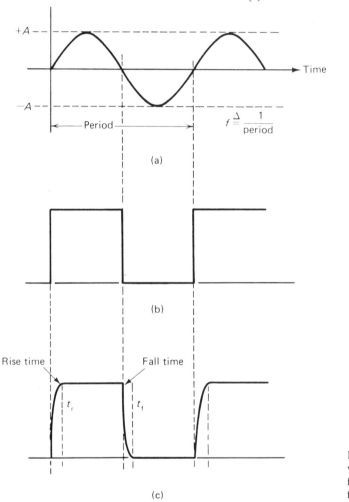

(a)

(b)

Rise time

Fall time

t_r

t_f

(c)

Fig. 1-4. Examples of (a) sinusoidal waveform. (b) An ideal square wave-form. (c) A nonideal square wave-form.

while in Figure 1-4(b) we have an ideal discrete signal, called a square wave signal, that is defined by an infinite series of sinusoidal expressions called a Fourier (four-yā) series. This ideal square wave is characterized by its square corners and infinitely short rise and fall times, and thus is classified distinctly as discrete. On the other hand, in Figure 1-4(c) we have the nonideal square wave, one that is much more closely related to the signals encountered in digital systems, and one in which its degree of ideality is determined by two figures of merit: the rise time (t_r)

and the fall time (t_f). Though certainly continuous, it is more often classified as a discrete signal. This is because its changes from one condition (high voltage state) to the other (low voltage state) are dominated by a series of rapid transitions. Thus, it is supposed that some reasonable criteria could be developed for classifying processes and signals as continuous or discrete by determining the time it takes to move from one condition in relation to the time spent in the new condition before the next condition must be moved to. However, we could go on philosophically trying to differentiate the two classes indefinitely and never come up with a general finite rule. This is particularly true when the ever-present NOISE is brought into the picture. Noise exists in different forms everywhere and finds its way into every process. Noise is a process that generally injects unwanted and undesirable responses in any process, be it continuous or discrete. For example, looking with microscopic accuracy at the sine wave which has heretofore been described as continuous, or the quasi-square wave that has been classified as discrete, we see little random "hairy spikes" (sometimes referred to as "grass") all over the waveforms, causing us to wonder if it is continuous or discrete, or what! We could go on bringing into play all sorts of interesting facets until your head hurts and end up with the results that almost any process can be classified as a mixture of:

(1) nonlinear
(2) linear
(3) continuous   } processes
(4) discrete

Thus we classify our first-order models based on the degree of dominance of these components.

As a reader, you are probably wondering, "what is this all about?" It is all about informing you that very few things come in nicely tied, well-defined packages. Thus it is up to the engineer to evaluate the conditions and make assignments and classifications to processes and to synthesize models and solution processes that will best suit solving a given problem. There are continuous methods for solving problems and there are discrete methods also. This is borne out by the fact that there are *differential* equations and there are *difference* equations in the field of mathematics. Differential equations deal with continuous processes and difference equations deal with discrete processes. Both are important because they both relate to solving problems, but in different ways. Because of this we have the digital vs. analog approaches to solving problems. Both have advantages; both have disadvantages. What the engineer must do is study the problem and make a decision whether to go

(1) continuous (analog),
(2) discrete (digital), or
(3) a mixture of both.

Obviously, it is safe to say that a mixture of both is the answer. The question is how much of each? This question can be answered using a knowledge of both approaches, and making value judgments as to whether one approach has advantages over the other for a given situation.

Now back to the original question: "Why digital?" There are several advantages that digital (two-valued discrete) systems have over the analog (continuous) systems. Some commonly named are:

(1) less sensitivity to device parameter changes;
(2) predetermined accuracy;
(3) better dynamic range;
(4) more applicable to nonlinear control;
(5) more predictable and less susceptible to variations of environment;
(6) more reliable;
(7) exact replicability (each system is *exactly* the same as the original);
(8) potential flexibility in terms of time-multiplexing significant portions of a given system.

Both digital and analog approaches have pitfalls. However, the pitfalls of digital are at times easier to identify and resolve than the associated pitfalls in the analog world. This advantage, as well as those mentioned above, answer much of the question, "why digital?" The rest of this text is devoted to the fifth of Kipling's honest men—HOW digital.

1-3 DIGITAL AND ITS SYMBOLOGY

As mentioned earlier, a person starting out in a new field of study is faced with expanding or at least extrapolating his present knowledge to encompass a new language. The language associated with digital design differs little in structure from other languages, for it too has the five basic components of symbolic languages, as shown in Table 1-1.

As we proceed through the study of digital practices, you will see each of the components of the digital language develop into an ordered symbolic language. This special symbolic language is used to maximize information transfer in short periods of time; however, like most symbolic languages it is traceable back to a basic science. For example, consider the symbolic evolution of the NAND gate symbol that is used frequently in digital design, shown in Figure 1-5.

As we study Figure 1-5 we can see that schematic diagrams could be drawn using the symbol set for quantum and semiconductor physics; however, the actual practicality of doing so is obviously remote. For, as mentioned earlier, we use specialized symbolic languages like the one associated with a NAND symbol and its rules pertaining to usage to augment the information transfer. Thus we can conclude that learning digital design is nothing more than learning to create with a new language.

TABLE 1-1

The Spoken and Written Language	The Digital Design Language
(1) Symbols—which are graphical characters and basic communicative representations. For example: $A, B, C, \ldots, Z$; $0, 1, 2, \ldots, 9$; $+, X, -, \div, \ldots, /$ Phonemes which are the communicative symbols for a spoken language	(1) Symbols:
(2) Words—which is the grouping of symbols into definitive sequences. For example: Spelling and enunciation, pronunciation, and the rules pertaining thereto. The rules pertaining to "i before e except after c," etc.	(2) Words:

(3) Semantics—assigning words definitions.
 	
Definitions: assigning words
            meanings or
            conceptualizations
 	
For example:
 	
LION   APPLE
	(3) Semantics—input/output specifications (commonly referred to as truth-table specifications) for the gates. For example:
	
	A B | C
	LV LV | LV
	LV HV | LV
	HV LV | LV
	HV HV | HV
	
	defines an AND function

(4) Grammar—proper word grouping structure and punctuation.	(4) Grammar—interconnection rules. (a) Outputs go to inputs, except under certain defined conditions. (b) Inputs can be tied together if both are to be driven by the same source (c) No output should be required to drive beyond its drive limit. (d) Etc.
(5) Syntax—the variation in word grouping order for the purpose of proper information transfer during communication. For example: "John hit Mary" conveys one message; however, the *same* words arranged differently, "Mary hit John" conveys quite a different message.	(5) Syntax—circuit/network/system synthesis (clearly the same "words" can be so used to convey two quite unique "messages"). For example, the same "gates" interchanged in sequence yield far different results. $\bar{A} + \bar{B} + C$ vs $\bar{A} \cdot \bar{B} + \bar{C}$

Fig. 1-5. An example of the use of a higher order symbology to represent a much more involved process stemming from a basic science.

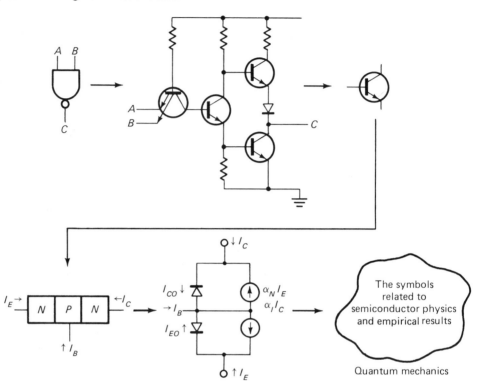

1-4 DIGITAL AND THE REAL WORLD

As mentioned earlier, the use of digital practices can be a viable method for solving design problems in the real world. The reason that design problems are emphasized stems from the fact that the major areas of involvement for electrical and digital engineers are the (1) measurement, (2) control, and (3) transmission of information and energy. Thus if we look at the "what we do," we find that we are continually trying to find solutions to problems related to the measurement, control, and transmission of information or energy in the domain of the real world. However, the real world tends to have a continuous nature. Because of this, the discrete domain needs to be buffered in some way. As a result of this buffering requirement, we should view the digital domain in the perspective shown in Figure 1-6.

However, Figure 1-6 does not completely describe the relation between the two domains because there are several important processes in the real world that are at least modeled as discrete processes. A few of these are: light, nuclear radiation, and the electric signals governing the human nervous system which are, interestingly enough, most definitely discrete phenomena. But for the most part, Figure 1-6 does depict the typical relation between the outside world and the digital domain.

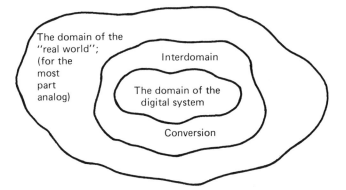

Fig. 1-6. The conceptualization of the digital system and its relation to the real world.

The interdomain converter depicted in Figure 1-6 is a specialized system that converts or translates information of one domain into information of another domain. For example, *you* will serve as a special interdomain converter shortly when you are asked to convert a decimal number to its binary equivalent This operation we define as an ANALOG-TO-DIGITAL CONVERSION.

You will remember that one of the reasons for "why digital" is that digital systems are theoretically more reliable and less subject to drift with time and temperature. This stems directly from the fact that digital systems are made up of arrays of simple and reliable single-pole/single-throw switches that are either open or closed. (These switches can exist as either mechanical, electromechanical or electronic devices, as is discussed later.) Thus we see a simple analog-to-digital conversion can be performed with a switch as shown in Figure 1-7.

Fig. 1-7. A rudimentary analog-to-digital conversion

Since pure digital systems are made up of arrays of simple and reliable switches with only two positions, a numerical system that already existed was adapted to serve as the "tool" needed for utilizing the basic concept. This numerical math system, called the *binary system*, is based on the two symbols "0" and "1" in contrast to the decimal system which has ten symbols: $0, 1, 2, \ldots, 9$. *Remember that we are talking about a numerical system, not to be confused with Boolean algebra, which is a deductive mathematics related to a logic process and not necessarily a numerical value process. This is mentioned to avoid the confusion created by inter-relations between Boolean algebra, computers, and binary arithmetic.*

We should see now that in order to use a digital system, such as a digital computer for mathematical computations, we must first convert our mathematical symbolisms (decimal in this case) into binary symbolisms to allow the computer to perform this mathematical operation. Once this is done, the inverse process must be performed to convert the binary results into a readable decimal representation.

The obvious question: "Is digital worth all of the conversion?" The answer cannot be simply stated in yes/no terms, but must be left to the individual and the particular situation. In certain instances, it may *not* in fact be worth the bother. Such would not be the case if we were able to create and use multiple-valued logic systems to create a "totally decimal machine." Obviously, if there were ten unique descriptors usable for our "decimal computer," there would be no need to convert any information into the now required two-valued binary system. However, practically speaking, binary systems presently dominate and will continue to be the dominant system for some years to come. Since such is the case, and man ultimately must learn how to communicate with his machine, it is necessary that we study the processes involved in number conversion and the different codes used to represent and convey information.

In the next section we cover some of the basics of the special interdomain converters called voltage/current analog-to-digital and digital-to-analog converters, which are used in large quantities in wide areas of application.

1-5 DIGITAL-TO-ANALOG/ANALOG-TO-DIGITAL CONVERTERS

Our discussion up to this point has brought us to the understanding that the *real world* inputs are mainly continuous and nonlinear, and digital systems operate on sequences of discrete information. Further, we have indicated that digital systems, in many cases, have distinct advantages over the more traditional analog systems. Thus it is important that the digital engineer be informed of the basics of inter-domain conversions and methods of transforming continuous signals into sequences of discrete information, which then can be processed, transformed, and reconverted back to a continuous signal if need be. The two conversion processes are commonly referred to as:

(1) analog-to-digital (A/D),
(2) digital-to-analog (D/A).

Consider the system shown in Figure 1-8, which illustrates the general model for a digital system used as a control system in the real world. We see from the figure that the single analog input fans-out into a multi-line definition for the digital system, which is quite simple to understand once the conversion technique is understood. For example, a voltage from the transducer as indicated in Figure 1-8 is sequentially sampled and held by the SAMPLE and HOLD network, then this sampled voltage is converted to digital words and displayed as a sequence of information in a parallel format acceptable to the digital system. Thus we see the A/D process as one of generating a time-spaced sequence of multi-digit information that is linearly related to the assigned value of the analog input. Likewise in a broad sense, the D/A process is one of linearly converting or transforming multi-line digital information to a single analog signal.

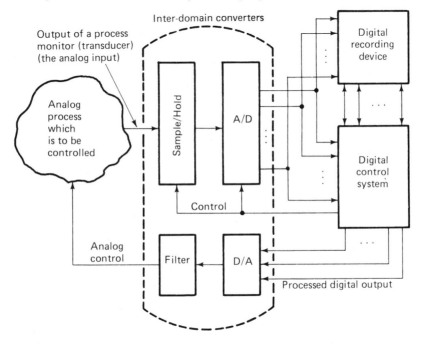

Fig. 1-8. A general model for a system that controls an analog process using digital methods.

It has just been mentioned that analog-to-digital converters require sampling the input signal if this signal is time varying. This immediately raises two questions related to the sampling process:

(1) "How often must the input signal be sampled?"
(2) "Given a sequence of samples, how is the original signal reconstructed?"

Without a lengthy mathematical development, the first question can be reasonably answered by the *Uniform Sampling Theorem*:

*A band-limited signal that has no frequency components above X Hz (cycles per second)
is uniquely determined by samples that are taken at the uniform rate of 2X Hz or greater.*

In short, this theorem, which is proven in many texts dealing with sampled data systems, states that any band-limited signal can be reconstructed by appropriate filtering if it is sampled at a frequency which is at least twice that of the highest frequency component contained in that signal. For example, the complex signals generated in a hi-fi stereo system are considered to be band limited between 20 Hz and 20,000 Hz. Theoretically this signal could be sampled at a rate of 40,000 samples per second ($2 \times 20,000$ Hz) and the discrete output of this sampling circuit could be filtered to completely recover the original signal. However, practically speaking, five times the highest frequency component is considered to be fairly standard.

The reconstruction of a sampled analog wave form which has been digitized is generally done with a combination of a digital-to-analog converter and a frequency-selective network called a *low-pass filter*, as shown in Figure 1-8. A low pass filter is a special network that stops the passage of frequency components which exceed some specified cutoff frequency f_c and passes all frequency components below f_c. It can be shown that if the data whose highest component is X Hz is sampled at the frequency f_0, then f_c can be specified as $X \leq f_c \leq f_0 - X$. It should be pointed out that the SAMPLE/HOLD is not always required. This is particularly true when the period of the highest frequency component of the input is much lower than the conversion time of the A/D. Likewise, many times the FILTER is left out when the frequency response of the system receiving this output of the D/A is appropriate.

D/A techniques are relatively simple in comparison to A/D techniques. However, the understanding of both requires considerable background in both the analog and digital fields. Two rather simple D/A methods are shown in Figure 1-9. Both require an understanding of the op-amp summer circuit shown in Figure 1-9(c). Once the summer concept is understood and coupled with the fact that digital signals can be simulated by simple switches, the operation of a voltage/current operated D/A is quite obvious.

D/A's are available in a wide variety of packages. See Figure 1-10 for some typical commercial D/A's. These and others similar are available from a number of manufacturers.

Voltage/current A/D converters are more complex, as has been mentioned, and there are two methods that can be used:

(1) simultaneous method;
(2) feedback method (requires an internal D/A):
    (a) counter method (similar to feedback method),
    (b) continuous method (similar to counter method with up/down counter),
    (c) successive approximation method.

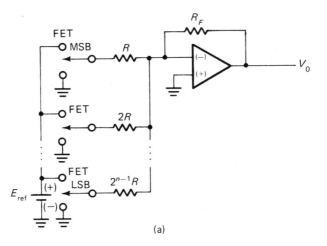

(a)

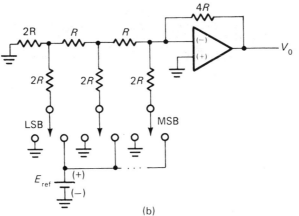

(b)

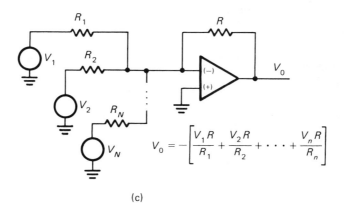

$$V_0 = -\left[\frac{V_1 R}{R_1} + \frac{V_2 R}{R_2} + \cdots + \frac{V_n R}{R_n}\right]$$

(c)

Fig. 1-9. (a), (b) Two "summing" types of D/A, both of which are based on the summing circuit (c).

Preferred Digital to Analog Converters

The "preferred" digital to analog converters listed in this table are selected from Datel Systems broad line of 74 different models. These models are selected for the best price-performance values and are the preferred devices used in over 80% of our customer requirements. All of the converters are proven designs backed up by volume production, as evidenced by the delivery of many thousands of units over the past five years.

The D/A converters listed here have a wide selection of performance parameters with a price range from $14.95 to $299.00. Units may be selected from either current or voltage output models, and by resolution, speed, tem-perature coefficient, and input coding. Output settling times span 500 to 25 nanoseconds for current output models and 30 microseconds down to 50 nanoseconds for voltage output models. Output resolution varies from 6 bits to 16 and includes 2 through 4 digit BCD models.

For a more detailed listing of all Datel Systems' D/A converters, request a copy of our Product Engineering Handbook. Individual data sheets are available on all models listed in this brochure. For complete ordering information contact your nearest Datel Systems sales representative, sales office, or the factory.

Converter Type	Model	Resolution	Error (1) (%FS max.)	Output	Settling Time, max.
Economy DAC's	DAC-98BI/8DI(5)	8 Bits/2 Dig.	.2/.5%	Current	500 nsec.
	DAC-198B/8D	8 Bits/2 Dig.	.2/.5%	Voltage	20 μsec.
	DAC-198BI/DI	8 Bits/2 Dig.	.2/.5%	Current	300 nsec.
	DAC-298B/8D	8 Bits/2 Dig.	.2/.5%	Voltage	5 μsec.
	DAC-4910B/10BI	10 Bits	.05%	Volt./Cur.	5 μsec./300 nsec.
	DAC-4912D/12DI	3 Digits	.05%	Volt./Cur.	5 μsec./300 nsec.
	DAC-6912B/12BI	12 Bits	.01%	Volt./Cur.	20 μsec./300 nsec.
High Performance DAC's	DAC-HB8B/10B/12B	8/10/12 Bits	.2/.05/.01%	Voltage	5 μsec.
	DAC-HB12D	3 Dig.	.05%	Voltage	5 μsec.
	DAC-I8B/10B/12B	8/10/12 Bits	.2/.05/.01%	Current	150 nsec.
	DAC-I8D/12D	2/3 Dig.	.5/.05%	Current	150 nsec.
	DAC-R8B/10B/12B	8/10/12 Bits	.2/.05/.01%	Voltage	5 μsec.
	DAC-R8D/12D	2/3 Dig.	.5/.05%		
	DAC-TR8B/10B/12B	8/10/12 Bits	.2/.05/.01%		
	DAC-TR8D/12D	2/3 Dig.	.5/.05%		
WITH DIGITAL INPUT REGISTER	DAC-V8B/10B/12B	8/10/12 Bits	.2/.05/.01%	Voltage	2 μsec.
	DAC-V8D/12D	2/3 Dig.	.5/.05%		
	DAC-VR8B/10B/12B	8/10/12 Bits	.2/.05/.01%		
	DAC-VR8D/12D	2/3 Dig.	.5/.05%		
High Resolution DAC's	DAC-169-16B	16 Bits	.005%	Volt., Cur.	30/.75 μsec.
	DAC-169-16D	4 Dig.	.005%	Volt., Cur.	30/.75 μsec.
	DAC-HR13B/14B/15B/16B	13/14/15/16 Bits	.0015%	Current	1 μsec.
Multiplying DAC's	DAC-MV8B/10B/12B	8/10/12 Bits	.2/.05/.01%	Voltage	4 μsec.
	DAC-MV8D/12D	2/3 Dig.	.5/.05%		
High Speed DAC's	DAC-HI8B/10B/12B	8/10/12 Bits	.2/.05/.01%	Current	25/25/50 nsec.
	DAC-HV6B/8B/10B-100	6/8/10 Bits	.8/.2/.05%	Voltage	50/50/100 nsec.

Fig. 1-10. Some typical commercial D/A's (Courtesy of Datel).

ALL DATEL SYSTEMS' D/A CONVERTERS ARE
COVERED UNDER GSA CONTRACT NO. GS-00S-27959,
FSC GROUP 66, PART II SECTION H, PERIOD 3-1-75
THROUGH 2-29-76.

NOTES:
(1.) Error after adjusting zero and full scale. Does not include
quantization error.
(2.) Coding: Bin = binary including offset binary for bipolar operation. BCD = binary coded decimal.
(3.) Over operating temperature range of $0°$ to $70°C$. Extended
temperature range versions are also available. Contact factory
for details.
(4.) Pins are .020" round, gold plated, with .100" DIP compatible
spacing.
(5.) Does not contain internal reference. For internal reference
models become DAC-98BIR/8DIR. Add $2.00 to price.

DAC-169: 16 Bits or 4 BCD Digits, $79 (100's).

Input Coding (2)	Analog Output Ranges	Gain Tempco, max. (3)	Power Requirement	Module Size (4)	Price (1-9)
Bin/BCD	+2.6/+1.6mA	±100ppm/°C		1" x 2" x .375"	$14.95/14.95
Bin/BCD	±5, +10V/+10V	±50ppm/°C	±15V	2" x 2" x .375"	$29/29
Bin/BCD	±1.25, +2.5/+1.54mA	±50ppm/°C		2" x 2" x .375"	$29/29
Bin/BCD	±5, +10/+10V				$39/39
Bin	±5, +10V/±1.25, +2.5mA	±50ppm/°C	±15V	2" x 2" x .375"	$49/49
BCD	+10V/+1.54mA				$49/49
Bin	±5, +10V/±1.25, +2.5mA				$59/59
Bin	±5, +10V	±30ppm/°C		1.5" x 2" x .375"	$65/79/89
BCD	+10V	±30ppm/°C	±15V	1.5" x 2" x .375"	$89
Bin	±1, +2mA	±15ppm/°C		1" x 2" x .375"	$69/79/89
BCD	+1.25mA	±15ppm/°C		1" x 2" x .375"	$69/89
Bin		±30ppm/°C			$69/75/79
BCD	±2.5, ±5, ±10, +5, +10V	±30ppm/°C	±15V, +5V	2" x 2" x .375"	$69/79
Bin		±7ppm/°C			$129/159/179
BCD		±7ppm/°C			$129/179
Bin	±5, ±10, +5, +10V		±15V		$79/99/119
BCD	+5, +10V	±20ppm/°C	±15V	2" x 2" x .375"	$79/119
Bin	±5, ±10, +5, +10V		±15V, +5V		$89/109/129
BCD	+5, +10V		±15V, +5V		$99/129
Bin	+10, 10, ±5V; ±1, +2mA	±10ppm/°C		2" x 2" x .375"	$109
BCD	+10, 10V, +1.25mA	±10ppm/°C	±15V	2" x 2" x .375"	$109
Bin	±1, +2mA	±1.5ppm/°C		2" x 4" x .4"	$249/263/276/299
Bin	±5 ±10V	±30ppm/°C	±15V	2" x 3" x .375"	$119/129/159
BCD					$119/159
Bin	±2.5, +5mA	±15/15/20ppm/°C	±15V	2" x 2" x .375"	$99/119/129
Bin	+5V @ 100mA	±60ppm/°C	±15V	2" x 3" x .375"	$169/179/189

As mentioned, most of these methods are very similar in the way they are modeled, but they do vary in the internal control of the actual conversion process. A fairly general model of a feedback A/D is shown in Figure 1-11.

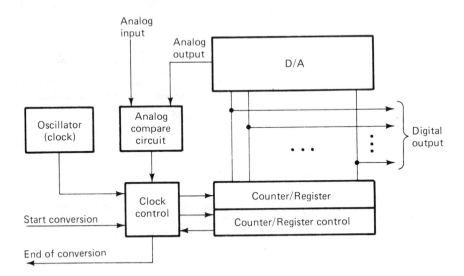

Fig. 1-11. Example model of an analog-to-digital converter.

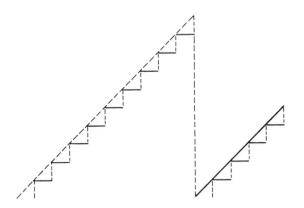

Fig. 1-12. Digitization of a ramp voltage.

We see the operation on a voltage/current A/D as one of issuing a START OF CONVERSION (SOC), at which time the CLOCK CONTROL starts directing clock signals to a special digital module called a counter/register module. The COUNTER or REGISTER operation starts formulating the digital equivalence of the analog input by counting the clock pulses. At the same time, the D/A is monitoring the conversion process (counting process) and once the count reaches the level equivalent to the analog input, the COMPARE CIRCUIT fires and the conversion process is halted. At that time, the digital outputs are valid and represent the digitization of the analog input. See Figure 1-12 for an example of the digitization of a ramp voltage input.

Granted, this is a rather cursory treatment of such an important subject. However, it does describe the general process and, further, it indicates that A/D processes require time to complete, hence their use requires frequency response considerations. See Figure 1-13 for typical A/D devices that are available commercially.

We will see that these A/D and D/A processes are closely related to the conversion of a number from one base system to another base system, which is a slick way to introduce and treat a rather trite and boring subject.

1-6 NUMBER SYSTEMS

Before we get into the special analog-to-digital conversion of a decimal number to its binary equivalent, let us first consider the makeup of number systems in general.

A number system is a language system consisting of an ordered set of symbols called digits with rules defined for addition, multiplication, and other mathematical operations The *radix* or *base* of a number system specifies the actual number of *digits* included in its ordered set. Further, a number system allows for numbers (collection of digits) to have an integer and a fractional part set apart by a radix point ".", that is,

$$(N)_r = \left[\begin{array}{c} \text{Radix Point} \\ \downarrow \\ \text{(integer part)}.\text{(fractional part)} \end{array} \right]_r$$

1-7 JUXTAPOSITIONAL NUMBERS

There are two common notations by which a general number can be represented. For example 1976.4, which we read in short-form notation as "nineteen-seventy-six point four" is a *juxtapositional* notation. Juxtapositional implies the placing of digits side by side.

Preferred Analog to Digital Converters

The "preferred" analog to digital converters featured in this table have been selected as the best price-performance values available. Out of Datel Systems' complete line of 62 different A/D converter models, these are the devices preferred in 80% of our customers' requirements. Each of these converters is a carefully engineered and conservatively specified product, produced in volume with proven performance.

The process of selecting the right analog to digital converter for an application is important. Performance, price, delivery, and reputation of the manufacturer are all important factors in the selection process. Datel Systems is an established leader in the manufacture of A/D converters, with a reputation based on tens of thousands of delivered units over the past five years.

The converters listed here cover the price range from $29.95 to $995.00 and span various types, from counter converters to successive approximation, dual slope, and parallel types. A broad selection of accuracy, speed, temperature stability, and other performance features is available to meet a wide range of application requirements.

For a more detailed listing of all Datel Systems' A/D converters, request a copy of our Product Engineering Handbook. Individual data sheets are available on all models listed in this brochure. For complete ordering information contact your nearest Datel Systems sales representative, sales office, or the factory.

Converter Type	Model	Resolution	Error (1) (%FS, max.)	Total Conv. Time, max.	Output Codes (2)
Economy Counter Type	ADC-Econoverter	6 Bits	0.78%	50 μsec.	Bin
	ADC-89A8B/8D	8 Bits/2 Dig.	.2/.5%	200/100 μsec.	Bin/BCD
General Purpose Succ. Approximation	ADC-MA10B2A/10B2B	10 Bits	.05%	40/20 μsec.	Bin, 2C
	ADC-MA12B2A/12B2B	12 Bits	.012%		
High Performance Successive Approximation	ADC-L8B/8D	8 Bits/2 Dig.	.2/.5%	12 μsec.	Bin, 2C/BCD
	ADC-L10B	10 Bits	.05%	16 μsec.	Bin, 2C
	ADC-L12B/12D	12 Bits/3 Dig.	.012/.05%	20 μsec.	Bin, 2C/BCD
High Resolution	ADC-149-14B	14 Bits	.005%	50 μsec.	Bin, 2C
Low Power CMOS (40mW dissipation) (5)	ADC-CM8B	8 Bits	.2%	250 μsec.	Bin
	ADC-CM10B	10 Bits	.05%	300 μsec.	
	ADC-CM12B	12 Bits	.012%	350 μsec.	
Economy Dual Slope	ADC-E8B/8D	8 Bits/2½ Dig.	.2/.5%	312/500 μsec.	Bin/BCD (7)
	ADC-E10B	10 Bits	.05%	1.25 msec.	Bin (7)
	ADC-E12B/12D	12 Bits/3½ Dig.	.05/.05%	5.0/5.0 msec.	Bin/BCD (7)
Ratiometric Dual Slope	ADC-ER8B/8D	8 Bits/2½ Dig.	.2/.5%	43.3/76.7 msec.	Bin/BCD (7)
	ADC-ER10B	10 Bits	.05%	43.3 msec.	Bin (7)
	ADC-ER12B/12D	12 Bits/3½ Dig.	.05/.05%	43.3/76.7 msec.	Bin/BCD (7)
Hi Res. Dual Slope	ADC-EP14B/16D	14 Bits/4½ Dig.	.01%	230 msec.	Bin/BCD (7)
High Speed Successive Approximation	ADC-EH8B1/8B2	8 Bits	0.2%	4.0/2.0 μsec.	Bin, 2C
	ADC-EH10B1/10B2	10 Bits	.05%	4.0/2.0 μsec.	
	ADC-EH12B1/12B2	12 Bits	.012%	8.0/4.0 μsec.	
	ADC-G8B	8 Bits	0.2%	800 nsec.	Bin, 2C
	ADC-G10B	10 Bits	.05%	1.0 μsec.	
A/D with Sample-Hold	ADC-SH4B	4 Bits	3.0%	500 nsec.	Bin
Ultra High Speed Parallel Type	ADC-VH4B/UH4B	4 Bits	3.0%	100/40 nsec.	Bin
	ADC-VH6B/UH6B	6 Bits	0.8%	200/100 nsec.	
	ADC-VH8B/UH8B	8 Bits	0.4%	200/100 nsec.	

Fig. 1-13. Some typical commercial A/D's (Courtesy of Datel).

ALL DATEL SYSTEMS' A/D CONVERTERS ARE
COVERED UNDER GSA CONTRACT NO. GS-00S-27959,
FSC GROUP 66, PART II SECTION H, PERIOD 3-1-75
THROUGH 2-29-76.

NOTES:
(1.) Error after adjusting zero and full scale. Does not include quantization error.
(2.) Coding: Bin = binary, including offset binary for bipolar operation BCD = binary coded decimal. 2C = two's complement for bipolar operation.
(3.) Over operating temperature range of 0° to 70°C. Extended temperature range versions are also available. Contact factory for details.
(4.) Pins are .020" round, gold plated, with .100" DIP compatible spacing.
(5.) Maximum dissipation for +12V supply and 1000 conversions per second.
(6.) Input buffer option is available giving 100 Megohm input impedance.
(7.) Sign-magnitude coding is used for both Binary and BCD.

ADC-UH8B: 8Bits, 10 Million Conversions per Second, $995.

Analog Input Ranges	Input Impedance	Gain Tempco, max. (3)	Power Requirement	Module Size (4)	Price (1-9)
±2.5, ±5, +10V	2.4, 4.2K	±100ppm/°C	±15V, +5V	2" x 2" x .375"	$29.95
±5, +10/+10V	4.25K	± 50ppm/°C	±15V, +5V	2" x 3" x .375"	$69/69
±5, ±10, +5, +10V	2.5, 5, 10K (6)	±30ppm/°C	±15V, +5V	2" x 4" x .4"	$95/125 $125/145
±5, ±10, +5, +10V	10K (6)	±10ppm/°C	±15V, +5V	2" x 4" x .4"	$135/135 $155 $175/175
±5, ±10, -10, -20V	5, 10K	±15ppm/°C	±15V, +5V	2" x 4" x .8"	$239
±5, ±10, -5, -10V	25, 50, 100K	± 30ppm/°C	+12 to +15V	2" x 3" x .8"	$149 $159 $169
1, ±5, ±10/±2, ±5, ±10V ±1, ±5, ±10V 1, ±5, ±10/±2, ±5, ±10V	100M, 10K	±50ppm/°C	±15V, +5V	2" x 4" x .4"	$79/79 $89 $99/99
±1/±2V	100M	±35ppm/°C	+5V	2" x 4" x .4"	$79/79 $89 $99/99
±2V	100M	±13ppm/°C	±15V, +5V	2" x 4" x .8"	$179/179
±5, +10V	4.45K 2.3K 2.3K	± 50ppm/°C ± 30ppm/°C ± 30ppm/°C	±15V, +5V	2" x 2" x .375" 2" x 3" x .375" 2" x 4" x .4"	$85/129 $149/189 $169/229
±5, ±10, -5, -10V	.5, 1, 2K	±50ppm/°C	±15V, +5V	2" x 4" x .4" 2" x 4" x .8"	$249 $349
+1V	50 Ohms	±200ppm/°C	±15V, +5V	2" x 2" x .375"	$79
±1.28, -2.56V	100Ω	±50ppm/°C	±15V, ±5V	3" x 5" x 1.15"	$795/895 $845/945 $895/995

In general, a collection of digits from a base $=r$ system, which we define as a number $(N)_r$, is written in juxtapositional notation as follows:

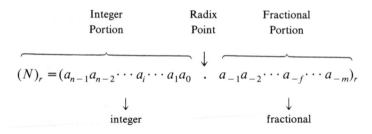

| | Integer Portion | Radix Point | Fractional Portion |

$$(N)_r = (\underbrace{a_{n-1}a_{n-2}\cdots a_i \cdots a_1 a_0}_{\text{integer}} \,.\, \underbrace{a_{-1}a_{-2}\cdots a_{-f}\cdots a_{-m}}_{\text{fractional}})_r$$

where

$$r \triangleq \text{radix of the number system}$$

$$a \triangleq \text{a digit in the set}$$

$$n \triangleq \text{number of digits in integer portion}$$

$$m \triangleq \text{number of digits in fractional portion}$$

$$a_{n-1} \triangleq \text{most significant digit}$$

$$a_{-m} \triangleq \text{least significant digit}$$

Keep in mind that since the actual number of digits in the set of a base "r" system is equal to r itself, we can deduce the following:

$$0 \le (a_i \text{ or } a_{-f}) \le r - 1$$

which says in plain terms that the largest valued digit in the decimal system is $10 - 1 = 9$, and in the binary system "1" is the largest valued digit.

From this we see that the juxtapositional notation is a system whereby the allowable digits of the base system are placed side by side and the integer and fractional portions are set apart by a radix point, and each position in the number is assigned a "weight" or an index of importance by some predesigned rule. For example

$$\$1976.40$$

could mean various things to us, but in particular it represents

1—one thousand dollar bill
plus 9—one hundred dollar bills
plus 7—ten dollar bills
plus 6—one dollar bills
plus 4—dimes

Thus we see by affixing the special dollar sign notation ($) to the number, we assign a special weight to each position, in this case $1,000 bills, $100 bills, and so forth.

By the same token a binary number in juxtaposition notation would be shown as follows:

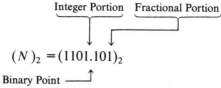

$$(N)_2 = (1101.101)_2$$

Binary Point ⟶

And if we lived in land where the currency was based on the binary monetary unit called the CROUTON signified by δ, then

$$\delta(1101.10)$$

would represent

> 1—8 crouton bill
> plus 1—4 crouton bill
> plus 0—2 crouton bill
> plus 1—1 crouton bill
> plus 1—$\frac{1}{2}$ crouton coin

1-8 POLYNOMIAL NOTATION

Another notation or representation of a number $(N)_r$ can be written as follows:

$$(N)_r = \sum_{j=-m}^{n-1} a_j r^j$$

Thus we see again, by expanding this expression, that each digit position is weighted by the (r^j) factor in each term:

$$(N)_r = a_{n-1}r^{n-1} + a_{n-2}r^{n-2}$$
$$+ \cdots + a_1 r^1 + a_0 r^0 + a_{-1}r^{-1} + a_{-2}r^{-2} + \cdots + a_{-m}r^{-m}$$

$$\therefore (1976.4)_{10} = 1 \times 10^3 + 9 \times 10^2 + 7 \times 10 + 6 \times 1 + 4 \times 10^{-1}$$

With respect to the binary system, the number $(1101.101)_2$ can be represented in the polynomial notation as:

$$(1101.101)_2 = 1 \times 2^3 + 1 \times 2^2 + 0 \times 2^1 + 1 \times 2^0 + 1 \times 2^{-1} + 0 \times 2^{-2} + 1 \times 2^{-3}$$

The polynomial representation is more formal and will be used to illustrate how numbers in the base 10 (decimal) system or any other system can be converted to their equivalent in the binary system.

1-9 BASE CONVERSION METHODS

Quite frequently conversions from one base system to another must be made. Therefore, it is necessary that we at least touch upon the process involved in base-to-base conversion, and, more specifically, in the conversion from base 10 to base 2 (binary), base 8 (octal), and base 16 (hexadecimal), and back again. A simple example will give you some idea why such conversions would be required.

Fig. 1-14. A characterization of a questionable A/D.

EXAMPLE 1-1: Suppose you were in charge of a system that is to record the dc voltage at some point in a special analog circuit and in turn record this voltage once each second and store these accumulated values in a digital computer. At a later time, this data is to be displayed on a print-out sheet. The system sketched in Figure 1-14 would, using an A/D converter, allow you to perform this task if you were sure it was functioning properly. This A/D system is to be under the control of the computer. The computer keeps track of the 1-sec periods, then signals the A/D to convert the value of the dc input voltage to its binary equivalent. When this conversion is completed, the value is to be stored in the memory of the computer. However, you have reason to believe that the A/D is *not* functioning properly, that is, it is not generating the proper voltage coded binary number for its output. What do you do? Naturally you perform a hand calculation of the conversion to check the A/D converter. For example, using a voltmeter we measure +19.75 volts at the input of the A/D. Now you must ask:

$$(19.75)_{10} \text{ volts} = (??)_2 \text{ volts}$$

1-10 NUMBER CONVERSION BY SUBSTITUTION

By definition, the number $(N)_r$ in base r may be represented as

$$(N)_r = a_{n-1}r^{n-1} + a_{n-2}r^{n-2} + \cdots + a_1 r^1 + a_0 r^0 + a_{-1}r^{-1} + a_{-2}r^{-2} + \cdots$$

and the weighting of the resulting juxtapositional number is assigned by r^j. Thus:

$$(19.75)_{10} = 1 \times 10^1 + 9 \times 10^0 + 7 \times 10^{-1} + 5 \times 10^{-2}$$

Now the real question is how does this number relate to its equivalent in the base 2 system? The answer lies in the fact that the base 2 system or any other base system has the identical operations $+$, $-$, $\times$, and $\div$ as defined in the decimal system that defines the results of a "binary operation" between two elements of the set of elements. Thus you can carry out a direct substitution for each term in the expanded polynomial notation if you have a base 10 to base 2 conversion table for each *digit in the decimal set (0, 1, 2, ..., 9) and the binary equivalent* of the number $(10)_{10}$ (see Table 1-2).

For example:

$$(19.75)_{10} = \left[(0001 \times 1010) + (1001 \times 0001) + \left(0111 \times \frac{1}{1010}\right) + \left(0101 \times \frac{1}{1010} \times \frac{1}{1010}\right) \right]_2$$

TABLE 1-2 A table for binary digit equivalents of decimal digits

	Decimal	Binary	
	0	0	binary digits
	1	1	
	2	10	
	3	11	
decimal digits	4	100	binary equivalents of decimal digits plus the decimal number 10
	5	101	
	6	110	
	7	111	
	8	1000	
	9	1001	
number	10	1010	

We can complete the conversion to the binary equivalent by carrying out the indicated mathematics in the base 2 system, which is a straightforward process but somewhat tedious.

Examples are given of the arithmetic operations for the binary system in Figure 1-15. We see from the figure that the mechanics are exactly the same as in the decimal system; therefore, the substitution is valid.

Fig. 1-15. The mechanics of performing mathematical operations on two multi-digit binary numbers.

+	0	1
0	0	1
1	1	10

(a) Addition table for binary

×	0	1
0	0	0
1	0	1

(b) Multiplication table for binary

```
  1 1 1
  0 1 1 1
+ 0 0 1 1
---------
  1 0 1 0
```

(c) Adding two binary numbers

```
    0 1 1 1
  × 0 0 1 1
  ---------
    0 1 1 1
  0 1 1 1
  ---------
  1 0 1 0 1
```

(d) Multiplying two binary numbers

```
  0 1 10 1
  1 0 1 0
- 0 0 1 1
--------
  0 1 1 1
```

(e) Subtracting two binary numbers

```
                1 1 1
  0 1 1 ) 1 0 1 0 1
          0 1 1
          -----
          1 0 0
          0 1 1
          -----
            0 1 1
            0 1 1
            -----
            0 0 0
```

(f) Division of two binary numbers

What we would like is some system whereby conversion could be made by carrying out the mathematics in the base 10 system for obvious reasons. To do this, consider the following.

The radix divide/multiply method. First we are assured at this point that

$$(19.75)_{10} = (a_{n-1})_2 2^{n-1} + \cdots + (a_1)_2 2^1 + (a_0)_2 + (a_{-1})_2 2^{-1} + \cdots$$

or

$$(19.75)_{10} = (\text{integer})_2 + (\text{fractional})_2$$

Thus

$$19 = (a_{n-1})_2 2^{n-1} + \cdots + (a_1)_2 2^1 + (a_0)_2 \tag{1}$$

The question is what are the binary values of $a_{n-1}, \ldots, a_1, a_0$ (which we know will be either 0 or 1)? Divide both sides of Eq. (1) by two, we see that

$$\underbrace{\frac{19}{2} = 9}_{\text{Quotient}} + \underbrace{\frac{1}{2}}_{\frac{\text{Remainder}}{2}} = \underbrace{\frac{(a_{n-1})_2(2^{n-1})}{2} + \cdots + \frac{(a_1)_2(2)}{2}}_{\text{Quotient}} + \underbrace{\frac{a_0}{2}}_{\frac{\text{Remainder}}{2}}$$

Therefore, by equating terms we see that

$$9 = (a_{n-1})_2(2^{n-2}) + \cdots + a_1$$

and

$$\frac{1}{2} = \frac{a_0}{2}$$

Therefore

$$a_0 = 1$$

Now, if we divide again,

$$\frac{9}{2} = 4 + \frac{1}{2} = \frac{(a_{n-1})_2(2^{n-2})}{2} + \cdots + \frac{a_1}{2}$$

we see that

$$4 = (a_{n-1})_2(2^{n-3}) + \cdots + a_2$$

and

$$\frac{1}{2} = \frac{a_1}{2}$$

$$\therefore a_1 = 1$$

Now you begin to see a pattern develop. Each successive division done on the number $(N)_{10}$ in base 10 by two results in the quotient plus a remainder, that remainder being the binary coefficient of the weight position determined by the numbered division just performed. This is more plainly described by carrying out this process to completion.

$$
\begin{array}{ll}
2\overline{)19} = 9+1 & \therefore a_0 = 1 \\
2\overline{)9} \ = 4+1 & \therefore a_1 = 1 \\
2\overline{)4} \ = 2+0 & \therefore a_2 = 0 \\
2\overline{)2} \ = 1+0 & \therefore a_3 = 0 \\
2\overline{)1} \ = 0+1 & \therefore a_4 = 1 \\
2\overline{)0} \ = 0+0 & \therefore a_5 = 0 \\
\quad\quad\ \ \vdots & \\
2\overline{)0} \ = 0+0 & \therefore a_{n-1} = 0
\end{array}
$$

From this successive division and from the knowledge that

$$(19)_{10} = (a_{n-1}\cdots a_4 a_3 a_2 a_1 a_0)_2$$

we see

$$(19)_{10} = (10011)_2$$

You now have a simple method by which you can convert the integer portion of a base 10 number to *any other base*.

But what about the fractional portion of $(19.75)_{10}$? Here again we know that

$$0.75 = (a_{-1})_2 2^{-1} + (a_{-2})_2 2^{-2} + \cdots + (a_{-m})_2 2^{-m} \tag{2}$$

Therefore, we multiply both sides of Eq. (2) by two, which gives us

$$(0.75\times2) = 1.50 = (a_{-1})_2(2^{-1})(2) + (a_{-2})(2^{-2})(2) + \cdots$$
$$= \underbrace{(a_{-1})_2\times1}_{\geq 0} + (a_{-2})(2^{-1}) + \cdots$$
$$\therefore (a_{-1})_2 = 1$$

By successive multiplications by the base (2 in this case), the fractional portion of the number can be evaluated as shown:

$$
\begin{array}{c}
0.75 \\
\underline{2} \\
a_{-1} \to \overline{1.50} \quad\quad \dfrac{(1+0.50)}{2} = 0.75\\
0.50 \\
\underline{2} \\
a_{-2} \to \overline{1.00} \\
0.00 \\
\underline{2} \\
a_{-3} \to \overline{0.00} \\
\vdots \\
a_{-m} \to 0.00
\end{array}
$$

Thus we see

$$(19.75)_{10} = (10011.110)_2$$

Now going back to the original problem where 19.75 volts were present on the input of our analog-to-digital converter, we would expect to see the voltage equivalent to the representation in Figure 1-16.

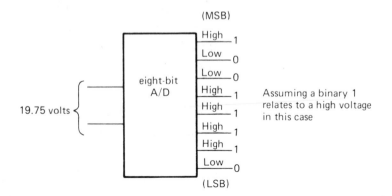

Fig. 1-16. The output voltage representation of 19.75 for an eight-bit A/D.

To this point we have illustrated two methods of number conversion:

(1) Direct Substitution: A technique whereby a number $(N)_r$ can be converted to base s by directly substituting into the following:

$$(N)_r = \sum_{j=-m}^{n-1} (a_j)_s \cdot (r^j)_s$$

and carrying out the indicated mathematics in base $= s$.

(2) Divide/Multiply by Radix: A technique whereby a number $(N)_r$ can be converted to base $= s$ by dividing (multiplying) $(N)_r$ by s using base $= r$ arithmetic.

These techniques have been generalized to any system-to-system conversion. However, when base systems other than 10 are encountered, there can be difficulty carrying out the mathematics in a different base system. To avoid this, both techniques can be used to convert a given number in any base to any other base and use only decimal arithmetic. For example:

$$(N)_r = (X)_s?? \quad \text{where} \quad r \neq 10$$
$$s \neq 10$$

First

$$(N)_r = (Y)_{10} \quad \text{by substitution}$$
$$(Y)_{10} = (X)_s \quad \text{by divide/multiply radix}$$

We see that $(N)_r$ is first converted to $(Y)_{10}$, a base 10 number, by direct substitution using only decimal arithmetic. Next $(Y)_{10}$ is converted to $(X)_s$, a base s number, by divide/multiply by radix s, which is another decimal arithmetic exercise. This procedure is best understood by examples.

EXAMPLE 1-2: Convert the decimal number $(105)_{10}$ into its: (a) binary, (b) trinary (base 3), (c) quinary (base 5) and (d) octal (base 8) equivalents by the divide method.

Solution:

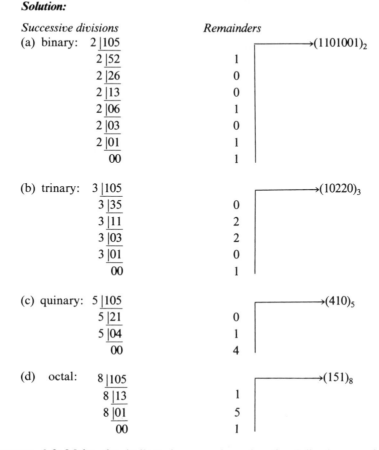

Successive divisions   *Remainders*

(a) binary: $2\,|\,105$ → $(1101001)_2$
$2\,|\,52$ 1
$2\,|\,26$ 0
$2\,|\,13$ 0
$2\,|\,06$ 1
$2\,|\,03$ 0
$2\,|\,01$ 1
00 1

(b) trinary: $3\,|\,105$ → $(10220)_3$
$3\,|\,35$ 0
$3\,|\,11$ 2
$3\,|\,03$ 2
$3\,|\,01$ 0
00 1

(c) quinary: $5\,|\,105$ → $(410)_5$
$5\,|\,21$ 0
$5\,|\,04$ 1
00 4

(d) octal: $8\,|\,105$ → $(151)_8$
$8\,|\,13$ 1
$8\,|\,01$ 5
00 1

EXAMPLE 1-3: Make the indicated conversions for the following numbers (substitution method).

  a. $(743)_8 = (?)_{10}$

Solution:

$$7 \times 8^2 + 4 \times 8^1 + 3 \times 8^0 = ? \times 10^2 + ? \times 10^1 + ? \times 10^0$$

The solution to this problem involves finding the equivalent decimal value of each of the terms on the left-hand side.

Coefficients	*Powers*	*Total*
$(7)_8 = (7)_{10}$	$(8^2)_8 = (64)_{10}$	$(7)_{10} \times (64)_{10} = (448)_{10}$
$(4)_8 = (4)_{10}$	$(8^1)_8 = (8)_{10}$	$(4)_{10} \times (8)_{10} = (32)_{10}$
$(3)_8 = (3)_{10}$	$(8^0)_8 = (1)_{10}$	$(3)_{10} \times (1)_{10} = \underline{(3)_{10}}$
		$(483)_{10}$

  b. $(432)_5 = (?)_7$

Solution:

$$4 \times 5^2 + 3 \times 5^1 + 2 \times 5^0 = ? \times 7^2 + ? \times 7^1 + ? \times 7^0$$

We can find the solution to this problem by performing an intermediate step of conversion to base 10.

Coefficients	Powers	Total
$(4)_5 = (4)_{10}$	$(5^2)_5 = (25)_{10}$	$(4)_{10} \times (25)_{10} = (100)_{10}$
$(3)_5 = (3)_{10}$	$(5^1)_5 = (5)_{10}$	$(3)_{10} \times (5)_{10} = (15)_{10}$
$(2)_5 = (2)_{10}$	$(5^0)_5 = (1)_{10}$	$(2)_{10} \times (1)_{10} = \underline{(2)_{10}}$
		$(117)_{10}$

This number can now be converted to base 7 by the division process.

Successive Division	Remainders
7 |117	
7 |16	5 →$(225)_7$
7 |02	2
00	2

Check:

$$(225)_7 = (2)_{10} \times (7^2)_{10} + (2)_{10} \times (7^1)_{10}$$
$$+ (5)_{10} \times (7^0)_{10} = 98 + 14 + 5 = (117)_{10}$$

Remember, symbol 7 in base 7 does not exist, but is conveyed by $(10)_7$. Likewise, the symbol 8 in base 8 does not exist, but the decimal value is represented as $(10)_8$; and so forth.

EXAMPLE 1-4: Convert the following numbers.

a. $(101101)_2 = (?)_{10}$

Solution (substitution method):

$$1 \times 2^5 + 0 \times 2^4 + 1 \times 2^3 + 1 \times 2^2 + 0 \times 2^1 + 1 \times 2^0 = (45)_{10}$$

*Solution (division method): ***

Successive Division	Remainders
1010 |101101	
1010 |100	$(101)_2 = 5$ →$(45)_{10}$
000	$(100)_2 = 4$

b. $(1101101)_2 = (?)_{10}$

Solution (substitution method):

$$1 \times 2^6 + 1 \times 2^5 + 0 \times 2^4 + 1 \times 2^3 + 1 \times 2^2 + 0 \times 2^1 + 1 \times 2^0 = (109)_{10}$$

Some other examples can be used to show the process involved with converting fractional values into equivalent bases.

---

*Remember: $(10)_{10} = (1010)_2$

EXAMPLE 1-5: Convert the number $(0.875)_{10}$ into its: (a) binary, (b) trinary, (c) quinary, and (d) octal equivalents using the multiplication method.

(a) binary:
$(0.875)_{10} \times 2$ $(0.111)_2$
1.750 $\times 2$
1.500 $\times 2$
1.000

(b) trinary:
$(0.875)_{10} \times 3$ $(0.2121...)_3$
2.625 $\times 3$
1.875 $\times 3$
2.625 $\times 3$
1.875 $\times 3$
$\vdots$

(c) quinary:
$(0.875)_{10} \times 5$ $(0.4141...)_5$
4.375 $\times 5$
1.875 $\times 5$
4.375 $\times 5$
1.875 $\times 5$
$\vdots$

(d) octal:
$(0.875)_{10} \times 8$ $(0.700)_8$
7.000

There exists a simple method for converting binary numbers into their equivalent octal representations. In fact, this process can be extended to the conversion of binary numbers into any base that is itself a power of 2; that is, 4, 8, 16, 32, and so forth. The number system that uses 16 as its base is referred to as hexadecimal, and uses the symbols 0 through 9 and the first six letters of the alphabet, A, B, C, D, E, and F, to represent the 16 values as shown in Table 1-3.

TABLE 1-3 Decimal-binary-octal-hexadecimal equivalence number representations

Decimal	Binary	Octal	Hexadecimal	Decimal	Binary	Octal	Hexadecimal
0	0000	0	0	8	1000	10	8
1	0001	1	1	9	1001	11	9
2	0010	2	2	10	1010	12	A
3	0011	3	3	11	1011	13	B
4	0100	4	4	12	1100	14	C
5	0101	5	5	13	1101	15	D
6	0110	6	6	14	1110	16	E
7	0111	7	7	15	1111	17	F

If a binary number is being converted to an octal representation, instead of the previously described processes, you need only to make groups of three bits each on either side of the radix point, and then find their equivalent total value to produce the octal number. For instance, from our previous examples:

EXAMPLE 1-6: $(1101001.111)_2 = (151.7)_8$

$$\underset{1}{\underbrace{001}} \quad \underset{5}{\underbrace{101}} \quad \underset{1}{\underbrace{001}} . \underset{7}{\underbrace{111}}$$

The binary to hexadecimal is similar and is done by grouping four bits at a time. See Example 1-7.

EXAMPLE 1-7: $(1101001.111)_2 = (69.E)_{16}$

$$\underset{6}{\underbrace{0110}} \quad \underset{9}{\underbrace{1001}} . \underset{E}{\underbrace{1110}}$$

More will be said about octal and hexadecimal number representations in a future section on codes.

1-11 COMPLEMENTS OF NUMBERS

There exists a mathematical relationship between numbers that allows numerical subtractions by performing addition operations. In the decimal system, using a number's complement and a pencil and paper to perform subtractions yields no savings whatsoever, as will be shown. However, in the binary system complements are easily obtained and using the same hardware to add and subtract represents a considerable savings.

r's complements. The definition of the r's complement of a number N is as follows:

$$(N)_{r,c} \triangleq r^n - N \quad \text{if } N \neq 0, \qquad 0 \text{ for } N = 0$$

where n = number of digits in the integer portion of N

and r = radix number

The following examples illustrate the process of finding the r's complement:

(a) $(147)_{10,c} = 10^3 - 147 = 853.00$
(b) $(0.53)_{10,c} = 1 - 0.53 = 0.47$
(c) $(147.53)_{10,c} = 10^3 - 147.53 = 852.47$
(d) $(1010)_{2,c} = 2^4 - 1010 = 10000 - 1010 = 00110$
(e) $(0.101)_{2,c} = 2^0 - 0.101 = 1.0 - 0.101 = 0.011$
(f) $(1010.101)_{2,c} = 2^4 - 1010.101 = 10000 - 1010.101 = 101.011$

Thus we see that determining an r's complement of a number N requires some subtraction process if the definition is followed explicitly. However, with binary numbers there are shortcut techniques that bypass the subtraction requirement.

The first of these techniques is done quite simply in a two-step process:

(1) Invert each digit of the number (referred to as the "logical complement"), then
(2) add 1 to the least significant digit of step (1).

For example, given: $\dots 00010110.0110$

$$
\begin{array}{rl}
\text{step (1)} \dots & 11101001.1001 \\
\text{step (2)}+ & \qquad\qquad 1 \\
\hline
\dots & 11101001.1010
\end{array}
$$

This technique is widely used in digital computers and can be quickly accomplished with any modest instruction set.

The other of these techniques can be done by examination as follows. Given: $\dots 00010110.0110000\dots$

Procedure: Start from the right end of the number scan to the left, leaving all digits unchanged until the first 1 is encountered. Leave this 1 unchanged and invert the rest of the digits to the left. Crossing the radix point has no effect.

Thus the 2's complement of $\dots 00010110.011000\dots = \dots 11101001.101000\dots.$

Subtraction with r's complements. The subtraction of two positive base r numbers M and S, $(M - S)$ goes as follows:

(1) Add M to the r's complement of S.
(2) Check the results for overflow carry:
    (a) If an overflow carry results, discard it. The rest of the result represents $(M - S)$.
    (b) If an overflow carry *does not* occur, the result of the first step is negative. Therefore, take the r's complement of the results and add a negative sign to the results.

Consider the following examples:

(a) $(M - S) = (1010 - 0111)$

$$
\begin{array}{rl}
& 1010 \\
& 1001 \rightarrow 2\text{'s complement of } 0111 \\
\text{overflow carry} \leftarrow 1\ & \overline{0011} \rightarrow +0011 \\
\text{discarded} & \qquad\quad \underbrace{} \\
& \qquad\quad \text{answer}
\end{array}
$$

(b) $(M - S) = (0111 - 1010)$

$$
\begin{array}{rl}
& 0111 \\
& 0110 \rightarrow 2\text{'s complement of } 1010 \\
\text{no overflow carry} \leftarrow 0\ & \overline{1101} \rightarrow -0011 \\
& \qquad\quad \underbrace{} \\
& \qquad\quad \text{answer}
\end{array}
$$

(c) $(M-S) = (1010.101000 - 111.01000)$

001010.101000

$\overline{111000.110000}$ → 2's complement of 00111.0100

overflow carry ←1 $\overline{000011.011000}$ → +11.0110

discarded

answer

Thus the 2's complement technique for subtracting two binary numbers employing the same hardware used to perform additions is simple and straightforward.

(r − 1)'s complement. The definition of the "r minus one" complement of a number N is as follows:

$$(N)_{r-1,c} \triangleq r^n - r^{-m} - N$$

where

n = number of digits in the integer portion of N

m = number of digits in the fractional portion of N

r = radix number

The following examples illustrate the process of finding the $(r-1)$'s complement:

(a) $(147)_{9,c} = 10^3 - 1 - 147 = 852.00$

(b) $(0.53)_{9,c} = 1 - 10^{-2} - 0.53 = 0.46$

(c) $(147.53)_{9,c} = 10^3 - 10^{-2} - 147.53 = 852.46$

(d) $(1010)_{1,c} = 2^4 - 1 - 1010 = 0101.$

(e) $(0.101)_{1,c} = 1 - 2^{-3} - 0.101 = 0.010111\ldots$

(f) $(1010.101)_{1,c} = 2^4 - 2^{-3} - 1010.101 = 0101.010111\ldots$

Again arriving at an $(r-1)$'s complement of a number N requires some subtraction processes if the definition is followed explicitly. However, there is also a shortcut method for finding 1's complements that requires no subtraction. This is done quite simply by complementing each digit (0 or 1) of the number up to the most significant digit specified.

$$(\ldots 0001010.101000\ldots)_{1,c} = \ldots 1110101.010111\ldots$$

Subtraction with (r − 1)'s complements. The subtraction of two positive base r numbers M and S, $(M-S)$, goes as follows.

(1) Add M to the $(r-1)$'s complement of S.

(2) Check results for overflow carry:

    (a) If an overflow carry exists, add it to the least significant digit.

    (b) If an overflow carry *does not* exist, the result is negative. Therefore, complement the results and add a minus sign in front.

Consider the following examples:

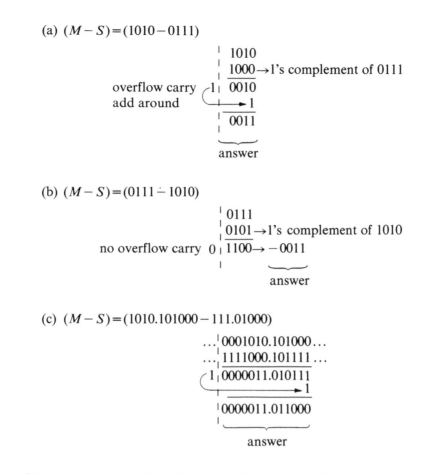

(a) $(M - S) = (1010 - 0111)$

$$1010$$
$$1000 \rightarrow \text{1's complement of 0111}$$
overflow carry $\overline{1}$ $\overline{0010}$
add around $\longrightarrow 1$
$$\overline{0011}$$

answer

(b) $(M - S) = (0111 - 1010)$

$$0111$$
$$0101 \rightarrow \text{1's complement of 1010}$$
no overflow carry 0 $1100 \rightarrow -0011$

answer

(c) $(M - S) = (1010.101000 - 111.01000)$

$$\dots 0001010.101000\dots$$
$$\dots 1111000.101111\dots$$
$$1\,0000011.010111$$
$$\longrightarrow 1$$
$$0000011.011000$$

answer

From this exercise we see that if the complement of a binary number is easily accomplished, the subtraction of this number from another is at most a three-step process, two of which use the same computer hardware required to perform a straight addition. The other (bit INVERSION) is a standard feature of most digital computers. Further, there are other special number notations related to digital computing. Those interested are referred to other references.

1-12 CODES

Coding and encoding is the process of assigning a group of binary digits, commonly referred to as "bits," to represent, tag, identify, or otherwise relate to multivalued items of information. By assigning each item of information a unique combination of bits (1's and 0's), we transform some given information into another form. In short, a CODE is a symbolic representation of an information transform. The bit combinations are referred to as "WORDS" or "CODE

WORDS." There are some other general definitions assigned to bit combinations, with which you should become familiar. These are:

> Bit—a binary digit (1 or 0)
> Bytes—usually a group of eight bits
> Nibbles—usually a group of four bits
> Words—a group of bytes; usually a word has two bytes or
> four nibbles

The encoding of information can be an intricate and involved process, particularly when data security is of importance. However, encoding is not nearly as difficult as *decoding* that same information without knowledge of the encoding scheme.

There are many different coding schemes, each having some particular advantages and characteristics. One of the main efforts in coding other than security is to standardize a set of universal codes that can be used by all. Some typical examples of codes are given as follows:

(1) binary codes
(2) binary coded decimal codes
(3) reflected codes
(4) unit distance codes
(5) alphameric codes
(6) error detecting codes

1-13 BINARY CODES

As illustrated in the analog-to-digital conversion example, there is a direct analogy among discrete signals, binary circuit elements (switches), and binary digits; and a combination of n binary digits can represent the conditions of n switching elements in a digital system. These conditions (voltage in electronic systems) can represent discrete elements of information other than simple numeric values. The assignment of "bit patterns" to discrete elements of information is generally referred to as binary coding. Two examples of binary coding schemes are illustrated in Figure 1-17. Note that Code X is a code for the decimal numbers 0 through 15 that assigns the binary codes which are equivalent to their numeric value. Code Y is encoded in yet another way.

If n elements of information in some form are to be coded with two-valued bits, the question arises as to how many bits are required to assign each element of the original information a unique code word (bit combination). It should be noted that *unique* is important, otherwise the code would be ambiguous. Probably the best way to approach the number of bits required to assign a unique code to any number of information elements is to evaluate how many unique code words can be derived from a combination of n bits.

Decimal Code	Four-bit Binary Code X	Four-bit Binary Code Y
0	0 0 0 0	0 0 0 0
1	0 0 0 1	0 0 1 0
2	0 0 1 0	0 1 0 0
3	0 0 1 1	0 1 1 0
4	0 1 0 0	1 0 0 0
5	0 1 0 1	1 0 1 0
6	0 1 1 0	1 1 0 0
7	0 1 1 1	1 1 1 0
8	1 0 0 0	1 1 1 1
9	1 0 0 1	1 1 0 1
10	1 0 1 0	1 0 1 1
11	1 0 1 1	1 0 0 1
12	1 1 0 0	0 1 1 1
13	1 1 0 1	0 1 0 1
14	1 1 1 0	0 0 1 1
15	1 1 1 1	0 0 0 1

Fig. 1-17. A simple example of binary codes assigned to the decimal numbers 0 through 15.

For example: Let n = number of bits in the code word and x = number of unique words.

$$\text{If } n=1, \text{ then } x = 2 \quad (0, 1)$$
$$n=2, \text{ then } x = 4 \quad (00, 01, 10, 11)$$
$$n=3, \text{ then } x = 8 \quad (000, 001, \ldots 111)$$
$$\vdots$$
$$n=j, \text{ then } x = 2^j$$

From this we can conclude that if we are given x elements of information to code into binary coded format, the following expression must hold:

$$x \leq 2^j$$
$$\text{or} \quad j \geq \log_2 x$$
$$\text{or} \quad j \geq 3.32 \log_{10} x$$

where j = number of bits in code word.

From this we can evaluate how many bits would be required to code the 26 alphabetic characters plus the 10 decimal digits as follows:

26 alphabetic symbols + 10 digits = 36 discrete elements of information

$$\therefore \ j \geq 3.32 \log_{10} \tag{36}$$
$$\text{or} \quad j \geq 5.16 \text{ bits}$$

Since bits are not defined in fractional parts, we know $j \geq 6$. In other words, a six-bit code would be required that leaves 28 unassigned code words out of the 64 which are possible.

1-14   BINARY CODED DECIMAL CODES

There are many Binary Coded Decimal codes (BCD), all of which are used to *represent decimal digits. Therefore, all BCD codes have at least four bits and at least six unassigned code words.* Some examples of BCD codes are shown in Table1-4. These are:

(1) 8421 BCD code, sometimes referred to as the Natural Binary Coded Decimal code (NBCD);
(2) Excess-3 code (XS3);
(3) 5421 code;
(4) $84 - 2 - 1$ code $(+8, +4, -2, -1)$;
(5) biquinary code.

TABLE 1-4   BCD codes

Decimal Value	8421 Code	Excess-3 Code (XS3)	5421 Code	$84 - 2 - 1^*$ Code	7421 Code	5311 Code	Biquinary
	8421	8421	5421	$84 - 2 - 1$	7421	5311	ABCDEFG
0	0000	0011	0000	0000	0000	0000	0100001
1	0001	0100	0001	0111	0001	0001	0100010
2	0010	0101	0010	0110	0010	0011	0100100
3	0011	0110	0011	0101	0011	0100	0101000
4	0100	0111	0100	0100	0100	0101	0110000
5	0101	1000	0101	1011	0101	1000	1000001
6	0110	1001	0110	1010	0110	1001	1000010
7	0111	1010	0111	1001	1000	1011	1000100
8	1000	1011	1011	1000	1001	1100	1001000
9	1001	1100	1100	1111	1010	1101	1010000

*Note: Dashes $(-)$ are minus signs.

There are many BCD codes that one can contrive by assigning each column or bit position in the code some weighting factor in such a way that all of the decimal digits can be coded by simply adding the assigned weights of the 1 bits in the code word.

For example: 9 is coded $\overset{8421}{1001}$ in NBCD, which is interpreted as

$$1 \times 8 + 0 \times 4 + 0 \times 2 + 1 \times 1 = 9$$

The NBCD code is a handy and widely used code for the representation of decimal quantities in a binary coded format.

For example: $(19.75)_{10}$ would be represented in NBCD as

$$(19.75)_{10} = (\overset{1}{\overbrace{0001}} \; \overset{9}{\overbrace{1001}} . \overset{7}{\overbrace{0111}} \; \overset{5}{\overbrace{0101}})_{NBCD}$$

It should be noted that on the per digit basis the NBCD code is the binary numeral equivalent of the decimal *digit* it represents.

As mentioned above, there are many possible weights that can be assigned in order to derive a BCD code; and because of this there are some desirable properties that one code has over another which makes it more applicable. At least two of these properties give some figure of merit to a given code. These are:

(1) The self-complementing property and
(2) the reflective property.

1-15 BCD CODE PROPERTIES

When arithmetic is to be performed, often an arithmetic "complement" of the numbers will be used in the computations. Certain codes have a distinct advantage in that their logical complement is the same as the arithmetic complement. For example, the 9's complement of an Excess-3 code word is the same as its logical complement. This has a particular advantage in machines that use decimal arithmetic. Some examples of this self-complementing feature in some BCD codes are shown in Table 1-5.

TABLE 1-5   Self-complementing BCD codes

Decimal Value	631 − 1 Code	2421 Code	Excess-3 Code
	631 − 1	2421	8421
0	0011	0000	0011
1	0010	0001	0100
2	0101	0010	0101
3	0111	0011	0110
4	0110	0100	0111
5	1001	1011	1000
6	1000	1100	1001
7	1010	1101	1010
8	1101	1110	1011
9	1100	1111	1100

The second property mentioned above was the "reflection" or "reflective" property. The 9's complement of a reflected BCD code word is formed simply by changing only one of its bits. A reflected code is characterized by the fact that it is imaged about the center entries with one bit changed. Some examples of reflective codes are shown in Table 1-6.

TABLE 1-6 Reflective BCD codes

Decimal Value	Code 1 ABCD	Code 2 WXYZ
0	0000	0100
1	0001	1010
2	0010	1000
3	0011	1110
4	0100	0000
5	1100	0001
6	1011	1111
7	1010	1001
8	1001	1011
9	1000	0101

The BCD codes are used widely and you should become familiar with their reason for existence and some of their applications. For instance, many of the hand-held calculators presently in use operate on NBCD representations of data.

1-16 UNIT DISTANCE CODES (UDC)

There are applications in which it is desirable to represent numerical as well as other information with a code that changes in only *one* bit position from one code word to the next adjacent word. This class of code is called a Unit Distance Code (UDC). The Unit Distance Codes are sometimes erroneously called "cyclic," "reflective," and "Gray Code" (a special case). As alluded to above, the unit distance property implies that only *one* bit changes in the next or adjacent code word independent of the direction taken in the code. See Table 1-7 for some examples of unit distance codes. The unit distance codes have special advantages in that they minimize what is termed "transitional" errors or "flashing," to which it is sometimes referred. These terms will be defined later in the text when unit distance codes are used for particular applications. The Gray Code shown in Table 1-8 is an interesting code that is both reflective and unit distance. Thus we see that the reflective and unit distance codes have overlap, as shown in Figure 1-18.

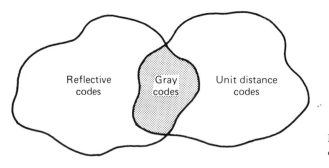

Fig. 1-18. An illustration of the overlap of reflective and unit distance codes.

TABLE 1-7   Unit distance codes

Decimal Value	Code I ABCD	Code II WXYZ	Code III RSTV
0	0000	0000	0000
1	0100	0001	1000
2	1100	0011	1001
3	1000	0010	0001
4	1001	0110	0011
5	1011	1110	0111
6	1111	1111	1111
7	0111	1101	1011
8	0011	1100	1010
9	0001	0100	0010

TABLE 1-8   Gray codes

Decimal Value	Three-bit Gray Code	Four-bit Gray Code
0	000	0000
1	001	0001
2	011	0011
3	010	0010
4	110	0110
5	111	0111
6	101	0101
7	100	0100
8	—	1100
9	—	1101
10	—	1111
11	—	1110
12	—	1010
13	—	1011
14	—	1001
15	—	1000

The Gray Code has some interesting applications in a special inter-domain converter called a positional or rotational encoder. A rotational encoder or shaft encoder is used to convert some angular position of a shaft to a digital format. A simple technique for this employs a photographic disk attached to the shaft. This disk has windows strategically placed in circular patterns through which light can pass and activate a photo sensor (light-sensitive switch). If these windows are arranged on the circumference of concentric circles around the center of the shaft, a digital code related to its angular position can be generated, as shown in Figure 1-19.

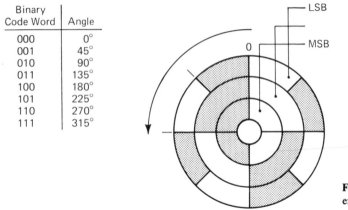

Binary Code Word	Angle
000	0°
001	45°
010	90°
011	135°
100	180°
101	225°
110	270°
111	315°

Fig. 1-19. Binary coded disk encoder (three bits).

From this figure we see that because of mechanical imperfections (improper photographic alignment), a straight binary code can lead to some errors. For example, note the transition from 45 to 90°. If, by some chance, at the transition from 001 to 010, a misalignment caused a transient code of 011 to appear, erroneous data would be received, that is, 001→011→010.

The Gray Coded disk will eliminate this by making certain that transition in one sensor's output takes place somewhere internal of the block of 1's or 0's in all the other columns or rings. Thus a Gray Coded disk shown in Figure 1-20 is much more forgiving than is the straight binary disk.

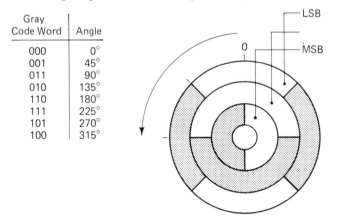

Gray Code Word	Angle
000	0°
001	45°
011	90°
010	135°
110	180°
111	225°
101	270°
100	315°

Fig. 1-20. Gray Coded disk encoder (three bits).

Another interesting thing about the Gray Code is that a *binary number sequence* can be converted to *a* Gray Code word by the following process:

(1) Place a leading zero before the most significant bit in the binary number in the sequence.
(2) Exclusive-OR adjacent bits together starting from the left of this number will result in the Gray Code equivalent of the binary number.*

---

*Definition of an EX-OR function is: If the two bits exclusive-OR'd are identical, the result is 0; if the two bits differ, the result is 1.

EXAMPLE *1-8:* Determine the Gray Code word for the binary representation of $(82)_{10}$ in the sequence of decimal numbers from 0 to 127.

$$(82)_{10} \rightarrow (1010010)_2$$

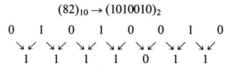

The inverse process (changing a Gray Coded word to its binary equivalent) is slightly more difficult. First, scan the Gray Code word from left to right. The first 1 encountered is copied exactly as it stands. From then on, 1's will be written until the next 1 is encountered, in which case a 0 is written. Then 0's are written until the next 1 is encountered, in which case a 1 is written, and so on. This is best illustrated with an example and the flow chart found in Figure 1-21. This flow chart is an excellent example of a sequential process and is given as an introductory example illustrating the important concept of sequential problem definition.

Fig. 1-21. A flow diagram illustrating the sequential procedure for the Gray Code to binary conversion.

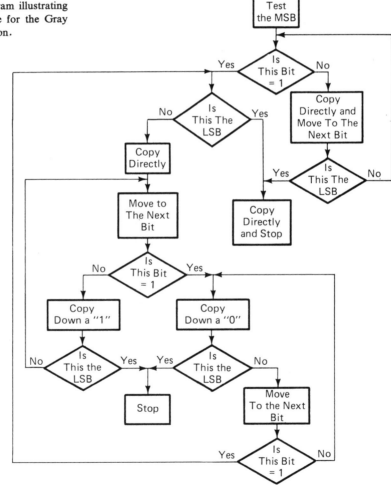

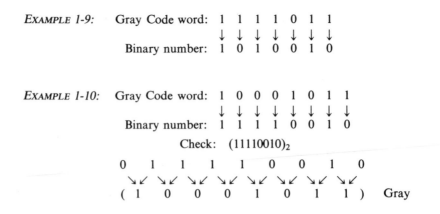

EXAMPLE 1-9:　Gray Code word: 1 1 1 1 0 1 1
　　　　　　　　　　　　　　↓ ↓ ↓ ↓ ↓ ↓ ↓
　　　　　　　Binary number: 1 0 1 0 0 1 0

EXAMPLE 1-10:　Gray Code word: 1 0 0 0 1 0 1 1
　　　　　　　　　　　　　　↓ ↓ ↓ ↓ ↓ ↓ ↓ ↓
　　　　　　　Binary number: 1 1 1 1 0 0 1 0

Check: $(11110010)_2$

0 1 1 1 1 0 0 1 0
(1   0   0   0   1   0   1   1) Gray

1-17 ALPHAMERIC CODES

When the information to be encoded includes entities other than numerical values, an expanded code is required. For example, alphabetic characters $(A, B, \ldots, Z)$ and special operation symbols like $+, -, /, *, ($, and other special symbols are used in digital systems. Codes that include alphabetic characters are commonly referred to as ALPHAMERIC CODES. These additional information entities can be encoded by simply adding extra bits to the code words. However, because there are a great number of schemes to encode information, the decoding process becomes a difficult problem when one man's machine is connected with another man's machine, both of which encode and decode a basic character set in different ways. Because of this problem, there have been attempts to standardize codes related to alphameric data. Furthermore, specific codes have been developed for specific information media. For example, there are specific codes for punched cards, paper tape, and so forth. The five-bit teletypewriter code is an example of a code developed for a particular data communication device. This five-bit code is sometimes referred to as the Baudot (baw-doe) code and uses only five data bits to encode 45 elements of information. This is done by using the special character (mode change) to separate alphabetic characters from the numeric related characters. The use of this mode-changes character creates the illusion that five bits can be used to encode 45 elements of information. However, if one looks more closely, the fundamentals still hold.

Another widely used alphameric code is the ASCII (ask-key) code, which stands for the *American Standard Code for Information Interchange*, and is shown in Table 1-9. ASCII is a seven-bit code and includes special informative control characters such as ACK, BEL, and so forth used for teletype and other data communication devices. Another alphameric code called the EBCDIC is shown in Table 1-10. EBCDIC (eb-sid-dic) stands for the *Extended Binary Coded Decimal Interchange Code.*

TABLE 1-9   The ASCII code*

b_4	b_3	b_2	b_1	b_7 → 0 b_6 → 0 b_5 → 0	0 0 1	0 1 0	0 1 1	1 0 0	1 0 1	1 1 0	1 1 1
				0	1	2	3	4	5	6	7
0	0	0	0	0	NUL	DLE	SP	0	@	P	'	p
0	0	0	1	1	SOH	DC1	!	1	A	Q	a	q
0	0	1	0	2	STX	DC2	"	2	B	R	b	r
0	0	1	1	3	ETX	DC3	#	3	C	S	c	s
0	1	0	0	4	EOT	DC4	$	4	D	T	d	t
0	1	0	1	5	ENQ	NAK	%	5	E	U	e	u
0	1	1	0	6	ACK	SYN	&	6	F	V	f	v
0	1	1	1	7	BEL	ETB	'	7	G	W	g	w
1	0	0	0	8	BS	CAN	(	8	H	X	h	x
1	0	0	1	9	HT	EM	)	9	I	Y	i	y
1	0	1	0	A	LF	SUB	*	:	J	Z	j	z
1	0	1	1	B	VT	ESC	+	;	K	[	k	{
1	1	0	0	C	FF	FS	,	<	L	\	l	|
1	1	0	1	D	CR	GS	-	=	M	]	m	}
1	1	1	0	E	SO	RS	.	>	N	∧	n	~
1	1	1	1	F	SI	US	/	?	O	—	o	DEL

*The code is read from this table as:

	b_7	b_6	b_5	b_4	b_3	b_2	b_1
$ =	0	1	0	0	1	0	0
A =	1	0	0	0	0	0	1

At the present time ASCII is becoming the standard code for most data communication networks. It is used with practically all data communication media except punched cards, which use a 12-bit Hollerith code. Therefore, the ASCII Code is one well worth becoming familiar with.

TABLE 1.10 The EBCDIC code

b_8					*1*	*1*	*1*	*1*	*0*	*0*	*0*	*0*
	b_7				*1*	*1*	*1*	*1*	*1*	*1*	*1*	*1*
		b_6			*0*	*0*	*1*	*1*	*0*	*0*	*1*	*1*
			b_5		*0*	*1*	*0*	*1*	*0*	*1*	*0*	*1*
b_4	b_3	b_2	b_1		C	D	E	F	4	5	6	7
0	0	0	0	0				0	Blank		−	
0	0	0	1	1	A	J		1			/	
0	0	1	0	2	B	K	S	2				
0	0	1	1	3	C	L	T	3				
0	1	0	0	4	D	M	U	4				
0	1	0	1	5	E	N	V	5				
0	1	1	0	6	F	O	W	6				
0	1	1	1	7	G	P	X	7				
1	0	0	0	8	H	Q	Y	8				
1	0	0	1	9	I	R	Z	9				
1	0	1	0	A								
1	0	1	1	B					.	$	,	
1	1	0	0	C						*		
1	1	0	1	D					(	)	'	
1	1	1	0	E					+			=

1-18 ERROR CODES

When information is transformed and transmitted from one medium to another, the possibility of a bit being lost (changed due to a transient failure) in the process becomes a point of interest. This is particularly true when considering that millions of bits per second are manipulated in a typical digital system. It is interesting to contemplate how complex digital systems function reliably. For example, a system with which the author was involved had a mixture of approximately 0.2 lb of silicon and 11 miles of wire, through which electron flow was directed. It almost boggles the mind to think that in order for that system to function properly, all those electrons had to be at the right place at the right time. Aside from this, because of high data rates, high data integrity is required, or at least a violation of data integrity must be detectable.

A simple process of adding a special code bit to a data word can improve the data integrity in digital systems. This extra bit will allow the detection of a single error in a given code word in which it is used, and it is called the PARITY BIT. The encoding of a simple parity bit is done on an odd or even basis. The odd or even designation of a code word may be determined by the actual number of 1's in the data word (including the parity bit) to which this parity bit is attached. For example, the A in ASCII is coded

$$(A) \rightarrow (100\ 0001)_{\text{ASCII}}$$

An *A* in ASCII when coded with odd parity could be shown as

Parity bit $\rightarrow$ 1100 0001} (A)<small>ASCII WITH ODD PARITY</small>

Note the actual number of 1's in the complete word equals three, an odd number. The ASCII *A* with even parity could be coded as

Parity bit $\rightarrow$ 0100 0001} (A)<small>ASCII WITH EVEN PARITY</small>

In this case the number of 1's in the complete code word is two, an even number. Thus, the parity encoding scheme is a simple one and requires only one extra bit. In a system using odd parity, if a code word is found that contains an even number of 1's, we know immediately that one or more of the data bits or the parity bit is incorrect. Hence, this is an erroneously transmitted piece of information, and we have achieved single-error detection. If two bits are transmitted incorrectly, however, the addition of a parity bit will not be of any use in detecting the error. Just how much does this extra bit buy us in terms of data integrity? It would be nice to know how much more reliable our information is because of the addition of this parity bit. This can be illustrated by an example.

> EXAMPLE 1-11: Suppose we have a digital system that transmits eight-bit data words and based on some previous statistical measurement it is determined that the probability of a *single* bit being lost (changed) is 1 in 10,000 operations (or $P_1 = 10^{-4}$). A parity bit is added to this system to detect this simple error. Now the question is, how much more reliable has our system been made by adding the parity bit? Or, in short, what is the probability of two errors existing together?
>
> To evaluate this we must know how many combinations of bits can be derived from an eight-bit word by changing two bits.
>
> **Answer:**
>
> $$_nC_m = \frac{n!}{(n-m)!(m!)} = \text{no. of combinations of } m \text{ elements in a total of} n$$
>
> $$_8C_2 = \frac{8!}{6!2!} = 28$$

Hence we see that there are 28 combinations involving two bits in an eight-bit word.

Now from probability theory if P_1 is the probability of one error occurring, then P_x (x errors) $= (P_1)^x (1-P_1)^{n-m} \cdot {_nC_m}$. Thus we see:

$$P_2 \text{ (probability of two errors existing)} = (P_1)^2 (1-P_1)^6 {_8C_2}$$

$$P_2 = (10^{-4})^2 (1-10^{-4})^6 (28)$$

$$\text{or } P_2 = 28 \times 10^{-8}$$

which says the probability of two errors is 28 in one hundred million.

From this we can conclude that by adding a simple bit to detect a single error the data integrity has been increased 357 times.

1-19 OTHER ERROR DETECTING AND CORRECTING CODES

Brief mention of parity checking has been made to illustrate the idea of improving data transmission through the process of adding redundant "checking bits" to a given code word. This process allows us to detect when an error has occurred, but we still don't know which of the bits has been transmitted in error. The addition of a "parity word" at the end of a block of information (a group of code words) can serve to provide parity check in another dimension. If we can identify the code word that has an error with the parity bit, and the column in which that error occurs by way of the parity word, we have the ability to correct the wrong bit of information. Hence, this scheme is referred to, in general, as a single error detecting, single error correcting, coding scheme. (It is also referred to as vertical and horizontal redundancy check, or cross-parity checking.) Figure 1-22 illustrates this idea.

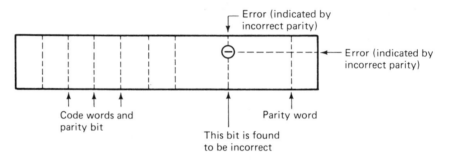

Fig. 1-22. Vertical and horizontal redundancy checking scheme.

Another single error detecting, single error correcting, code is one invented by Hamming. It is a distance-3 code; that is, there are at least three bits that differ from any given code word to any other given code word. This allows the detection/correction feature. Many more codes could be discussed that are used in data encription and encoding to preserve data integrity. These are left for you to pursue on your own, with only this brief mention to incite interest.

1-20 ONCE OVER LIGHTLY

You undoubtedly, through your experience, have been introduced to one of the major digital applications, *the digital computer*. Certainly the digital computer includes just about every facet of digital design and thus it serves as an excellent example of, as well as a monument to, the application of digital principles. It is not our task to design a computer, but the hardware aspects related to a computer design are covered. To this point, you have covered the introductory aspects of some of the language systems in general, number systems and inter-domain conversion. The purpose of this section is to further familiarize you with things to come and to help you determine the direction of your studies.

Digital design is like any other design methdology in which a logical sequence of steps is followed, tried, reviewed, compromised, modified, and finalized. Keep in mind that compromises and trade-offs are natural and necessary exercises in any design effort. In general, meeting-the-spec in digital design is developing a system that performs the desired task under a prescribed set of input conditions. The input/output relation dictates the type of design approach to be taken. For example, if an output is to be generated strictly on the basis of the present input conditions, then we have what is commonly referred to as a COMBINATIONAL SYSTEM. On the other hand, if the output is dependent on a *sequence* of input conditions, then we have what is called a SEQUENTIAL SYSTEM. Of course, the majority of task performing systems will require a mixture of both combinational and sequential subsystems. A good deal more will be covered with regard to these two systems.

(1) AND gates
(2) OR gates
(3) NAND gates
(4) NOR gates
(5) INVERTERS
(6) DECODERS
(7) ENCODERS
(8) MULTIPLEXERS
(9) FLIP/FLOPS
(10) REGISTERS–COUNTERS
(11) READ-ONLY-MEMORIES
(12) RANDOM-ACCESS-MEMORIES
(13) PROGRAMMABLE-LOGIC-ARRAYS
(14) MICROPROCESSORS

16-LEAD HERMETIC DUAL IN-LINE PACKAGE TYPE C

18-LEAD HERMETIC DUAL IN-LINE PACKAGE TYPE C

22-LEAD HERMETIC DUAL IN-LINE PACKAGE TYPE C

28-LEAD HERMETIC DUAL IN-LINE PACKAGE TYPE C

24-LEAD HERMETIC DUAL IN-LINE PACKAGE TYPE C

40-LEAD HERMETIC DUAL IN-LINE PACKAGE TYPE C

Fig. 1-23. Logic design device packages. (Courtesy of Intel)

Once the system specifications are understood and the appropriate word statement to logic notation transformations are made, the designer must translate the specifications to a hardware realization. At this point he must be familiar with hardware device operational characteristics, device symbology, and digital signal generation. This entails being familiar with integrated circuit (IC) logic design devices, some of which are shown in Figure 1-23. Being familiar with symbology entails visual recognition of the distinctively shaped symbols like the ones shown in Figure 1-24. The actual operational characteristics of the hardware devices these symbols represent are introduced in Chapter 2. It should be noted that these schematic symbols are to be referred to as graphical depictions of logic *functions*, NOT depictions of logic *gates*. A great deal of effort is spent drawing the distinction between *functions* and *gates* in Chapter 2. By doing this, some interesting hardware synthesis techniques are developed.

(a)   (b)

Fig. 1-24. Some example symbology for two standard logic operators.

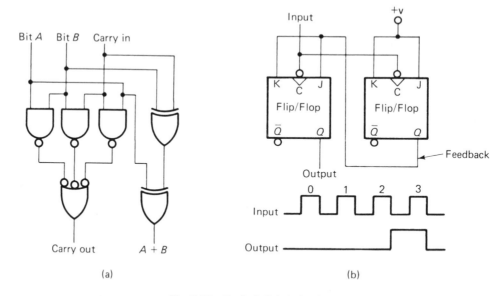

(a)   (b)

Fig. 1-25. Typical digital circuits.

As mentioned earlier, the two major segments of logic design are combinational design and sequential design. To illustrate the application of digital design, consider the two circuits shown in Figure 1-25. Shown in Figure 1-25(a) is a typical example of a combination circuit, which is used to arithmetically add two single-bit binary digits along with the carry-in from the next least significant column of digits and generate a column sum and a carry-out, which becomes the carry-in for the next significant column adder circuit. Circuits such as these are cascaded to build *n* bit adders in digital computers. It is true that circuits like the adder are presently developed and packaged ready for interconnection, so little or no adder design is required. However, there are many other applications where actual grass root design is required, resulting in combinational circuits with complexity similar to that of the adder.

The circuit shown in Figure 1-25(b) is a typical example of a SEQUEN-TIAL circuit. This circuit is designed with *feedback* (from output to input) in order to cause the output function to be a sequential function of its input. This four-pulse counter is designed to cause the output to make a complete transition after four input pulses are received. It is quite plain to see that this circuit has some memory capability, illustrated by its ability to store the occurrence of the first three input pulses.

We find that sequential circuits are of great interest in digital design. Further, we find that a digital computer when viewed from a global aspect is by definition a sequential system. Thus considerable time is spent on the application and design of sequential circuits.

The word LOGIC and its application is closely allied with digital design, which may or may not be entirely correct, based on its definition. In a general sense *logic is a process of classifying information*, which is countered with the two rather humorous definitions:

> Logic is the study of the workings of the mind when the mind is working the way it ought to work.
>
> *A. R. Turquette*

> Digital logic is the study of the workings of the mind that can only count to 2!
>
> *Bitter Analog Designer*

In any case, the proper design of digital systems requires thought processes that are both combinational and sequential in nature. To test your ability to interpret a problem, think logically and organize your thought processes such that these exercises result in a meaningful solution. Consider the following examples.

EXAMPLE 1-12: Suppose you were incarcerated in some strange, far-off land, and one day the ruthless leader of this land had you brought into a room with two doors in it. By each door stands a man. The leader says to you: You have two choices to determine your destiny. They are: (1) You can stay in prison for the rest of your life, or (2) you can ask one question directed to *one* of these men...not both, just one. One man is standing by the door of freedom; the other is standing by a door behind which is a firing squad. One wants you to die, the other wants you to go free. But you don't know which is which.

Further, there is no guarantee that the man who wants you to die is standing by the door of death. Also, one man is bound to always lie and the other is bound to always tell the truth. What single question can you ask to guarantee freedom?

This example, the next example, and several problem exercises come from a collection of brain-teasers the author has accumulated over the years. Unfortunately, the authors are unknown, but whoever they are the author gives credit. The previous example is a classic combinational problem. The next example is one of sequential nature.

> EXAMPLE 1-13:   You are given seven identical looking rings of golden color. Six of these rings are identical brass rings and the other is gold. Further, you are given a weighing balance. Find the gold ring in two weighings. Work out a foolproof algorithm (set of processing steps) for finding the gold ring.

It has been found that students that do well with problems such as these also find digital design fun and exciting. How did you do?

1-21   SUMMARY

Chapter 1 has given a general introduction to the topic of digital systems. Advances in technology over the years have given rise to a tremendous growth in the industry incorporating more and more "ability" for fewer and fewer dollars, and consuming smaller and smaller physical space. Such is the trend at present also. We have covered the background of where it all comes from; some of the details involved with the number systems used internally to computers were discussed as well as means of conveying alphabetic information with similar representations—namely codes. It is hoped that this brief introduction will serve as a basis for a more detailed examination of the fundamental entities involved in digital systems, which is the topic of discussion in Chapter 2.

BIBLIOGRAPHY

1.   *Analog-Digital Conversion Handbook*, the Engineering Staff of Analog Devices, Inc., edited by Daniel H. Sheingold. Analog Devices, Norwood, Mass. 1972.

2.   CHU, Y. *Digital Computer Design Fundamentals*. New York: McGraw-Hill, 1962.

3.   DAVENPORT, WILLIAM P. *Modern Data Communication: Concepts, Language and Media*. Rochelle Park, N. J: Hayden, 1971.

4.   FIXX, JAMES F. *Games for the Super-intelligent*. Popular Library, 1972.

5.   FLORES, I. *The Logic of Computer Arithmetic*. Englewood Cliffs, N. J.: Prentice-Hall, 1963.

6.   HAMMING, R. W. Error Detecting and Error Correcting Codes. *BSTJ*, **29**, no. 2 (1950), pp. 147–160.

7. HOESCHELE, DAVID F., JR. *Analog to Digital / Digital to Analog Conversion Techniques.* New York: Wiley, 1968.

8. MARCUS, MITCHELL P. *Switching Circuits for Engineers*, Englewood Cliffs, N.J.: Prentice-Hall, 1967.

9. MCCLUSKEY, E. J. *Introduction to the Theory of Switching Circuits.* New York: McGraw-Hill, 1965.

10. PHISTER, MONTGOMERY, JR. *Logical Design of Digital Computers.* New York: Wiley, 1968.

11. STEPHENSON, BARBERA W. *Analog-Digital Conversion Handbook.* Maynard, Mass.: Digital Equipment Corporation, 1964.

PROBLEMS AND EXERCISES

1-1. Define a "system."

1-2. Define a (a) continuous and (b) discrete process and outline the basic differences between the two.

1-3. Define a (a) linear system and (b) nonlinear system and outline the basic difference between the two.

1-4. List six of the most important advantages digital (discrete) systems have over analog (continuous) systems.

1-5. List the five basic components of any language. Give examples of each (not those in the text).

1-6. What are the major areas of involvement for electrical and digital engineers?

1-7. Define an inter-domain converter. Give at least two specific examples.

1-8. You are asked to build an A/D converter whose output is $\pm 0.1\%$ accurate.
(a) How many bits will be required if a standard binary code is used if the converter has been designed for a range from 0 to 10 volts maximum signal?
(b) What will be the digital output if a 6.5-volt signal is the analog input?

1-9. Write the first ten digits of base 2, base 4, and base 7.

1-10. Convert 421.6095 to binary, octal, and hexadecimal.

1-11. Perform the following conversions.
(a) 34567_8 to _____ $_{10}$
(b) 143112_5 to _____ $_7$
(c) $A98B_{12}$ to _____ $_3$
(d) $EF64H_{20}$ to _____ $_6$

1-12. Complete the following conversions between the number systems.
(a) 42_5 to _____ $_7$
(b) 101011.1011_2 to _____ $_{10}$
(c) 1001100110_2 to _____ $_8$
(d) $7E2C_{16}$ to _____ $_2$
(e) 38.65_{10} to _____ $_2$
(f) 347_8 to _____ $_{16}$

1-13. Perform the following operations.

(a) 1001_2
1101_2
$+1111_2$
$(?)_2$

(b) 41531_8
$+ 3641_8$
$(?)_8$

(c) 234.5_6
$+ 34.2_6$
$(?)_6$

(d) 100.1011_2
$- 11.11_2$
$(?)_2$

(e) 75.63_8
$- 14.36_8$
$(?)_8$

(f) 1343.11_5
$- 332.21_5$
$(?)_5$

(g) 40862_9
$\times 3746_9$
$(?)_9$

(h) 11.1001001001_2
$\times 10.11_2$
$(?)_2$

(i) $A96_{12}$
$\times 68_{12}$
$(?)_{12}$

(j) $1011_2 \div 11010010_2$

(k) $210_3 \div 12_3$

(l) $98BC_{14} \div 87_{14}$

1-14. Convert:
(a) 226.978_{10} to binary, octal, hexadecimal
(b) 1101100101.11011011_2 to octal, hexadecimal
(c) $7AD.EF_{16}$ to binary, octal
(d) 126.76_8 to binary, hexadecimal

1-15. Convert the following decimal numbers to binary and find the 1's and 2's complements:
(a) 15   (c) 846   (e) 349.786
(b) 123   (d) 115.74

1-16. Perform the subtraction on the following decimal numbers by using 9's and 10's complements.
(a) $6251 - 433$ (c) $3674 - 598$
(b) $834 - 562$ (d) $347 - 491$

1-17. Using 1's and 2's complement perform the following subtractions.
(a) $100110 - 11011$ (c) $10011.1101 - 101.11$
(b) $1101010 - 110100$ (d) $1010 - 11011$

1-18. (a) Describe the process of coding.
(b) Define bit, byte, nibble, and word.
(c) List the six common codes.

1-19. How many bits would be required to encode:
(a) 56 elements of information?
(b) 131 elements of information?

1-20. Represent the number 6820_{10} in
(a) NBCD   (c) 2421
(b) XS3   (d) as a binary number

1-21. Develop two different four-bit unit distance codes.

1-22. How many four-bit unique Gray Codes can you derive?

1-23. Develop six different three-bit code sequences (with eight code words) that are both unit distance and reflective.

1-24. Determine the Gray Code for
(a) 42_{10} (b) 97_{10}

1-25. Write your complete name in
(a) ASCII
(b) EBCDIC

1-26. (a) Develop an eight-bit ASCII code sequence for your name with odd parity.
(b) Convert that sequence to Hex.

1-27. If the probability of one error occurring in a digital transmission system is 1 in 10^6 bits, this system transmits 16-bit words. What would be the data integrity improvement made by adding a parity bit check?

1-28. Develop a six-bit, four-word block of data with horizontal and vertical redundancy scheme. Then introduce an error in your block of data and demonstrate how your error-correcting scheme can be used to find the error.

1-29. Find and correct the error in the following code sequence:

$$\text{Parity bit} \rightarrow 10110$$
$$00001$$
$$11111$$
$$10100$$
$$10000$$
$$01110$$
$$11001$$
$$10101$$
$$01110$$
$$11101 \leftarrow \text{parity word}$$

1-30. Suppose you were out walking one day, looking for a good-looking mate. You come upon a junction in the road. One of the roads leads to the land of the UGLIES and the other leads to the land of the CUTIES, but there are no signs indicating which road leads to which land. Under bilateral agreement, the leaders of the two kingdoms station one of their men at the junction, but you don't know if the man is from the land of the uglies or the cuties. All you do know is that a man from the land of the uglies always *lies* and a man from the land of the cuties always tells the truth. You are allowed but one question to find your way to the land of the cuties. What would your question be?

1-31. Given the following data and the knowledge that Dwight has been killed, determine who killed him. You have three suspects, named Al, Bill, and Charlie. Two of them are lawyers. They each make two statements, for a total of six statements. There are only two true statements. A lawyer killed Dwight.

Statements:

Al: I am not a lawyer.
I did not kill Dwight.

Bill: I am a lawyer.
I did not kill Dwight.

Charlie: I am not a lawyer.
A lawyer killed Dwight.

1-32. Who owns the Zebra? The facts essential to solving the problem—which can be solved by combining deduction, analysis, and sheer persistence—are as follows:

1. There are five houses, each a different color and inhabited by men of different nationalities, with different pets, drinks, and cars.
2. The Englishman lives in the red house.
3. The Spaniard owns the dog.
4. Cocoa is drunk in the green house.
5. The Ukrainian drinks eggnog.
6. The green house is immediately to the right (your right) of the ivory house.
7. The Oldsmobile owner owns snails.
8. The owner of the Ford lives in the yellow house.
9. Milk is drunk in the middle house.
10. The Norwegian lives in the first house on the left.
11. The man who owns a Chevrolet lives in the house next to the house where the man owns a fox.
12. The Ford owner's house is next to the house where the horse is kept.
13. The Mercedes-Benz owner drinks orange juice.
14. The Japanese drives a Volkswagen.
15. The Norwegian lives next to the blue house.

Now, who drinks water? And who owns the zebra?

1-33. You are given nine identical-looking rings of golden color. Eight of these rings are identical brass rings and the other is gold. You are given a weighing balance. Find the gold ring in two weighings on the balance scales.

1-34. This time you are given 12 rings and one of these rings is different from the others, but you don't know if it is lighter or heavier than the others. Identify the special ring in three weighings and determine whether it is lighter or heavier than the others.

CHAPTER **2**

DIGITAL DESIGN FUNDAMENTALS

2-1 INTRODUCTORY COMMENTS

Experience has shown that the material presented in this chapter requires a proper introduction. Without this introduction, some difficulty has been experienced at times in instructing others in the proper use of a special schematic notation designed for developing the sound thought processes and the readable circuit diagrams required in digital design. You will find that if you have little or no digital design background, this special notation should present no particular problem provided you grasp the real intent of concepts set forth and use these concepts for the purposes for which they were intended. However, to those of you who have digital design backgrounds and are unfamiliar with this notation, you are asked to submit yourself to a significant relearning process. Figure 2-1 illustrates this special notation contrasted with the more traditional notation. From this

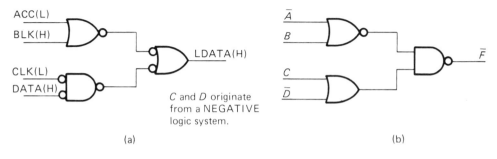

(a)

(b)

Fig. 2-1. An example contrasting (a) the schematic notation developed in this chapter with (b) the more traditional notation.

illustration you see that the two circuit representations are quite different in appearance even though the function is identical for both. Further, you will find that the notation presented here is widely accepted by industry, as a survey of manufacturer's device data sheets and industrial schematic diagrams will reveal. Because of this and the fact that the rest of this text is developed around this notation, it is strongly recommended that this material *not* be taken lightly.

In the next section we introduce the concepts that underpin this notation. Read them carefully.

2-2 INTRODUCTORY CONCEPTS OF DIGITAL DESIGN

George Boole, in his work entitled *An Investigation of the Laws of Thought, on which are Founded the Mathematical Theories of Logic and Probability* (1854), introduced the fundamental concepts of a two-valued (binary) system called Boolean Algebra. This work was later organized and systemized by Claude Shannon in *Symbolic Analysis of Relay and Switching Circuits* (1938). Digital design since that time has been pretty much standard, following Boole's and Shannon's fundamentals, with added refinements here and there as new knowledge has been unearthed and more exotic logic devices have been developed.

Digital design as treated in this text is the field of study relating the adaptation of LOGIC concepts to the design of recognizable, realizable, and reliable digital hardware. The following discussion is an introduction to some engineering approaches to applied thought processes or at least some different conceptualizations of practical logic processes. It is not a direct head-to-head confrontation with the more traditional approaches, but is merely a presentation of different ways of looking at the same old things. These concepts have been considered worthy of mention because they have been found, when properly applied, to aid the digital designer in reaching his goals in a straightforward manner.

These concepts are also an attempt to standardize a logic "ACTION" description and definition for the purpose of improving the designer's insight to logic design and documentation. When used properly, these concepts transfer the idea of a "dynamic" or action-related approach to logic thought.

Through experience it has been found that the main advantages of using the concepts set forward here lie in the field of higher level digital system design, and the larger the design task, the more applicable these concepts become. However, if these techniques are practiced *and applied* to the more traditional "small scale designs," they become natural and easy to extend to system level design application. They also lend themselves very nicely to the DIGITAL DESIGN LANGUAGE AND PROGRAMMED LOGIC approaches to system design. The DIGITAL DESIGN LANGUAGE approach to digital design is presently gaining prominence and is described nicely by the following description of DIDL taken as a quote from Dr. A. M. Despain's paper, *DIDL: A Multi-level Digital Hardware Design Language.*

DIDL is an acronym for "DIGITAL INTEGRATED DE-SIGN LANGUAGE." It is a specialized language system for use in the design, design automation, documentation, and simulation of all digital systems including digital computers. It is a formal, block-structured, multi-level, register transfer type language. Separation of the control and the data path of a system is allowed so that either software or hardware control implementation can be employed. DIDL also has macro definition and procedure capabilities. It is useful for initial system specification, various levels of design, and simulation down to the logic level.

This quote leads you to understand that sophisticated digital design capabilities and techniques do, in fact, exist. However, before you can grasp the real impact of these powerful techniques, you should gain considerable practical experience. Therefore, when we begin a study of logic, digital logic, binary systems, switching circuits, or any other field of study that can be classified as being related to digital design, we must concern ourselves with learning some philosophical premises from which we must launch our studies. In order to reach a desirable theoretical, as well as conceptual, understanding of digital design, you must grasp some fundamental definitions and insight-giving concepts. This is true independent of the field of study and it is particularly important in the field of digital design, because often slanted meanings and feelings are adopted early and these, though not completely wrong, tend to lead to some confusion and frustration later.

Concepts. Generally speaking, being involved in digital design is dealing in "LOGIC," a term that certainly needs some definition. LOGIC, by definition, *is a process of classifying information. Information is intelligence related to ideas, meanings, and actions which can be processed or transformed into other forms.* For example, NEWS is information by virtue of the fact that it is intelligence related to ACTIONS, be it good news or bad news. News can be heard, read, seen, even felt or any combination of all four, indicating the possibility of its transformation into different forms. "BINARY LOGIC," or two-valued logic, *is a process of classifying information into two classes.* Traditionally, binary arguments, or that information which can be definitely classified as two-valued, has been deemed either TRUE or FALSE. Thus, the Boolean variable is unlike the algebraic variables of the field of real numbers in that any Boolean variable can take on only *two* values, the TRUE or the FALSE. Though certainly applicable to *arguments* and *conditions*, this TRUE/FALSE classification for digital design is *not* really optimal. This nonoptimal classification stems from the fact that digital hardware design is generally a process of organizing hardware for the express purpose of classifying information ACTIONS. What this statement implies is that the hardware in a digital system should be organized to process the input information entities defined as "binary input actions" and in turn generate some "binary output actions," which is to be thought of as a dynamic process.

What is implied here by ACTION is that most hardware responses are directly related to some *physical operation* or some *condition* resulting from a *physical operation*. For example, the operation of manually changing the position of a switch on the front panel of a computer is to be considered an ACTION. This ACTION in turn changes a voltage condition at the input of some hardware device somewhere in the internal workings of the computer. This action-related voltage change in turn is to be interpreted by the hardware as a transformed physical action equivalent to the actual switch movement on the front panel. The voltage change can be interpreted as the representation of the *physical action*. Further, once this action-related voltage is received by the hardware, it is to be conditioned by this hardware for the purpose of generating some resultant binary output actions.

Once the concept of binary ACTIONS is understood, it can be seen that classifying an ACTION as TRUE or FALSE somehow does not "ring clear." This is because grammatically an adjective should not modify a verb. To illustrate this rather clumsy TRUE/FALSE classification for action-related signals, consider for a moment that you have a "Register" which is a multi-bit storage element in your system. See Figure 2-2. This register is "loaded" (data stored) when a high to low voltage transition is seen at its LOAD control input. Further, consider that this loading signal is given the title of: "LOAD REGISTER A," which will be shortened subsequently. Certainly this phrase, LOAD REGISTER A, is an action-related statement that creates some image of the actual edge-loading of the register. Therefore, to say LOAD REGISTER A IS TRUE as is done traditionally seems somewhat clumsy and void of the intended message. However, the intended message becomes much clearer if the loading signal is given the following label: "LOAD REGISTER A IS ASSERTED LOW," *which is to be interpreted as: The action "LOAD REGISTER A" is to be invoked when the signal so described transfers to the low voltage level.* The verb IS ASSERTED enhances the action description more appropriately than does the adjective TRUE. The actual definition of ASSERT is to avow or affirm or in some way *declare a position*. The word ASSERTED, though not strictly applicable to a hardware concept, does most aptly *declare a voltage position*, and does so with more clarity than does the adjective TRUE. But certainly we cannot be expected to fill out schematic diagrams with lengthy messages such as: "LOAD REGISTER A IS ASSERTED LOW." However, we can adopt a special shortened format for all our signal "names"; this format will be

(ACTION)(ASSERTED signal condition)

These special shortened names we call *"Polarized Mnemonics"* (nem-on-ik). To illustrate the use of a polarized mnemonic, consider the equivalence of

LOAD REGISTER A	IS ASSERTED LOW	and	LDREGA(L)
DESCRIPTION OF THE LOGIC ACTION	SIGNAL LEVEL AT which the ACTION takes place		

where the shortened message is broken down as follows:

$$\underbrace{\text{LDREGA}}_{\substack{\text{de-} \\ \text{scribes} \\ \text{ACTION} \\ \text{(mnemonic)}}} \qquad \underbrace{\text{(L)}}_{\substack{\text{defines} \\ \text{signal} \\ \text{level} \\ \text{(Polarizing} \\ \text{Element)}}} \qquad \text{where} \quad \text{(L) implies} \quad \text{LOW}$$

An alternate polarized mnenomic like

LDREGA (0), where (0) implies LOW

could also be defined; however this style is not often used.

Figure 2-2 demonstrates the schematic use of the polarized mnemonic LDREGA(L).

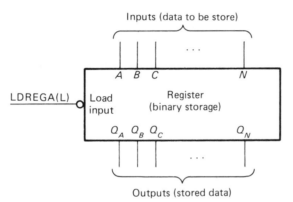

Fig. 2-2. The schematic usage of a polarized mnemonic.

From this we can see that the use of verbs such as ASSERTED, EXCITED, or INVOKED can be used to modify an ACTION related logic message and does so by directing your attention to the signal condition under which the ACTION is to be performed. There will be more discussion concerning the use of action-related mnemonics or polarized mnemonics throughout this chapter.

In summary, *"ASSERTED" as it relates to digital design is defined as: the affirmative position of an ACTION related Boolean variable (mnemonic)*. Further, in order to realize the true value of a polarized mnemonic it *must* be synthesized (spelled, if you wish) in such a way as to explicitly or implicitly describe a specific logic operation. For example, a logic operation describing a physical action of "DELAY DATA" would be given a mnemonic like "DD" or "DLAY D." or "D DAT." Therefore, when generating a mnemonic, be as creative as you wish, but remember that the spirit of the process is to create a shortened name that will jog the memory to recall the logic ACTION it was designed to emulate. Now, if the logic operation is *being performed* (data is being delayed), we say that the Boolean variable is ASSERTED. It follows that if the logic operation is *not being performed*, we say that the Boolean variable is NOT-ASSERTED. Traditionally, it is standard to use the shorthand symbols 1 for TRUE and 0 for FALSE. *In this text we will adopt 1 to imply ASSERTED and 0 to imply NOT-ASSERTED.* However, keep in mind that 1's and 0's are also used for numeric values (binary numbers) and as high and low voltage indicators as well. For the experienced, being able to discern the implied meaning of a 1 or 0 is no real problem, but for the beginner it can be a bit confusing. Because of this, the alternate polarized mnemonic style,

LDREG(0) or LDREG 0

will be used sparingly, giving way to the more obvious mnemonics that are polarized (H) or (L). For example:

DLAYD(H) and LDREG(L)

Before we leave the subject of comparing the TRUE/FALSE classification with the ASSERTED/NOT-ASSERTED classification, it is interesting to note that there is one pivotal point around which TRUE/FALSE interacts with ASSERTED/NOT-ASSERTED and this is encountered when one considers a comparison between a logic ACTION and a logic CONDITION. When considering only CONDITIONS, the TRUE/FALSE modification is proper, for the word CONDITION is a noun and nouns are properly modified by adjectives. However, upon the realization that any CONDITION is the direct result of some ACTION, and a CONDITION can be grammatically enhanced by the modification of a verb (ASSERTED), the concept of using ASSERTED becomes doubly applicable to both ACTIONS and CONDITIONS. Thus the ASSERTED concept is consistent, independent of whether it is modifying a CONDITION or an ACTION. Hopefully, you can gain a feel for the action-related logic ideas set forth here—how these ideas relate to the "mixed-logic" approach to digital design*—and continue to investigate their interesting applications to hardware design. In the next few sections we examine more closely the nature of digital signals and hardware, which will further your understanding of digital design.

2-3 THE TRUTH-TABLE

We have, up to this point, established that a Boolean variable (mnemonic) can take on only two values, not an infinite number as its kindred associate, the variable of the real number system, can. This basic difference allows us to illustrate *all* possible logic conditions of a Boolean variable or a collection of Boolean variables using a finite tabular format called a TRUTH-TABLE. Further, the nontrivial decisions in digital design are based on more than one two-valued variable. Thus, if an output is to be completely specified as a function of two inputs, there are four input combinations that must be considered. If there are three inputs, then eight combinations must be considered and from this we see that n inputs will require 2^n combinations to be considered.

---

*A mixed-logic system is one in which no particular effort is made to maintain a strict adherence to a standard or unique ASSERTED level assignment, and further, it is a system in which all the different circuit elements, called gates, are mixed freely.

Inputs	Outputs
A B C D	
0 0 0 0	
0 0 0 1	
0 0 1 0	
0 0 1 1	
0 1 0 0	
0 1 0 1	
0 1 1 0	
0 1 1 1	
1 0 0 0	
1 0 0 1	
1 0 1 0	
1 0 1 1	
1 1 0 0	
1 1 0 1	
1 1 1 0	
1 1 1 1	

Inputs	Outputs
A B C	
0 0 0	
0 0 1	
0 1 0	
0 1 1	
1 0 0	
1 0 1	
1 1 0	
1 1 1	

	A B	F
Row 0:	0 0	0
Row 1:	0 1	0
Row 2:	1 0	0
Row 3:	1 1	1

(a) (b) (c)

Fig. 2-3. (a) An example two-variable TRUTH-TABLE (b) The three-variable TRUTH-TABLE. (c) The four-variable TRUTH-TABLE.

A TRUTH-TABLE as suggested is a tabular or graphic technique for listing *all* possible combinations of input variables, arguments, or whatever they may be called, in a vertical order, listing each input combination one row at a time (see Figure 2-3). When every possible combination is recorded, each combination can be studied to determine whether the "output" or "combined interaction" of that combination should be ASSERTED or NOT-ASSERTED. Of course the information used to determine the combined interaction or output must come from studying arguments of the logic problem. Figure 2-3(a) illustrates the use of a two-variable TRUTH-TABLE and how the output or combined interaction is normally listed to the right of each possible input combination. Figures 2-3(b) and 2-3(c) show the standard form for three and four variable TRUTH-TABLES. In review, what is suggested here is that after all of the input variables have been identified, and all the possible combinations of these variables have been listed in the TRUTH-TABLE on the left, then each row should be studied to determine what output or combined interaction is desired for that input combination. Further, note that the input combinations are listed in ascending order, starting with the binary equivalent of zero. The TRUTH-TABLE also allows us to establish or prove Boolean identities without detailed mathematical proofs, as will be shown later.

The TRUTH-TABLE came into existence during the early years of logic study when logicians used them to validate their thinking. It is somewhat unfortunate that its TRUE/FALSE connotation has been carried over into digital hardware design. In digital design, the TRUTH-TABLE is used primarily to specify an INPUT/OUTPUT relation for a digital network, not to determine the truth value of an argument. You will find it closely related to the "functional tables" used in algebra to tabulate data from which we plot curves on an (x,y)

coordinate system (see Figure 2-4(a)). Realistically speaking, the TRUTH-TABLE can be considered analogous to the "transfer function" specification for an electronic amplifier system, where one is given a nonlinear amplifier specification in an INPUT/OUTPUT TABLE and then is asked to tailor the response of the amplifier system to meet the "best-fit" for the values specified in the table (see Figure 2-4(b)).

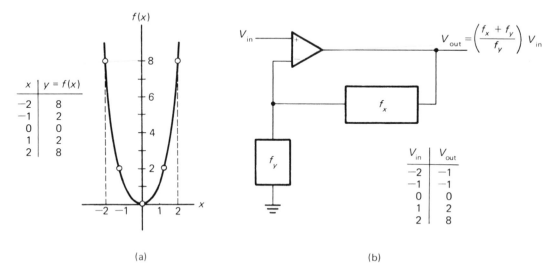

x	$y = f(x)$
-2	8
-1	2
0	0
1	2
2	8

V_{in}	V_{out}
-2	-1
-1	-1
0	0
1	2
2	8

$$V_{out} = \left(\frac{f_x + f_y}{f_y}\right) V_{in}$$

(a)   (b)

Fig. 2-4. (a) An illustration of the use of a functional table to describe a mathematical function. (b) An illustration of the use of an INPUT/OUTPUT table to describe the transfer function of an amplifier.

The analog designer then goes about selecting components, designing, analyzing, breadboarding, and "tweeking" until he meets the design criteria set forth in the INPUT/OUTPUT SPECIFICATION TABLE. In the same manner, the digital designer uses a TRUTH-TABLE as a set of discrete conditions that have to be met by a circuit design. However, in the interest of preserving tradition we will continue to refer to the INPUT/OUTPUT SPECIFICATION TABLES as TRUTH-TABLES. On the other hand, we will change the interpretation of the 0 entry from FALSE to NOT-ASSERTED and the 1 entry from TRUE to ASSERTED.

To illustrate the use of a TRUTH-TABLE in this manner, consider the following example.

EXAMPLE 2-1: Let E=ENABLE, F=FLIP, where ENABLE and FLIP are logic mnemonics describing some definite action in a digital system. The TRUTH-TABLE describing the combined interaction of these two is defined as the output FLEN and is shown in Figure 2-5. The specification for FLEN, it will be assumed at this time, has been filled-in from some known specification. Once the output is specified in a TRUTH-TABLE, you must learn how to interpret the discrete nature of this INPUT/OUTPUT definition. This is done almost instinctively by considering each input combination (row) and inserting the conjunction AND between each input variable condition for that combination, then in turn inserting the conjunction OR between each row statement. This technique is demonstrated in Figure 2-5.

Fig. 2-5. An example TRUTH-TABLE and its interpretation.

	E F	FLEN
Row 0:	0 0	0
Row 1:	0 1	0
Row 2:	1 0	0
Row 3:	1 1	1

It becomes obvious by examining the TRUTH-TABLE in Figure 2-5 that the combined interaction of ENABLE and FLIP (FLEN) can be defined in two ways:

(1) FLEN is ASSERTED if and only if ENABLE *and* FLIP are ASSERTED
   or
(2) FLEN is NOT-ASSERTED if ENABLE *and* FLIP are NOT-ASSERTED, *or* ENABLE is NOT-ASSERTED *and* FLIP is ASSERTED, or ENABLE is ASSERTED *and* FLIP is NOT-ASSERTED

Now, as you study these two statements abstracted from the TRUTH-TABLE, you should become aware of two points:

(1) The same or identical information resides in both statements, a point that is covered later in this chapter.
(2) The clarity of both statements relies heavily on the two conjunctions AND and OR. This is a very important point, and one on which a great deal of emphasis will be placed.

It will be shown that the grammatical usage of AND and OR serves as a bridge between a problem stated in words and a hardware realization of that same problem. Also, it will be found that AND and OR are associated with "gates" and "functions," which are discussed in the next section.

2-4 A WORD ABOUT GATES AND FUNCTIONS

It will be shown shortly that the foundation of logic design is seated in a well-founded axiomatic system called Boolean algebra, which will be shown to be what is known as a "Huntington system." In this axiomatic system the definition of the AND and OR *operators* is set forth, and these are found to be well-defined operators having certain properties that allow us to extend their definition to hardware applications. However, for the time being, note again the grammatical usage of the conjunctions AND and OR in Example 2-1. These conjunctions, sometimes referred to as connectives, actually suggest a function that can be emulated by some hardware logic device. This connection between grammar and hardware is mentioned again because of its importance in formulating a word statement that can be related directly to a hardware logic network.

The logic hardware devices just mentioned are commonly referred to as "gates." There are four basic "gates" used in varying degrees in logic hardware design. They are known as:

(1) the AND gate,
(2) the OR gate,
(3) the NAND gate,
(4) the NOR gate.

Keep in mind that the usage of "gate" refers to an actual piece of hardware, where "function" or "operation" refers to a logic operator. Thus, when we refer to an "AND function," we are referring to the logic operator AND. On the other hand, when we refer to an "AND gate," we are referring directly to a piece of hardware called an AND gate. This distinction is presented at this point because each of the four *gates* mentioned can be used for both AND and OR logic *operators* or *functions*.* This is demonstrated shortly and used throughout the text.

In the author's opinion, it is unfortunate that the names given to the *logic gates* are so closely associated with the basic logic operators (AND, OR). This leads one to believe they are *single function devices*, which they most emphatically are *not*! For example, because an AND gate is called such, it is easy to believe that it provides only an AND function. Likewise, it is easy to believe that OR gates provide only OR functions, leading to bewilderment when an AND gate is used for an OR operator and an OR gate is recommended for an AND operator. For example, mathematical statements, sometimes referred to as Boolean expressions, are synthesized from a word statement using AND and OR connectives, and then in turn this expression is implemented with hardware gates, and this process should be straightforward. However, it has been found that confusion sets in when it is suggested that the AND functions be implemented with OR gates and the OR function is implemented with AND gates.

To illustrate at least in part how a word statement can be formulated into a mathematical statement (Boolean expression), consider Example 2-2.

EXAMPLE 2-2: The following is an example of how a conditional statement can be symbolized into a mathematical statement.

Bob will go to school *if* Carol *and* Ted go to school, *or* Carol *and* Alice go to school.

This statement can be symbolized as a Boolean expression as follows:

$$\text{B } \textit{IF} \text{ C } \textit{AND} \text{ T } \textit{OR} \text{ C } \textit{AND} \text{ A}$$

$$\text{or} \quad \downarrow \qquad \downarrow \qquad \downarrow \qquad \downarrow$$

$$\text{B} = (\text{C} \quad \cdot \quad \text{T}) + (\text{C} \quad \cdot \quad \text{A})$$

---

*The words "operator" and "function" are used interchangeably throughout our discussions.

Thus the information in the word statement is transformed into a mathematical expression by assigning the AND and OR connectives the following symbols.

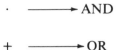

The next step is to transform this Boolean expression into a hardware network, and this is where the rub comes. Since AND and OR connectives are used, the AND and OR gates *should* always be used—right? WRONG! Maybe AND and OR gates should be used, but, on the other hand, it might be better to use *OR gates for the AND functions and NAND gates for the OR functions.*

The actual hardware implementation for this example is not demonstrated at this time because we have not introduced the symbology for gates as yet. The main point to remember is *don't confuse gates with logic operators and remember that the four gates mentioned can be used for both AND and OR functions.*

2-5 THE LOGIC OPERATORS

In the last section you were assured that a well-founded system exists that is based on some well-defined AND and OR operators. Further, it was illustrated how a word statement can be symbolized and transformed into a mathematical-looking expression (Boolean) using these same operators. Then it was postulated that gates could be used as a hardware operator to transcend the "paper domain." With this importance placed on the operator coupled with our faith that all four basic gates exhibit both AND and OR operator capabilities, it is best that we define the AND and OR operators in terms of the ASSERTED response of a gate.

It should be remembered that in order for a logic variable to be completely defined, a "level" position associated with the ASSERTED conditions must be made. This level position can be associated with properties such as light, pressure levels of air and fluids, sound intensity levels, voltage levels, or any other measurable physical evidence. This point is made because we will be dealing mainly with devices that are voltage level responsive in this text, and because of this the level information related from this point on will be treated in terms of voltage levels.

Definition: A "gate" is defined as a multi-input (≥ 2) hardware device that has a two-level output. The output level (HIGH/LOW) of this gate is a strict and repeatable function of the two-level combinations applied to its inputs. See Figure 2-6 for a general model of a gate.

In reference to "level" and ASSERTED, we see that the "levels" assigned to ASSERTED determine the variability referred to as "exhibiting both AND and OR operator capabilities."

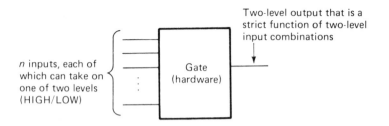

Fig. 2-6. The general model of a gate.

Definition: A gate whose output transfers to one of its two possible output levels when *ALL* of its input are brought to a *common level* (Lx)*, and maintains this output level ONLY under this input condition, is said to exhibit the Boolean AND function. Any gate which exhibits the Boolean AND function is assigned a schematic distinctive-shaped symbol, as shown in Figure 2-7.

Fig. 2-7. The distinctive-shaped symbol for any gate that exhibits the Boolean AND function.

Other schematic symbols are added to this distinctive-shaped symbol based on the number of inputs and assigned ASSERTED levels.

Definition: A gate whose output transfers to one of the two possible output levels when *ANY* of its inputs are brought to a *common level* (Lx), and this output level is held under *all* input conditions where any one input or any combination of inputs remain at the input level (Lx), is said to exhibit the Boolean OR function. Any gate which exhibits the Boolean OR function is assigned a schematic distinctive-shaped symbol, as shown in Figure 2-8.

Fig. 2-8. The distinctive-shaped symbol for any gate that exhibits the Boolean OR function.

Like the AND operator symbol, other schematic symbols are added to this distinctive-shaped symbol based on the number of inputs and assigned ASSERTED levels.

To clarify these two definitions, consider the following. If a gate has three inputs (*A*, *B*, and *C*) and this gate's output transfers to either one of the two possible levels *only* when *A and B and C* are *all* at the same level (Lx), it is said to exhibit the Boolean AND function. Note that it is assumed that the *other* output level is the output under the other seven input conditions. Further, if a gate has three inputs (*A*, *B*, and *C*) and this gate's output transfers to either one of the two

---

*Note: The level Lx can be assigned either high or low.

possible levels when *A or B or C* is at a particular level (Lx), *or* when any two or all three are at this same level (Lx), this gate is said to exhibit the Boolean OR function.

From these definitions it seems that if a gate is not exhibiting an AND function, it must be exhibiting an OR function. But this is not the case, for there are 256 different output specifications that *can* be made for a gate with three inputs, of which only four exhibit AND and OR characteristics. *However, it is true that if an AND characteristic is identified for a gate, this same gate has an OR characteristic also.* To illustrate this, we consider a two-input device whose output can take on one of two voltage levels (a high voltage level and a low voltage level) based on all possible input voltage level combinations. We show this representation in an INPUT/OUTPUT SPECIFICATION TABLE; see Figure 2-9.

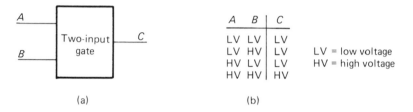

A	B	C
LV	LV	LV
LV	HV	LV
HV	LV	LV
HV	HV	HV

LV = low voltage
HV = high voltage

(a)   (b)

Fig. 2-9. (a) Some two-input gate. (b) The INPUT/OUTPUT specification for that two-input gate.

By studying the INPUT/OUTPUT SPECIFICATION TABLE for this gate, we see that the output transfers to a high voltage (HV) under the unique input combination of *A AND B* being at the same or common input level. In this case, both inputs must be at the high voltage level. Thus we can say the output of this gate is ASSERTED HIGH when *A* is ASSERTED HIGH *AND B* is ASSERTED HIGH. From this we make the following definition. This gate is defined as the two-input AND gate and has been assigned the modified distinctive-shaped schematic symbol shown in Figure 2-10 *when it is used for an AND operator or function.*

Fig. 2-10 The distinctive-shaped symbol for the two-input AND gate when it is used for an AND operation.

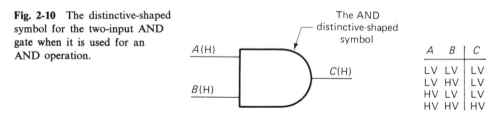

A	B	C
LV	LV	LV
LV	HV	LV
HV	LV	LV
HV	HV	HV

The mathematical function descriptor (symbol) for the AND operator has not been standardized. Some of the symbols which are commonly used are:

$$A \text{ AND } B = A \cdot B = AB = A \wedge B$$

The first and second symbols ($A \cdot B$ and AB) are used in this text.

Remember the earlier statement that the AND gate can also be used for an OR operation or function. In fact, we were assured that if an AND existed, the OR was automatic. To illustrate this, consider the first three entries in the INPUT/OUTPUT SPECIFICATION TABLE. We see the output of this gate transfers to a low voltage (LV) under the conditions of *A OR B OR* BOTH being at a low voltage. From this we can say that this gate exhibits a Boolean OR function with the output ASSERTED LOW when *A* is ASSERTED LOW *OR B* is ASSERTED LOW *OR* BOTH are ASSERTED LOW. Thus the OR distinctiveshaped symbol can be assigned to the AND gate when it is used for an OR operator or function. *However, some added symbology must be given to help one identify the number of inputs and at what voltage levels the OR function is invoked (see Figure 2-11).* Here we see a *low ASSERTION level indicator,* O, sometimes referred to as simply a state indicator or "ninny" or bubble (slang), has been added to the inputs and outputs of the basic symbol.

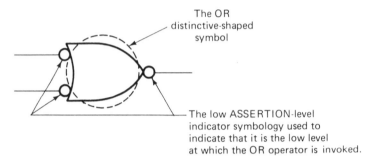

The OR distinctive-shaped symbol

The low ASSERTION-level indicator symbology used to indicate that it is the low level at which the OR operator is invoked.

Fig. 2-11. The distinctive-shaped symbol for the two-input AND gate when it is used for an OR operation.

To interpret schematic symbols such as the one shown in Figure 2-11:

First: Look for the distinctive-shaped symbol to identify the logic operator. In this case we see it as an OR function.

Second: Look at the output. If a low ASSERTION level indicator O is present, the operator indicated by the symbol is ASSERTED LOW. If no low-level ASSERTION indicator is present, the operator indicated by the symbol is ASSERTED HIGH. In this case the output is ASSERTED LOW.

Third: Look at the inputs. If low-level ASSERTION indicators are present at the inputs, the operator indicated by the symbol is invoked when the *inputs* are ASSERTED LOW. If no low-level ASSERTION indicator is present, the operator indicated by the symbol is invoked when the *inputs* are ASSERTED HIGH. In this case we see the inputs are ASSERTED LOW.

Taking another example that illustrates the ease of the interpretation of distinctive-shaped symbols, consider that you were given the following symbol.

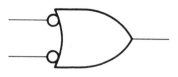

First: You see an OR operator suggested by the basic symbol.

Second: You see that the OR operator is ASSERTED HIGH (i.e., no bubble at the output).

Third: You see that either one *or* both of the inputs must be LOW before the output is to go HIGH, that is, the output is ASSERTED HIGH when one *or* the other *or* both inputs are at a LOW level.

Thus we see that we have a simple analysis process for quickly interpreting these schematic symbols. Also, it is obvious that one should be able to adapt these to a design process. Take it on faith that becoming familiar with the concepts of distinctive-shaped symbols will pay dividends in the future, for it allows you to do much of your work by simple inspection processes.

For now, let us get back to the problem at hand, which is learning about the OR and AND operators of gates.

Like the AND connective, the OR is also a conjunction and its position in a verbal statement is important. Since the statement regarding the OR includes the case where all inputs are ASSERTED, it is common practice to define this function as the "INCLUSIVE-OR." The commonly used functional descriptor symbols for the OR operator are

$$A \text{ OR } B = A + B = A \vee B$$

The $A + B$ symbology is used in this text.

Let us consider another two-input gate with an INPUT/OUTPUT SPECIFI-CATION TABLE illustrated in Figure 2-12.

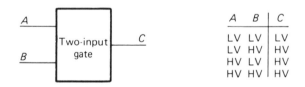

A	B	C
LV	LV	LV
LV	HV	HV
HV	LV	HV
HV	HV	HV

Fig. 2-12. Another two-input gate and INPUT/OUTPUT SPECIFICATION TABLE.

We see from the last three entries in the table that this gate exhibits an OR function ASSERTED HIGH when *A OR B OR* BOTH are ASSERTED HIGH. This gate is defined as the two-input OR gate and has been assigned the distinctive-shaped symbol shown in Figure 2-13 *when it is used for an OR operator or function.*

Note the first entry in the INPUT-OUTPUT SPECIFICATION TABLE. Here we see this same gate exhibiting an AND function ASSERTED LOW when *A*

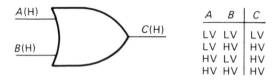

A	B	C
LV	LV	LV
LV	HV	HV
HV	LV	HV
HV	HV	HV

Fig. 2-13. The distinctive-shaped symbol for the two-input OR gate when it is used for an OR operation.

AND B are both ASSERTED LOW. Thus the AND distinctive-shaped symbol is used with the addition of the LOW-LEVEL ASSERTION indicators when an OR gate is used for an AND operation or function (see Figure 2-14).

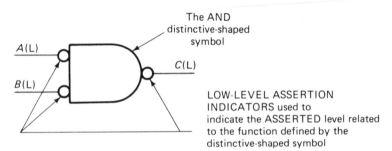

Fig. 2-14. The symbol used for an OR gate when used for an AND operation.

A special note regarding the general usage of low-level ASSERTION indicators: Refer to Figure 2-2. Here we see a ○ affixed to the LOAD input of the register. This ○ indicates the LOAD operation of this device is performed when a low-level signal is applied to this input. This is considered to be a *general* schematic notation for the more complex devices that have each input function defined directly on their symbol.

In summary, we have demonstrated that both the AND gate and the OR gate can be used as AND and OR operators if you are free to choose the ASSERTED levels for your signals. Many applications are used throughout this text that illustrate this very important point. Also, you are reminded once more of the distinction between gate and operator or function. *It should be noted that a strict avoidance of using a TRUTH-TABLE with 1's and 0's to describe the IN-PUT/OUTPUT specification of a gate was maintained. This was done to preserve the previous assignment of 1 = ASSERTED and 0 = NOT-ASSERTED.* Using 1's and 0's to describe a gate operation masks out its dual application. Thus, TRUTH-TABLES with 1's and 0's are used only to specify problem statements throughout this text. From this it is assumed that "problems" are something more than a single gate situation.

Also, it is important to note that gates come in more than two inputs, but before arbitrarily using an *n* input gate for some operator, check a manufacturer's data book to determine what gates are available.

In the next section more is covered regarding voltage levels and the practical application of gates used to transform word statements into hardware realizations.

2-6 HARDWARE ASPECTS RELATED TO ASSERTED AND NOT-ASSERTED CONDITIONS

It is time now to talk about some more of the real-life hardware concepts related to logic gates. Again let us restrict our discussion to the semiconductor type of devices.

It is a fact that once an electronic logic hardware family has been selected such as Transistor-Transistor-Logic (TTL), or Complementary-Metallic-Oxide-Semiconductor (CMOS), there is a definite set of voltage ranges that determine the INPUT/OUTPUT relationship for each gate. For example: The SN7408, which is a TTL quad-AND gate package, requires both inputs of each selected gate to be at a voltage >2.0 volt before the output is guaranteed to transfer from $\simeq0.0$ to 3.6 volts. Also, it requires at least one of its inputs to be <0.8 volt to assure the output voltage to be at, or approximately, 0.0 volt. This means that once you, the designer, have selected a gate from a particular logic family (TTL, CMOS, etc.) the input voltage ranges required to achieve a switching response at the output must be determined. Then as you select that gate for a logic operator you should define, *for that gate*, the voltage range assigned to the ASSERTED condition. *It is important that you DO NOT get into the rut of thinking that ASSERTED always implies the relatively high voltage range and the relatively low voltage is automatically assigned to the NOT-ASSERTED condition* (see Figure 2-15). There will be times when you will find it to be an advantage to assign the low voltage range to an ASSERTED level of some mnemonic. Other times you will find it advantageous to assign the high voltage range as the ASSERTED level. What is important is that you remember what the ASSERTED condition voltage assignment range is. You do this by adding (L) or (H) to the mnemonic. Also, keep in mind if the ASSERTED condition voltage range is defined, the NOT-ASSERTED condition voltage range assignment is automatic. For instance, if the ASSERTED range is the relatively high voltage range, it then follows automatically that the NOT-ASSERTED must be the relatively low range.

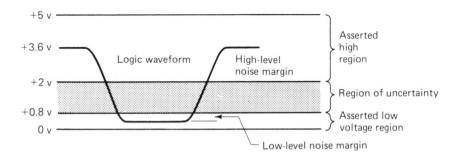

Fig. 2-15. An illustration of a logic voltage waveform showing ASSERTED voltage regions and noise margin.

As just mentioned, you will find at times you have the choice as to what voltage level you would like to assign to the ASSERTED condition. Other times the ASSERTED levels are forced on you by the inputs given to you from some other system. Historically, phrases such as POSITIVE LOGIC and NEGATIVE LOGIC have been relegated to the concepts of TRUE=HIGH for POSITIVE LOGIC systems and TRUE=LOW for NEGATIVE LOGIC systems. Further, you will find that once a designer has chosen a logic system, be it POSITIVE or NEGATIVE, he will stick with the system throughout his design and seldom, if ever, will he mix POSITIVE and NEGATIVE LOGIC. This fact, coupled with an apparent aversion to NEGATIVE LOGIC, has contributed largely to the fact that most basic material is treated from a POSITIVE LOGIC point of view. Then somewhere, at an appropriately chosen juncture, the NEGATIVE LOGIC is introduced quite modestly and then quickly forgotten, as far as actual applications are concerned. In this text it is found that "MIXED LOGIC SYSTEMS" are used freely, and that many times by using MIXED LOGIC, hardware savings can be achieved. It is therefore important to formally define POSITIVE and NEGATIVE LOGIC in terms of ASSERTED. These are the simple definitions:

> POSITIVE LOGIC is defined by logic variables or mnemonics that are
> ASSERTED *HIGH*.
> NEGATIVE LOGIC is defined by logic variables or mnemonics that are
> ASSERTED *LOW*.

Within any given system it is entirely valid to use both ASSERTED levels, and in most cases it is impossible to have strictly a POSITIVE or NEGATIVE LOGIC system if you are considering the system at the gate level rather than system level. Therefore, logic *systems* in general are truly MIXED, but few refer to them as such.

As mentioned above, the ASSERTED voltage range assignment to be chosen or given must be remembered; therefore, we add the extra element to the mnemonic of each logic argument to aid the designer in remembering the ASSERTED voltage range. Keep in mind that this "extra element" is really only an aid when the logic family has been selected and the logic operator identified, and schematic diagrams are being drawn. The aid mentioned we defined as the *POLARIZING ELEMENT* and placed it at the end of the mnemonic as previously outlined.

The use of polarized mnemonics is a great aid to you as a designer using mixed logic, allowing you to use mixed logic assertion levels throughout your design without having to worry if the system is strictly a positive or negative logic system. This is why it is felt that these concepts should be introduced at the inception of logic studies so that they can be used freely and without the painful relearning that seems to accompany the process after becoming familiar with the more traditional positive and negative logic studies.

To further strengthen the case for polarized mnemonics, consider another illustration of their value in clarifying an interface design problem.

EXAMPLE 2-3: Consider that you are to design a system (your system) to operate in some prescribed manner, which at this time is not important. What is important is that your system is to receive inputs from two other systems, one of which is a POSITIVE LOGIC system (A) and the other is a NEGATIVE LOGIC system (B) (see Figure 2-16).

At the outset of your design, it will pay great dividends to translate system A's and system B's outputs into polarized mnemonic form in such a way that you can continue with your design without regard to whether any particular mnemonic has its origin in a positive logic or negative logic system. This is done, as shown in Figure 2-16, by drawing a boundary around your system and making your translation to the right of the boundary as shown. Make certain that you *avoid* redefining the mnemonic portion in your translation because this usually creates confusion or at best retranslation later.

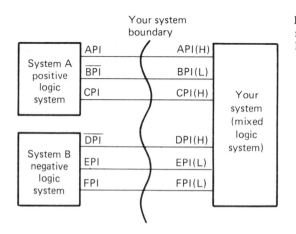

Fig. 2-16. An illustration of how polarized mnemonics can be derived from traditional logic variables.

We see that API, $\overline{\text{BPI}}$, and CPI are all mnemonics having origins in the positive logic system.* Therefore, API and CPI are to be interpreted as API(H) and CPI(H), and $\overline{\text{BPI}}$ is to be interpreted as BPI(L). In other words, API and CPI are logic signals that are to be interpreted as being ASSERTED HIGH. On the other hand, BPI is to be interpreted as ASSERTED LOW.

Now the mnemonics, $\overline{\text{DPI}}$, EPI, and FPI have their origin in a negative logic system. Therefore, EPI and FPI are translated to EPI(L) and FPI(L), respectively. $\overline{\text{DPI}}$ is, on the other hand, translated to DPI(H).

It should now be apparent that once this translation is completed, you then work only with the boundary mnemonics of your system, thereby reducing your "mental baggage" by never having to worry about whether or not any given variable stems from a negative logic system or a positive logic system. Further, it will be shown that a knowledge of the input assertion levels is necessary to make an optimal choice of gates to implement a design.

---

*Traditionally the bar over a variable is read as "NOT," that is, $\overline{\text{BPI}}$ is read as "BPI NOT" or "NOT BPI." In this text, variables such as $\overline{\text{BPI}}$ are read as: "BPI NOT-ASSERTED."

2-7 USING MECHANICAL SWITCHES FOR SIGNAL SOURCES

Most digital systems incorporate mechanical switches for generating signals as well as inputting data. Typical switches found on a control panel are: RESET (SANITY), which initializes the system, RUN/START, which initiates the operation, SINGLE-STEP, which allows the slow single-step operation of an otherwise high-speed system as well as other special function switches. The use of a switch as a signal source requires special consideration regarding switch properties and schematic documentation. For example, you first should understand that one of the physical switch positions must be declared as the ASSERTED position. This position is typically the "IN" or "UP" position. Then once the physical position has been established the proper connections must be made to the switch to assure the proper signal ASSERTION level is derived. Another important property to remember is that most switches suffer from "contact-bounce" upon closure. This contact-bounce is the result of the springlike operation of the switch mechanism and the microscopic irregularity of the switch contacts. The results of contact-bounce can be simulated by the repeated random operation of an *ideal* SPST switch and can take several milliseconds to die out. There are several methods of "debouncing" a switch, which are discussed in Chapter 5. However, at this time assume that the switches are ideal and dwell more on the schematic application of the switch. This application is demonstrated in Example 2-4.

> EXAMPLE 2-4: It is required that a control panel have two control switches. The first switch is the "RESET" switch, which is a SPST switch, and is to generate the signal SANITY(L). The second switch is the RUN/STOP switch, which is a SPDT switch and is to generate the START(H) signal. Figure 2-17 illustrates the schematic drawing for these two switches. Note the use of the "Pull-up" resistor, which is used to guarantee the high voltage level and avoids leaving any device input to "float." From Figure 2-17 we see that working out the physical location of the contact-pole positions first and then making the appropriate electrical connection to the switch makes the use of a switch for an input signal to a digital system a simple process.

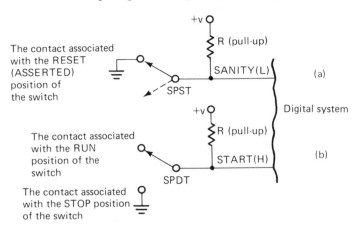

Fig. 2-17. The schematic documentation of the switch requirements specified in Example 2-4.

2-8 THE CONCEPT OF THE INVERTER

Once you understand that ASSERTED conditions and voltage levels are interrelated, and further understand that the conjunctions AND and OR in a word statement relate directly to some hardware operator, you are well on your way to design. However, once under way you will find that the set of conjunctions AND and OR is not sufficient, for there will be times when the word NOT is necessary to describe a condition for a problem. NOT means NOT-ASSERTED. Further, you will find when you are selecting operators (by selecting gates) that the hardware set of AND/OR gates also comes up short, for there will be times when a voltage level inversion is necessary. To illustrate this necessary function, consider the following problem statement.

EXAMPLE 2-5: There are three people who man a critical rocket launch control panel. Each of the three men has a two-position switch he must operate in some prescribed pattern (note pattern, not sequence) in order that the rocket can be launched (Figure 2-18). Because of special psychological studies made on these men, those in control found that each responded differently to the same stress. Based on this study, those in control prescribed the following conditions for rocket launch: If Kay has his switch in the ASSERTED position *and* Jim has his switch in the ASSERTED position *and* A.T. has his switch in the ASSERTED position, *or* if Kay has his switch in the ASSERTED position *and* Jim has his switch in the ASSERTED position *and* A. T. has his switch in the NOT-ASSERTED position.

Fig. 2-18. Rocket launch control panel.

Now, by assigning mnemonics as described previously (remember we have not selected hardware yet and therefore we will not assign the polarizing elements at this time), let:

LNCH RKT = Launch rocket
K SWCH = Kay's switch in the ASSERTED position
JM SWCH = Jim's switch in the ASSERTED position
AT SWCH = A.T.'s switch in the ASSERTED position

Put into a Boolean expression, we have

LNCH RKT = (K SWCH · JM SWCH · AT SWCH) + (K SWCH · JM SWCH · (?))

We can see thus far that we haven't described the case for the situation where A.T.'s switch is in the NOT-ASSERTED position or where the output of an AND function must be ASSERTED if one of the *system* inputs is in a NOT-ASSERTED condition. In other words, if the rocket is to be launched under the conditions where Kay's switch is ASSERTED *and* Jim's switch is ASSERTED *and* A.T.'s switch is NOT-ASSERTED, something must be done to condition the signal of A.T.'s switch in order to ENABLE the AND function. This is because all inputs to a gate used for an AND operator must be at the same voltage level before its output is ASSERTED.

Therefore, we introduce the logic INVERTER. *The function of the IN-VERTER is simply to complement or INVERT the logic voltage level of its incoming signal.* Keep in mind that it changes *only* the voltage level associated with the ASSERTED condition. For example: If the voltage level associated with A.T.'s switch being in the NOT-ASSERTED position is $\simeq 0$ volts, then passing this signal through an INVERTER simply changes the same logic condition (A.T.'s switch NOT-ASSERTED) from $\simeq 0$ volts to 3.6 volts. It will be assumed here that an AND gate is used for the AND operator. Therefore, before the output of the AND gate can yield an ASSERTED condition for its AND operator, *all* of its inputs must be ASSERTED at a relatively high voltage. Hence, we see an INVERTER could transform the NOT-ASSERTED low voltage at the output of A.T.'s switch ($\simeq 0$ volts) to a high voltage at the input of the AND gate, thus enabling the AND gate to ASSERT its output on the condition:

K SWCH · JM SWCH · $\overline{\text{AT SWCH}}$

The definition given here for an INVERTER differs considerably from the traditional definition of the INVERTER. However, it more accurately describes the physical function that it really performs. *Since an INVERTER is a single input device,* it performs *no logic interaction function between two variables; and to say that merely changing a voltage level constitutes a logic operation would be misleading.* Therefore, we define it as an INVERTER function rather than a logic-operator like the AND operator or OR operator. The distinctive-shaped symbol for the INVERTER is shown in Figure 2-19.

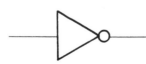

Fig. 2-19. The distinctive-shaped symbol for the INVERTER.

To further discuss the statement "The INVERTER merely changes the assertion voltage level," consider Figure 2-20, which illustrates this statement using "polarized mnemonics."

Fig. 2-20. Using the INVERTER to change the assertion voltage level of a given logic mnemonic.

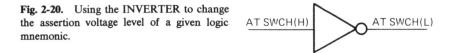

The point of having "mixed" ASSERTED levels can become confusing when reading other texts because most of these make the assumption that the ASSERTED levels are always within the *same* voltage range. As will be shown later, this can be a relatively expensive assumption. Therefore, don't become confused by a schematic symbol as shown in Figure 2-21(a), and remember the schematic symbol in Figure 2-21(b) is equivalent.

Fig. 2-21. (a) The traditional positive logic inverter symbology. (b) Using polarized mnemonic symbology.

It certainly is true that $\overline{\text{AT SWCH(H)}}$ = AT SWCH(L), but it is of no real value when reading or interpreting drawings. So don't spend time worrying about the overbar that traditionally reads NOT. One simply has to look at the polarizing element to determine the voltage level the signal line will be at when the logic operation defined by the mnemonic is ASSERTED. If the voltage level is different from the polarizing element, then it is immediately known that the operation is NOT-ASSERTED. As simple as that! The reverse argument is made when one is designing a circuit, which is very handy.

Now, if we are dealing with NOT-ASSERTED conditions at the expression level, it is possible to synthesize these NOT-ASSERTED logic requirements, such as the one in Example 2-5, in the following manner:

$$\text{LNCH RKT} = \text{K SWCH} \cdot \text{JM SWCH} \cdot \text{AT SWCH}$$
$$+ \text{K SWCH} \cdot \text{JM SWCH} \cdot \overline{\text{AT SWCH}}$$

By adding the polarizing elements we get:

$$\text{LNCH RKT(H)} = [\text{K SWCH} \cdot \text{JM SWCH} \cdot \text{AT SWCH}$$
$$+ \text{K SWCH} \cdot \text{JM SWCH} \cdot \overline{\text{AT SWCH}}\,](H)$$

The implementation of this logic expression is shown in Figure 2-22.

Here we see the inverter was added in such a way that when A.T.'s switch is in the NOT-ASSERTED position, AT SWCH(L) will be in the high voltage range, which allows the AND function (K SWCH · JM SWCH · $\overline{\text{AT SWCH}}$) to transfer to its ASSERTED level, in this case the high voltage level.

The specific point made here leads the way to a general implementation concept, which is covered in the next section.

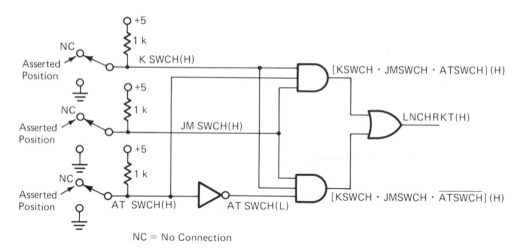

Fig. 2-22. The unsimplified implementation of the rocket launch problem.

2-9 GENERAL IMPLEMENTATION PROCEDURES

Consider the mixed input assertion level notation illustrated in Figure 2-23. The validity of the output expression indicated in Figure 2-23 can be established quite easily from your knowledge of two things:

    (1) The functional AND operation of the AND gate, that is, the output, is HIGH *only* when all inputs are high.
    (2) The given assertion level for the *A* variable is low. Keep in mind that in general you may or may not have control over the assertion levels of your inputs.

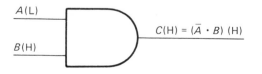

Fig. 2-23. A notational illustration of mixed input assertion levels.

Therefore, from an empirical standpoint the output *C* can only be high when the *B* variable is ASSERTED *and* the *A* variable is NOT-ASSERTED. Thus we derive the expression

$$C(\text{H}) = (\overline{A} \cdot B)(\text{H})$$

which is interpreted as: *C* (the output) is ASSERTED High when *A* is NOT-ASSERTED *and B* is ASSERTED.

Note that the assertion levels of the individual inputs were deleted from this interpretation leaving only the logic message of the expression and its assertion level. This is always done, for several reasons. One important reason is that it reduces the sheer bulk of the output expression. Another, and probably the most important, reason is that carrying these assertion levels to the output expression is a superfluous operation. This can be seen by realizing that *each logic symbol definition automatically establishes the input conditions under which the logic function specified by the symbol is carried out*. Therefore, to specify the output of the AND function of an AND gate as

$$C(\text{H}) = \left[\, \overline{A}(\text{H}) \cdot B(\text{H}) \,\right](\text{H})$$

is an unnecessary operation if we have the definition of the symbol in mind. We simply say

$$C(\text{H}) = \left[\, \overline{A} \cdot B \,\right](\text{H})$$

Attaching the polarizing element to the overall expression is done for diagnostic purposes as well as for information pertaining to the possible later use of this expression as an input to some other symbol.

Another key point related to the output notation specified in Figure 2-23 *is logic expressions with complemented variables can be implemented in hardware simply by assigning the complemented variables with low polarizing elements to symbol inputs without low-level indicators or those complemented variables with high polarizing elements to symbol inputs with low-level indicators*. See Figure 2-22. Here we see that the operation just prescribed results in output expressions with complemented variables. This very important concept is re-demonstrated by the following example. Suppose you were given the following expression and asked to implement this expression in hardware:

$$F = A \cdot \overline{B} + \overline{A} \cdot C$$

The method of attack is as follows:

(1) First recognize that the circuit represented by this expression is to receive its inputs (A, B, and C) from some other system.
(2) Recognize that the output of this circuit (F) is to drive some other system.

Therefore, you must be sensitive to the given ASSERTED levels for the inputs and the required ASSERTED level for the output.

(3) Based on the restrictions imposed on you by the input and output ASSERTION levels, make a selection of gates that will perform the indicated AND/OR functions.

Make this choice in such a way that INVERTER functions are minimized. The reason we do this is that INVERTERS exhibit no logic operator, they merely change voltage levels, use power, and take up room. Therefore, their use should be minimized.

To illustrate the process of implementing the given function

$$F = A \cdot \overline{B} + \overline{A} \cdot C$$

based on the following input and output restrictions,

F must be ASSERTED LOW
A, B, and C are all ASSERTED HIGH

consider the following steps to an implementation:

(1) Select a gate that exhibits an OR function ASSERTED LOW for the OR operator. The only one we have studied thus far is the AND gate which has the OR function symbol shown:

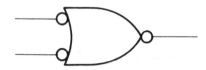

(2) Select a gate for the AND functions that complements (matches) the inputs to the selected OR operator. The only one we have studied thus far is the OR gate which has the AND function symbol shown:

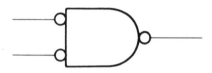

(3) Bring these two operators together and match the input variables ASSERTED LEVELS to the AND operator using an INVERTER only when needed. This is done in Figure 2-24.

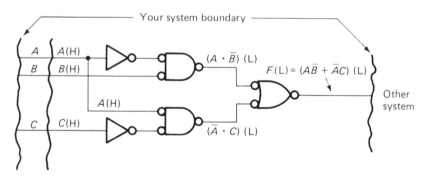

Fig. 2-24. An illustration of the circuit which receives A(H), B(H), and C(H) and generates F(L)=($A\bar{B}$ + $\bar{A}C$)(L).

Had you not used the mixed logic concepts you have studied thus far, your circuit would more than likely have looked like the one in Figure 2-25. In this figure you see that an extra INVERTER is required—tsk, tsk.

Thus it is hoped that you recognize some merit in the mixed logic concepts, since it has been positively reinforced by an example that illustrates a circuit savings. Granted, these concepts are somewhat subtle, but their use does make circuit design a little more exciting as well as making circuit saving more obvious.

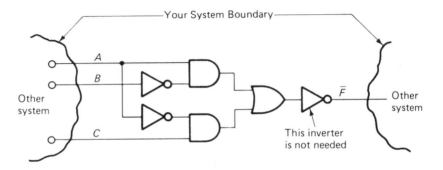

Fig. 2-25. A traditional implementation of the function $\bar{F}$.

2-10 AXIOMATIC SYSTEMS AND BOOLEAN ALGEBRA

Thus far we have discussed the AND, OR, and INVERTER functions and stated that it can be proven that these functions make up a sufficient set to define a two-valued Boolean algebra. However, we have attacked the introduction to Boolean algebra in a slightly reversed manner purposely, to develop some physical insight into what this axiomatic system might be about. It is time to introduce some formal treatment of this two-valued Boolean algebra.

When contemplating the origin of new knowledge, you soon come to the realization that this new knowledge must originate from some sound basis if it is to be meaningful. To be meaningful it need not include total or even partial usefulness, for there is much knowledge that may not be of immediate use. However, if the foundation of this knowledge is couched in sound reasoning and it has certain basic properties, its usefulness may only be hidden from view by the shortsightedness of its interpreters, and may well be brought into view by related studies at any time.

An illustration of how later studies bring to light the usefulness of new knowledge unearthed by the pure research of yesteryear is shown almost daily. Hardly a day goes by in which applied research does not uncover ways and means whereby pure research can be brought into application. For example, the theoretical work of Boole done in the mid-1800's was not applied to hardware until Shannon extended this knowledge in the late 1930's. Had Boole not done his work properly and had those who followed him not nurtured his work, it might well be that it would have gone unnoticed; and its applications as we know them today, and as those in the future will know them, would be unknown or at best channeled into some other area. Thus we see that the responsibility rests heavily on those doing pure research to make certain that the knowledge unearthed is properly founded and documented. To support this, great thinkers have given us principles on which to base the formulation of new thoughts related to axiomatic systems.

Axiomatic systems are founded on some fundamental statements referred to as *axioms* or *postulates*. As you delve deeper into the origin of axioms and postulates, you find these to be predicated on a set of undefined objects that are accepted on *faith*.

Faith is defined in many ways, one of which is taken from the Bible, Hebrews 11:1. "Faith is the substance of things hoped for, the evidence of things not seen." Though generally applicable, this definition of faith is not quite the one required. For one to accept something on faith he has to accept the fact that not every object is definable, yet statements must be made regarding these objects. Thus it is assumed that those of us involved have a conceptualization of what those objects are without further definitions; *this we will call faith*. An example of faith as it is defined here and how it is arrived at can be cited as follows: When you were a baby it is most likely that your mother pointed at a table and repeated the word "table" to you, and on various other occasions she pointed out other objects and said again, "table." Thus you accepted a conceptualization of an object you associated with the word "table", and now you have the faith that those same-looking objects are still tables, which is another indication that nobody can really define "things" to babies who have no set of objects (other definitions) on which to base their understanding. They merely accept things on faith.

Thus we are called on to exercise faith when we define objects in terms of more primitive objects and in turn define these more primitive objects in terms of still more primitive objects; continuing until we find that, practically, we must have some place from whence we can start. From this place there exist no further primitive objects on which we can base definitions. Therefore, from this place the logician selects objects on faith and builds from there. For example, in geometry one starts from the basis of statements regarding the undefined objects, the point and the line, which are accepted on faith and, from these, elegant axiomatic systems are developed.

Axioms and postulates are statements about undefined objects that are believed by faith. They are the statements that make up the framework from which new systems can be developed. They are the basis from which theorems and the proofs of these theorems are derived. For example, proofs are justified on the basis of a more primitive proof. Thus we use the statement: From this we justify this. Again, we find a process that is based on some point for which there exists no further primitive proofs. Hence we need a starting point and that starting point is a set of axioms or postulates.

Axioms are formulated by combining intelligence and empirical evidence and should have some basic properties in order for them to be useful. These properties are:

(1) They are statements about a set of undefined objects.
(2) They must be consistent, that is, they must not be self-contradictory.
(3) They should be simple but useful, that is, not lengthy or complex.
(4) They should be independent, that is, these statements should not be interdependent.

In regards to the strict adherence to (3) and (4), these should be modified in such a way that they facilitate ease of use.

The study of axiomatic systems related to logic motivated the creation of the set of postulates known as the *Huntington Postulates*.* (At this point it is assumed that you are at a sufficiently fundamental level that you are willing to accept a conceptualization of an object rather than any further definition.) These postulates as set forth can be used to evaluate proposed systems and those systems that meet the criteria set forth by these postulates become known as Huntington Systems. *Further, once a proposed system meets the criteria set forth by the Huntington Postulates, automatically all theorems and properties related to other Huntington Systems become immediately applicable to the new system.* Thus, if we define some set of black and white "chicken feed" and define some operators over this set of chicken feed which meet the criteria of the Huntington Postulates, we have immediately established that those things true about other Huntington Systems are also true about the chicken feed system.

Thus we propose a Boolean algebra and test it with the Huntington Postulates to determine its structure. We do this so that we can utilize the theorems and properties of other Huntington Systems for a new system that is defined over a set of *voltage levels* and hardware operators. Boolean algebra, like other axiomatic systems, is based on several operators defined over a set of undefined elements. *A SET is any collection of elements having some common property*; and these elements need not be defined. The set of elements we will be dealing with is {0,1}. The 0 and 1, as far as we are concerned, are some special symbols and have no numerical connotation whatsoever. They are simply some objects we are going to make some statements about. *An OPERATOR $(\cdot, +)$ is defined as a rule defining the results of an operation on two elements of the set.* Because these operators operate on *two* elements, they are commonly referred to as "binary operators." However, this has nothing to do with the fact that we are presently dealing with "binary systems."

Huntington's Postulates

(1) A set of elements S is closed with respect to an operator if for every pair of elements in S the operator specifies a unique result (element) which is also in the set S.

In other words: For the operator $+$ the results of $A + B$ must be found in S if A and B are in S; and for the operator $\cdot$ the results of $A \cdot B$ must also be found in S if A and B are elements in S.

(2a) There exists an element 0 in S such that for every A in S, $A + 0 = A$.
(2b) There exists an element 1 in S such that for every A in S, $A \cdot 1 = A$.

---

*E.V. Huntington (1904) formulated this set of postulates that have the basic properties described desirable, consistent, simple, and independent.

(3a) $A + B = B + A$ ⎫
(3b) $A \cdot B = B \cdot A$ ⎬ commutative laws
(4a) $A + (B \cdot C) = (A + B) \cdot (A + C)$ ⎫
(4b) $A \cdot (B + C) = (A \cdot B) + (A \cdot C)$ ⎬ distributive laws

(5) For every element A in S, there exists an element $\overline{A}$ such that $A \cdot \overline{A} = 0$ and $A + \overline{A} = 1$.

(6) There exist at least two elements A and B in S such that A is not equivalent to B.

Therefore, if we propose the following two-valued Boolean algebra system, that is, if we define the set $S = \{0, 1\}$ and prescribe the rules for $\cdot$, $+$ and INVERTER as follows:

Rules for "·"

·	0	1		A	B	A·B
0	0	0	or	0	0	0
1	0	1		0	1	0
				1	0	0
				1	1	1

Rules for "+"

+	0	1	A	B	A+B
0	0	1	0	0	0
1	1	1	0	1	1
			1	0	1
			1	1	1

INVERT Function

A	$\overline{A}$
0	1
1	0

and test our system with the postulates, we find:

(1) Closure is obvious—no results other than the 0 and 1 are defined.

(2) From the tables:
  (a) $0 + 0 = 0$ $0 + 1 = 1 + 0 = 1$
  (b) $1 \cdot 1 = 1$ $1 \cdot 0 = 0 \cdot 1 = 0$

(3) The commutative laws are obvious by the symmetry of the operator tables.

(4a) The distributive laws can be proven by a TRUTH-TABLE

A	B	C	$B + C$	$A \cdot (B + C)$	$A \cdot B$	$A \cdot C$	$(A \cdot B) + (A \cdot C)$
0	0	0	0	0	0	0	0
0	0	1	1	0	0	0	0
0	1	0	1	0	0	0	0
0	1	1	1	0	0	0	0
1	0	0	0	0	0	0	0
1	0	1	1	1	0	1	1
1	1	0	1	1	1	0	1
1	1	1	1	1	1	1	1

(4b) Can be shown by a similar table.

(5) From the INVERTER function table:

$$1 \cdot \bar{1} = 1 \cdot 0 = 0, \qquad 0 \cdot \bar{0} = 0 \cdot 1 = 0$$
$$1 + \bar{1} = 1 + 0 = 1, \qquad 0 + \bar{0} = 0 + 1 = 1$$

(6) It is obvious that the set $S = \{0, 1\}$ fulfills the minimum requirements of having at least two elements where $0 \neq 1$.

From this study the following identities in Table 2-1 can be listed:

TABLE 2-1 Identities

(1a) $0 \cdot A = 0$	(1b) $1 + A = 1$	
(2a) $1 \cdot A = A$	(1b) $0 + A = A$	
(3a) $A \cdot A = A$	(1b) $A + A = A$	(Note the duality*)
(4a) $A \cdot \bar{A} = 0$	(1b) $A + \bar{A} = 1$	
(5a) $\bar{\bar{A}} = A$		

*Duality is defined for Huntington Systems, just as it is for other axiomatic systems, and the dual of a given expression can be derived by simply replacing the $\cdot$'s with $+$'s and $+$'s with $\cdot$'s and 0's with 1's and 1's with 0's in that expression.

From the identities in Table 2-1 the theorems in Table 2-2 can be developed and proven.

TABLE 2-2 Theorems

(1) $A + AB = A$ (absorption)

(2) $A + \bar{A}B = A + B$

(3) $AB + A\bar{B} = A$ (logic adjacency)

(4) $AC + \bar{A}BC = AC + BC$

(5) $AB + AC + \bar{B}C = AB + \bar{B}C$

(6) $\overline{A \cdot B \cdot C} \ldots = \bar{A} + \bar{B} + \bar{C} + \cdots$ ⎫
(7) $\overline{A + B + C} \ldots = \bar{A} \cdot \bar{B} \cdot \bar{C} \ldots$ ⎬ DeMorgan

Each of these theorems and many others can be proven mathematically using the postulates and identities, or by a TRUTH-TABLE, as will be shown. However, since these theorems and relations have been previously established for other Huntington Systems, we need not put forth the effort; but in the interest of developing some valuable experience in manipulating Boolean expressions, some of these theorems will be proven as follows. It should be noted that each theorem does have a dual that is not listed but is left for an exercise.

Theorem 1 (*Absorption*):

$$A + AB = A(1 + B)$$
$$= A(1)$$
$$= A$$
$$\therefore A + AB = A$$

A	B	AB	$A + AB$
0	0	0	0
0	1	0	0
1	0	0	1
1	1	1	1

Theorem 2:

$$A + \overline{A}B = A \cdot 1 + \overline{A}B$$
$$= A(B + \overline{B}) + \overline{A}B$$
$$= AB + A\overline{B} + \overline{A}B$$
$$= AB + AB + A\overline{B} + \overline{A}B$$
$$= A(B + \overline{B}) + B(A + \overline{A})$$
$$= A + B$$
$$\therefore A + \overline{A}B = A + B$$

A	B	$\overline{A}$	$\overline{A}B$	$A + \overline{A}B$	$A + B$
0	0	1	0	0	0
0	1	1	1	1	1
1	0	0	0	1	1
1	1	0	0	1	1

Theorem 3 (*Logic-adjacency*):

$$AB + A\overline{B} = A(B + \overline{B})$$
$$= A(1)$$
$$= A$$
$$\therefore AB + A\overline{B} = A$$

A	B	AB	$A\overline{B}$	$AB + A\overline{B}$	A
0	0	0	0	0	0
0	1	0	0	0	0
1	0	0	1	1	1
1	1	1	0	1	1

Now that we have shown the proposed Boolean algebra to be a Huntington System, the properties related to other Huntington Systems become applicable to the Boolean system. It is interesting to note that the 0 and 1 elements in the Boolean set can be redefined by using the = and those properties which are true for 1 and 0 then become true for ASSERTED and NOT-ASSERTED. Thus we can show the ASSERTED and NOT-ASSERTED concepts are consistent. These results can be further extended to voltage levels and voltage operators, which we call gates. In other words, we can define two voltage levels that are elements of a set and design hardware which have one-to-one correspondence with the operators defined in the Boolean system. We then have a hardware system about which we can say that those things true for the other Huntington Systems are true for our hardware system. Now we see that we have a postulative basis for the digital hardware system based around the AND/OR gates and INVERTERS.

It is important to note that we have developed our hardware system around AND/OR operators and INVERTER functions, which will require some further adaptation for the other hardware gates (NAND and NOR) in order for these to be used consistently. This will be illustrated shortly.

With reference to the ASSERTED and polarized mnemonic format, it can be shown by inspection that the following are identities:

(1a) $\overline{F(H)} = F(L)$ (most important)

(1b) $\overline{F(L)} = F(H)$

(2a) $\overline{F(H)} = \bar{F}(H)$

(2b) $\overline{F(L)} = \bar{F}(L)$

From these it can be proven that:

$$F(H) = \bar{F}(L)$$
$$F(L) = \bar{F}(H)$$

Proof:

$$F(H) = \overline{\overline{F(H)}}$$

from (1a) $\quad \overline{\overline{F(H)}} = \overline{F(L)}$

from (1b) $\quad \overline{F(L)} = \bar{F}(L)$

$\quad \therefore \quad F(H) = \bar{F}(L)$

Therefore we introduce the following table of relations (Table 2-3).

TABLE 2-3   Useful relations

(1a) $F(H) = \bar{F}(L)$	(1b) $F(L) = \bar{F}(H)$
(2a) $\overline{F(H)} = F(L)$	(2b) $\overline{F(L)} = F(H)$
(3a) $\overline{F(H)} = \bar{F}(H)$	(3b) $\overline{F(L)} = \bar{F}(L)$

We see from (1a) and (1b) that a given function F ASSERTED at either level has an exact equivalent which is arrived at by complementing both the function and the polarizing element.

From (2a) and (2b) we see that the complement of a function can be derived by simply complementing the polarizing element. *These are the ones most often used in design.*

From (3a) and (3b) we see an alternate way of arriving at the complement of a function using DeMorgan's theorem on the function F and leaving the polarizing element as it was. *This identity is used generally when some functional transformation is desired and plays no real part in the design process.*

TABLE 2-4   Useful relations

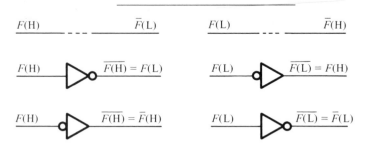

A hardware illustration of these useful relations is shown in Table 2-4. Pay special attention to the alternate symbol for the INVERTER introduced in Table 2-4. This new symbol is supported by the same rules set forth regarding the low-level ASSERTION indicator for the AND and OR basic distinctive-shaped symbols. In short, the symbols in Table 2-4 support the rule set down earlier stating that a function stemming from an output without a low-level indicator yields an output mnemonic that is ASSERTED HIGH. Conversely, a function stemming from an output with a low-level indicator yields an output mnemonic which is ASSERTED LOW. Likewise, when the input mnemonic polarizing element does not match the assignment of the state indicator at the input, then that variable appears at the output as a complemented variable. We find later that this is a very useful concept for schematically generating complemented functions.

The theorems listed in Table 2-2 serve an important function in that they are used to reduce the number of variables in a given Boolean expression. In particular, Theorem 3, the logic adjacency theorem, is a key theorem used in the development of a graphical simplification method called "MAPPING," which is treated in Chapter 3.

To illustrate how you can use these theorems for simplification, consider the following two examples:

GIVEN:

$$F = X + YXZ \quad + Z\bar{X} \quad \text{(to be simplified)}$$
$$\overbrace{\uparrow \text{Thm 1} \uparrow}$$
$$F = \bar{X} + Z\bar{X}$$
$$\overbrace{\uparrow \text{Thm 2} \uparrow}$$
$$\therefore F = X + Z$$

$$S = \underbrace{Y + Z + \overline{Y}X} + \overline{X} \quad \text{(to be simplified)}$$
$$= Y + Z + \underbrace{X + \overline{X}}$$
$$= (Y + Z) + 1$$
$$\therefore S = 1$$

More is said concerning the use of theorems for reduction in Chapter 3.

DeMorgan's theorem are also very important; in particular, they yield some important insight into the use of AND-INVERTER and OR-INVERTER logic functions, which is presented in the next section. In general, the results of these theorems are summed up in Figures 2-26(a) and 2-26(b).

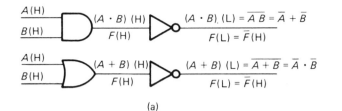

(a)

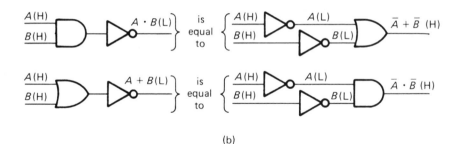

(b)

Fig. 2-26. Illustrations of the applications of DeMorgan's theorems in relation to AND-INVERTER and OR-INVERTER applications.

Thus we have seen several useful applications for the theorems.

2-11 OTHER GATES AND THEIR FUNCTIONS

Now that we have formally established the theoretical basis for the AND and OR operators and the INVERTER function, and have further demonstrated the application of these operators in terms of hardware AND and OR gates, it should prove interesting to examine the other 14 possible output specifications for an arbitrary two-input gate. Consider Table 2-5.

TABLE 2-5 Input/output specifications for the 16 possible outputs derived from two-input gates

A	B	$\perp$	F_1	F_2	F_3	F_4	F_5	F_6	F_7	F_8	F_9	F_{10}	F_{11}	F_{12}	F_{13}	F_{14}	$+v$
LV	LV	LV	HV	LV	HV	LV	HV	LV	HV	LV	HV	LV	HV	LV	HV	LV	HV
LV	HV	LV	LV	HV	HV	LV	LV	HV	HV	LV	LV	HV	HV	LV	LV	HV	HV
HV	LV	LV	LV	LV	LV	HV	HV	HV	HV	LV	LV	LV	LV	HV	HV	HV	HV
HV	HV	LV	LV	LV	LV	LV	LV	LV	LV	HV	HV	HV	HV	HV	HV	HV	HV

Scanning the table for gates that exhibit the Boolean AND and OR operator, we see that F_1 (NOR), F_7 (NAND), F_8 (AND), and F_{14} (OR) are the only outputs from gates which manifest the AND and OR operators. Because of this, they are found in integrated circuit form. All the rest are more complex and deemed unuseful for AND/OR implementation and are not normally found in gate form, with two exceptions: They are F_6 and F_9. F_6 is the INPUT/OUTPUT specification for a gate called the EXCLUSIVE OR gate and F_9 is the specification for the COINCIDENCE, EQUIVALENCE, or NEXOR gate, also referred to as an EXCLUSIVE NOR.

2-12 NAND AND NOR GATES

As mentioned previously, the NAND and NOR gates are widely used and are readily available from most integrated circuit manufacturers. A major reason for the widespread use of these gates is that they are both UNIVERSAL gates, universal in the sense that both can be used for AND operators, OR operators, as well as an INVERTER. Thus we see that a complex digital system can be completely synthesized using only NAND gates or NOR gates. At present there are computer-aided design techniques that can be used to design all-NAND/all-NOR digital systems, indicating that these are truly important logic devices.

From Table 2-5 we see the INPUT/OUTPUT specification that defines a two-input NAND gate as shown below.

A	B	C
LV	LV	HV
LV	HV	HV
HV	LV	HV
HV	HV	LV

By examining this SPECIFICATION TABLE we see that this gate exhibits an AND operation which is ASSERTED LOW when both inputs are ASSERTED HIGH. *From this we can develop the distinctive-shaped schematic symbol shown in Figure 2-27.* This symbol is to be used when a NAND gate is used for an AND operator.

Fig. 2-27. The distinctive-shaped symbol for the NAND gate used for an AND operator.

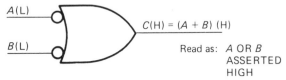

A(H)

B(H)

C(L) = $(A \cdot B)$ (L)

Read as: A AND B
ASSERTED
LOW

If we study the INPUT/OUTPUT TABLE for the NAND gate further, we see that it exhibits an OR function ASSERTED HIGH if the input A is ASSERTED LOW *OR* B is ASSERTED LOW *OR* BOTH are ASSERTED LOW. *From this we can develop the distinctive-shaped schematic symbol for the NAND gate when it is to be used for an OR operator or function* (see Figure 2-28).

Fig. 2-28. The schematic symbol used when a NAND gate is used for an OR operator.

A(L)

B(L)

C(H) = $(A + B)$ (H)

Read as: A OR B
ASSERTED
HIGH

A frequently used functional descriptor symbol for the NAND function is ($\uparrow$), which indicates

$$A \text{ NAND } B = A \uparrow B$$

However, by treating the NAND gate as either an AND operator or an OR operator, we totally disregard the existence of the NAND function. There are good reasons for this since we are geared to interpret expressions such as

$$F = AB + BC$$

not

$$F = (A \uparrow B) \uparrow (B \uparrow C)$$

These two expressions are equivalent; however, it is not at all obvious at the first glance. By repeated use of DeMorgan's theorems we can prove this:

$$A \uparrow B = \overline{AB} = \bar{A} + \bar{B}$$

and

$$B \uparrow C = \overline{BC} = \bar{B} + \bar{C}$$

$$\therefore \quad (A \uparrow B) \uparrow (B \uparrow C) = (\bar{A} + \bar{B}) \uparrow (\bar{B} + \bar{C})$$

and

$$(\bar{A} + \bar{B}) \uparrow (\bar{B} + \bar{C}) = \overline{(\overline{A + B})(\overline{B + C})}$$

$$= AB + BC$$

One can imagine the burden of the repeated use of DeMorgan's theorems as a task that should be avoided simply because algebraic manipulations lead to human errors. Therefore, from here on out we will strive to keep our functional development in terms of AND, OR, and INVERTERS; and further strive to avoid the introduction of any other functional descriptors such as ($\uparrow$).

We have mentioned that the NAND gate can be used universally and to this point we have illustrated the AND and OR functions, so let's get on to the INVERTER application. Consider Figure 2-29. Little need be said about this figure. The end result is obvious if you understand that

$$(A \cdot A)(\text{L}) = A(\text{L})$$

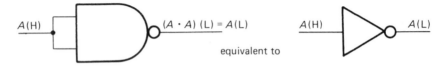

Fig. 2-29. The illustration of the use of a NAND gate for an INVERTER function.

In summary, you should be reminded that the main objective of this study of the NAND gate is intended to convince you that the use of functional descriptors, such as (↑), should be avoided; and that the NAND gate should be thought of in terms of its AND, OR, and INVERTER function in keeping with developed Boolean algebra and its defined operators.

2-13 THE AND, OR, AND INVERTER FUNCTIONS OF THE NOR GATE

As mentioned earlier, both NAND and NOR gates are readily available and both are classified as "universal" gates. Therefore, studies parallel to the NAND gate are covered for the NOR gate. The INPUT/OUTPUT specification for the NOR gate is

A	B	C
LV	LV	HV
LV	HV	LV
HV	LV	LV
HV	HV	LV

By examining this SPECIFICATION TABLE we see this gate exhibits an OR operation that is ASSERTED LOW when A is ASSERTED HIGH *OR B* is ASSERTED HIGH *OR* BOTH are ASSERTED HIGH. *From this we can develop the distinctive-shaped schematic symbol shown in Figure 2-30 for the NOR gate when it is used for an OR operator or function.*

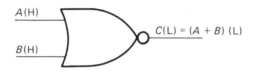

Fig. 2-30. The schematic symbol for the NOR gate used for an OR operator.

Now as we study the INPUT/OUTPUT TABLE for the NOR gate further, we see that it exhibits an AND function ASSERTED HIGH when the input A is ASSERTED LOW *AND B* is ASSERTED LOW. *From this we can derive the distinctive-shaped schematic symbol for the NOR gate when it is to be used for an AND operator or function* (see Figure 2-31).

Fig. 2-31. The schematic symbol for a NOR gate when it is used for an AND function.

A functional descriptor symbol frequently used for the NOR function is ($\downarrow$), which indicates

$$A \text{ NOR } B = A \downarrow B$$

However, it is best to avoid using the ($\downarrow$) as much as possible.

In order to gain a little more insight into the NOR gate, examine the results of the illustration in Figure 2-32.

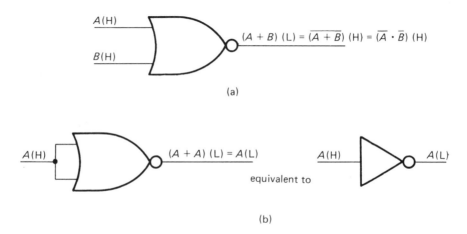

(a)

(b)

Fig. 2-32 (a) An illustration of the algebraic justification of the AND distinctive-shaped symbol used for the NOR gate as shown in Figure 2-31.-32(b) The NOR gate used as an INVERTER.

Looking at Figure 2-32(a), the output expression $(\overline{A} \cdot \overline{B})$(H) serves as theoretical support for the distinctive-shaped symbol shown in Figure 2-31.

To this point we have proven both practically and theoretically that each of the four gates (AND, OR, NAND, and NOR) all exhibit both Boolean AND and OR functions, and each is assigned a distinctive-shaped symbol as summarized in Figure 2-33. Figure 2-34 summarizes some of the examples of outputs generated by mixed ASSERTED levels at the input of the distinctive-shaped symbols. You should remember that, in general, an input that does not match the required input ASSERTED level called for by the distinctive-shaped symbol does in fact appear as a NOT-ASSERTED variable in the output expression.

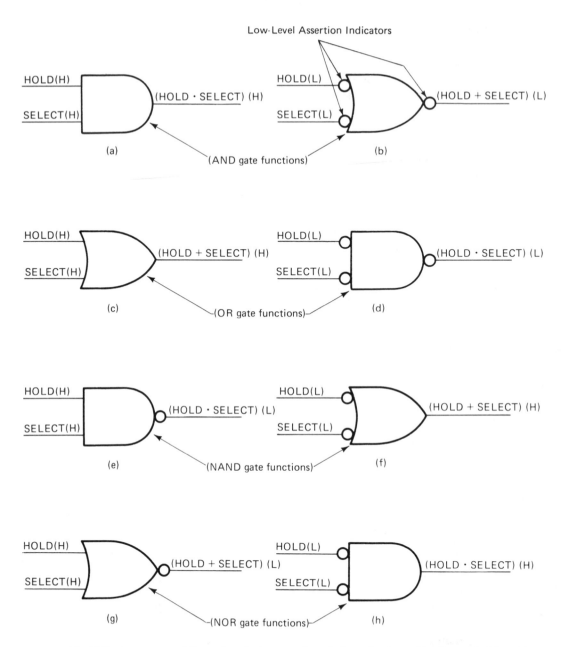

Fig. 2-33 A summary of the various logic expressions that can be derived by the symbol for: (a) an AND gate when used for an AND function; (b) an AND gate when used for an OR function; (c) an OR gate when used for an OR function; (d) an OR gate when used for an AND function; (e) a NAND gate when used for an AND function; (f) a NAND gate when used for an OR function; (g) a NOR gate when used for an OR function; (h) a NOR gate when used for an AND function.

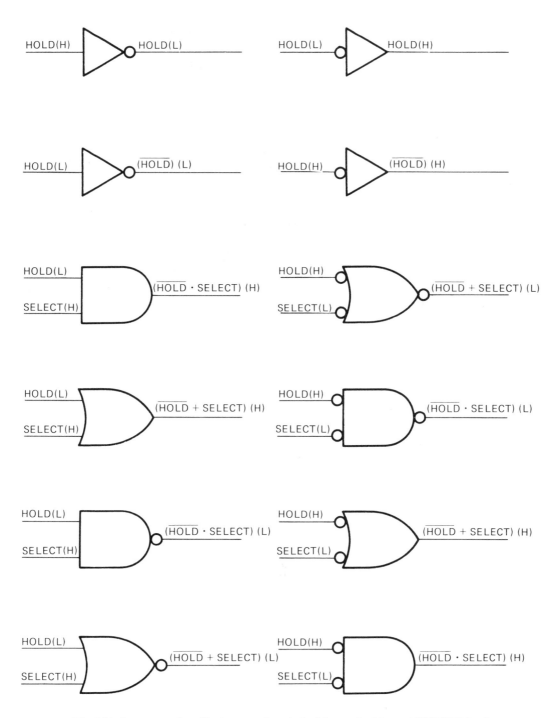

Fig. 2-34 Some examples of logic expressions derived from mixed input ASSERTED levels.

2-14 JUSTIFICATION OF DISTINCTIVE-SHAPED SYMBOL SET

The justification of the distinctive-shaped symbol set is as follows:

(1) It aids in the implemention of AND/OR Boolean expressions by allowing you to visualize the familiar AND and OR operators and INVERTER functions directly.
(2) It aids in reading or analyzing logic networks by allowing you to visualize the familiar AND and OR operations and INVERTER functions.

We have introduced the synthesis procedure in several examples; however, we have not shown directly how the distinctive-shaped symbol set can aid you in an analysis process. To do this, consider the simple examples shown in Figure 2-35 and note how the mental errors resulting from the repeated application of DeMorgan's theorems can be avoided by a simple inspection process.

Much more will be discussed about both analysis and design of combinational circuits. This example is given merely to help justify the use of the distinctive-shaped symbol set shown in Figure 2-33.

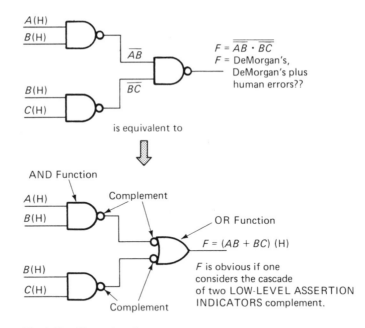

Fig. 2-35. Illustrating the equivalence of two circuits: one easy to read in AND/OR format, the other potentially fraught with human errors.

2-15 EXOR AND EQUIVALENCE GATES

The EXOR and EQUIVALENCE (EXNOR) gates are widely used and are found in binary adders, subtractors, comparators, and controlled inverters. Also, special map techniques have been developed to utilize the devices. The distinctive-shaped symbol for the two-input EXOR is shown in Figure 2-36. The accepted connective for the EXCLUSIVE-OR is $A \oplus B$. Since the $\oplus$ function includes both AND and OR functions, it cannot be treated as a single Boolean operator.

However, it does derive its name from the fact that its output is ASSERTED when A is ASSERTED *or* B is ASSERTED and it is *exclusive* of both. Further, it could also be referred to as an INCLUSIVE AND function, since its output is ASSERTED LOW when A and B are both ASSERTED at either voltage level.

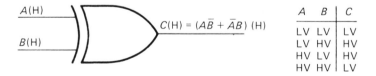

A	B	C
LV	LV	LV
LV	HV	HV
HV	LV	HV
HV	HV	LV

Fig. 2-36. The distinctive-shaped symbol for the EXOR gate and its INPUT/OUTPUT SPECIFICATION TABLE.

It is interesting to note that by inverting either input or the output, an EXOR function can be converted to an EQUIVALENCE function $\odot$.

$$A \odot B = AB + \overline{A}\,\overline{B}$$
$$\overline{A \oplus B} = \overline{A\overline{B} + \overline{A}B} \quad = (\overline{A} + B)(A + \overline{B})$$
$$= AB + \overline{A}\,\overline{B}$$

$$\text{or} \quad \overline{A} \oplus B = \overline{A}\,\overline{B} + AB \quad = A \odot B$$
$$\text{or} \quad A \oplus \overline{B} = AB + \overline{A}\,\overline{B} \quad = A \odot B$$

There is no accepted $\odot$ distinctive-shaped symbol as yet; however, one that is quite widely used is shown in Figure 2-37.

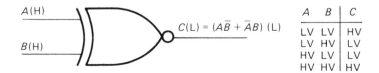

A	B	C
LV	LV	HV
LV	HV	LV
HV	LV	LV
HV	HV	HV

Fig. 2-37. The widely accepted distinctive-shaped symbol for the EQUIVALENCE or EXNOR gate.

The switch-LED equivalent circuit for the two-input EXOR and EQUIVA-LENCE circuits is shown in Figure 2-38.

An interesting electric light switch problem can be implemented with EXOR functions using switches. If a room has three separate light switches from which a single light can be turned on or off from any switch, it so happens that

$$\text{LIGHT ON} = (A \oplus B) \oplus C$$
$$= (A \odot B)C + (A \oplus B)\overline{C}$$

This implementation is shown in Figure 2-39. If you closely examine the circuit in Figure 2-39, the ⊙, ⊕, and AND functions can be plainly seen. There is an alternate switch configuration for this problem that results in a "cheaper" implementation (see Problem 2-37).

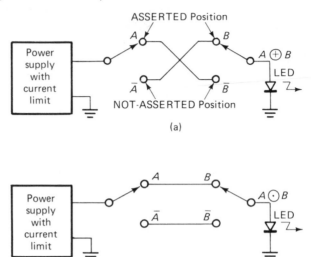

(a)

(b)

Fig. 2-38 (a) The switch-LED equivalent circuit for the function $A \oplus B$. (b)The switch-LED equivalent circuit for the function $A \odot B$.

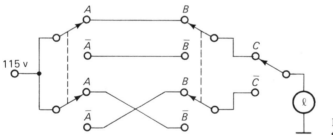

Fig. 2-39. The switch implementation of the three-switch room lighting problem.

This concludes our study of the basic gates and their INPUT/OUTPUT functions. Further, your attention is directed to Figure 2-49, which will give you an idea of the typical small-scale-integrated (SSI) "gate" devices that are available.

2-16 MINTERM AND MAXTERM REALIZATIONS

Up to this point the major effort has been devoted to building up an understanding of Boolean algebra, ASSERTED/NOT-ASSERTED logic gates, and logic functions. We next cover some systematic techniques for transforming a problem specification into a nonsimplified combinational logic expression.

Any Boolean variable, which we call a mnemonic, can take on only one of two values. Therefore, if n Boolean mnemonics are defined as inputs to some given "combinational" circuit, it can be shown that only 2^n distinct possible combinations exist for these n inputs. Further, we have introduced the TRUTH-TABLE as a tabular scheme for systematically listing all of these 2^n combinations. Also, we have illustrated a process of considering *each* entry (row) in the TRUTH-TABLE, one at a time, for the purpose of determining if the output is to be ASSERTED or NOT-ASSERTED for this input condition. For each ASSERTED output condition, a "1" is to be entered in the output column, leaving the 0 for the NOT-ASSERTED cases. To illustrate this, reconsider Example 2-5, where K SWCH, JM SWCH, and AT SWCH were defined as inputs and LNCH RKT was defined as the single output. From this a TRUTH-TABLE can be constructed as shown in Figure 2-40.

Fig. 2-40. The TRUTH-TABLE for the rocket launch problem listing all possible input conditions.

K SWCH	JM SWCH	AT SWCH	LNCH RKT
0	0	0	Output
0	0	1	column
0	1	0	
0	1	1	
1	0	0	
1	0	1	
1	1	0	
1	1	1	

Based on some initial bad results, those in charge have decided to modify the input condition combinations. In other words, it was found that the conditions

$$[\text{K SWCH} \cdot \text{JM SWCH} \cdot \text{AT SWCH}] + [\text{K SWCH} \cdot \text{JM SWCH} \cdot \overline{\text{AT SWCH}}]$$

were not exactly the conditions desired; and the terms

$$[\text{K SWCH} \cdot \overline{\text{JM SWCH}} \cdot \overline{\text{AT SWCH}}] + [\overline{\text{K SWCH}} \cdot \text{JM SWCH} \cdot \text{AT SWCH}]$$

needed to be added, resulting in the TRUTH-TABLE found in Figure 2-41.

Fig. 2-41. The TRUTH-TABLE for the rocket launch including output assignment.

	K SWCH	JM SWCH	AT SWCH	LNCH RKT
m_0	0	0	0	0
m_1	0	0	1	0
m_2	0	1	0	0
m_3	0	1	1	1
m_4	1	0	0	1
m_5	1	0	1	0
m_6	1	1	0	1
m_7	1	1	1	1

We see that by considering each row entry in the TRUTH-TABLE and comparing these to the given desired operational specification, LNCH RKT is to be ASSERTED in rows m_3, m_4, m_6, and m_7. This leads to an *unsimplified* expression for LNCH RKT expressed in terms of AND and OR operators and INVERTER functions and one in which each term of the expression contains every input variable either in its ASSERTED *or* NOT-ASSERTED condition.

$$\text{LNCH RKT} = \left.\begin{array}{l} \overline{\text{K SWCH}} \cdot \text{JM SWCH} \cdot \text{AT SWCH} + \\ \text{K SWCH} \cdot \overline{\text{JM SWCH}} \cdot \overline{\text{AT SWCH}} + \\ \text{K SWCH} \cdot \text{JM SWCH} \cdot \overline{\text{AT SWCH}} + \\ \text{K SWCH} \cdot \text{JM SWCH} \cdot \text{AT SWCH} \end{array}\right\} \begin{array}{l} \text{the four} \\ \text{MINTERMS} \\ \text{defining the} \\ \text{ASSERTION of} \\ \text{LNCH RKT} \end{array}$$

Each term in this expression is defined as a MINTERM, and the complete expression itself is defined as a CANONICAL SUM-OF-MINTERMS, or as the CANONICAL SUM-OF-PRODUCTS (SOP) form for a Boolean expression. *Further, it can be stated that given a TRUTH-TABLE specifying the IN-PUT/OUTPUT relations for any given problem, that problem can be expressed in SOP form.* However, there is no guarantee that this SOP expression will be a minimal expression. In other words, CANONICAL SOP expressions are likely to have redundancies that lead to systems which require more hardware than is necessary. This is where the role of theorems and other reduction techniques come into play as will be shown.

Let

$$\begin{aligned} \text{LR} &= \text{Launch rocket} \\ \text{K} &= \text{Kay's switch in the ASSERTED position} \\ \text{J} &= \text{Jim's switch in the ASSERTED position} \\ \text{A} &= \text{A.T.'s switch in the ASSERTED position} \end{aligned}$$

Then

$$\text{LR} = \overline{\text{K}}(\text{JA}) + \text{K}\overline{\text{J}}\overline{\text{A}} + \text{K}\text{J}\overline{\text{A}} + \text{K}(\text{JA})$$

$$\text{Thm 3} \qquad \text{Thm 3}$$

$$\therefore \text{LR} = \text{JA} + \overline{\text{K}}\overline{\text{A}}$$

Here we see that the repeated application of Theorem 3 is used to simplify the original SOP expression. This simplified expression is commonly defined as a STANDARD SOP expression.

We can see that the reduction process has apparently reduced the hardware list from four 3-input AND functions, one 4-input OR function and four IN-VERTERS to two 2-input AND functions, one 2-input OR function, and one INVERTER.

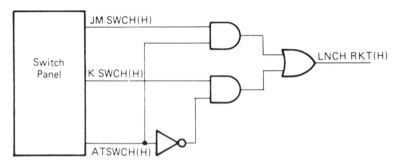

Fig. 2-42. The simplified implementation of the rocket launch problem.

To continue, we select some hardware and assign some polarizing elements and consider a possible implementation of the design as shown in Figure 2-42. Suppose the rocket launch was to take place when LNCH RKT moved from the low condition to the high condition, as the following expression suggests:

$$(\text{LNCH RKT})(\text{H}) = (\text{JM SWCH} \cdot \text{AT SWCH} + \text{K SWCH} \cdot \overline{\text{AT SWCH}})(\text{H})$$

Had the ASSERTED specification for LNCH RKT been in the low voltage range, that is, (LNCH RKT)(L), the implementation could be as shown in Figure 2-43.

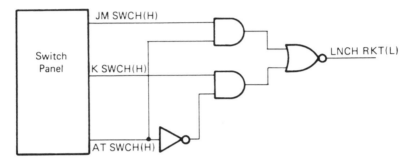

Fig. 2-43. An implementation of LNCH RKT ASSERTED LOW.

As mentioned previously, any TRUTH-TABLE INPUT/OUTPUT specification can be expressed in a SOP expression. To facilitate this, a shorthand symbology has been developed to specify such expressions. This is done by giving each row (MINTERM) in the TRUTH-TABLE a decimal number that is equivalent to the binary code of that row, and specifying the expression thus:

$$\text{LNCH RKT} = \Sigma m_3, m_4, m_6, m_7$$

which reads: LNCH RKT = the Sum-of-products of MINTERMS 3, 4, 6, and 7. This shorthand notation can be further shortened by the following acceptable symbology:

$$\text{LNCH RKT} = \Sigma 3, 4, 6, 7$$

Expressions such as these serve as great aids to the simplification process, as shown in Chapter 3.

Thus far, we see that the general combinational design steps are:

(1) Specify the problem and classify the arguments into ASSERTED and NOT-ASSERTED cases.
(2) Generate a TRUTH-TABLE specifying the INPUT/OUTPUT relations.
(3) Generate a SOP expression.
(4) Simplify the expression.
(5) Implement, keeping in mind the *given* input ASSERTED levels and the *desired* output ASSERTED levels.

2-17 MAXTERM REPRESENTATION

It seems only logical that if an output expression can be generated from the ASSERTED entries in a TRUTH-TABLE, an equally valid expression can be generated from the NOT-ASSERTED entries in the TRUTH-TABLE. Consider the cases where LNCH RKT is NOT-ASSERTED in the TRUTH-TABLE shown in Figure 2-41. We can see that

$$\overline{\text{LNCH RKT}} = \Sigma m_0, m_1, m_2, m_5$$

which written out and reordered reads

$$\overline{\text{LNCH RKT}} = \overline{K}\overline{J}\overline{A} + \overline{K}J\overline{A} + \overline{K}\overline{J}A + KJ\overline{A}$$

Now by using DeMorgan's theorems, we see that

$$\text{LNCH RKT} = \overline{\overline{\text{LNCH RKT}}} = \overline{\overline{K}\overline{J}\overline{A} + \overline{K}J\overline{A} + \overline{K}\overline{J}A + KJ\overline{A}}$$

$$\therefore \text{LNCH RKT} = (K + J + A)(K + \overline{J} + A)(K + J + \overline{A})(\overline{K} + J + \overline{A})$$

By definition, this is the "CANONICAL PRODUCT-OF-SUMS" expression for LNCH RKT. Like the SOP expression, it too can be simplified to the following STANDARD PRODUCT-OF-SUMS expression by using the theorems:

$$\text{LNCH RKT(H)} = (K + A)(J + \overline{A})(H)$$

An implementation of this expression is shown in Figure 2-44.

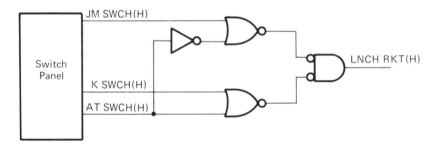

Fig. 2-44. The implementation of the STANDARD PRODUCT-OF-SUMS expression for the rocket launch problem.

The shorthand symbology for canonical POS expressions is as follows:

$$\text{LNCH RKT} = \prod M_0, M_1, M_2, M_5$$

$$\text{or} \quad \text{LNCH RKT} = \prod 0, 1, 2, 5$$

Consider the table shown in Figure 2-45 to help you establish the relationship between the MAXTERM and MINTERM numbers.

From Figure 2-45 we see that:

$$mj = \overline{Mj}$$

$$Mj = \overline{mj}$$

which indicates that MAXTERM j can be derived by complementing MINTERM j.

Fig. 2-45. The MINTERM and MAXTERM designations.

$\bar{A}\bar{B}\bar{C} \rightarrow m_0$	$A + B + C \rightarrow M_0$
$\bar{A}\bar{B}C \rightarrow m_1$	$A + B + \bar{C} \rightarrow M_1$
$\bar{A}B\bar{C} \rightarrow m_2$	$A + \bar{B} + C \rightarrow M_2$
$\bar{A}BC \rightarrow m_3$	$A + \bar{B} + \bar{C} \rightarrow M_3$
$A\bar{B}\bar{C} \rightarrow m_4$	$\bar{A} + B + C \rightarrow M_4$
$A\bar{B}C \rightarrow m_5$	$\bar{A} + B + \bar{C} \rightarrow M_5$
$AB\bar{C} \rightarrow m_6$	$\bar{A} + \bar{B} + C \rightarrow M_6$
$ABC \rightarrow m_7$	$\bar{A} + \bar{B} + \bar{C} \rightarrow M_7$

An interesting point can be made in the relationship between MAXTERM lists and MINTERM lists. The subscript numbers of the terms in the MAXTERM list correspond to the same subscript numbers for MINTERMS that are *not* included in the MINTERM list. From this we can say the following.

Given:

$$\prod \text{(set of MAXTERM numbers)}$$

We know that the function derived from this list will yield precisely the same results as the following:

$$\Sigma \text{ (set of MINTERM numbers that are not included in the MAXTERM list)}$$

For example,

Given:

$$F(A, B, C) = \prod(0, 1, 4, 6)$$

we know immediately that

$$F(A, B, C) = \Sigma(2, 3, 5, 7)$$

It is shown in Chapter 4 that this is a worthwhile bit of information when implementing circuits with fixed building blocks.

In summary, it should be pointed out that at times a POS implementation will result in a simpler form, and therefore, both cases should always be examined. Also, it should be obvious that SOP and POS Boolean implementations fall into one of two basic *two-level models*, as shown in Figure 2-46.

A very important point and one well worth remembering is that canonical forms reduced by standard techniques result in two-level standard forms, which are sometimes referred to as "disjunctive (SOP)" and "conjunctive (POS)" forms. This is not to say that these simplified forms cannot be factored into other forms such as

$$F = A\bar{B} + A\bar{C} + D = A(\bar{B} + \bar{C}) + D$$
$$\text{or} \quad F(\text{H}) = \left[A(\bar{B} + \bar{C}) + D \right](\text{H})$$

This expression can be implemented in a three-level implementation as shown in Figure 2-47.

Generally speaking, the extra delay in some of the signal paths is not always desirable and this type of implementation is not often encountered except when trying to limit the number of gate inputs. However, note that reading the expression for $F(H)$ from the circuit in Figure 2-47 is made quite obvious by using the distinctive-shaped symbol set.

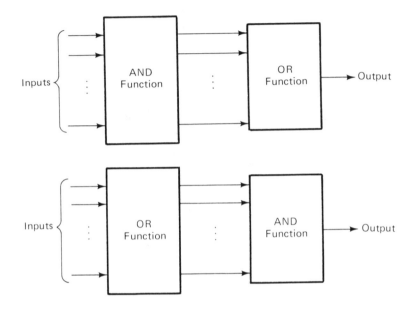

Fig. 2-46 The basic two level models for combinational circuits. (a) Standard SOP AND/OR. (b) Standard POS OR/AND.

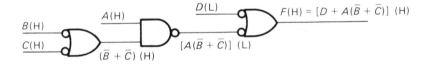

Fig. 2-47 A three-level implementation of the two-level expression $F = A\bar{B} + A\bar{C} + D$.

However, most of our implementations will be of the two-level forms, and as an aid, Table 2-6 provides the resultant two-level forms that can be arrived at by cascading the two-level combinations of AND, OR, NAND, and NOR gates.

It is interesting to note that of the 16 possible combinations, eight yield both SOP and POS implementations. The kicker, however, is the ASSERTED conditions for the inputs and outputs. The other eight provide expanded input AND or OR functions. More is discussed about the application of these combinations in Chapter 4. To aid in your understanding of Table 2-6, Figure 2-48 should be referred to. Figure 2-49 is provided to help you get an idea of the variety of types of gates that are available.

TABLE 2-6   Resultant two-level forms arrived at by cascading the four basic gates in two levels

1st Level / 2nd Level	Possible Two-level Implementations
AND/OR	AND/OR—OR/AND
OR/AND	OR/AND—AND/OR
AND/AND	Expanded AND—Expanded OR
AND/NAND	Expanded AND—Expanded OR
NAND/AND	OR/AND—AND/OR
AND/NOR	AND/OR—OR/AND
NOR/AND	Expanded AND—Expanded OR
OR/OR	Expanded OR—Expanded AND
OR/NAND	OR/AND—AND/OR
NAND/OR	Expanded OR—Expanded AND
OR/NOR	Expanded OR—Expanded AND
NOR/OR	OR/AND—AND/OR
NAND/NAND	AND/OR—OR/AND
NAND/NOR	Expanded AND—Expanded OR
NOR/NAND	Expanded AND—Expanded OR
NOR/NOR	AND/OR—OR/AND

Fig. 2-48.   Examples of resultant two-level forms taken from Table 2-6.

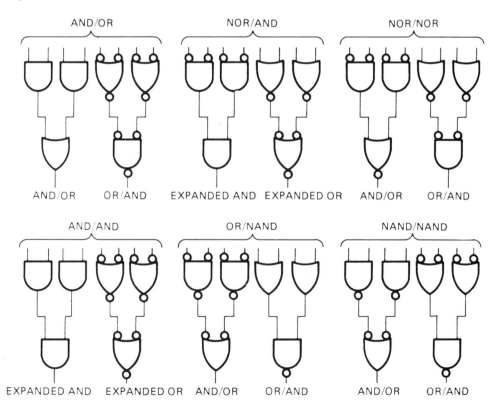

	TTL			CMOS	
AND					
2 input	7408 74S08	74LS08		MC14081B	74C08
3 input	74S11	74LS11		MC14073B	
4 input				MC14082B	
OR					
2 input	74S32 74LS32	7432		MC14071B	74C32
3 input				MC14075B	
4 input				MC14072B	
NOR					
2 input	74S02 74LS02	7402		MC14001B	74C02
3 input	7427	74LS27		MC14000	4025
4 input	7425			MC14002B	
5 input	74S260				
NAND					
2 input	74S00	74LS00	7400	MC14011B	74C00
3 input	74S10	74LS10	7410	MC14023B	74C10
4 input	74S20	74LS20	7420	MC14012B	74C20
8 input	74S30	74LS30	7430	MC14068B	74C30
13 input	74S133				
INVERTERS	74S04	7404	74LS04	MC14069B MC14049B	74C04
EXCLUSIVE NOR				MC14077B	
EXCLUSIVE OR	74S86	74LS86	7486	MC14070B	74C86

Fig. 2-49. A listing of SSI gates available in TTL and CMOS.

2-18 ONCE OVER LIGHTLY

Up to this point we have developed most of the background necessary to design combinational networks using integrated circuit devices. However, the important aspects of *combination reduction* have been treated rather lightly; these are developed more fully in Chapter 3 and integrated to the formal design process. Therefore, at this time let us review some of the *documentation* methods (schematic drawing notation) developed thus far and then extend and use these methods for strengthening our analytic powers. Keep in mind that the material to be presented here might seem a little "heavy" at this time, but the author feels that good habits should be developed early, and it is intended that you will be referring to this material throughout your studies in this text.

2-18.1 POLARIZED MNEMONICS
REVISITED

A thorough treatise of the "whys" for the specialized notation, Polarized Mnemonics and State Indicators, has been given. We now carry this concept on to the "wheres" and "hows" of its uses.

Boolean algebra as used presently was developed around AND, OR, and INVERT logic. We are also aware of the utility of NAND and NOR *gates*. However, to bring these two facts together, some specialized techniques must be employed. The real problem is, given some Boolean SOP/POS expression, how can we implement this expression using NAND or NOR gates? Better yet, how can a mixture of AND, OR, NAND, and NOR gates be arranged to minimize the use of INVERTER functions? Another important question is: How can we draw schematic diagrams in some format that does not require theorem (DeMorgan's) application each time the schematics are read? As the author views it, there seems to be a good deal of confusion with regard to logic symbology and digital gate usage. This confusion further compounds the problems related to digital system design because little is taught about formal documentation techniques. It is generally agreed that the design of digital systems, particularly large designs, without some formal format for signal line identification, logic level indicators, source and destination descriptors, can be one great big tangled mess. By their nature, digital systems tend to become large before they become useful, and because of this, documentation standards are an absolute must. Nothing can be more frustrating to someone than troubleshooting or debugging some digital system with poorly documented and hard-to-read schematics. Thus it is important to use a standard and approved technique when drawing your schematics, even the small three-gate designs you often do. This is good practice, because most of your small designs will become part of a bigger system.

Thus we have hit upon some key reasons for using Polarized Mnemonics coupled with what we call MIXED LOGIC and cross-reference schematic drawings. Keep in mind that a *MIXED LOGIC system is one in which no special efforts are made to keep the system totally POSITIVE LOGIC (all signals ASSERTED HIGH) or totally NEGATIVE LOGIC (all signals ASSERTED LOW).* Cross-referenced schematic drawings are simply schematic drawings, drawn on paper, that have ZONAL-COORDINATES like a road map. By using cross-referenced drawings, you avoid the jungle of lines criss-crossing back and forth across drawings. This jungle is avoided by simply giving an output (source) signal a unique mnemonic and the zone coordinate of its destination, and giving the input of the gate that receives this signal the same mnemonic along with the zone coordinate of the source. When this is done, you can read your schematics quickly without becoming entangled in a maze of lines. For more information related to schematic drawing and system documentation, see Appendix A.

In summary, we can list the following criteria for any digital design schematic documentation. Any schematic documentation system should yield diagrams that are:

(1) drawn with standard and readable symbols;
(2) drawn in such a way that they can be quickly interpreted;
(3) documented to allow easy signal tracing from one sheet to another sheet and back;
(4) documented to allow subsystem identification;
(5) documented to allow component identification to a pin or lead level;
(6) documented to identify loading and fan-out information.

Further, the system should be flexible for use with any of the logic families available and, more importantly, the system should serve as an aid to the designer by making much of the design and analysis work an inspection process. Designing by inspection is certainly a dream, but a good schematic system will minimize much of the voltage level analysis and algorithmic or axiomatic Boolean expression-to-hardware conversions. The documentation system called POLARIZED MNEMONICS, LOGIC STATE INDICATORS, and CROSS REFERENCED DRAWINGS has been developed to incorporate the above mentioned criteria and will be discussed and used throughout the remainder of this text.

The fourfold premise of this documentation system is:

(1) Leads or logic lines are given unique shortened names (MNEMONICS), which implicitly or explicitly suggest a logic operation to be performed.
(2) The logic level (high or low) is also attached to each mnemonic, indicating the level at which the logic operation is ASSERTED or *performed*.
(3) The use of a logic symbology called *logic state indicators* (bubbles), which schematically support the use of polarized mnemonics.
(4) Schematics are drawn on paper with zonal coordinates with all leads cross-referenced.

2-18.2 MNEMONICS REVISITED

Remember, *a mnemonic is a short adaptive notation given to a logic line which suggests the logic operation performed by the signal on that line.* Table 2-7 illustrates some typical logic operations to be performed and suggested mnemonics. Generally, mnemonics should be as short as possible and still convey some indication of the operation they are meant to identify. One technique used extracts all vowels from the functional description leaving the sounds of the consonants to carry the meaning, that is, HOLD=HLD. It is very important to keep mnemonic assignments unique. Confusion is created by the assignment of the same mnemonic to more than one functionally different lead.

TABLE 2-7   Example polarized mnemonics

Function Performed	Asserted Voltage Level	Suggested Mnemonic	Optional Mnemonic
Load Bus	Low	LDBS(L)	LDBS0
Lock Address	High	LKADR(H)	LKADR1
Strobe	Low	STRB(L)	STRB0
Busy	High	BSY(H)	BSY1
Transmit	Low	XMT(L)	XMT0
Load Accumulator	Low	LDACC(L)	LDACC0
Set Flip-Flop	Low	SETFF(L)	SETFF0
Fill Buffer	High	FLBUFR(H)	FLBUFR1
Clear Register	High	CLRREG(H)	CLRREG1
Set Index	Low	SETNDX(L)	SETNDX0
Gate Data	High	GATDAT(H)	GATDAT1
Request to Send	Low	RTS(L)	RTS0
Data Carrier Detect	High	DCD(H)	DCD1

2-18.3   POLARIZATION REVISITED

It should be noted that the mnemonics found in Table 2-7 are polarized with either a (H) or a (L) or optionally with a "1" or "0", conveying the information that the ACTION described by the mnemonic is ASSERTED at a high or low voltage, respectively. Thus when you assign a polarizing element to a mnemonic, it identifies the voltage level at which the operation or action described by the mnemonics is to be performed.

It is true that there are cases where some action is not explicitly suggested by a polarized mnemonic. An example of this follows. The main clock oscillator of a synchronous system could be given the mnemonic CLK or OSC and at first glance it might appear that the use of CLK(L) or OSC(L) as opposed to CLK(H) or OSC(H) would be of little significance. However, consider the case when both phases of that clock are used for different purposes. The OSC(H) or CLK(H) could be used to identify clock lines that trigger operations on the rising edge (LOW to HIGH transition) of the main clock, while OSC(L) or CLK(L) could be used to identify clock lines that initiate operations on the falling edge (HIGH to LOW transition) of the main clock waveform. Another example occurs in assigning mnemonics to a set of lines that carry parallel numeric data. In this case things become confusing because the data is valid independent of the voltage level. In short, a particular *line is low or high because of its inherent numerical value.* In cases such as these a mnemonic like the following could be used:

$$DBIT6 = 1(L)$$

which conveys the information that data bit 6 is equal to the numerical value of 1 when its signal line is at a low voltage level. Therefore, in general, with a little thought you can always generate an appropriate mnemonic to fit any given problem if you keep in mind the descriptive nature of mnemonics.

One of the real advantages of a polarized mnemonic notation is the aid it can lend in troubleshooting. This feature can be best illustrated by Example 2-6.

EXAMPLE 2-6: Consider the following. A technician is troubleshooting a system and has at hand several schematic diagrams. He suspects that the system isn't loading the binary address 15 into an address register (see Figure 2-50).

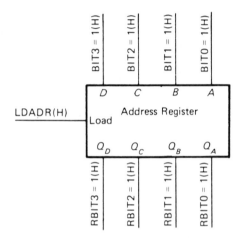

Fig. 2-50. Address register illustrating use of polarized mnemonics.

He first checks the inputs: BIT3 = 1(H), BIT2 = 1(H), BIT1 = 1(H), and BIT0 = 1(H), finds them all high. He then knows by the mnemonics BIT3 = 1(H)...BIT0 = 1(H) that the binary address 15 is present at the register inputs. He then sets up the condition for loading the register and checks LDADR(H) lead and finds it low. By examining the mnemonic LDADR(H) he can determine that the LOAD ADDRESS line has a fault (it is low and it should be high). If there were no polarizing symbol with the mnemonic, he would have no information, except experience, regarding whether the register is loaded with a low or high voltage on its load input. Thus we see another useful advantage of using polarized mnemonics in the interpretation of schematic diagrams for troubleshooting.

2-18.4 LOGIC POLARITY INDICATORS REVISITED

The study of the basic logic gates revealed that *any* of the AND, OR, NAND, and NOR *gates* can be used as either AND or OR *functions*. Also it was noted that the LOGIC STATE INDICATORS at the inputs and outputs schematically carry information concerning the ASSERTED polarity of the signal on the connecting logic line. This significance is established by the following criteria.

When a state indicator is present at an *output* it serves as a schematic symbol conveying the information *that the function performed by the gate or any other complex logic function block is ASSERTED LOW*. As shown in Figure 2-33(e), the NAND gate performs an AND logic operation with its output ASSERTED LOW. Likewise, the NOR gate as shown in Figure 2-33(g) performs an OR operation with its output ASSERTED LOW. When there is no state indicator at the output of a gate or complex logic block, then this is a schematic representation conveying the information *that the function performed by the gate or complex network is ASSERTED HIGH*. As shown in Figure 2-33(f), the NAND gate, drawn differently, will perform an OR operation with its output ASSERTED HIGH whenever either or both of its inputs are ASSERTED LOW. Similarly, the NOR gate, redrawn in Figure 2-33(h), will perform an AND operation with its output ASSERTED HIGH, when both of its inputs are ASSERTED LOW.

Consider now the two schematic symbols for the inverter shown in Figure 2-34. The presence of the state indicator at the output conveys the idea that the information ASSERTED HIGH at the input is ASSERTED LOW at the output. Conversely, when the state indicator is present at the input, the output is ASSERTED HIGH when the input is ASSERTED LOW, following the defined logic function of the INVERTER.

The all-important concept emphasized here is concerned with the connection between the *compatibility* of the *polarizing element of the mnemonic* and an associated state indicator. The definition of compatibility: *An output with a state indicator must have a corresponding mnemonic with a low polarizing element. An output with no state indicator must have a corresponding mnemonic with a high polarizing element. A mnemonic with a low polarizing element normally connects to an input with a state indicator. A mnemonic with a high polarizing element normally connects to an input with no state indicator.*

Note the distinction drawn between *must* and *normally*. This leads us to the next question to be answered: What is to be done if an *incompatibility* at an input occurs? For example, what is to be done when a mnemonic with a *low* polarizing element is joined with an input with *no* state indicator or conversely when a mnemonic with a *high* polarizing element is joined with an input with a state indicator? This situation was found to be necessary and desirable in combination design and analysis. However, if the norm is to strive for compatibility, how then do we properly document incompatibilities? The answer follows: First, this type of problem should be properly tagged by some suitable symbol like a small triangle (▼, ▲). Second, determine what kind of logic function this incompatibility is associated with. These incompatible situations will occur in one of two situations: (a) at the input of an AND function, or (b) at the input of an OR function. Let an INHIBIT operation be defined if the incompatibility exists at the input of an AND function and an ENABLE operation be defined if the incompatibility exists at the input of an OR function. The ▼ symbol will be used to identify an INHIBIT operation and the ▲ symbol will identify an ENABLE operation.

You will see these ▼, ▲ symbols attached to symbol inputs on schematic drawings. These are used for two reasons.

(1) It serves as a notation indicating, *"this variable is to appear complemented in the output expression."*

(2) It serves as a visual aid to those interpreting your schematics that you recognize the deviation from the norm.

Example 2-7 illustrates another use of the INHIBIT and ENABLE schematic symbols.

> EXAMPLE 2-7: It is desired that the HOLD logic operation inhibit or disable the logic operation SELECT. The implementation of this problem is illustrated in Figure 2-51(a). It is of particular importance that the INHIBIT operation be denoted as a special case, hence the use of the small INVERTED triangle on the lead named HOLD(L). It should be noticed that there exists an incompatibility between the mnemonic HOLD(L) and the input without a state indicator. This incompatibility is the very essence of the INHIBIT operation and should be used as a design aid in INHIBIT implementations. Figure 2-51(b) illustrates another implementation of the INHIBIT function.

Fig. 2-51. An illustration of the use of INHIBIT notation for Example 2-7.

A similar example illustrating the ENABLE function is shown in Figures 2-52(a) and 2-52(b). Here the logic function HOLD is to ENABLE or permit the logic operation of SELECT.

Examination of the conditions presented in Figure 2-52(a) shows that the logic function HOLD(L) *ENABLES* the function SELECT. Likewise, in Figure 2-52(b) HOLD(H) *ENABLES* the function of SELECT. In both cases a triangle ▲ was used to denote the use of the ENABLE function. Aside from this, the important aspect of the compatible/incompatible mnemonic input relation is that it allows you to quickly select the gates needed to implement a design from a Boolean expression by matching mnemonics to inputs for uncomplemented variables and mismatching mnemonics to inputs for complemented variables.

Fig. 2-52. An illustration of the use of ENABLE notation for Example 2-7.

2-18.5 OTHER USES FOR THE STATE INDICATOR

The author recognizes that the type of notation used here is not completely in agreement with similar standards set forth in the IEEE publication *Graphic Symbols for Logic Diagrams ANSI Y32, Vol. 14 (1973)*. For those who are interested in the symbology set forth in this publication, the following symbols are introduced in Figure 2-53.

▷: *POLARITY INDICATOR SYMBOL*, which denotes the ASSERTED state of an input/output with respect to the symbol is the less positive level.

▷: *DYNAMIC INDICATOR SYMBOL*, which denotes that the ASSERTED state of an input is a *transition* from a NOT-ASSERTED to the ASSERTED state, not merely the presence of the ASSERTED state.

○▷: *DYNAMIC INDICATOR AND NEGATION INDICATOR SYMBOL*, which denotes that the ASSERTED state of an input is a *transition* from the ASSERTED state to the NOT-ASSERTED state.

Fig. 2-53. Explanation of the IEEE standard symbols.

It can be seen from this that the low-level ASSERTION indicator ○ is used for a dual purpose, serving both as a negation indicator symbol as well as the polarity indicator symbol. This approach is consistent when the standard inverter symbol is used.

As mentioned above, the state indicator is used to indicate the polarity of the signal at which the function is ASSERTED. This concept can apply equally well for logic devices that are more complex than simple AND, OR, NAND, NOR, and INVERTER gates. For example, consider the schematic symbols for D Flip-Flops and PARALLEL IN/PARALLEL OUT SHIFT REGISTERS shown in Figure 2-54.

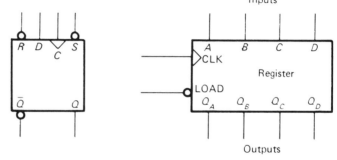

Fig. 2-54. Examples of state indicator usage.

In this case, the state indicator notation, although not completely accepted by industry, serves as an additional aid. The interpretation is as follows: The Flip-Flop is SET by taking its *S* input low; it is RESET by taking its *R* input low. The register is LOADED by taking its LOAD input low. Examples of mnemonics that could be used for these functions are: SETFF(L), RESETFF(L), and LDREG(L). Many other devices are in use which also employ state indicator notation; for example, DECODER and MULTIPLEXER enables, ROM chip selects, COUNTER clear and load inputs, and so forth. *Polarized mnemonics and state indicators* can serve the logic designer as valuable tools rather than misunderstood inconveniences.

2-18.6 CROSS-REFERENCED DRAWINGS

Cross-referenced drawing is the use of the addressable sectors (zones) on special drafting paper for the purpose of identifying "geographical" locations. The special drafting paper that has this addressable sector feature is similar to topographical road maps. The address of any sector is made up from (a) systems identification, (b) schematic sheet numbers, (c) a number for the vertical coordinates, and (d) an alphabetic character for the horizontal coordinate. Zonal coordinates coupled with polarized mnemonics and state indicators simplify crossreferencing for signal tracing in a multi-schematic sheet system (see Figure 2-55). The drafting rules for zonal coordinated schematics are given in Appendix A.

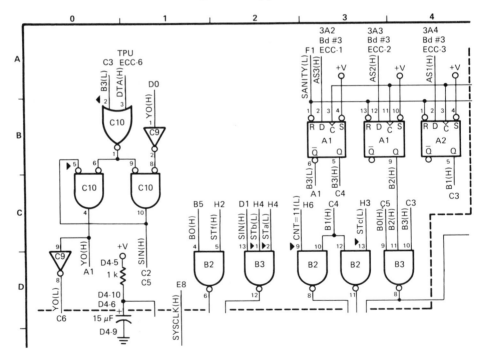

Fig. 2-55. (a) Inset of (b).

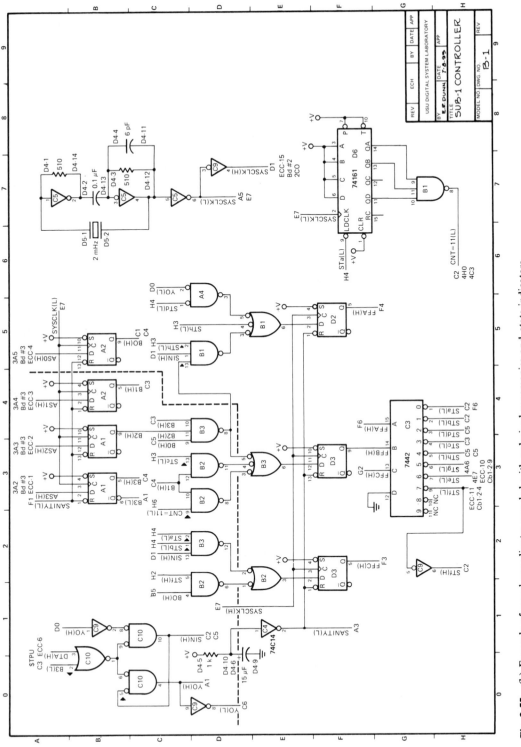

Fig. 2-55. (b) Example of zonal coordinates coupled with polarized mnemonics and state indicators.

117

2-19 ANALYSIS OF COMBINATIONAL CIRCUITS

Your studies up to this point have been primarily devoted to the understanding and applying of concepts related to design, somewhat contrary to the natural development of a science, which is:

(1) first, to understand, which is unearthing new knowledge;
(2) second, to predict, which is analysis;
(3) third, to control, which is design.

Now let us reverse this direction and treat some analysis concepts. The analysis of combinational circuits is an easy process and particularly so using the polarized-mnemonics mixed schematic symbology. There are at least two reasons for analyzing a circuit:

(1) to determine if an error exists in a given design, or to see if the thing works as you think it should, or
(2) to determine if the circuit is truly in its minimal form, or in general, if you want the Boolean expression for the circuit.

Many times you will be confronted with arrays of NAND and NOR gate circuits drawn in the standard way. Unless you have trained yourself to recognize NAND/NAND, NOR/NOR, NAND/NOR, and NOR/NAND patterns, you are normally confronted with a detailed successive application of DeMorgan's theorems. If you are like most, the repetitive application of anything precipitates errors. Besides that, repeated applications of DeMorgan's theorems is just plain boring. This is where the mixed symbology you have learned can spare you from the trials of DeMorgan. The following steps will aid you in your reduction tasks.

The steps to analysis: Given a circuit drawn up with standard NAND and NOR symbols, mixed or otherwise:

(1) Label each input of the circuit with a mnemonic and an ASSERTION level polarizing element. The inputs that require these mnemonics are primarily those that are considered the OUTSIDE WORLD INPUTS.
(2) Strive to develop the output expression in SOP standard form. To do this, form the output gate into an *OR FUNCTION*, be it ASSERTED HIGH or LOW.
(3) Working back from the output through the logic levels, strive to match input and output state indicators at all times. Special note: This may at times require a slight re-drawing of the same gate or gates in both of its functional representations.
(4) Once you have your diagram at the point where you can read it in AND/OR notations, write the Boolean expression for the output by inspection.

Several examples will be shown illustrating this process and its advantages over successive applications of De Morgan's theorems. Again, this advantage stems from minimizing the mathematical manipulation of large expressions, thus reducing the chance for introducing errors.

EXAMPLE 2-8: Analyze the circuit shown in Figure 2-56.

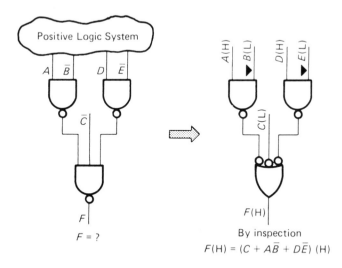

Fig. 2-56. Example of analysis by inspection.

EXAMPLE 2-9: Analyze the circuit shown in Figure 2-57, that is, find the output expression ASSERTED LOW.

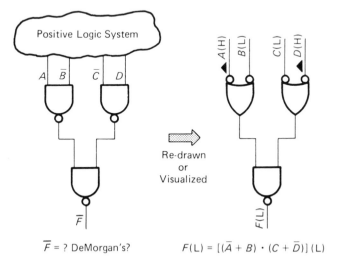

Fig. 2-57. An example analysis problem illustrating the use of mixed symbology.

EXAMPLE 2-10:   Analyze the circuit shown in Figure 2-58.

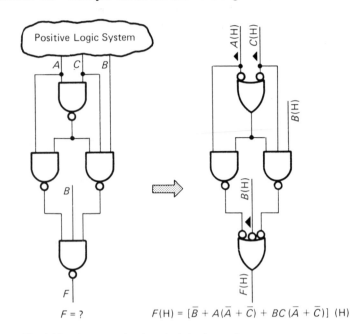

$$F(H) = [\bar{B} + A(\bar{A} + \bar{C}) + BC(\bar{A} + \bar{C})] \ (H)$$

Fig. 2-58.   An example of analysis by inspection.

EXAMPLE 2-11:   Analyze the circuit shown in Figure 2-59.

Fig. 2-59.   (a) The circuit to be analyzed.

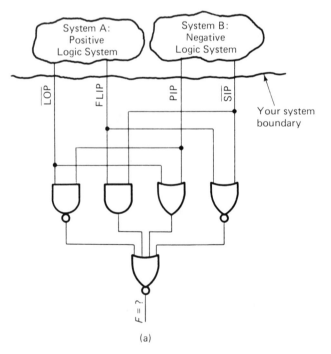

(a)

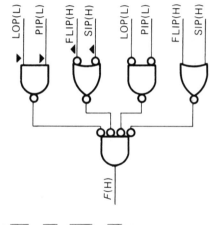

$$F(H) = [(\overline{LOP} \cdot \overline{PIP})(\overline{FLIP} + \overline{SIP})(LOP \cdot PIP)(FLIP + SIP)] \ (H)$$

(b)

Fig. 2-59. (b) The resultant mixed logic schematic of the circuit in Part a.

2-20 SUMMARY

The salient points and concepts of this chapter are listed as follows:

(1) Concepts of ASSERTED and NOT-ASSERTED
(2) ASSERTED HIGH/LOW polarized mnemonics
(3) Electronic INPUT/OUTPUT relations of gates
(4) The distinction drawn between gates and functions
(5) Distinctive-shaped symbols for logic gates
(6) The development of a two-valued Boolean algebra and accompanying identities and theorems
(7) Use of theorems for minimization of expressions
(8) The development of a total AND, OR and INVERTER philosophy even when using NAND and NOR gates
(9) The systematic techniques of using a TRUTH-TABLE, canonical forms, and theorems to develop the AND/OR or OR/AND combinational circuit models.
(10) The systematic technique for analyzing combinational circuits using mixed logic symbology.

In total, a good deal of information concerning combinational circuit design has been introduced. It is important that the reader understand these salient concepts before proceeding further, for all the material that follows is predicated upon the information presented here.

BIBLIOGRAPHY

1. AMERICAN NATIONAL STANDARDS INSTITUTE. *Graphic Symbols for Logic Diagrams (Two-State Devices)*. New York: IEEE, 1973.

2. BIRKHOFF, G., AND T. C. BARTEE, *Modern Applied Algebra*. New York: McGraw-Hill, 1970.

3. BOOLE, G. *An Investigation of the Laws of Thought, on Which are Founded the Mathematical Theories of Logic and Probability* (1849). New York: Dover (reprint), 1954.

4. DEMPSEY, JOHN A. *Basic Digital Electronics with MSI Applications*. Reading, Mass.: Addison-Wesley, 1977.

5. HOHN, F. E. *Applied Boolean Algebra*, 2nd ed., New York: Macmillan, 1966.

6. HUNTINGTON, E. V. Sets of Independent Postulates for the Algebra of Logic. *Trans. Am. Math. Soc.*, **5** (1904), pp. 288–309.

7. KINTER, PAUL M. How to Succed in MIL-STD 806-B Without Half-Trying. *Computer Design*, (July 1967), pp. 18–21.

8. PHISTER, MONTGOMERY, JR. *Logical Design of Digital Computers*. New York: Wiley, 1968.

9. PRATHER, RONALD E. *Introduction to Switching Theory: A Mathematics Approach*. Boston, Mass.: Allyn and Bacon, 1967.

10. SHANNON, C. E. *Symbolic Analysis of Relay and Switching Circuits. Trans. AIEE*, **57** (1938), pp. 713–723.

PROBLEMS AND EXERCISES

2-1. Define:
(a) Information
(b) Logic
(c) Binary logic

2-2. In your own words, describe the word ACTION as it relates to the definition and clarification of logic variables.

2-3. (a) Define or describe ASSERTED as it is used in this chapter.
(b) Why does ASSERTED relate to ACTIONS more clearly than TRUE?

2-4. (a) What is a MNEMONIC?
(b) What is a POLARIZED MNEMONIC?
(c) Illustrate two formats for a polarized mnemonic.

2-5. The use of the symbols '1' and '0' is extensive in design in various capacites. List four different interpretations for each of these symbols.

2-6. (a) What is a TRUTH-TABLE?
(b) List two uses for TRUTH-TABLES.

2-7. In this chapter it was specifically mentioned that a 1 entered in a TRUTH-TABLE was a shorthand notation for ___ ?

2-8. Given the following TRUTH-TABLE:

BIF	KZ	SIB
0	0	0
0	1	1
1	0	0
1	1	1

Interpret this table and write a logic statement using the words IF, AND, OR, ASSERTED and NOT-ASSERTED.

2-9. Using ASSERTED and other phraseology, describe:
(a) The general AND gate
(b) The general OR gate

2-10. The OR gate is commonly referred to as a ___ gate. Why?

2-11. Illustrate the three- and four-input OR gate INPUT/OUTPUT specification table.

2-12. Illustrate the three- and four-input AND gate INPUT/OUTPUT specification table.

2-13. You are given the following INPUT/OUTPUT specification for some gates:
(a) Identify those that exhibit an AND/OR operation.
(b) Using the technique illustrated in Section 2-5, develop the two proper distinctive-shaped symbols for these gates.

A	B	C		A	B	C		A	B	C		A	B	C
LV	LV	LV		LV	LV	HV		LV	LV	LV		LV	LV	HV
LV	HV	HV		LV	HV	HV		LV	HV	HV		LV	HV	LV
HV	LV	HV		HV	LV	HV		HV	LV	HV		HV	LV	LV
HV	HV	LV		HV	HV	LV		HV	HV	HV		HV	HV	LV

2-14. (a) Define positive logic.
(b) Define negative logic.

2-15. (a) Given Figure 2P-1, convert the given mnemonic to polarized mnemonics.
(b) Why is this conversion recommended?

Fig. 2P-1

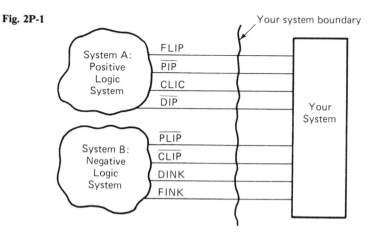

2-16. You are to design a switch panel using two SPST switches that generate the LOAD(L) and CLEAR(H) signals. Make certain that, at no time during or after a switch operation, these signal lines are allowed to "float." Draw schematics and label properly.

2-17. Define the function of an INVERTER and describe its practical application. Why is the INVERTER more appropriately referred to as a "function" rather than an "operator?"

> *Note:* The next several problems are word problems relating to logic. They are to be reviewed and studied, then a Boolean Expression (unsimplified) is to be defined which reflects the information contained in these statements.

2-18. Consider the following logic statements:
(a) Harriet never drinks.
(b) Von drinks if and only if Harriet and Keffer are present.
(c) Steinitz drinks under all conditions—even by himself.
(d) Keffer drinks if and only if Harriet is not present.
If A represents Harriet's presence in the bar, B Keffer's presence, C Steinitz's, and D Von's, determine the Boolean function defining the state of NO drinking.

2-19. Using a logic expression, define the conditions for issuing Form 104 (hookup notice) from the Power and Light Company. According to the company manual, Form 104 is to be issued if the applicant:
(a) has been issued prior service and is a married man, or
(b) has been issued Form 103 and is married and under 25, or
(c) has not been issued prior service and is a married female, or
(d) is a male under 25, or
(e) is married and is 25 or over.

2-20. A local swimming pool is trying to hire lifeguards for the next summer. There are several groups of people to choose from. The first of these is men and women. The second is lifeguards who either can or can't swim. Experience is also a factor. This has been broken down into two groups of more than or less than five years of experience. The final breakdown is those who are good-looking and those who aren't. Write the logic expressions defining those who would be hired if the pool manager hired anyone who can swim with five years experience, all good-looking women and good-looking men with more than five years experience, and good-looking lifeguards with less than five years experience.

2-21. Draw the logic diagrams using AND and OR and INVERTERS for the following (refer to Section 2-9):
(a) $F = (AB + C\overline{D})$(H); if all inputs are ASSERTED HIGH
(b) $F = (AB + C\overline{D})$(L); if all inputs are ASSERTED LOW
(c) $F = (A\overline{B} + C\overline{D})$(H); if A and C are ASSERTED HIGH and B and D are ASSERTED LOW
(d) $F = (\overline{A}\,\overline{B} + CD)$(L); if A, B ASSERTED HIGH, and C, D ASSERTED LOW

2-22. A proposed deductive system for the set $S = \{0, 1, 2\}$ is shown below.

*	0	1	2
0	0	0	0
1	0	1	1
2	0	1	2

/	0	1	2
0	0	1	2
1	1	1	2
2	2	2	2

Analyze this proposed system using Huntington's postulates.

2-23. Choose your own set having three elements and define two binary operators. Test your system using Huntington's postulates.

2-24. Derive the "dual theorems" for the theorems in Table 2-2.

2-25. Prove two ways that:
(a) $AB + ABC = AB$
(b) $\bar{A} + AB = \bar{A} + B$
(c) $AB + A\bar{B} = A$

2-26. Reduce the following Boolean expressions using the theorems and identities:
(a) $F = AB(C + \bar{C}) + A\bar{B}$
(b) $F = C + AB + AD(B + \bar{C}) + CD$
(c) $F = A\bar{B} + A\bar{C} + \bar{B}\bar{C}$
(d) $F = A + ABC + \bar{A}C$
(e) $F = AB + C\bar{D}B + \bar{A}C\bar{D}$
(f) $F = (\bar{X} + \bar{Y})(\bar{X} + \bar{Z})$

2-27. Simplify the following using theorems:
(a) the Boolean expression derived for Problem 2-18;
(b) the Boolean expression derived for Problem 2-19;
(c) the Boolean expression derived for Problem 2-20.

2-28. Evaluate the following:
(a) $\overline{A \cdot B \cdot C}$
(b) $\overline{A + B + C}$
(c) $\overline{A \cdot \bar{B} \cdot \bar{C}}$
(d) $\overline{(\bar{A} + \overline{AC} + B)}$
(e) $\overline{A(\overline{B + C})D}$

2-29. Evaluate the following:
(a) $(A \cdot B \cdot C)(L) = ($? $)(H)$
(b) $(A + B)\underline{(H)} = ($? $)(L)$
(c) $(XY + \overline{ZW})(L) = ($? $)(H)$

2-30. Implement Problem 2-21(a) using only NAND gates to illustrate the universality of the NAND gate.

2-31. Implement Problem 2-21(b) using all NAND gates to illustrate the universality of the NAND gate.

2-32. Repeat Problem 2-30 using all NOR gates to illustrate the universality of the NOR gate.

2-33. Repeat Problem 2-31 using all NOR gates to illustrate the universality of the NOR gate.

2-34. Implement the circuit in Figure 2-24 using:
(a) all NAND gates,
(b) all NOR gates,
(c) all AND and INVERTERS only.

2-35. Assume that LNCH RKT(L) was desired for the implementation of the circuit in Figure 2-22. Implement using:
(a) all NAND,
(b) all NOR,
(c) all OR and INVERTERS only.

2-36. Show:
(a) $\overline{AB + \overline{A}\overline{B}} = A \oplus B$
(b) $\overline{A} \oplus B = A \odot B$
(c) $\overline{A \odot B} = A \oplus B$
(d) $[(C \oplus D) + C](L) = (\overline{CD})(H)$
(e) $(A \oplus B)(L) = (A \odot B)(H)$

2-37. Derive an alternate switch configuration for the three-way light problem shown in Figure 2-39.

2-38. Given the following TRUTH-TABLES, which are several functions of the same variables. Express each in terms of:
(a) the Σ notation,
(b) the Π notation.

A	B	F_1	F_2	F_3
0	0	0	1	0
0	1	1	0	1
1	0	0	0	1
1	1	0	0	1

A	B	C	F_4	F_5	F_6
0	0	0	0	0	0
0	0	1	1	1	0
0	1	0	0	1	0
0	1	1	1	1	1
1	0	0	1	0	0
1	0	1	0	1	1
1	1	0	1	0	1
1	1	1	1	0	0

2-39. Generate the TRUTH-TABLE and canonical SOP and POS expression for:
(a) Problem 2-18
(b) Problem 2-19
(c) Problem 2-20
(d) Generate the MINTERM and MAXTERM list using Σ and Π notation.

2-40. If $F(A,B,C,D) = \Sigma\ 0,2,4,7,11,12,15$, then $F(A,B,C,D)$ expressed as a POS list includes what MAXTERM number?

2-41. The following MINTERMS relate to what MAXTERMS?

minterm	maxterm
$\overline{A}\,B\overline{C}\,D$	_____
$A\overline{B}\,C\overline{D}$	_____
$AB\overline{C}\,D$	_____
$\overline{A}\,BC\overline{D}$	_____

2-42. Suppose you have need for a five-input OR function ASSERTED LOW, but you only have several two-input AND gates. Can you develop the OR function needed? How many AND gates does it take?

2-43. Given: Jones, Baker, Harris, and Johnson are members of the board of trustees of C. I. G. Investment Co. Decisions are made by the following criteria.

A "buy" order is placed if:

Jones, Baker, and Johnson vote no and Harris votes yes,

or Jones and Harris vote no and the rest vote yes,

or Baker and Harris vote yes and the rest vote no,

or Jones votes no and the others vote yes,

or Baker votes no and the others vote yes,

or Baker and Jones vote yes and the others vote no,

or Johnson votes no and the others vote yes,

or they all vote yes.

Design a simplified switch panel and logic circuit (both SOP and POS) that will make the buy decision for these obviously confused stock brokers. Use any combination of gates, but minimize your use of INVERTERS.

2-44. The following circuits (Figures 2P-2(a)–2P-2(d)) are actual schematics taken from various sources. It is desired that you analyze these circuits and determine F(H) and F(L) by two ways:

(a) using DeMorgan reduction;
(b) by redrawing, using the alternate symbols to your advantage, such that the Boolean expressions for F can be read by inspection.
(c) Compare the two results.

Fig. 2P-2 Note that A, B, 5¢ and Coin are from a positive logic system, C, D, and CLK are from a negative logic system.

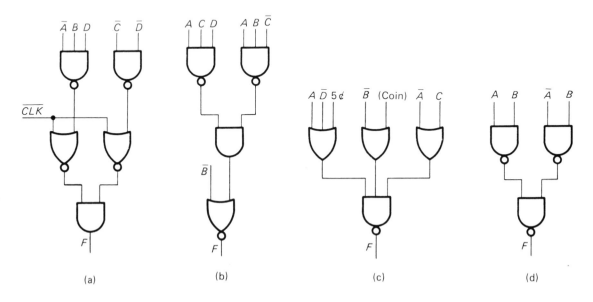

(a)   (b)   (c)   (d)

2-45. Repeat the process of Problem 2-44 for the following circuits (Figures 2P-3(a)–2P-3(c)). Avoid using DeMorgan's theorem. Assume A, B, and C come from a positive logic system; all others come from a negative logic system. In Figure 2P-3(a), find $F(L)$ and $F(H)$. In Figure 2P-3(b), find $F(L)$ and $F(H)$. In Figure 2P-3(c), find $F(L)$ and $F(H)$.

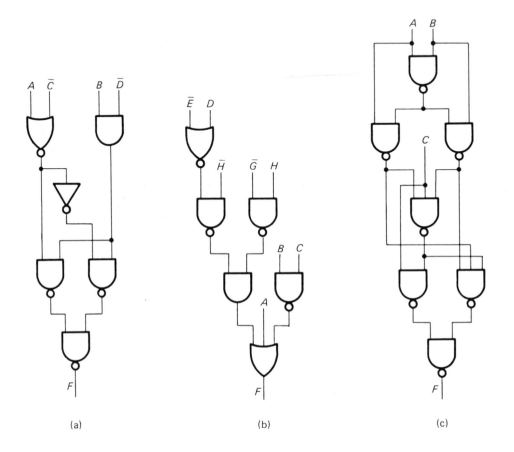

(a)   (b)   (c)

Fig. 2P-3.

CHAPTER 3

MINIMIZATION AND DESIGN

OF COMBINATIONAL CIRCUITS

3-1 INTRODUCTION

It was pointed out in Chapter 2 that the minimization of combinational expressions is considered to be one of the major steps in the digital design process. This emphasis on minimization stems from the time when logic gates were very expensive and required a considerable amount of physical space and power. However, times have changed with the new advances in semiconductor processes to the point where the actual gate count for a system is no longer the most important consideration. The major emphasis now is on the physical space allocation and reliability aspects of systems designed around the combination of small scale integrated circuits (SSI), medium scale integrated circuits (MSI), large scale integrated circuits (LSI), and extra large scale integrated circuits (XLSI). Even though the actual emphasis on the traditional minimization processes has lessened somewhat, there is still a reasonable degree of correlation between minimizing gate count and reduced package count, enough so that treating the basics of combinational reduction is not considered to be a complete waste by any stretch of the imagination.

Because of the reason mentioned above, the emphasis in this chapter is directed toward developing an understanding of how modern reduction techniques have evolved from the time-consuming mathematical approach (theorem reduction) to quick graphical techniques called "MAPPING." Next we extend the standard map process to what is called VARIABLE-ENTERED MAPPING (VEM), increasing our map reduction powers to encompass problems of many variables. It should be noted that this VEM technique is used extensively throughout the rest of this text for both combinational and sequential circuits developed around modern MSI and LSI devices. Last, we examine a Computer-Aided Method that extends our ability to reduce very large problems should the case ever arise. As you proceed, keep in mind that the central theme of the material presented here is to develop time-efficient reduction techniques that minimize time-consuming and error-generating "table-making steps" and can be readily and realistically applied to present-day digital design.

3-2 MINIMIZATION WITH THEOREMS

At the outset it is important to point out that the reduction processes covered in this chapter deal strictly with Boolean expressions that are *not* assigned ASSERTED levels. This is in keeping with previously established processes in which the polarizing element is not added until the simplified expression has been derived and a hardware implementation is being considered. Therefore, we will be involved with developing ways to simplify expressions with little regard to the ASSERTION levels specified. With this in mind, let us get on with learning some valuable methods for minimizing Boolean expressions.

The keys to Boolean minimization lie in the theorems introduced in Chapter 2. The ones of major interest are:

$$\text{Thm 1a.} \quad A + AB = A \qquad \text{1b.} \quad A(A + B) = A \quad \text{(absorption)}$$
$$\text{Thm 2a.} \quad A + \overline{A}B = A + B \qquad \text{2b.} \quad A(\overline{A} + B) = AB$$
$$\text{Thm 3a.} \quad A\,B + A\overline{B} = A \qquad \text{3b.} \quad (A + B)(A + \overline{B}) = A \quad \text{(logic adjacency)}$$

Each of these theorems can have application in the minimization of Boolean expressions. Theorems 1 and 2 have special significance when applied to expressions in standard form, whereas Theorem 3, the logic adjacency theorem, is of particular importance in simplifying canonical form expressions. Once you become familiar with these three mathematical relations, their application becomes somewhat automatic by applying an associated word statement that relates to each. For example, Theorem 1 has a word statement which aids the user: *"If a smaller term or expression is found entirely in a larger term, then the larger term is superfluous."* Theorem 1 can be applied only when an expression is in a STANDARD FORM, that is, one that has at least one term which is not a MIN or MAX term. Once given an expression such as this, you need only select one of the smaller terms and examine the larger terms which contain this smaller term. See Example 3-1.

EXAMPLE 3-1:

$$F = CD + A\overline{B}C + AB\overline{C} + B\overset{\nearrow}{C}D$$
$$\underset{\text{Thm 1}}{\underline{\qquad\qquad\qquad\qquad}}$$

The application of Theorem 2 directly parallels that of Theorem 1; but this time, the larger terms are scanned looking for the smaller in its complemented form. See Example 3-2.

Example 3-2:

$$F = AB + BEF + \overline{A}\,CD + \overline{B}\,CD$$

At first glance we can see no immediate application for Theorem 2. However, consider:

$$F = AB + BEF + CD(\overline{A} + \overline{B})$$

By DeMorgan's theorem we see

$$\overline{A} + \overline{B} = \overline{AB}$$

$$\therefore \quad F = AB + BEF + CD(\overline{AB})$$

$$\underbrace{\qquad\qquad \text{Thm 2} \qquad\qquad}$$

and

$$F = AB + BEF + CD$$

As pointed out earlier, the logic adjacency theorem is the key to the minimization process of canonical forms. In fact, it will be shown that this theorem is the basis from which the Karnaugh map simplification technique is developed.

The word statement that applies to the logic adjacency theorem goes as follows: *"If any two terms in a canonical or standard form expression vary in only one variable, and that variable in one term is the complement of the variable in the other term then that variable is superfluous to both terms."* See Example 3-3.

Example 3-3:

$$F = \overline{A}\,\overline{B}\,\overline{C} + \overline{A}\,\overline{B}\,C + AB\overline{C} + AB\,\overline{C}$$

$$\underbrace{\quad \text{Thm 3} \quad} \qquad \underbrace{\quad \text{Thm 3} \quad}$$

$$F = \overline{A}\,\overline{B} + A\overline{C}$$

We see the first two terms are adjacent, that is, C is the variable. Therefore,

$$F = \overline{A}\,\overline{B} + \overline{A}\,\overline{B} + \cdots$$

$$F = \overline{A}\,\overline{B}(1+1) + \cdots$$

$$F = \overline{A}\,\overline{B} + \cdots$$

Likewise considering the second group:

$$F = \cdots + A\overline{C} + A\overline{C}$$

$$F = \cdots + A\overline{C}$$

Thus we see the application of the logic adjacency theorem is quite automatic. Further, it will be shown that given an expression in canonical form, this theorem is the *only* theorem needed to simplify that expression. However, it must be applied in an appropriate manner. Consider the following expression:

$$F = \overline{A}\,\overline{B}\,\overline{C} + A\overline{B}\,\overline{C} + AB\overline{C} + \overline{A}\,\overline{B}\,C$$

If at first glance you recognize that $\overline{A}\,\overline{B}\,\overline{C}$ and $A\overline{B}\,\overline{C}$ are adjacent and you group these first, the following expression results:

$$F = \overline{B}\,\overline{C} + AB\overline{C} + \overline{A}\,\overline{B}\,C$$

which is not the simplest form!

Now in order to arrive at the simplest expression, we will have to use another theorem that seems a little inconsistent in regards to the statement: "If you have a canonical form, *all* you need is Theorem 3." This is why the statement "If you do it right!" has been added. Now let us reconsider the example and show all possible applications of Theorem 3:

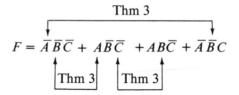

$$F = \overline{A}\,\overline{B}\,\overline{C} + A\overline{B}\,\overline{C} + AB\overline{C} + \overline{A}\,\overline{B}C$$

Now you are faced with deciding which grouping to take, and the major point on which you must decide is: How to minimize the number of groupings (applications of Theorem 3) and at the same time maximize the number of terms affected by each of the groups. This is based on the knowledge that each time the theorem is applied to two terms, a single reduced term is the result, which is in the spirit of reduction. However, if the theorem is applied more than once to the same two terms, a redundant or unnecessary term may result. *From this you learn quickly that terms which will group with no other terms are to be extracted first. The terms that group with only one other term are extracted next, and terms that will group more than one way must be given special attention to avoid redundancy.* So from our expression we find that $AB\overline{C}$ and $\overline{A}\,\overline{B}C$ are terms that will group only with one other term:

$$A\overline{B}\,\overline{C} + AB\overline{C} + \overline{A}\,\overline{B}C + \overline{A}\,\overline{B}\,\overline{C} = A\overline{C} + \overline{A}\,\overline{B}$$
$$\uparrow\text{Thm 3}\uparrow \qquad \uparrow\text{Thm 3}\uparrow$$

Now we see that each term in the expression has been covered at least once and our reduction process is complete. Had we grouped $\overline{A}\,\overline{B}\,\overline{C}$ with $A\overline{B}\,\overline{C}$ also, the result would have been:

$$F = \overline{A}\,\overline{B} + A\overline{C} + \left(\overline{B}\,\overline{C}\right) \quad \rightarrow \text{ redundant or unnecessary term}$$

To illustrate further, consider the following expression.

$$F = \overline{A}\,\overline{B}\,\overline{C} + \overline{A}\,B\overline{C} + AB\overline{C} + A\overline{B}\,\overline{C}$$

From this we see that this expression has a chained application of Theorem 3. With expressions such as this, the reduction process can be attacked in one of two ways. One way is by selecting two terms and reducing them using Theorem 3, then selecting the other two terms and reducing them using Theorem 3, and then using Theorem 3 once more on the resultants of the first two applications. This process is illustrated as follows:

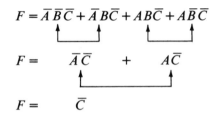

$$F = \overline{A}\,\overline{B}\,\overline{C} + \overline{A}\,B\overline{C} + AB\overline{C} + A\overline{B}\,\overline{C}$$

$$F = \qquad \overline{A}\,\overline{C} \qquad + \qquad A\overline{C}$$

$$F = \qquad \overline{C}$$

Another way to simplify expressions such as these is to use Theorem 3 in a *chain* application. This is done by selecting any term in the chain and writing this term down. We will call this the STARTING TERM. Then begin applying Theorem 3, and as you move from one term to the next, strike the changing variable from the STARTING TERM for each successive application of Theorem 3. We will now demonstrate this process.

Given:

$$F = \overline{A}\,B\overline{C} + \overline{A}\,B\overline{C} + AB\overline{C} + A\overline{B}\,\overline{C}$$

Let us select $\overline{A}B\overline{C}$ as our STARTING TERM. Now as we move right we see the application of Theorem 3 eliminates the A variable. Thus we strike the $\overline{A}$ from our starting term:

$$\cancel{\overline{A}}B\overline{C}$$

Continuing on to $A\overline{B}\,\overline{C}$ we see that the B variable changes from $AB\overline{C}$ to $A\overline{B}\,\overline{C}$, therefore the B variable is struck from the STARTING TERM leaving:

$$\cancel{\overline{A}}\cancel{B}\overline{C}$$

Continuing on in the chain until we arrive back at our STARTING TERM, striking the changing variable each time results in the simplified expression $\overline{C}$. Now we see that all seems well, but before we accept this method let us try another example.

Given:

$$F = \overline{A}\,\overline{B}\,\overline{C}D + \overline{A}\,\overline{B}\,CD + \overline{A}\,BCD + \overline{A}\,B\overline{C}D + AB\overline{C}D + ABCD$$

Here we see two chains of four terms each meshed together by the shared terms $\overline{A}BCD$ and $\overline{A}B\overline{C}D$. By applying Theorem 3 systematically, we find the following:

$$F = \overline{A}D + BD$$

By now it should become obvious that another technique is needed because the arrows and theorem application is becoming a bit tedious. Therefore, if we could develop some graphical technique whereby the application of the logical adjacency theorem is made obvious and where the desired grouping could be plainly displayed, we would be in a much better position to visualize the proper application of this theorem.

3-3 THE KARNAUGH MAP

The Karnaugh map developed by M. Karnaugh in his paper titled *The Map Method for Synthesis of Combinational Logic Circuits* (1953) does what we have just determined as desirable. *Karnaugh's map orders and displays the minterms in a geometrical pattern such that the application of the logic adjacency theorem becomes obvious.* Consider what are called Karnaugh maps shown in Figure 3-1.

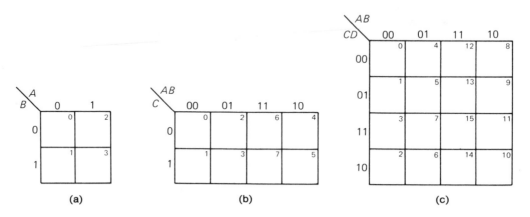

Fig. 3-1. (a) Two-variable map. (b) Three-variable map. (c) Four-variable map.

If we examine the two-, three-, and four-variable TRUTH-TABLES as shown in Figure 2-3, we can make some general observations that support the geometric layout of the Karnaugh maps.

Karnaugh organized a map, as shown in Figure 3-1, such that the cells in each map were assigned a MINTERM number and then he arranged these such that the geographic location of each cell places it adjacent to the cells as prescribed by the itemized lists shown in Figure 3-2.

For the two-variable TRUTH-TABLE:

MINTERM	is adjacent to
0	1,2
1	0,3
2	0,3
3	1,2

For the three-variable TRUTH-TABLE:

MINTERM	is adjacent to
0	1,2,4
1	0,3,5
2	0,3,6
3	1,2,7
4	0,5,6
5	1,4,7
6	2,4,7
7	3,5,6

For the four-variable TRUTH-TABLE:

MINTERM	is adjacent to
0	1,2,4,8
1	0,3,5,9
2	0,3,6,10
3	1,2,7,11
4	0,5,6,12
5	1,4,7,13
6	2,4,7,14
7	3,5,6,15
8	0,9,10,12
9	1,8,11,13
10	2,8,11,14
11	3,9,10,15
12	4,8,13,14
13	5,9,12,15
14	6,10,12,15
15	7,11,13,14

Fig. 3-2. An illustration of the MINTERMS that are logically adjacent in two-, three-, and four-variable problems.

As we study Figure 3-2 we see that any given minterm (M) is adjacent to a set of other minterms $\{S\}$. This series can be generated by inspection or with the following expression:

$$S_i = M + [2^{(i-1)}][(-1)^{M/2^{(i-1)}}]$$

for $i = 1, 2, \ldots, n$ where $n =$ the number of variables and $M/2^{(i-1)}$ is defined as an integer divide. Also, it should be mentioned that this expression proved to be a valuable tool in a computer program developed to use numerical methods for reducing combinational expressions.

Now, once the adjacent minterms are identified, they must be arranged such that they are physically adjacent in some geometric pattern. With the two-variable map, we see that the physical adjacencies are obviously in a planar display. However, the adjacencies for the end cells (0, 1, 4, and 5) of a three-variable map cannot be visualized in a planar organization. Therefore, you must visualize the map bent into a cylinder with the left and right edges (row ends) of the planar map touching. Now it can be visualized that cell 0 is adjacent to cell 4 and cell 1 is adjacent to cell 5 [see Figure 3-3(a)].

Fig. 3-3. Three-dimensional configurations of three- and four-variable maps.

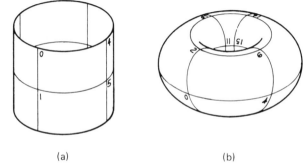

(a)   (b)

The four-variable map is even more oblique in that not only do the left and right edges have to be adjacent, but so do the top and bottom edges. This configures the map into a toroid or a "doughnut" [see Figure 3-3(b)]. Five variables?? See "Star Trek" to find that extra dimension! No, it's easier than that; the five and six-variable maps are discussed in Section 3-7.

3-4 PLOTTING A KARNAUGH MAP

It is interesting to note that a Karnaugh map, referred to from here on out as a K-map, is nothing more than an interesting-looking TRUTH-TABLE, and it simply provides a graphical display of the implicants (MINTERMS) involved in any SOP canonical or standard form expression. Therefore, when using a K-map for the purpose of simplifying an expression, you need only enter into each cell (MINTERM) some mark indicating that this MINTERM is implicated in the expanded SOP expression. Keep in mind that each cell is to be considered OR'ed with the others. The marks normally made are 1's in the implicated cells

(MINTERMS ASSERTED) and 0's in those cells not implicated (MINTERMS NOT-ASSERTED). Consider the examples of maps plotted from TRUTH-TABLES and shorthand expressions in Figure 3-4.

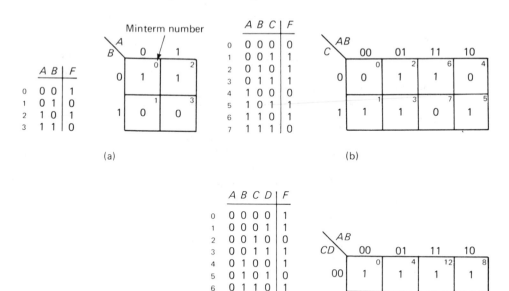

(a)

(b)

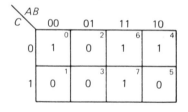

$F(A, B, C) =$
$\Sigma\,(0, 4, 6, 7)$

(c)

(d)

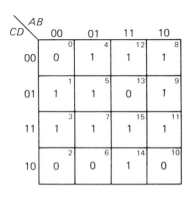

$F(A, B, C, D) = \Sigma\,(1, 3, 4, 5, 7, 8, 9, 11, 12, 14, 15)$

(e)

Fig. 3-4. Examples of map plotting.

3-5 LABELING A K-MAP

Consider the K-MAPS shown in Figure 3-5 for the purpose of gaining an understanding of the labeling of a K-MAP and, also, how to add the variable lettering. Note the order in which the MINTERM is read into or out of the map.

The boundaries indicated in Figures 3-5(k), 3-5(1), and 3-5(m) are directly related to the codes at the ends of the columns and rows. These codes and boundaries are particularly important when READING the map, which will be treated shortly. To preface this task, you should be aware that *each time a boundary is cut or crossed* as you move from one cell to another, *one* variable changes. In other words, as you move from one cell to another, the boundary cut, be it $A, B, C, D, \dots$, tells you what variable differs between the two cells. It is because of this that you draw "loops" around the entries in adjacent cells and each boundary cut indicates that a boundary variable has changed; thus the theorem $AB + A\bar{B} = A$ is mechanized, and automatically you know that this changing variable is to be dropped.

Fig. 3-5. Maps marked to illustrate the markings' meanings and variable boundaries.

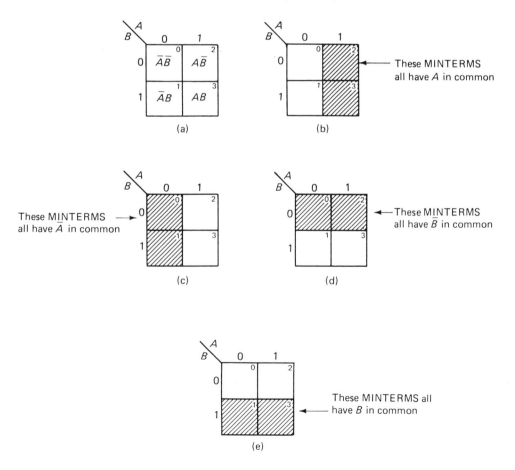

Fig. 3-5. (Cont.)

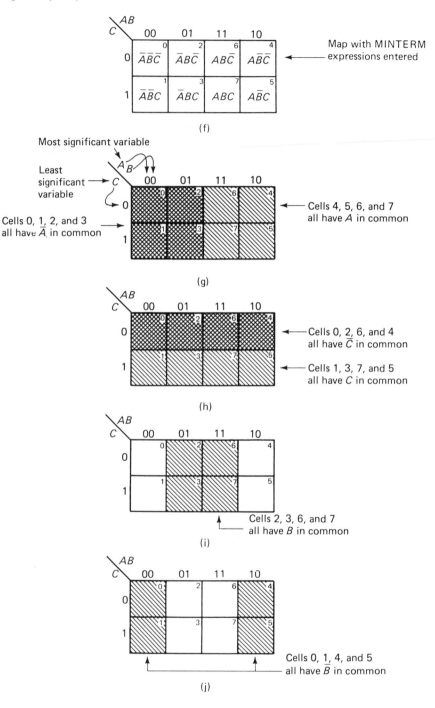

Map with MINTERM expressions entered

(f)

Most significant variable

Least significant variable

Cells 0, 1, 2, and 3 all have $\overline{A}$ in common

Cells 4, 5, 6, and 7 all have A in common

(g)

Cells 0, 2, 6, and 4 all have $\overline{C}$ in common

Cells 1, 3, 7, and 5 all have C in common

(h)

Cells 2, 3, 6, and 7 all have B in common

(i)

Cells 0, 1, 4, and 5 all have $\overline{B}$ in common

(j)

Fig. 3-5. (Cont.)

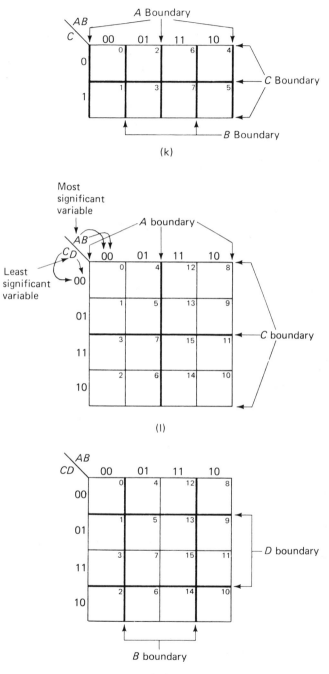

(k)

(l)

(m)

3-6 READING THE K-MAP

We have alluded to the map-reading process in the previous section as a process of grouping MINTERMS in the map with loops, and at the same time keeping track of the boundaries cut by the loop in order to determine what variables are to be dropped from each term of the original expression. Remember that each cell is representative of a MINTERM and if each cell is looped separately, by itself, then the map-reading process should result in the original expression in canonical form. When two cells are grouped together, at least one variable changes. When this happens, the theorem $AB + \overline{A}B = B$ has been invoked once. If a group of four *adjacent* cells can be grouped or looped, then the theorem has been invoked twice. It was at this point that we found the order in which the logic adjacency theorem was invoked to be of extreme importance when we were using the theorems. Also, it was pointed out earlier that the process of reducing Boolean expressions requires some method of attack. The key to the map technique of minimization is one of graphical pattern recognition. This suggests that you must recognize the graphical application of Theorem 3 and, further, you must recognize the order of its application. This all might sound somewhat imposing, but it is quite easy once you get the hang of it. Keep in mind that what you are trying to do is: *Minimize the number of groupings required to cover all entries in the map and at the same time maximize the number of entries covered in each grouping.* This is termed a *minimal cover.* We do this because minimizing the number of groupings reduces the number of AND functions required and at the same time reduces the number of inputs required for the OR function, and by maximizing the number of entries covered by each grouping we reduce the input requirements of the AND functions. By striving to uphold this criterion we will arrive at what we define as a "minimal cover" solution.

The following steps are offered to provide you with a general single-pass sequential method for arriving at a minimal cover solution for a Boolean reduction problem. Even though these steps are presently directed at a map-reading process, they are equally applicable to other methods also. In fact, this algorithm, with some modification, is the basis of the computer-aided reduction method introduced later in this chapter. In short, they are designed to avoid some unnecessary operational and sorting steps common to other reduction methods. We will also find shortly that with a little experience we can reduce these steps to a single sentence statement. To effectively apply these steps they should be applied as they pertain to a *single entry.*

Suggested map-reading steps.

(1) Search your map, considering each entry one at a time, and loop and extract those single entries that will *not* group with any other entry. These essential implicants we will call "islands."

(2) After all islands have been grouped and extracted, scan your map one entry at a time for those entries that will group with only *one* other entry. Loop and extract these "duals."

As you scan the map in steps 1 and 2 you are likely to find single entries that will group into larger groups (4, 8, etc.). Likewise you are likely to find single entries which will group into a dual in *more than one* way. The grouping of these entries requires special attention and should be left for the later steps.

(3) Once all entries that will group into a dual in only one way have been grouped and extracted, re-examine your map, one entry at a time, for uncovered entries that will group several ways but *cannot* be grouped into a group of 4 or larger. Study these entries and first group, one at a time, those entries that will group with *only one other uncovered entry*. Then go back and group and extract the similar entries which group with one other *covered* entry.

(4) Once steps 1, 2, and 3 are completed, search your map, one entry at a time, for those *single* uncovered entries that will group into a group of four (quad) and no larger, in only one way with three other *uncovered* entries. Then go back and search out those single uncovered entries that will group into a quad in *only* one way with other covered entries.

(5) Once step 4 has been completed, re-examine your map, one entry at a time, for those single uncovered entries that will group into a quad in *more than one* way, but will not group into a group of 8 or larger. Study and group these quads in the identical fashion as outlined in step 3, but this time look for quads rather than duals.

Practically speaking, by the time step 5 is completed your map-reading process should be fairly complete; in other words, given a map for six or fewer variables, by the time step 5 is completed the rest of the grouping should be obvious.

(6) Continue to scan your map in a fashion similar to steps 2–5, looking for groups of 8, 16, and so forth *until every entry has been covered at least once.*

⋮

Final Step
Give your map a quick check to determine if, by mistake, *all* of the entries of any group happen to be covered by other valid groupings. If so, that particular group is redundant and should be removed.

Special note: Should you find that you have a map that places you in a loop on these steps, you have what is called a "cycle map." The key to breaking the cycle map is to *pick* a grouping at the step which you loop back. Once this grouping has been taken, go back to step 3 and continue. See Figure 3-12.

Final note: Keep in mind that there is no real substitute for using your mind and thinking about the desired "minimal cover" criterion set forth earlier. "Minimize the number of groupings and maximize their size." You will find that your mind has tremendous "pattern recognition" ability and your need for reference to these rules will diminish with practice.

Let us now consider several examples illustrating the use of these mapping rules. See Figure 3-6.

EXAMPLE 3-4:   Mapping examples (Figure 3-6).

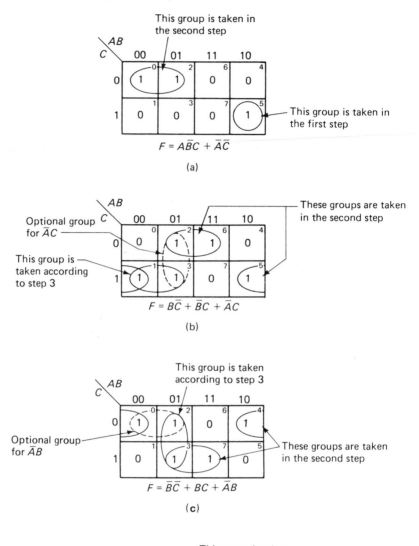

(a)

(b)

(c)

(d)

Fig. 3-6. Mapping examples for Example 3-4.

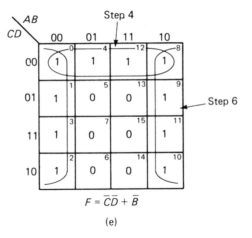

$$F = \overline{C}\overline{D} + \overline{B}$$

(e)

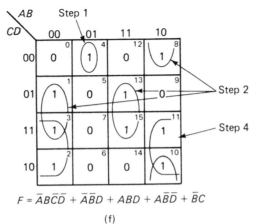

$$F = \overline{A}B\overline{C}\overline{D} + \overline{A}\,\overline{B}D + ABD + A\overline{B}\overline{D} + \overline{B}C$$

(f)

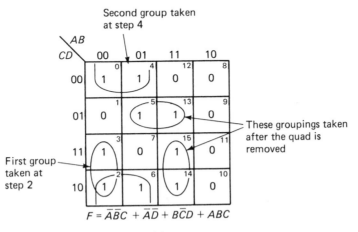

$$F = \overline{A}\overline{B}C + \overline{A}\overline{D} + B\overline{C}D + ABC$$

(g)

Fig. 3-6. (Cont.)

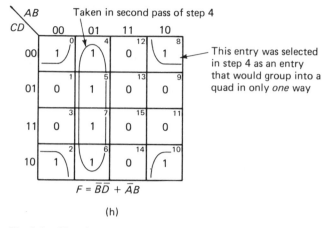

This entry was selected in step 4 as an entry that would group into a quad in only *one* way

$F = \overline{B}\overline{D} + \overline{A}B$

(h)

Fig. 3-6. (Cont.)

3-7   FIVE- AND SIX-VARIABLE MAPS

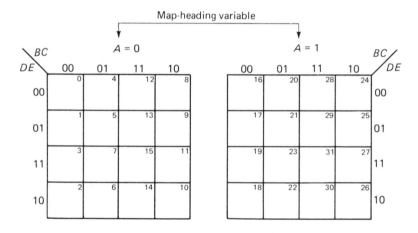

Fig. 3-7.   Example of a blank five-variable map.

A blank five-variable map is shown in Figure 3-7. It is important to note that in order to identify the adjacent looping in the five-variable map, you must imagine the two maps *superimposed* on one another; not "hinged" or "mirror imaged." An example five-variable map-reading problem is shown in Figure 3-8.

Maps greater than six variables are so cumbersome that tabular or other techniques are required. However, in problems containing many variables, some of the variables are likely to be what is termed "infrequently used variables." These infrequently used variables are those variables that appear in a relatively few terms of a given expression. For example:

$$F(A,B,C,D,E,F,G) = ABCD\overline{F} + A\overline{B}\,\overline{C}DG + \overline{A}\,B\overline{C}DFG + \overline{A}\,\overline{B}\,\overline{C}\,\overline{D}\,\overline{G} + ABCDF$$

In this expression it appears that we are faced with a seven-variable map reduction problem. But in fact this expression can be reduced quite easily with a four-variable map. This technique will be introduced in the section on VARIABLE-ENTERED-MAPS.

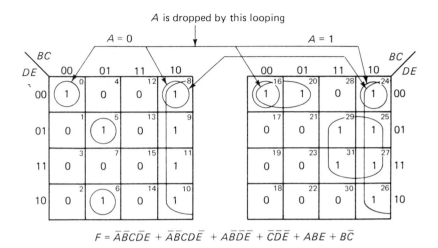

A is dropped by this looping

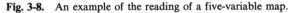

$$F = \overline{A}\overline{B}C\overline{D}\overline{E} + \overline{A}\overline{B}CD\overline{E} + A\overline{B}\overline{D}\overline{E} + C\overline{D}\overline{E} + ABE + B\overline{C}$$

Fig. 3-8. An example of the reading of a five-variable map.

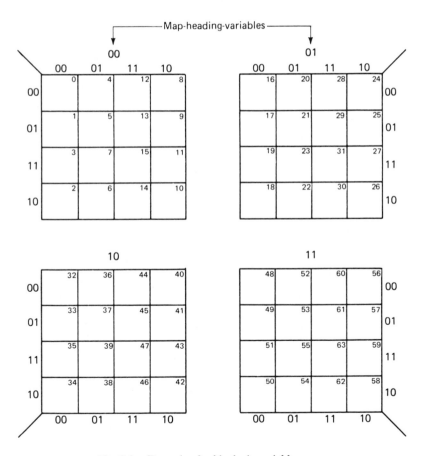

Fig. 3-9. Example of a blank six-variable map.

A blank six-variable map is shown in Figure 3-9. This map has four cells constructed from four-variable maps. The adjacencies between entries in each cell (four-variable map) are visualized identical to that of a four-variable map. However, the adjacencies between the cells (four-variable maps) are visualized as the groupings in a two-variable map. Note special labeling of the map where the MOST-SIGNIFICANT-VARIABLE moves up to become the overall map label, which is an indication that as one loops cells *between the maps* on five- and six-variable maps, the map heading variable changes, and therefore it drops with the application of the logic adjacency theorem.

An example of a six-variable map reading is illustrated in Figure 3-10.

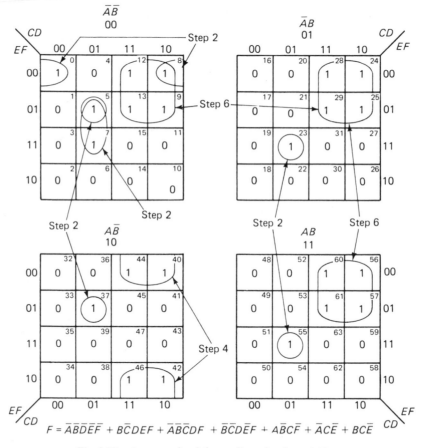

$$F = \overline{A}\overline{B}\overline{D}\overline{E}\overline{F} + B\overline{C}DEF + \overline{A}\overline{B}CDF + \overline{B}C\overline{D}\overline{E}F + A\overline{B}C\overline{F} + \overline{A}C\overline{E} + BC\overline{E}$$

Fig. 3-10. An example of the reading of a six-variable map.

3-8 PRIME AND ESSENTIAL IMPLICANTS

Now that we have established a method for reading Karnaugh maps in such a way that unnecessary (redundant) groupings can be avoided, let us take a moment to establish some important definitions basic to this method and others to come. To do this, let us analyze the grouping shown in the map in Figure 3-11. Here we see that all realistic groupings are shown. Note further that each group is sufficiently large that it cannot be completely covered by any other *single* grouping. Each of these *groupings* is defined as a *PRIME IMPLICANT*.

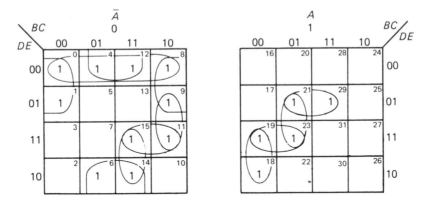

Fig. 3-11. An example map illustrating the prime implicant cover for some functions of $F(A, B, C, D, E)$.

As we examine the set of prime implicants that covers this map, it becomes obvious that some of the entries can be grouped in only one way (single way groupings). For example, the groups that enclose cell 1, cell 6, cell 18, and cell 29 are groups of this nature. The resultant terms from these groupings are defined as *ESSENTIAL IMPLICANTS*. Note further that the single group that covers cells 15 and 11 is the only possible grouping which can be defined that covers these two entries with a *single grouping*. The resultant terms from groupings of this nature are called *NECESSARY IMPLICANTS*. The two possible groupings that cover cell 23 are called *OPTIONAL IMPLICANTS* with arbitration generally directed toward minimizing the number of inverters required. The term resulting from the two groups covering cells 14 and 15 and cells 9 and 11 as well as the quad $(0, 4, 12, 8)$ can be classed as *REDUNDANT IMPLICANTS*; and it is these implicants which should never be included in the *minimal cover implicant list*. Thus we see that the complete *prime implicant* list (set) includes sub-sets of essential, necessary, optional, and redundant implicants. The heuristic scheme outlined by the map-reading steps is designed to help you extract the essential implicants first, then the necessary, leaving the optional implicants until last without requiring an exhaustive search for all prime implicants followed by an optimizing search after. However, there will be times when, in cases of *cycles*, an optional grouping will be the first group taken, requiring you to re-initiate your search for necessary implicants. This is illustrated in Figure 3-12. Here we see at first glance that there are no essential implicants and no obvious necessary implicants, leaving only an optional implicant for our first choice. In this case, we optionally pick the group which includes cells 0 and 1. Now, once this cycle breaking group is taken, the rest of the groupings become necessary implicants. These concepts will be integrated into a single line reduction criterion, which is introduced in the next section and also serves as the basis of a computer-aided reduction scheme.

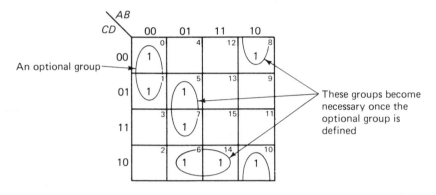

Fig. 3-12. A map illustrating a cycle.

3-9 DON'T CARE MAP ENTRIES

Many times in digital system design, code converter design in particular, some input codes must be considered as cases that "just don't happen", and there are cases when the occurrence of particular codes will have no effect on the system, and if those codes do happen, "you don't care." For example, consider the case where the outputs of a four-bit *decimal counter*, which happens to have a *possible* counting range from 0000 to 1111, is to be converted to a decimal display having the range of $0, 1, 2, \ldots, 9$. In this particular case, the output codes 1010, 1011, 1100, 1101, 1110, and 1111 are to be considered as codes that just cannot be issued by a decimal counter if it is functioning properly. Therefore, when the combinational decoding logic is being designed, these MINTERMS in the map are treated in a special way. That is, a $\emptyset$ is entered into each cell to signify "don't care" MIN/MAX terms. There are other cases related to sequential machine design, where the $\emptyset$ entries in a map have a great deal of significance.

Reading a map with $\emptyset$ entries is a simple process summed up by the statement: *"Loop the $\emptyset$ with a 1 grouping if and only if this looping will result in greater simplification; otherwise treat it as if it were a 0 entry."* Some specific $\emptyset$ entry mappings are illustrated in the following examples.

EXAMPLE 3-5: Examples illustrating $\emptyset$ entry mapping are shown in Figure 3-13. The input list notation using $\emptyset$'s is shown as:

$$F(A, B, C) = \Sigma 0, 2, 7, \emptyset(3, 4)$$

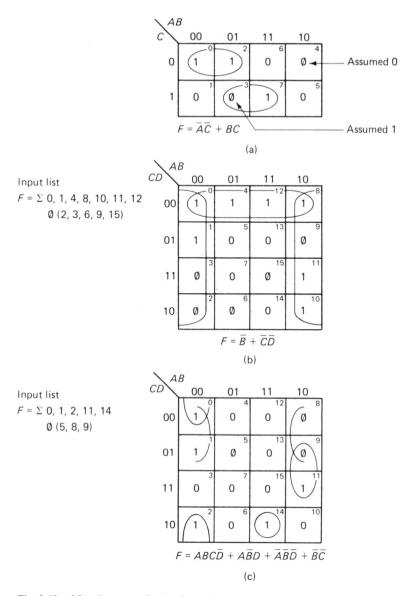

Input list

$F = \Sigma\ 0, 1, 4, 8, 10, 11, 12$

$\emptyset\ (2, 3, 6, 9, 15)$

Input list

$F = \Sigma\ 0, 1, 2, 11, 14$

$\emptyset\ (5, 8, 9)$

Fig. 3-13. Mapping examples for Example 3-5.

Now that you are familiar with the use of $\emptyset$'s in the map-reading process, we can introduce a single statement reduction criterion that will lead to a minimal cover implicant list. This single statement criterion is based on your knowledge that $\emptyset$ entries are never grouped with 1 entries if the 1 entry can be grouped with other 1 entries, resulting in a group of size equal to or greater than the group resulting from grouping with adjacent $\emptyset$'s.

Now if we properly stage our map-reading attack, we can sum up the optimal map-reading algorithm in one statement: *At any given point in the reading process, always search out and extract the smallest essential or necessary implicant that is presently available, then replace the 1's in that grouping with Ø's and repeat the process until each 1 entry has been covered at least once.* Extracting the smallest available essential or necessary implicant implies that single entries that will not group with another entry are sequentially extracted first, then you should sequentially group and extract those entries that will group into a dual in one way next, then a prime implicant resulting from a single entry that will group into a quad in only one way is taken *if this quad is the smallest single way grouping available.* Each time a group is taken, the 1's in the group are replaced with Ø's and the search is started over. This algorithm is defined by the flow chart shown in Figure 3-14. This reading process is illustrated by several example maps shown in Examples 3-6 and 3-7.

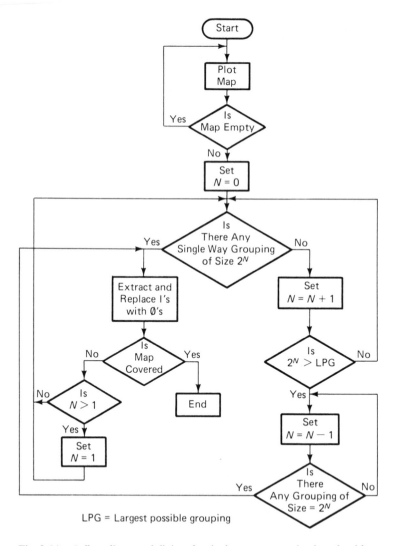

LPG = Largest possible grouping

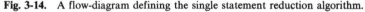

Fig. 3-14. A flow-diagram defining the single statement reduction algorithm.

EXAMPLE 3-6: Given the map shown in Figure 3-15(a):

(1) We find no islands.
(2) We find no single entries that group into a dual in only one way.
(3) See Figure 3-15(b). We do find that the entry in cell 1 groups into a quad in only one way. This was found by starting at cell 0 and scanning down the column.
(4) See Figure 3-15(c). Now we resume our search for the *smallest single way grouping* and find cell 11 groups only one way with cell 15.
(5) See Figure 3-15(d). Again we search for those single entries that will group into the smallest single way grouping available. Since there are no duals, we select cell 14 as the single entry that will group into the smallest available single way grouping.
(6) See Figure 3-15(e). Next we see cell 2 is the only one left uncovered. Again we see that this entry groups into a quad if we utilize the $\emptyset$ entries in cells 0, 4, and 6, which covers the map.

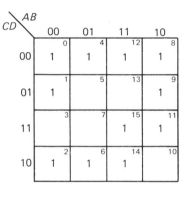

(a)

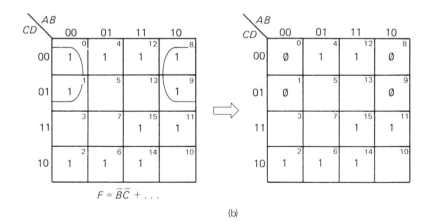

(b)

Fig. 3-15. An example illustrating the single statement map-reading criterion.

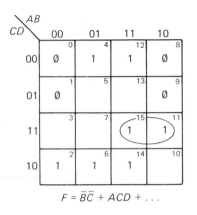

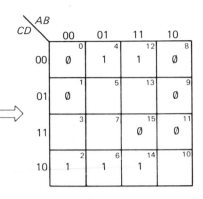

$$F = \overline{B}\,\overline{C} + ACD + \ldots$$

(c)

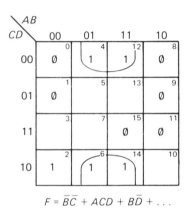

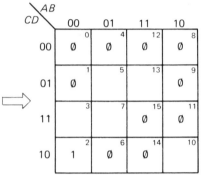

$$F = \overline{B}\,\overline{C} + ACD + B\overline{D} + \ldots$$

(d)

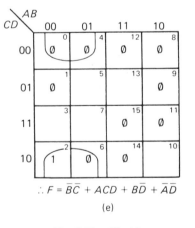

$$\therefore F = \overline{B}\,\overline{C} + ACD + B\overline{D} + \overline{A}\,\overline{D}$$

(e)

Fig. 3-15. (Cont.)

EXAMPLE 3-7:   Given the map shown in Figure 3-16(a), reduce according to the single statement reduction criterion.

(1) We find no islands.
(2) We find no single entries that group into a dual in only one way.
(3) We do find the entry in cell 0 groups into a quad in only one way. Therefore, we extract it and replace the 1's in this group with $\emptyset$'s. See Figure 3-16(b).
(4) We now resume our search for the smallest single way grouping we can find, which is obviously the four remaining duals involving the entries in cells 5, 6, 8, and 11, which yield the following simplified expression:

$$F = \overline{A}\,\overline{B} + B\overline{C}D + BC\overline{D} + A\overline{C}\,\overline{D} + ACD$$

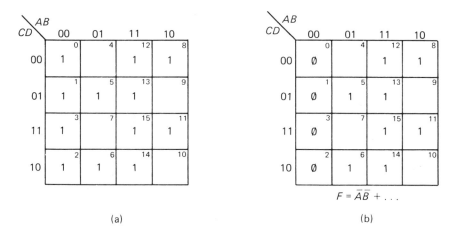

(a)   (b)

Fig. 3-16.   Another illustration of the use of single statement reduction criterion.

3-10   MAP REDUCTION RESULTING IN PRODUCT-OF-SUM EXPRESSIONS

As mentioned earlier, a designer should examine both the sum-of-products and product-of-sum reductions to ascertain which has the implementation advantage. The technique for using maps for POS reductions is a simple step-by-step process:

(1) Plot map as for SOP; include the 0 entries.
(2) Loop 0 entries as you loop 1 entries for a SOP reading, to determine the simplified SOP expression for $\overline{F}$.
(3) Use DeMorgan's theorem on $\overline{F}$ to produce the simplified expression in POS form.

EXAMPLE 3-8:   Examples illustrating mapping for POS reductions. See Figures 3-17(a) and 3-17(b).

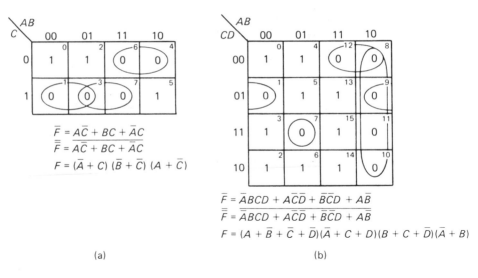

$$\overline{F} = A\overline{C} + BC + \overline{A}C$$
$$\overline{\overline{F}} = \overline{A\overline{C} + BC + \overline{A}C}$$
$$F = (\overline{A} + C)(\overline{B} + \overline{C})(A + \overline{C})$$

(a)

$$\overline{F} = \overline{A}BCD + A\overline{C}\overline{D} + \overline{B}\overline{C}D + A\overline{B}$$
$$\overline{\overline{F}} = \overline{\overline{A}BCD + A\overline{C}\overline{D} + \overline{B}\overline{C}D + A\overline{B}}$$
$$F = (A + \overline{B} + \overline{C} + \overline{D})(\overline{A} + C + D)(B + C + \overline{D})(\overline{A} + B)$$

(b)

Fig. 3-17. Mapping examples for Example 3-8.

3-11 USING THE MAP FOR SIMPLIFYING PARTIALLY SIMPLIFIED EXPRESSIONS

There are times when you will be confronted with an expression that is already partially simplified or is in some sort of STANDARD form that still has redundancies. The question then arises: "If a K-Map is based on the logic adjacency theorem and this theorem guarantees results only if the expression is in CANONICAL form, what should be done?" The answer to this question is given by illustration. Consider one of the simplified expressions covered in the map-reading section, for instance the three-variable problem in Example 3-4(b). The simplified results are:

$$F = B\overline{C} + \overline{A}C + \overline{B}C$$

Now pretend for a moment that you are unaware that this is a simplified expression and proceed to re-plot the K-map:

> *PROCEDURE:*
> Consider the first term $B\overline{C}$. See Figure 3-18(a).
>
> > 1's are entered into the map in the boundary intersection of B and $\overline{C}$
>
> Next consider $\overline{A}C$. See Figure 3-18(b).
>
> > 1's must be entered into the boundary intersections of $\overline{A}$ and C.
>
> > Next consider $\overline{B}C$. See Figure 3-18(c).
>
> > 1's must be entered into the boundary intersection of $\overline{B}$ and C.
>
> The result of all this is the original map in Example 3-4(b), as shown in Figure 3-18(d).

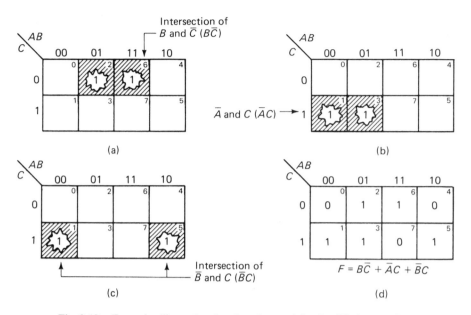

Fig. 3-18. Examples illustrating the plot of a partially simplified expression.

From this example we see that the K-map can be used to expand partially simplified expressions into a canonical form, as well as to further simplify those expressions.

3-12 MULTI-OUTPUT MINIMIZATION

Finding the optimal cover for a system of output expressions all of which are a function of the same variables is generally considered to be a rather tedious task. This task is basically one of identifying all possible prime implicants that cover each implicated minterm in each output expression, then carrying out a search for the minimal cost cover by using "shared" terms. The most widely used approach is one of extending the tabular Quine–McCluskey method for reducing expressions, which is generally considered a possible method for reducing expressions of more than six variables. However, since this text introduces a different approach to reducing expressions of more than six variables, a simple heuristic method is outlined here, leaving the drudgery of multi-output reduction to a computer-aided approach treated later.

> EXAMPLE 3-9:   Suppose you were given the following system of expressions and asked to find the optimal cover for the complete system, implying that you must find how to optimally share terms between the expressions.
>
> $$F_1(A,B,C) = \Sigma 0,2,3,5,6$$
> $$F_2(A,B,C) = \Sigma 1,2,3,4,7$$
> $$F_3(A,B,C) = \Sigma 2,3,4,5,6$$

First generate the maps for these expressions, as shown in Figure 3-19. Then make up an implicant table, as shown in Table 3-1, showing how each minterm can be covered.

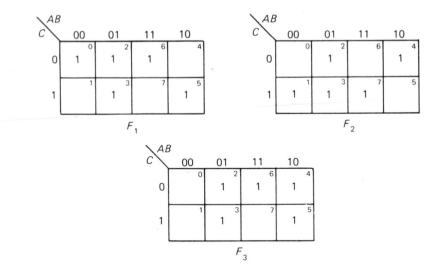

Fig. 3-19. Maps for Example 3-9.

TABLE 3-1   The Implicant Table for Example 3-9

Minterm	F_1	F_2	F_3
m_0	$\overline{A}\,\overline{B}\,\overline{C}\,/\,\overline{A}\,\overline{C}$	—	—
m_1	—	$\overline{A}\,\overline{B}\,C\,/\,\overline{A}\,C$	—
m_2	$\overline{A}\,B\overline{C}\,/\,\overline{A}\,\overline{C}\,/\,\overline{A}\,B\,/\,B\overline{C}$	$\overline{A}\,B\overline{C}\,/\,\overline{A}\,B$	$\overline{A}\,B\overline{C}\,/\,\overline{A}\,B\,/\,B\overline{C}$
m_3	$\overline{A}\,BC\,/\,\overline{A}\,B$	$\overline{A}\,BC\,/\,\overline{A}\,B\,/\,\overline{A}\,C\,/\,BC$	$\overline{A}\,BC\,/\,\overline{A}\,B$
m_4	—	$A\overline{B}\,\overline{C}$	$A\overline{B}\,\overline{C}\,/\,A\overline{C}\,/\,A\overline{B}$
m_5	$A\overline{B}\,C$	—	$A\overline{B}\,C\,/\,A\overline{B}$
m_6	$AB\overline{C}\,/\,B\overline{C}$	—	$AB\overline{C}\,/\,B\overline{C}\,/\,A\overline{C}$
m_7	—	$ABC\,/\,BC$	—

First scan the table for rows with only a single entry. These are related to essential implicants (m_0, m_1, m_7). Take the largest grouping and update your table and maps as shown in Table 3-1 and Figure 3-20. Next scan the rows for those which have two entries, selecting the functions that have only a single way grouping *option* (m_4 under F_2 and m_5 and m_6 under F_1). Group and extract these essential implicants and also remove from them the other maps. These groups are shown boxed in Table 3-1. Next those rows with three entries are examined, groupings are selected based on single groups that can be taken. In this case the $\overline{A}B$ grouping is determined by the single way group under F_2. This process is continued until the maps are completely covered. For this example:

$$F_1 = \overline{A}\,\overline{C} + B\overline{C} + \overline{A}B + A\overline{B}C$$

$$F_2 = \overline{A}C + BC + A\overline{B}\,\overline{C} + \overline{A}B$$

$$F_3 = B\overline{C} + \overline{A}B + A\overline{B}\,\overline{C} + A\overline{B}C$$

Here we see F_3 is totally generated from shared terms from F_1 and F_2 with considerable savings over a conventional function by function reduction.

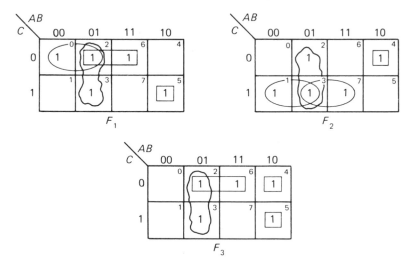

Fig. 3-20. The optimal cover for the multi-output system for Example 3-9.

In summary, it is acknowledged that this approach is heuristic and tedious. However, it does generally produce good results, though as mentioned earlier a computer-aided method will be introduced which produces optimal multi-function cover.

3-13 VARIABLE-ENTERED MAPPING

The Variable-Entered-Map (VEM) technique, introduced in this section, adds yet another dimension to the simplification powers of the K-map and, if used properly, reduces the work required for plotting and reading maps. It will be shown that the VEM technique can reduce the map size for three-, four-, five-, six-, and seven-variable maps. To allow for this desirable feature, the list of map entries will be expanded to include not only 1's, 0's, and Ø's, but also Boolean variables, even Boolean expressions for the bold and experienced. The processes of plotting and reading are simple and straightforward, as will be illustrated by several examples. You will find that VEM will be one of the most useful design aids discussed and its use permeates the rest of this text in a wide variety of applications. It is introduced here from a conceptual point of view and its application may not be easy to envision. However, in future chapters it will be used for both the simplification and documentation of systems designed with LSI devices.

3-14 VEM PLOTTING THEORY

It should be remembered that the simplification power of the K-map stems from the basic theorem: $XY + \overline{X}Y = Y$, which we have referred to as the logic adjacency theorem. As mentioned above, the VEM plotting technique is an extension of the standard K-map technique. Therefore, let us back up for a moment and consider what is assumed when a K-map is plotted from a TRUTH-TABLE. Consider the three-variable TRUTH-TABLE and the general expression for F as shown in Figure 3-21.

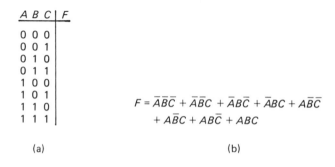

$$F = \overline{A}\overline{B}\overline{C} + \overline{A}\overline{B}C + \overline{A}B\overline{C} + \overline{A}BC + A\overline{B}\overline{C}$$
$$+ A\overline{B}C + AB\overline{C} + ABC$$

(a)   (b)

Fig. 3-21. (a) Three-variable TRUTH-TABLE. (b) General sum-of-product expression for F.

The process of generating a *specific* Boolean expression for F is one of selecting the appropriate minterms from the *general* expression for F. This can be thought of as a process of assigning some dummy-variable ANDed with each minterm for the purpose of minterm selection or de-selection, whichever the case may be. For example, consider the following development:

$$F \cdot F = F$$

$$= \overline{A}\,\overline{B}\,\overline{C}F + \overline{A}\,\overline{B}CF + \overline{A}\,B\overline{C}F + \overline{A}\,BCF + A\overline{B}\,\overline{C}F + A\overline{B}CF + AB\overline{C}F + ABCF$$

Here both sides of the general Boolean expression are ANDed with the same Boolean literal F and no algebraic rules are violated. To generate a specific expression for F we need only supply the prescribed value for F for each minterm in the general expression, F being 1 for those minterms desired and F being 0 for those minterms not desired. Then when plotting the K-map, we enter these same desired values of F for each minterm. This is nothing new, but many times it becomes so automatic that we tend to become somewhat mechanical when plotting a map. Consider Example 3-10, which illustrates the process just described.

EXAMPLE 3-10: Example of VEM plotting. See Figure 3-22.

$$F \cdot F = F = \overline{A}\,\overline{B}\,\overline{C}(0) + \overline{A}\,\overline{B}C(0) + \overline{A}B\overline{C}(1)$$
$$+ \overline{A}BC(1) + A\overline{B}\,\overline{C}(1) + A\overline{B}C(0)$$
$$+ AB\overline{C}(\emptyset) + ABC(\emptyset)$$

Given:

A B C	F
0 0 0	0
0 0 1	0
0 1 0	1
0 1 1	1
1 0 0	1
1 0 1	0
1 1 0	$\emptyset$
1 1 1	$\emptyset$

From this we plot the values of F in a three-variable map as shown:

Fig. 3-22. Mapping example for Example 3-10.

To develop the VEM plotting technique, we need only expand on the idea of plotting the ASSERTED value of a variable associated with each minterm to one of plotting the ASSERTED value of some *expression* associated with each minterm. To illustrate this idea, consider grouping the least significant variable with the variable F in the general expression for F. Consider the following expression:

$$F \cdot F = F$$
$$= \overline{A}\,\overline{B}(\overline{C}F) + \overline{A}\,\overline{B}(CF) + \overline{A}B(\overline{C}F) + \overline{A}B(CF)$$
$$+ A\overline{B}(\overline{C}F) + A\overline{B}(CF) + AB(\overline{C}F) + AB(CF)$$

or

$$F = \overline{A}\,\overline{B}(\overline{C}F + CF) + \overline{A}B(\overline{C}F + CF) + A\overline{B}(\overline{C}F + CF) + AB(\overline{C}F + CF)$$

Through a process parallel to the example illustrating the map plotting using the truth value of the literal F, it can be seen that the ASSERTED value for the term $(\overline{C}F + CF)$ (which is called the *Map-Entered Function*), can be plotted in a two-variable (A,B) map. Before continuing, let us define the *sub-minterms* as the terms made up of all possible combinations of the two most significant variables (A,B) ANDed together $(\overline{A}\,\overline{B}, \overline{A}B, A\overline{B}, AB)$. Now consider the development in Example 3-11 using the same TRUTH-TABLE in Example 3-10. In this example the original TRUTH-TABLE is partitioned such that the factoring of the output expression is made obvious. See Figure 3-23(a).

EXAMPLE 3-11: We can plot the map with the ASSERTED value for each $(\overline{C}F + CF)$, resulting in the map shown in Figure 3-23(b).

With practice you will find that plotting a VEM can be as simple as plotting a standard K-map. To further illustrate the plotting process from the partitioned TRUTH-TABLE shown in Example 3-11, first consider the process to be one of performing a row partition of the TRUTH-TABLE for each sub-minterm, then one

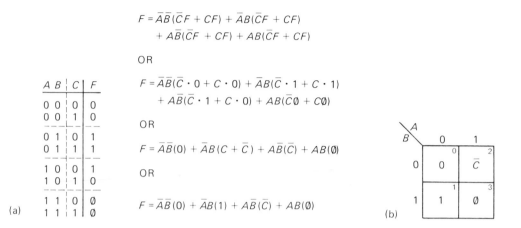

$$F = \overline{A}\overline{B}(\overline{C}F + CF) + \overline{A}B(\overline{C}F + CF)$$
$$+ A\overline{B}(\overline{C}F + CF) + AB(\overline{C}F + CF)$$

OR

$$F = \overline{A}\overline{B}(\overline{C}\cdot 0 + C \cdot 0) + \overline{A}B(\overline{C}\cdot 1 + C \cdot 1)$$
$$+ A\overline{B}(\overline{C}\cdot 1 + C \cdot 0) + AB(\overline{C}\text{Ø} + C\text{Ø})$$

OR

$$F = \overline{A}\overline{B}(0) + \overline{A}B(C + \overline{C}) + A\overline{B}(\overline{C}) + AB(\text{Ø})$$

OR

$$F = \overline{A}\overline{B}(0) + \overline{A}B(1) + A\overline{B}(\overline{C}) + AB(\text{Ø})$$

A B	C	F
0 0	0	0
0 0	1	0
0 1	0	1
0 1	1	1
1 0	0	1
1 0	1	0
1 1	0	Ø
1 1	1	Ø

(a)

(b)

Fig. 3-23. Variable-entered-mapping example for Example 3-11.

of examining the truth value of F, and associate this with the truth values of C within the partition. For example, we see that, in the first partition of the TRUTH-TABLE $(\overline{A}\,\overline{B})$, F is NOT-ASSERTED independent of C. Therefore, a 0 is plotted in the $\overline{A}\,\overline{B}$ cell of the two-variable map. Next, the second partition $(\overline{A}\,B)$ is examined. Here it is found that F is ASSERTED independent of C. Therefore, a 1 is plotted in the $\overline{A}\,B$ cell of two-variable map. Next, the third partition is examined; here it is found that F is ASSERTED only with $\overline{C}$. Therefore, a $\overline{C}$ is plotted in cell $A\overline{B}$. Last, we examine the fourth partition and find that F is a "don't care" condition independent of C. Therefore, a Ø is plotted in the last cell. It should be pointed out once more that it is the value of $(\overline{C}F + CF)$ for each sub-minterm that is plotted into the appropriate cell in the reduced size map. To further illustrate the VEM plotting process, consider the following examples:

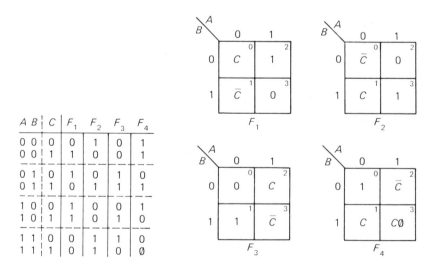

A B	C	F_1	F_2	F_3	F_4
0 0	0	0	1	0	1
0 0	1	1	0	0	1
0 1	0	1	0	1	0
0 1	1	0	1	1	1
1 0	0	1	0	0	1
1 0	1	1	0	1	0
1 1	0	0	1	1	0
1 1	1	0	1	0	Ø

Fig. 3-24. VEM examples for Example 3-12.

EXAMPLE 3-12:   More examples of VEM plotting shown in Figure 3-24. Note the special entry in cell AB for F_4 in the figure. Here a "don't care" condition existed with C. Because "don't care" entries are used only when they enhance the simplification of a problem, a special notation $(C\emptyset)$ is introduced to indicate that when reading the map this cell should be used only if its use results in further simplification.

It should be obvious that n variable problems can also be plotted in a $n-1$ variable map by using the same partitioning technique as Example 3-13 illustrates where $n=4$.

EXAMPLE 3-13:

A B C D	F_1	F_2
0 0 0 0	0	1
0 0 0 1	0	1
0 0 1 0	1	1
0 0 1 1	1	0
0 1 0 0	0	1
0 1 0 1	0	0
0 1 1 0	1	0
0 1 1 1	0	0
1 0 0 0	1	0
1 0 0 1	1	1
1 0 1 0	0	1
1 0 1 1	1	1
1 1 0 0	0	0
1 1 0 1	0	0
1 1 1 0	0	0
1 1 1 1	0	0

F1

C \ AB	00	01	11	10
0	0	$\bar{D}\emptyset$	$\bar{D}\emptyset$	1
1	1	$\bar{D}$	0	D

F2

C \ AB	00	01	11	10
0	1	$\bar{D}$	$\emptyset$	D
1	$\bar{D}+D\emptyset$	$\bar{D}\emptyset$	0	1

Fig. 3-25.   Mapping examples for Example 3-13. Note: A 1 entry can be and should be thought of as $1 = D + \bar{D}$.

Another interesting feature is that the four-variable TRUTH-TABLES in Example 3-13 could be partitioned in such a manner as to include both C and D as map-entered variables and reduce the map size to a two-variable map. In this case an *expression* of C and D would be inserted in the map. For example, consider the plot of F_2 of Example 3-13 as shown in Example 3-14.

EXAMPLE 3-14:   Let $F_2 = F$. Then

$$F = \bar{A}\bar{B}(\bar{C}\bar{D}F + \bar{C}DF + C\bar{D}F + CDF) + \bar{A}B(\bar{C}\bar{D}F + \bar{C}DF + C\bar{D}F + CDF)$$
$$+ A\bar{B}(\bar{C}\bar{D}F + \bar{C}DF + C\bar{D}F + CDF) + AB(\bar{C}\bar{D}F + \bar{C}DF + C\bar{D}F + CDF)$$

This results in the expression-entered map shown in Figure 3-26.

Fig. 3-26. The variable-entered expression map for F_2 of Example 3-13.

It should now be obvious that an n variable problem can be partitioned in any manner as long as the resulting map is of reduced size. However, it has been found by experience that *reading* maps with *map-entered expression*s can be a bit tedious. Therefore, don't get overzealous with this technique for plotting maps. The *reading* of a VEM is covered in the next section.

3-15 VEM READING THEORY

Considerable effort has been spent in dealing with the concepts of plotting variable-entered maps. Now the time has come to develop the techniques for *reading* them.

We first introduce a map-reading algorithm, then justify its use by noting that it closely parallels the development of the algorithm given for reading a standard K-map. Keep in mind that the variable entered into the map will be defined as the Map-Entered Variable (MEV).

Step 1: First imagine that all 1 entries in the map are replaced by the map-entered variables ORed with its complement, that is, $1 = D + \bar{D}$. Then perform a looping over the single entry MEV's as prescribed by the following rules:*

Looping rules

> (a) First loop all *single* MEV entries that will *not* loop with another identical MEV in an adjacent cell or with a 1 or a $\emptyset$ (island). Remember that a C and $\bar{C}$ in adjacent cells cannot be looped because they are not identical MEV's.
> (b) Loop all MEV's that will loop into duals only with another identical MEV in an adjacent cell.
> (c) Loop all MEV's that will loop into a dual only with a 1.
> (d) Loop all MEV's that will loop into a dual only with a $\emptyset$.
> (e) Any MEV that will loop two ways with another identical MEV, 1, or $\emptyset$ but won't loop into a quad, leave until later.
> (f) Continue looping in similar fashion for quads and groups of eight until every MEV has been looped at least once. This completes step 1.

---

*It is intended that the single statement grouping rule introduced in Section 3-9 be integrated into these rules.

Step 2: Once all *single* MEV entries have been covered, transform the map according to the following transformations:

(a) Replace the MEV and $\overline{\text{MEV}}$ with 0, that is, MEV and $\overline{\text{MEV}} \rightarrow 0$.

(b) $0 \rightarrow 0, \varnothing \rightarrow \varnothing$.

(c) $1 \begin{cases} \nearrow 1 \text{ \{if not completely covered} \\ \searrow \varnothing \begin{cases} \text{if completely covered, i.e., looped with both} \\ \text{the MEV and } \overline{\text{MEV}} \end{cases} \end{cases}$

(d) $\text{MEV}\varnothing$ and $\overline{\text{MEV}}\varnothing \rightarrow 0$

(e) $(\text{MEV} + \overline{\text{MEV}}\varnothing)$ and $(\overline{\text{MEV}} + \text{MEV}\varnothing) \begin{cases} \nearrow 1 \begin{cases} \text{if not covered at all or} \\ \text{if just the } \varnothing \text{ is covered} \end{cases} \\ \searrow \varnothing \begin{cases} \text{if completely covered or} \\ \text{if just the necessary term} \\ \text{is covered} \end{cases} \end{cases}$

necessary variable

Then proceed as if a standard K-map was being used.

Example 3-15: See Figure 3-27 for VEM reading examples.

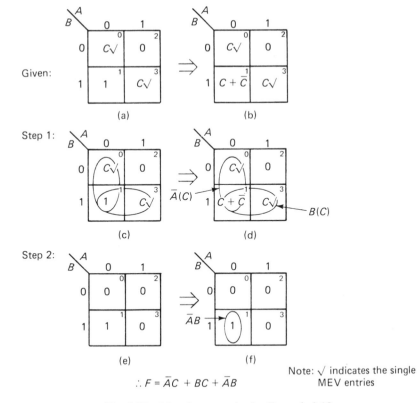

Given: (a) (b)

Step 1: (c) (d) $\overline{A}(C)$ $B(C)$

Step 2: (e) (f) $\overline{A}B$

$$\therefore F = \overline{A}C + BC + \overline{A}B$$

Note: $\sqrt{}$ indicates the single MEV entries

Fig. 3-27. Mapping examples for Example 3-15.

Keep in mind that when you are reading a map in the map-entered format, part of the complete minterm resides within the cell. For example, the minterms $A\bar{B}C$ and $A\bar{B}\bar{C}$ are found in the map, as shown in Figure 3-28. Therefore, when you are extracting the simplified terms, the variable looped within the cell must be attached to the standard K-map reduced term. Hence, you read the looping in K-map notation, disregarding the MEV first, then adding it later. For example, the map in Figure 3-28 reads first as $\bar{B}$ in K-map notation, and then the MEV is added, resulting in the term $\bar{B}C$.

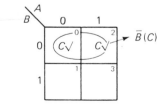

Fig. 3-28. An illustration of how the reduced term is read from a VEM.

The following examples are given to further illustrate the VEM reading process.

EXAMPLE 3-16:   More examples of VEM plotting and reading (Figure 3-29).

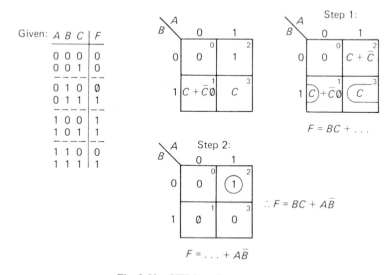

Fig. 3-29. VEM reading process.

EXAMPLE 3-17:   Steps 1 and 2 can be combined as shown in Figure 3-30.

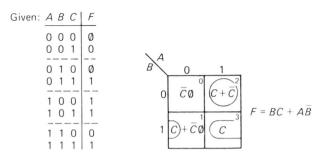

Given:

A B C	F
0 0 0	Ø
0 0 1	0
0 1 0	Ø
0 1 1	1
1 0 0	1
1 0 1	1
1 1 0	0
1 1 1	1

$$F = BC + A\bar{B}$$

Fig. 3-30. An illustration of combining steps 1 and 2 in a single VEM.

EXAMPLE 3-18: A four-variable MEV example is illustrated in Figure 3-31.

A B C D	F_1	F_2
0 0 0 0	Ø	0
0 0 0 1	Ø	0
0 0 1 0	1	1
0 0 1 1	0	1
0 1 0 0	1	0
0 1 0 1	1	1
0 1 1 0	Ø	1
0 1 1 1	0	1
1 0 0 0	0	0
1 0 0 1	0	0
1 0 1 0	1	Ø
1 0 1 1	1	Ø
1 1 0 0	0	0
1 1 0 1	1	Ø
1 1 1 0	0	1
1 1 1 1	Ø	0

$$F_1 = B\bar{C}D + \bar{A}\bar{D} + A\bar{B}C$$

$$F_2 = \bar{A}BD + C\bar{D} + \bar{A}C$$

Fig. 3-31. An illustration of a four-variable reduction using the VEM technique.

The mapping examples in Example 3-19 illustrate how two maps can be used to graphically illustrate the two-step reading process, thus reducing confusion for the beginner.

EXAMPLE 3-19: See Figures 3-32(a)–3-32(c).

The MEV technique can also be used to minimize given Boolean expressions which involve what were defined earlier as *infrequently used variables*. This is shown in Example 3-20.

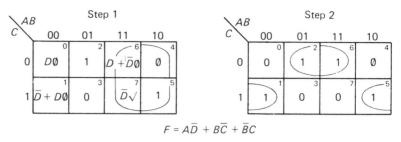

$$F = A\bar{D} + B\bar{C} + \bar{B}C$$

(a)

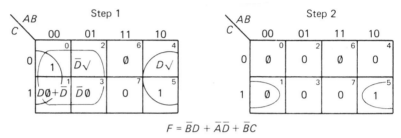

$$F = \bar{B}D + \bar{A}\bar{D} + \bar{B}C$$

(b)

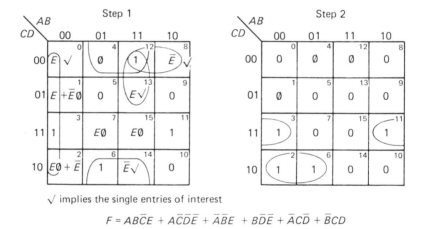

√ implies the single entries of interest

$$F = AB\bar{C}E + A\bar{C}\bar{D}\bar{E} + \bar{A}\bar{B}E + B\bar{D}\bar{E} + \bar{A}C\bar{D} + \bar{B}CD$$

(c)

Fig. 3-32. Example maps illustrating the process of reading VEM's with ∅ entries.

EXAMPLE 3-20: Given:

$$F(A,B,C,G,H) = \bar{A}\,\bar{B}\,\bar{C}\,\bar{H} + \bar{A}\,\bar{B}\,C\bar{H} + \bar{A}\,BC + A\bar{B}\,\bar{C}\,\bar{G} + A\bar{B}\,C\bar{G} + AB\bar{C} + ABC$$

where G and H are the infrequently used variables, which can be grouped as:

$$F(A,B,C,G,H) = (\bar{A}\,\bar{B}\,\bar{C})(\bar{H}) + (\bar{A}\,\bar{B}\,C)(\bar{H}) + (\bar{A}\,BC) + (A\bar{B}\,\bar{C})(\bar{G})$$
$$+ (A\bar{B}\,C)(\bar{G}) + (AB\bar{C}) + (ABC)$$

From this we can plot the map shown in Figure 3-33.

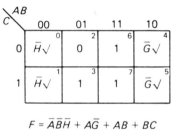

Fig. 3-33. The VEM technique to an expression involving infrequently used variables.

$$F = \overline{A}\,\overline{B}\overline{H} + A\overline{G} + AB + BC$$

From this example we see that a simple three-variable map can be used to reduce an expression that would normally require a five-variable map.

These examples illustrate that the MEV mapping technique is a powerful and useful tool, one that can be used in a wide variety of problems. The chapters covering sequential circuits show that the MEV opens a new vista in which the drudgery of traditional sequential design is greatly reduced by using the techniques set forth here. However, the two-step reading process given can create a little confusion when Ø entries are present. Because of this you might choose to continue to use the two-map scheme until you gain the necessary experience.

In the next section we illustrate how minimization is integrated into the design process.

3-16 MINIMIZATION AND COMBINATIONAL DESIGN

Now that the mechanics of minimization have been developed, consider how these principles are effectively applied in the design process.

The design of combinational circuits is generally considered to be one of starting with a set of operational specifications, which can be written, verbal or imagined, and ending with a *well-documented functional* circuit. Generally the design procedure follows, formally or informally, some set of design steps. The following steps and remarks are offered to aid you in your development of combinational circuits.

RECOMMENDED STEPS AND PROCEDURES

(1) Receive specifications. It is during this step that you develop a global understanding of what your circuit is to do, and make certain a combinational circuit of some variety is needed.

(2) Draw a block diagram (if needed) of your system (circuit) and illustrate its relation to the systems providing inputs for your system. Likewise illustrate where the system is receiving your outputs. *Document clearly the ASSERTION LEVELS of the inputs given to you and the ASSERTION LEVELS required for your outputs.* This documentation implies that appropriate mnemonics be developed for inputs and outputs.

(3) Determine the magnitude of your design problem. In short, determine how many input variables and outputs you are dealing with. It may in fact be required that you revert to some sort of partitioning (modularization) of your design into linked sub-systems if the design requirements are too large.

(4) Develop a TRUTH-TABLE or map defining the combinational requirements of your design. *Be certain to treat the 1 entries as ASSERTED and the 0 entries as NOT-ASSERTED without trying to assign any voltage level.*

(5) Reduce your problem using the techniques previously outlined.

(6) Now using the given ASSERTION levels of the inputs and the required ASSERTION levels for the outputs, develop the optimal circuit diagram according to the following procedure.

    (a) Examine the simplified expressions developed in step 5 and determine output ASSERTION level. Then select the *output function symbol* (OR/AND) which meets the following requirements: (i) It has the required ASSERTION level and (ii) it has sufficient inputs to implement the complete expression.

    (b) Select the *input symbols* that *complement* (match) the inputs of the selected output symbol as well as optimally meet the requirements of the given input ASSERTION levels. In short, the input symbols selection is one of first meeting the ASSERTION level requirements of the selected output symbol, and secondly these should be selected if possible such that no INVERTERS are required to change the system input ASSERTION levels.

(7) Wire-up your circuit and debug if necessary, keeping your documentation updated.

In step 2 you must determine and identify the sources of your inputs as to whether or not they originate from a positive or negative logic system, or more importantly what are the ASSERTION levels of each input. Likewise the same exercise must be carried out for the outputs of your system. Remember that this helps in making decisions as to what types of *gates* should be used to implement the design and to reduce the number of INVERTERS. This will be demonstrated shortly and throughout the text. In step 3 you determine the magnitude of the design problem and make the decision as to whether or not the problem is too large for a traditional TRUTH-TABLE approach. There are practical limits for the number of input variables that can be entertained because there are 2^n entries in an n variable TRUTH-TABLE, or map. A practical limit is $n=6$; anything greater than six becomes quite cumbersome and it is time to consider another approach. One approach is that of re-examining the specifications to determine if the problem can be subdivided in two or more mutually exclusive problems. Another approach is to determine if maybe the problem can be synthesized by interconnecting an array of more simple modules. Also, maybe an infrequently used MEV approach can be used. Each of these techniques is a viable alternative to solving a large single problem and therefore should be kept in mind.

It is during step 6 that the art of using the polarized mnemonics approach has its biggest impact on the final design. Several examples of this process will be illustrated shortly.

During steps 6 and 7 the actual selection of gates is made and a well-documented circuit diagram is drawn using the appropriate symbols in such a way that the AND/OR (OR/AND) levels are immediately perceived by inspection. This process is reviewed as another step-by-step process.

(1) Select the appropriate *output* gate or gates by considering two things.
    (a) Is your Boolean expression in SOP or POS form?
    (b) What ASSERTED level is desired for your output or outputs?
(2) Select the appropriate first-level gates after considering two things.
    (a) Which input variables are complemented in the output expression?
    (b) What are the ASSERTED levels of the inputs?

These design steps will be illustrated by several design examples.

EXAMPLE 3-21:

Step 1: You are to design a special combinational circuit having two inputs (LD and BRK). These inputs originate in a positive logic system. Your circuit is to have one output that must be ASSERTED high. This output (FX DAT) is to be ASSERTED if and only if LD and BRK are not *identical*.

Step 2: See Figure E3-1.

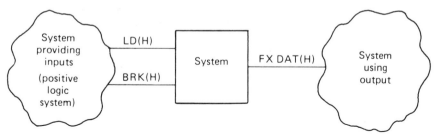

Fig. E3-1.

Step 3: Problem is certainly within limits of TRUTH-TABLE approach:

Number of inputs = 2

Number of outputs = 1

Step 4: Make a TRUTH-TABLE.

LD	BRK	FX DAT
0	0	0
0	1	1
1	0	1
1	1	0

Step 5: Plot and reduce the map. See Figure E3-2.

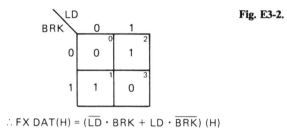

Fig. E3-2.

$\therefore$ FX DAT(H) = ($\overline{\text{LD}}$ · BRK + LD · $\overline{\text{BRK}}$) (H)

Step 6: See Figure 3-34 for possible circuit implementations.

As you study the steps leading to a completed design for Example 3-21, observe that steps 1 through 5 are straightforward and quite easy to follow. However, step 6 requires more thought. Therefore, go back and again analyze what needs to be considered.

From the specifications, the output FXDAT must be ASSERTED HIGH and the expression for FXDAT must be in SOP form. This was illustrated by selecting the OUTPUT symbol to be an OR function ASSERTED HIGH. Therefore, in your selection of gates you have but two choices: (a) an OR gate, or (b) a NAND gate (see Figure 3-34).

Next, once the output symbol is selected, you must select the AND function level of your circuit so that its output is compatible with the inputs to the output gate. You observe from Figure 3-34 that you can use AND or NOR gates with an OR output gate or NAND or OR gates with a NAND output gate. In each of these four combinations the *same* number of inverters (two) is required to condition the inputs from the outside world. Thus, there are four options for the implementation. The choice of implementation will depend on several factors such as: (1) relative cost of different gates, (2) personal prejudices, and (3) availability of the gates. This last choice is an important one, particularly if your circuit is to be part of a larger system built up on the circuit board. Typically, in larger designs a selection of gates will be available to be used freely throughout the design. Therefore, the chances of having all four types of gates available to use without worry or waste is quite large, unless you work for a company that stresses all NAND or all NOR implementations. Even in this case the techniques described above are applicable and useful.

Before continuing, take one more look at Example 3-21. You recognize by now that this is an EXOR function and could be implemented by simply buying an EXOR gate. However, this particular problem illustrates an interesting technique whereby *mixed gate designs and insight* can save inverter functions. In short, by using this technique, many circuits, like the EXOR, can be designed *without using gates* for inverter functions! For example, if we take the expression for FXDAT:

$$\text{FXDAT(H)} = (\overline{\text{LD} \cdot \text{BRK}} + \text{LD} \cdot \overline{\text{BRK}})(\text{H}) = (\text{LD} \cdot \text{BRK} + \overline{\text{LD}} \cdot \overline{\text{BRK}})(\text{L})$$

From F(H) = ($\overline{\text{F}}$)(L)

Note that both first-level gates generate a homogeneous or nonmixed product term, that is, LD·BRK and $\overline{\text{LD}} \cdot \overline{\text{BRK}}$. Therefore, you can take advantage of

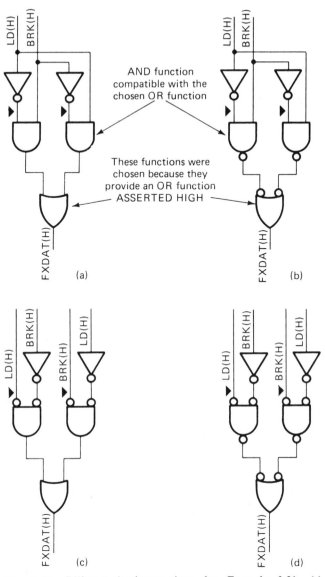

Fig. 3-34. Different implementations for Example 3-21. (a) AND/OR gates and inverters. (b) NAND gates and inverters. (c) NOR/OR gates and inverters. (d) OR/NAND gates and inverters.

this situation and implement the expression for FXDAT(H) without need for any inverters (see Figures 3-35(a) and 3-35(b)).

There are several other alternate inverter-free circuits for the EXOR. These will be left for exercises.

It is hoped that by now you realize that using mixed-logic approaches has some definite advantages, both in saving hardware and in creating a stimulating thought pattern allowing for some creative thinking.

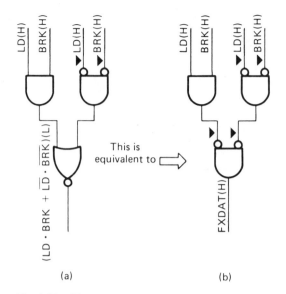

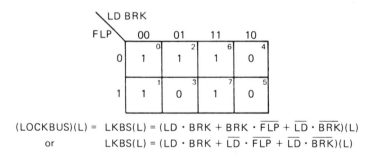

Fig. 3-35. The implementation of an EXOR without inverters.

Let's try another example to investigate further our understanding of the design step.

EXAMPLE 3-22: Given the following map of some problem specification, derive the Boolean expression for the output ASSERTED LOW and implement it based on all three inputs being ASSERTED HIGH (see map in Figure 3-36).

$(LOCKBUS)(L) =$ $LKBS(L) = (LD \cdot BRK + BRK \cdot \overline{FLP} + \overline{LD} \cdot \overline{BRK})(L)$

or $LKBS(L) = (LD \cdot BRK + \overline{LD} \cdot \overline{FLP} + \overline{LD} \cdot \overline{BRK})(L)$

Fig. 3-36. Map for Example 3-22.

Two equally valid expressions can be derived for LKBS(L), depending on which way cell 2 is grouped with the others. However, you will notice that the second expression will be the easiest to implement because of the nonmixed nature of each of its terms. Each term has two variables, both of which are either complemented or uncomplemented. Figure 3-37 illustrates two possible implementations for Example 3-22. At first the expression is SOP for ASSERTED LOW, dictating that a three-input NOR gate or AND gate be used. Once a NOR gate is selected, the AND level gates must be selected.

Observe that you have the choice of mixing AND gates and NOR gates. Figure 3-37(a) illustrates a mixed choice of gates for the AND level. This saves on inverter requirements. Figure 3-37(b) illustrates an alternate solution.

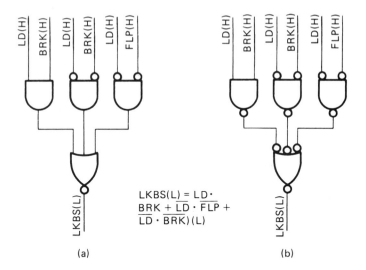

$$LKBS(L) = LD \cdot BRK + \overline{LD} \cdot \overline{FLP} + \overline{LD} \cdot \overline{BRK})(L)$$

(a)   (b)

Fig. 3-37. Two implementations of the second expression of LKBS(L).

Had the first expression been chosen, one extra inverter would have been required. Therefore, you have learned to group optional grouping in such a way that the variables in the simplified terms are all complemented or all uncomplemented for single rail systems.

Let's work one more example in which a POS type of expression is desired.

EXAMPLE 3-23: Using the same map as in Example 3-22, derive the POS expression for LKBS(H) and implement with mixed logic. See Figure 3-38.

FLP \ LD BRK	00	01	11	10
0	1 ^{0}	1 ^{2}	1 ^{6}	0 ^{4}
1	1 ^{1}	0 ^{3}	1 ^{7}	0 ^{5}

$\overline{LKBS} = LD \cdot \overline{BRK} + \overline{LD} \cdot BRK \cdot FLP$

Fig. 3-38. Map for Example 3-23. $\therefore LKBS(H) = [(\overline{LD} + BRK) \cdot (LD + \overline{BRK} + \overline{FLP})](H)$

Our choice for the output gate is restricted to either a two-input AND gate or a two-input NOR gate. Once a two-input AND gate is selected for the output, the OR level function must be selected, one with ASSERTED HIGH outputs. OR gates or NAND gates are the only choice. Figure 3-39(a) illustrates the NAND gate choice. Figure 3-39(b) illustrates an alternate solution.

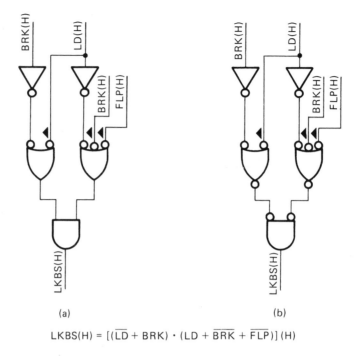

(a)   (b)

$$LKBS(H) = [(\overline{LD} + BRK) \cdot (LD + \overline{BRK} + \overline{FLP})](H)$$

Fig. 3-39. Alternate implementations of Example 3-23.

Thus you have a general approach to combinational circuit implementation which yields several alternative solutions to a given problem from which you can select the one you prefer or the one that best fits the overall requirements. This concludes the directed studies of hand reduction and combinational circuit design procedures. In the next several sections we introduce some computer-aided reduction methods suitable for design requirements beyond six variables.

3-17 MINIMIZING FUNCTIONS OF MORE THAN SIX VARIABLES

With the exception of using variable-entered mapping processes, the "hand" minimization of expressions involving more than six variables is a tedious and time-consuming task. Furthermore, many times the task is hardly worth the effort. This is particularly true when one-of-a-kind systems are being designed, and LSI components are available for use. Even if high volume production is anticipated, the lengthy minimization processes can be bypassed or traded for what might be termed a wasteful but cost-effective implementation centered around products of the LSI technology. For example, a single package Read-Only-Memory (ROM) (see Chapter 8) can be used to generate multiple functions of many variables at a very low cost without regard to any sort of minimization. Generally speaking, the use of ROM's is a widely accepted practice even though the wasted on-chip-logic hardware is often enormous. Philosophically this waste is accepted because the use of ROM's for random logic generation is both cost effective and reliable. Therefore, the traditional need for absolute minimization has been diminished somewhat by the products of the LSI technology. However, those involved in LSI circuit development and use still have occasions to use large scale minimization processes.

Two important areas are: (1) "chip level" LSI design, where the efficient use of silicon real estate is of prime importance; (2) the use of Programmed-Logic-Arrays (PLA) (see Chapter 8), which require optimal utilization of the limited on-chip logic power. Aside from these applications there are still occasions where the typical logic designer could use large scale minimization processes on a day-by-day basis if they were quick and low cost. Obviously the quick and low cost requirement eliminates the human hand reduction methods and strongly suggests that computer methods be used.

At present there are well over fifty technical references dealing with the problem of minimizing Boolean expressions. The most widely publicized is the Quine–McCluskey method and variations of this approach. Others include a variety of topological and mathematical approaches related to the same process.

Basically the process is one of finding all prime implicants and then processing this set to find some sort of cover that may or may not be a minimal cover. Although the past work in this area has been thorough and productive, this author has struck out on his own in hopes of finding the better way. Through research, work, and practice in the field, a set of desirable attributes has been developed. These attributes, some of which are indicated as immeasurable qualities, are listed as follows:

(1) Fast, in comparison to a presently used system
(2) Efficient, in comparison to a presently used system
(3) Guaranteed minimal cover
(4) Flexible data input formatting:
 (a) Standard minterm list
 (b) Map-entered-variable notation
 (c) Partially simplified expressions
 (d) Free use of "don't cares"
 (e) Process time mainly related to problem complexity, not strictly on variable number
(5) Selectable output options:
 (a) All or any possible SOP or POS minimal cover listings
 (b) A complete prime implicant listing if desired for transient hazard analysis*
 (c) All or any optimal solutions based on desired prime implicant constraints
 (d) All or any optimal solution constrained to minimal use of inverters
 (e) All or any optimal solutions for multi-output

---

*Normally this process developed does not produce a complete prime implicant list in the interest of improving the speed and efficiency.

3-18 INTRODUCTION TO THE "BOOZER" PROGRAM

BOOZER is an acronym for BOOlean ZEro-one Reduction. The BOOZER computer program is based on a modified extension of the single statement map-reading algorithm and is basically broken into three major processes:

(1) DATA INPUT processing;
(2) A folding array algorithm is used to identify pertinent information related to group location and size, which is then used by a "walking variable elimination" scheme to produce a list of essential and optional implicants, including some special constraint data;
(3) A modified zero-one optimization process that processes the product of step 2 into the desired optimal cover.

The first process of the BOOZER program facilitates the desirable input data formats allowing for (1) a standard minterm listing, (2) a standard map-entered or factored input notation, (3) a partially reduced expression entry format, and (4) the free use of "don't care" entries. Basically the first process step does nothing more than generate an implicated minterm array from the data input. The second process of BOOZER is itself a two-step process. The first of these processes performs a simple mathematical manipulation on the minterm array which produces the following:

(1) All islands (minterms that will not group in any way) are identified.
(2) All single way duals (minterms that will group in only one way) are identified.
(3) Information is derived that indicates the largest possible grouping every implicated minterm can be involved in.
(4) Information is derived that indicates the largest possible grouping which must be looked for in the complete problem. For example, if a quad is the largest possible grouping which can be taken anywhere in an eight-variable problem, then this information is made available so as to eliminate unnecessary searches.
(5) Information is derived that indicates which variables are to be eliminated by each grouping.

The second step in process 2 of BOOZER then takes the information made available from the first step and searches out all prime implicants, using a *"walking variable elimination"* if they are desired, otherwise a modified "walking search" for the essential implicants and necessary implicants is carried out. This is done to improve efficiency and process time. In short, after a grouping has been identified and extracted $\emptyset$'s are inserted for the 1's in this grouping. Further, the grouping data is prepared with constraint information that is pertinent to the *zero-one optimization process* carried out in the third and final process of BOOZER.

The third process of BOOZER as mentioned uses a numerical optimization subroutine known as the *zero-one optimization algorithm* modified specifically to facilitate the optimal cover selection from the data generated in the second process.

Though it is not the intent to completely discuss BOOZER in detail, we will work through a problem that will illustrate and simulate the processes carried out by the actual program. Keep in mind that the processes are fully intended for computer operation and in no way should they be construed as hand operation methods.

Example 3-24: This example is aimed at demonstrating (simulating) processes 2 and 3 of BOOZER using a four-variable map problem as the problem source. This map is shown in Figure 3-40. First the minterm array is generated as shown in Figure 3-41. Next the implicated minterm array (the $F(A,B,C,D)$ array) is processed by a method that produces results identical to those produced by folding the map over (flat) on each variable boundary and multiplying the vertically adjacent cells, then generating a new map (array) with the 1's plotted in those cells where the product equals 1. This is demonstrated in Figure 3-42 for a simple three-variable problem. Observe that the original map is folded flat on each of the three variable boundaries (A, B, and C) and the resultant maps or partition arrays ($P(A)$, $P(B)$, and $P(C)$) are generated from the folding process.

Fig. 3-40. An example map to be reduced by the processes of the BOOZER program.

CD \ AB	00	01	11	10
00	0: 1	4: 1	12: Ø	8:
01	1: 1	5: Ø	13:	9:
11	3:	7: 1	15: 1	11:
10	2:	6:	14:	10: 1

Fig. 3-41. The implicated minterm array generated from the input data for Example 3-24.

Minterm No.	$F(ABCD)$
0	1
1	1
2	0
3	0
4	1
5	Ø
6	0
7	1
8	0
9	0
10	1
11	0
12	Ø
13	0
14	0
15	1

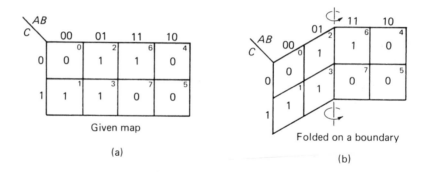

Given map

(a)

Folded on a boundary

(b)

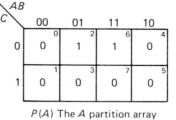

Entries in this map
are derived from
multiplying the
vertical adjacent
entries in the folded
map

$P(A)$ The A partition array

(c)

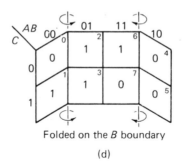

Folded on the B boundary

(d)

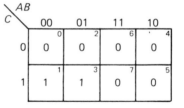

$P(B)$ The B partition array

(e)

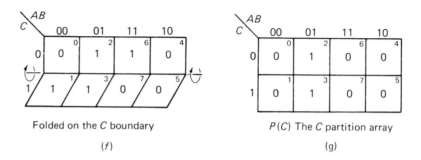

Folded on the C boundary

(f)

$P(C)$ The C partition array

(g)

Fig. 3-42. An illustration of the map folding process and resultant data.

Minterm No.	$F(A, B, C)$	$P(A)$	$P(B)$	$P(C)$	Row Sum
0	0	0	0	0	0
1	1	0	1	0	1
2	1	1	0	1	2
3	1	0	1	1	2
4	0	0	0	0	0
5	0	0	0	0	0
6	1	1	0	0	1
7	0	0	0	0	0

The composite array results observed by folding
the map including a ROW sum array.

(h)

Fig. 3-42. (Cont.)

Once the folding process is completed it produces some very useful data. For example, notice that from the maps for partition arrays $P(A)$, $P(B)$, and $P(C)$ the groupings that involve the elimination of the folding variable are immediately exposed. From $P(A)$ observe that the $B\overline{C}$ group stripped away from the rest of the map. Likewise the $\overline{A}C$ term is exposed in the $P(B)$ map and $\overline{A}B$ term is exposed in the $P(C)$ map. *In short, the 1 entries in the partition arrays identify a possible grouping involving the minterm at that position and at the same time indicate the variable that is to be eliminated.* We see from Figure 3-42(h) that when the partition array maps are portrayed in an array notation and the sum of the entries in the rows (row sum) of $P(A)$, $P(B)$, and $P(C)$ is taken, even more information can be extracted. It is from this row sum array we identify the islands, the single-way duals, and the other information related to maximum possible group size and the number of ways each minterm will group. This information is quickly gleaned from the row sum data by the following process:

(1) Any implicated minterm with a row sum $=0$ is an island.
(2) Any implicated minterm with a row sum $=1$ is an essential dual (see Figure 3-42(h) for minterms 1 and 6).
(3) A row sum $=n$ indicates the implicated minterm could possibly group into a group of 2^n, that is, the largest possible grouping the minterm can group into. For example, if $n=2$, then this minterm could possibly group into a quad.
(4) If n equals the largest row sum entry and iff there are 2^n row sum entries that equal n, the largest possible grouping in the cover for the problem is a 2^n sized group. For example, if $n=3$ is the largest row sum entry, then there must be $2^n=8$ entries of three to assure the possibility of a group of eight.

Thus a great deal of preliminary reduction information can be gleaned from the results of the simulated folding process. However, keep in mind that this folding process is merely a simulated process for the actual process carried out in the BOOZER program.

Now let us return to the reduction of the problem specified in Example 3-24. We will do this by presenting the composite array for the problem as shown in Figure 3-43. Note that the $\emptyset$ entries were treated as 1's where the partition arrays $(P(A), P(B), P(C),$ and $P(D))$ were generated.

Minterm No.	$F(A, B, C, D)$	$P(A)$	$P(B)$	$P(C)$	$P(D)$	Row Sum
0	1	0	1	0	1	2^a
1	1	0	1	0	1	2^b
2	0	0	0	0	0	0
3	0	0	0	0	0	0
4	1	1	1	0	1	3^c
5	$\emptyset$	0	1	1	1	3
6	0	0	0	0	0	0
7	1	1	0	1	0	2
8	0	0	0	0	0	0
9	0	0	0	0	0	0
10	1	0	0	0	0	0^d
11	0	0	0	0	0	0
12	$\emptyset$	1	0	0	0	1
13	0	0	0	0	0	0
14	0	0	0	0	0	0
15	1	1	0	0	0	1^e

[a] m_0 groups two ways eliminating B or D

[b] m_1 groups two ways, may be a Quad

[c] m_4 groups three ways, but no Octet

[d] m_{10} is an island

[e] m_{15} is a single way dual

Fig. 3-43. The composite data array for Example 3-24.

To summarize the relevant data obtained from Figure 3-43, observe that minterm 10 is an island; *it will not reduce at all.* Minterms 12 and 15 will group into duals in one way and one way only. Minterms 0, 1, and 7 will group into duals two ways or possibly into a quad. Minterms 4 and 5 will group into duals three ways, groups of four or possibly into groups of eight. However, there is an insufficient number of $n \geq 3$ entries to support a group of eight, so the largest possible group for this problem is a quad.

Now the first step of process 2 is complete. The next procedure is to identify the grouping that will cover the problem using the information generated by the simulated folding process. Basically this is done by selecting the first implicated minterm, examining the composite array information related to this minterm, and extracting the appropriate grouping or groupings.

Once an implicated minterm M is identified it must be remembered that it can only be grouped with a selected set of other minterms to form a group of any particular size. This set of minterms $\{S\}$ can be identified by the following relation:

$$S_i = M + \left[2^i\right]\left[(-1)^{M/2^i}\right], \qquad i = 0, 1, 2, \ldots, n-1$$

where $n =$ the number of variables and $M/2^i$ is defined as an integer division. *Also, it should be noted that each particular value of i used indicates what variable boundary is being crossed.* For example, when $i = 0$ the search for a grouping that will eliminate the variable D is being carried out; when $i = 1$ the groupings that will eliminate the variable C are being sought after. Likewise, $i = 2$ relates to the variable B and $i = 3$ relates to the variable A. Therefore, for each power of 2 in a group size there must be another boundary variable defined in the group. For example, groups of two are defined by only cutting a single variable boundary, groups of four (quads) are defined by cutting two boundaries, groups of eight by three cuttings. In essence, the value of i establishes a *variable elimination search direction.* In order to clarify this explanation the minterms that will group together alone with the dropping variable are shown in Figure 3-44. For example, Figure 3-44 shows that minterm 5 (m_5) will group with m_{13} resulting in the elimination of the column heading variable A. Likewise, m_5 will group with m_7, resulting in the elimination of the column heading variable C. Now examine how this information might be used to help in reducing the problem posed in Example 3-24. But first:

Variable that is
eliminated by grouping

Minterm No.	A	B	C	D	
m_0	8	4	2	1	← Minterm numbers that
m_1	9	5	3	0	group with minterm 0
m_2	10	6	0	3	
m_3	11	7	1	2	
m_4	12	0	6	5	
m_5	13	1	7	4	
m_6	14	2	4	7	
m_7	15	3	5	6	
m_8	0	12	10	9	
m_9	1	13	11	8	
m_{10}	2	14	8	11	
m_{11}	3	15	9	10	
m_{12}	4	8	14	13	
m_{13}	5	9	15	12	
m_{14}	6	10	12	15	
m_{15}	7	11	13	14	

Fig. 3-44. A table illustrating all possible groupings for each minterm.

Let's take a moment to review the data available in the composite array shown in Figure 3-43. Observe that m_0 can possibly group into a quad, and a quad is the largest possible grouping involved in the problem. Further, we know from $P(B)$ in Figure 3-43 that the variables B and D can possibly be eliminated by a group involving m_0. Therefore, if we start at m_0 we are assured a "walk" to m_4 will successfully define a dual. Now once at m_4 we see a walk to m_5 defines a dual that eliminates the variable D. Therefore, a simulated two-step walk has successfully defined a quad involving m_0, m_4, and m_5 and our search is complete. In essence we started with $\overline{A}\,\overline{B}\,\overline{C}\,\overline{D}(m_0)$, took two steps, and found the term $\overline{A}\,\overline{C}$, which terminated our search for quads or any other larger grouping. Now that all quads have been removed, a search begins for the next size smaller group, in this case, duals. The search is continued in a similar fashion until the problem is covered, resulting in a prime implicant list as follows:*

minterms 0, 1, 4, and 5	covered by $\overline{A}\,\overline{C}$
minterms 5 and 7	covered by $\overline{A}\,BD$
minterms 7 and 15	covered by BCD
minterm 10	covered by $A\overline{B}\,C\overline{D}$

Next an *objective function* is generated from this output with each term of the function assigned a weighting constant related to its size. For example, terms with four variables are assigned a weight of four, terms with three variables are assigned a weight of three, and so forth. The objective function for our problem is:

$$F = 4(A\overline{B}\,C\overline{D}) + 2(\overline{A}\,\overline{C}) + 3(\overline{A}\,BD) + 3(BCD)$$

Now the task is to find the minimum numeric value for this objective function subject to the following value constraints:

$[\overline{A}\,\overline{C}] \geq 1$ because of single way cover for m_0, m_1, m_4, and m_5
$[BCD] \geq 1$ because of single way cover for m_{15}
$(A\overline{B}CD] \geq 1$ because of single way cover for m_{10}
$[\overline{A}BD] + [BDC] \geq 1$ because of the two optical groups covering m_7

This information is then turned over for processing by the simplified and modified *Balas zero-one* subroutine that proceeds to find any or all of the absolute minimal solutions to the objective function subject to the prescribed constraints. The algorithm used here was first defined by Egon Balas as a procedure for solving zero-one linear programming problems. It is a procedure that guarantees the absolute minimal solution to the problem using an efficient and ingenious scheme. We can see by inspection that the optimal solution to the given objective function subject to the constraints given is:

$$F(ABCD) = A\overline{B}\,C\overline{D} + BCD + \overline{A}\,\overline{C}$$

Thus a simulated execution of the BOOZER program listed in Appendix B has been demonstrated.

The BOOZER program listed in Appendix B is written in Burroughs Extended Algol operating on a near minimal configuration B6700. BOOZER can

---

*A complete prime implicant list is generated only if requested.

easily be adapted to block structured Algol or PL-1 type languages, with conversion to BASIC or FORTRAN being more difficult. BOOZER basically has all the attributes listed earlier with the exception of the multioutput minimization.

All process time comparisons with BOOZER have been made against reduction programs written in the same Algol running on the same machine. Although these comparisons have not been exhaustive, typical results show BOOZER winning the process time race by an order of magnitude on all problems with a considerably larger margin with problems involving more than seven variables.

However, since the process time of BOOZER is a function of the complexity of the problem rather than a direct function of the number of variables, it is difficult to gain an exact measure of the figure of merit. BOOZER has been used to simplify problems up to 18 variables without excessive process time expenditures on the near minimal B6700 configuration. It is forecasted that larger problems can be run on larger systems.

The following examples illustrate a short user introduction to BOOZER and two example runs. One run illustrates the use of BOOZER with a minterm list including Øs. The second example illustrates the use of map-entered variables.

3-19 USING BOOZER

All inputs are free format when map-entered variables are entered. They are listed one per line as they will be used in the problem. The list is terminated with a #.

Terms are input also one per line, terminated with #. The format is:
⟨minterm or minterm range⟩ ⟨expression⟩ ⟨value⟩

Each item in the format is separated by a delimiter. A delimiter is any nonalphanumeric character other than ., ', +, −, (, or). The minterm or minterm range is a number or number-number. The expression is optional. If used, it is a Boolean expression allowing one level of parentheses with no precedence assumed. In other words, the expression $AB + CD$ will be evaluated $(((A \cdot B) + C) \cdot D)$. If some other value is intended, parentheses must be used. All terms are assumed to be not-asserted when the program starts. They can be changed as often as necessary. The value 1 means asserted. The value Ø is "don't care" and any other number returns the term to not-asserted. If the input were

$$
\begin{array}{ll}
1-15 & 1 \\
13 & 5
\end{array}
$$

The program would have terms 1–15 asserted then change 13 to not-asserted. No reduction takes place until after the input list is terminated.

EXAMPLE 3-25: Simplify:

$$F(ABCDE) = \sum 1,4,7,14,17,20,21,22,23$$

$$Ø\,(0,3,6,19,30)$$

```
RUN(874003)BOOZER
#RUNNING 7495
NUMBER CF STATE VARIABLES?    #?
5
ARE YOU USING MAP ENTERED VARIABLES?    NO
THERE WERE  0 MAP ENTERED VARIABLES  5 VARIABLES TOTAL

ENTER TERMS
TERMINATE LIST WITH '#'

1  1
4  1
7  1
14 1
17 1
20-23 1
0  0
3  0
6  0
19 0
30 0
#
DC YOU WANT THE PRIME IMPLICANTS?
YES
(B') (C') (E)
(B') (C) (E')
(B') (D) (E)
(B') (C) (D)
(C) (D) (E')
(A) (B') (E)
(A) (B') (C)


THE MINIMIZED EXPRESSION IS

(A) (B') (C)
(B') (C') (E)
(B') (C) (E')
(B') (D) (E)
(C) (D) (E')
```

$$F(A,B,C,D,E) = A\overline{B}C + \overline{B}\,\overline{C}E + \overline{B}C\overline{E} + \overline{B}DE + CD\overline{E}$$

The following is another example of a map-entered-variable run using BOOZER.

EXAMPLE 3-26: Given the following VEM. (Figure E3-3). Simplify using BOOZER. Here we have a run for a ten-variable problem with a process time of 8.2 sec.

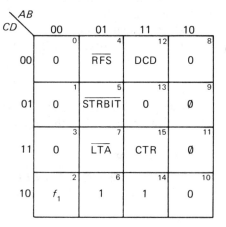

(ten-variable problem)

Figure E3-3

```
'
RUN (874003) BOOZER
'RUNNING 4388
NUMBER OF STATE VARIABLES?   '?
4
ARE YOU USING MAP ENTERED VARIABLES?     YES
LIST MAP ENTERED VARIABLES.
TERMINATE LIST WITH ''''
FI
RFS
STRBIT
LTA
DCD
CTR
'
THERE WERE  6 MAP ENTERED VARIABLES 10 VARIABLES TOTAL

ENTER TERMS
TERMINATE LIST WITH ''''

2 FI 1
4 RFS' 1
5 STRBIT' 1
7 LTA' 1
12 DCD 1
15 CTR 1
6 1
14 1
9 0
11 0
'
DO YOU WANT THE PRIME IMPLICANTS?
NO

\ DEL
BYE


THE MINIMIZED EXPRESSION IS

(B) (C) (D')
(A') (C) (D') (FI)
(A') (B) (D') (RFS')
(A') (B) (C') (D) (STRBIT')
(A') (B) (C) (LTA')
(A) (B) (D') (DCD)
(A) (C) (D) (CTR)
'ET= 12:21.8 PT=16.7 IO=0.9


BYE
'END SESSION 4367   ET=15:55.9 PT=17.4 IO=1.4
'USER = 834553011   12:18:39   03/07/79
```

3-20 SUMMARY

This chapter covers what are considered to be the basics of combinational minimization and how minimization relates to the digital design process. This is done by first illustrating the use and importance of the fundamental theorems and how they relate to the graphical means of minimization called mapping. Then mapping is extended to variable-entered mapping, which is used extensively in the later chapters. Considerable effort is spent developing a reading algorithm that is then extended into a computer-aided scheme which culminates in a reduction program called BOOZER. In short, the basics of minimization have been covered and an attempt has been made to put this process in the proper perspective relative to present-day importance.

BIBLIOGRAPHY

1. BALAS, E. An Additive Algorithm for Solving Linear Programs with Zero-one Variables. *Operations Research*, **13** (1965), 517–546.

2. CLARE, CHRISTOPHER R. *Designing Logic Systems Using State Machines*. New York: McGraw-Hill, 1973.

3. DIETMEYER, D. L. *Logic Design of Digital Systems*. Boston: Allyn and Bacon, 1971.

4. HILL, FREDRICK J., and PETERSEN, GERALD R. *Introduction to Switching Theory and Logical Design*. New York: Wiley, 1974.

5. KARNAUGH, M. The Map Method for Synthesis of Combinational Logic Circuits. *Trans. AIEE*, **72**, Pt. I (1953), 593–598.

6. LOGAN, J. ROBERT. Congruent Partitioning and Network Synthesis. *Computer Design*, **13**, No. 12 (1974), 53–60.

7. MCCLUSKEY, E. J. Minimization of Boolean Functions. *Bell System Tech. J.*, **35**, No. 5 (1956), 1417–1444.

8. MCCLUSKEY, E. V. *Introduction to the Theory of Switching Circuits*. New York: McGraw-Hill, 1965.

9. MCMILLAN, CLAUDE. *Mathematical Programming*, 2nd ed. New York: Wiley, 1975.

10. MANO, M. MORRIS. *Computer Logic Design*. Englewood Cliffs, N. J.: Prentice-Hall, 1972.

11. NAGLE, H. TROY, JR., CARROLL, B. D., and IRWIN, J. DAVID. *An Introduction to Computer Logic*. Englewood Cliffs, N. J.: Prentice-Hall, 1975.

12. PETRICK, S. R. On the Minimization of Boolean Functions, in *Proc. Symp. on Switching Theory*, ICIP, Paris, France, June, 1959.

13. QUINE, W. V. The Problem of Simplifying Truth Functions. *Am. Math. Monthly*, **59**, No. 8 (1952), 521–531.

14. —— *Mathematical Logic*. Cambridge, Mass.: Harvard Univ. Press, 1955.

15. REUSCH, B. Generation of Prime Implicants from Subfunctions and a Unifying Approach to the Covering Problem. *IEEE Trans. Computer*, **C-24**, (1975), 924–930.

16. ROTH, CHARLES H., JR. *Fundamentals of Logic Design*. St. Paul, Minn., West, 1975.

17. ROTH, J. P. Algebraic Topological Methods for the Synthesis of Switching Systems I. *Trans. Am. Math. Soc.*, **88** (1958), 301–326.

18. TANANA, E. J. The Map Method. *A Survey of Switching Circuit Theory*, E. J. McCluskey and T. G. Bartee (eds). New York: McGraw-Hill, 1962.

19. VEITCH, E. W. A Chart Method for Simplifying Truth Functions, in Proc. ACM, Pittsburgh, Penn., (May, 1952), pp. 127–133.

PROBLEMS AND EXERCISES

3-1. Reduce or minimize the following using theorems:
(a) $F(A,B,C) = A + \bar{B} + \bar{A}B + \bar{C}$

(b) $F(A,B) = A + \bar{B} + \bar{A}B + (A + \bar{B})\bar{A}B$
(c) $F(X,Y,Z,W) = X + XYZ + WX + \bar{X}Y + \bar{W}X + \bar{X}YZ$

3-2. Simplify with theorems:
(a) $F(A,B,C,D,E) = \bar{A} + ACD\bar{E} + \bar{D}E$
(b) $F(A,B,C) = (A + \bar{B})AB + \bar{C}$
(c) $F(A,B,C,D) = A\bar{B}C + ABCD + \bar{C}A$
(d) $F(X,Y,Z) = (\bar{X} + \bar{Y})(XY + Z)$

3-3. Simplify with theorems:
(a) $F(A,B,C,D,E) = AE + AB\bar{C}D + B\bar{C}E$
(b) $F(A,B,C,D,E) = \bar{A}B\bar{C} + \bar{A}D + BC\bar{D}$
(c) $F(A,B,C,D) = \bar{A}B\bar{C} + \bar{A}BD + CD$

3-4. Expand the following expressions into canonical SOP form, then use only the logical adjacency theorem to simplify:
(a) $F(A,B,C) = \bar{A}C + A\bar{B}C + ABC + A\bar{B}C$
(b) $F(A,B,C) = \bar{A}B + AB\bar{C} + ABC + AB$
(c) $F(A,B,C) = \bar{A}\bar{B}C + A\bar{B}C + \bar{A}B + \bar{B}C + A\bar{B}C$
(d) $F(A,B,C) = \bar{A}C + \bar{A}B + AC + BC$

3-5. Expand the following expressions into canonical SOP form, then use only the logical adjacency theorem to simplify:
(a) $F(A,B,C,D) = \bar{B}\bar{C}D + \bar{A}BC + A\bar{B}C + \bar{A}BD + ABD$
(b) $F(A,B,C,D) = BD + \bar{A}\bar{B}D + ACD + \bar{A}BD + AB\bar{C}D$
(c) $F(A,B,C,D) = \bar{A}BC + AB + A\bar{B}\bar{C}$
(d) $F(A,B,C,D) = \bar{A}\bar{B}CD + \bar{A}CD + AB\bar{C}D + A\bar{B}CD + AB\bar{C}D + A\bar{B}C$

3-6. Make and label an appropriate map, then plot the following in the K-map:
(a) $F(A,B) = AB + \bar{A}B$
(b) $F(A,B) = \Sigma 0,3$
(c) $F(A,B,C) = \bar{A}B\bar{C} + \bar{A}BC + \bar{A}BC + ABC$
(d) $F(A,B,C) = \Sigma 1,2,3,6$
(e) $F(A,B,C) = \Sigma 0,1,2,3$
(f) $F(A,B,C) = \Sigma 4,5,6,7$

3-7. Make a K-map for each of the following, then plot the indicated functions:
(a) $F(A,B,C,D) = \Sigma 0,5,6,13,14$
(b) $F(A,B,C,D) = \Sigma 0,5,7,13,14,15$
(c) $F(A,B,C,D) = \Sigma 2,5,6,7,8,12$
(d) $F(A,B,C,D) = \Sigma 1,4,6,8,11,13,15$

3-8. Simplify the following using K-maps:
(a) $F(A,B,C) = \Sigma 0,6,7$
(b) $F(A,B,C) = \Sigma 0,5,6,7$
(c) $F(A,B,C) = \Sigma 1,2,6,7$
(d) $F(A,B,C) = \Sigma 1,2,4,6,7$
(e) $F(A,B,C) = \Sigma 0,2,3,4,6,7$
(f) $F(A,B,C) = \Sigma 0,2,3,5,6,7$

3-9. Plot the maps for the following then reduce the expression:
(a) $F(A,B,C,D) = \Sigma 0,5,6,13,14$
(b) $F(A,B,C,D) = \Sigma 0,5,7,13,14,15$
(c) $F(A,B,C,D) = \Sigma 2,5,6,7,8,12$
(d) $F(A,B,C,D) = \Sigma 1,4,6,8,11,13,14$

(e) $F(A,B,C,D)=\Sigma 1,2,4,5,7,8,10,11,13,14$

(f) $F(A,B,C,D)=\Sigma 0,5,7,8,9,10,11,13$

3-10. Simplify the following using a K-map:

(a) $F(A,B,C,D)=\Sigma 0,2,3,5,7,8,12,13$

(b) $F(A,B,C,D)=\Sigma 1,3,4,5,6,11,13,14,15$

(c) $F(A,B,C,D)=\Sigma 1,2,4,5,6,7,12,15$

(d) $F(A,B,C,D)=\Sigma 0,4,5,8,9,10,13,14,15$

(e) $F(A,B,C,D)=\Sigma 0,2,3,4,5,11,13,14,15$

3-11. Simplify the following:

(a) $F(A,B,C,D,E)=\Sigma 0,4,8,12,16,20,24,28$

(b) $F(A,B,C,D,E)=\Sigma 0,2,5,10,13,15,16,20,21,26,27,31$

(c) $F(A,B,C,D,E)=\Sigma 0,2,5,8,13,15,18,21,24,29,31$

(d) $F(A,B,C,D,E)=\Sigma 8,9,10,11,13,15,16,18,21,24,25,26,27$

(e) $F(A,B,C,D,E)=\Sigma 0,4,5,6,7,11,12,13,14,15,21,23,27,28,29,30,31$

(f) $F(A,B,C,D,E)=\Sigma 1,2,3,4,5,7,8,10,12,15,16,18,19,21,22,23,24,26,27,31$

3-12. Simplify the following:

(a) $F(A,B,C,D,E,F)=\Sigma 6,9,13,18,19,25,27,29,41,45,57,61$

(b) $F(A,B,C,D,E,F)=\Sigma 4,5,6,7,8,9,14,21,23,29,31,37,38,39,45,47,49,51,52,53,55$

(c) $F(A,B,C,D,E,F)=\Sigma 0,1,5,6,9,15,16,18,21,25,29,30,35,37,39,40,45,48,49,50,55,58,$
    $60,61,63$

(d) $F(A,B,C,D,E,F)=\Sigma 4,5,6,7,8,18,20,23,25,26,27,28,37,38,42,44,49,51,58,59,60,63$

(e) $F(A,B,C,D,E,F)=\Sigma 0,1,2,3,9,10,11,14,15,20,23,24,26,27,29,30,31,33,36,41,42,47,$
    $48,49,52,58,59,62,63$

3-13. Find the set of ALL prime implicants, then identify the essential, necessary, optional, and redundant implicants in this set for the following:

(a) Problem 3-8

(b) Problem 3-10

(c) Problem 3-11

(d) Problem 3-12

3-14. "Don't care" problems. Simplify:

(a) $F(A,B,C,D)=\Sigma 1,3,5,8,9,11,15,\emptyset,(2,13)$

(b) $F(A,B,C,D)=\Sigma 4,5,7,12,14,15,\ \emptyset,(3,8,10)$

(c) $F(A,B,C,D)=\Sigma 0,4,5,6,7,\ \emptyset,\ (12,14)$

(d) $F(A,B,C,D)=\Sigma 3,7,8,12,13,15,\emptyset,(9,14)$

(e) $F(A,B,C,D)=\Sigma 4,5,6,12,13,\ \emptyset,(2,9,15)$

(f) $F(A,B,C,D,E,F)=\Sigma 5,7,13,15,19,27,28,29,30,31,32,37,39,45,47,51,53,55,61,63,$
    $\emptyset,(2,8,10,16,26,40,41,42,43,56,57,58,59)$

3-15. Reduce the following using the single statement reduction criteria:

(a) Problem 3-8

(b) Problem 3-9

(c) Problem 3-11

(d) Problem 3-12

3-16. Simplify the following using a K-map:

(a) $F(A,B,C,D,E)=CDE+\overline{A}B\overline{C}\overline{E}+\overline{A}BDE+\overline{A}BC\overline{E}$

(b) $F(A,B,C,D,E)=\overline{A}BC\overline{E}+BD\overline{E}+BCDE+ABDE$

(c) $F(A,B,C,D,E)=\overline{A}BC+BC\overline{D}+BE+\overline{C}\overline{E}$

(d) $F(A,B,C,D,E)=\overline{A}B\overline{C}+A\overline{D}E+CD\overline{E}+\overline{B}C$

(e) $F(A,B,C,D,E,F) = A\bar{B}CDE + \overline{ACD} + BD\bar{E} + AB\overline{CD} + \overline{ABEF}$

3-17. Using the expressions of Problem 3-4, plot maps and reduce.

3-18. Using the expressions of Problem 3-5, plot maps and reduce.

3-19. Find the simplified POS expressions for Problem 3-7 and compare with SOP form.

3-20. Find the simplified POS expressions for Problem 3-8 and compare with SOP form.

3-21. Find the simplified POS expressions for Problem 3-9 and compare with SOP form.

3-22. Find the simplified POS expressions for Problem 3-14 and compare with SOP form.

3-23. Find the minimal cover for the following multiple-output problems:

(a) $F_1(A,B,C,D) = \Sigma 11,12,13,14,15$
$F_2(A,B,C,D) = \Sigma 3,7,11,12,13,15$
$F_3(A,B,C,D) = \Sigma 3,7,12,13,15$

(b) $F_1(A,B,C,D) = \Sigma 2,3,5,7,8,9,10,11,13,15$
$F_2(A,B,C,D) = \Sigma 2,3,5,6,7,10,11,14,15$
$F_3(A,B,C,D) = \Sigma 6,7,8,9,13,14,15$

3-24. Simplify using two-variable VEM for each of the output functions:

A	B	C	F_1	F_2	F_3	F_4	F_5	F_6
0	0	0	0	1	Ø	0	1	1
0	0	1	1	0	Ø	1	0	1
0	1	0	1	1	0	1	1	0
0	1	1	1	1	1	0	0	Ø
1	0	0	1	0	1	1	1	0
1	0	1	1	0	0	1	0	1
1	1	0	0	0	1	1	Ø	Ø
1	1	1	0	1	1	1	1	Ø

3-25. Simplify F_1, F_2, and F_3 using a three variable VEM. Simplify F_4 using a two-variable VEM at your own risk.

	A	B	C	D	F_1	F_2	F_3	F_4
0	0	0	0	0	0	1	0	1
1	0	0	0	1	1	1	0	1
2	0	0	1	0	1	0	1	0
3	0	0	1	1	1	0	0	1
4	0	1	0	0	0	0	1	0
5	0	1	0	1	1	1	1	1
6	0	1	1	0	1	1	0	1
7	0	1	1	1	0	1	0	0
8	1	0	0	0	1	1	0	1
9	1	0	0	1	0	0	Ø	1
10	1	0	1	0	0	1	Ø	1
11	1	0	1	1	1	0	Ø	1
12	1	1	0	0	1	1	Ø	1
13	1	1	0	1	1	1	Ø	0
14	1	1	1	0	1	1	1	0
15	1	1	1	1	1	0	1	0

3-26. Using the MEV technique, simplify the exercises set forth in Problem 3-10 using three-variable maps.

3-27. Simplify F_1 and F_2 using a four-variable VEM.

A	B	C	D	E	F_1	F_2
0	0	0	0	0	0	1
0	0	0	0	1	1	1
0	0	0	1	0	1	0
0	0	0	1	1	0	1
0	0	1	0	0	1	0
0	0	1	0	1	1	1
0	0	1	1	0	1	1
0	0	1	1	1	1	0
0	1	0	0	0	0	1
0	1	0	0	1	0	1
0	1	0	1	0	0	0
0	1	0	1	1	0	1
0	1	1	0	0	1	1
0	1	1	0	1	1	1
0	1	1	1	0	0	0
0	1	1	1	1	1	0
1	0	0	0	0	0	0
1	0	0	0	1	0	0
1	0	0	1	0	1	0
1	0	0	1	1	0	1
1	0	1	0	0	1	1
1	0	1	0	1	1	0
1	0	1	1	0	1	1
1	0	1	1	1	ø	1
1	1	0	0	0	ø	0
1	1	0	0	1	ø	1
1	1	0	1	0	ø	1
1	1	0	1	1	ø	0
1	1	1	0	0	ø	1
1	1	1	0	1	ø	1
1	1	1	1	0	ø	0
1	1	1	1	1	ø	1

3-28. Using the MEV technique, simplify the exercise set forth in Problem 3-11 using four-variable maps.

3-29. Using the MEV technique, simplify the expression set forth in Problem 3-16 using four-variable maps.

3-30. Write the simplified expressions for the maps in Figure P3-1.

3-31. Write the simplified expressions for the maps in Figure P3-2.

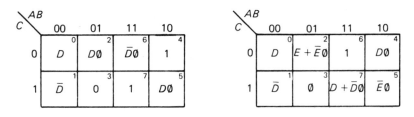

Figure P3-1

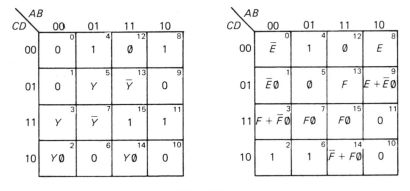

Figure P3-2

3-32. Using MEV techniques, simplify the following expressions:

(a) $F(A,B,C,D,W,X,Y,Z) = \overline{A}\overline{B}C\overline{D} + \overline{A}\overline{B}C\overline{D}(X) + \overline{A}BC\overline{D}(Z+W) + \overline{A}BC\overline{D}(XY)$
$+ \overline{A}BCD(\overline{X}) + AB\overline{C}\overline{D}[(X+Y)Z] + ABCD(Z \oplus Y)$
$+ ABC\overline{D}(W) + A\overline{B}\overline{C}\overline{D} + A\overline{B}C\overline{D}$

(b) $F(A,B,C,D,W,X,Y,Z) = \overline{X}\overline{Y}\overline{Z}WA + \overline{X}\overline{Y}ZW + \overline{X}Y\overline{W}A\overline{B} + X\overline{Y}\overline{Z}W$
$+ X\overline{Y}\overline{Z}W[(A+B)C] + \overline{X}YZW + \overline{X}YZ\overline{W}(C+D) + X\overline{Y}Z\overline{W}(D \odot B)$

(c) $F(A,B,C,D,Q,R,S,T) = \overline{A}B\overline{C}\overline{D}(\overline{R}+S) + AB\overline{C}\overline{D} + \overline{A}\overline{B}CD + AB\overline{C}DQR$
$+ A\overline{B}\overline{C}D + \overline{A}\overline{B}CD(\overline{Q}+T) + ABCD\overline{S}T + A\overline{B}CD + \overline{A}BCD$

(d) $F(A,B,C,D,E,F,G,H,K) = \overline{A}B\overline{C}\overline{D}E + A\overline{B}\overline{C}\overline{D}E(F \oplus K) + A\overline{B}C\overline{D}E + \overline{A}\overline{B}C\overline{D}E$
$+ \overline{A}\overline{B}C\overline{D}EFGH + \overline{A}\overline{B}C\overline{D}EK + \overline{A}BCDEF\overline{G} + ABC\overline{D}E[G(F+K)] + ABC\overline{D}EHF$
$+ ABC\overline{D}EHK + ABCDE + \overline{A}B\overline{C}DEF + \overline{A}BCDE\overline{G} + A\overline{B}\overline{C}DE$

3-33. Given the following four-variable map (Figure P3-3):

(a) Compress this map into a three-variable VEM and reduce it.

(b) Compress the three-variable map done into a two-variable VEM, then reduce this function. Check your results.

Note: Problems 3-34 through 3-38 are special implementation problems given for you to practice drawing neat and well-documented schematic diagrams using mixed logic and polarized mnemonic notation. These are considered an important prerequisite to the rest of the problem set.

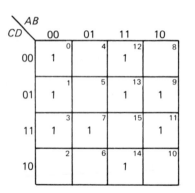
Figure P3-3

3-34. Given the following expression:

$$F(A,B,C,D) = A\bar{B}C + \bar{A}BC + D$$

(a) Verify minimal solution.

(b) Find eight different two-level implementations of this expression.

3-35. You are given the following logic expressions:

$$F_1(L) = (D + A\bar{B}F + \bar{C}E)L$$

BDF   ASSERTED LOW

ACE   ASSERTED HIGH

Show a neat drawing of your implementation based on the fact that you have only the following devices:

2	two-input OR gates
1	three-input AND gate
1	three-input OR gate
three	inverters available

Minimize your use of inverters.

3-36. Implement the following expression without changing the form, that is, using DeMorgan's theorem. Use mixed logic, assuming all inputs are ASSERTED HIGH:

$$F(L) = \left[\overline{BC} + A + \left(\overline{GH + H(\bar{E} + \bar{F})} \right) \right](L)$$

Based on OR and AND gates having only two inputs and NAND and NOR gates having two, three, four, and eight inputs, implement the expression, minimizing your use of inverters.

3-37. Using a mixed logic approach, implement the following expression *directly* and *minimize the use of INVERTERS.* Fully document your implementation:

$$F = \left[\bar{A}B\bar{C}(\alpha + \beta) + \bar{A}\bar{B}C(\bar{\alpha}\bar{\beta}) + AC D(X + \bar{Y}) + \bar{B}C \right]$$

Special note: You work for a company that *uses only four-input gates:* (AND, OR, NAND, NOR). Given:

A, B, C, and D are double rail inputs
$(\alpha + \beta)$ is an input function ASSERTED LOW
X is ASSERTED LOW
Y is ASSERTED HIGH

3-38. Implement the following control equations minimizing the use of inverters. Show implementations in full polarized mnemonic notation. You can use:

(a) two- and three-input AND gates
(b) two-input OR gates
(c) two-, three-, four-, and eight-input NAND gates
(d) two- and three-input NOR gates

Inputs: A, B, C, D, 10¢, and 5¢ are double rail input
Inputs: NICKEL, DIME, QURTR, CR, COIN are single rail ASSERTED HIGH

(a) $F = A\bar{B}D + BCD + \bar{B}C(\text{DIME}) + \bar{A}BD(10¢ + 5¢)$
(b) $F = \bar{A}BCD + \bar{A}\bar{B}\bar{C}D(\text{NICKEL}) + \bar{A}BD(5¢ + \overline{10¢}) + A\bar{B}\bar{D}(\overline{10¢} + \overline{5¢})$
$\qquad + \bar{B}\bar{A}CD(CR) + ABC(\overline{CR})$
(c) $F = \bar{A}B\bar{D} + \underline{CD} + \bar{B}CD(\text{COIN}) + \bar{A}D\,(\overline{10¢} + \overline{5¢}) + \bar{B}\bar{C}D(5¢)$
(d) $F = BCD + \bar{B}\bar{C}D(\text{DIME}) + BD(5¢ + \underline{10¢}) + A\bar{C}$
(e) $F = AB + A(5¢ + 10¢) + B(10¢ + \overline{5¢}) + \bar{A}\bar{B}\bar{D}(\text{QURTR})$

Note: The following problems are a selection of combinational design exercises. It is intended that the full design process be carried out including fully documented schematics done in mixed logic format.

3-39. Design a combinational circuit with four inputs (A,B,C,D) and one output (f). The output will be ASSERTED when the following conditions prevail: (1) all inputs are ASSERTED; (2) none of the inputs are ASSERTED; (3) an odd number of inputs are ASSERTED.

(a) Obtain the TRUTH-TABLE.
(b) Find the output function in SOP.
(c) Find the output function in POS.
(d) Draw logic diagrams for both functions ASSERTED HIGH and LOW. Use mixed logic format. Minimize your use of INVERTERS. Assume inputs A and B are ASSERTED HIGH and C and D are ASSERTED LOW.

3-40. Use the variables W, X, and Y to represent a three-digit number with Z representing the sign of the number. If Z is ASSERTED, the number is positive; if Z is NOT-ASSERTED, the number is negative. Design a circuit such that the following specifications are met.

When the number is negative, the output equals that number minus two.

When the number is positive, the output equals that number plus two.

(a) Obtain the TRUTH-TABLE; plot maps for SOP and POS realization.
(b) Draw the logic diagram using mixed logic with output ASSERTED HIGH and LOW. Minimize your use of INVERTERS. Assume all inputs are ASSERTED LOW.

3-41. With a three-digit binary number, design a circuit that generates an output code equal to the square of that number.

(a) Define the TRUTH-TABLE.
(b) Show all maps for SOP and POS.
(c) Draw the logic diagram with output ASSERTED HIGH, minimizing use of INVERTERS. Assume all inputs are ASSERTED HIGH.

3-42. Design a combinational system with inputs A(H), B(L), and C(H) and two outputs $X = 1$(H) and $y = 1$(L), where x and y are to be interpreted as the binary number $(xy)_2$. This number $(xy)_2$ is to represent the decimal value of the number of ASSERTED inputs present at any time.

(a) You are to carry out a complete design process culminating in a well-documented schematic diagram for the minimal cover SOP solution.

(b) Repeat (a) for POS solution.

3-43. There are four adjacent parking slots in the XYZ Inc. executive parking area. Each slot is equipped with a special sensor whose output is ASSERTED LOW when a car is occupying the slot. Otherwise the sensor's output is at a high voltage. You are to design and draw schematics for a decoding system that will generate a low output voltage if and only if there are two (or more) adjacent vacant slots. Do a complete well-documented minimal cover design.

3-44. You are to design a special combinational system controlled by three switches (A, B, and C). This system is to function as follows: The output is to be NOT-ASSERTED when all three switches are in their NOT-ASSERTED position. Then the output (H) is to change levels any time a switch is changed in position. Assume only a single switch can be changed at a time.

(a) Define a TRUTH-TABLE for this problem.

(b) Reduce the problem using a map.

(c) Draw schematics using the full documentation procedure and a two-level implementation using AND, OR, NAND, NOR, and INVERTERS.

(d) Re-examine your solution for the possibility of using EXOR gates.

3-45. Design a combinational system that produces the product of two binary numbers $A = (a_1 a_2)_2 \times B = (b_1 b_2 b_3)_2$. The range of values that A has is from 0 to 3; B has the range from 0 to 5. Therefore, max product $A \times B = 15$. This is a five (5) input four output problem. You are to carry out a fully documented design process through schematic diagrams. a_1 and a_2 are ASSERTED LOW while b_1, b_2, and b_3 are ASSERTED HIGH. Outputs with a numerical value of 1 are to be ASSERTED HIGH.

3-46. Using the seven segment LED display shown below in Figure P3-4, design a decoder that will convert a binary code into the control logic for the display so that the display shows the decimal equivalent of the binary number. Beware of "don't care" conditions. Carry out the complete design process including schematics drawings in

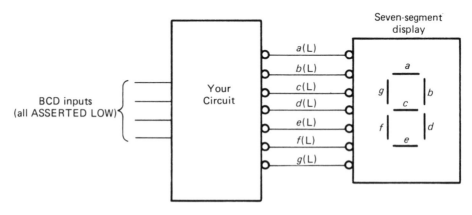

Figure P3-4

mixed logic and polarized mnemonic notation. (Try for a multi-function minimal cover.)

3-47. For the LED seven segment display treated in Problem 3-46, re-design the display decoder such that any time a code outside the range of 0000 to 1001 is present the letter E is displayed indicating Error. Assume BCD inputs are ASSERTED LOW. Carry out the complete process including schematics drawings in mixed logic and polarized mnemonic notation.

3-48. For the LED seven segment display shown in Problem 3-46, design a decoder that will perform according to the following specifications. Assume BCD inputs are ASSERTED LOW. Carry out the complete design process including schematic drawings in mixed logic and polarized mnemonic notation.

A	B	C	D	Seven Segment Output
0	0	0	0	0
0	0	0	1	1
0	0	1	0	2
0	0	1	1	3
0	1	0	0	4
0	1	0	1	5
0	1	1	0	6
0	1	1	1	7
1	0	0	0	8
1	0	0	1	9
1	0	1	0	A
1	0	1	1	B = lower case b
1	1	0	0	C
1	1	0	1	D = lower case d
1	1	1	0	E
1	1	1	1	F

3-49. Design a minimal cover two-level combinational system that converts the XS-3 code to NBCD. Note that this is a multi-function minimization problem involving $\emptyset$ entries. (All inputs and outputs ASSERTED HIGH.) Carry out the complete design process including schematic drawings in mixed logic and polarized mnemonic notation.

3-50. Design a minimal cover two-level combinational system that has five inputs, $SABCD$, which are ASSERTED as follows:

$$S = +(H) \quad \text{sign bit}$$
$$A = 1(L) \quad (MSB)$$
$$B = 1(L)$$
$$C = 1(L)$$
$$D = 1(L) \quad (LSB)$$

Your system is to decode these inputs as a signed binary number and in turn convert it to its 2's complement. Outputs are to be ASSERTED LOW. Carry out the complete design process including schematic drawings in mixed logic and polarized mnemonic notation.

3-51. A logic network is to be designed to implement the seat belt alarm that is required on all new cars. A set of sensor switches is available to supply the inputs to the network. One switch will be turned on if the gear shift is engaged (not in neutral). A switch is placed under each front seat and each will turn on if someone sits in the corresponding seat. Finally, a switch is attached to each front seat which will turn on if and only if that seat belt is fastened. An alarm buzzer is to sound (LED display light) when the ignition is turned on and the gear shift is engaged, provided that either of the front seats is occupied and the corresponding seat belt is not fastened.

Alarm (sound)—A(H)
Ignition (on)—I(L)
Gearshift (engaged)—G(H)
Left front seat (occupied)—L(H)

Right front seat (occupied)—R(H)
Left seat belt (fastened)—BL(H)
Right seat belt (fastened)—BR(H)

Carry out a complete and well-documented design including schematic drawings done in mixed logic and polarized mnemonic notation.

3-52. First National Bank needs to be equipped with the latest burgular alarm system. It consists of various switches and sensors located in the Bank and tied into the Logan City Police Station. The main switch is located at the police station, and it is turned on at night after banking hours. When this switch is activated, anyone wanting to enter the bank has to turn on a secret switch located near the front door before entering or the alarm will sound. Also, so the bank president can get a little cash after hours when the police station switch is on, he can turn on the second floor switch located by the president's desk which de-activates the system and allows him to get into the vault. Each teller has a switch by her foot that she can press if the bank is being robbed. The teller switch will turn on the alarm unless the switch by the president's desk is turned on, which will de-activate the teller's switch. This is in case the president wants to rob the bank himself. Also, during the day when the police station switch is off, the bank vault can be opened without an alarm sounding if the switch by the president's desk is on.

Let: Police station switch—P(L)
President's desk switch—D(H)
Bank vault door sensor—V(L)
Bank front door sensor—F(L)
Secret switch at front door—S(H)
Teller window switch—T(L)

Carry out a complete and well-documented design including schematic drawings done in mixed logic and polarized mnemonic notation.

3-53. Given the following map (Figure P3-5):

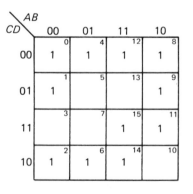

Figure P3-5

(a) Find $P(A)$, $P(B)$, $P(C)$, and $P(D)$ by using the folding algorithm.

(b) Make a composite array and summarize the data available.

(c) Find $P(A,B)$, $P(A,C)$, and $P(A,D)$ by taking the $P(A)$ array and folding it on the B, C, and D boundaries.

(d) Similar to part (c) above, find $P(B,C)$, $P(B,D)$, and $P(C,D)$ and make a new composite array $P(A,B)$, $P(A,C)$, $P(A,D)$, $P(B,C)$, $P(B,D)$, and $P(C,D)$. Summarize the data extracted from the second-order folding process.

(e) Are essential quads identified by this second-order folding?

MSI AND LSI CIRCUITS AND THEIR APPLICATIONS

4-1 INTRODUCTION

The previous chapters covered the basics of combinational circuit design, demonstrating the steps taken to gate-level implementations. This chapter presents some of the more complex integrated circuits and their application to combinational system design.

The integrated circuit revolution has left in its wake an almost innumerable variety of developed and proven devices that are more than single function circuits. These devices, depending on the circuit complexity and internal gate count, have been dubbed as Medium Scale Integrated (MSI) and Large Scale Integrated (LSI) circuits, when compared to the single gate function circuits called Small Scale Integrated (SSI) circuits. The equivalent gate count complexity for SSI is 12 gates and under, for MSI is under 100 gates, and for LSI is greater than 100 gates. At the present rate of chip-size expansion, you should prepare for Extra Large Scale Integration (XLSI) acronyms.

The wake as mentioned has left a most attractive array of devices such as multiplexers, decoders, priority encoders, parity generators, checkers, adders, multipliers, comparators, code converters, read only memories, programmable read only memories, and logic arrays, to mention a few combinational-type circuits. There is also an equivalent number of sequential or storage circuits, such as registers of all varieties, counters, and random access memories. Table 4-1 lists some of the more popular MSI and LSI circuits presently available.

TABLE 4-1 MSI and LSI device listing

Adders	Shift registers
Multipliers	Register files
Comparators	Multi-mode registers
Parity generators/checkers	Pulse synchronizers
Other arithmetic operators	Latches
Read only memories (ROM's, PROM's)	Read/write memories (RAM's)
Code converters	Asynchronous counters (Ripple
Data selectors/multiplexers	Clock)—Negative-edge
Decoders/demultiplexers	Triggered
Open-collector display decoders/	Synchronous counters—Positive-
Drivers	Edge triggered
Open-collector display decoders/	Multi-mode counters
Drivers with counters/latches	
Priority encoders	

As a logic designer, you are faced with a veritable supermarket of relatively low cost devices. You must only decide how to configure a design in order to satisfy your design goals using these devices and at the same time utilize space and dollars efficiently. The general usage philosophy in regard to using MSI and LSI circuits is: *"The internal circuitry exists and is wired in a proven reliable form; therefore, use it wherever possible."* This author chooses to moderate this philosophy somewhat. It is true that the circuitry exists and that there are purposes for which it can be utilized other than its most obvious application, which the name and data book describe. It is felt, however, that a designer should *not* use these devices to the end that general design techniques *cannot* be adapted or general system configurations (models) developed. By not considering the alternatives, you run the risk of producing one of those "IT PERFORMS THE FUNCTION" type designs. The same goes for using the microprocessor in this day when marketing people are screaming, "I don't care what it is or what it does, just as long as it has a microprocessor in it." As a good design engineer you should strive to generalize a design and its documentation and use the appropriate devices for the design, in order to make it cost effective over its lifetime. Imagine what happens if a not-so-good engineer leaves his present job, leaving behind a trail strewn with ill-documented nonstandard designs.

Remember, on one hand it is ingenious to dream up different uses for any given device, and yet again, it is even more ingenious to adapt this device to fit a general system configuration.

Therefore, keep in mind that using MSI and LSI devices can significantly reduce a systems packaging cost by reducing the IC package count and also improve the reliability by reducing the number of external wired connections. However, there are no sweeping statements saying this will always be true. This is where real-life engineering judgment is to be used. In general, it has been said and will be said again: "Know your devices, know their limitations, and use good judgment when you bring them together." To this end we introduce some general design ideas in this chapter that can be widely adapted. In the next section we introduce the major categories of useful combinational MSI and LSI devices.

4-2 EXAMPLES OF USEFUL DIGITAL CIRCUITS

There are several categories of combinational circuits that over the years have become general building blocks in digital systems. The purpose of this section is to help you become familiar with these circuits and at the same time gain more practice in combinational design and analysis. The four major divisions of the circuits to be studied are:

(1) arithmetic circuits
(2) comparators and parity generators
(3) multiplexers and demultiplexers
(4) decoders and encoders

4-3 ARITHMETIC CIRCUITS

Digital computers are designed to perform a variety of arithmetic instructions on binary numerical data. In fact, computers have a major subdivision called the Arithmetic-Logic-Unit (ALU) that is used to perform a variety of data processing operations. A typical instruction is to ADD two eight-bit binary numbers in parallel as shown in Figure 4-1.

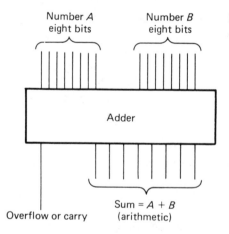

Number A eight bits   Number B eight bits

Adder

Overflow or carry   Sum = A + B (arithmetic)

Fig. 4-1. A block diagram of an eight-bit binary ADDER.

Arithmetic circuits are the result of an interesting redefinition of 1 and 0. Until now 1 and 0 have been defined to be shorthand symbols for ASSERTED and NOT-ASSERTED, but in arithmetic circuits they take on an actual numerical value. However, even though the numeric value is implied, the use of TRUTH-TABLES still holds, as will be demonstrated shortly.

As mentioned above, a TRUTH-TABLE can be used to develop the solution for the eight-bit adder circuit shown in Figure 4-1. This implies that the TRUTH-TABLE becomes a LOOK-UP TABLE for each of the $2^{16} = 65536$ entries! That's right, to design a composite eight-bit adder it would take a TRUTH-TABLE with 65536 rows. This is one of those times to consider some other approach to design, such as the modular or iterative technique. Modular design is based on the idea of building one simple module that can be used in an array and that will give results comparable to a composite design. Thus, let's examine the design of a circuit called the HALF-ADDER which is designed to add two bits by receiving inputs BIT A and BIT B and generating two outputs SUM and CARRY. For example:

$$\begin{array}{r} 1 \\ +\,1 \\ \hline 10 \end{array}$$

$$\text{CARRY} \longrightarrow 10 \longleftarrow \text{SUM}$$

The TRUTH-TABLE for the HALF-ADDER is shown in Figure 4-2. From the TRUTH-TABLE for the HALF-ADDER we see:

$$\text{SUM(H)} = (\overline{A}\cdot B + A\cdot \overline{B})(\text{H}) = (A \oplus B)(\text{H})$$

and

$$\text{CARRY(H)} = (A\cdot B)(\text{H})$$

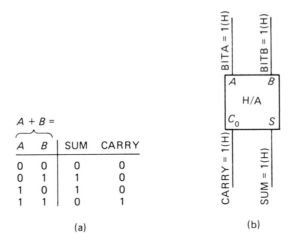

Fig. 4-2. (a) The TRUTH-TABLE for a binary HALF-ADDER (b) The block diagram of a HALF-ADDER.

The logic circuit for a system which interprets input voltages as equivalences to numeric values and in turn generates output voltages representative of numeric values is shown in Figure 4-3.

A little study of the modular application of a HALF-ADDER shows that it has little function in an array because it has no input that will allow it to ADD the carry bit from the bit column to the right. Therefore, what is needed is a FULL-ADDER, a circuit with three inputs: BIT A, BIT B, and CARRYIN and two outputs SUM and CARRYOUT. See Figure 4-4 for the TRUTH-TABLE and block diagram of a FULL-ADDER. The design of the FULL-ADDER is developed in Figure 4-5.

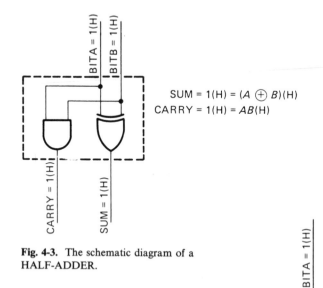

$$SUM = 1(H) = (A \oplus B)(H)$$
$$CARRY = 1(H) = AB(H)$$

Fig. 4-3. The schematic diagram of a HALF-ADDER.

$$A + B + C_i =$$

A	B	C_i	S	C_0
0	0	0	0	0
0	0	1	1	0
0	1	0	1	0
0	1	1	0	1
1	0	0	1	0
1	0	1	0	1
1	1	0	0	1
1	1	1	1	1

(a)

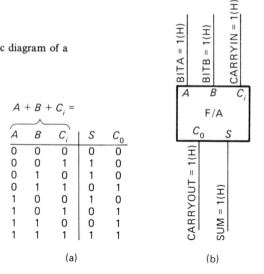

(b)

Fig. 4-4. (a) The TRUTH-TABLE for the FULL-ADDER. (b) The block diagram of a FULL-ADDER.

The utility of a FULL-ADDER as a modular block is shown in Figure 4-6. Note further that the carry must ripple through each FULL-ADDER to the succeeding unit. This ripple-through-carry can be a problem when high speed operation with a large number of bits is required. However, there are special circuits called CARRY-LOOK-AHEAD ADDER units that reduce the time required for a stable n-bit SUM to settle in. See Problem 4-1.

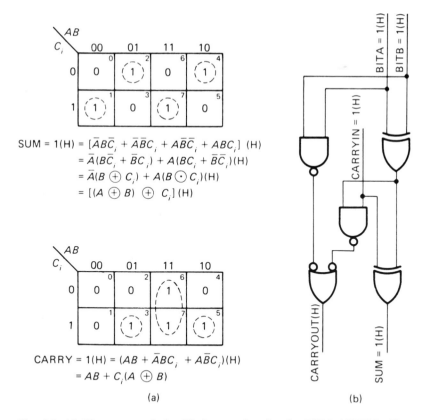

$$SUM = 1(H) = [\bar{A}B\bar{C}_i + \bar{A}\bar{B}C_i + A\bar{B}\bar{C}_i + ABC_i] \; (H)$$
$$= \bar{A}(B\bar{C}_i + \bar{B}C_i) + A(BC_i + \bar{B}\bar{C}_i)(H)$$
$$= \bar{A}(B \oplus C_i) + A(B \odot C_i)(H)$$
$$= [(A \oplus B) \oplus C_i] \, (H)$$

$$CARRY = 1(H) = (AB + \bar{A}BC_i + A\bar{B}C_i)(H)$$
$$= AB + C_i(A \oplus B)$$

(a)

(b)

Fig. 4-5 (a) The maps and simplified expression for the FULL-ADDER. (b) Circuit diagram for a FULL-ADDER.

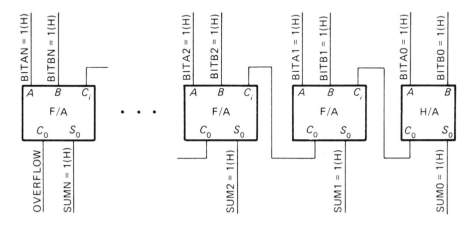

Fig. 4-6. An n-bit ADDER implemented with one HALF-ADDER and $n-1$ FULL ADDERS.

Fig. 4-7. The specification sheet of a four-bit FULL-ADDER. (Courtesy of Texas Instruments, Inc.)

- **Full-Carry Look-Ahead across the Four Bits**
- **Systems Achieve Partial Look-Ahead Performance with the Economy of Ripple Carry**
- **Supply Voltage and Ground on Corner Pins to Simplify P-C Board Layout**

TYPE	TYPICAL ADD TIMES		TYPICAL POWER DISSIPATION PER 4-BIT ADDER
	TWO 8-BIT WORDS	TWO 16-BIT WORDS	
'283	23 ns	43 ns	310 mW
'LS283	25 ns	45 ns	95 mW

description

The '283 and 'L283 adders are electrically and functionally identical to the '83A and 'LS83A respectively; only the arrangement of the terminals has been changed.

These improved full adders perform the addition of two 4-bit binary numbers. The sum (Σ) outputs are provided for each bit and the resultant carry (C4) is obtained from the fourth bit. These adders feature full internal look ahead across all four bits generating the carry term in ten nanoseconds typically. This provides the system designer with partial look-ahead performance at the economy and reduced package count of a ripple-carry implementation.

The adder logic, including the carry, is implemented in its true form meaning that the end-around carry can be accomplished without the need for logic or level inversion.

Designed for medium-speed applications, the circuits utilize transistor-transistor logic that is compatible with most other TTL families and other saturated low-level logic families.

function table and schematics of inputs and outputs

Same as SN5483A/SN7483A and SN54LS83A/SN74LS83A, see pages S-115 and S-116.

SN54283, SN54LS283 . . . J OR W PACKAGE
SN74283, SN74LS283 . . . J OR N PACKAGE
(TOP VIEW)

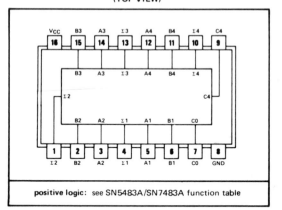

positive logic: see SN5483A/SN7483A function table

functional block diagram

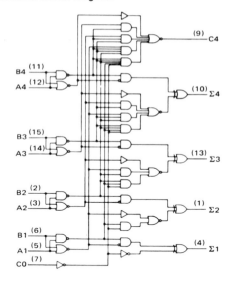

absolute maximum ratings over operating free-air temperature range (unless otherwise noted)

Supply voltage, V_{CC} (see Note 1) . . . . 7 V
Input voltage: '283 . . . . 5.5 V
               'LS283 . . . . 7 V
Interemitter voltage (see Note 2) . . . . 5.5 V
Operating free-air temperature range: SN54283, SN54LS283 . . . . $-55°$C to $125°$C
                                SN74283, SN74LS283 . . . . $0°$C to $70°$C
Storage temperature range . . . . $-65°$C to $150°$C

NOTES: 1. Voltage values, except interemitter voltage, are with respect to network ground terminal.
       2. This is the voltage between two emitters of a multiple-emitter transistor. This rating applies for the '283 only between the following pairs: A1 and B1, A2 and B2, A3 and B3, A4 and B4.

Modular ADDER devices are available in integrated circuit form, which can be cascaded as shown in Figure 4-6. See Figure 4-7 for the specifications of the SN74283 four-bit BINARY FULL-ADDER. There are several exercises in the problem set that illustrate the general usage of a four-bit ADDER.

As just mentioned, most ADDER circuits like the one in Figure 4-6 are relatively slow because the final sum is not stable until the carry ripples through each module. The device shown in Figure 4-7 is a FULL-ADDER with full look-ahead CARRY across the four bits. However, each additional four-bit module added to the cascade slows the ADDER system by one delay unit.

4-3.1 SUBTRACTORS

Though not commonly used, the hardware SUBTRACTOR is an interesting circuit. The subtraction of two binary numbers is normally accomplished by adding the 2's or 1's complement of the subtrahend to the minuend, as outlined in Chapter 1. Since the process of subtraction is one of addition, the subtraction hardware is not normally incorporated in computers. However, should the need arise, the same design processes used for the ADDER circuits can be implemented. The design of a HALF-SUBTRACTOR is illustrated in Figure 4-8.

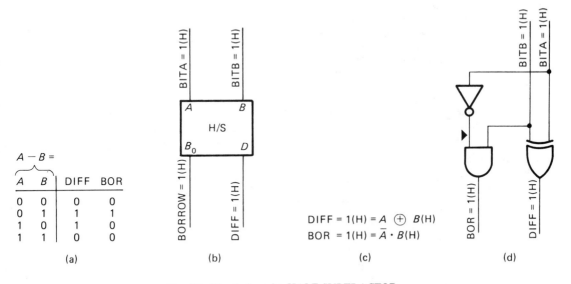

$A - B =$

A	B	DIFF	BOR
0	0	0	0
0	1	1	1
1	0	1	0
1	1	0	0

(a)

(b)

$$DIFF = 1(H) = A \oplus B(H)$$
$$BOR = 1(H) = \bar{A} \cdot B(H)$$

(c)

(d)

Fig. 4-8. The design of a HALF-SUBTRACTOR.

There are other hardware — arithmetic circuits, like binary MULTIPLIERS —also available in IC form (see Figure 4-9).

- 'S274 Provides 8-Bit Product in Typically 45 ns
- 'S274 Can Provide Sub-Multiple Products for n-Bit-by-n-Bit Binary Numbers
- 'S275 Accepts 7 Bit-Slice Inputs and 2 Carry Inputs for Reduction to 4 Lines in Typically 45 ns
- These New High-Complexity Functions Can Reduce Package Count by Nearly 50% in Most Parallel Multiplier Designs
- When Combined With SN74H183 and Schottky Look-Ahead Adders, Multiplication Times Are Typically:
  16-Bit Product in 75 ns
  32-Bit Product in 116 ns

description

These high-complexity Schottky-clamped TTL circuits are designed specifically to reduce the delay time required to perform high-speed parallel binary multiplication and significantly reduce package count. The 'S274 is a basic 4-bit-by-4-bit parallel multiplier in a single package, and as such, no additional components are required to obtain an 8-bit product. The 'S275 expandable bit-slice Wallace tree has been designed to accept up to seven bit-slice inputs and two carry inputs from previous slices for reduction to four lines. For word lengths longer than 4 bits, a number of 'S274 multipliers can be combined to generate sub-multiple partial products. These partial products can then be combined in Wallace trees to obtain the final product. See Typical Application Data.

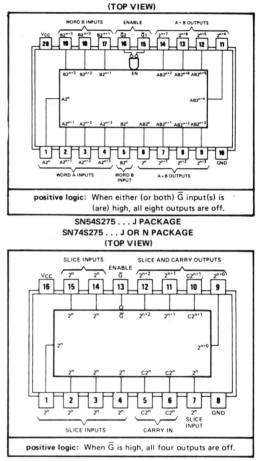

positive logic: When either (or both) $\overline{G}$ input(s) is (are) high, all eight outputs are off.

positive logic: When $\overline{G}$ is high, all four outputs are off.

functional block diagram

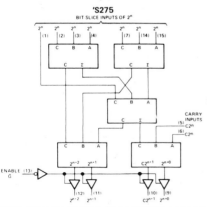

schematics of inputs and outputs

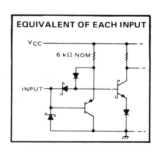

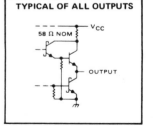

NOTE: When one of the C_2^n carry inputs is not used, it must be grounded. If neither C_2^n carry input is used, both C_2^n inputs are grounded and the C_2^{n+1} output is normally left open.

4-4 COMPARATORS

A comparator is a special combinational circuit designed primarily to compare the relative magnitude of two binary numbers. See Figure 4-10 for the description of a two-bit comparator design.

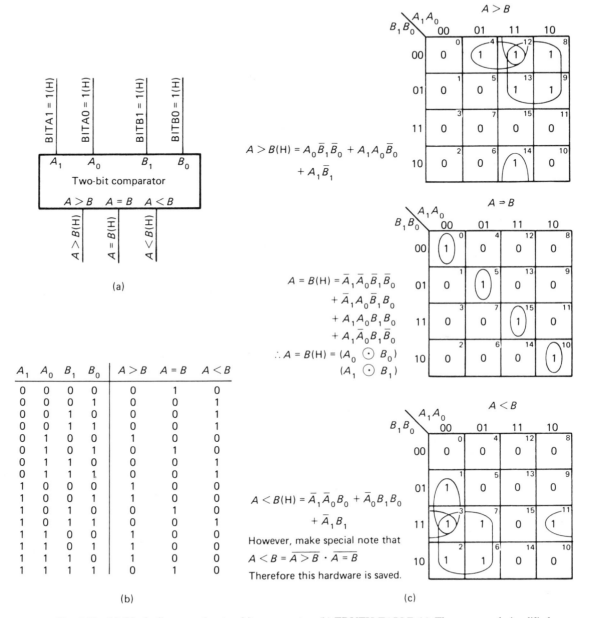

Fig. 4-10. (a) Block diagram of a two-bit comparator. (b) TRUTH-TABLE (c) The maps and simplified expressions for the comparator. The design of a two-bit comparator.

Fig. 4-10. (Cont.)

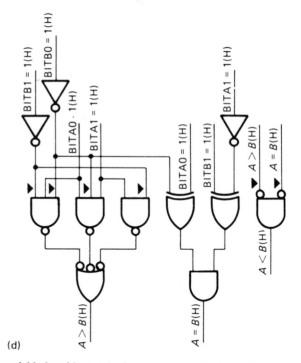

(d)

Fig. 4-11. Below the data sheet for an expandable four-bit magnitude comparator. (Courtesy of Texas Instruments, Inc.)

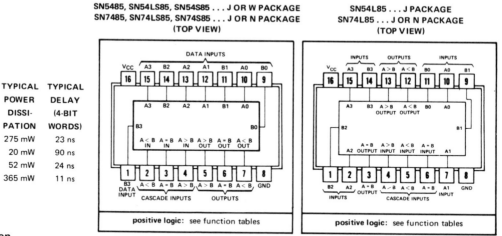

TYPE	TYPICAL POWER DISSI- PATION	TYPICAL DELAY (4-BIT WORDS)
'85	275 mW	23 ns
'L85	20 mW	90 ns
'LS85	52 mW	24 ns
'S85	365 mW	11 ns

description

These four-bit magnitude comparators perform comparison of straight binary and straight BCD (8-4-2-1) codes. Three fully decoded decisions about two 4-bit words (A, B) are made and are externally available at three outputs. These devices are fully expandable to any number of bits without external gates. Words of greater length may be compared by connecting comparators in cascade. The A > B, A < B, and A = B outputs of a stage handling less-significant bits are connected to the corresponding A > B, A < B, and A = B inputs of the next stage handling more-significant bits. The stage handling the least-significant bits must have a high-level voltage applied to the A = B input and in addition for the 'L85, low-level voltages applied to the A > B and A < B inputs. The cascading paths of the '85, 'LS85, and 'S85 are implemented with only a two-gate-level delay to reduce overall comparison times for long words. An alternate method of cascading which further reduces the comparison time is shown in the typical application data.

Fig. 4-11. (Cont.)

FUNCTION TABLES

COMPARING INPUTS				CASCADING INPUTS			OUTPUTS		
A3, B3	A2, B2	A1, B1	A0, B0	A > B	A < B	A = B	A > B	A < B	A = B
A3 > B3	X	X	X	X	X	X	H	L	L
A3 < B3	X	X	X	X	X	X	L	H	L
A3 = B3	A2 > B2	X	X	X	X	X	H	L	L
A3 = B3	A2 < B2	X	X	X	X	X	L	H	L
A3 = B2	A2 = B2	A1 > B1	X	X	X	X	H	L	L
A3 = B3	A2 = B2	A1 < B1	X	X	X	X	L	H	l
A3 = B3	A2 = B2	A1 = B1	A0 > B0	X	X	X	H	L	L
A3 = B3	A2 = B2	A1 = B1	A0 < B0	X	X	X	L	H	L
A3 = B3	A2 = B2	A1 = B1	A0 = B0	H	L	L	H	L	L
A3 = B3	A2 = B2	A1 = B1	A0 = B0	L	H	L	L	H	L
A3 = B3	A2 = B2	A1 = B1	A0 = B0	L	L	H	L	L	H

'85, 'LS85, 'S85

A3 = B3	A2 = B2	A1 = B1	A0 = B0	X	X	H	L	L	H
A3 = B3	A2 = B2	A1 = B1	A0 = B0	H	H	L	L	L	L
A3 = B3	A2 = B2	A1 = B1	A0 = B0	L	L	L	H	H	L

'L85

A3 = B3	A2 = B2	A1 = B1	A0 = B0	L	H	H	L	H	H
A3 = B3	A2 = B2	A1 = B1	A0 = B0	H	L	H	H	L	H
A3 = B3	A2 = B2	A1 = B1	A0 = B0	H	H	H	H	H	H
A3 = B3	A2 = B2	A1 = B1	A0 = B0	H	H	L	H	H	L
A3 = B3	A2 = B2	A1 = B1	A0 = B0	L	L	L	L	L	L

H = high level, L = low level, X = irrelevant

'85, 'S85

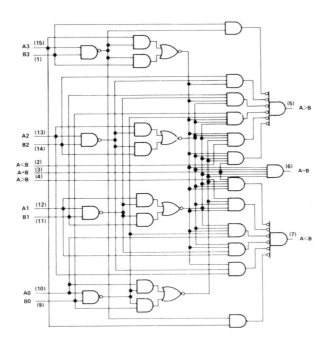

Fig. 4-11. (Cont.)

'L85

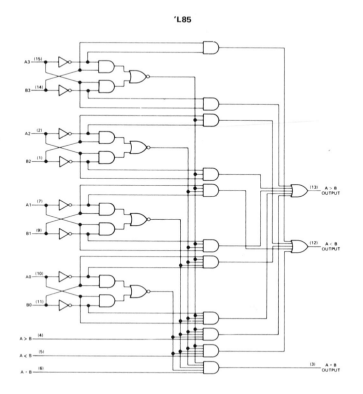

The useable comparators are designed to be cascadable modules much like the FULL-ADDER which can be expanded into an *n*-bit unit. The design of a two-bit cascadable comparator module will be left as a problem exercise. Comparators are also available in IC form (see Figure 4-11).

4-5 MULTIPLEXERS

The *multiplexer (MUX)* sometimes referred to as *DATA SELECTOR* is a special combination circuit that is one of the most widely used standard circuits in digital design. By definition *the multiplexer is a combinational circuit designed to gate one out of several inputs to a single output.* The input selected for connection to the output is controlled by a set of "SELECT INPUTS." See Figure 4-12 for an illustration of the schematic symbol and switch model of a 4 to 1 multiplexer.

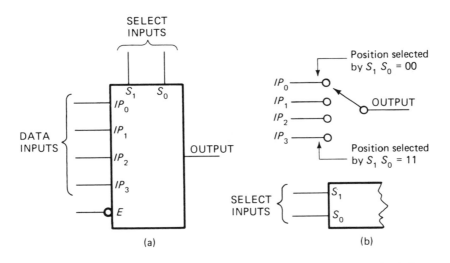

Fig. 4-12. (a) The schematic symbol for a 4-to-1 MUX. (b) The mechanical switch for a 4-to-1 MUX.

EXAMPLE 4-1:   The design of a 2-to-1 MUX is illustrated in Figure 4-13.

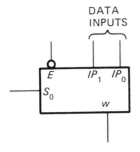

(a)

S_0	IP_1	IP_0	W
0	0	0	0
0	0	1	0
0	1	0	1
0	1	1	1
1	0	0	0
1	0	1	1
1	1	0	0
1	1	1	1

(b)

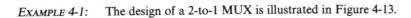

$$W(H) = (IP_0 S_0 + IP_1 \overline{S}_0)(H)$$

(c)

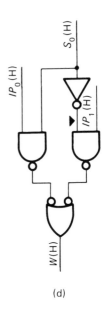

(d)

Fig. 4-13. The design of a 2-to-1 MUX.

4-5.1 USING A MUX FOR COMBINATIONAL LOGIC DESIGN

The schematic model for the general 2^n-to-1 MUX is shown in Figure 4-14. The traditional use of the multiplexer is one of time-division gating several data lines through some medium using the SELECT lines and a single data transmission line. This is done by using a MUX as the sender unit and a demultiplexer (DMUX) as a receiver unit as shown in Figure 4-15.

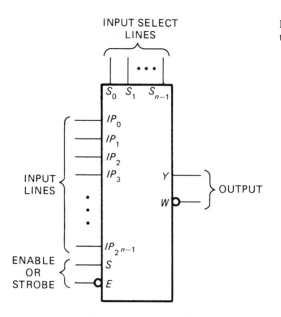

INPUT SELECT LINES

Fig. 4-14. The general schematic model for the 2^n-to-1 MUX.

However, the MUX in Figure 4-14 has the output expression that is of interest:

$$\text{OUTPUT} = m_0(IP_0) + m_1(IP_1) + m_2(IP_2) + \cdots + m_j IP_j + \cdots + m_{2^n-1}(IP_{2^n-1})$$

where m_j is the general MINTERM made up from the SELECT INPUTS (S_0, S_1, $S_2, \cdots, S_{n-1}$) and IP_j is the variable, or expression, connected to the jth input.

From this general expression for the output of a 2^n-to-1 MUX, we can derive the output expressions for some of the more typical and widely used multiplexers. These are shown in Table 4-2.

Table 4-2 shows that the general canonical SOP expression can be generated by using a MUX.* Now all the designer must do is derive some technique whereby the desired minterms can be selected. There are several techniques used, including some clumsy map methods, for logic realization using multiplexers. However, a different and hopefully easier technique will now be introduced using the map-entered-variable type philosophy.

---

*Keep in mind that one of the main reasons for considering using a MUX for logic is to minimize a package count. The logic exists and it is wired up; why not use it?

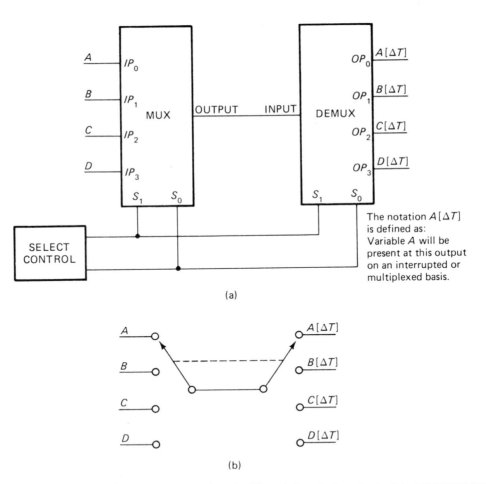

(a)

(b)

Fig. 4-15. (a) MUX/DEMUX configuration. (b) The switch equivalent circuit of the MUX/DEMUX configuration.

TABLE 4-2   Output and notation for some typical multiplexers

No. of Inputs	No. of Select Lines	Max Select Line Subscript
$2^n = 4$	$n = 2$	$n - 1 = 1$

$$\text{OUTPUT} = \bar{S}_1\bar{S}_0(IP_0) + \bar{S}_1S_0(IP_1) + S_1\bar{S}_0(IP_2) + S_1S_0(IP_3)$$

$2^n = 8$	$n = 3$	$n - 1 = 2$

$$\text{OUTPUT} = \bar{S}_2\bar{S}_1\bar{S}_0(IP_0) + \bar{S}_2\bar{S}_1S_0(IP_1) + \cdots \qquad \cdots + S_2S_1S_0(IP_7)$$

$2^n = 16$	$n = 4$	$n - 1 = 3$

$$\text{OUTPUT} = \bar{S}_3\bar{S}_2\bar{S}_1\bar{S}_0(IP_0) \quad + \bar{S}_3\bar{S}_2\bar{S}_1S_0(IP_1) + \cdots \qquad \cdots + S_3S_2S_1S_0(IP_{15})$$

EXAMPLE 4-2: Given the following TRUTH-TABLE in Figure 4-16, implement the expression using the 8-to-1 MUX. The process here will be to connect the three most significant input variables (A, B, C) to the *input select* lines of the MUX $(S_2S_1S_0)$ as follows: $A{\rightarrow}S_2$, $B{\rightarrow}S_1$, and $C{\rightarrow}S_0$, and then to connect the least significant input variable D in some manner or pattern to the *data inputs* of the MUX $(IP_0, IP_1, \cdots)$. The trick, then, is to discover how to easily recognize this connection pattern. Consider the map shown in Figure 4-16. Treat each cell in this map as "INPUT SELECTED." Now each cell of the map needs to be supplied with the input conditions (D or $\bar{D}$) required for that selected input.

	A B C D	F
0	0 0 0 0	1
1	0 0 0 1	1
2	0 0 1 0	0
3	0 0 1 1	1
4	0 1 0 0	0
5	0 1 0 1	1
6	0 1 1 0	0
7	0 1 1 1	0
8	1 0 0 0	1
9	1 0 0 1	0
10	1 0 1 0	0
11	1 0 1 1	0
12	1 1 0 0	0
13	1 1 0 1	1
14	1 1 1 0	1
15	1 1 1 1	0

Fig. 4-16. Example TRUTH-TABLE and map for a circuit to be implemented with a MUX.

$S_2 S_1 S_0$

	A B C	D	F
0	0 0 0	0	1
1	0 0 0	1	1
2	0 0 1	0	0
3	0 0 1	1	1
4	0 1 0	0	0
5	0 1 0	1	1
6	0 1 1	0	0
7	0 1 1	1	0
8	1 0 0	0	1
9	1 0 0	1	0
10	1 0 1	0	0
11	1 0 1	1	0
12	1 1 0	0	0
13	1 1 0	1	1
14	1 1 1	0	1
15	1 1 1	1	0

(a)

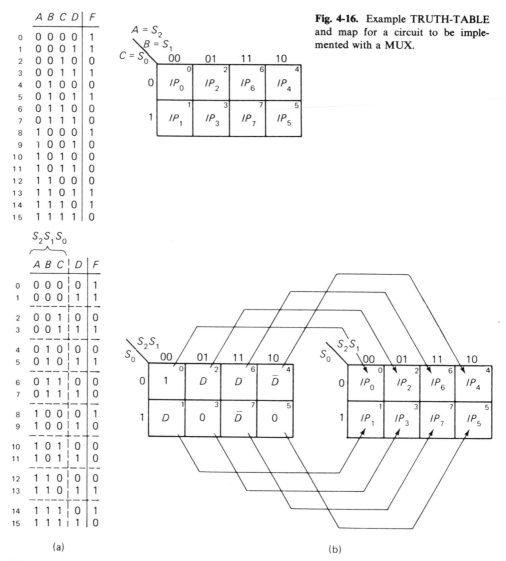

(b)

Fig. 4-17. (a) An illustration of the TRUTH-TABLE-PARTITION for the MUX input assignment for Example 4-2. (b) An illustration of map plotting for the MUX input assignment for Example 4-2.

For instance, if the MINTERM $(\bar{A}B\bar{C})(D)$ is desired, this relates to $(\bar{S}_2 S_1 \bar{S}_0)(IP_2)$. Now determine what is to be connected to IP_2: D, $\bar{D}$, or 1. In this case it is D; 0 is used to de-select any of the MINTERMS not desired.

An easy method for determining the entries has been devised. First partition the TRUTH-TABLE just as for the MEV problems and plot a map in exactly the same manner as shown in Figure 4-17(a). However, do not simplify the map. *Then use the entered variable to indicate what is to be connected to the various data inputs as Figure 4-17(b) illustrates.*

This map technique provides an easy method for determining the data input connection, as shown in Figure 4-18.

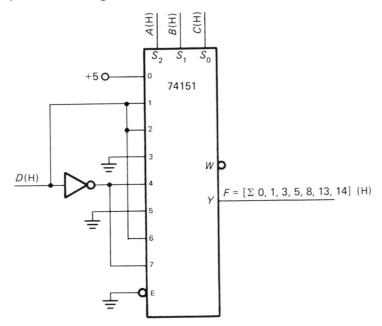

Fig. 4-18. The MUX implementation of Example 4-2.

It is interesting to note that this technique has resulted in an implementation requiring one IC package, where a discrete gate implementation would require two packages. That is a 2-to-1 savings which should be of interest to anybody.

In summary of multiplexer usage, we see that a general design technique has emerged and, in general, an n input variable problem can be implemented with a 2^{n-1} input to 1 MUX, which says any four-variable problem can be implemented with a $2^3 = 8$-to-1 MUX, five-variable with a 16-to-1 MUX, and so forth. Further, it should be noted that no attempt was made to simplify the function F. There is no need; the hardware already exists. It can't be reduced, so why bother? Note further that the MUX combinational logic model is an AND/OR.

Remember the process:

(1) Partition the TRUTH-TABLE as for a MEV problem.
(2) Plot a map as for a MEV problem.
(3) Use the entries in the map to connect the data inputs appropriately.

Figure 4-19 illustrates some data sheets for some of the typical integrated circuit multiplexers presently available. The next section illustrates how multiplexers can be used with mixed-rail input systems.

features

- Buffered Inputs and Outputs
- Three Speed/Power Ranges Available

TYPES	TYPICAL AVERAGE PROPAGATION TIME	TYPICAL POWER DISSIPATION
'157	9 ns	150 mW
'L157	18 ns	75 mW
'LS157	9 ns	49 mW
'S157	5 ns	250 mW
'LS158	7 ns	24 mW
'S158	4 ns	195 mW

applications

- Expand Any Data Input Point
- Multiplex Dual Data Buses
- Generate Four Functions of Two Variables (One Variable Is Common)
- Source Programmable Counters

description

These monolithic data selectors/multiplexers contain inverters and drivers to supply full on-chip data selection to the four output gates. A separate strobe input is provided. A 4-bit word is selected from one of two sources and is routed to the four outputs. The '157, 'L157, 'LS157, and 'S157 present true data whereas the 'LS158 and 'S158 present inverted data to minimize propagation delay time.

FUNCTION TABLE

INPUTS				OUTPUT Y	
STROBE	SELECT	A	B	'157, 'L157, 'LS157, 'S157	'LS158 'S158
H	X	X	X	L	H
L	L	L	X	L	H
L	L	H	X	H	L
L	H	X	L	L	H
L	H	X	H	H	L

H = high level, L = low level, X = irrelevant

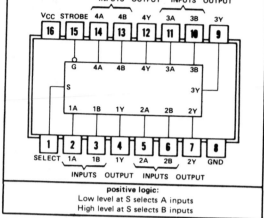

SN54157, SN54LS157, SN54S157 . . . J OR W PACKAGE
SN54L157 . . . J PACKAGE
SN74157, SN74L157, SN74LS157, SN74S157 . . . J OR N PACKAGE
(TOP VIEW)

positive logic:
Low level at S selects A inputs
High level at S selects B inputs

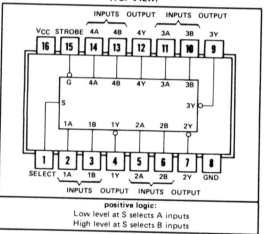

SN54LS158, SN54S158 . . . J OR W PACKAGE
SN74LS158, SN74S158 . . . J OR N PACKAGE
(TOP VIEW)

positive logic:
Low level at S selects A inputs
High level at S selects B inputs

absolute maximum ratings over operating free-air temperature range (unless otherwise noted)

Supply voltage, V_{CC} (see Note 1) . . . . 7 V
Input voltage: '157, 'L157, 'S158 . . . . 5.5 V
     'LS157, 'LS158 . . . . 7 V
Operating free-air temperature range: SN54', SN54L', SN54LS, SN54S' Circuits . . . . −55°C to 125°C
    SN74', SN74L', SN74LS, SN74S' Circuits . . . . 0°C to 70°C
Storage temperature range . . . . −65°C to 150°C

NOTE 1: Voltage values are with respect to network ground terminal.

Fig. 4-19. Data sheet for some typical IC multiplexers. (Courtesy of Texas Instruments, Inc.)

functional block diagrams

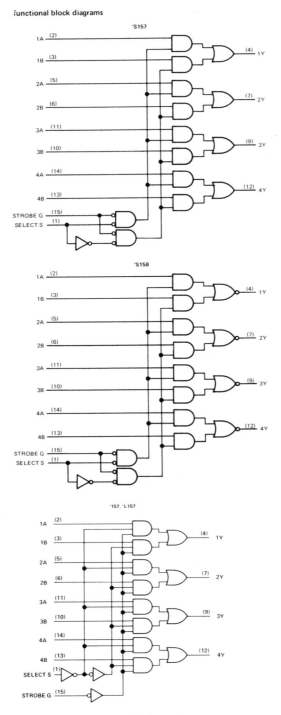

Fig. 4-19. (Cont.)

- '150 Selects One-of-Sixteen Data Sources
- Others Select One-of-Eight Data Sources
- Performs Parallel-to-Serial Conversion
- Permits Multiplexing from N Lines to One Line
- Also For Use as Boolean Function Generator
- Input-Clamping Diodes Simplify System Design
- Fully Compatible with Most TTL and DTL Circuits

TYPE	TYPICAL AVERAGE PROPAGATION DELAY TIME DATA INPUT TO W OUTPUT	TYPICAL POWER DISSIPATION
'150	11 ns	200 mW
'151A	8 ns	145 mW
'152A	8 ns	130 mW
'LS151	11 ns†	30 mW
'LS152	11 ns†	28 mW
'S151	4.5 ns	225 mW

†Tentative data

description

These monolithic data selectors/multiplexers contain full on-chip binary decoding to select the desired data source. The '150 selects one-of-sixteen data sources; the '151A, '152A, 'LS151, 'LS152, and 'S151 select one-of-eight data sources. The '150, '151A, 'LS151, and 'S151 have a strobe input which must be at a low logic level to enable these devices. A high level at the strobe forces the W output high, and the Y output (as applicable) low.

The '151A, 'LS151, and 'S151 feature complementary W and Y outputs whereas the '150, '152A, and 'LS152 have an inverted (W) output only.

The '151A and '152A incorporate address buffers which have symmetrical propagation delay times through the complementary paths. This reduces the possibility of transients occurring at the output(s) due to changes made at the select inputs, even when the '151A outputs are enabled (i.e., strobe low).

Fig. 4-19. (Cont.)

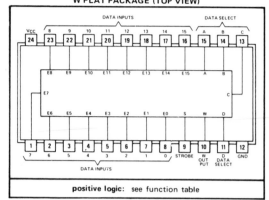

'150
J OR N DUAL-IN-LINE OR
W FLAT PACKAGE (TOP VIEW)

positive logic: see function table

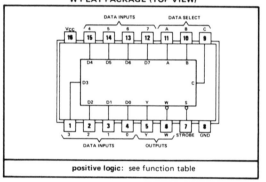

'151A, 'LS151, 'S151
J OR N DUAL-IN-LINE OR
W FLAT PACKAGE (TOP VIEW)

positive logic: see function table

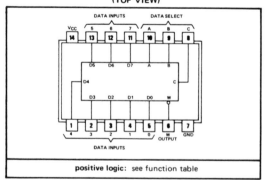

'152A, 'LS152
W FLAT PACKAGE
(TOP VIEW)

positive logic: see function table

'150
FUNCTION TABLE

INPUTS				INPUTS	OUTPUT
SELECT				STROBE	W
D	C	B	A	S	
X	X	X	X	H	H
L	L	L	L	L	$\overline{E0}$
L	L	L	H	L	$\overline{E1}$
L	L	H	L	L	$\overline{E2}$
L	L	H	H	L	$\overline{E3}$
L	H	L	L	L	$\overline{E4}$
L	H	L	H	L	$\overline{E5}$
L	H	H	L	L	$\overline{E6}$
L	H	H	H	L	$\overline{E7}$
H	L	L	L	L	$\overline{E8}$
H	L	L	H	L	$\overline{E9}$
H	L	H	L	L	$\overline{E10}$
H	L	H	H	L	$\overline{E11}$
H	H	L	L	L	$\overline{E12}$
H	H	L	H	L	$\overline{E13}$
H	H	H	L	L	$\overline{E14}$
H	H	H	H	L	$\overline{E15}$

'151A, 'LS151, 'S151
FUNCTION TABLE

INPUTS			INPUTS	OUTPUTS	
SELECT			STROBE	Y	W
C	B	A	S		
X	X	X	H	L	H
L	L	L	L	D0	$\overline{D0}$
L	L	H	L	D1	$\overline{D1}$
L	H	L	L	D2	$\overline{D2}$
L	H	H	L	D3	$\overline{D3}$
H	L	L	L	D4	$\overline{D4}$
H	L	H	L	D5	$\overline{D5}$
H	H	L	L	D6	$\overline{D6}$
H	H	H	L	D7	$\overline{D7}$

'152A, 'LS152
FUNCTION TABLE

SELECT INPUTS			OUTPUT
C	B	A	W
L	L	L	$\overline{D0}$
L	L	H	$\overline{D1}$
L	H	L	$\overline{D2}$
L	H	H	$\overline{D3}$
H	L	L	$\overline{D4}$
H	L	H	$\overline{D5}$
H	H	L	$\overline{D6}$
H	H	H	$\overline{D7}$

H = high level, L = low level, X = irrelevant
$\overline{E0}, \overline{E1} \ldots \overline{E15}$ = the complement of the level of the respective E input
D0, D1 . . . D7 = the level of the D respective input

functional block diagrams

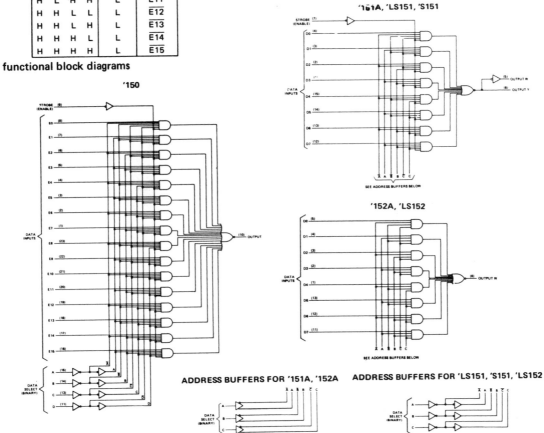

ADDRESS BUFFERS FOR '151A, '152A   ADDRESS BUFFERS FOR 'LS151, 'S151, 'LS152

Fig. 4-19. (Cont.)

- Permits Multiplexing from N lines to 1 line
- Performs Parallel-to-Serial Conversion
- Strobe (Enable) Line Provided for Cascading (N lines to n lines)
- High-Fan-Out, Low-Impedance, Totem-Pole Outputs
- Fully Compatible with most TTL and DTL Circuits

'153, 'LS153, 'S153 . . . J, N, OR W PACKAGE
'L153 . . . J OR N PACKAGE
(TOP VIEW)

positive logic: see function table

TYPE	TYPICAL AVERAGE PROPAGATION DELAY TIMES			TYPICAL POWER DISSIPATION
	FROM DATA	FROM STROBE	FROM SELECT	
'153	14 ns	17 ns	22 ns	180 mW
'L153	27 ns	34 ns	44 ns	90 mW
'LS153	14 ns	19 ns	22 ns	31 mW
'S153	6 ns	9.5 ns	12 ns	225 mW

FUNCTION TABLE

SELECT INPUTS		DATA INPUTS				STROBE	OUTPUT
B	A	C0	C1	C2	C3	G	Y
X	X	X	X	X	X	H	L
L	L	L	X	X	X	L	L
L	L	H	X	X	X	·L	H
L	H	X	L	X	X	L	L
L	H	X	H	X	X	L	H
H	L	X	X	L	X	L	L
H	L	X	X	H	X	L	H
H	H	X	X	X	L	L	L
H	H	X	X	X	H	L	H

Select inputs A and B are common to both sections.
H = high level, L = low level, X = irrelevant

description

Each of these monolithic, data selectors/multiplexers contains inverters and drivers to supply fully complementary, on-chip, binary decoding data selection to the AND-OR-invert gates. Separate strobe inputs are provided for each of the two four-line sections.

absolute maximum ratings over operating free-air temperature range (unless otherwise noted)

Supply voltage, V_{CC} (see Note 1) . . . . 7 V
Input voltage: '153, 'L153, 'S153 . . . . 5.5 V
              'LS153 . . . . 7 V
Operating free-air temperature range: SN54', SN54L', SN54LS', SN54S' Circuits . . . . −55°C to 125°C
                              SN74', SN74L', SN74LS', SN74S' Circuits . . . . 0°C to 70°C
Storage temperature range . . . . −65°C to 150°C

NOTE 1: Voltage values are with respect to network ground terminal.

Fig. 4-19. (Cont.)

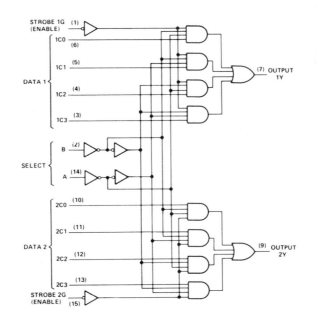

STROBE 1G (1)
(ENABLE)

1C0 (6)

1C1 (5)

DATA 1

1C2 (4)

1C3 (3)

B (2)

SELECT

A (14)

2C0 (10)

2C1 (11)

DATA 2

2C2 (12)

2C3 (13)

STROBE 2G
(ENABLE) (15)

(7) OUTPUT 1Y

(9) OUTPUT 2Y

Fig. 4-19. (Cont.)

4-5.2 USING MULTIPLEXERS WITH MIXED-RAIL INPUTS

The last section demonstrated how a MUX can be used to develop combinational logic requirements. However, each example illustrated its use with a single-rail system (ASSERTED HIGH). The question is: "Can the MUX be used in a straightforward manner in an input-rail system that has a mixture of inputs, some ASSERTED HIGH and some ASSERTED LOW?" The answer is yes, and all it requires is a quick shift of the rows and columns in the input assignment map. This is demonstrated by an example.

EXAMPLE 4-3: Suppose you were given the map in Figure 4-20 with the ASSERTED levels of the inputs defined as indicated.

Fig. 4-20 The map for $F(L)$ with input ASSERTED levels assigned.

Given:

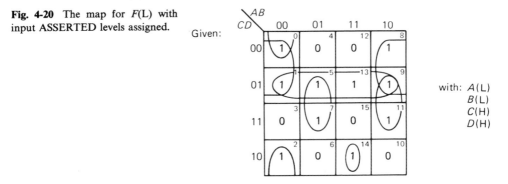

with: $A(L)$
$B(L)$
$C(H)$
$D(H)$

The standard realization is:

$$F(L) = (ABC\overline{D} + A\overline{B}D + \overline{A}\,\overline{B}\,\overline{D} + \overline{A}BD + \overline{B}\,\overline{C} + \overline{C}D)(L)$$

which requires seven gates plus four INVERTERS. Practically speaking, this implementation would require four IC packages using 7400 series logic.

To implement this with a MUX, first re-assign the columns in the map to compensate for A(L) and B(L). This is done as shown in Figure 4-21. Using the three-variable input assignment map shown in this figure, the expression for F(L) can be implemented with a 74151 (8-to-1) MUX as shown in Figure 4-22.

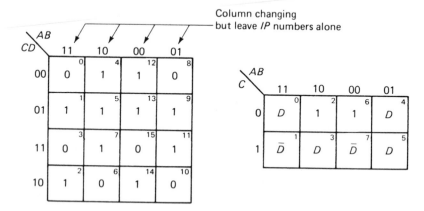

Fig. 4-21. Input assignment maps with re-assigned columns.

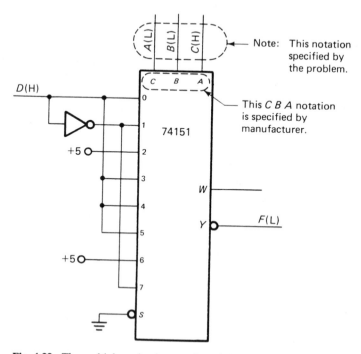

Fig. 4-22. The multiplexer implementation of F(L) for example 4-3.

In Figure 4-22 the MUX implementation of F(L) requires one IC package and a single INVERTER. Generally speaking, that will be all that is ever needed (worst case) for any four-variable problem. Thus the mixed logic concepts can be utilized with multiplexers and still minimize INVERTER requirements. There are other variations of this method which will be left for exercises.

4-5.3 OTHER IDEAS RELATED TO MUX USAGE

At present, 16-to-1 MUX's are the largest readily available devices. However, the manufacturers have provided ENABLE/STROBE inputs to allow for expansion to meet multiplexer input needs. Using these inputs, a "MUX STACK" or a "MUX TREE," as they are sometimes called, can be designed. Two methods are illustrated in Figure 4-23.

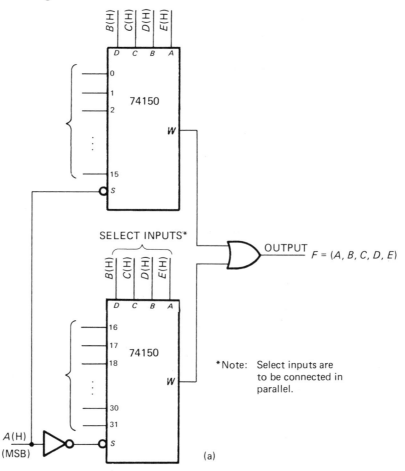

Fig. 4-23. (a) An illustration of how the ENABLE/STROBE inputs can be used to expand two 16-to-1 MUX's to a 32-to-1 MUX. (b) The MUX STACK or MUX TREE for expanding 16-to-1 MUX's to a 32-to-1 MUX.

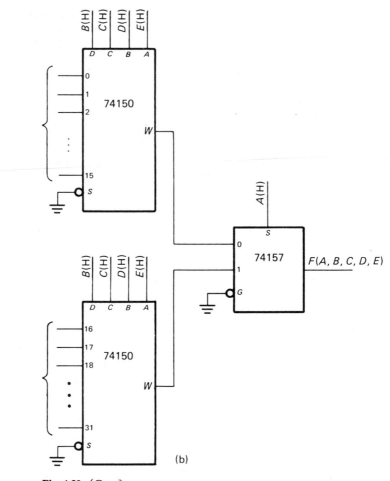

Fig. 4-23. (Cont.)

These two general techniques can expand to an *n* input MUX with little trouble. It is interesting to note that the MUX in Figure 4-23(b) could also be developed from four 8-to-1 MUX's and one 4-to-1 MUX. There will be times when you should consider this variation over the 16-to-1 implementation if you are using PC boards that will not facilitate 24-pin packages.

Further, it is interesting to note how an expression of four variables can be implemented with 4-to-1 MUX's. Consider the MAP shown in Example 4-3 and partition off variables *C* and *D* as shown in the maps in Figure 4-24. See Figure 4-25 for implementation.

This is obviously not a very good choice for this problem. However, this idea can be used to simplify and implement the function of infrequently used variables as discussed previously. Where the most frequently used variables are gated to the

MUX, select inputs and the infrequently used variables functions are sread along the data inputs. This method is used extensively in Chapter 8 for sequential machines (see Example 4-4).

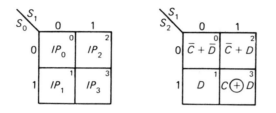

Fig. 4-24. The input assignment maps for a 4-to-1 MUX implementation of Example 4-3.

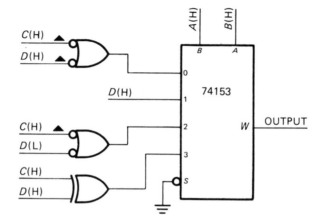

Fig. 4-25. Implementation of Example 4-3 using a 4-to-1 MUX and some input forming logic.

EXAMPLE 4-4: An illustration of how a MUX can be used to implement expressions having infrequently used variables (shown in Figure 4-26).

Given: $F = (A,B,C,\underline{D,E,F,G}) = \overline{A}\,\overline{B}\,\overline{C}(D) + A\overline{B}C(E)$

Infrequently $+ \overline{A}\,\overline{B}C(E+F) + ABC(G)$
used
variables $+ A\overline{B}\,\overline{C}(\overline{E}\,\overline{G}) + \overline{A}\,BC(\overline{D}+\overline{G})$

Viewing the new ways in which a MUX can be used, you might tend to forget its traditional uses; but all in all, the MUX is a most versatile device, one that no designer can afford to soft-pedal or neglect. The next section introduces the MSI decoder, which has similar applications.

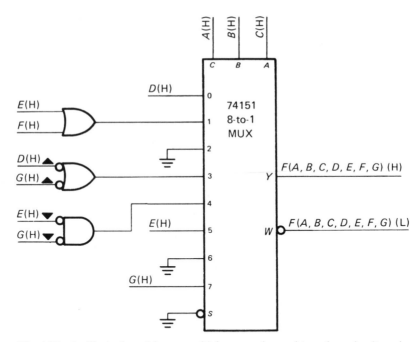

Fig. 4-26. An illustration of how a multiplexer can be used to reduce circuitry when implementing functions with infrequently used variables.

4-6 CODE CONVERTERS

In the previous study of codes, coding or encoding was defined as the use of groups of bits to represent, tag, identify, or otherwise designate items of information that are multivalued. Assigning each item of information a unique combination of bits makes an interinformational transformation of the original information. This you recognize as information being processed into another form. Because code usage is so prevalent, general code converters are available in integrated circuit form. These IC code converters are classified as decoders with labels such as:

   (1) Four line-to-16, three line-to-8, and two line-to-4
   (2) BCD-to-decimal (four line-to-10)
   (3) EXCESS 3-to-DECIMAL
   (4) BCD-to-SEVEN SEGMENT

These decoders, as mentioned, are commonly found in integrated circuit form (see Figure 4-27) and can be used for a variety of applications as is shown in the next section.

- Designed Specifically for High-Speed:
  Memory Decoders
  Data Transmission Systems

- 'S138 and 'LS138 3-to-8-Line Decoders
  Incorporate 3 Enable Inputs to Simplify
  Cascading and/or Data Reception

- 'S139 and 'LS139 Contain Two Fully
  Independent 2-to-4-Line Decoders/
  Demultiplexers

- Schottky Calmped for High Performance

TYPE	TYPICAL PROPAGATION DELAY (3 LEVELS OF LOGIC)	TYPICAL POWER DISSIPATION
'LS138	22 ns	32 mW
'S138	8 ns	245 mW
'LS139	22 ns	34 mW
'S139	7.5 ns	300 mW

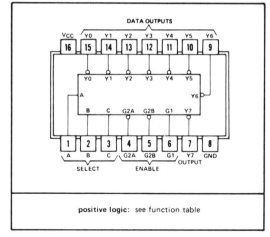

'LS138, 'S138
J OR N DUAL-IN-LINE OR
W FLAT PACKAGE (TOP VIEW)

positive logic: see function table

description

These Schottky-clamped TTL MSI circuits are designed to be used in high-performance memory-decoding or data-routing applications requiring very short propagation delay times. In high-performance memory systems these decoders can be used to minimize the effects of system decoding. When employed with high-speed memories utilizing a fast-enable circuit the delay times of these decoders and the enable time of the memory are usually less than the typical access time of the memory. This means that the effective system delay introduced by the Schottky-clamped system decoder is negligible.

The 'LS138 and 'S138 decode one-of-eight lines dependent on the conditions at the three binary select inputs and the three enable inputs. Two active-low and one active-high enable inputs reduce the need for external gates or inverters when expanding. A 24-line decoder can be implemented without external inverters and a 32-line decoder requires only one inverter. An enable input can be used as a data input for demultiplexing applications.

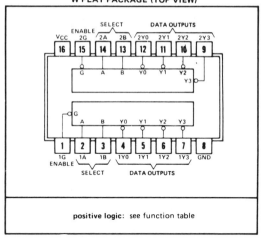

'LS139, 'S139
J OR N DUAL-IN-LINE OR
W FLAT PACKAGE (TOP VIEW)

positive logic: see function table

The 'LS139 and 'S139 comprise two individual two-line-to-four-line decoders in a single package. The active-low enable input can be used as a data line in demultiplexing applications.

All of these decoders/demultiplexers feature fully buffered inputs each of which represents only one normalized Series 54LS/74LS load ('LS138, 'LS139) or one normalized Series 54S/74S load ('S138, 'S139) to its driving circuit. All inputs are clamped with high-performance Schottky diodes to suppress line-ringing and simplify system design. Series 54LS and 54S devices are characterized for operation over the full military temperature range of −55°C to 125°C; Series 74LS and 74S devices are characterized for 0°C to 70°C industrial systems.

Fig. 4-27. Examples of integrated circuit decoders. (Courtesy of Texas Instruments, Inc.)

functional block diagrams and logic

'LS138, 'S138

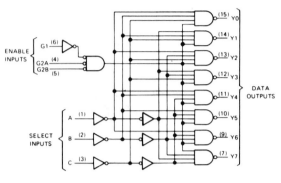

'LS138, 'S138 FUNCTION TABLE

INPUTS					OUTPUTS							
ENABLE		SELECT										
G1	G2*	C	B	A	Y0	Y1	Y2	Y3	Y4	Y5	Y6	Y7
X	H	X	X	X	H	H	H	H	H	H	H	H
L	X	X	X	X	H	H	H	H	H	H	H	H
H	L	L	L	L	L	H	H	H	H	H	H	H
H	L	L	L	H	H	L	H	H	H	H	H	H
H	L	L	H	L	H	H	L	H	H	H	H	H
H	L	L	H	H	H	H	H	L	H	H	H	H
H	L	H	L	L	H	H	H	H	L	H	H	H
H	L	H	L	H	H	H	H	H	H	L	H	H
H	L	H	H	L	H	H	H	H	H	H	L	H
H	L	H	H	H	H	H	H	H	H	H	H	L

*G2 = G2A + G2B
H = high level, L = low level, X = irrelevant

'LS139, 'S139

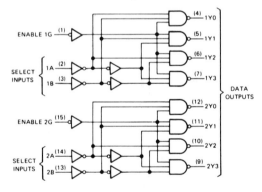

'LS139, 'S139 (EACH DECODER/DEMULTIPLEXER) FUNCTION TABLE

INPUTS			OUTPUTS			
ENABLE	SELECT					
G	B	A	Y0	Y1	Y2	Y3
H	X	X	H	H	H	H
L	L	L	L	H	H	H
L	L	H	H	L	H	H
L	H	L	H	H	L	H
L	H	H	H	H	H	L

H = high level, L = low level, X = irrelevant

Fig. 4-27. (Cont.)

'42A, 'L42, 'LS42 . . . BCD-TO-DECIMAL
'43A, 'L43 . . . EXCESS-3-TO-DECIMAL
'44A, 'L44 . . . EXCESS-3-GRAY-TO-DECIMAL

- **All Outputs Are High for Invalid Input Conditions**

- **Also for Application as 4-Line-to-16-Line Decoders 3-Line-to-8-Line Decoders**

- **Diode-Clamped Inputs**

TYPES	TYPICAL POWER DISSIPATION	TYPICAL PROPAGATION DELAYS
'42A, '43A, '44A	140 mW	17 ns
'L42, 'L43, 'L44	70 mW	49 ns
'LS42	35 mW	17 ns

description

These monolithic decimal decoders consist of eight inverters and ten four-input NAND gates. The inverters are connected in pairs to make BCD input data available for decoding by the NAND gates. Full decoding of valid input logic ensures that all outputs remain off for all invalid input conditions.

The '42A, 'L42, and 'LS42 BCD-to-decimal decoders, the '43A and 'L43 excess-3-to-decimal decoders, and the '44A and 'L44 excess-3-gray-to-decimal decoders feature inputs and outputs that are compatible for use with most TTL and other saturated low-level logic circuits. D-c noise margins are typically one volt.

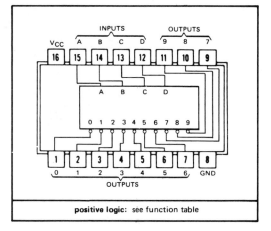

SN5442A THRU SN5444A, SN54LS42 . . . J OR W PACKAGE
SN54L42 THRU SN54L44 . . . J PACKAGE
SN7442A THRU SN7444A,
SN74L42 THRU SN74L44, SN74LS42 . . . J OR N PACKAGE
(TOP VIEW)

positive logic: see function table

Series 54, 54L, and 54LS circuits are characterized for operation over the full military temperature range of -55°C to 125°C; Series 74, 74L, and 74LS circuits are characterized for operation from 0°C to 70°C.

FUNCTION TABLE

NO.	'42A, 'L42, 'LS42 BCD INPUT				'43A, 'L43 EXCESS-3-INPUT				'44A, 'L44 EXCESS-3-GRAY INPUT				ALL TYPES DECIMAL OUTPUT									
	D	C	B	A	D	C	B	A	D	C	B	A	0	1	2	3	4	5	6	7	8	9
0	L	L	L	L	L	L	H	H	L	L	H	L	L	H	H	H	H	H	H	H	H	H
1	L	L	L	H	L	H	L	L	L	H	H	L	H	L	H	H	H	H	H	H	H	H
2	L	L	H	L	L	H	L	H	L	H	H	H	H	H	L	H	H	H	H	H	H	H
3	L	L	H	H	L	H	H	L	L	H	L	H	H	H	H	L	H	H	H	H	H	H
4	L	H	L	L	L	H	H	H	L	H	L	L	H	H	H	H	L	H	H	H	H	H
5	L	H	L	H	H	L	L	L	H	H	L	L	H	H	H	H	H	L	H	H	H	H
6	L	H	H	L	H	L	L	H	H	H	L	H	H	H	H	H	H	H	L	H	H	H
7	L	H	H	H	H	L	H	L	H	H	H	H	H	H	H	H	H	H	H	L	H	H
8	H	L	L	L	H	L	H	H	H	L	H	H	H	H	H	H	H	H	H	H	L	H
9	H	L	L	H	H	H	L	L	H	L	H	L	H	H	H	H	H	H	H	H	H	L
INVALID	H	L	H	L	H	H	L	H	H	L	L	H	H	H	H	H	H	H	H	H	H	H
	H	L	H	H	H	H	H	L	H	L	L	L	H	H	H	H	H	H	H	H	H	H
	H	H	L	L	H	H	H	H	H	L	L	L	H	H	H	H	H	H	H	H	H	H
	H	H	L	H	L	L	L	L	L	L	L	L	H	H	H	H	H	H	H	H	H	H
	H	H	H	L	L	L	L	H	L	L	L	H	H	H	H	H	H	H	H	H	H	H
	H	H	H	H	L	L	H	L	L	L	H	H	H	H	H	H	H	H	H	H	H	H

H = high level, L = low level

Fig. 4-27. (Cont.)

Code Converters **229**

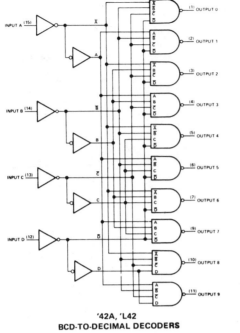

'42A, 'L42
BCD-TO-DECIMAL DECODERS

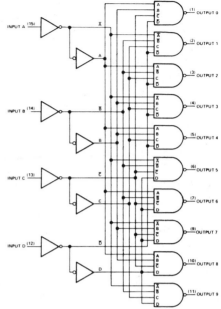

'43A, 'L43
EXCESS-3-TO-DECIMAL DECODERS

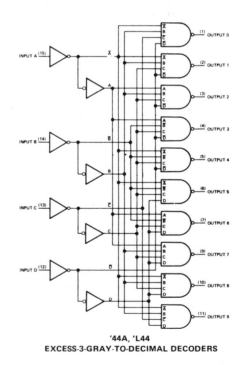

'44A, 'L44
EXCESS-3-GRAY-TO-DECIMAL DECODERS

Fig. 4-27. (Cont.)

4-6.1 DECODERS

The decoder/demultiplexer is another MSI device available to the logic designer, which can be used in a variety of applications. The device is a combinational circuit designed in such a way that at least one of several outputs will respond to a unique input code. The n to 2^n decoder, not the code converter, is sometimes referred to as the MINTERM RECOGNIZER. In other words, for each possible input code (MINTERM) applied to the decoder, *one* of the outputs will differ (become ASSERTED) from all the rest because of this input condition. When the code is changed, another output will respond and the original output will return to its NOT-ASSERTED condition.

Formally speaking, a decoder is a combinational circuit with n inputs and m outputs where $m \leq 2^n$. Each output will transfer from a NOT-ASSERTED condition to an ASSERTED condition in response to a specific, unique, and pre-assigned input code. See Figure 4-28 for a switch analog.

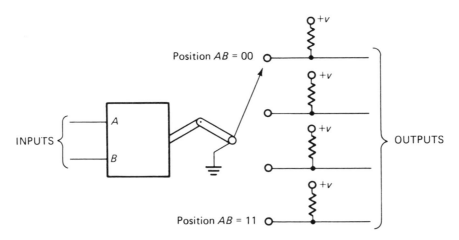

Fig. 4-28. Switching model for 2-line to 4-line binary decoder, sometimes referred to as an n to 2^n decoder.

Traditional uses of the decoder include code converters or read only memories where an input code, such as binary, is converted to yet another code, say EXCESS-3. Another traditional use is the demultiplexer seen in Figure 4-15(a). The circuit implementation of a 2-to-4 line decoder is shown in Figure 4-29. Pay particular attention to expressions attached to each output. Note further that the INPUTS have been buffered; this is done to assure a single load input drive. Also, an ENABLE input has been added for reasons to be discussed later. What is important is the understanding that the ENABLE *must* be ASSERTED in order for the decoder to function. An acceptable symbol for a 3-line to 8-line binary decoder (74LS138) is shown in Figure 4-30. Pay particular attention to the ENABLE inputs on the 74LS138.

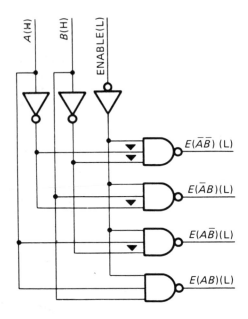

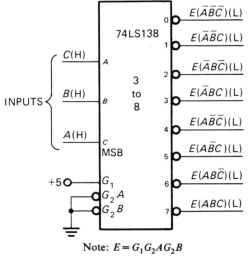

Fig. 4-29. A practical 2-line to 4-line binary decoder with ENABLE input.

Fig. 4-30. A 3-line to 8-line ASSERTED LOW binary decoder with ENABLE.

Note: $E = G_1 G_2 A G_2 B$

4-6.2 USING A DECODER FOR COMBINATIONAL DESIGN

Unlike the MUX, the decoder does require some SSI support in order to generate Boolean expressions in canonical SOP form. This can be seen from Figure 4-31 in which there is no inherent OR function related with a decoder's output. Therefore, in order to generate a canonical SOP expression, this OR function must be supplied externally. However, even in light of this apparent handicap, the DECODER can be more economical in cases where nontrivial *multiple output* expressions of the same input variables are called for. In cases such as these, one MUX is required for each output, but in turn it is likely that only one DECODER will be required, supported with a few SSI gates. Therefore, using a DECODER could have possible advantages over using a MUX. To illustrate how a DECODER can be utilized to implement a multiple output logic problem, consider Example 4-5.

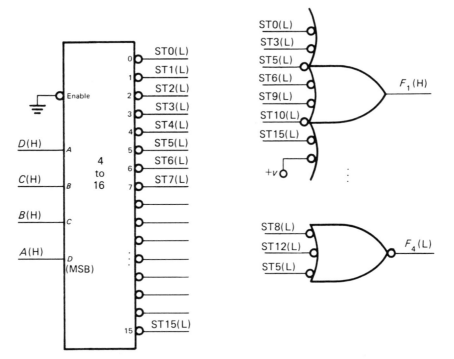

Fig. 4-31. The decoder implementation of Example 4-5.

EXAMPLE 4-5: Use a 74154 decoder to implement the following multi-output requirement of the variables A, B, C, and D ASSERTED HIGH.

$$F_1(H) = [\Sigma 0, 3, 5, 6, 9, 10, 15](H)$$
$$F_2(H) = [\Sigma 1, 2, 7, 13](H)$$
$$F_3(H) = [\Sigma 3, 4, 7, 15](H)$$
$$F_4(L) = [\Sigma 8, 12, 5](L)$$

This example shows, in Figure 4-31, that this multi-output problem requires one decoder, one eight-input NAND gate, two four-input NAND gates, and one three-input AND gate, totaling 3 2/3 packages; where the MUX implementation would require a minimum of four packages.

Note that this DECODER/NAND configuration forms an AND/OR model, with the AND's supplied by the decoder and the OR functions supplied by the NAND gates.

4-6.3 MIXED LOGIC DECODERS

The circuit shown in Figure 4-31 is referred to as a hard-wired READ ONLY MEMORY. READ ONLY MEMORIES (ROM's) are LSI devices that have many applications related to DECODER functions and random logic generation. These devices, along with the PROGRAMMABLE-LOGIC-ARRAY (PLA), are discussed in Chapter 8. However, it is recommended that you refer to Section 8-6 and read about these interesting system components.

4-6.4 USING DECODERS WITH MIXED-RAIL INPUTS

The decoder, like the multiplexer, can be quickly adapted to logic generation in mixed-rail systems by simply changing the row and column assignment for the output maps for each function. This will be demonstrated by example.

  EXAMPLE 4-6: Use the 74154 decoder to implement the $F_2(H)$ logic function of Example 4-5. Assuming the inputs available are:

$$A(L)$$
$$B(L)$$
$$C(H)$$
$$D(H)$$

First let us plot the map for $F_2(H)$ as shown in Figure 4-32.

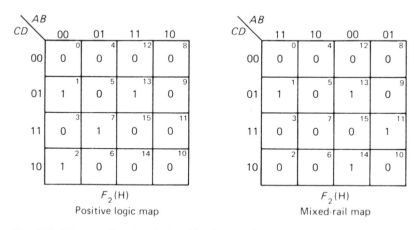

Fig. 4-32. The maps for the mixed rail implementation of $F_2(H)$ of Example 4-6.

  Thus it is a simple process to implement mixed-rail logic functions using a decoder. Another interesting application of decoders used for implementing logic expressions is derived from the example in which the number of minterms in the output list is greater than $2^n/2$. This illustrated in Example 4-7.

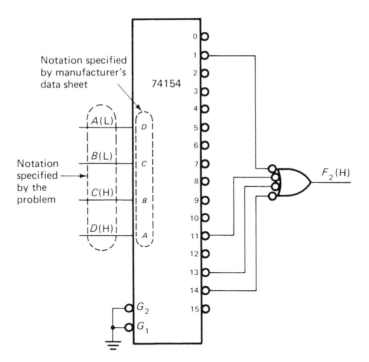

Fig. 4-33. The mixed-rail implementation of the F_2(H) using a 4-to-16 decoder.

EXAMPLE 4-7: You are to implement a function F_1(L) described by the TRUTH-TABLE and map shown in Figure 4-34.

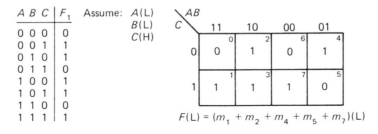

A B C	F_1
0 0 0	0
0 0 1	1
0 1 0	1
0 1 1	0
1 0 0	1
1 0 1	1
1 1 0	0
1 1 1	1

Assume: A(L)
B(L)
C(H)

$$F(L) = (m_1 + m_2 + m_4 + m_5 + m_7)(L)$$

Fig. 4-34. TRUTH-TABLE and converted output assignment map for Example 4-7.

Using the information in Figure 4-34, you see that the minterm list equals 5 minterms, which is greater than 8/2. Therefore, consider an alternate solution:

$$\text{Since:} \quad F_1 = m_1 + m_2 + m_4 + m_5 + m_7$$

$$\text{we know} \quad \overline{F}_1 = m_0 + m_3 + m_6$$

$$\therefore \quad F_1(L) = (\overline{m}_0 \cdot \overline{m}_3 \cdot \overline{m}_6)(L)$$

which can be implemented as shown in Figure 4-35 with a 74LS138. Again,

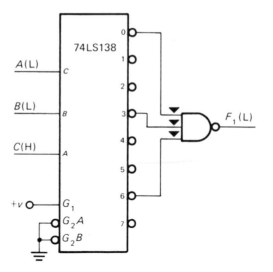

Fig. 4-35. The mixed-rail implementation of $F_1(L)$ for Example 4-7.

observe that implementation of combinational logic is quite easy using MSI decoders. Keep in mind, however, that the real benefit of using decoders occurs when multi-output functions of the same inputs are called for.

4-6.5 OTHER USES FOR DECODERS

Many times in computer systems, the input/output (I/O) devices are selected for data transfers to and from the computer by a code on a set of device address lines. This set of lines is commonly referred to as the ADDRESS BUS. It is not uncommon to find eight or more lines in the ADDRESS BUS, and this situation can create some decoding problems at the I/O device. Consider a system with eight lines in the ADDRESS BUS, which goes to each I/O device. Each I/O device is to be assigned a unique address (code) by which the computer selects it. Hence, when the computer, under software control, addresses I/O device number 127 by placing the code 0111 1111 on the ADDRESS BUS, the I/O device must decode the 0111 1111 in order to recognize selection.

Consider that 4-line to 16-line decoders are the largest available. The question arises: "Is a decoder stack or tree like the one in Figure 4-36 required for each I/O device?" The answer is probably no. In general, when only a few (< 10) codes of a large number need be recognized, the alternative MATRIX approach can be used, such as the one shown in Figure 4-37.

The question arises, "If the address is unique for the I/O device, why not hardwire a simple decoder from SSI gates that recognizes only 127 (0111 1111)?" The answer is twofold:

(1) The simple circuit talked about will require approximately two packages to implement, whereas the circuit in Figure 4-37 requires only 2 1/4 packages.

(2) Most I/O equipment must have a flexible address selection circuit because addresses are changed by computer center personnel from time to time, and to have a fixed hardwired limited address decoder would be most unhandy.

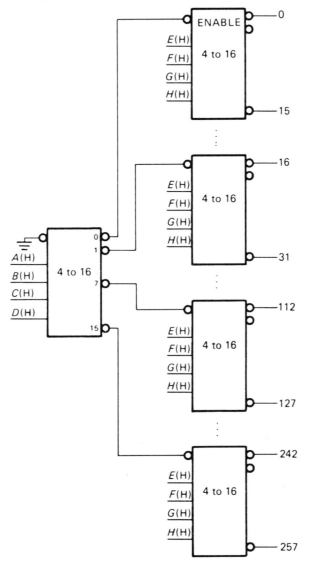

Fig. 4-36. An example of 8-line to 256-line decoders using 4-line to 16-line decoders in a stack or tree.

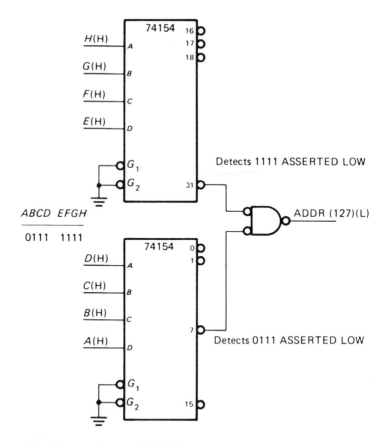

Fig. 4-37. An alternate MATRIX approach to the decode of address 127.

In defense of the circuit in Figure 4-36, many times decoders such as these are required when it is imperative that every INPUT MINTERM or at least a large number of the INPUT MINTERMS must be decoded. However, the designer must decide which of these will best suit the purpose when faced with something in between. As always, there are no hard and fast rules governing the selection process other than keep your design clean.

The decoders available today are also used widely as DEMULTIPLEXERS as mentioned earlier. The idea here is to use the ENABLE input as the RECEIV-ING INPUT and the normal inputs (A,B,C,D) as the channel select inputs as shown in Figure 4-38.

In order to understand the operation of this MUX/DMUX system, consider a specific case where the $S_2S_1S_0$ code $= 110$. This addressed IP_6 has the logic variable $F(H)$ (F ASSERTED HIGH). The output of the MUX will be $F(L)$ (F ASSERTED LOW). Now, over at the decoder, the MINTERM m_6 (110) is being selected and the total decoder is being ENABLED by $F(L)$. Further, remember the Boolean expression for OUTPUT 6 of the decoder as:

$$(\text{OUTPUT 6})(\text{L}) = \left[\text{ENABLE}\,(AB\overline{C})\right](\text{L})$$

Since m_6 being selected means that $AB\overline{C} = 1$:

$$(\text{OUTPUT 6})(\text{L}) = \left[\text{ENABLE}(1)\right](\text{L})$$

Since:

$$\text{ENABLE} = F$$

then

$$(\text{OUTPUT 6})(\text{L}) = F(\text{L})$$

Hence, OUTPUT 6 of the decoder logically follows the INPUT 6 of the MUX; only the ASSERTED voltage range is different. All this can be done using standard MSI devices.

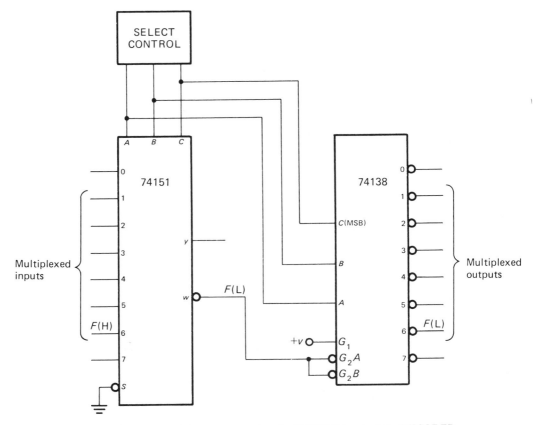

Fig. 4-38. A Multiplexer/Demultiplexer system using the ENABLE input of the DECODER.

Up to this point nothing has been said about the SELECT CONTROL circuit. The reason for this is that this circuit can be any sequential machine like a counter, which steps from one selected input to another in any desired fashion and hence little more need be said.

Reviewing multiplexers and decoders, it should be no real wonder that these devices are widely used and are manufactured as standard integrated circuits. Because of the flexibility of these devices, a designer should at least consider them for just about every combination logic design problem encountered, since most combinational logic circuits have basic decoder attributes.

4-6.6 ENCODERS

The encoder is another example of a combinational circuit that is designed to generate a different output code for each input which becomes ASSERTED. *In general, the ENCODER is a circuit with n inputs, one for each information element to be encoded, which generates an identifying code for each of these inputs.* Thus for n elements of information to be uniquely encoded, the output code width m must satisfy the following relation:

$$2^m \geq n$$

It should be noticed that the definition of the ENCODER *allows only one* input to be ASSERTED at any given time. An illustration of an ENCODER is shown in Figure 4-39.

It should be noted that the ENCODER shown in Figure 4-39 was designed to generate

$$C_1 C_0 = 00$$

for any input code that could not be deemed a single element ASSERTED code.

ENCODERS are not normally considered general circuits because of the single element code problem described above. However, there is an integrated circuit PRIORITY ENCODER available which is an extremely useful device and which is discussed in the next section.

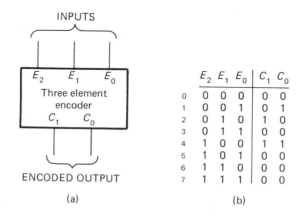

	E_2	E_1	E_0	C_1	C_0
0	0	0	0	0	0
1	0	0	1	0	1
2	0	1	0	1	0
3	0	1	1	0	0
4	1	0	0	1	1
5	1	0	1	0	0
6	1	1	0	0	0
7	1	1	1	0	0

(a)   (b)

Fig. 4-39. The design of a specialized three-element ENCODER.

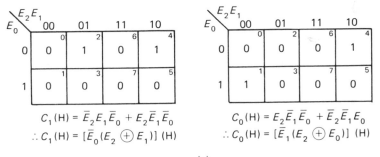

$C_1(H) = \bar{E}_2 E_1 \bar{E}_0 + E_2 \bar{E}_1 \bar{E}_0$

$\therefore C_1(H) = [\bar{E}_0 (E_2 \oplus E_1)]\ (H)$

$C_0(H) = E_2 \bar{E}_1 \bar{E}_0 + \bar{E}_2 \bar{E}_1 E_0$

$\therefore C_0(H) = [\bar{E}_1 (E_2 \oplus E_0)]\ (H)$

(c)

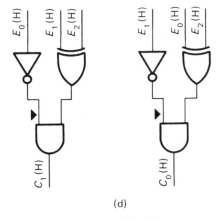

(d)

Fig. 4-39. (Cont.)

4-6.7 PRIORITY ENCODERS

The **PRIORITY ENCODER** is also a combinational circuit designed much the same as the general **ENCODER** described above, with the exception that the inputs are assigned a priority. This priority assignment in turn allows the device to identify a particular element when several inputs are ASSERTED simultaneously. Therefore, the general concept here is that each input is assigned a priority with respect to the other inputs, and the output code generated at any time is the code assigned to the *highest* priority input ASSERTED at that particular instant of time. An illustration of a **PRIORITY ENCODER** is shown in Figure 4-40, one in which the priority is established by: E_2 highest, E_1 middle, and E_0 lowest:

E_2 is to be encoded to 01
E_1 is to be encoded to 10
E_0 is to be encoded to 11
and 00 is to be assigned to the inactive state

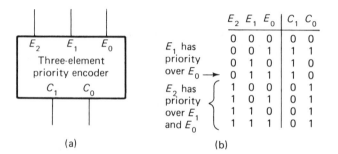

	E_2	E_1	E_0	C_1	C_0
	0	0	0	0	0
E_1 has	0	0	1	1	1
priority	0	1	0	1	0
over $E_0 \rightarrow$	0	1	1	1	0
E_2 has	1	0	0	0	1
priority	1	0	1	0	1
over E_1	1	1	0	0	1
and E_0	1	1	1	0	1

(a)   (b)

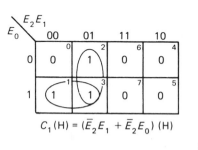

$C_1(\text{H}) = (\bar{E}_2 E_1 + \bar{E}_2 E_0)\,(\text{H})$

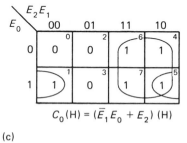

$C_0(\text{H}) = (\bar{E}_1 E_0 + E_2)\,(\text{H})$

(c)

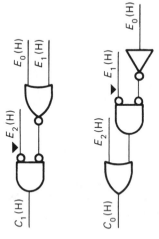

Fig. 4-40. The illustration of the implementation of a **PRIORITY ENCODER**.

SN54147, SN74147

- Encodes 10-Line Decimal to 4-Line BCD
- Applications Include:
    Keyboard Encoding
    Range Selection
- Typical Data Delay . . . 10 ns
- Typical Power Dissipation . . . 225 mW

SN54148, SN74148

- Encodes 8 Data Lines to 3-Line Binary (Octal)
- Applications Include:
    N-Bit Encoding
    Code Converters and Generators
- Typical Data Delay . . . 10 ns
- Typical Power Dissipation . . . 190 mW

J OR N DUAL-IN-LINE OR
W FLAT PACKAGE (TOP VIEW)

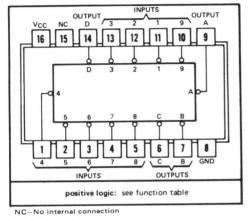

positive logic: see function table

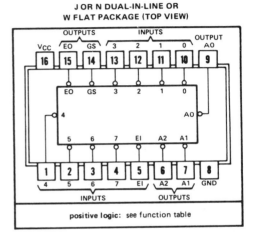

positive logic: see function table

NC—No internal connection

description

These TTL encoders feature priority decoding of the inputs to ensure that only the highest-order data line is encoded. The SN54147 and SN74147 encode nine data lines to four-line (8-4-2-1) BCD. The implied decimal zero condition requires no input condition as zero is encoded when all nine data lines are at a high logic level. All inputs are buffered to represent one normalized Series 54/74 load. The SN54148 and SN74148 encode eight data lines to three-line (4-2-1) binary (octal). Cascading circuitry (enable input EI and enable output EO) has been provided to allow octal expansion without the need for external circuitry. For all types, data inputs and outputs are active at the low logic level.

SN54147, SN74147 FUNCTION TABLE

INPUTS									OUTPUTS			
1	2	3	4	5	6	7	8	9	D	C	B	A
H	H	H	H	H	H	H	H	H	H	H	H	H
X	X	X	X	X	X	X	X	L	L	H	H	L
X	X	X	X	X	X	X	L	H	L	H	H	H
X	X	X	X	X	X	L	H	H	H	L	L	L
X	X	X	X	X	L	H	H	H	H	L	L	H
X	X	X	X	L	H	H	H	H	H	L	H	L
X	X	X	L	H	H	H	H	H	H	L	H	H
X	X	L	H	H	H	H	H	H	H	H	L	L
X	L	H	H	H	H	H	H	H	H	H	L	H
L	H	H	H	H	H	H	H	H	H	H	H	L

SN54148, SN74148 FUNCTION TABLE

INPUTS									OUTPUTS				
EI	0	1	2	3	4	5	6	7	A2	A1	A0	GS	EO
H	X	X	X	X	X	X	X	X	H	H	H	H	H
L	H	H	H	H	H	H	H	H	H	H	H	H	L
L	X	X	X	X	X	X	X	L	L	L	L	L	H
L	X	X	X	X	X	X	L	H	L	L	H	L	H
L	X	X	X	X	X	L	H	H	L	H	L	L	H
L	X	X	X	X	L	H	H	H	L	H	H	L	H
L	X	X	X	L	H	H	H	H	H	L	L	L	H
L	X	X	L	H	H	H	H	H	H	L	H	L	H
L	X	L	H	H	H	H	H	H	H	H	L	L	H
L	L	H	H	H	H	H	H	H	H	H	H	L	H

H = high logic level, L = low logic level, X = irrelevant

Fig. 4-41. The data sheets for two priority encoders. (Courtesy of Texas Instruments, Inc.)

functional block diagrams

SN54147, SN74147 SN54148, SN74148

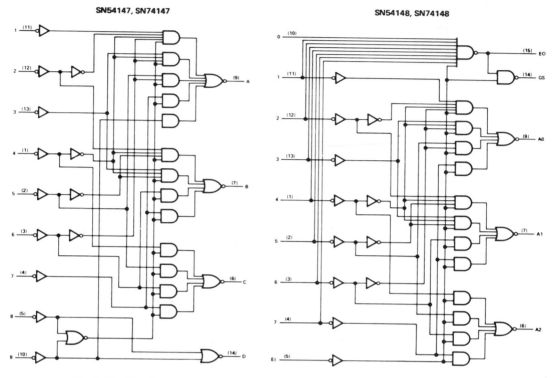

Fig. 4-41. (Cont.)

The PRIORITY ENCODER has some very specific applications in many digital systems that have sub-systems attached to the main system, in particular, a computer with several I/O devices attached to it. Because of the importance of the I/O devices to the overall operation, they are assigned priority addresses. For example, a high speed disk unit would typically receive higher priority than a slow speed paper tape reader. Thus, when both the disk and the tape reader are making application for the main computer's attention via some address code, a PRIORITY ENCODER can be used to select the disk over the paper tape unit. There are a variety of other uses for this device, including logic implementation in sequential circuits, which will be shown in a later chapter. See Figure 4-41 for the data sheets of two integrated circuit priority encoders.

The next two sections treat the usage of the EXOR and the AND-OR-IN-VERT devices. It is true that these do not fall into MSI or LSI categories; however, they have some interesting application in combinational logic generation.

4-7 EXOR AND AND-OR-INVERT GATES

The EXOR gate is used quite often throughout this text, and since this function exists as an integrated circuit, it seems fitting that we spend a little time and effort in learning how to recognize map patterns that indicate EXOR or NEXOR = $\overline{EXOR}$ functions. There is a special map, called the RING MAP, to be used for reducing logic requirements to EXOR/NEXOR implementations. However, this author chooses to inspect the standard K-map and detect map patterns that give an indication that EXOR functions are applicable. These patterns just mentioned are quite easy to detect, watching for:

(1) kitty-corner adjacencies;
(2) offset adjacencies.

Kitty-corner adjacencies are grouping singles, duals, and so forth that are not logically adjacent but can be viewed adjacent through a corner of a map cell:

Offset adjacencies are groups that are displaced by one column or row in a map:

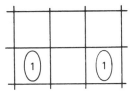

See Figure 4-42(a) for further definition of these adjacencies.

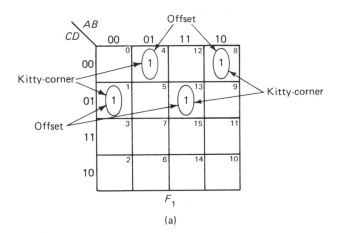

(a)

Fig. 4-42. Example maps illustrating EXOR GATES and applications.

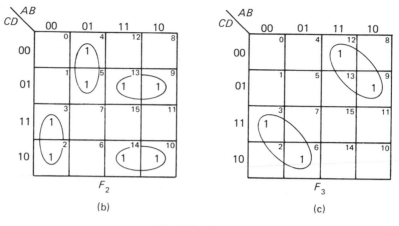

Fig. 4-42. (Cont.)

Here you should recognize a kitty-corner and/or offset grouping in the K-map. Once you recognize these, you know that there is either an EXOR or NEXOR function involved. You then hunt it out by factoring your expression as shown for the example maps in Figure 4-42.

$$F_1 = \bar{A}B\bar{C}\bar{D} + A\bar{B}\bar{C}\bar{D} + \bar{A}B\bar{C}D + AB\bar{C}D$$

$$\text{or} \quad F_1 = \bar{C}\bar{D}(A \oplus B) + \bar{C}D(A \odot B)$$

$$F_1 = \bar{C}\left[(\bar{D})(A \oplus B) + (D)(\overline{A \oplus B})\right]$$

$$\therefore F_1(\text{H}) = \bar{C}\left[(D) \oplus (A \oplus B)\right](\text{H})$$

which when implemented with EXOR gates turns out much simpler than a conventional logic. The EXOR implementation for F_1 is shown in Figure 4-43.

$$F_2 = \bar{A}B\bar{C} + \bar{A}\bar{B}C + A\bar{C}D + AC\bar{D}$$

$$\text{or} \quad F_2(\text{H}) = \left(\bar{A}(B \oplus C) + A(C \oplus D)\right)(\text{H})$$

and

$$F_3 = AB\bar{C}\bar{D} + A\bar{B}\bar{C}D + \bar{A}\bar{B}CD + \bar{A}BC\bar{D}$$

$$\text{or} \quad F_3(\text{H}) = (B \oplus D)(A \oplus C)(\text{H})$$

Thus using an EXOR gate, at times, can reduce package count. Again, let us review the concept related to EXOR recognition.

(1) If standard K-map groupings occur in a kitty-corner or offset pattern, you should recognize that either EXOR or $\overline{\text{EXOR}}$ functions exist in the K-map simplified expression. Therefore:

(2) Rather than learning a whole new mapping concept just for EXOR, you should *examine* the simplified expression and factor out the EXOR and $\overline{\text{EXOR}}$ function and implement directly.

Fig. 4-43. An example of EXOR implementation for F_1 in Figure 4-4.

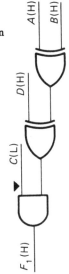

4-8 HINTS FOR READING EXOR AND NEXOR EXPRESSIONS DIRECTLY FROM THE MAP

In the last section you were given information related to recognizing offset and kitty-corner groupings as indicators of EXOR and NEXOR sub-expressions. You were given a foolproof but laborious method for finding these expressions, which you should not forget. In this section you are given some simple mapping rules that will allow you to extract these expressions automatically, but you are likely to forget them. Thus, these rules are treated as an interesting approach and introduced in example form.

> *EXAMPLE 4-8:* Given the two maps in Figure 4-44, it will be demonstrated how the EXOR and NEXOR rules apply (see Figure 4-45). Mapping steps referring to Figure 4-45:

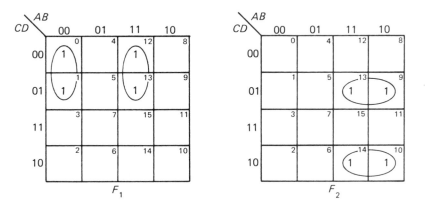

Fig. 4-44. Offset adjacencies examples.

(1) Make loops that group entries in standard K-map fashion as illustrated.

(2) Draw a line connecting the two groups, keeping track of the boundaries cut by this line, as shown.

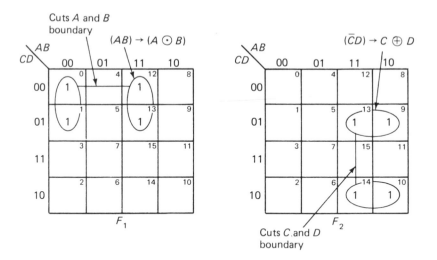

Fig. 4-45. Offset adjacency read examples.

(3) The variables associated with the boundaries cut by these lines are the variables connected with either an EXOR or a NEXOR connective, but you must determine which it will be. This is done by picking one of the groups, either one, and determining if these variables go with an EXOR or NEXOR. For example, if A and B boundaries are cut, do you have $A\bar{B}$ or $\bar{A}B$ in one of the groupings? If so, it is an EXOR connective. If it is an AB or $\bar{A}\bar{B}$, then it is a NEXOR $(\overline{A \oplus B})$ connective. Thus we see:

$$F_1 = (?)(\overline{A \oplus B})$$
$$F_2 = (?)(C \oplus D)$$

(4) Now fill in the (?) with the map variable associated with the area in the map in which both groups are common. This is easily done by looking at the map. Looking at the F_1 map observe that both groups are common to $\bar{C}$, or both are within the $\bar{C}$ boundaries. For F_2, both groups are within the A boundaries.

$$\therefore F_1 = \bar{C}(\overline{A \oplus B}) = \bar{C}(A \odot B) \quad \text{and} \quad F_2 = A(C \oplus D)$$

These same rules apply to the kitty-corner grouping also. For example, see maps in Figures 4-46 and 4-47.

EXAMPLE 4-9:

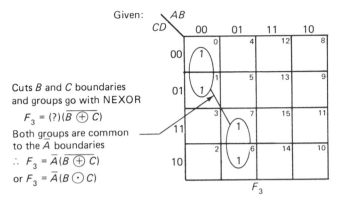

Given:

Cuts B and C boundaries and groups go with NEXOR

$$F_3 = (?)(\overline{B \oplus C})$$

Both groups are common to the $\overline{A}$ boundaries

$$\therefore F_3 = \overline{A}(\overline{B \oplus C})$$

or $F_3 = \overline{A}(B \odot C)$

Fig. 4-46. Example of a kitty-corner adjacency.

EXAMPLE 4-10:

Given:

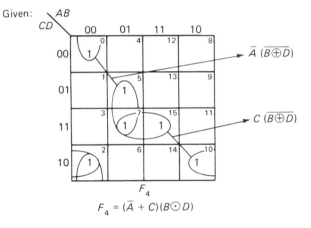

$\overline{A}(B \oplus D)$

$C(\overline{B \oplus D})$

$$F_4 = (\overline{A} + C)(B \odot D)$$

Fig. 4-47. Example of a kitty-corner adjacency.

Summary.

(1) We first group the map in standard K-map fashion.

(2) Scan the map for offset and kitty-corner groupings.

(3) Connect these groups appropriately with a line, keeping track of the boundaries cut by this line and knowing that these cut boundaries give information related to what variables are connected with the EXOR or NEXOR connective.

(4) Examine one of the groups to determine if the term associated with the boundary-cut variables goes with an EXOR or a NEXOR.

(5) Determine the variable ANDed with the EXOR or NEXOR by finding what variable is common to the area in which the groups are found.

As has been mentioned before, rules and steps are designed to be forgotten, but for the interested student these rules add an interesting dimension to his map-reading expertise and at least make interesting conversation.

4-9 AND-OR-INVERT GATE (A-O-I)

The semiconductor industry has provided the designer with an array of different devices that are relatively simple in construction but widely applicable. For example, the EXOR and NEXOR gates are not complex but generally useful. The AND-OR-INVERT gate shown in Figure 4-48 is another of this type of circuit available in integrated circuit form, and it is used quite widely. These A-O-I devices do have some interesting aspects related to their use. If you are interested in the use of A-O-I gates, you should consult the manufacturer's data books to determine exactly what A-O-I configurations exist, along with the A-O-I expanders that add a degree of flexibility to these devices.

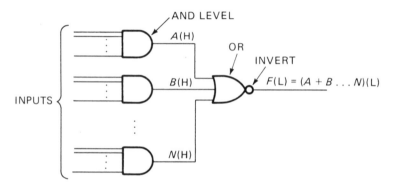

Fig. 4-48. The general logic diagram of A-O-I gate.

The circuit in Figure 4-48 and the A-O-I name indicate at least one immediate application for the type of device. This is in the implementation of SOP expressions which are to be ASSERTED LOW:

$$F(L) = (\text{simplified SOP expression})\ (L)$$

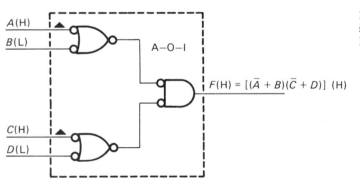

Fig. 4-49. A-O-I device used to implement an ASSERTED HIGH function.

$F(H) = [(\bar{A} + B)(\bar{C} + D)]\ (H)$

On the other hand, there are other interesting applications for these devices. Note that in Figure 4-49 an A-O-I gate is drawn in a POS symbolic notation. This figure demonstrates that it is possible to implement a function ASSERTED HIGH with A-O-I gates. However, the actual A-O-I device used for an ASSERTED HIGH application need not be exactly the same as the device that would be used for an ASSERTED LOW application, though it could be. An example will be given illustrating the use of an A-O-I implementation.

EXAMPLE 4-11: Given the map in Figure 4-50, implement F(L) and F(H) with an A-O-I device. See Figure 4-51 for the implementation.

Fig. 4-50. An example map illustrating the use of the A-O-I gate.

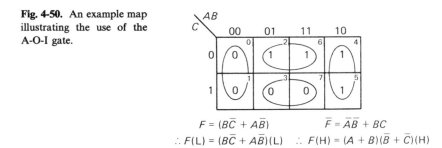

$$F = (B\bar{C} + A\bar{B})$$
$$\bar{F} = \bar{A}\bar{B} + BC$$
$$\therefore F(L) = (B\bar{C} + A\bar{B})(L) \quad \therefore F(H) = (A + B)(\bar{B} + \bar{C})(H)$$

Fig. 4-51. A-O-I implementation of F(H) specified in Figure 4-50.

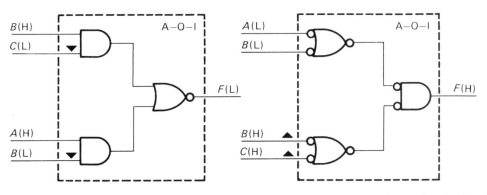

In the next section we cover yet another method of implementing logic using what is called "wired logic."

4-10 WIRED LOGIC

The phrase "wired logic" is frequently used in contemporary digital design. It is a phrase describing the condition where two or more outputs of special "busable" gates or devices are tied together on a common line. This line is commonly called a "bus line" or more simply a "bus." Those gates that drive this bus line are referred to as "bus drivers," naturally; and those gates that receive levels from this bus line are referred to as bus receivers.

Two widely used devices for implementing wired logic are:

(1) "open collector" output devices;
(2) "TRI-STATE" output devices.*

Before launching into the subtleties of using the open collector and tri-state devices, examine how one might conceptually use these devices. A typical open collector device is shown in Figure 4-52.

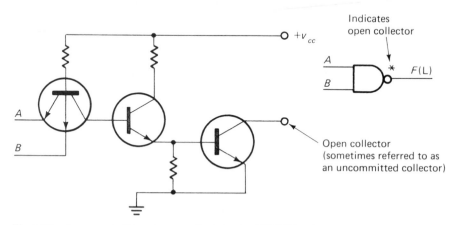

Fig. 4-52. An example 2-input open-collector output NAND gate.

To illustrate the application of the open collector devices, consider Figure 4-53.

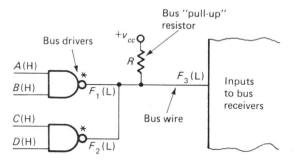

Fig. 4-53. An illustration of a bus arrangement for "wired logic."

From this figure we see that a bus "pull-up" resistor is necessary because open collector devices have no current drive capability for raising the voltage of the bus. Therefore, the resistor R is used to "pull the bus up" and the outputs of the drivers "pull the bus low." From this we see that the output signal F_3:

$$F_3(L) = F_1(L) + F_2(L)$$

In short, F_3 is ASSERTED LOW if F_1 is ASSERTED OR F_2 is ASSERTED. It is because of the OR relationship that wired logic networks like the one in Figure

———————————

*TRI-STATE is a registered trademark of the National Semiconductor Corporation.

4-53 are called "wired-OR" (OR-TIE) systems. However, closer examination reveals that the following symbol describes the expression $F_3(L) = F_1(L) + F_2(L)$, as shown in Figure 4-54, indicating the OR function of an AND gate. Therefore, the network in Figure 4-53 is most commonly referred to as a wired-AND and is symbolized as shown in Figure 4-55.

Fig. 4-54. The schematic symbol for a wired-OR network.

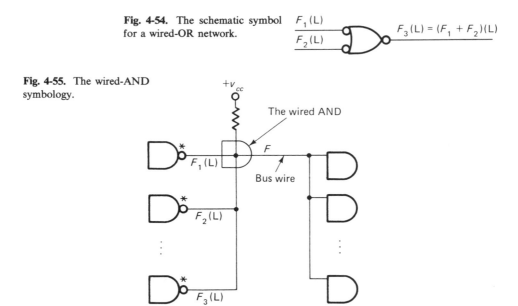

Fig. 4-55. The wired-AND symbology.

How you refer to these networks is your choice, be it wired-OR or wired-AND, but those familiar with mixed logic symbology will logically refer to it as an OR function ASSERTED LOW or wired-OR. See Figure 4-56 for an alternate OR symbology.

Fig. 4-56. Alternate symbols for a wired-AND circuit.

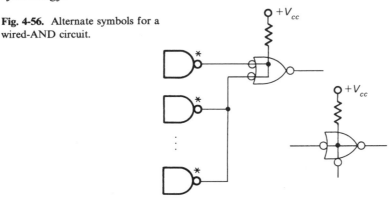

Wired logic is of particular interest in large bus-oriented digital systems when many separate systems are to input and receive data and information from a single source system. For example, a digital computer can have many peripheral I/O devices dedicated to it, each of which must send and receive data to and from the host computer. It is plain to see that it is impractical for each I/O device to have its own set of control and data lines, particularly if the number of these devices becomes large. Therefore, most computers communicate with the I/O units on a set or several sets of lines called bus structures or bus systems, and each I/O device hangs its inputs and outputs on these bus systems in parallel with the other I/O devices, similar to clothes hanging on a line. This illustrates that only one device at a time can utilize the bus system in a multiplexed type of operation. It is usually the host computer software that directs the traffic on the bus system in order to prevent overlapping interaction.

4-11 PRACTICAL ASPECTS OF WIRED LOGIC AND BUS-ORIENTED STRUCTURES

To preface this discussion, let us define some terms. Let:

$I_{out}(1) =$ the max leakage current required from the bus system by the output of a driver when the bus is pulled high.

$I_{in}(1) =$ the max current required from the bus by an input to a receiver when the bus is pulled high.

$I_{out}(0) =$ the max current a driver output can sink when this output is pulling the bus low.

$I_{in}(0) =$ the max current delivered to the bus by a receiver input when the bus is pulled low.

$V_0(1) =$ the minimum acceptable high voltage level for the bus.

$V_0(0) =$ the maximum value for the low voltage level of the bus.

The currents and voltages defined above are parameters that set constraints on the size of the pull-up resistor R shown in Figure 4-53. Should a very large R arbitrarily be chosen, the combination of the leakage current of the drivers and the inputs of the receiver would cause a voltage drop across R resulting in the inability to raise the bus wire to an acceptable level. Further, if the choice of resistor is arbitrarily small, the bus drivers will be unable to pull the bus wire low. Therefore, the number of drivers wired together, combined with the number of receivers, sets constraints on the size of the resistor to be used for the pull-up. Consider Figure 4-57 and the associated development to learn about how to size the pull-up resistor. We see:

$$V_{bus} = V_{cc} - [nI_{out}(1) + mI_{in}(1)]R \geq V_0(1)$$

Thus:

$$\boxed{R \leq \frac{V_{cc} - V_0(1)}{nI_{out}(1) + mI_{in}(1)}}$$

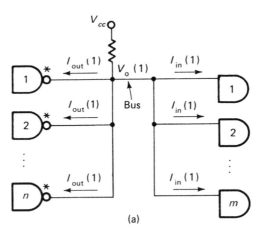

(a)

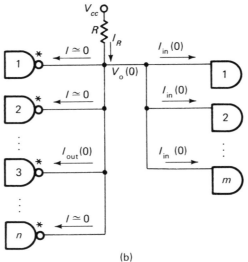

(b)

Fig. 4-57(a). An illustration of the current flow for a wired-logic circuit when the bus wire is HIGH. (b). Figure used to calculate the minimum value of R.

Similarly, when the bus is pulled low by *one* of the drivers, Figure 4-57(b) shows that the sink current for driver 3 is:

$$I_{out}(0) \geq - \left(mI_{in}(0)\right) + \left(\frac{V_{cc} - V_0(0)}{R}\right)$$

Thus:

$$R \geq \frac{V_{cc} - V_0(0)}{I_{out}(0) + mI_{in}(0)}$$

For the TTL family:

$$I_{out}(1) \simeq 250 \ \mu a$$

$$I_{in}(1) \simeq 40 \ \mu a$$

$$I_{out}(0) \simeq 15 \ ma$$

$$I_{in}(0) \simeq -1.6 \ ma$$

$$V_0(1) \geq 3.0 \ volt$$

$$V_0(0) \leq 0.4 \ volt$$

From these values the required value for R can be derived.

One further practical note: Bussed or wired logic systems tend to be slower than the active pull-up systems, because the stray capacitance associated with the bus must be charged through the pull-up resistor. Thus, when the bus is released by a driver, the low to high transitions on the bus are constrained by the time constant: RC_{stray}. Because of this and other limitations associated with wired logic, this author recommends that it be used only with bus systems and feels that it should not be considered a replacement for interconnecting gates in a standard logic network. The next section introduces the TRI-STATE approach to bus systems.

4-12 TRI-STATE BUS SYSTEMS

Special logic devices have been developed to minimize the loading and speed problems caused by using open-collector devices on bus systems. This family of devices is referred to as TRI-STATE and a typical TTL SN 74XX device is shown in Figure 4-58. Tri-state devices, as their name suggests, have three output states:

(1) High (output driving current to bus)
(2) Low (output sinking current from bus)
(3) Off (output disconnected from bus)

We see from Figure 4-58 that when the ENABLE input is at a low voltage, Q_1 cuts off Q_2 and Q_3 and there is no restriction in the basic inverter operation. However, when the ENABLE is raised to a high voltage, Q_2 and Q_3 turn on and shunt the drive current for the output stage to ground, thus leaving Q_4 and Q_5 in a cut-off condition, giving rise to the off or disconnected condition associated with tri-state logic systems. Note that a diode is added to the output to *overcompensate* for the leakage current of Q_5 and thus yields an almost ideal bussable device. As an added feature, to reduce the sinking requirement caused by large $I_{in}(0)$, input configurations have been developed, like the one shown in Figure 4-59, for reducing the input loading as much as a factor of 5 over standard T^2L.

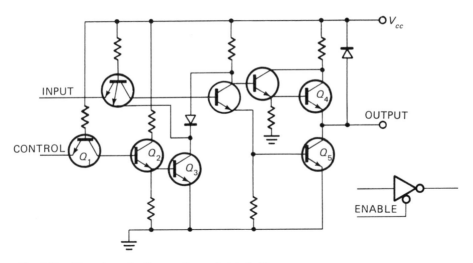

Fig. 4-58. The schematic diagram for a tri-state buffer.

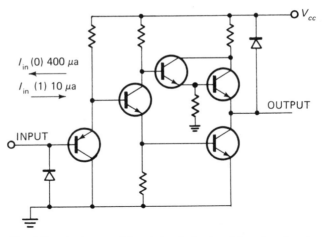

Fig. 4-59. An improved input circuit developed to reduce input loading.

Thus we can conclude that tri-state devices have marked advantages over their open collector counterparts on most counts including speed, loading factors, and flexibility. For example, a tri-state device such as the Signetics 8T26 transceiver circuit, whose information sheet is shown in Figure 4-60, is a tri-state device that will drive as well as receive information on and off a *bi-directional* bus system. Further information and application ideas related to tri-state devices can be obtained from most manufacturers' data books.

INTRODUCTION

The 8T26 Quad Bus Driver/Receiver is a Schottky TTL integrated circuit that has been designed for high speed bus applications. The device is particularly useful in bi-directional* data busses since it increases speed and reduces hardware compared to conventional implementations. Because of its unique design features, the 8T26 can be used in many other interface applications.

Tri-state outputs permit data bussing without the need for pull-up resistors. With an active pull-up structure with high current drive capability, line driving is facilitated even if bussing techniques are not required. In addition, low current high breakdown PNP input transistors eliminate the design constraints imposed by multiple emitter transistor inputs. This feature allows up to 200 8T26's to be driven on the same bus and also permits interfacing with data sources that cannot sink TTL input currents, particularly MOS.

Applications such as high speed I/O multiplexing, memory busses, MOS interface and various transmission line characteristics will be discussed.

LOGIC DESCRIPTIONS

The 8T26 consists of four driver/receiver pairs together with their enable logic as shown in Figure 1. For maximum versatility bus enable and receiver enable controls are brought out separately and buffered. A "1" on the bus enable input (B/E) allows D_{IN} data to pass through the bus driver and appear inverted at the D_{OUT} terminals. A "0" on the B/E input will force the driver output to the high impedance state and will also disable the PNP input resulting in negligible input current. The receivers are enabled by a "0" on the receiver enable (I/E) allowing data from the bus to appear inverted at the receiver output (R_{OUT}). The receiver may be forced to the high impedance state by a "1" on the I/E terminal, effectively disabling the receiver input and output. For convenience Table 1 summarizes the logic operation of the control lines.

TRUTH TABLE FOR 8T26 CONTROL LINES

TABLE 1		
B/E	I/E	OPERATION
0	0	Driver Disabled, Receiver Enabled
0	1	Driver Disabled, Receiver Disabled
1	0	Driver Enabled, Receiver Enabled
1	1	Driver Enabled, Receiver Disabled

DEVICE CHARACTERISTICS

The 8T26 is a Schottky TTL design that like the 82S MSI series has PNP input transistors. As shown in Figure 2, PNP emitter followers require very little "0" level input current which is specified at max $-200\mu A$. This is significantly lower than that of standard TTL (i.e., 1.6mA) giving the systems designer a great degree of freedom when driving a large number of 8T26 inputs or when interfacing with circuits that have a low drive capability. The maximum "1" level input current is $25\mu A$, a little lower than the $40\mu A$ of standard TTL. In addition the PNP inputs are Schottky-diode clamped to eliminate any negative ringing that may occur in systems usage.

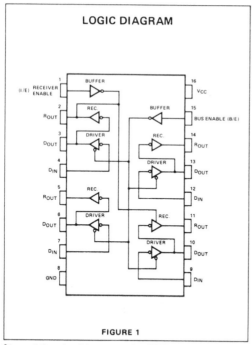

LOGIC DIAGRAM

FIGURE 1

*for uni-directional busses see also 8T09 applications memo

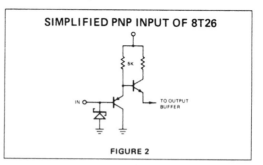

SIMPLIFIED PNP INPUT OF 8T26

FIGURE 2

Fig. 4-60. Data sheet for 8T26. (Courtesy of Signetics, copyright 1974, Sunnyvale, California, Signetics Digital Linear MOS Applications, P. 2–62.)

4-13 PRACTICAL ASPECTS RELATED TO COMBINATIONAL LOGIC DESIGN

Up to this point we have covered a variety of different techniques for arriving at possible implementations for combinational logic circuits. However, little has been said about how to begin specifying the actual hardware for a design. There are many engineers who have technicians who worry about the nitty-gritty aspects of putting a given design into a working hardware system. However, this author feels that digital designers should be familiar with such hardware related information as:

(1) electronic characteristics of the logic families used;
(2) power requirements;
(3) loading fan-out;
(4) logic voltage and current levels specifications and definitions and noise margins;
(5) effect of open inputs and outputs;
(6) propagation delay.

There are many good texts available in which you will find information related to the electronics of the TTL and CMOS gate. This information should be used as a guide to the important aspects related to any electronic logic family as they become available, as they most certainly will. However, in general, the data and application books from the semiconductor distributors are to be considered necessary. These publications help you become familiar with the subtle characteristics related to each logic family. In short, it is intended that this book be augmented by semiconductor data books.

4-14 FAN-IN FAN-OUT

As mentioned above, the particular electronic aspects of logic gates are covered in other sources; however, the concepts of FAN-IN, FAN-OUT, STANDARD LOADS, and propagation delay are important enough and general enough to define and mention at this time.

Consider the "black box" model of the general logic device shown in Figure 4-61.

Definitions:

(1) FAN-IN is a numeric merit figure assigned to a gate that defines the number of *inputs* the *gate* has, that is, a TTL SN7400 two-input NAND gate has a fan-in that equals 2.
(2) FAN-OUT is a numeric merit figure defining the number of STANDARD LOADS a given device output can drive without degrading its operation.

(3) STANDARD LOAD is defined as the load equivalence of a single input stage.

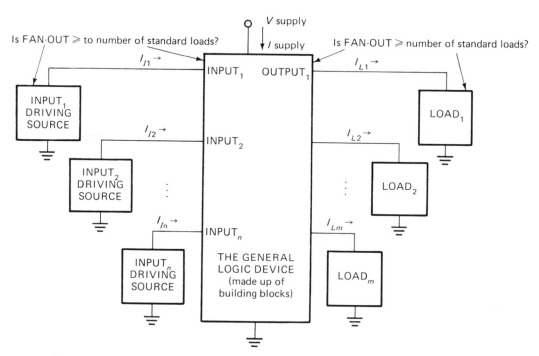

Fig. 4-61. The "black box" model of the general logic device.

Generally speaking, a logic family (TTL, CMOS, etc.) is based on a basic switching circuit configuration that has a particular input stage. This input stage is the stage which interfaces the rest of the device to the outside world (see Figure 4-62). Also, quite often this input stage is joined with other devices as shown in Figure 4-62 to make what is called a building block. This building block then becomes a fundamental module from which higher order integrated circuits are derived. In any case, it is the load of the *interface stage input* that is used to define the loading factor.

In terms of this input stage loading concept, it is possible to define the *loading* of an input for a more complex device. This is done by summing the number of equivalent input stages connected to this input. For example, assume $INPUT_2$ shown in the black box model in Figure 4-61 has four input stage inputs attached to it (that is, internal to the device). We then define the "loading" of this complex device input as *FOUR STANDARD LOADS.* Since any given device *output stage* can only supply or sink a finite amount of current, you must be concerned about the "loading" attached to it.

A word of warning: It is easy to be trapped at times by assuming that each input of a more complex device represents one STANDARD LOAD. This is not always the case, so check the specifications for *all* of your device inputs and outputs to determine STANDARD LOAD equivalence and FAN-OUT capability. For example, the "clock" input (single line) for a SN74LS112 has a *loading factor of 4*. Since the fan-out of a typical 74LSXX gate ≤ 10 standard loads, only two clock inputs can be driven by a standard gate.

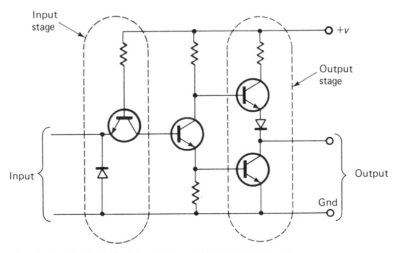

Fig. 4-62. The basic building block of the TTL logic family.

4-15 PROPAGATION DELAY

More will be said about the effects, both negative and positive, of propagation delay throughout this text. However, it is an important specification that sets the speed or high frequency limits for a logic device. Fact has it that the movement of electrons is not instantaneous; quick, yes, but they are slowed, or at least the effects of current flow is slowed, by things like stray capacitance, diffusion, properties of semiconductor material, and inline inductance. *Thus we define PROPAGATION DELAY as the time difference between cause and effect, or, in more specific terms, it is the time difference between the change of an input and the precipitated output change.* For example, see a typical example illustration of propagation delay through an INVERTER as shown in Figure 4-63.

You should always consult the manufacturer's data sheets to determine the "worst case" propagation delay specification and, more importantly, keep a running knowledge of all "ball park timing specs" relative to different logic families for ready reference.

As discussed previously, combinational logic circuits are circuits whose present output conditions are dependent only on the *present* input conditions; in other words, any change in an output variable is strictly dependent on some input change; or any time any given input code is applied to a combinational circuit, the same predetermined output code is always generated. This makes a combinational circuit a basic "look-up" type system in which a prescribed output is generated by the circuit each time a given input code is applied, independent of the timed spaced applications of other different input codes. However, remember the propagation delay and settling time constraints and allow the circuit to adjust to any new input condition. This look-up facet of combinational circuits can be reinforced by remembering that TRUTH-TABLES are used to design combinational circuits, and further by remembering that there are no conditions other than the input conditions considered to specify an output or outputs should several outputs be specified as a function of the same input variables.

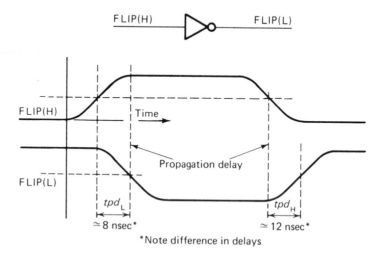

Fig. 4-63. An illustrated example of propagation delay.

switching characteristics at $V_{CC} = 5$ V, $T_A = 25°$C

TYPE	TEST CONDITIONS#	t_{PLH} (ns) Propagation delay time, low-to-high-level output			t_{PHL} (ns) Propagation delay time, high-to-low-level output		
		MIN	TYP	MAX	MIN	TYP	MAX
'00, '10			11	22		7	15
'04, '20	$C_L = 15$ pF, $R_L = 400$ Ω		12	22		8	15
'30			13	22		8	15
'H00			5.9	10		6.2	10
'H04			6	10		6.5	10
'H10	$C_L = 25$ pF, $R_L = 280$ Ω		5.9	10		6.3	10
'H20			6	10		7	10
'H30			6.8	10		8.9	12
'L00, 'L04, 'L10, L20	$C_L = 50$ pF, $R_L = 4$ kΩ		35	60		31	60
'L30			35	60		70	100
'LS00, 'LS04 'LS10, 'LS20	$C_L = 15$ pF, $R_L = 2$ kΩ		9	20		10	20
'LS30			9	20		25	35
'S00, 'S04	$C_L = 15$ pF, $R_L = 280$ Ω	2	3	4.5	2	3	5
'S10, 'S20	$C_L = 50$ pF, $R_L = 280$ Ω		4.5			5	
'S30, 'S133	$C_L = 15$ pF, $R_L = 280$ Ω	2	4	6	2	4.5	7
	$C_L = 50$ pF, $R_L = 280$ Ω		5.5			6.5	

Fig. 4-64. Typical T²L propagation delay schedule. (Courtesy of Texas Instruments, Inc.)

The general model of a combinational circuit including the effects of propagation delay is illustrated in Figure 4-65. Here the output code is specified as a function of the input codes and the propagation delay. This model is made up from ideal gates, those mythical devices without propagation delay and with a lumped time delay element. The output functions $F_1, F_2, \ldots, F_n$ are assumed to respond simultaneously with input changes, and the functions $f_1, f_2, \ldots, f_n$ will *equate* themselves with $F_1, F_2, \ldots, F_n$, respectively, after the specified propagation delays $\Delta t_1, \Delta t_2, \ldots, \Delta t_n$ have elapsed. Because of the inherent differences in the propagation delays $\Delta t_1, \Delta t_2, \ldots, \Delta t_n$, there is some settling time required before the output *code* becomes stable. Considering that the combination of $F_1, F_2, \ldots, F_n$ makes up an N-bit code, this settling time is then equal to the maximum $\Delta t (\Delta t \max)$. Therefore, when you consider a code settling time, you can imagine the output code adjusting to a new input code as a "100 yard dash" where each runner comes in at different times but the race is not over (code stable) until the last runner is in.

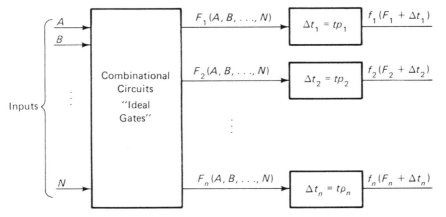

Fig. 4-65. The general model of a combinational circuit including the propagation delay.

The circuit and timing diagrams shown in Figure 4-66 illustrate the effects of propagation delay on a combinational circuit's performance; study it closely. Consider further the circuit shown in Figure 4-67 where f_a and f_b, each having different Δt's, are fed into an OR gate. Again the output function cannot be considered stable until the worst-case delay time has elapsed, including the delay of the combining function, in this case the OR gate. It is therefore standard to consider the worst-case delay path as the limiting factor of the response time of a combinational circuit, and it will be a relatively easy task to spot these worst-case situations by sight alone if you recognize their existence. Consult the data sheets for the logic family you are designing around and use the worst-case conditions specified to help you make the critical decisions regarding response time. An example of a data sheet specification of propagation delay is shown in Figure 4-64. This tabulation is a typical propagation delay schedule for some of the TTL logic gates. Pay special attention to the difference in times between the low-to-high and high-to low propagation true specifications. Note that the worst case low-to-high transition timing for the 7404 is 22 nsec, while the worst case high-to-low transition is 15 nsec.

Thus to here we have separately demonstrated some of the effects of propagation delay with AND and OR hardware functions. Now we should consider the combined effect this delay has on the performance of a two-level (AND/OR) combinational circuit, in short, what effects are derived from combining the circuit in Figure 4-66 with the OR operation in Figure 4-67. This study will illustrate that undesirable *transient output conditions* can be generated without proper design. The analysis of the effects of propagation delay on two-level or more combinational circuits is covered by several important exercises.

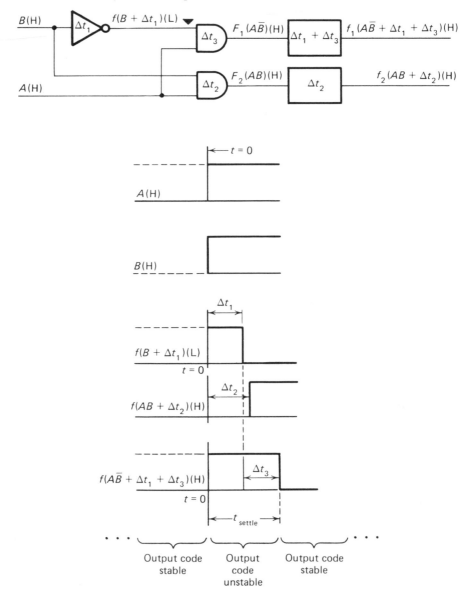

Fig. 4-66. An illustration of the effects of propagation delay.

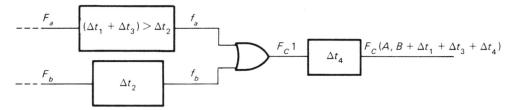

Fig. 4-67. An illustration of the ORing of signals with unequal propagation delays.

It might seem that we are belaboring the timing aspects related to combinational logic (what's a nanosecond or two?), but this author has witnessed many cases where ill-timing design or total disregard for timing considerations has dealt with untold grief, particularly when dealing with sequential circuits. Therefore, be certain *not* to take propagation delay constraints lightly.

4-16 SUMMARY

In this chapter we have covered a good deal related to the practical application of integrated circuit devices, including the use of MSI decoders and multiplexers as devices to be used to implement random logic requirements. Further, we have introduced a technique for utilizing AOI, EXOR, and NEXOR gates for random logic implementation. Along with this we have treated the practical aspects of wired logic, fan-out, and propagation delay.

BIBLIOGRAPHY

1. BLAKESLEE, THOMAS R. *Digital Design with Standard MSI and LSI*. New York: Wiley, 1975.

2. CARR, W. N, and MIZE, J. P *MOS/LSI Design and Application*. New York: McGraw-Hill, 1972.

3. FEMLING, DON. Enhancement of Modular Design Capability by Use of Tri-State Logic. *Computer Design*, 10:6 (1971), 59–64.

4. FRONEK, DONALD K. Ring Map Minimizing Logic Circuit. *Electronic Design*, **17** (1972).

5. KOHONEN, T. *Digital Circuits and Devices*. Englewood Cliffs, N. J.: Prentice-Hall, 1972.

6. LEE, SAMUEL C. *Digital Circuits and Logic Design*. Englewood Cliffs, New Jersey: Prentice-Hall, 1976.

7. MCCLUSKEY, E. J. *Introduction to the Theory of Switching Circuits*. New York: McGraw-Hill, 1965.

8. MANO, M. MORRIS. *Computer Logic Design*. Englewood Cliffs, New Jersey: Prentice-Hall, 1972.

9. NAGLE, H. TROY, JR., CARROL, B. D., and IRWIN, J. DAVID. *An Introduction to Computer Logic*. Englewood Cliffs, N. J.: Prentice-Hall, 1975.

10. PRIEL, URY. Take a Look Inside the TTL IC. *Electronic Design*, **8** (1971).

11. ROTH, CHARLES H., JR. *Fundamentals of Logic Design*. St. Paul, Minn.: West, 1975.

12. SHEETS, JOHN. Three State Switching Brings Wired-OR to TTL. *Electronics*, 43:19 (1970), 78–84.

13. *Signetics Digital Linear MOS Data Book*. Sunnyvale, Ca. Signetics Corporation, 1974.

14. *The TTL Data Book for Design Engineers*, 2nd ed. Dallas Texas Instruments, Incorporated, 1976.

15. WICKES, WILLIAM E. *Logic Design with Integrated Circuits*. New York: Wiley, 1968.

PROBLEMS AND EXERCISES

It is intended that full design processes be carried out on the problems of this set unless otherwise specified. This includes schematic drawings in mixed logic and polarized mnemonic notation.

4-1. Using Figures 4-5 and 4-6 as references:
  (a) Show that the full adder circuit can be generalized as the ith stage of a cascaded series of adders as:

$$\text{sum}_i = (A_i \oplus B_i) \oplus C_{i-1}$$
$$\text{Carryout}_i = C_i = A_i B_i + C_{i-1}(A_i \oplus B_i)$$

  where C_{i-1} is defined as the carryout from the preceding stage.
  (b) Now, using the TRUTH-TABLE for a full adder, show that a carryout is ASSERTED under distinct conditions.
   (1) A carryout is *generated* by the ith stage as the result of adding A_i and B_i together.
   (2) A carryout is to be *propagated* through the ith stage. In short, effectively no carry is generated in the ith stage. The carryin is merely propagated to the carryout.
  (c) Now show that a carry is generated by

$$CG_i = A_i \cdot B_i$$

  and a carry is propagated by

$$CP_i = A_i \oplus B_i$$

  Therefore,

$$\text{Sum}_i = CP_i \oplus C_{i-1}$$

  ∴ In general

$$\text{Sum}_i = CP_i \oplus C_{i-1}$$
$$C_i = CG_i + C_{i-1}(CP_i)$$

  (d) Now, using this information, design a four-bit ADDER circuit which minimizes the time necessary for the total sum to become valid, that is, design a four-bit ADDER with CARRY-LOOK-AHEAD over the four bits. Compare your answer with the SN74283 shown in Figure 4-7.

4-2. Design a four-bit-nibble control system that performs the bit manipulation defined in the control table (Figure P4-1).

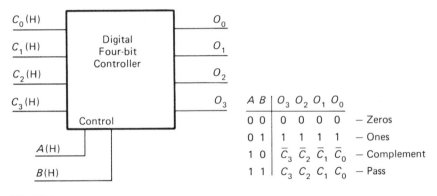

A B	O_3 O_2 O_1 O_0	
0 0	0 0 0 0	— Zeros
0 1	1 1 1 1	— Ones
1 0	$\bar{C}_3$ $\bar{C}_2$ $\bar{C}_1$ $\bar{C}_0$	— Complement
1 1	C_3 C_2 C_1 C_0	— Pass

Fig. P4-1.

4-3. Design a combinational circuit that will compare two bits A and B and produce one of three outputs:

$$A > B$$
$$A = B$$
$$A < B$$

This circuit must be designed such that it can be used as a module in a circuit which compares the relative magnitude of two eight-bit words (i.e., it must be modular so that it can be cascaded). Illustrate the interconnection of your modules.

4-4. The following problem is a modular design problem. You are to design a cascadable module defined as in Figure P4-2.

Binary code for $0_1 0_2 0_3$:
  0 $F_1 = A, F_2 = B$
  1 $F_1 = \bar{A}, F_2 = \bar{B}$
  2 $F_1 = A$ plus $B, F_2 = $ CARRY OUT
  3 $F_1 = A + B, F_2 = A \cdot B$
  4 $F_1 = \bar{A} \cdot B, F_2 = A \cdot \bar{B}$
  5 $F_1 = \bar{A} + B, F_2 = A + \bar{B}$
  6 $F_1 = A \otimes B, F_2 = A \odot B$
  7 $F_1 = 0, F_2 = 0$

Design this module so that it will perform the desired ALU functions of two N-bit words (i.e., make it modular).

Fig. P4-2.

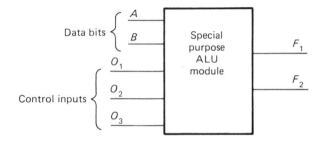

4-5. Show how the half subtractor shown in Figure 4-8 can quickly be modified to convert it into a controllable ADDER-SUBTRACTOR using a single control line.

4-6. Design a full subtractor equivalent to the full ADDER shown in Figure 4-5.

4-7. Convert the full ADDER shown in Figure 4-5 into a controllable ADDER/SUBTRACTOR.

4-8. Design a controlled 2's complement four-bit ADDER/SUBTRACTOR using 1-74283, four EXOR gates and one inverter. Show that your circuit can be slightly modified to make a 1's complement ADDER/SUBTRACTOR.

4-9. Design a circuit using 74283 ADDERS that will perform two-digit BCD ADDITION. (*Hint:* $(A)_{BCD}+(B)_{BCD}=(C)_{BCD}$ if carryout results. Add $(0110)_2$ to sum and send carry to next ADDER. Show how your circuit can be extended to an N-digit BCD ADDER.)

4-10. Design a circuit using a 74283 that will perform two-digit NBCD subtraction. (*Hint:* Develop a circuit (another 74283) which yields the 9's complement and then ADD. Show how your circuit can be extended to an N-digit subtractor.)

4-11. Show design of a four-bit magnitude comparator circuit using the 74283 ADDER.

4-12. Show how two SN74283's can be used to make an eight-bit magnitude comparator.

4-13. (a) Design a module that will check for even or odd parity on two input bits.
(b) Extend your design such that it can be cascaded to check the parity over an eight-bit word.

4-14. Design a four-bit parity checker/generator, that is, a circuit that can be used to check parity over a five-bit word as well as generate the parity bit over a four-bit word.

4-15. Using the technique outlined in Section 4-5.1, implement the problem specified in Figure 3-15(a).

(a) Using a 16-to-1 multiplexer.
(b) Using an 8-to-1 multiplexer.
(c) Compare your package count to the gate level implementation of the same problem.

4-16. (a) Using 8-to-1 multiplexers, implement the problems specified for Problem 3-9.
(b) Compare the package count with the gate level implementation.

4-17. (a) Using 16-to-1 multiplexers, implement the problem specified in Problem 3-11.
(b) Compare your package count with the gate level implementation.

4-18. Implement the following functions of four variables using eight-input multiplexers. (*Hint:* Partition your TRUTH-TABLE and use MEV techniques. Some residue gates may be needed.)

(a) $F(A,B,C,D)=\Sigma m(0,1,3,6,8,15)$; A and B are ASSERTED LOW
C and D are ASSERTED HIGH
(b) $F(A,B,C,D,RDY,CLR)=\bar{A}\,\bar{B}\bar{C}\bar{D}\cdot RDY+\bar{A}\,\bar{B}CD+\bar{A}\,BC\bar{D}+\bar{A}\,B\bar{C}D+\bar{A}\,BC\bar{D}$
$+A\bar{B}\bar{C}D\cdot RDY+AB\bar{C}D+ABCD\cdot CLR$
A,C,RDY are ASSERTED HIGH
B,D,CLR are ASSERTED LOW.

4-19. Implement a gray code to BCD converter as defined by the following TRUTH-TABLE:

Inputs				Outputs			
A	B	C	D	F_1	F_2	F_3	F_4
0	0	0	0	0	0	0	0
0	0	0	1	0	0	0	1
0	0	1	1	0	0	1	0
0	0	1	0	0	0	1	1
0	1	1	0	0	1	0	0
0	1	1	1	0	1	0	1
0	1	0	1	0	1	1	0
0	1	0	0	0	1	1	1
1	1	0	0	1	0	0	0
1	1	0	1	1	0	0	1

(a) Use two dual four-input multiplexers and residue gates.
(b) Use four eight-input multiplexers.
(c) Use a quad two-input multiplexer and residue gates.
(d) Which implementation requires the smallest number of IC packages?

4-20. Treat the expressions specified in Problem 3-8 as a multiple output (6) specification for the variables A, B, C. Implement these as a system of outputs using a 3-to-8 decoder (74LS138) and an assortment of NAND gates.

4-21. Implement the following functions using one 74154 (4-to-16 decoder with LOW ASSERTED outputs).
(a) $F_1(A, B, C, D) = \Sigma(0, 1, 4, 7, 9, 12, 14)$
(b) $F_2(A, B, C, D) = \Sigma(0, 1, 2, 3)$

4-22. Implement the following Boolean functions using only one 7442 (BCD to decimal decoder with LOW ASSERTED outputs) and some extra gates (ANDing and ORing functions).
(a) $F_1(A, B, C) = AB\bar{C} + A\bar{B} + \bar{B}C$
(b) $F_2(A, B, C) = \bar{A}\bar{B} + AB$
(c) $F_3(A, B, C, D) = ABC + A\bar{B}C\bar{D} + \bar{A}B\bar{C}D + \bar{A}\bar{B}CD$
Assume all function outputs are to be ASSERTED HIGH with A and B ASSERTED LOW and C and D ASSERTED HIGH.

4-23. Use a 3-to-8 (74138) decoder with other combinational logic to implement the following functions shown in the K-maps. GO and TEST are ASSERTED HIGH with STOP ASSERTED LOW. See Figure P4-3.

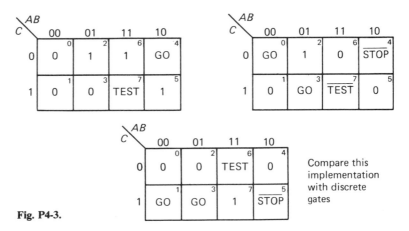

Fig. P4-3.

4-24. (a) Design a TRUTH-TABLE that defines a three-input priority encoder. Assume the A input has a priority of 3, the B input has a priority of 2, and the C input has a priority of 1. The device is to have an INACTIVE output, an output that is to indicate the device is not being used to prioritize the inputs.

(b) Assume the inputs and outputs are all ASSERTED HIGH except INACTIVE. Implement the device with a 74138 (3-to-8) decoder and other logic you may need. Avoid the use of inverters if possible.

(c) Implement the device with a 74153 (4-to-1) MUX.

(d) Compare the package count and other virtues/drawbacks of each of your designs.

4-25. The following problem is an example of a particular problem in which one does not want to consider an exhaustive TRUTH-TABLE approach.

(a) Design a seven-line priority encoder with inputs to be ASSERTED LOW. This device is to have an ENABLE input ASSERTED LOW. The outputs are to be ASSERTED HIGH and represent the binary code of the highest ASSERTED input at any point in time. Also, this encoder is to have an inactive output ASSERTED LOW that indicates *no* input is ASSERTED. The device model is as shown in Figure P4-4.

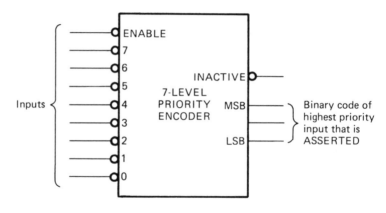

Fig. P4-4.

(b) Illustrate how you can use two of these priority encoders to realize a 16-level priority encoder.

(c) Illustrate how you can use four of these priority encoders to realize a 32-level priority encoder.

4-26. Suppose you are given a plastic credit card/badge reader to design. This card reader is to be designed such that it will yield a single output when a card with five rows of hole patterns each row, having ten holes possible in each row. (See Figure P4-5.) Assume the optoelectronic sensors are in proper position for reading one row at a time. Outputs of the sensors are ASSERTED LOW. Your circuit is to indicate a row is under the sensors and generate a four-bit code word representative of the hole pattern of that row using a 74147 priority encoder.

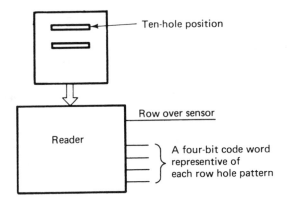

Fig. P4-5.

4-27. Design a priority multiplexer that can be used to connect the appropriate output line (OA, OB, OC, OD) from any one of four devices to a system output line (OUTPUT) subject to the following priority schedule (see Figure P4-6):

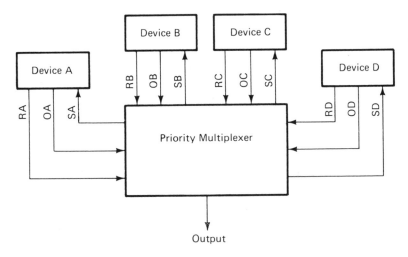

Fig. P4-6.

> Device A—1st (highest priority)
> Device B—2nd
> Device C—3rd
> Device D—4th (lowest priority)

Each device also has request line (RA, RB, RC, RD) that is asserted when the system output line is requested by that device. The priority multiplexer must also return a signal to each device (SA, SB, SC, SD) indicating whether the device request was accepted. These signals should be asserted only if a request has been received from the device and the device output has been connected to the system output. Assume all input signals to the multiplexer are ASSERTED HIGH and output signals from the multiplexer are ASSERTED LOW. You can use standard multiplexers or decoders and any standard logic gates (AND, OR, NAND, NOR). Your design should use a minimum number of inverters.

4-28. The maps in Figure P4-7 have built-in EXOR implementations. Read these maps with this in mind and illustrate your circuits.

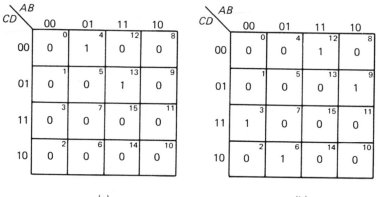

(a)   (b)

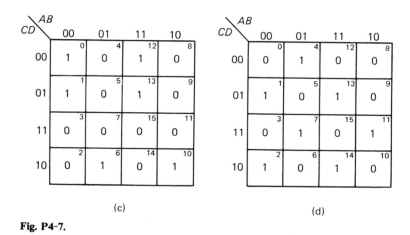

(c)   (d)

Fig. P4-7.

4-29. Re-work Problem 3-44 with the EXOR map technique in mind.

4-30. The map in Figure P4-8 has been modified by simply interchanging the last two rows and columns ($11 \rightleftarrows 10$). By doing this, EXOR and EXNOR functions can be readily recognized. You are to work up a map-reading algorithm that can be used to read EXOR and EXNOR functions directly.

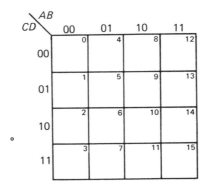

Fig. P4-8.

4-31. You are given an A-O-I with an expander input x and x', as shown in Figure P4-9, where

$$F(L) = (AB + CD + X)(L)$$
$$X(H) = (Y \cdot Z \cdot W \cdot S)(H)$$

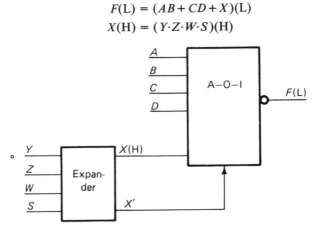

Fig. P4-9.

Use this gate and others if necessary to implement the following:
(a) $(\overline{A}\,\overline{B} + CD)(L)$
(b) $(\overline{G}\,\overline{H} + IJ + KL\overline{M})(L)$
(c) $[GH + IJ + KL(\overline{M} + N)](L)$
(d) $(\overline{A}\,\overline{B} + AB + A\overline{C})(H)$
Assume all inputs are double rail.

4-32. You are to determine the PULL-UP RESISTOR SIZE for a bus wire that has ten open-collector (TTL) outputs and 15 TTL inputs. Use the data for current voltages found in Section 4-11. $V_{cc} = 5$ volts.

4-33. Determine the maximum number of open collector outputs (TTL) that can be tied to a single bus wire which drives 10 other inputs (TTL). Find both n and the value of R_{pullup}.

4-34. Make a comparison between open collector and tri-state bus systems. Consider loading, speed, and so forth.

4-35. Define fan-out, fan-in, and standard load.

4-36. Define propagation delay.

4-37. Given the network in Figure P4-10, what is the worst case propagation delay?

$$\Delta t_1 = 10 \text{ nsec}$$
$$\Delta t_2 = 20 \text{ nsec}$$
$$\Delta t_3 = 25 \text{ nsec}$$
$$\Delta t_4 = 10 \text{ nsec}$$

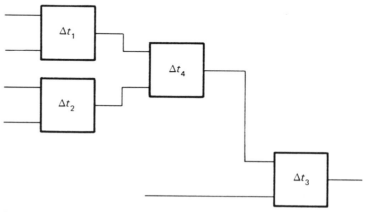

Fig. P4-10.

4-38. Calculate the worst case propagation delay for your implementation of Problem 3-36. Use the worst case propagation delay specification for the devices you choose to use. Consult the manufacturer's data book to obtain this data.

4-39. Calculate the worst case propagation delay for the ADD time for the design called in Problem 4-1. Assume you are implementing your design with the Schottky TTL family.

CHAPTER **5**

SEQUENTIAL MACHINE FUNDAMENTALS

5-1 INTRODUCTION

Thus far our studies have been directed toward combinational circuit design and analysis. Though very important to digital system design, combinational aspects constitute only a portion of digital design. The other major segment of logic design, as you might have surmised from the title, is SEQUENTIAL CIRCUIT design and analysis. Figure 5-1 shows the related divisions in digital system design. This illustration differentiates the major divisions in logic design, and indicates that there is a definite difference between combinational and sequential circuits. However, sequential circuit design depends to a large extent on combinational techniques; this is demonstrated throughout the next six chapters.

A good deal of effort is put forth in this chapter to familiarize you with the underlying concepts related to designing sequential circuits. The chapter covers the following: needs for sequential circuits, the definition of a sequential circuit, combinational aspects of sequential machines, sequential circuit models, distinction between asynchronous and synchronous machines, binary cells, Flip-Flop models, design of Flip-Flops, and other fundamental concepts that are important to a good understanding of sequential circuits.

It is also interesting to note in Figure 5-1 that multiple-valued logic directly parallels the binary logic practices studied thus far. In short, multiple-valued logic differs from binary logic in that any given variable can take on more than *two* values.

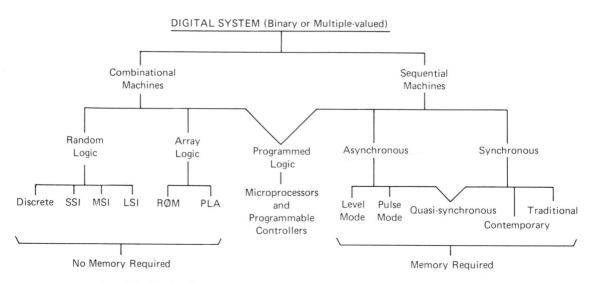

Fig. 5-1. The breakdown and relations of logic design.

5-2 THE NEED FOR SEQUENTIAL CIRCUITS

There are many and varied problems to which digital techniques can be applied. One of the more important applications is "control," where digital signals are received and interpreted by a digital system and control outputs are generated in accordance with the *sequence* in which the input signals are received. Applications such as these cannot be satisfied using a combinational logic system. These applications require some system that generates control outputs, which are a function of the present input conditions and, just as important, the past history of these inputs. The past history of the inputs of a controlled system is provided by a *feedback* path from the output back to the input. A model of a controlled system with feedback is shown in Figure 5-2. By using this feedback, *ideally the output of a controlled system at some time t_0 is the resultant of both the input conditions at t_0, combined with all the input conditions leading up to t_0.* In other words, the output of a controlled system at any time is what it is not only because of the present input but also because of the series of input conditions that have prevailed previous to this time.

We can see by examining Figure 5-2 that the present inputs and outputs are transformed and mixed to form the modified or controlled inputs for the controlled system. The manner in which these signals are mixed, coupled with the response (input/output relationship) of the *controlled system*, determines to what degree the system is actually controlled. Using this general model we can generate the traditional *linear* feedback control system models shown in Figures 5-3(a) and 5-3(b).

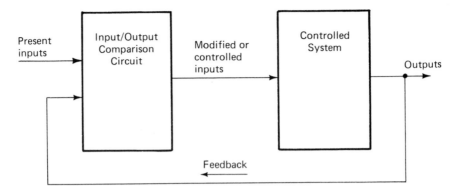

Fig. 5-2. The general model for a controlled system.

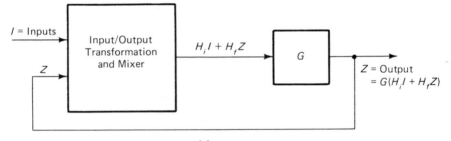

(a)

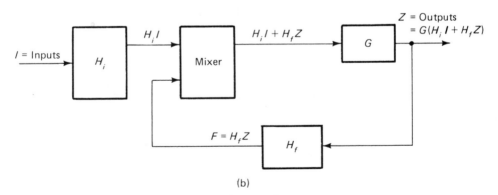

(b)

Fig. 5-3. Traditional models for a simple linear control system.

The following mathematical relationship can be derived from these models:

$$Z = G(H_iI + H_fZ) = GH_iI + GH_fZ \qquad (1)$$

Thus the output (Z) at any point in time is a function of its present inputs $(H_i I)$ as well as its present outputs $(H_f Z)$. Equation (1), after some further mathematical manipulation, can be represented in its traditional form:

$$Z = \frac{GH_i I}{1 - H_f G} \qquad (2)$$

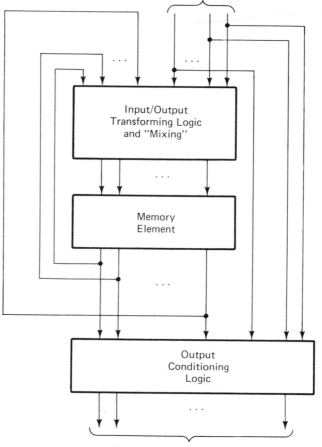

Fig. 5-4 The general model for a controlled digital system, or a sequential machine, or a finite machine.

Using a parallel thought process, we can generate the feedback controlled digital or discrete system model shown in Figure 5-4. In this diagram we see that the memory element, in essence, is the controlled system, and for now we will concentrate on this model.* This model has basic importance and we will refer to

---

*The memory element in this system is used to store information related to the past history of the inputs.

it as a SEQUENTIAL MACHINE or a FINITE-STATE MACHINE (FSM). It is shown in later chapters that a controlled system such as the one in Figure 5-4 can control yet another system. Figure 5-5 illustrates this. Note that in Figure 5-5 the controlled memory element system that we call a sequential machine is coupled with yet a larger controlled system. This particular system is analogous to the multiple-loop linear control system studied in a linear control discipline.

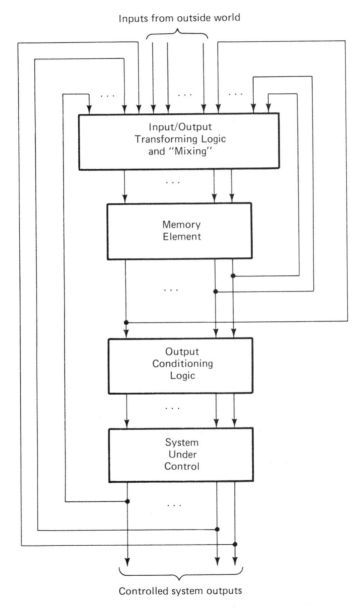

Fig. 5-5. A higher order digital control system.

These general digital models can be readily applied to traditional control problems as well as to many other algorithmic or sequential problems. The solution of algorithmic or sequential problems requires that before a desired single output or output sequence can be generated, the processing system must be plied with an appropriate and predesigned set of input conditions in some sequential manner, with time being a variable. Here again the processing system must generate output sequences in accordance with some function of the past history of the inputs and the present input conditions. It should be evident from our studies that combinational circuits cannot provide "past history" information, and therefore another dimension must be added to our logic design capabilities.

As a result of this, the study of sequential machines or finite-state machines is an important endeavor. It is hoped that you will find the study of sequential design to be fun and challenging. In presenting the sequential machine, the function of each block of the model shown in Figure 5-4 is covered in depth.

5-3 BASIC ARCHITECTURAL DISTINCTIONS BETWEEN COMBINATIONAL AND SEQUENTIAL CIRCUITS

Turn your attention to Figures 4-65 and 5-4 and note the two basic architectural differences between combinational and sequential circuits. First it should be noticed in Figure 5-4 that a MEMORY element is added to an otherwise combinational circuit. Second, it should be noticed that the outputs of this so-called memory element are fedback into the same logic block as the inputs from the OUTSIDE WORLD. From this we generally categorize the sequential system or circuit by the existence of two properties.

Sequential Properties:

(1) The system must have some memory capability or memory element.
(2) The system must have at least one feedback path from the memory element to the system inputs.

Likewise, we categorize the combinational circuit by the existence of two similar properties.

Combinational Properties:

(1) The output of the system must be strictly a function of the inputs.
(2) No feedback path can exist from the output to the input.

A word of warning: The two basic identifying properties for sequential circuits are necessary but they are not sufficient. It will be found later that sequential circuits all have a common basic *operational* property as well as common architectural properties. This common operational property is *that sequential circuits are cyclic in nature as the name suggests*, and if you wait long enough making operational observations of a truly sequential machine, you will observe that it repeats operations over and over again.

A sequential machine can be defined in esoteric terms as well as practical terms. The practical definition of a sequential machine is: *A circuit having the two basic sequential properties described above, and in addition to these properties it must, under an input condition control, exhibit a "cyclic" nature.* A finite-state machine is defined as: *A sequential circuit that has some practical bounds governing the number of different conditions (STATES) in which a sequential machine can reside.* To illustrate the difference between a general sequential machine and a finite-state machine, consider the following example.

> *EXAMPLE 5-1:* A programmable digital computer is by definition a sequential machine. However, given a modest 16-bit mini-computer with 4096 16-bit words of memory, it can be shown that even though it is sequential the number of states in which this machine can reside is *for practical purposes not finite.* If we imagine all 4096 memory locations stretched out into a single string, we see that there exist 65536 variables for a TRUTH-TABLE. A TRUTH-TABLE with 65536 input variables will have 2^{65536} rows! This means that the mini-computer can take on $2^{65536} = 10^{19728}$ different states. Changing these states at the rate of 1 per microsecond, it would take 3.17×10^{19714} years to step that computer through every possible condition. Therefore, normally a computer is not defined as a finite-state machine, though it is a sequential machine.

However, in dealing with finite-state sequential machines, it is possible to design, accidentally or not, circuits which have the two basic architectural properties mentioned above, and yet they are not sequential (cyclic) in nature, for they can and will hang-up so to speak, and will not cycle under any input condition. Anyone who has programmed a computer using an ill-formatted "Do-loop" can identify with a hang-up. There is just no way for an output to be generated while the computer is endlessly incrementing and decrementing itself into an operator's intervention. More will be said concerning *hardware* hang-ups in the next chapter.

5-4 THE CONCEPT OF MEMORY

Before launching into the effects derived from feedback coupled with memory and combinational circuits, consider the concept of MEMORY, which Figure 5-4 illustrates as an essential element of sequential circuits and digital systems in general.

Examining the memory unit illustrated in Figure 5-4, you should have the illusion that this unit is a multiple-input device, and that the binary value of the signal on each one of these inputs makes up a code when all are considered together. Now consider that this memory element can be directed or commanded to *store this input code and transfer this code to its outputs at any given time it is deemed desirable, and once this command is given and the storing and transfer of the input code is completed, no input change can alter the outputs of the memory until the command is issued again.*

Herein lies the fundamental concept of memory: that memory is some medium in which the binary values of 0 or 1 can be stored or retained until commanded to replace its present contents with some new value. In a sense, a 0 or 1 is stored in some medium which by some translation or manipulation can be converted into a voltage level. For instance, an output may go to a high voltage range when a 1 is stored, or a magnetic medium can be polarized in some manner so that a voltage level can be generated in a reading operation. At any rate, it will be assumed that the storing process will be one of "locking a voltage level" and associating that level with a 1 or 0.

"Memory" is a word that is used extensively in digital circles. We hear various terms such as: Random-Access-Memories (RAMS), Read-Only-Memories (ROMS), Programmable-Read-Only-Memories (PROMS), Read-Mostly-Memories (RMMS), Content-Addressable-Memories (CAMS), Sequential-Accessed-Memory (SAMS), Erasable-Programmable-Read-Only-Memory (EPROMS), and various other acronyms associated with memory types. We sometimes hear of the Write-Only-Memory (WOM), the humorous spoof memory long heralded for its boundless uselessness. We cover the ROM, PROM, and RMM in Chapter 8 and we find them to be nothing more than "array"-type combinational circuits.

However, the RAMS, SAMS, and CAMS fall into a READ/WRITE class of memory that is generally more complex. These complex memory units, the kind which are found in computers, are quite general in their configurations and for the most part are a multiple-location type configured from arrays of "BINARY CELLS." Each BINARY CELL is a small sequential circuit that has the capacity of storing one bit, locking either a high voltage *or* a low voltage upon command. These "cells" are generally arranged into commonly gated groups which make up "registers" and each register becomes a word location in memory. These registers are combined with combinational logic for steering the input codes to proper "memory locations" (registers) and also for directing the stored information to the common output terminals. In other words, the combinational logic is added to address (locate) a location (register) and to route incoming data to that location for storage or to connect the output of an addressed location (register) to the output terminals.* These multiple-location memories, though interesting, are not generally the type found (although they could be) in a typical small scale sequential circuit. However, the type of memory found in the sequential circuits covered in this text have something in common with the more complex array-type memory, and that is that they are generally made from single location arrays of "BINARY CELLS."

---

*A note of general interest is that when a group of bits (word) is stored in memory, the process is referred to as "WRITING IN MEMORY." When a group of bits (word) is located and taken from memory, the process is referred to as "READING FROM MEMORY."

5-5 THE BINARY CELL

The binary cell, as mentioned above, is the fundamental building block of memory and it can be fabricated from a number of manufacturing processes such as: bipolar, MOS, and other semiconductor processes, as well as made from magnetic materials such as ferrite cores and magnetic bubbles. However, independent of the manufacturing process involved in generating the binary cell, its purpose and fundamental operation remains the same—it is meant to store one bit of binary information and it must be SET to store a 1 and RESET to store a 0.

Remembering that binary cells differ in construction but are identical in functional properties, a general symbology for the cell is shown in Figures 5-6(a) and 5-6(b). The circuits in Figure 5-6 are referred to as the *cross-coupled-NAND* gate cell and the *cross-coupled-NOR* gate cell. Examining these cross-coupled gate cells shows that they have the basic property preserved for sequential circuit, which is feedback (see Figure 5-8). The memory element is not at all obvious unless you understand that the lumped propagation delay of the gates (a) and (b) provide "temporary memory." This concept of using propagation delay to simulate memory is the main subject treated later in Chapter 10 dealing with asynchronous circuits. For the time being, take it on faith that the "basic cell" is the most rudimentary of all memory elements, and from this bit of faith we will build the concepts on which sequential circuits are predicated.

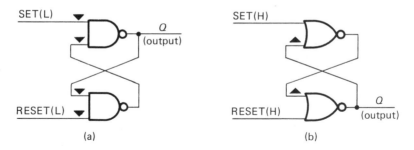

Fig. 5-6. (a) The cross-coupled-NAND gate cell. (b) The cross-coupled-NOR gate cell.

It is believed that a more conceptual picture of the operation of these cells can be obtained by re-drawing the configuration, as shown in Figure 5-7, which will be the standard configuration used throughout this text. Also, it should be noted that these configurations are drawn in a polarized-mnemonic or mixed logic format.

Consider Figure 5-7(a). Let us develop the memory operation of the cell. We see that if the SET INPUT is ASSERTED *and* the RESET line is NOT-ASSERTED, Q(H) will go to an ASSERTED condition. This ASSERTED condition on Q(H), together with the $\overline{\text{RESET}}$ condition, drives Q(L) to its ASSERTED condition, which comes back around and reinforces the SET condition. Once this reinforcement has taken place, the SET condition can be removed and the circuit will remain stable. Hence, the cell is "loaded" with the binary bit 1. Once this 1 is loaded, repeated SET operations have no effect. However, if a RESET operation is ASSERTED and the SET operation is NOT-ASSERTED, Q(L) goes to its NOT-ASSERTED condition which drives Q(H) to its NOT-ASSERTED condition. When Q(H) falls to its NOT-ASSERTED condition, it comes back around and reinforces the RESET condition. Once this reinforcement takes place, the RESET condition can be removed and the circuit will remain stable. Hence the cell is loaded with the binary bit 0. Once the cell is loaded with the binary bit 0, repeated RESET operations have no effect. Now you should be able to see the basic memory operation of the cell.

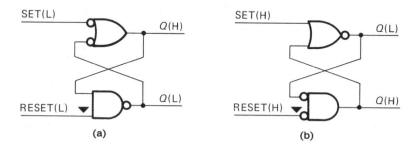

Fig. 5-7. (a) The cross-coupled-NAND cell re-drawn in a polarized mnemonic format to better illustrate basic operation. (b) The cross-coupled-NOR cell re-drawn in a polarized mnemonic format to better illustrate basic operation.

Let us now formally define the SET and RESET operations that are fundamental to the further understanding of the cell's operations.

When the SET operation is ASSERTED, the output defined as Q(H) will be driven to an ASSERTED condition.

When the RESET operation is ASSERTED, the output defined as Q(H) will be driven to its NOT-ASSERTED condition.

More specifically, when working with an electronic logic family, for example TTL, a SET drives Q(H) to a high voltage and a RESET drives Q(H) to a low voltage. It is also interesting to note that the output defined as Q(L) is the complement of Q(H), indicating that a SET operation drives Q(L) to its ASSERTED condition (low); likewise the RESET operation drives Q(L) to its NOT-ASSERTED condition (high), subject to one restriction. That restriction is that the conditions related to Q(L) above are valid if and only if both a SET and RESET operation *are not* ASSERTED simultaneously.

Examining the cell more closely in order to gain some insight into its actual operation, first consider the circuit for the NAND cell re-drawn in Figure 5-8, which better illustrates the logic expression for Q(H). We see that:

$$Q(H) = \left[SET + \overline{RESET} \cdot Q \right](H) \tag{3}$$

$$Q(L) = (Q \cdot \overline{RESET})(L) \tag{4}$$

It should be noted that Eq. (3) is strikingly similar to the equation defining the output for a linear control system [Eq. (1)]:

$$Z = GH_I I + GH_F Z$$

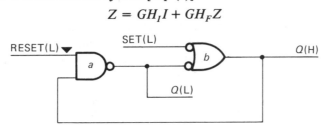

Fig. 5-8. The cross-coupled-NAND cell drawn to better identify the single feedback path and to aid in writing the Boolean expression for Q(H).

This similarity supports the sequential nature of the binary cell and should give added insight into the operation of this basic circuit.

Now look at these expressions in a TRUTH-TABLE as shown in Figure 5-9. In the TRUTH-TABLE it is assumed that the SET and RESET functions remain static for each entry. Remembering that the entries 1 and 0 represent ASSERTED and NOT-ASSERTED, we see in this TRUTH-TABLE that Q(L) is ASSERTED for all the conditions of SET, RESET, and Q that Q(H) is ASSERTED, *except* where SET and RESET are ASSERTED at the same time. In other words, the final value of Q(L) is LOW for all conditions where the final value of Q(H) is HIGH except for the last two entries, where *both* are *HIGH*. This feature can lead to some problems if not properly understood. Note that if the SET and RESET inputs are ASSERTED simultaneously, the outputs are completely defined; both are HIGH. However, when both are released simultaneously, the final output from this action is *not* predictable because of the indeterminability of the propagation delays. To illustrate this indeterminable condition, consider Figure 5-10, where both the SET and RESET inputs are driven from a common source SIG(L).

	SET	RESET	Q	$(\overline{RESET \cdot Q})$(L)	$(\overline{SET + RESET\, Q})$(H)	
0	0	0	0	$1 \cdot 0 = 0$	$0 + 0 = 0$	left alone
1	0	0	1	$1 \cdot 1 = 1$	$0 + 1 = 1$	
2	0	1	0	$0 \cdot 0 = 0$	$0 + 0 = 0$	RESET operation
3	0	1	1	$0 \cdot 1 = 0$	$0 + 0 = 0$	
4	1	0	0	$1 \cdot 0 = 0 \rightarrow 1$	$1 + 0 = 1$	SET operation
5	1	0	1	$1 \cdot 1 = 1$	$1 + 1 = 1$	
6	1	1	0	$0 \cdot 0 = 0$	$1 + 0 = 1$	don't do
7	1	1	1	$0 \cdot 1 = 0$	$1 + 0 = 1$	

Fig. 5-9. A TRUTH-TABLE illustrating the comparison between Q(H) and Q(L) under different static, SET, and RESET conditions.

We see in Figure 5-10 that the final state of the output condition of a cell is a direct function of the propagation delay of the gates used to implement it. In one case where gate b has a greater propagation delay than gate a, the output state after a simultaneous release of a SET and RESET operation is Q(H) HIGH and Q(L) LOW. On the other hand, if the propagation delay of gate b is less than gate a, the final state is Q(H) LOW and Q(L) HIGH. From a practical point of view, it is nearly impossible to select gates in order to force a desired outcome, since typically the rise and fall propagation delay differ randomly from one gate to the next. Further, the propagation delay of a piece of wire used in making connections for a cell will vary with the length of the wire, further complicating the picture.

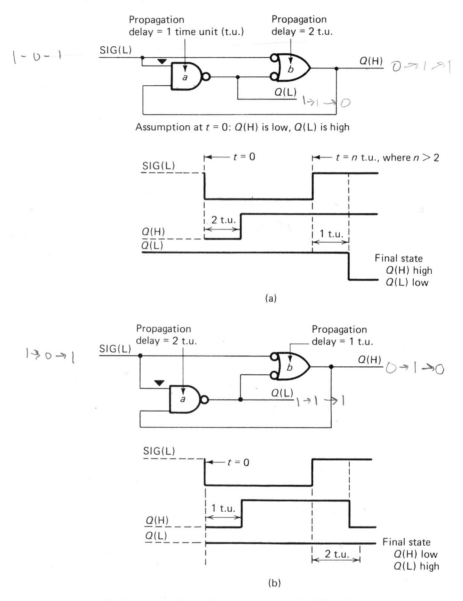

Fig. 5-10. An illustration of the indeterminability of the output of a cell after receiving a simultaneous SET and RESET.

Because of all this, it is generally understood that the condition of a simultaneous SET and RESET operation is to be treated as a condition that should *never be exercised*, that is, a $\emptyset$ condition.

Note that the TRUTH-TABLE shown in Figure 5-9 has been specially labeled with "Leave alone," "RESET operation," "SET operation," and "don't do." This is done to instill a fundamental design technique that is used throughout this text, as far as sequential circuits are concerned, with phrases like "SET that cell on this condition," or "RESET this cell on that condition" used quite often. This is done in order that a more conceptual understanding of sequential circuit behavior can be realized. Therefore, don't be surprised when you read first-person statements such as: "I want to SET cell A and RESET cell B if the *xyz* input is ASSERTED." This technique will be demonstrated in Section 5-17 when the design of a "Flip-Flop" is treated.

As mentioned, the cell makes up the important portion of memory elements shown in Figure 5-4. It is therefore important that a good understanding of its operation be achieved before moving on to the next several sections. Further, it is important to visualize that propagation delay can and does serve a memory function in the cell and classifies the cell as an *asynchronous sequential circuit*. In the next section some elementary but practical applications of a cell are illustrated.

5-6 THE CELL AND THE BOUNCING SWITCH

In Chapter 2 it was pointed out that mechanical switches exhibit a contact bounce when closed. The bounce is the result of the spring-loaded impact of the switch throw contact and the pole contacts. Almost every mechanical switch suffers from this problem unless its contacts are specifically designed and "wetted" with mercury. In most general switch applications contact bounce is no real problem. However, it can be very much a problem in digital circuits. This is particularly true when sequential circuits are involved, and each switch closure-bounce sequence is interpreted as an independent input sequence. You can imagine that a bouncing START/STOP switch for a computer could create all sorts of short start-stop sequences before the switch contact came to rest. The circuit shown in Figure 5-11 illustrates how a cross-coupled NAND cell can be used to de-bounce a SPDT mechanical switch.

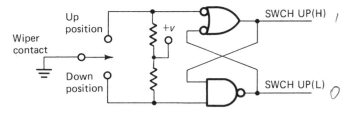

Fig. 5-11. The switch debouncer centered around a cross-coupled-NAND cell.

A quick analysis of the circuit shown in Figure 5-11 reveals that the initial contact of the wiper with the up-position contact sets the cell within nanoseconds. Then *milliseconds* later when the first mechanical bounce occurs the cell is firmly locked into the SET condition and subsequent bounces have no further effect. This is true providing the switch design is *not* so sloppy that it will allow a bounce to carry the wiper contact from up-position contact clear back to the down position contact. Figure 5-12 illustrates two other alternative switch de-bounce circuits centered around a set of cross-coupled INVERTERS. Figure 5-13 shows the data sheet for the DM8544 TRI-STATE QUAD-SWITCH DEBOUNCER centered around NOR gate cells. It should be noticed that this device has a strobe input that can be used to disable the complete circuit. This is an important disabling feature when accidental or unauthorized switch flipping can lead to catastrophic results.

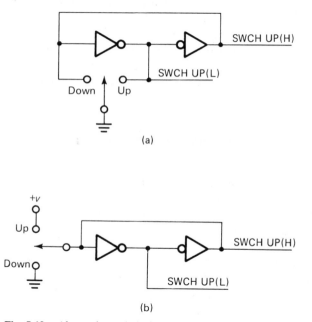

(a)

(b)

Fig. 5-12. Alternative switch debouncing circuits utilizing INVERTERS.

Fig. 5-13. (facing page) The data sheet for DM8544 switch debouncer. (Courtesy of National Semiconductor).

TRI-STATE Quad Switch Debouncers

General Description

These circuits are for use in front panels, and similar applications where contact bounce must be eliminated. Within the single package, these circuits do the job of four R-S latches plus pull-up resistors. A strobe is also available which permits sampling of the switch information at a predetermined time. TRI-STATE outputs are also provided for direct connections to the switch line bus.

Features

- Replaces SN54279/74279
- Eliminates push-button noise
- Allows clocked devices to be operated from switches
- Maximum power dissipation   250 mW
- Bus-line connectable
- TRI-STATE outputs
- Typical propagation delay   18 ns

Connection Diagram

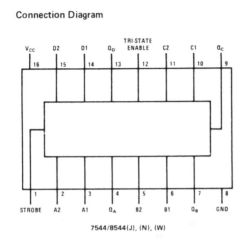

7544/8544 (J), (N), (W)

Truth Table

A1	A2	TRI-STATE ENABLE	STROBE	$Q_{A(t)}$
X	X	H	X	Hi-Z
X	X	L	L	$Q_{A(t-1)}$
L	L	L	L	Indeterminate
L	H	L	H	L
H	L	L	H	H
H	H	L	H	$Q_{A(t)}$

Logic Diagram

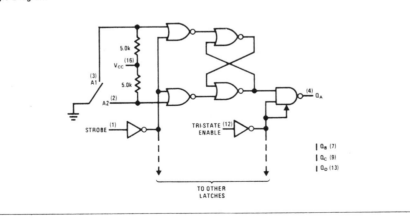

5-7 FUNDAMENTAL DIFFERENCES BETWEEN SEQUENTIAL MACHINES

In the past few sections we have dedicated a good deal of effort to developing an understanding of the functional behavior of the blocks of the sequential machine model shown in Figure 5-4. We have introduced the concepts of using a cell for memory, even using propagation delay for memory, and we have discussed some of the timing and operational aspects of combinational circuits that are important to the understanding of sequential machines.

Now let us establish a major distinction between *sequential* circuits. Introducing the concepts of sequential machines presents an interesting dichotomy; on one hand there are *asynchronous* sequential and on the other hand there are *synchronous* sequential circuits. For all intents and purposes asynchronous circuit concepts should be discussed first, because asynchronous concepts are fundamental to all sequential machines. However, the actual uses of asynchronous circuits are somewhat more limited than synchronous; further, asynchronous design tends to be more tedious and difficult for most people, leading to the probable reason why synchronous design techniques seem to have gained considerable domination over asynchronous during the relatively short history of digital design. This results in the trend to teach few or no asynchronous concepts and to deal strictly with synchronous circuits. This author feels that both should be treated, and the order in which they should be treated is: first, a little asynchronous, enough to understand the operation of the "Basic Cell" and traditional Flip-Flops, then a good dose of synchronous circuits, followed by a good dose of asynchronous circuits, and finally at the system level a good mixture of the applications of both.

To make certain that we all have a common understanding, *asynchronous sequential circuits are basically combinational logic with direct feedback and are "paced" or cycled by transitions of EACH input and strictly use the propagation delay of the NEXT STATE DECODER for memory. Synchronous circuits, on the other hand, use hardware devices called Flip-Flops for memory and are paced or cycled by a special single sychronizing input waveform commonly called the SYSTEM CLOCK.* This CLOCK is the "command signal" mentioned earlier that causes the memory element (Flip-Flop) to *READ* and *STORE* the code at its inputs. Though this distinction is drawn between the two types of sequential circuits, we find that the Flip-Flop, by itself, is an asynchronous circuit specifically designed to provide the memory requirements of a synchronous circuit. Therefore, other than some subtle distinctions, the operation of both types is basically the same, and the model shown in Figure 5-14 is equally applicable to both. Hence, the following discussions related to the functional operation of a sequential machine is applicable to both. Note further that Chapter 10 is devoted to the study of asynchronous circuits.

5-8 FUNDAMENTALS OF SEQUENTIAL MACHINE OPERATION

Figure 5-14 is a block diagram of a fully labeled general model of a sequential or finite-state machine. The labeling is important because it defines or identifies pertinent signal lines and variables that are used to define the operation of the machine. This figure is nothing more than an expanded version of Figure 5-4, expanded to help develop a conceptual picture of the machine's operation as well as to spatially position the basic blocks and signal lines.

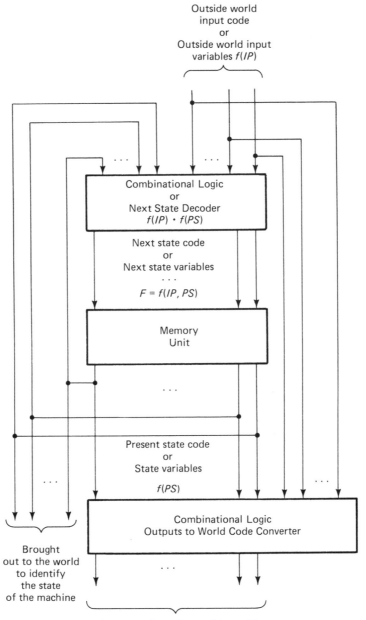

Fig. 5-14. The general model of the sequential or finite-state machine.

Sequential machines were first classified as such by Huffman and Moore when they introduced the concept of the "STATE" of a machine as a means of characterizing the memory of these circuits. They did this by defining the output code (bit pattern) of the memory at appropriately chosen times as the STATE of the machine. The appropriately chosen time is any time the circuit is *NOT* in a transient condition, that is, changing STATES. To say it again, we define the STATE of a sequential circuit according to the code presented to us directly *from* the output of the memory element. It should be noted that other names have been given to the STATE of the machine. They are the PRESENT STATE or the STATE VARIABLES. These will be used interchangeably throughout this text.

The following definition of a STATE is rather formal; however, it supports the Huffman–Moore concept as well as the control concept of the sequential machine related earlier.

The STATE of a machine is the property of that machine which relates the inputs to the output in such a way that knowledge of the input time function (f) for $t \geq t_o$ and the state at $t = t_o$ completely determines the output for all $t > t_o$.

By defining the state of the machine in this manner, sequential circuit design is found to be nothing more than *combinational design with certain constraints*, as illustrated through the rest of this text. Further, it is possible to describe the operation in a discrete step-by-step process by using a graphical aid called a STATE DIAGRAM. The STATE DIAGRAM and its uses are treated thoroughly in Chapter 6.

Now turn your attention to Figure 5-14 and consider the function of the combinational block labeled the *NEXT STATE DECODER*, sometimes called the *INPUT or NEXT STATE FORMING LOGIC*. The function of this logic network is to decode the inputs from the outside world and the *PRESENT STATE* of the machine (stored by the memory) and to generate as its output a code called the *NEXT STATE CODE*. This *NEXT STATE CODE* will become the *PRESENT STATE CODE* when the memory loads and stores it.* This process is defined as a *STATE CHANGE* or a *CHANGE OF STATE*. State changing is a continual process with each new state and the *PRESENT INPUT CONDITIONS* being decoded to form the new NEXT STATE CODES (bit patterns). After being convinced that the *PRESENT STATE* of the machine really reflects its past history you realize that each new succeeding state is a function of the present inputs and the past history of these inputs. This is relatively easy to see when examining the process of getting to any given state. It can be determined that this process is one of repeatedly determining which input conditions were required to cause the machine to transfer to its present state from the state or states just previous. This then provides a simple process of tracing back through each successive state and input conditions to some beginning. By doing this the history of all the input conditions required to place the circuit into any arbitrary state can be determined.

The combinational logic block in Figure 5-14 labeled the *OUTPUTS TO THE OUTSIDE WORLD CODE CONVERTER* has the basic function of decoding

---

*This is true only when special memory elements are used, otherwise the NEXT STATE CODE is further decoded in the memory element to generate the true PRESENT STATE CODE.

the PRESENT STATE of the machine and the PRESENT INPUT CONDITION for the purpose of generating the desired control outputs to the outside world. In many texts this logic block is included with the NEXT STATE decoder block; however, it is felt that a more conceptual picture of the machine's operation can be had if these blocks are shown separately, particularly when one starts to break the model down into classes of machines, as will be done in the next section.

In review, a sequential machine is one that steps through STATES (memory output codes) in a sequential manner. The STATE CODES of the machine are generated by the NEXT STATE DECODER that converts the OUTSIDE WORLD INPUTS combined with the PRESENT STATE CODE into bit patterns called the NEXT STATE CODES of the machine.

5-9 USING VARIATIONS OF THE GENERAL MODEL TO CLASSIFY SEQUENTIAL MACHINES

The following models can be derived from the basic model shown in Figure 5-14 by a process of degeneration, as shown in Figures 5-15 through 5-19.

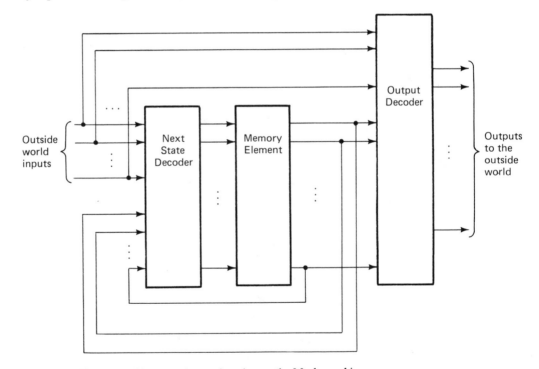

Fig. 5-15. Class A machine sometimes referred to as the Mealy machine.

For the most part these machine classes are self-explanatory; however, there are three classes worth mentioning. They are the class *A*, *B*, and *C*. The class A machine is defined as a MEALY machine named after G. H. Mealy, one of the pioneers in sequential design. *The basic distinction of a Mealy machine is that the outputs to the outside world are a function of two sets of variables: (1) the present input conditions and (2) the present state of the machine.*

The class B and C machines are defined as MOORE machines, named after E. F. Moore, another pioneer in sequential circuits. The basic distinction of a Moore machine is that its output is *strictly a function of the state of the machine.* Both the Mealy and Moore machines are widely used and it is possible to derive machines that are mixtures of both; in other words, some outputs are conditional on both the inputs and the state of the machine, where others are dependent only on the state of the machine.

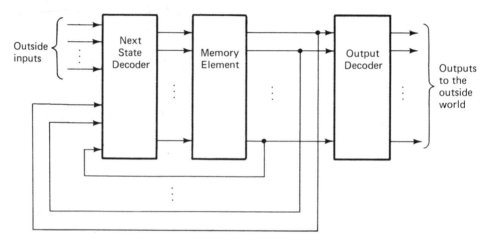

Fig. 5-16. Class B machine, sometimes referred to as the Moore machine.

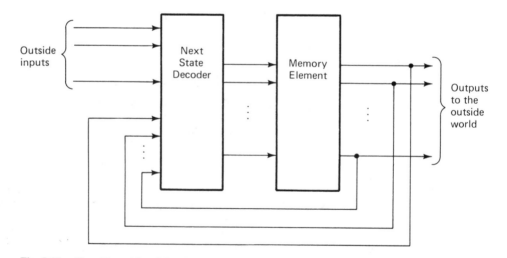

Fig. 5-17. Class C machine: Moore machine without an output decoder.

The class A, B, and C circuits with a *single input* are interesting machines. These form the general model for a counter circuit in which the events to be counted are entered directly into the memory element or through the NEXT STATE DECODER logic. These special circuits and many others will be covered in depth in the following chapters.

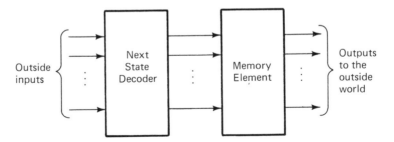

Fig. 5-18. Class D machine: look-up memory.

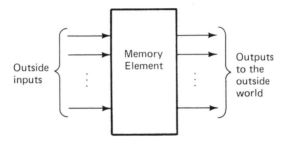

Fig. 5-19. Class E machine.

In review, it is important to note again that the class A, B, and C machines are equally applicable for both asynchronous as well as synchronous circuits, and the *minimum number of INPUTS* to any of these machines is *ONE*. For synchronous machines, that *ONE* input must be the *System Clock*.

5-10 THE FLIP-FLOP

To this point, the memory element in the sequential machine model has been considered to be one of two things: (1) a propagation delay or (2) some special hardware device that includes a binary cell capable of storing the PRESENT STATE of the machine. At this time we introduce the *Flip-Flop* as the special hardware device that is widely used in *synchronous* finite-state machines. We do this as an introduction to the detailed study of the analysis and design of synchronous sequential circuits covered in Chapter 6. Though the Flip-Flop is used widely as the memory element in sequential circuits, there are other memory applications for this fundamental device, as demonstrated throughout the rest of this text.

The name for the Flip-Flop stems from the days when basic cells were implemented with cross-coupled *relays*. The SET and RESET operations of this electromechanical cell gave rise to distinctive audible Flip and Flop sounds.

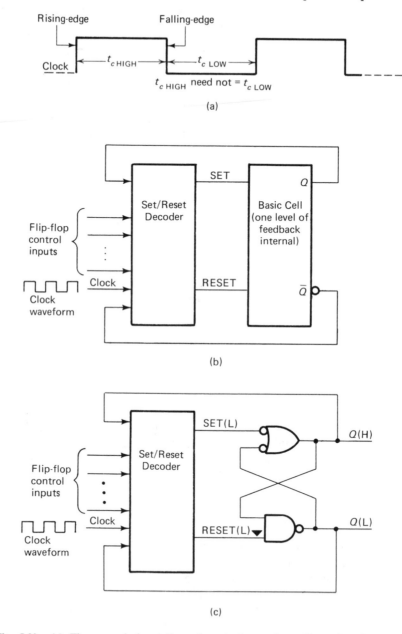

Fig. 5-20. (a) The general description of a clock waveform illustrating the rising-edge and falling edge and relative HIGH and LOW timing periods $t_{c\ HIGH}$ and $t_{c\ LOW}$. (b) The general model of the Flip-Flop. (c) A more specific Flip-Flop model using cross-coupled NAND cell.

The CLOCKED FLIP-FLOP is a sequential circuit designed basically to perform the fundamental process of conditionally storing the binary bits 0 and 1. This operation is accomplished by using a binary cell coupled with some combinational SET/RESET decoding logic to allow some input control over the SET and RESET operations of the cell. One of these inputs is the CLOCK (see Figure 5-20(a)). Because of this structure, the general model of the Flip-Flop fits a class C machine configuration. Thus the general model for the clocked Flip-Flop is shown in Figure 5-20(b).

We observe in Figure 5-20(b) that the general Flip-Flop can have at least two levels of feedback. Further, it should be interesting to note, in passing, that in every synchronous machine design using clocked Flip-Flops there are multiple levels of feedback controlling the circuits. For example, the clocked Flip-Flop itself is a sequential machine with two levels of feedback. When this Flip-Flop is utilized in a class A, B, or C machine, there is yet another overall feedback, and if the class A, B, or C machines are used to control yet another system, then there is still one more level of feedback. Therefore, when using a class A, B, or C machine to control another system, there are no less than *four* levels of feedback. This points to a real need for sound design practices, or some erratic-behaving systems will result.

The combinational logic block in Figure 5-20, labeled as the SET/RESET DECODER, has a basic and important function. This function is the decoding of the Flip-Flop *control* inputs, including the CLOCK and the PRESENT STATE of the basic cell, and from this ASSERTING *one* of the two output lines, SET or RESET. Here we see a fundamental design procedure emerging: When we are given a specification for a Flip-Flop's operation based on some control inputs and the design is left up to us, we must consider each input condition along with the PRESENT STATE of the cell and answer one of the three basic questions for each and every possible condition.

(1) Do I want to SET the cell with the next clock pulse on this condition?
(2) Do I want to RESET the cell with the next clock pulse on this condition?
(3) Do I leave it as it is with the next clock pulse on this condition?

This design procedure is interesting and straightforward and is demonstrated many times throughout the remainder of this text. The next section introduces some special circuits that can be used to generate the all-important CLOCK.

5-11 CLOCK AND OSCILLATORS

In this section we touch upon some circuits that can be used to generate the CLOCK (CLK) or SYSTEM CLOCK (SYSCLK) for synchronous sequential circuits and systems. It is not intended that all the theory be developed relative to oscillator circuits and their applications. It is merely intended that enough material be presented so that you can put a clock circuit together and have it work.

However, generally speaking, transient circuit analysis and some knowledge of device electronics is all that is required to derive the expressions given for f_o.

As mentioned, clock circuits are rectangular waveform generators and their output need not be square waves, as illustrated in Figure 5-20(a). Clock oscillators are mainly specified by the following criteria:

(1) Frequency (f_o) in Hz (cycles per second)
(2) Frequency stability equals the percent of f_o drift due to temperature changes and device aging
(3) Duty cycle $= t_{c\,\text{HIGH}}/[(t_{c\,\text{HIGH}}) + (t_{c\,\text{LOW}})] \times 100\%$

For example: A square wave duty cycle equals 50%. Thus we see that the particular oscillator circuit chosen should allow the designer to carry out some mathematical calculations to develop an oscillator which will meet specifications. The oscillator circuits shown in Figure 5-21 are offered as a reasonable selection of circuits which can fulfill a wide variety of clock needs. Many of these circuits are developed around CMOS devices for the following reasons:

(1) inherent threshold symmetry,
(2) good temperature stability, and
(3) high input impedance.

However, these CMOS circuits are somewhat limited at high frequencies.

Special Note: Since there is quite a wide variation in device characteristics and parameters, the expressions given for f_o are only *approximately true* (i.e., in the ball park), typically $\pm 15\%$. This is true in all cases except the crystal controlled circuits.

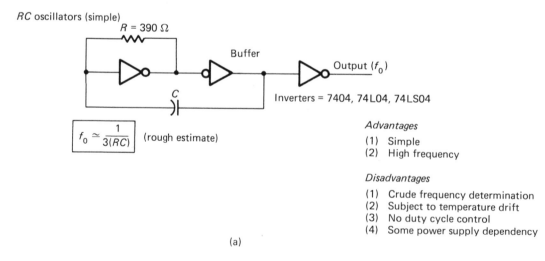

RC oscillators (simple)

$R = 390\ \Omega$

Buffer

Output (f_0)

Inverters = 7404, 74L04, 74LS04

$$f_0 \simeq \frac{1}{3(RC)}$$ (rough estimate)

Advantages
(1) Simple
(2) High frequency

Disadvantages
(1) Crude frequency determination
(2) Subject to temperature drift
(3) No duty cycle control
(4) Some power supply dependency

(a)

Fig. 5-21. A collection of oscillator circuits suitable for digital system clocks.

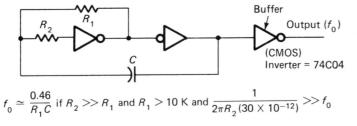

$$f_0 \simeq \frac{0.46}{R_1 C} \text{ if } R_2 \gg R_1 \text{ and } R_1 > 10 \text{ K and } \frac{1}{2\pi R_2 (30 \times 10^{-12})} \gg f_0$$

Advantages

(1) Simple
(2) Reasonably close frequency determination
(3) Reasonably square output
(4) Relatively temperature stable with good R and C
(5) Power supply independent

Disadvantages

(1) Frequency limit $\leqslant 100$ K
(2) No duty cycle control
(3) May not start if C is very small

(b)

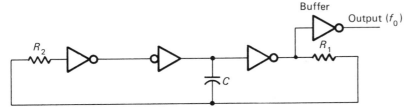

CMOS Inverters

$$f_0 \simeq \frac{0.46}{R_1 C} \text{ if } R_2 \gg R_1, R_1 \geqslant 10 \text{ k and } \frac{1}{2\pi R_2 (30 \times 10^{-12})} \gg f_0$$

Advantages

(1) Simple
(2) Close to square wave output
(3) Reasonable temperature stability
(4) Reasonably insensitive to power supply variation
(5) Will always start

Disadvantages

(1) High frequency limits
(2) No duty cycle control

(c)

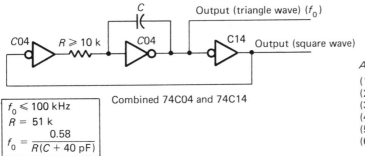

Combined 74C04 and 74C14

| $f_0 \leqslant 100$ kHz |
| $R = 51$ k |
| $f_0 = \dfrac{0.58}{R(C + 40 \text{ pF})}$ |

Advantages

(1) Simple (1 capacitor, 1 resistor)
(2) Schmitt output (clean edges)
(3) Good temperature stability
(4) Good predictability
(5) Reasonable (50%) duty cycle
(6) Symmetrical triangle-wave output also

Disadvantages

(1) $f_0 \leqslant 100$ kHz
(2) No duty cycle adjustment
(3) Requires two different IC's

(d)

Fig. 5-21. (Cont.)

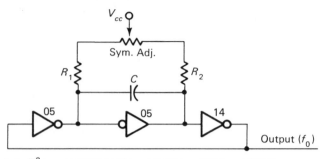

Hybrid T^2L and CMOS (7405 and 74C14 or 7405 and 7414)

For 74C14
$f_0 \simeq 0.50/RC$
where $R = R_1 = R_2$

For 7414
$f_0 \simeq 1/RC$
where $R = R_1 \doteq R_2$

Advantages

(1) Duty cycle adjustable
(2) Good temperature stability
(3) Good power sensitivity
(4) One capacitor

Disadvantages

(1) Reasonably complex
(2) High frequency limited unless 74C is replaced with 7414
(3) Required two IC's

(e)

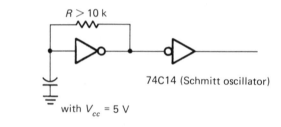

74C14 (Schmitt oscillator)

with $V_{cc} = 5$ V

$T_0 \simeq 1.89\ RC$
$f_0 \simeq \dfrac{0.53}{RC}$

Advantages

(1) Simple
(2) Temperature stable (reasonably) with good R and C
(3) Self-starting

Disadvantages

(1) Frequency limited
(2) No duty cycle control

(f)

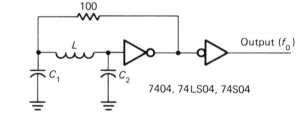

7404, 74LS04, 74S04

$f_0 \simeq \dfrac{1}{2\pi\sqrt{LC_T}}$; $\quad C_T = \dfrac{C_1 C_2}{C_1 + C_2}$

Advantages

(1) High frequency capability

Disadvantages

(1) Reasonably complex
(2) No duty cycle control

(g)

Fig. 5-21. (Cont.)

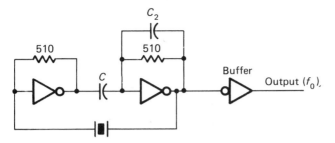

Quartz crystal frequency = f_0 Inverter 7404, 74LS04, 74S04

$$X_{c1} \to 0 \text{ at } f_0$$
$$X_{c2} \simeq 510 \ \Omega \text{ at } f_0 \quad \text{(overtone suppression)}$$

Advantages

(1) Frequency stability
(2) Simple crystal oscillator
(3) High frequency
(4) Will always start

Disadvantages

(1) Cost
(2) No symmetry adj.

(h)

Crystal controlled oscillator

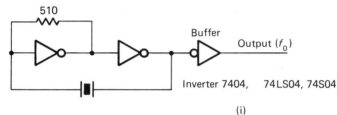

Inverter 7404,   74LS04, 74S04

(i)

Advantages

(1) Frequency stability
(2) More simple than circuit (h)
(3) High frequency

Disadvantages

(1) No overtone suppression
(2) No symmetry adj.
(3) Might require starting

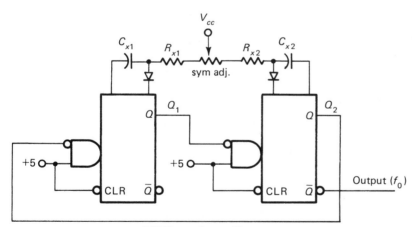

74123 one shot oscillator

$$t_{c \ \text{HIGH}} = 0.25 \ (R_{x1} C_{x1}) \text{ if } R_{x1} \gg 700 \ \Omega$$
$$t_{c \ \text{LOW}} = 0.25 \ (R_{x2} C_{x2}) \text{ if } R_{x2} \gg 700 \ \Omega$$
$$T_0 = (t_{c \ \text{HIGH}} + t_{c \ \text{LOW}}) \text{ sec}$$
$$f_0 = 1/T_0$$

Advantages

(1) Duty cycle adj.
(2) Reasonably temperature stable
(3) One IC package

Disadvantages

(1) Complex (two capacitors/two resistors)
(2) Power supply sensitive

(j)

Fig. 5-21. (Cont.)

5-12 TYPES OF TRADITIONAL CLOCKED FLIP-FLOPS

The design procedure just outlined in Section 5-10 allows you to design all varieties of Flip-Flops if you so choose. However, there are several basic types that are readily available in integrated circuit forms. These are the "DELAY" or "D" Flip-Flop and the "JK" Flip-Flop, both of which can be converted to a TOGGLE or "T" Flip-Flop or any of several other types. Other types of Flip-Flops do exist, but they seem to have very limited use. These are the "SR" (SET/RESET), which has been replaced by the JK, the JK-T Flip-Flop, and other similar exotic devices. For the most part, let us concern ourselves with the five basic types:

    (1) Clocked SET/RESET
    (2) Clocked D-Latch
    (3) Clocked T
    (4) Clocked JK
    (5) Clocked JK MASTER/SLAVE

5-13 THE SET/RESET FLIP-FLOP

To initiate the study of Flip-Flop operation and design, first consider the clocked *SR* and its characteristics, as shown in Figure 5-22.

Figure 5-22(a) shows the accepted schematic symbol for the SR Flip-Flop to be used when drawing schematics for a design using the SR Flip-Flop. Note that the *S* input is just above the *Q* output on the same line. The *R* input is on the same line with the $\overline{Q}$ output, with the clock input centered between *S* and *R*.

In Figure 5-22(b) we begin to see the building block approach to the design of the clocked Flip-Flop. In this logic diagram it can be seen that if *S*(H) is ASSERTED at the rising-edge of the clock, the SET(L) is ASSERTED and the basic cell is SET, thus *Q*(H)→HIGH. Further, it can be seen that if *R*(H) is ASSERTED, the cell is RESET on the rising-edge of the clock, thus *Q*(H)→LOW. At this point it should be noted that when *the clock is high, the cell is vulnerable to changes on the S(H) and R(H) inputs.* In other words, the inputs *S*(H) and *R*(H) have a straight shot at the basic cell when the clock is high, allowing changes in these inputs to alter the information that was gated into the cell on the rising-edge of the clock. This may or may not be a problem in some cases. More will be discussed later about this feature and the effects it can have on sequential machine design.

The CHARACTERISTIC TABLE shown in Figure 5-22(c) is a special TRUTH-TABLE for specifying the operational characteristic of the SR Flip-Flop. The *Qn* and *Qn+1* notation is added to illustrate the sequential nature of the device. *Qn* is to be interpreted as the PRESENT STATE OF *Q*(H) and *Qn+1* is to be interpreted as the NEXT STATE OF *Q*(H) or the STATE after the rising-edge of the clock. Note further that the bracketed notation to the side of the characteristic table suggests the ACTION taken on the basic cell on the rising-edge of the clock. This is important information to those who are interested in designing some other type of Flip-Flop using the model shown in Figure 5-20(b). How to use this information is illustrated in a later section.

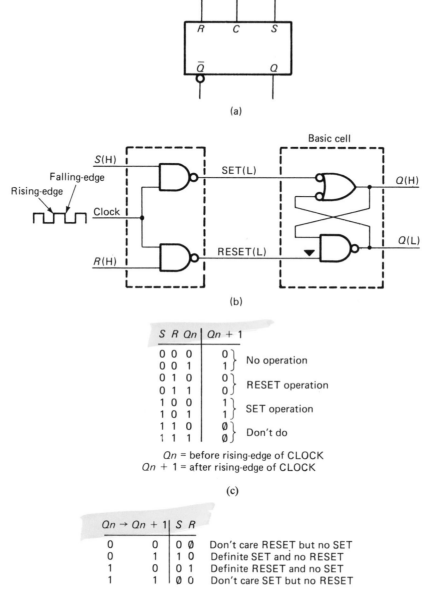

(a)

(b)

S R Qn	Qn + 1	
0 0 0	0	No operation
0 0 1	1	
0 1 0	0	RESET operation
0 1 1	0	
1 0 0	1	SET operation
1 0 1	1	
1 1 0	Ø	Don't do
1 1 1	Ø	

Qn = before rising-edge of CLOCK
Qn + 1 = after rising-edge of CLOCK

(c)

Qn → Qn + 1	S R	
0 0	0 Ø	Don't care RESET but no SET
0 1	1 0	Definite SET and no RESET
1 0	0 1	Definite RESET and no SET
1 1	Ø 0	Don't care SET but no RESET

(d)

Fig. 5-22. The documentation related to the *RS* Flip-Flop. (a) Schematic symbol. (b) Logic diagram showing the two major blocks SET/RESET DECODER and the BASIC CELL. (c) The characteristic table. (d) The excitation table for the clocked SR Flip-Flop.

The EXCITATION TABLE shown in Figure 5-22(d) is also an important design aid, and the information plotted in this table is derived from the CHARACTERISTIC TABLE in Figure 5-22(c). The EXCITATION TABLE graphically answers the question: What input conditions must prevail to cause the indicated transitions? For example, what input conditions must exist prior to the rising-edge of the clock in order to produce $Qn=0 \rightarrow Qn+1=0$? By looking in the CHARACTERISTIC TABLE for the entries where $Qn=0$ and $Qn+1=0$, we find that $S=0$, $R=0$ and $S=0$, $R=1$ are the only conditions where $Qn=Qn+1=0$. Thus $S=0$ is a completely specified condition and $R=\emptyset$ is the other condition. From this we can state that for an SR Flip-Flop to make a $Qn=0 \rightarrow Qn+1=0$ transition, S must *not* be ASSERTED and R is a *don't care* ($\emptyset$). The rest of the entries in the EXCITATION TABLE are filled out in a similar manner. This covers the important information related to the SR Flip-Flop, and will serve as the guide to developing similar documentation for the following Flip-Flop circuits.

5-14 THE "D"-LATCH FLIP-FLOP

The D-Latch is an interesting device used quite extensively for temporary data storage. It is important to draw a distinction between the D-LATCH and the edge-triggered D Flip-Flop. Though they are similar in their operation, the LATCH is designed in such a way that when the *clock is high*, the Q(H) output will follow the data or D_L input, while the edge-triggered D Flip-Flop loads on the edge of the clock waveform, usually the rising-edge, and locks out the effects of any further changes at the D input until the next rising-edge. These edge-triggered devices and their operation are discussed in the edge-triggered Flip-Flop section. Figure 5-23 illustrates the schematic symbol, logic diagram, CHARACTERISTIC, and EXCITATION TABLES for the D-Latch Flip-Flop.

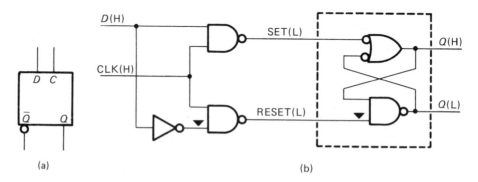

Fig. 5-23. The CLOCKED D-LATCH Flip-Flop. (a) The schematic symbol. (b) The logic diagram.

D	Qn	Qn + 1			Qn → Qn + 1		D
0	0	0	Ø RESET cell*		0	0	0
0	1	0	RESET cell		0	1	1
1	0	1	SET cell		1	0	0
1	1	1	Ø SET cell**		1	1	1

(c)   (d)

*Ø RESET is read as: Don't care if a RESET operation is performed.
**Ø SET is read as: Don't care if a SET operation is performed.

(c) The characteristic table. (d) The excitation table.

Fig. 5-23. (Cont.)

Considering the schematic shown in Figure 5-23(b), observe that when the clock is ASSERTED or HIGH the input logic is ENABLED and the output will follow the input (D_L) if it changes during this time. As mentioned earlier, this feature may or may not be a desirable one, depending on the application for the device.

5-15   THE "CLOCKED T" FLIP-FLOP

The "T" Flip-Flop derives its name from its operation, which is "toggle." *The word toggle implies a change of state when the T input is ASSERTED.* The T Flip-Flop, even though it does not exist in integrated circuit form, can be quickly generated by slight modifications on the D and JK Flip-Flop. Figure 5-24 illustrates the characteristic information regarding the use and function of the T Flip-Flop.

It should be noticed in Figure 5-24 that the T Flip-Flop is a multiple-feedback system and is one in which the outputs are fed directly back into the SET/RESET decoder, unlike the RS and D Flip-Flops just discussed. This multiple feedback leads to several undesirable modes of operation under certain conditions. One of these undesirable modes is oscillation.

If the propagation delays of gates a and c are slightly longer than the propagation delays of b and d, the Flip-Flop will break into oscillation with the rising-edge of the clock and will remain in oscillation for the period of time the clock is at its high level. This oscillation mode is intuitively obvious from the control definition of the T input, that is, if T and CLK are both ASSERTED the Flip-Flop is to change states. Once the state is changed, conditions are such that another change is called for. Thus if T and CLOCK are held high and the propagation delays of a and $c > b$ and d, oscillations will prevail. The other undesirable mode of operation develops when the combined propagation delay of a and c is less then b and d. Under these conditions the Flip-Flop will revert into a simultaneous SET and RESET mode with both outputs held HIGH and will remain there until the falling edge of the clock.

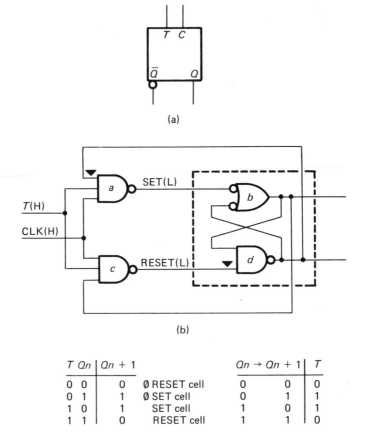

Fig. 5-24. The CLOCKED "T" Flip-Flop. (a) The schematic symbol of the T Flip-Flop. (b) The logic diagram for the T Flip-Flop. (c) The characteristic table. (d) The excitation table.

Neither of these modes of operation is desirable; however, if extremely short clock pulses are used to trigger the circuit, it will perform the normal operations. This clock high duration should be slightly longer than $\Delta t_c + \Delta t_b$ or $\Delta t_d + \Delta t_b$. This clock timing constraint was commonly used in the early days of digital design.

5-16 THE "CLOCKED JK" FLIP-FLOP

The "JK" Flip-Flop is probably the most functional and interesting of all Flip-Flop types. Its origin undoubtedly stems from an extension of the RS Flip-Flop. It will be shown that the JK is functionally identical to the RS except for the case where J and K are both ASSERTED together. It should be remembered that when using an RS Flip-Flop the case where R and S are both ASSERTED is one that must be avoided because of the indeterminability problem. A JK Flip-Flop is designed in such a way as to cause the basic cell to simply toggle or change states with the rising-edge of the clock waveform should both J and K be ASSERTED.* This is the only difference between the JK and the RS Flip-Flops, and as a result of this the J input can be thought of as the SET input and the K as the RESET input. Thinking this way can reduce a good deal of the mental baggage associated with Flip-Flop nomenclature. Figure 5-25 illustrates the necessary descriptive and functional features concerned with JK Flip-Flops. Note that the logic diagram in Figure 5-25(b) has been modified somewhat. Two extra inputs have been added to the cell. These are the asynchronous SET and RESET inputs that completely *override* the CLOCKED inputs to the cell. These inputs are standard for most integrated Flip-Flops and are normally added in order to make the device more flexible. They are not to be included in the clocked operational description for the Flip-Flop; they are to be thought of as a separate and independent function. However, the use of these asynchronous SET and RESET is restricted to the low period of the clock in order to avoid simultaneous SET and RESET conditions.

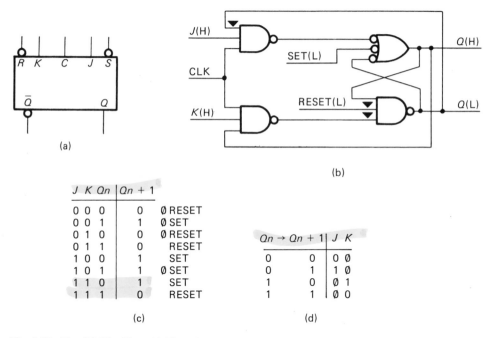

(a)

(b)

J	K	Qn	$Qn + 1$	
0	0	0	0	Ø RESET
0	0	1	1	Ø SET
0	1	0	0	Ø RESET
0	1	1	0	RESET
1	0	0	1	SET
1	0	1	1	Ø SET
1	1	0	1	SET
1	1	1	0	RESET

(c)

$Qn \rightarrow Qn + 1$		J	K
0	0	0	Ø
0	1	1	Ø
1	0	Ø	1
1	1	Ø	0

(d)

Fig. 5-25. The JK Flip-Flop. (a) The schematic symbol. (b) The logic diagram. (c) The characteristic table. (d) The excitation table.

There is yet another type of Flip-Flop called the JK MASTER/SLAVE, which is discussed after the next section along with some of the devices that are presently found in integrated circuits. These devices are designed in such a way

---

*Watch out again when the CLOCK J and K inputs are ASSERTED; because this JK Flip-Flop has the same two anomalous modes the T has.

that the undesirable modes are avoided. In the next section we discuss a design procedure which will hopefully yield some insight into the actual design of a Flip-Flop. Further, this design technique will allow you to design special purpose Flip-Flops should the need ever arise.

5-17 THE DESIGN OF A CLOCKED FLIP-FLOP

It is important to note that the design philosophy illustrated in this section is an introduction to a general design approach used throughout the following chapters on sequential design. Specifically, general models are defined and the function of each block of the model are designed based on the interaction required between the blocks of the model by calling out such sequential circuit actions as: "SET the cell on this condition" or "RESET the cell on that condition."

The past section defined or specified the operation of the different Flip-Flops *from a given circuit* without regard to where the circuit came from or how it was designed. In this section it will be illustrated how to go about designing a Flip-Flop given a CHARACTERISTIC TABLE and using the Flip-Flop model shown in Figure 5-20(b). It is true that most of the circuits described exist in integrated circuit packages; however, there may come a time when it becomes necessary for you to define and design a different type of Flip-Flop. Besides, it is comforting to know that the Flip-Flops shown in the past section didn't just come from thin air, that there really is a definite design technique used to develop them. Again, it should be pointed out that the following technique is just one of several possible techniques. This particular process was chosen because it carries over into other areas of design, where its use provides a decisive advantage over the more traditional approaches.

STEPS TO FLIP-FLOP DESIGN

Step 1: Given a CHARACTERISTIC TABLE prescribing some desired operation, examine each entry of this table (both inputs and the output desired), and answer the following questions for each row of the table:

(1) Does the cell need to be SET for this condition, or would a SET cause the wrong transition (SET or $\emptyset$ SET)?
(2) Does the cell need to be RESET for this condition, or would a RESET cause the wrong transition (RESET or $\emptyset$ RESET)?
(3) Does the cell need to be left alone?

REMEMBER, a simultaneous SET and RESET is NEVER TO OCCUR.

After each row in the CHARACTERISTIC TABLE has been examined and the questions above have been answered, a TRUTH-TABLE can be plotted with SET and RESET as output variables.

Step 2: Based on the answer to the questions above and the resultant TRUTH-TABLE, plot a SET MAP and RESET MAP and derive the combinational logic for the SET/RESET DECODER block in Figure 5-20(b).

Example 5-2: Using the technique just described, design a clocked SR Flip-Flop given the CHARACTERISTIC TABLE and the maps shown in Figure 5-26.

	CLK	S	R	Q_n	Q_n+1	SET	RESET	
0	0	0	0	0	0	0	Ø	{No SET, Ø RESET
1	0	0	0	1	1	Ø	0	{Ø SET, No RESET
2	0	0	1	0	0	0	Ø	.
3	0	0	1	1	1	Ø	0	.
4	0	1	0	0	0	0	Ø	.
5	0	1	0	1	1	Ø	0	
6	0	1	1	0	0	0	Ø	Input can happen with
7	0	1	1	1	1	Ø	0	no CLK ∴ optional
8	1	0	0	0	0	0	Ø	.
9	1	0	0	1	1	Ø	0	.
10	1	0	1	0	0	0	Ø	.
11	1	0	1	1	0	0	1	{No SET, Yes RESET
12	1	1	0	0	1	1	0	{Yes SET, No RESET
13	1	1	0	1	1	Ø	0	{Ø SET, No RESET
14	1	1	1	0	Ø	Ø	Ø	Input conditions must
15	1	1	1	1	Ø	Ø	Ø	not happen

CHARACTERISTIC   TRUTH-TABLE
TABLE   for SET/RESET
DECODER

Step No. 2: Plot maps:

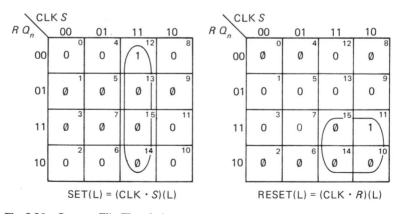

SET(L) = (CLK · S)(L)   RESET(L) = (CLK · R)(L)

Fig. 5-26. Steps to Flip-Flop design.

Thus we see that the circuit resulting from this design is the same as that shown in Figure 5-22(b).

The design of a D-LATCH and a T Flip-Flop is equally easy, as demonstrated in the following examples.

EXAMPLE 5-3:   Design the D-LATCH as prescribed by the CHARACTERISTIC TABLE and SET and RESET map shown in Figure 5-27.

CLK	D	Qn	Qn+1	SET	RESET	
0	0	0	0	0	$\emptyset$	{No SET, $\emptyset$ RESET
0	0	1	1	$\emptyset$	0	{$\emptyset$ SET, No RESET
0	1	0	0	0	$\emptyset$	.
0	1	1	1	$\emptyset$	0	.
1	0	0	0	0	$\emptyset$	.
1	0	1	0	0	1	{No SET, Yes RESET
1	1	0	1	1	0	.
1	1	1	1	$\emptyset$	0	.

<table>
<tr><td>CHARACTERISTIC
TABLE</td><td>SET/RESET
DECODER TRUTH-TABLE</td></tr>
</table>

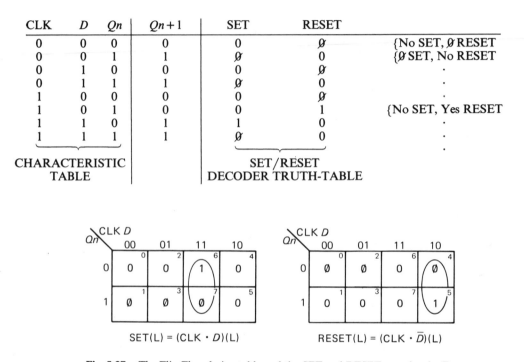

$$SET(L) = (CLK \cdot D)(L) \qquad RESET(L) = (CLK \cdot \overline{D})(L)$$

Fig. 5-27.   The Flip-Flop design table and the SET and RESET map for the D Flip-Flop.

Thus we see again that when the logic for SET(L) and RESET(L) is designed and coupled with the basic cell, we have the D-LATCH Flip-Flop shown in Figure 5-23(b).

It should be noted that both the RS and D-LATCH Flip-Flops required no feedback from the cell itself to SET/RESET DECODER. However, the T Flip-Flop does, as illustrated by the following.

EXAMPLE 5-4:   Design a T Flip-Flop as prescribed by the following characteristic table and the map shown in Figure 5-28.

	CLK	T	Qn	$Qn+1$	SET	RESET
0	0	0	0	0	0	Ø{No SET, Ø RESET
1	0	0	1	1	Ø	0{Ø SET, No RESET
2	0	1	0	0	0	Ø·
3	0	1	1	1	Ø	0·
4	1	0	0	0	0	Ø·
5	1	0	1	1	Ø	0
6	1	1	0	1	1	0{Yes SET, No RESET
7	1	1	1	0	0	1{No SET, Yes RESET

T CHARACTERISTIC TABLE   SET/RESET DECODER TRUTH-TABLE

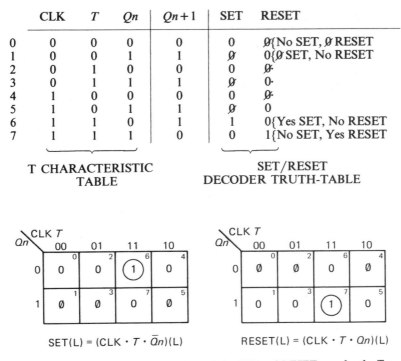

$$SET(L) = (CLK \cdot T \cdot \bar{Q}n)(L) \qquad RESET(L) = (CLK \cdot T \cdot Qn)(L)$$

Fig. 5-28. The Flip-Flop design table and the SET and RESET map for the T Flip-Flop.

Thus again we see that the circuit resulting from this design gives rise to a Flip-Flop that functions as prescribed by a CHARACTERISTIC TABLE and fits the Flip-Flop model shown in Figure 5-24(b). Exactly the same steps are followed to design the other Flip-Flops described in this text.

5-18 FLIP-FLOP CONVERSION FROM ONE TYPE TO ANOTHER

There are times when one type of Flip-Flop must be converted to another in order to fulfill some design obligation. However, more importantly, the process of conversion provides an insight into the process of recognizing which Flip-Flop is the optimum or the best choice for a particular task. Note again that the same SET/RESET attack is used in keeping with the design philosophy previously described. To illustrate the conversion process, consider the following example.

EXAMPLE 5-5: Convert the RS Flip-Flop to a (a) D-LATCH, (b) T, and (c) a D-LATCH to a T Flip-Flop.

Solution: The general attack on a problem like this is to use the model shown in Figure 5-29. Here we see that the process of converting one type of Flip-Flop to another is very similar to that of converting a basic cell into one of the general types. In other words, some combinational logic decoder must be designed for converting new input definitions into input codes which will cause the given Flip-Flop to perform as desired.

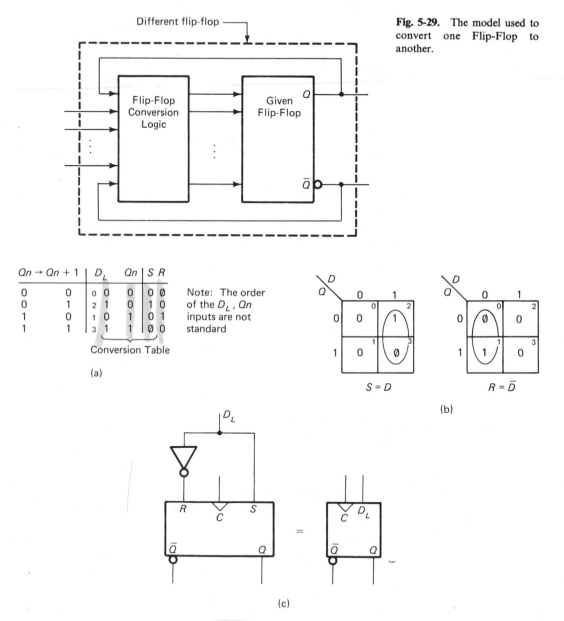

Different flip-flop

Fig. 5-29. The model used to convert one Flip-Flop to another.

Conversion Table

(a)

Note: The order of the D_L, Qn inputs are not standard

$S = D$

$R = \bar{D}$

(b)

(c)

Fig. 5-30. (a) The conversion table for converting an RS Flip-Flop to a D. (b) The SET and RESET conversion map. (c) The circuit conversion of an RS to a D.

Therefore, to convert an RS Flip-Flop to a D-LATCH, you need only combine the EXCITATION TABLES for both Flip-Flops as shown in Figure 5-30(a) and make a TRUTH-TABLE (CONVERSION TABLE) for each of the inputs for the Flip-Flop to be converted. To construct this TRUTH-TABLE, arrange the tabulation in the same order as the EXCITATION TABLE and show the inputs to be controlled as a function of the Qn present state of the machine and the inputs of the new Flip-Flop desired. This conversion process is shown in Figure 5-30. From the model (Figure 5-30(a)) we know in general that S and R must be a function of D and Qn. Therefore we have the map shown in Figure 5-30(b). Hence the circuit follows, as shown in Figure 5-30(c).

To convert an RS Flip-Flop to a T, we do the same thing. However, this time R and S are functions of both T and Qn (the present state). This is shown in Figure 5-31.

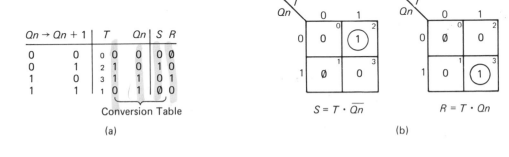

$Qn \to Qn + 1$		T		Qn	S	R
0	0	0	0	0	0	Ø
0	1	2	1	0	1	0
1	0	3	1	1	0	1
1	1	1	0	1	0	0

Conversion Table

(a)

$S = T \cdot \overline{Qn}$ $R = T \cdot Qn$

(b)

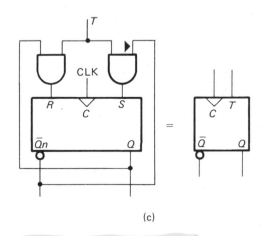

(c)

Fig. 5-31. The conversion of an RS Flip-Flop to a T Flip-Flop.

Another example could be the conversion of a D-LATCH to a T Flip-Flop. Using a method similar to the last two examples generates the circuit shown in Figure 5-32. The conversion of a D-LATCH to a T is shown in Figure 5-32(c).

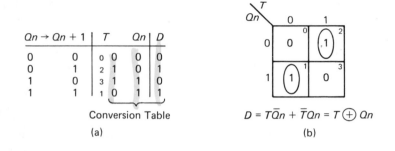

$Qn \rightarrow Qn+1$		T		Qn	D
0	0	0	0	0	0
0	1	2	1	0	1
1	0	3	1	1	0
1	1	1	0	1	1

Conversion Table

(a)

$$D = T\overline{Q}n + \overline{T}Qn = T \oplus Qn$$

(b)

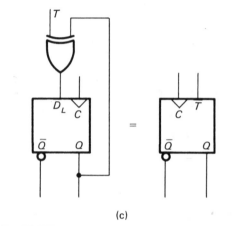

(c)

Fig. 5-32. The conversion of a D Flip-Flop to a T Flip-Flop.

These examples show that there is a simple and straightforward technique for converting one Flip-Flop type to any of the other types.

5-19 PRACTICAL CLOCKING ASPECTS CONCERNING FLIP-FLOPS

In a previous section we discussed some of the interesting concepts related to operational characteristics of four different types of Flip-Flops. Actually, with one exception, the devices we have studied are rather limited in their use. The one exception mentioned is the D-LATCH, which is often used to latch and hold data. The common problem that all these devices have is the vulnerability of the cell when the clock is ASSERTED (high). This feature makes these devices undesirable for finite-state machine design for the following reason: The lack of a lock-out or edge-triggering feature can cause erratic state transitions in finite-state machines! The same problem was also alluded to previously. To further illustrate this problem, consider the following example.

EXAMPLE 5-6: Given the finite-state machine model as shown in Figure 5-33, consider at the indicated time frame (before rising-edge of clock) that the

NEXT STATE CODE is STABLE. Now, when the rising-edge of the clock does occur, the NEXT STATE CODE is transferred into the Flip-Flops and a "NEW" PRESENT STATE CODE is generated. At this instant this NEW PRESENT STATE CODE presents itself to the NEXT STATE DECODING LOGIC where a whole NEW NEXT STATE CODE is generated. This occurs, of course, after an appropriate propagation delay has elapsed. If this NEW NEXT STATE CODE or even a change in an INPUT variable is generated *while the clock is still ASSERTED*, the basic cell in the Flip-Flop can be changed from the condition loaded into it on the rising-edge, presenting an anomaly. If this anomaly does take place, erratic machine behavior will result. What this means is that a multiple-state change can be effected with one clock pulse, contrary to the basic concept of the machine being paced or stepped from STATE to STATE by one clock pulse at a time. To better illustrate this anomaly, consider the next example.

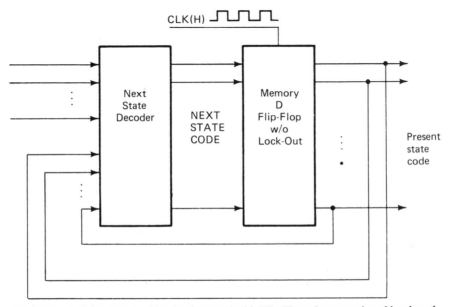

Fig. 5-33. A finite-state machine implemented with Flip-Flops that are vulnerable when the clock waveform is ASSERTED.

EXAMPLE 5-7: An example of the anomaly described above can be illustrated by analyzing one state variable X (one Flip-Flop output) in the machine proposed in Figure 5-34.

We can see by studying the proposed sequence that the variable X is supposed to step with the clock from a 0 condition to a 1 condition with the first clock pulse, then from a 1 to a 0 on the next clock pulse. What really happened is: Assuming an initial stable 0 condition for X, on the rising-edge of the clock a 1 (NEXT STATE) is loaded into the Flip-Flop. After t_1 seconds, this 1 appears at the output of the Flip-Flop. This 1 is then coupled back around into the NEXT STATE DECODER designed to form the NEXT STATE of 0 as the sequence indicated. Now after t_2 seconds this new 0 NEXT STATE condition is generated and this condition RESETS the basic cell to 0 again after t_1 seconds.

We see that a chain reaction of sorts is initiated by the rising-edge of the clock. Of particular interest in this example is the STATE of variable X at the falling-edge of the clock. We see from the figure that the falling-edge catches the NEXT STATE variable at a 0 condition and hence the new present state is 0 rather than 1. The net effect of all this is that the next state, which should be a 1, is a 0 and a good deal of oscillating is taking place while the clock pulse is high.

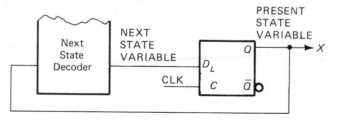

(a)

(b)

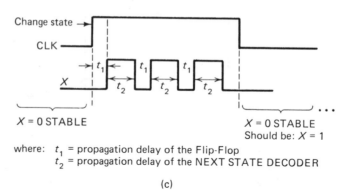

where: t_1 = propagation delay of the Flip-Flop
t_2 = propagation delay of the NEXT STATE DECODER

(c)

Fig. 5-34. The state transition anomaly caused by using a Flip-Flop (D-LATCH) that is vulnerable when the clock is ASSERTED. (a) One Flip-Flop of a finite-state machine. (b) The desired four-step sequence for the state variable X indicated in (a). (c) Timing diagram of Clock and X.

There are two obvious solutions to the anomaly described in Example 5-7.

(1) Use very narrow clock pulses, as prescribed earlier.
(2) Use Flip-Flops that exhibit some sort of blocking operation. In other words, use a Flip-Flop like a pulse-triggered JK MASTER/SLAVE Flip-Flop which triggers on the falling-edge of the clock waveform and in

turn blocks the changing data from modifying its output. A pulse-triggered JK MASTER/SLAVE Flip-Flop is shown in Figure 5-35. This
Flip-Flop is designed specifically to avoid the dual mode anomaly discussed in Section 5-15, allowing for its use in finite-state machine designs
under certain constraints.

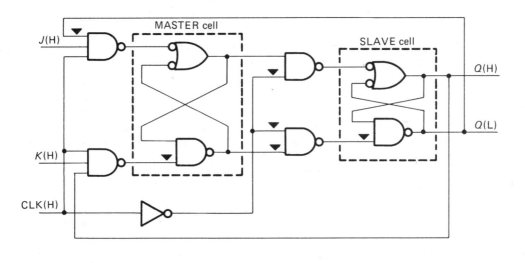

$Qn \rightarrow Qn + 1$		J K
0	0	0 Ø
0	1	1 Ø
1	0	Ø 1
1	1	Ø 0

Excitation Table

Fig. 5-35. A JK MASTER/SLAVE Flip-Flop and EXCITATION TABLE.

To analyze this circuit, consider the MASTER section first. We see that the
MASTER CELL and the associated SET/RESET DECODER is exactly the same
as the JK Flip-Flop shown in Figure 5-25(b) without the asynchronous SET/RE-
SET inputs. Therefore, we see that on the rising-edge of the clock waveform the
MASTER CELL is loaded in accordance to the J, K, Q(H), and Q(L) conditions.
At this same time and during the complete period, the clock is high and the
SLAVE CELL is inhibited. Now, on the falling-edge of the clock waveform the
data stored in the MASTER is dumped to the SLAVE and the outputs are
updated.* This is why this Flip-Flop is called a *pulse-triggered device*. Further, we
can see from Figure 5-35 that the MASTER CELL of a JK MASTER/SLAVE is
vulnerable during the period when the clock is high and therefore can be SET or

---

*Remember, in general, MASTER/SLAVE devices change state on the falling-edge of the clock. If this is
forgotten, timing problems will result.

RESET by input changes, giving rise to the *1's and 0's catching feature of a JK MASTER/SLAVE Flip-Flop.* This 1's and 0's catching feature of the JK MASTER/SLAVE Flip-Flop can be illustrated by a closer look at Figure 5-35. Note that when the Flip-Flop is RESET Q(H) is LOW and Q(L) is HIGH and the clock comes high *and*, while still high, the J input comes high, the MASTER CELL will SET and the Q(H) output will catch a 1 *on the falling-edge of the clock.* Conversely, if the Flip-Flop is SET (Q(H) is HIGH; Q(L) is LOW) and the clock comes high and then the K input comes high after the clock, the MASTER CELL will RESET and the Q(H) output will catch a 0 on the falling-edge of the clock. A practical note: This is of particular importance because a good deal of the MSI and LSI sequential devices such as counters and shift registers that use JK Flip-Flops exhibit this problem. What is even more important is that the manufacturers' specifications for these devices make indirect references to this malady, and therefore it is up to the designer to be aware of these problems.

When using the pulse-triggered JK MASTER/SLAVE Flip-Flop in a finite-state machine design in which the state changes take place on the falling-edge of the clock and the MASTER section is locked out at the same time, the anomalies described above apparently are avoided; and everything looks fine. However, what happens to the data loaded into the MASTER CELL when an *asynchronous outside world input changes after the rising-edge of the clock?* Input changes such as these are to be designed out in some way so they do not cause trouble. See Figure 5-36 for data sheets for pulse-triggered JK Flip-Flops.

The pulse-triggered JK MASTER/SLAVE, introduces at least a partial solution to the anomalies previously described. This device guarantees stability against oscillatory state changes and the dual mode anomalies but does not prevent the 1's and 0's catching problem. This leads to the third solution to the triggered problem.

(3) Use devices which are edge-triggered or have a feature called "data lock-out." These types of devices are available in integrated circuit form and are widely used. The edge-triggering or data lock-out features allow the device to load the NEXT STATE information into the Flip-Flop on an *edge* of the clock waveform and once this operation is complete, the *effects of input changes* are locked out until the next corresponding edge of the clock waveform as shown in Figure 5-37.

Some of the typical devices that are available that exhibit the lock-out operation are the SN74110 and the SN74111 JK Flip-Flops. Typical data sheets and logic diagrams for these devices are shown in Figure 5-38. Also, included in Figures 5-39 and 5-40 is a collection of data sheets for some of the common *edge-triggered devices*, both JK and D Flip-Flops. Figure 5-41 includes important operational definitions and specifications related to Flip-Flop usage. These specifications and definitions are reasonably standard and should be studied and understood when using the devices they specify. *Pay particular attention to the definitions for set-up and hold times.*

PULSE-TRIGGERED DUAL FLIP-FLOPS

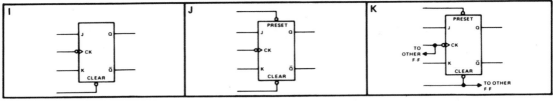

PULSE-TRIGGERED SINGLE FLIP-FLOPS

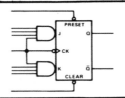

DWG. REF.	TYPICAL CHARACTERISTICS		DATA TIMES		DEVICE TYPE AND PACKAGE				PAGE REFERENCES	
	f_{max} (MHz)	Pwr/F-F (mW)	SETUP (ns)	HOLD (ns)	−55°C to 125°C		0°C to 70°C		PIN ASSIGNMENTS	ELECTRICAL
I	30	80	0↑	0↓	SN54H73	J, W	SN74H73	J, N	5-22	6-50
	20	50	0↑	0↓	SN5473	J, W	SN7473	J, N	5-22	6-46
	20	50	0↑	0↓	SN54107	J	SN74107	J, N	5-32	6-46
	3	3.8	0↑	0↓	SN54L73	J, T	SN74L73	J, N	5-22	6-54
J	30	80	0↑	0↓	SN54H76	J, W	SN74H76	J, N	5-23	6-50
	20	50	0↑	0↓	SN5476	J, W	SN7476	J, N	5-23	6-46
K	30	80	0↑	0↓	SN54H78	J, W	SN74H78	J, N	5-24	6-50
	3	3.8	0↑	0↓	SN54L78	J, T	SN74L78	J, N	5-24	6-54
L	30	80	0↑	0↓	SN54H71	J, W	SN74H71	J, N	5-21	6-50
M	30	80	0↑	0↓	SN54H72	J, W	SN74H72	J, N	5-22	6-50
	20	50	0↑	0↓	SN5472	J, W	SN7472	J, N	5-22	6-46
	3	3.8	0↑	0↓	SN54L72	J, T	SN74L72	J, N	5-22	6-54
N	3	3.8	0↑	0↓	SN54L71	J, T	SN74L71	J, N	5-21	6-54

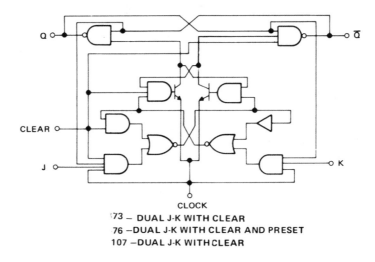

'73 – DUAL J-K WITH CLEAR
76 –DUAL J-K WITH CLEAR AND PRESET
107 –DUAL J-K WITH CLEAR

Fig. 5-36. Data sheets for pulse-triggered JK Flip-Flops. (Courtesy of Texas Instruments, Inc.)

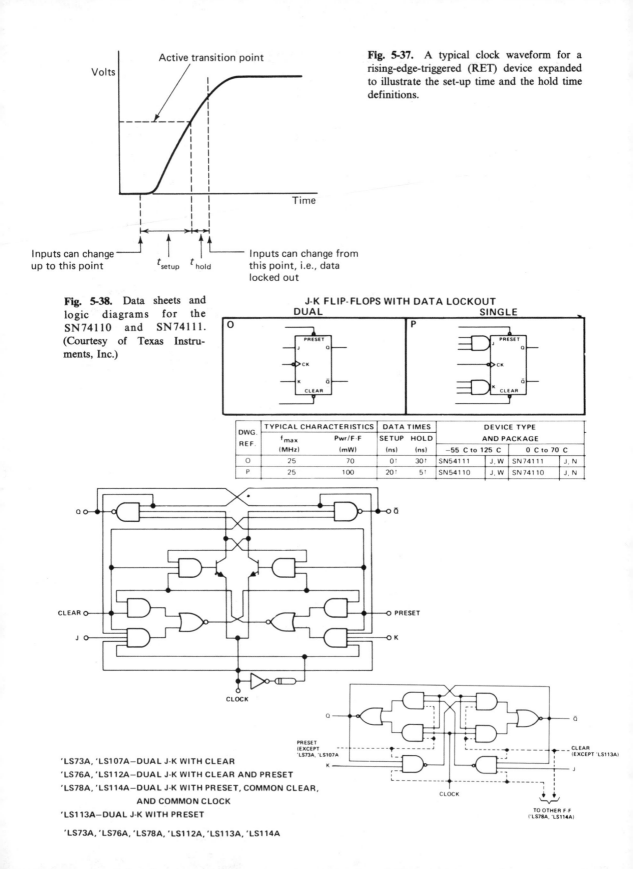

Volts

Active transition point

Time

Inputs can change up to this point — t_{setup} t_{hold} — Inputs can change from this point, i.e., data locked out

Fig. 5-37. A typical clock waveform for a rising-edge-triggered (RET) device expanded to illustrate the set-up time and the hold time definitions.

Fig. 5-38. Data sheets and logic diagrams for the SN74110 and SN74111. (Courtesy of Texas Instruments, Inc.)

J-K FLIP-FLOPS WITH DATA LOCKOUT

DUAL   SINGLE

O

PRESET
J   Q
CK
K   Q̄
CLEAR

P

PRESET
J   Q
CK
K   Q̄
CLEAR

DWG. REF.	TYPICAL CHARACTERISTICS		DATA TIMES		DEVICE TYPE AND PACKAGE			
	f_{max} (MHz)	Pwr/F·F (mW)	SETUP (ns)	HOLD (ns)	−55 C to 125 C		0 C to 70 C	
O	25	70	0↑	30↑	SN54111	J, W	SN74111	J, N
P	25	100	20↑	5↑	SN54110	J, W	SN74110	J, N

Q

Q̄

CLEAR

PRESET

J

K

CLOCK

Q

Q̄

PRESET (EXCEPT 'LS73A, 'LS107A)

K

CLEAR (EXCEPT 'LS113A)

J

CLOCK

TO OTHER F·F ('LS78A, 'LS114A)

'LS73A, 'LS107A—DUAL J-K WITH CLEAR

'LS76A, 'LS112A—DUAL J-K WITH CLEAR AND PRESET

'LS78A, 'LS114A—DUAL J-K WITH PRESET, COMMON CLEAR, AND COMMON CLOCK

'LS113A—DUAL J-K WITH PRESET

'LS73A, 'LS76A, 'LS78A, 'LS112A, 'LS113A, 'LS114A

DUAL J-K EDGE-TRIGGERED FLIP-FLOPS

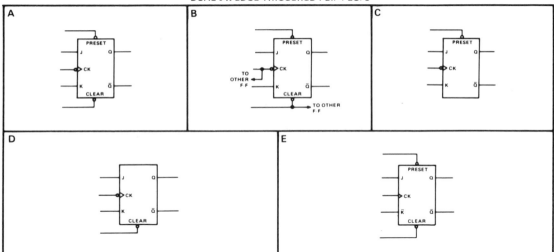

SINGLE J-K EDGE-TRIGGERED FLIP-FLOPS

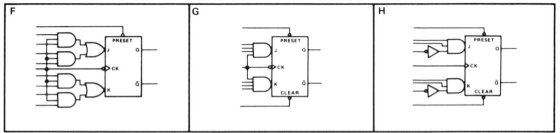

DWG REF.	TYPICAL CHARACTERISTICS		DATA TIMES		DEVICE TYPE AND PACKAGE				PAGE REFERENCES	
	f_{max} (MHz)	Pwr/F-F (mW)	SETUP (ns)	HOLD (ns)	−55°C to 125°C		0°C to 70°C		PIN ASSIGNMENTS	ELECTRICAL
A	125	75	3↓	0↓	SN54S112	J, W	SN74S112	J, N	5-34	6-58
	50	100	13↓	0↓	SN54H106	J, W	SN74H106	J, N	5-32	6-52
	45	10	20↓	0↓	SN54LS76A	J, W	SN74LS76A	J, N	5-23	6-58
	45	10	20↓	0↓	SN54LS112A	J, W	SN74LS112A	J, N	5-34	6-56
B	125	75	3↓	0↓	SN54S114	J, W	SN74S114	J, N	5-34	6-58
	50	100	13↓	0↓	SN54H108	J, W	SN74H108	J, N	5-32	6-52
	45	10	20↓	0↓	SN54LS78A	J, W	SN74LS78A	J, N	5-24	6-56
	45	10	20↓	0↓	SN54LS114A	J, W	SN74LS114A	J, N	5-34	6-56
C	125	75	3↓	0↓	SN54S113	J, W	SN74S113	J, N	5-34	6-58
	45	10	20↓	0↓	SN54LS113A	J, W	SN74LS113A	J, N	5-34	6-56
D	50	100	13↓	0↓	SN54H103	J, W	SN74H103	J, N	5-31	6-52
	45	10	20↓	0↓	SN54LS73A	J, W	SN74LS73A	J, N	5-22	6-56
	45	10	20↓	0↓	SN54LS107A	J	SN74LS107A	J, N	5-32	6-56
E	33	10	20↑	5↑	SN54LS109A	J, W	SN74LS109A	J, N	5-33	6-56
	33	45	10↑	6↑	SN54109	J, W	SN74109	J, N	5-33	6-46
F	50	100	13↓	0↓	SN54H101	J, W	SN74H101	J, N	5-31	6-52
G	50	100	13↓	0↓	SN54H102	J, W	SN74H102	J, N	5-31	6-52
H	35	65	20↑	5↑	SN5470	J, W	SN7470	J, N	5-21	6-46

↑↓ The arrow indicates the edge of the clock pulse used for reference: ↑ for the rising edge, ↓ for the falling edge.

Fig. 5-39. Data sheet for RET and FET. JK Flip-Flops. (Courtesy of Texas Instruments, Inc.)

D-TYPE FLIP-FLOPS
DUAL

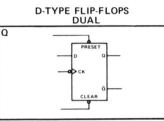

DWG. REF.	TYPICAL CHARACTERISTICS		DATA TIMES		TEMPERATURE RANGE	
	f_{max} (MHz)	Pwr/F-F (mW)	SETUP (ns)	HOLD (ns)	−55°C to 125°C	0°C to 70°C
Q	110	75	3↑	2↑	SN54S74	SN74S74
	43	75	15↑	5↑	SN54H74	SN74H74
	33	10	25↑	5↑	SN54LS74	SN74LS74
	25	43	20↑	5↑	SN5474	SN7474
	3	4	50↑	0↑	SN54L74	SN74L74

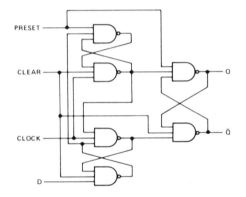

Fig. 5-40. Data and specification sheets for RET D Flip-Flops. (Courtesy of Texas Instruments, Inc.)

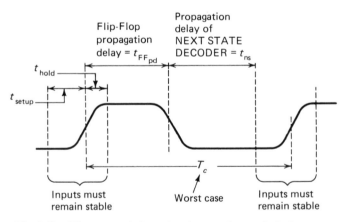

Fig. 5-41. Worst case timing related to maximum clock frequency determination.

The logic diagrams for the devices shown in Figures 5-36, 5-37, 5-38, and 5-39 are vastly different from those developed earlier. The reason for this is twofold:

(1) These devices incorporate the edge-trigger or lock-out features.
(2) The actual integrated circuit manufacturing processes many times dictate a particular logic form.

However, the EXCITATION TABLES for these IC devices are identical to those we have developed. Also, note that the rising-edge of the clock for the SN74111 locks the data into the master cell and the falling-edge transfers this data to the outputs, providing advantages or disadvantages depending on the circumstances.

We see in Chapter 10 how Flip-Flops with edge-triggering and data lock-out features can be designed in a straightforward manner. However, we use these devices and other similar devices to our advantage in the next several chapters to implement a variety of finite-state machines.

5-20 TIMING AND TRIGGERING CONSIDERATIONS

It should be noted that two important timing constraints are listed in the typical data sheet listing shown in Figures 5-38, 5-39, and 5-40. These are SET-UP and HOLD times. The definition of *SET-UP time is the time required for the input data to settle in before the triggering edge of the clock*. If you choose to ignore this specification, you should expect unpredictable behavior. This unpredictable behavior manifests itself in several ways:

(1) missed data or ignored actions;
(2) possible partial transient outputs.

These partial transient outputs are referred to as "partial SET" and "partial RESET" outputs. In other words, it is possible to start a RESET or SET operation, causing the output to start to change, but to fall back to its original state. Worse yet, a metastable condition can be precipitated in which the Flip-Flop is neither SET nor RESET for some undeterminable time. These concepts are fundamental in nature and are discussed at length in Chapter 7.

The definition of *HOLD time is the time required for the data to remain stable after the triggering edge of the clock*. Again, if you choose to ignore this specification, unpredictable behavior will result.

In keeping with this odd behavior constraint, these critical timing specifications also help determine the maximum allowable clock frequency for a finite-state machine. With all constraints included, Figure 5-41 illustrates how the worst case t_{SET-UP}, t_{HOLD}, Flip-Flop propagation delay and propagation delay of the NEXT STATE DECODER add together to determine the maximum clock frequency.

From this figure we see that if:

$$T_{c_{wc.}} \geq t_{su} + t_{FFpd} + t_{ns}$$

$$\therefore f_c \triangleq \frac{1}{T_c} \leq \frac{1}{t_{su} + t_{FFpd} + t_{ns}}$$

where $t_{su} \triangleq$ worst case SET-UP time

$t_{FFpd} \triangleq$ worst case Flip-Flop propagation delay from clock edge

$t_{ns} \triangleq$ worst case propagation delay through the NEXT STATE DE-CODER

5-21 CLOCK SKEW

Clock skew is effectively a time shift in a triggering edge of the system clock to various devices caused by delay introduced by buffer devices and the propagation delay of conducting paths (wires). Skew is of particular importance when shift register operation is involved. For example, there are many times when one memory device (destination device) is intended to load the output of another driving device (source device) on the rising-edge of the clock, when this same rising-edge is in turn changing the output of the source device (see Figure 5-42).

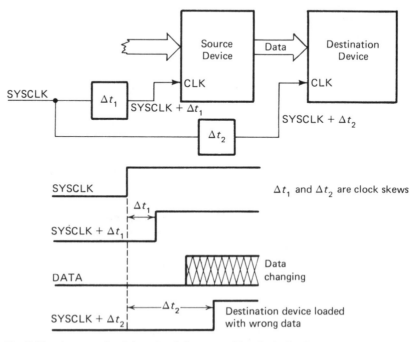

Fig. 5-42. An example of the missed data caused by clock skewing.

Now, if there is clock skew which tends to delay the loading of the destination device for a period of time greater than it takes to change the present output of the source device, reliable operation no longer prevails. In short, if the clock skew violates the HOLD time requirements of the destination device, you have trouble. Thus if clock drivers (buffers) are used in systems which incorporate this source/ destination relationship, added delay (inverters) may have to be added to assure reliable operation.

One more warning: When using any device, integrated or not, be certain to spend some time dwelling on the specification sheets for that device. Many times there are hidden messages in these sheets that will make or break your design. *Hence, know your devices and their limitations and use good sense when bringing them together.*

Table 5-1 presents a listing of symbols, terms, and definitions for digital integrated circuits. You should study these closely in order to facilitate your interpretation of manufacturers' data sheets.

GLOSSARY
TTL TERMS AND DEFINITIONS

INTRODUCTION

These symbols, terms, and definitions are in accordance with those currently agreed upon by the JEDEC Council of the Electronic Industries Association (EIA) for use in the USA and by the International Electrotechnical Commission (IEC) for international use.

PART I — OPERATING CONDITIONS AND CHARACTERISTICS (INCLUDING LETTER SYMBOLS)

Clock Frequency

Maximum clock frequency, f_{max}
The highest rate at which the clock input of a bistable circuit can be driven through its required sequence while maintaining stable transistions of logic level at the output with input conditions established that should cause changes of output logic level in accordance with the specification.

Current

High-level input current, I_{IH}
The current into* an input when a high-level voltage is applied to that input.

High-level output current, I_{OH}
The current into* an output with input conditions applied that according to the product specification will establish a high level at the output.

Low-level input current, I_{IL}
The current into* an input when a low-level voltage is applied to that input.

Low-level output current, I_{OL}
The current into* an output with input conditions applied that according to the product specification will establish a low level at the output.

Table 5-1. (Courtesy of Texas Instruments, Inc.)

Off-state output current, $I_{O(off)}$

The current flowing into* an output with input conditions applied that according to the product specification will cause the output switching element to be in the off state.

Note: This parameter is usually specified for open-collector outputs intended to drive devices other than logic circuits.

Off-state (high-impedance-state) output current (of a three-state output), I_{OZ}

The current into* an output having three-state capability with input conditions applied that according to the product specification will establish the high-impedance state at the output.

Short-circuit output current, I_{OS}

The current into* an output when that output is short-circuited to ground (or other specified potential) with input conditions applied to establish the output logic level farthest from ground potential (or other specified potential).

Supply current, I_{CC}

The current into* the V_{CC} supply terminal of an integrated circuit.

Hold Time

Hold time, t_h

The interval during which a signal is retained at a specified input terminal after an active transition occurs at another specified input terminal.

NOTES: 1. The hold time is the actual time between two events and may be insufficient to accomplish the intended result. A minimum value is specified that is the shortest interval for which correct operation of the logic element is guaranteed.

2. The hold time may have a negative value in which case the minimum limit defines the longest interval (between the release of data and the active transition) for which correct operation of the logic element is guaranteed.

Output Enable and Disable Time

Output enable time (of a three-state output) to high level, t_{PZH} (or low level, t_{PZL})[†]

The propagation delay time between the specified reference points on the input and output voltage waveforms with the three-state output changing from a high-impedance (off) state to the defined high (or low) level.

Output enable time (of a three-state output) to high or low level, t_{PZX}[†]

The propagation delay time between the specified reference points on the input and output voltage waveforms with the three-state output changing from a high-impedance (off) state to either of the defined active levels (high or low).

Output disable time (of a three-state output) from high level, t_{PHZ} (or low level, t_{PLZ})[†]

The propagation delay time between the specified reference points on the input and output voltage waveforms with the three-state output changing from the defined high (or low) level to a high-impedance (off) state.

Output disable time (of a three-state output) from high or low level, t_{PXZ}[†]

The propagation delay time between the specified reference points on the input and output voltage waveforms with the three-state output changing from either of the defined active levels (high or low) to a high-impedance (off) state.

Propagation Time

Propagation delay time, t_{PD}

The time between the specified reference points on the input and output voltage waveforms with the output changing from one defined level (high or low) to the other defined level.

Propagation delay time, low-to-high-level output, t_{PLH}

The time between the specified reference points on the input and output voltage waveforms with the output changing from the defined low level to the defined high level.

Table 5-1. (Cont.) (Courtesy of Texas Instruments, Inc.)

Propagation delay time, high-to-low-level output, tPHL
The time between the specified reference points on the input and output voltage waveforms with the output changing from the defined high level to the defined low level.

Pulse Width

Pulse width, t_w
The time interval between specified reference points on the leading and trailing edges of the pulse waveform.

Recovery Time

Sense recovery time, t_{SR}
The time interval needed to switch a memory from a write mode to a read mode and to obtain valid data signals at the output.

Release Time

Release time, $t_{release}$
The time interval between the release from a specified input terminal of data intended to be recognized and the occurrence of an active transition at another specified input terminal.

Note: When specified, the interval designated "release time" falls within the setup interval and constitutes, in effect, a negative hold time.

Setup Time

Setup time, t_{su}
The time interval between the application of a signal that is maintained at a specified input terminal and a consecutive active transition at another specified input terminal.
NOTES: 1. The setup time is the actual time between two events and may be insufficient to accomplish the setup. A minimum value is specified that is the shortest interval for which correct operation of the logic element is guaranteed.
2. The setup time may have a negative value in which case the minimum limit defines the longest interval (between the active transition and the application of the other signal) for which correct operation of the logic element is guaranteed.

Transition Time

Transition time, low-to-high-level, t_{TLH}
The time between a specified low-level voltage and a specified high-level voltage on a waveform that is changing from the defined low level to the defined high level.

Transition time, high-to-low-level, t_{THL}
The time between a specified high-level voltage and a specified low-level voltage on a waveform that is changing from the defined high level to the defined low level.

Voltage

High-level input voltage, V_{IH}
An input voltage within the more positive (less negative) of the two ranges of values used to represent the binary variables.
NOTE: A minimum is specified that is the least positive value of high-level input voltage for which operation of the logic element within specification limits is guaranteed.

High-level output voltage, V_{OH}
The voltage at an output terminal with input conditions applied that according to the product specification will establish a high level at the output.

Table 5-1. (Cont.) (Courtesy of Texas Instruments, Inc.)

Input clamp voltage, V_{IK}

An input voltage in a region of relatively low differential resistance that serves to limit the input voltage swing.

Low-level input voltage, V_{IL}

An input voltage level within the less positive (more negative) of the two ranges of values used to represent the binary variables.

NOTE: A maximum is specified that is the most positive value of low-level input voltage for which operation of the logic element within specification limits is guaranteed.

Low-level output voltage, V_{OL}

The voltage at an output terminal with input conditions applied that according to the product specification will establish a low level at the output.

Negative-going threshold voltage, V_{T-}

The voltage level at a transition-operated input that causes operation of the logic element according to specification as the input voltage falls from a level above the positive-going threshold voltage, V_{T+}.

Off-state output voltage, $V_{O(off)}$

The voltage at an output terminal with input conditions applied that according to the product specification will cause the output switching element to be in the off state.

Note: This characteristic is usually specified only for outputs not having internal pull-up elements.

On-state output voltage, $V_{O(on)}$

The voltage at an output terminal with input conditions applied that according to the product specification will cause the output switching element to be in the on state.

Note: This characteristic is usually specified only for outputs not having internal pull-up elements.

Positive-going threshold voltage, V_{T+}

The voltage level at a transition-operated input that causes operation of the logic element according to specification as the input voltage rises from a level below the negative-going threshold voltage, V_{T-}.

Table 5-1. (Cont.) (Courtesy of Texas Instruments, Inc.)

5-22 SUMMARY

Fundamental and practical information concerning sequential and finite-state machines has been discussed in this chapter. It is imperative that you understand these concepts, for the rest of this text is strongly dependent on your understanding of:

(1) combination timing aspects of sequential machines;
(2) the concept of memory;
(3) the concept of control;
(4) the general model of the sequential machine;
(5) the distinction between combinational and sequential machines;
(6) propagation delay;
(7) the binary cell;
(8) classes of sequential machines;
(9) Flip-Flop design;
(10) the practical aspects of modern Flip-Flops.

BIBLIOGRAPHY

1. HARTMANIS, J. and R. E. STEARNS. *Algebraic Structure Theory of Sequential Machines.* Englewood Cliffs, N. J.: Prentice-Hall, 1966.

2. HILL, FREDRICK J. and PETERSEN, GERALD R. *Introduction to Switching Theory and Logical Design.* New York: Wiley, 1974.

3. McCLUSKEY, E. J. *Introduction to the Theory of Switching Circuits.* New York: McGraw-Hill, 1965.

4. MANO, M. MORRIS. *Computer Logic Design.* Englewood Cliffs, N. J.: Prentice-Hall, 1972.

5. MEALY, G. H. A Method for Synthesizing Sequential Circuits. *Bell System Tech. J.,* 34:5 (1955), 1045–1080.

6. MOORE, E. F. *Sequential Machines: Selected Papers.* Reading, Mass.: Addison-Wesley, 1964.

7. *The TTL Data Book for Design Engineers,* 2nd ed. Dallas: Texas Instruments, Inc., 1976.

8. TORNG, H. C. *Introduction to the Logical Design of Switching Systems.* Reading, Mass.: Addison-Wesley, 1964.

9. WICKES, WILLIAM E. *Logic Design with Integrated Circuits.* New York: Wiley, 1968.

10. WILLIAMS, GERALD E. *Digital Technology.* Chicago: Science Research Associates, Inc., 1977.

PROBLEMS AND EXERCISES

5-1. In your own words, define a controlled system.

5-2. The XYZ Elevator Company has need for a system that will position an elevator threshold level with the hall floor each time it stops. Use a block diagram approach and any sensors you like, and define a closed-loop (feedback) control system that you believe will solve this positioning problem.

5-3. Figure P5-1 is a schematic of a digital circuit that employs feedback. Assume the devices called out as FLIP-FLOPS combined together form the memory element.
   (a) Redraw the circuit.
   (b) Identify the portion of this circuit which can be considered to be the IN-PUT/OUTPUT transforming logic.
   (c) Identify the portion of this circuit which can be considered to be the output conditioning logic.

5-4. Discuss in your own words how a digital system utilizing feedback differs from a strictly combinational circuit. Include in your discussion how the past history of the input sequences is provided by this feedback.

5-5. (a) In your own words define the basic operational characteristics of a sequential machine.
   (b) What single word is basic to the description of a sequential circuit?
   (c) Draw a distinction between a sequential machine and a finite-state machine.

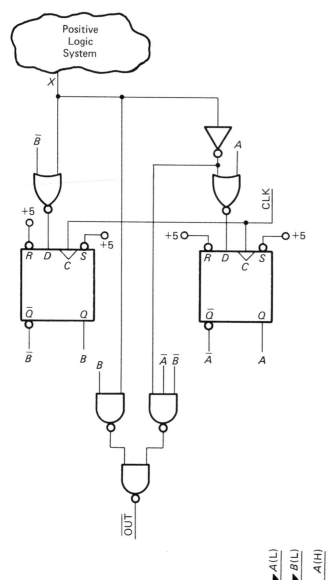

Fig. P5-1.

Fig. P5-2.

5-6. (a) List the two essential properties that a digital system must have in order to be classed as a SEQUENTIAL CIRCUIT.

(b) Classify the circuit shown in Figure P5-2.

(c) If you have classified this circuit as sequential, identify the MEMORY ELEMENT in this circuit.

5-7. In your own words discuss the concept of memory as it applies to digital circuits.

5-8. (a) Discuss, using timing diagrams, the operation of a binary cell developed around NOR gates.

(b) Draw a distinction between a NAND and NOR cell.

(c) Why is it unadvisable to ASSERT both the SET and RESET input of any binary cell?

(d) What should be the direct consequence of a SET OPERATION (RESET OPERATION)?

5-9. Using timing diagrams, analyze the switch debouncer shown in Figure 5-11.

5-10. Design and document a switch debouncer centered around a two-input NOR gate.

5-11. Using timing diagrams, analyze the switch debouncers shown in Figure 5-12. Discuss any potential problems that might be caused by using these "debouncers."

5-12. Discuss the basic difference between ASYNCHRONOUS and SYNCHRONOUS sequential circuits. Classify the binary cell. What function does the CLOCK perform?

5-13. Discuss the concept of the STATE of a machine introduced in Section 5-8. In doing so, relate the concept of the past history discussed in Section 5-2 to the definition of the STATE.

5-14. Without looking back into the text, *draw and fully label* the general model of a sequential finite-state machine.

5-15. What is the basic difference between a MEALY machine and a MOORE machine?

5-16. Taken as a stand alone device, is a Flip-Flop a synchronous or asynchronous device?

5-17. Without looking back into the text, draw the general model of a simple Flip-Flop.

5-18. (a) Analyze the following CLOCK OSCILLATOR (Figure P5-3) using timing diagrams and determine the frequency of oscillation if the propagation delay through each INVERTER = 30 nsec.

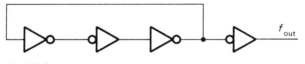

Fig. P5-3.

(b) What three basic circuit properties make this circuit oscillate?

5-19. Design a clock oscillator that will oscillate at 50 KHz.

(a) Use the circuit in Figure 5-21(b).

(b) Use the circuit in Figure 5-21(d).

(c) Use the circuit in Figure 5-21(e).

(d) Use a 74C14 as the output buffer and an adjustable resistor sufficiently large to obtain ±20% symmetry adjustment.

5-20. Using timing diagrams analyze the operation of:
(a) The clocked RS Flip-Flop shown in Figure 5-22.
(b) The clocked D-Latch shown in Figure 5-23.

5-21. Discuss why the avoidance of the indeterminability of a binary cell becomes increasingly important where clocked RS Flip-Flops are being used.

5-22. By making a simple transformation, convert the RS Flip-Flop shown in Figure 5-22 to support the following schematic symbol (Figure P5-4).

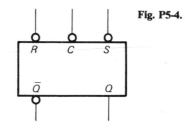

Fig. P5-4.

5-23. Using a timing diagram approach, analyze the T Flip-Flop shown in Figure 5-24. Include propagation delay in your analysis, illustrating the undesirable mode of operation (oscillation or hang) discussed in Section 5-15.

5-24. Using the steps set forth in Section 5-17:
(a) Design a NAND cell centered LM Flip-Flop specified by the following characteristic table and schematic symbol (Figure P5-5).

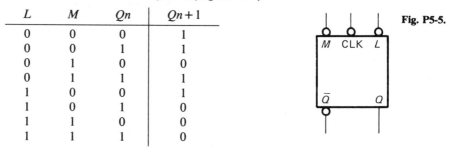

Fig. P5-5.

L	M	Qn	$Qn+1$
0	0	0	1
0	0	1	1
0	1	0	0
0	1	1	1
1	0	0	1
1	0	1	0
1	1	0	0
1	1	1	0

(b) Define the excitation table for the LM Flip-Flop.

5-25. Using the steps set forth in Section 5-17:
(a) Define the characteristic table.
(b) Design a NAND cell-centered Flip-Flop.
(c) Define the excitation table for a SET dominant clocked SR Flip-Flop. This Flip-Flop is to always leave the basic cell in a SET condition if S and R are asserted together. Design in asynchronous SET and RESET functions.

5-26. Repeat the steps specified in Problem 5-25 for the following design problem: Design a RESET dominant clocked RS Flip-Flop. This Flip-Flop is to always leave the basic cell in a RESET condition if S and R are ASSERTED together. Design in asynchronous SET and RESET functions.

5-27. Repeat the steps specified in Problem 5-25 for the following design problem: Design a RS Flip-Flop that will leave the basic cell unchanged if the S and R are ASSERTED together.

5-28. Design a Flip-Flop specified by the following characteristic table. Check your circuit with Figure 5-25(b).

	J	K	Qn	Qn+1
0	0	0	0	0
1	0	0	1	1
2	0	1	0	0
3	0	1	1	0
4	1	0	0	1
5	1	0	1	1
6	1	1	0	1
7	1	1	1	0

5-29. Using all the information available, design a NOR cell centered POOPS-DINK (P,D) Flip-Flop that operates as specified by the following table and schematic symbol (Figure P5-6):

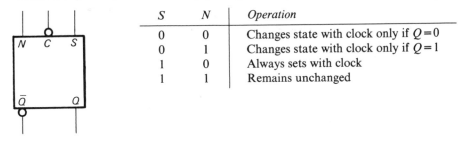

P	D	Operation
0	0	Changes state with clock only if $Q=1$
0	1	Changes state with clock only if $Q=1$
1	0	Always sets the Flip-Flop with clock
1	1	Changes state with clock.

Fig. P5-6.

(a) Show general model of your Flip-Flop.
(b) Define the characteristic table.
(c) Define the excitation table.
(d) Show completely documented schematic diagram.

5-30. Repeat Problem 5-29 for the SN Flip-Flop that is specified by the following table and schematic symbol (use NAND cell) (see Figure P5-7).

S	N	Operation
0	0	Changes state with clock only if $Q=0$
0	1	Changes state with clock only if $Q=1$
1	0	Always sets with clock
1	1	Remains unchanged

Fig. P5-7.

5-31. Is it possible to design a T Flip-Flop that triggers on the rising-edge of the clock and within reasonable limits avoid the oscillation or hang problems associated with T Flip-Flops? Outline your method of attack for solving the problem.

5-32. Using the method outlined in Section 5-18, carry out the following conversions.
(a) Convert a D-Latch to a JK.
(b) Convert a JK Flip-Flop to a D-Latch.
(c) Convert a JK Flip-Flop to a T.
(d) Convert a T Flip-Flop to a JK.

5-33. Using the method outlined in Section 5-18, carry out the following conversions.
(a) Convert a D Flip-Flop to the PD Flip-Flop specified in Problem 5-29.
(b) Convert a JK Flip-Flop to the SN Flip-Flop specified in Problem 5-30.

5-34. In your own words discuss the "hows" and "whens" the 1's and 0's catching problem arises when using a MASTER/SLAVE Flip-Flop. How does the asynchronous input create a problem?

5-35. Design, using the methods outlined, a D MASTER/SLAVE Flip-Flop.

5-36. In your own words discuss the three types of JK Flip-Flops triggering discussed in Section 5-19. Draw comparisons between the three and list what you see as advantages and disadvantages of each.

5-37. Draw a timing diagram and illustrate your understanding of SETUP and HOLDING time. Give a qualitative description of each and how these specifications relate to the hardware of the Flip-Flop.

5-38. In your own words discuss clock skew. Discuss why clock skew can create data transmission problems.

5-39. Consider you are far off in Futz-a-too and you have burned out your last J-K falling-edge trigger Flip-Flop which was used as a T Flip-Flop with T ASSERTED LOW. But all is not lost—you have one rising-edge triggered D Flip-Flop, and the following gates (not packages) on your board: one INVERTER, one two-input OR gate, and two two-input NAND gates.
(a) Using these devices *design* (show all design work) a circuit which will replace your burned out T Flip-Flop. (i) Draw your conversion model. (ii) Draw your circuit.
(b) You are given the following propagation delay parameters:

Inverter—10 nsec
All two-input gates—20 nsec
D Flip-Flop
  —set up time = 20 nsec
  —hold time = 5 nsec

What is the set up and hold time for your new Flip-Flop?

TRADITIONAL APPROACHES TO
SEQUENTIAL ANALYSIS AND DESIGN

6-1 INTRODUCTION

Chapter 5 introduces the general concepts of sequential machines and their nature and behavior at a systems level and covers the operational characteristics of Flip-Flops. This chapter presents a detailed study of the *synchronous* sequential machine in order that you may gain an insight into the fundamental aspects of the analysis and design of some of the more traditional synchronous sequential circuits. In particular, special methods of attack are illustrated for both the analysis and design of small scale sequential machines. Further, the use of design aids such as STATE DIAGRAMS and special maps are covered. More importantly, some basic design philosophy and concepts are hammered out that hopefully go a long way toward helping you to conquer a structured approach to sequential problem solutions. These concepts are treated through the use of many example and problem exercises concerned with some general and widely used sequential machines. Generally, these sequential machines are classed as follows:

(1) Code sequence detectors
(2) Standard counters and registers
(3) Sequential code generators
(4) Multi-input system controllers

The analysis and design of the first three classifications are discussed in this chapter, leaving the fourth classification to be treated in Chapters 7, 8, and 9.

6-2 THE STATE DIAGRAM

The success of analysis or design of sequential machines depends largely on the aids and systematic techniques used in these processes. Although all designers do not use the techniques outlined in this chapter, *some* systematic techniques such as these are certainly desirable. One of the aids mentioned previously was the *state diagram*. This aid is a widely accepted pictorial guide used to describe or graphically define the STATE-TO-STATE transitions of a sequential machine. It will be illustrated shortly that the STATE DIAGRAM is to sequential design what the TRUTH-TABLE is to combinational design. An example of a state diagram is given in Figure 6-1 illustrating the STATE-OF-INTEREST and five important and required pieces of information related to *each STATE* of the machine. As shown, the state diagram is an array of "bubbles" connected by directed line segments with arrowheads. Each bubble represents a STATE of the machine and the line segments are graphical indications of STATE changes. By further study of Figure 6-1, you discover that five important and descriptive pieces of information for each STATE are given and labeled as follows:

(1) some STATE identifying symbol or code;
(2) the previous STATE of the STATE OF INTEREST;
(3) the INPUT conditions leading to the STATE OF INTEREST;
(4) the OUTPUT specification for the STATE OF INTEREST;
(5) the NEXT STATES and NEXT STATE branching conditions for the STATE OF INTEREST.

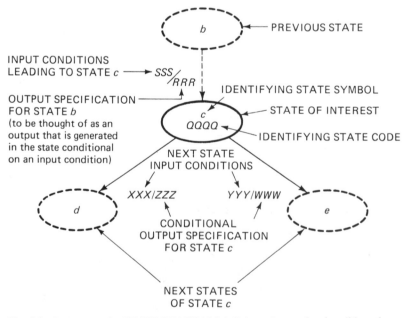

Fig. 6-1. A segment of a STATE DIAGRAM defining a format for describing the five important pieces of information for *each* STATE of a machine.

Chapter 6 shows how a state diagram can be put to a definite use in the description of the operation of a sequential machine. Chapter 7 demonstrates the power of a well-documented state diagram by illustrating that this diagram and maps are essentially *all* that are required to develop the schematics for a sequential design.

To further illustrate the use of a state diagram, consider the following example.

> *EXAMPLE 6-1:* Suppose you were given the following word specification describing the sequential operation of some machine. This machine has a single control input X and the CLOCK, and two outputs A and B. On consecutive rising edges of the CLOCK the code on A and B changes from 00 to 01 to 10 to 11 and then repeats itself if X is ASSERTED; if at any time X is DE-ASSERTED, this machine is supposed to hold its present STATE. The pictorial description of this sequential machine is shown in Figure 6-2.

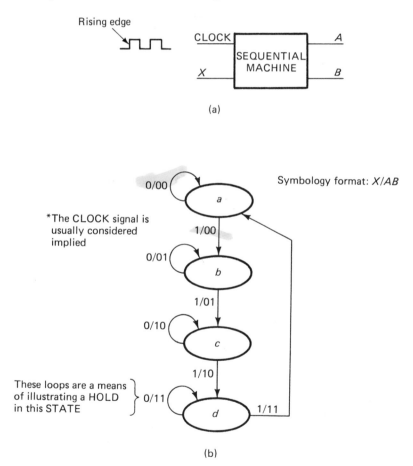

(a)

(b)

Fig. 6-2. The pictorial description of the machine described in Example 6-1. (a) The block diagram. (b) The state diagram defining the operation of the sequential machine.

The machine is obviously described much more clearly by the state diagram than by the word statement. As you scan the state diagram you can examine each STATE and obtain the information required to determine the previous STATE, the conditions for the NEXT STATE, and the output for each STATE.

The descriptive features of the state diagram make it an invaluable aid in the following three major areas: (1) the definition of sequential systems, (2) the analysis of sequential circuits, and (3) the design of sequential circuits. The state diagram shown in Figure 6-2 for Example 6-1 illustrates the use of a state diagram for a sequential system definition. Here the word description of the circuit's operation is replaced by a picture. Example 6-2 illustrates yet another system with more complex branching requirements. Also, a code is assigned to the STATE VARI-ABLES (see Figure 6-3(b)).

EXAMPLE 6-2: See Figure 6-3.

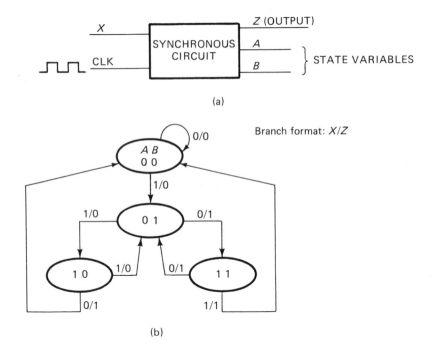

(a)

(b)

Fig. 6-3. An illustration of block and state diagrams for defining the sequential behavior of a sequential circuit. (a) A proposed sequential machine whose input controlled operation is described by the state diagram in (b).

Here again the sequential behavior of a circuit can be visualized without a cumbersome word description. Thus, as far as descriptive properties go, the state diagram is to sequential circuits what the TRUTH-TABLE is to combinational circuits.

How the state diagram can be used in the analysis of a sequential machine is illustrated in the next few sections.

6-3 ANALYSIS OF SYNCHRONOUS SEQUENTIAL CIRCUITS

Imagine that you were given the circuit shown in Figure 6-4 and asked to analyze it. Without some method of attack it would be difficult to get started; furthermore, it would not be obvious what the results of an analysis should be.

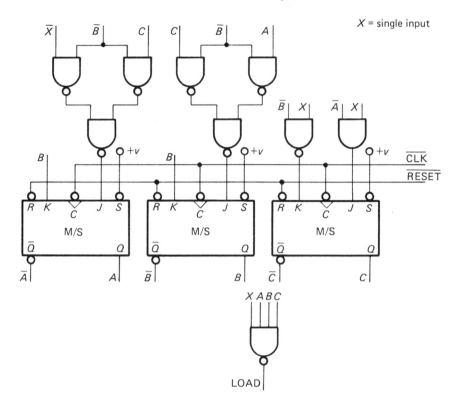

Fig. 6-4. A circuit to be analyzed.

For this reason, an analysis procedure is developed in the next section. Another reason for treating analysis at this time is that comprehending the design process is probably easier once an analysis technique is understood. Still another important reason for your learning analysis is that there might be cases in which you are given a circuit designed by some other party and asked to answer questions such as: "How does it work?", "Does it work?" and "If it doesn't work, what needs to be done to make it work?"

When faced with any analysis problem you must first determine: (1) What class of circuit is the one that you are to analyze; and (2) What are to be the results of the analysis process. In other words, is it a combinational circuit or sequential circuit? If it is a sequential circuit, is it asynchronous or synchronous? Once the class of machine has been established, what exactly is to be the information derived from the analysis? The analysis of *synchronous* sequential circuits and the answers to specific questions concerning the resultant information are best answered by examples. There are some basic questions, however, that should be addressed before any analysis process is undertaken. These basic questions are given as follows:

(1) What STATES (codes) are involved in postulated cyclic behavior of the circuit to be analyzed?
(2) What are the input conditions associated with the postulated state changes of the circuit to be analyzed?
(3) What are the output sequences associated with the postulated cyclic or sequential behavior of the circuit to be analyzed?

Note that a cyclic behavior criterion is postulated in each question to be answered, and based on this, the first assumption is that the machine will reside in more than *one* STATE. Also, note the general overriding question: "How will this circuit respond under *all* or *selected* input conditions?"

6-4 A SYNCHRONOUS ANALYSIS PROCESS

Chapter 5 demonstrates that the operation of a sequential machine can be nicely characterized by the STATE OF THE MACHINE concept, with the STATE OF THE MACHINE defined as the code present at the outputs of the memory element of a sequential machine. Further, Chapter 5 introduces the concept of tracing the STATE TO STATE behavior of a sequential machine by selecting some STATE (code) and input conditions and deriving the NEXT STATE and the OUTPUT of the machine in *that particular STATE*. This concept is the very essence of the analysis procedure to be followed. In short, when given a synchronous sequential circuit to analyze, start the process by selecting some possible STATE for that machine, combine this STATE variable code with *all* or some *selected* INPUT conditions, and derive the NEXT STATE and the OUTPUT conditions for that *STATE*. Then continue this process until all possible STATES for the machine have been covered. Understanding this process is based on understanding the NEXT STATE DECODER, Flip-Flop characteristics, and the OUTPUT DECODER sections of the class *A*, *B*, and *C* sequential machines. Remember that the NEXT STATE DECODER has the function of decoding the STATE OF THE MACHINE *and* the present input conditions and generating a NEXT STATE CODE. This NEXT STATE CODE is further decoded by the combinational logic internal to the particular Flip-Flop (RS, D, T, or JK) before the TRUE NEXT STATE is generated. To illustrate this, consider Figure 6-5.

In this figure it should be obvious that the logic required for the NEXT STATE DECODER is *directly dependent* on the *type* of Flip-Flop used for the memory element. Therefore, complete knowledge of Flip-Flop characteristics is required before the TRUE NEXT STATE code can be determined. This TRUE NEXT STATE decoding will be demonstrated shortly using special tables filled out from the information provided by maps and the Flip-Flop NEXT STATE tables.

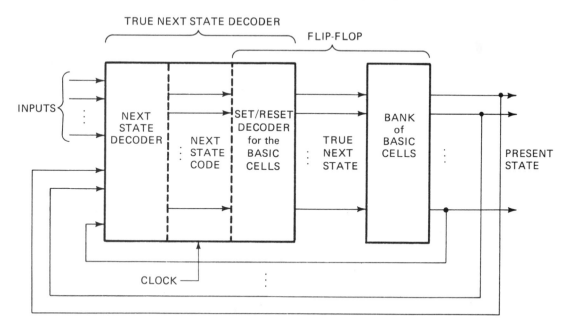

Fig. 6-5. An illustration of how the TRUE NEXT STATE for a sequential machine is generated.

The OUTPUT DECODER block in a sequential machine may or may not be present, based on whether the machine is a class C or not. However, its general function is to decode the STATE of the machine combined with the PRESENT INPUT condition and to generate an OUTPUT accordingly.

With this basic understanding, the circuit shown in Figure 6-4 can be analyzed to determine the cyclic behavior of this machine under *all* possible input conditions as shown in the following example.

> *EXAMPLE 6-3:* Given the circuit in Figure 6-6, which is the circuit in Figure 6-4 re-drawn in a mixed-logic format, completely analyze its sequential behavior.
>
> *Step 1*: Indentify the functional block of the sequential machine as shown in Figure 6-5, that is, NEXT STATE DECODER, MEMORY ELE-MENT, and OUTPUT DECODER. Note: This is a class *A* machine.
>
> *Step 2*: Write the Boolean expression for each of the outputs of the NEXT STATE DECODER. This six-bit CODE makes up the inputs for the JK Flip-Flops. Once these are known, they can be coupled with the JK Flip-Flop characteristics to determine the TRUE NEXT STATE code.

Thus we derive:

$$J_A(\text{H}) = (\bar{B}C + \bar{B}\bar{X})(\text{H})$$

$$K_A(\text{H}) = B(\text{H})$$

$$J_B(\text{H}) = (A\bar{B} + \bar{B}C)(\text{H})$$

$$K_B(\text{H}) = B(\text{H})$$

$$J_C(\text{H}) = (\bar{A}X)(\text{H})$$

$$K_C(\text{H}) = (B + \bar{X})(\text{H})$$

and the output:

$$\text{LOAD}(\text{L}) = (ABCX)(\text{L})$$

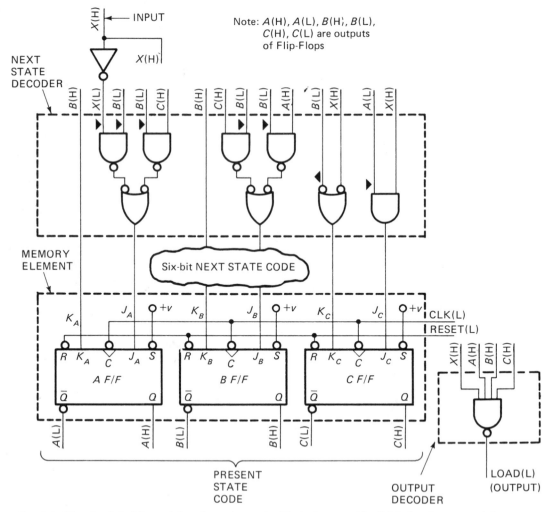

Fig. 6-6. The circuit in Figure 6-4 re-drawn in a mixed-logic format with all blocks of a sequential machine indicated.

Step 3: Plot the map for each of the NEXT STATE variables shown in Figure 6-7. These maps serve as a useful tool for tabulating the NEXT STATE code, as shown in this example.

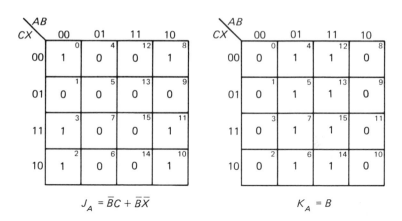

$$J_A = \bar{B}C + \bar{B}\bar{X}$$

$$K_A = B$$

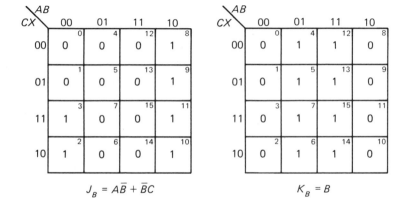

$$J_B = A\bar{B} + \bar{B}C$$

$$K_B = B$$

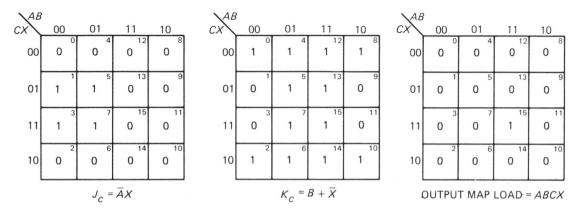

$$J_C = \bar{A}X$$

$$K_C = B + \bar{X}$$

OUTPUT MAP LOAD = $ABCX$

Fig. 6-7. NEXT STATE VARIABLE MAPS and OUTPUT MAP.

Step 4: Using the entries in these maps, plot the values for the Flip-Flop inputs $(J_A, K_A, J_B, K_B, J_C, K_C)$ in a PRESENT and NEXT STATE TABLE as shown in Table 6-1. Hint: Note that the entries for the J_A, K_A, J_B, K_B, J_C, and K_C in the PRESENT and NEXT STATE TABLE can be readily taken from the maps for J_A, K_A, J_B, K_B, J_C, and K_C. This can be seen by examining the actual maps as shown in Figure 6-8.

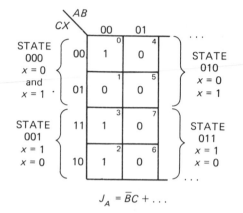

$$J_A = \bar{B}C + \ldots$$

Fig. 6-8. A partial map illustrating how the map may be partitioned to aid in plotting the PRESENT and NEXT STATE TABLE entries for the Flip-Flop inputs.

Another possible analysis map format that can be used is the one shown in Figure 6-9. These maps use the MAP-ENTERED-VARIABLE approach in that each cell entry indicates the action to be taken for each Flip-Flop for each of the possible states under the different input conditions. The NEXT STATE TABLE shown in Figure 6-10 is used to plot these so-called ACTION MAPS.*

A Flip-Flop ACTION MAP

Each cell represents a STATE

B Flip-Flop ACTION MAP

C Flip-Flop ACTION MAP

Fig. 6-9. An alternate analysis to be used to determine the next STATE for each state of the machine.

*These Flip-Flop tables are introduced as an aid for beginners. Once you become completely familiar with Flip-Flops, these tables serve no real purpose.

Fig. 6-10. The NEXT STATE TABLE for a JK Flip-Flop.

INPUTS J K	ACTION	NEXT STATE
0 0	Do nothing (D)	Unchanged
0 1	RESET(R)	0
1 0	SET(S)	1
1 1	TOGGLE(T)	Change state (0 → 1, 1 → 0)

Step 5: Using the entries for the NEXT STATE CODE in the TABLE and a Flip-Flop NEXT STATE TABLE for the Flip-Flop, determine the TRUE NEXT STATE for *each* Flip-Flop one row at a time. See the TRUE NEXT STATE column in Table 6-1.

TABLE 6-1   The present and next state table and map for example 6-2

Present State A B C	Inputs X	Next State Code $J_A K_A J_B K_B J_C K_C$	Output Load	True Next State A B C
State 0 0 0 0	0	1 0 0 0 0 1	0	1 0 0
0 0 0 0	1	0 0 0 0 1 0	0	0 0 1
State 1 0 0 1	0	1 0 1 0 0 1	0	1 1 0
1 0 0 1	1	1 0 1 0 1 0	0	1 1 1
State 2 0 1 0	0	0 1 0 1 0 1	0	0 0 0
2 0 1 0	1	0 1 0 1 1 1	0	0 0 1
0 1 1	0	0 1 0 1 0 1	0	0 0 0
0 1 1	1	0 1 0 1 1 1	0	0 0 0
1 0 0	0	1 0 1 0 0 1	0	1 1 0
1 0 0	1	0 0 1 0 0 0	0	1 1 0
1 0 1	0	1 0 1 0 0 1	0	1 1 0
1 0 1	1	1 0 1 0 0 0	0	1 1 1
1 1 0	0	0 1 0 1 0 1	0	0 0 0
1 1 0	1	0 1 0 1 0 1	0	0 0 0
State 7 1 1 1	0	0 1 0 1 0 1	0	0 0 0
7 1 1 1	1	0 1 0 1 0 1	1	0 0 0

Entries indicate NEXT STATE

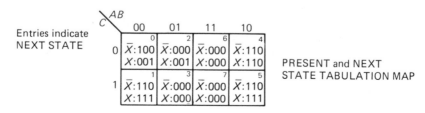

PRESENT and NEXT STATE TABULATION MAP

Using the NEXT STATE TABLE for a JK Flip-Flop shown in Figure 6-10, fill in the NEXT STATE column of Table 6-1, one row at a time, considering every possible STATE and all possible conditions for the *outside world inputs*. This is done by examining the codes in the $J_A K_A$, $J_B K_B$, and $J_C K_C$ columns and relating this information to the NEXT STATE TABLE in order that the NEXT STATE CODE can be derived (see Table 6-1). Likewise the PRESENT and NEXT STATE tabulation MAP can be filled out from the ACTION map in Figure 6-9.

Once the PRESENT and NEXT STATE table and/or map is completed, a state diagram can be developed directly from this information. This is done by selecting a PRESENT STATE (say 000) and drawing vectors to the appropriate NEXT STATES as indicated in the TRUE NEXT STATE column for $x = 0$ and $x = 1$. This procedure is repeated until all of the STATES have been analyzed as shown in Step 6.

Step 6: Using the PRESENT STATE, INPUT, and NEXT STATE data plotted in the PRESENT and NEXT STATE TABLE, develop a state diagram to graphically illustrate the circuit's STATE TO STATE behavior (see Figure 6-11).

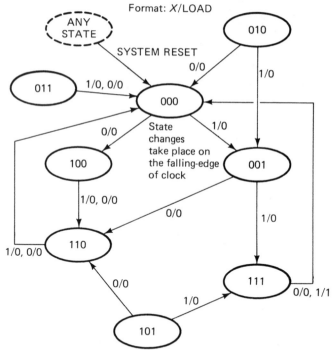

Fig. 6-11. The state diagram for the circuit shown in Figure 6-6.

Figure 6-11 shows that there are some interesting aspects concerning the cyclic behavior of the circuit. Observe that STATES 000, 001, 100, 110, and 111 are the sequential STATES and that the STATES 010, 011, and 101 are conditions which can never be reached unless NOISE or a POWER CONDITION forces the circuit into these STATES. However, further note that these states are not "hang" STATES,* because if the circuit happens to be jammed to one of these STATES by some abnormal conditions such as NOISE or POWER transients, it will not stay there for more than *one* clock cycle. This is a good feature to incorporate into most designs because unwanted STATES are undesirable, but unwanted STATES that hang the machine must be avoided. Therefore, designs should be carefully analyzed to insure that hang states are not possible. At times, situations may require building some programmed hang STATES into advanced designs. Programmed hang STATES differ from inadvertent hang STATES because programmed hang STATES are STATES into which a machine can be placed with a *specific input* condition (not NOISE). Once placed by an input condition in such a STATE, the machine will hang and no input condition except for a special reserved input will release the machine. This temporary hanging or holding operation is a useful debugging trick and is paralleled by a PAUSE feature built into a software or computer program, whereby the programmer can execute a program to some specific point or until some condition exists, signalling the machine (computer) to go into a PAUSE or temporary HOLD condition and remain in this condition until commanded to CONTINUE.

More is said in a later chapter about designs that have these debug features. For now, consider another analysis example in order to sharpen your ability to attack and analyze synchronous sequential circuits.

To aid in further analysis, the NEXT STATE TABLES for the D, T, and RS clocked Flip-Flops are given in Figures 6-12, 6-13, and 6-14.

Fig. 6-12. NEXT STATE TABLE for a D Flip-Flop.

INPUT D	ACTION	NEXT STATE
0	RESET	0
1	SET	1

Fig. 6-13. NEXT STATE TABLE for a T Flip-Flop.

INPUT T	ACTION	NEXT STATE
0	Do nothing	Unchanged
1	Toggle	Change states $(0 \rightarrow 1, 1 \rightarrow 0)$

Fig. 6-14. NEXT STATE TABLE for an SR Flip-Flop.

INPUT SR		ACTION	NEXT STATE
0	0	Do nothing	Unchanged
0	1	RESET	0
1	0	SET	1
1	1	Avoided	?

---

*A hang STATE is defined as a STATE in a machine in which *no input condition can cause a transition from that STATE.*

EXAMPLE 6-4: Analyze the circuit shown in Figure 6-15(a).
    Step 1:   Circuit

Step 1: Circuit

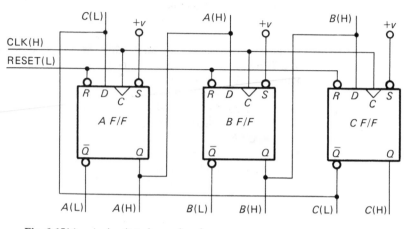

Fig. 6-15(a). A circuit to be analyzed.

Step 2: Flip-Flop equations

$$D_A = \bar{C}, \qquad D_B = A, \qquad D_C = B$$

Step 3: NEXT STATE MAPS

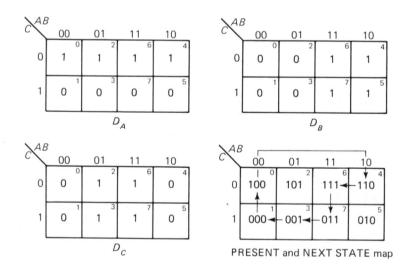

Fig. 6-15 (b).

Steps 4 and 5: PRESENT and NEXT STATE Tabulation

PRESENT STATE A B C	INPUTS $\emptyset$	NEXT STATE CODE D_A D_B D_C	OUTPUTS $\emptyset$	TRUE NEXT STATE A B C
0 0 0	–	1 0 0	–	1 0 0
0 0 1	–	0 0 0	–	0 0 0
0 1 0	–	1 0 1	–	1 0 1
0 1 1	–	0 0 1	–	0 0 1
1 0 0	–	1 1 0	–	1 1 0
1 0 1	–	0 1 0	–	0 1 0
1 1 0	–	1 1 1	–	1 1 1
1 1 1	–	0 1 1	–	0 1 1

Fig. 6-15(c).

Steps 6: The state diagram is derived as shown in Figure 6-16. We see by examining the state diagram in Step 6 that this sequential circuit has two states (010 and 101) that are isolated from the main sequence states. This type of operation is typical of a "twisted-ring counter" circuit such as the one in Figure 6-15(a). Another example of this twisted-type ring circuit is shown in Example 6-5.

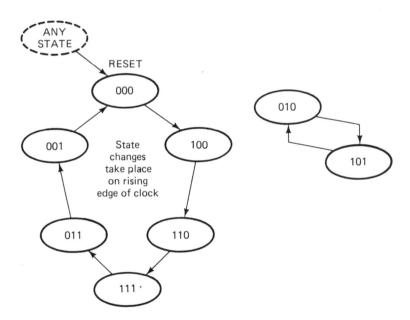

Fig. 6-16. The state diagram for the circuit shown in Figure 6-15(a).

EXAMPLE 6-5: Analyze the twisted-type ring counter of circuit shown in Figure 6-17(a).

Step 1: Circuit

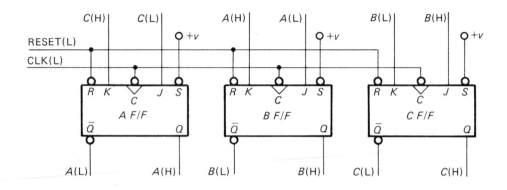

Fig. 6-17(a). Twisted ring counter circuit.

***Step 2*:** Flip-Flop equations

$$J_A = \overline{C}, \qquad J_B = \overline{A}, \qquad J_C = B$$
$$K_A = C, \qquad K_B = A, \qquad K_C = \overline{B}$$

***Step 3*:** NEXT STATE MAPS

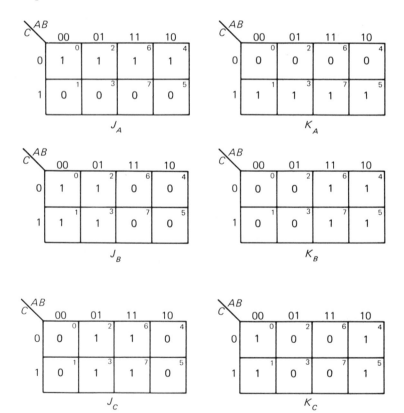

Fig. 6-17(b).

Steps 4 and 5:   PRESENT and NEXT STATE MAP and TABLE.

C \ AB	00	01	11	10
0	110 [0]	111 [2]	101 [6]	100 [4]
1	010 [1]	011 [3]	001 [7]	000 [5]

PRESENT STATE A B C	INPUT $\emptyset$	NEXT STATE CODE J_A K_A J_B K_B J_C K_C	OUTPUT $\emptyset$	TRUE NEXT STATE A B C
0 0 0	—	1 0 1 0 0 1	—	1 1 0
0 0 1	—	0 1 1 0 0 1	—	0 1 0
0 1 0	—	1 0 1 0 1 0	—	1 1 1
0 1 1	—	0 1 1 0 1 0	—	0 1 1
1 0 0	—	1 0 0 1 0 1	—	1 0 0
1 0 1	—	0 1 0 1 0 1	—	0 0 0
1 1 0	—	1 0 0 1 1 0	—	1 0 1
1 1 1	—	0 1 0 1 1 0	—	0 0 1

Fig. 6-17(c) and (d). NEXT STATE TABLE and MAP.

Step 6:   The state diagram is shown in Figure 6-17(e).

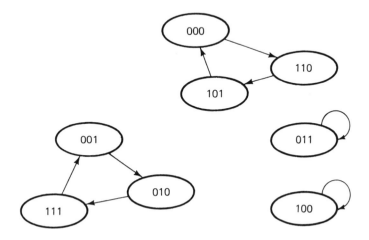

Fig. 6-17(e).   The steps taken to analyze the circuit shown in (a).

Figure 6-17(e) shows that this ring-type circuit definitely has problems.

SUMMARY OF ANALYSIS

We see from these examples that the analysis of synchronous sequential circuits is a straightforward process that can be summarized by the following steps:

(1) The given circuit must first be classified as a Class *A*, *B*, or *C* machine. Then the major blocks of the machine must be identified. If the observations required in this step can be enhanced by redrawing the circuit given in mixed logic format, do so. It has been found that the analysis of a synchronous machine's operation can be augmented by viewing it from the point of view shown in Figure 6-18 first, and then later by breaking it down into its functional blocks. In this way you can readily identify the pertinent variables associated with the machine's sequential behavior, namely: INPUTS, CLOCK, OUTPUTS, and STATE VARIABLES.

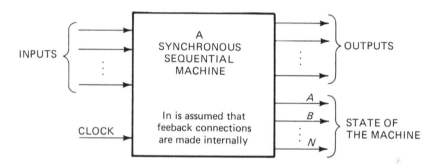

Fig. 6-18. A view of a synchronous sequential machine illustrating the pertinent variables associated with its behavior.

(2) Once NEXT STATE DECODER is identified, develop the Boolean expressions for *each of its outputs*.
(3) Plot the NEXT STATE MAPS from the expressions derived from the NEXT STATE DECODER outputs. If using the map methods, develop the ACTION MAPS.
(4) Develop a PRESENT and NEXT STATE TABLE or MAP that includes *all of the possible* PRESENT STATE CODES, NEXT STATE CODES, INPUT and OUTPUT CODES. Use the maps plotted in Step 3 to derive the NEXT STATE CODE.
(5) Complete the PRESENT and NEXT STATE TABLE or MAP by filling in the TRUE NEXT STATE code by using the Flip-Flop NEXT STATE TABLE for the particular Flip-Flop used.
(6) Develop a state diagram from the completed PRESENT and NEXT STATE TABLE or MAP. This is done simply by starting with the *first* PRESENT STATE entry and determining what the NEXT STATE is to be. Once a NEXT STATE has been documented in the state diagram, use this NEXT STATE code and the TABLE to derive the third STATE.

Continue this process until all STATES and input conditions have been documented.

(7) (Optional) From the state diagram a word description of the circuit can be derived.

As you develop an understanding of the analysis steps, you should begin to develop an important insight into the *design* processes. The next section shows that the traditional approach to designing synchronous sequential machines is closely allied with the analysis process, the major difference being that design processes start with Step 7 of the analysis steps and work backwards through these steps toward Step 1, with some extra embellishments added along the way. The insight gained by analyzing circuits should solidify your understanding of the functional requirements of the NEXT STATE DECODER, Flip-Flops, and OUTPUT DE-CODER circuits. This understanding is imperative in order for you to be able to effectively design other circuits, for it is generally true that *creativity stems from familiarity*.

6-5 APPROACHES TO THE DESIGN OF SYNCHRONOUS SEQUENTIAL FINITE-STATE MACHINES

The last several sections demonstrate some specific techniques for analysis of synchronous sequential machines. These techniques, though they seem somewhat algorithmic in nature, were specifically outlined to reinforce your conceptual understanding of the functional contribution made by each of the major blocks of an FSM.

This and the following sections introduce the steps leading to the design and implementation of synchronous circuits. These circuits will be of a simple variety, having a restricted number of INPUTS (≤ 2) and a possible number of states ≤ 16. The techniques introduced here are general, but it has been found through experience that the actual tabular documentation (dog work) required by traditional techniques for circuits having more than two OUTSIDE WORLD INPUTS and more than 16 STATES becomes impractical. This is particularly true when there are other easier and more straightforward design techniques available. Since these more advanced techniques are merely an extension of the traditional approaches, it is felt that a good understanding of the traditional approaches is desirable before going on to the so-called contemporary or advanced concepts treated in Chapter 7.

6-6 DESIGN STEPS FOR TRADITIONAL SYNCHRONOUS SEQUENTIAL CIRCUITS

The design of small scale and limited input sequential circuits is a straightforward algorithmic process, as the following 12 steps indicate. However, there is room for creativity, and some of these steps require a good deal of penetrating thought.

DESIGN STEPS

Step 1: Receive design specifications.

Step 2: Spend time studying specifications sufficient to gain an insight into the "real" operational behavior of the circuit.

Step 3: Make a block diagram model of your design. Identify all inputs and outputs. Note: Make certain that you completely understand *when and under what conditions outputs are to be generated*.

Step 4: Design a primitive state diagram based on the information obtained from Steps 2 and 3.

Step 5: Develop a primitive state table from the primitive state diagram and check this table systematically for possible redundant states in the state diagram.

Step 6: If necessary, develop a simplified state diagram from the simplified primitive state table.

Step 7: Make a state assignment using rules assigned to the states in the simplified diagram. Document your state assignment in a state map. This step may be optional if a state assignment is specified in the design.

Step 8: Develop a PRESENT/NEXT STATE TABLE using assignments from the simplified state diagram with state assignments.

Step 9: Develop the NEXT STATE maps using the PRESENT/NEXT STATE TABLE with state assignments. From these maps derive the NEXT STATE DECODER logic for D, T, and JK Flip-Flops.

Step 10: Make a selection for your memory elements (Flip-Flops).

Step 11: From Step 3 and state diagram with state assignments, develop the output decoder logic by plotting the output maps.

Step 12: Draw the schematic diagram.

The 12 design steps just outlined could constitute a rather lengthy process, and many times this is true if the solution to the problem requires a large number of STATES and input variables. However, two examples (6-6 and 6-7) are given to demonstrate that these steps can be carried out quite quickly for simple sequential problems. The first example is intended to illustrate the mechanics of the design process; therefore only short comments are given to each step. See Figure 6-19. The second example is more lengthy because it includes considerable commentary on the significance and importance of each step of the design process.

EXAMPLE 6-6: Figure 6-19 encapsulates a design requirement and solution for a simple sequential circuit.

The circuit shown in Figure 6-19(a) is to control the code on the outputs Z and W based on the position of the control switch (CS). This control is prescribed as follows: When the switch is in the UP position (CSUP(L) ASSERTED) the ZW code equals 00. When the circuit senses that the switch has been moved to the down position (CSUP(L) NOT-ASSERTED), the output is to *sequence*, with the rising-edge of the CLK, from $ZW=00$ to $ZW=01$ to

$ZW = 11$ to $ZW = 10$ and then stop and hold until the switch is moved back to the up position once more, at which time the ZW code reverts to $ZW = 00$.

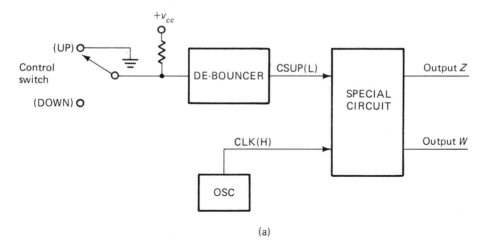

(a)

Fig. 6-19. An encapsulated illustration of the traditional sequential design process.

Design steps: A state diagram and state table are generated to define the sequential behavior of the circuit as shown in Figure 6-19(b). Next the state diagram and state table are checked for possible state redundancy, that is, checked to determine if any unnecessary states have been introduced during the state diagram design. By inspection you find that each state prescribed is necessary.

Format: CSUP/ZW

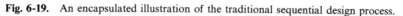

This table is made directly from the state diagram.

PRESENT STATE	INPUT CS UP	NEXT STATE	OUTPUTS Z W	
a	0	b	0	0
	1	a	0	0
b	0	c	0	1
	1	c	0	1
c	0	d	1	1
	1	d	1	1
d	0	d	1	0
	1	a	1	0

Fig. 6-19(b).

Next a *STATE ASSIGNMENT* is made on the state diagram such that each *STATE* is uniquely defined.* From this state diagram the state table with state assignments is filled out (see Figure 6-19(c)). Note the TRUTH TABLE FORM.

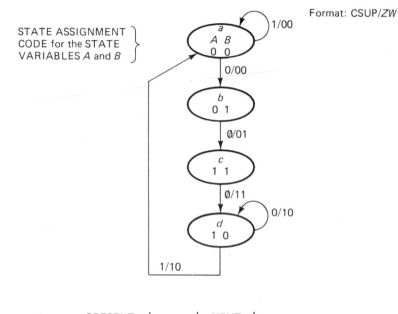

PRESENT STATE		INPUT	NEXT STATES	OUTPUT
A	B	CS UP	A B	Z W
(a) 0 0	0	0	0 1	0 0
1 0	0	1	0 0	0 0
(b) 2 0	1	0	1 1	0 1
3 0	1	1	1 1	0 1
(c) 6 1	1	0	1 0	1 1
7 1	1	1	1 0	1 1
(d) 4 1	0	0	1 0	1 0
5 1	0	1	0 0	1 0

Fig. 6-19(c).

Assuming two RET D Flip-Flops are to be used, the NEXT STATE MAPS are filled out directly from the state table with the state assignment (Figure 6-19(d)).

---

*Note that the STATE ASSIGNMENT CODE was made identical to the OUTPUT CODE.

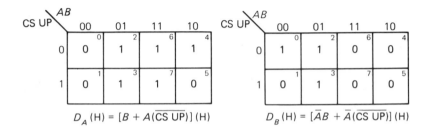

$$D_A(H) = [B + A(\overline{\text{CS UP}})] \, (H) \qquad D_B(H) = [\overline{A}B + \overline{A}(\overline{\text{CS UP}})] \, (H)$$

Fig. 6-19(d).

Next the schematic diagram (Figure 6-19(e)) is drawn showing that the outputs Z and W are taken directly from the STATE VARIABLES A and B using a special notation for the required re-definition of $A = Z$ and $B = W$.

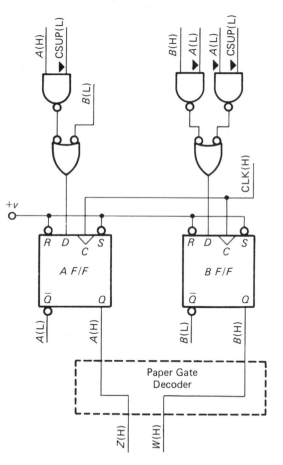

Fig. 6-19(e).

Now consider Example 6-7 keeping in mind that this example is lengthy and it includes other illustrative examples. Therefore, it is important that you closely follow the developments as they unfold.

EXAMPLE 6-7: **Step 1:** *Receive Circuit Specifications.* You are to design a special circuit that will produce an output pulse if a sampled data input is tested *three* times and found to be at a relatively high voltage level an *odd* number of times, and will then return to an initial condition and start the testing process over again.

Step 2: *Study of Specifications.* According to these specifications our design is to be sequential and it is apparently meant to sample some data line asynchronously with respect to the information on that line. Further, it is apparently meant to sample this data three times, generate an output if necessary, and then start over again, repeating this operation indefinitely. However, this should all be done in some SYNCHRONOUS fashion with respect to the machine which is to be designed.

Step 3: *Make a Circuit Model.* A block diagram and output-specification-timing diagram are shown in Figure 6-20.

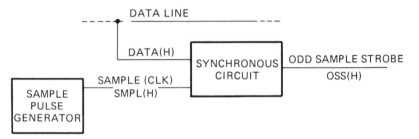

Fig. 6-20(a). A block diagram of the data sampling system.

Input Definitions: *DATA(H)* is defined as the input from the data line and is assigned a polarizing element because we are to sample "looking" for a high voltage.

SAMPLE (SMPL(H)) is defined as the sampling input which paces the sequential circuit through the cyclic sequence. It can also be thought of as the system clock, with the sampling done on the rising-edge.

Output Definitions: *ODD SAMPLE STROBE (OSS(H))* is defined as the output from this circuit which is to be generated after three samples have been taken and an odd number of high samples have been found. The output-specification-timing diagram illustrating some of the possible options available for specifying this output is shown in Figure 6-20(b).

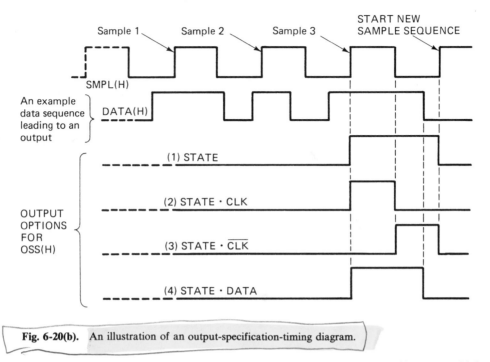

Fig. 6-20(b). An illustration of an output-specification-timing diagram.

The choice of output option will affect the formatting of your state diagram, which is discussed next.

Step 4: *Design Primitive State Diagram.* As pointed out earlier, the state diagram is an important tool in digital design. However, it can be documented or formatted in several ways, possibly confusing the user if he doesn't understand exactly what the special branch notations imply. Basically, the confusion is related to when, or within what time frame, and under what INPUT conditions the output should be generated. For example, consider the special example state diagram shown in Figure 6-21.

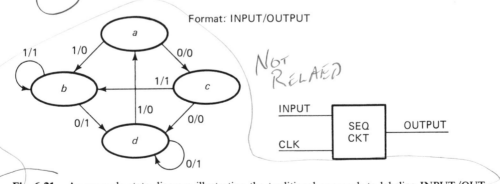

Fig. 6-21. An example state diagram illustrating the traditional approach to labeling INPUT/OUTPUT designations.

With this form of state diagram, it is important to understand that the *output notation* on each branching vector *leaving* a given state refers to output conditions for that *same* state, not for the NEXT STATE. Thus observe that the output from State *a* is NOT-ASSERTED under any conditions. A similar situation exists for state *b* where the OUTPUT is definitely ASSERTED under all branch conditions. This implies that an output is to be generated during the period of time the machine resides in state *b* independent of the INPUT conditions. It is this "some time" that can create confusion. From this the question arises: "Is the output ASSERTED for the complete time the machine resides in *b*, or is it gated out with some segment of the system clock or some other condition?" This important question must be addressed and answered in detail before a hardware design is ever started. Because of this, *never leave output generation to chance*. To continue, note that state *c* has an interesting assignment; if the machine is in state *c*, the output may or may not be generated, *depending on the input*, as indicated by the notation on the branching vectors (1/1,0/0). If the input is ASSERTED, then an output is generated during some portion of the time the machine resides in state *c*. State *d* has a similar type assignment with the output being generated some time during state *d* if the INPUT is NOT-ASSERTED. Outputs such as these are referred to as CONDITIONAL OUTPUTS.

The INPUT/OUTPUT relations just discussed are typical of the *conditional output generation encountered in the design of sequential circuits*, and it is important that you recognize the *different possible output specifications* for branching conditions from any state. In short, when you recognize mixed branching conditions like those of states *c* and *d*, you should realize that you are faced with a conditional OUTPUT, and that this output must be a function of the *state and the inputs*, a requirement of a Mealy machine. Therefore, in general, any state diagram that calls for conditional outputs will employ a Mealy machine, and any state diagram whose outputs are specified independent of the input will employ a Moore machine.

The example information just represented regarding output generation covers the different situations that can been countered in sequential design. However, not every possible case has been covered, and, therefore, when specifying an output assignment, make certain that you define when and under what conditions your output is to be ASSERTED and document this information in some way, possibly by using a timing diagram as shown in Figure 6-20(b).

The actual development of a state diagram is an interesting sequential problem in itself, and, as is usually the case, those just beginning have some difficulty. Experience shows that the most difficulty with state diagram design is encountered in finding a logical place or state to start, and in thinking the problem through in a sequential manner.

Making what is called a tight state diagram is closely akin to designing a compact computer program, one in which there are no unnecessary or extra program steps. Those of you who have had programming experience know the thrill of putting together a good, clean, and compact (tight) software package that efficiently does the job it was called upon to do. This same feeling is derived from designing compact and efficient state diagrams.

Designing a state diagram is undoubtedly the most fun part of sequential design, for it is in this step that you must think through your problem sequentially, relating input conditions to NEXT STATE assignments and output generation, thus allowing you to be creative and imaginative. Though a challenge, state diagram design provides the digital designer with an important creative outlet in an otherwise relatively structured discipline.

The greatest creative design challenge is to devise a state diagram without redundant states. If you spend the time necessary to think through your state diagram design in a step-by-step manner, *utilizing previously generated states whenever possible*, you can virtually eliminate the time-consuming steps of searching for redundant states and the subsequent work of reducing the primitive state table and state diagram. In short, if you make your state diagram as tight as you possibly can, it will save you time and effort. However, making a tight state diagram requires an in-depth feeling for the circuit's sequential operation. As the state diagram for the example develops, this process is illustrated. Consider the so-called loose state diagram shown in Figure 6-22 for the data sampling example.

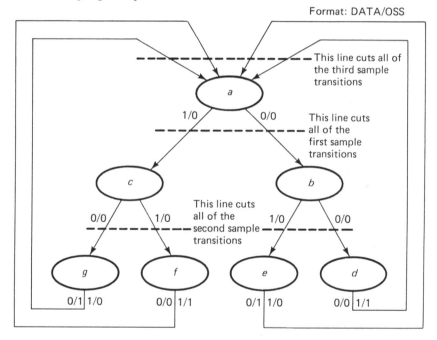

Fig. 6-22. The so-called "loose" state diagram for the data sampling example.

Examining the state diagram in Figure 6-22, observe that the NEXT STATE for each STATE in the state diagram is specified *independent* of other existing STATES. In short, a separate STATE was generated for each possible branching condition from each STATE. By doing this, some unnecessary STATES were introduced. How could we have avoided these unnecessary STATES that eventually cause us to use extra time and effort eliminating them?

Even though there is no completely general approach to avoiding the introduction of redundant states, there are some thought processes which certainly reduce the possibilities. These are: (a) start your state diagram with a single *particular INPUT/OUTPUT sequence* in mind and follow this sequence through to completion, and (b) for each state to be added thereafter, examine the possibility of using one of the existing states instead. For example, start in state a and develop the states that will lead to the proper output with the $1, 1, 1$ input sample sequence (see leftmost states a, c, and f in Figure 6-23).

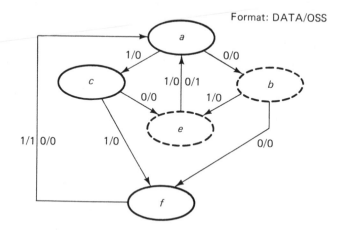

Fig. 6-23. An example of how to select some input sequence and follow it through to completion.

Now, once the complete initial sequence is documented, go back to the initial state (state a) and start another sequence, keeping in mind the input sequence requirements it takes to get into the already existing states c and f. This implies that each level of the state diagram is related to a particular sample number. Now observe that a 0 data condition must lead to another state b. Once states b and c are established, there is an "odd number of 1's" path and an "even number of 1's" path. Consider the branching from states b and c and note that only one more state (state e) is needed to complete the tight state diagram shown in Figure 6-23. By thinking through the problem, states d and g have been eliminated from the original loose state diagram in Figure 6-22. As mentioned above, there is no general approach to designing tight state diagrams other than thinking the problem through once one sequence path has been established. This thinking-through process is a challenge, but it is the common thread that makes designing tight state diagrams a general process. However, for the less experienced, there is the straightforward process that always yields an accurate state diagram, but that has possible redundant states which must be removed in a later step. This straightforward process is one of generating 2^n branches ($n =$ number of inputs) from the initial STATE, and following each of these 2^n branches to their NEXT STATES and from each of these NEXT STATES taking another 2^n branches until the problem is completely specified. This was the process used to develop the so-called loose state diagram in Figure 6-22.

Now turn your attention to the output specifications for the state diagrams shown in Figures 6-22 and 6-23. In particular, consider the states e and f in Figure 6-23, which are the same states as e and f in Figure 6-22. Notice that the output specification for the states is CONDITIONAL. OSS is generated conditionally according to the state of the machine and the condition of the DATA input. Therefore, when and where in relation to the clock this output time frame must be worked out will be specified. "Time frame" implies that a segment of time is to be specified relative to the system clock in which a conditional output may be generated. Referring to Figure 6-20(b), Option 4 or a modified Option 2 would be selected. The modified Option 2, which is referred to now as Option 5, is one in which the output is a function of the STATE·INPUT·CLK; in other words an output will be generated during the high segment of CLK conditional on the input. We see from our state diagram specification the OSS output is to be the function:

$$\text{OPTION 4:} \quad \text{OSS} = (\text{state } e \cdot \overline{\text{DATA}}) + (\text{state } f \cdot \text{DATA})$$
$$\text{OPTION 5:} \quad \text{OSS} = (\text{state } e \cdot \overline{\text{DATA}} \cdot \text{SMPL}) + (\text{state } f \cdot \text{DATA} \cdot \text{SMPL})$$

This specification appears to be harmless except for the *asynchronous nature of DATA* that will affect the width of the OSS pulse. This output pulse width variation can be a problem. Therefore, think about some way to freeze the level of DATA during the output generation time frame. This freezing or synching of input conditions during an output time frame is the subject of considerable discussion in Chapter 7. Therefore, for the present, assume that Option 5 is to be utilized for the data sampling example, keeping in mind that conditional outputs require special attention when they are encountered in designs.

Step 5: *Develop a Primitive State Table.* In this step we develop a primitive state table for the state diagram shown in Figure 6-22 to illustrate the process of eliminating redundant states, then we compare this result with the primitive state table derived from the tight state diagram in Figure 6-23. This is done to illustrate the value of trying to accomplish a tight state diagram at the start.

The process of developing a primitive state table is a simple one of tabulating the information found in the primitive state diagram in the form shown in Figure 6-24.

PRESENT STATE	NEXT STATE		OUTPUT	
	DATA = 0	DATA = 1	DATA = 0	DATA = 1
a	b	c	0	0
b	d	e	0	0
c	g	f	0	0
d	a	a	0	1
e	a	a	1	0
f	a	a	0	1
g	a	a	1	0

Fig. 6-24. The traditional primitive state-table for the state diagram shown in Figure 6-22.

Figure 6-25 illustrates an alternative primitive state table for the state diagram shown in Figure 6-22. It is felt that this type of table is a more descriptive way to illustrate a TRUTH-TABLE representation of the NEXT STATE and OUTPUT specifications than is the traditional table shown in Figure 6-24. Thus, this type of table will be used throughout the remainder of the text.

PRESENT STATE	INPUTS DATA	NEXT STATE	OUTPUTS OSS
a	0	b	0
a	1	c	0
b	0	d	0
b	1	e	0
c	0	g	0
c	1	f	0
d	0	a	0
d	1	a	1
e	0	a	1
e	1	a	0
f	0	a	0
f	1	a	1
g	0	a	1
g	1	a	0

Fig. 6-25. An alternate primitive state table for the state diagram shown in Figure 6-22.

6-7 STATE REDUCTION

State reduction is the process of recovering from mental errors incurred during the state diagram design. It has been stressed that you should strive to develop tight state diagrams and avoid the introduction of redundant states. Also, it is the author's opinion that the reduction techniques used traditionally are limited to a particular class of problems, all of which are similar to the present example; this class is somewhat limited in its application. However, the state reduction process is covered lightly, utilizing the following definitions and theorem.

Definition: *If two states p and q are equivalent, then state q is defined as REDUNDANT.*

Definition: *Two states p and q of a finite-state machine are defined to be equivalent when the machine is started in these states, and identical output sequences are generated from every possible set of input sequences that can be applied.*

From these definitions it can be proven that the following theorem is true:

Two states p and q are equivalent (q EQ p) iff: (1) the output specification for both are identical and (2) both have the identical NEXT STATE specifications.

Therefore once an equivalence between p and q has been established, state q can be replaced by p in the state diagram and table. Basically there are four reduction methods predicated on the above. These are: (1) inspection, (2) logical reasoning, (3) mathematical partitioning, and (4) using an implication table. These methods are generally applied in a two-step process: (1) first identify the candidates for equivalence by identifying and grouping together those states that have identical output assignments and then (2) systematically relate the next state specifications of each state in each group. For example, consider the table in Figure 6-25. Here states a, b, and c are candidates for equivalence as well as states d and f; likewise states e and g are candidates. Therefore, partition these states into groups according to their output specifications.

The partitions are $((a), b, c)$, $((d),f),((e),g)$, with the circled entries arbitrarily chosen as the necessary state of the group. To illustrate the equivalent determination process, consider the (e,g) group. We see:

$$g \text{ EQ } e \text{ iff } a \text{ EQ } a \quad \text{and} \quad a \text{ EQ } a$$

Therefore we can say

$$g \text{ EQ } e$$

We then go back and strike g from the group and strike row g from the table and replace g by e elsewhere in the table. Continuing we see:

$$b \text{ EQ } a \text{ iff } d \text{ EQ } b \quad \text{and} \quad e \text{ EQ } c \quad \text{but} \quad d \overline{\text{ EQ }} b \text{ (outputs differ)}$$

Therefore

$$b \overline{\text{ EQ }} a$$

From this we see that b is a necessary state; therefore we circle b in the first grouping : $((a), (b), c)$.

The same systematic search can be carried out for *each grouping* to identify the equivalences within that grouping. However, there are cases when the equivalence argument reverts to a linked argument or to an argument equivalent to the following:

$$c \text{ EQ } d \text{ iff } e \text{ EQ } f, \quad \text{but} \quad e \text{ EQ } f \text{ iff } c \text{ EQ } d$$

In cases such as this keep in mind that by using the *rules of inference* the following statement can be proven to be valid:

$$c \text{ EQ } d \quad \text{and} \quad e \text{ EQ } f$$

All this is interesting; however, the actual application of classic state reduction, as mentioned earlier, is limited in contemporary digital design. Therefore we leave the study here as merely a short introduction.

Steps 6 and 7: *State Assignment.* Once the tight state diagram has been developed, a STATE ASSIGNMENT is made. This state assignment process, in keeping with the state classification concept set forth by Huffman and Moore, classifies each state by assigning it a unique n-bit code. The numerical value for n is in turn determined by the number of states. For example, if a given state diagram has r states, then:

$$2^n \geq r$$

or

$$n \geq \frac{\log\ r}{\log\ 2} \qquad\qquad (1)$$

Thus the state assignment problem is definitely a coding problem, as outlined in Chapter 1.

The choice of state assignment has a significant effect on the amount of hardware required to implement the combinational circuits associated with a sequential machine, which are the NEXT STATE and OUTPUT DECODER sections. This statement suggests that there must be at least one optimal choice for a state assignment for any given machine, but examining the processes involved indicates that an optimal or even a good assignment must be based on some predetermined criteria. The following is a list of some of the criteria commonly used.

(1) Minimize the number of gates/packages required to implement the NEXT STATE DECODER.
(2) Minimize the number of gates/packages required to implement the OUTPUT DECODER.
(3) Minimize the number of gates/packages overall required to implement both the NEXT STATE and OUTPUT DECODER.
(4) Minimize the overall cost of circuit implementation by reducing engineering time, power supply requirements, and printed circuit allocation, and so forth.

Once one of the first three criteria is selected, the search for an optimal state assignment is generally a very tedious process. Before taking a closer look at the state assignment problem, take a moment to develop some insight into what effects various state assignments have on the NEXT STATE DECODER and how hardware is actually derived from a state assignment. It should be remembered that the NEXT STATE DECODER of a sequential machine is a combinational circuit that decodes the INPUT VARIABLES and the PRESENT STATE VARIABLES in order to generate the NEXT STATE CODE, which is further decoded by the logic internal to the Flip-Flops, in order to develop the TRUE NEXT STATE. Thus the combinational design of the NEXT STATE DECODER is a function of three factors, which are:

(1) outside world inputs;
(2) the state assignment;
(3) the type of Flip-Flop to be used in the machine.

Little can be done about the outside world inputs; they come with the problem. Therefore, a Flip-Flop must be selected and then some state assignment prescribed to knit these three factors together in such a manner that a minimal amount of hardware is required to synthesize the NEXT STATE DECODER.

Similarly, the OUTPUT DECODER must decode the STATE OF THE MACHINE and the INPUT VARIABLES in order to generate the OUTPUTS TO THE OUTSIDE WORLD. However, the choice of the Flip-Flop does not directly influence its design. As just pointed out, the derivation of an optimal state assignment is at best a two-variable problem, and each of these variables is usually a multi-variable function in itself, further complicating the problem. So complicated is the state assignment problem that at present there is no general technique guaranteed to yield an optimal state assignment without some sort of exhaustive search, implying that you CUT AND TRY! However, there are some redeeming factors such as: (1) Any arbitrary unique assignment will work—it may not be optimal but it will at least work, insuring that the system's sequential performance is not strictly dependent on an optimal state assignment*; (2) There is a relatively easy technique available that gives reasonably good results, maybe not optimal results, but typically results much better than random assignments. Also, along this line, there are several computer programs available, or at least some algorithms, which can be used to develop state assignment computer programs.† However, the techniques developed in articles such as these fall short of a comprehensive address of the problem of the *multi-input* machines that makes up a large segment of contemporary design efforts or that are at least presently far more wide-reaching in application than a machine with only one or two inputs.

To illustrate the complexity of the state assignment problem, consider a state diagram with 16 states (four state variables) and four input variables from the outside world. For any given present state condition code, say (PS_i), the NEXT STATE code (NS_i) must be a function of PS_i combined with the 16 possible input codes derived from the four input variables. In other words, for each of the 16 present states there are 16 possible NEXT STATES, implying that there are 256 possible NEXT STATES. Further, there is an almost infinite number of possible state assignments for these 256 NEXT STATES. For example, the number of possible state assignments can be derived from the following expression:

$$N_{PA} = \frac{(i^{N_{sv}})!}{(2^{N_{sv}} - N_{ns})!} \tag{2}$$

where N_{sv} = number of state variables (Flip-Flops)
N_{ns} = number of NEXT STATES

Thus for the example with 16 states and four state variables:

$$N_{PA} = \frac{(2^4)!}{0!} = 16! \simeq 2.09 \times 10^{13}$$

It is interesting to note that if it were possible to try a new state assignment once every 100 microseconds, it would take approximately 66 years to try all the

---

*We will find in Chapter 7 that this statement is *not* generally true, but for the time being assume it is.
†One of these is titled: "Optimal State Assignments for Synchronous Sequential Circuits" by J. R. Story, H. J. Harrison, and E. A. Reinhard; *IEEE Trans. Computers, C-21* (1972), 1365-1373.

possible state assignments for a simple 16 state machine. Therefore, the cut and try method for finding an optimal assignment is out of the picture even if one uses a computer. However, not all the possible state assignments specified by Eq. (2) are unique; for example, there is no real difference in two state assignment sequences if one is generated from the other by simply exchanging two columns. Therefore, the number of unique assignments is given as follows:

$$UA = \frac{(2^{N_{sv}} - 1)!}{(2^{N_{sv}} - N_{ns})!(N_{sv})!}$$

For our 16-state four-input problem:

$$UA = \frac{15!}{0!\,4!} \simeq 5.45 \times 10^{10}$$

This is not a realistic big savings over the 16! derived from Eq. (2). Therefore, some process must be developed that will aid the designer in recognizing what conditions should exist to constitute a good state assignment.

6-8   MINIMIZING THE NEXT STATE DECODER

Keep in mind that the design of the NEXT STATE DECODER is a combinational design problem to be reduced by using maps, and that minimal nontrivial combinational designs are in concept acheived by MINIMIZING THE NUMBER OF REQUIRED GROUPINGS IN THE MAP AND MAXIMIZING THE SIZE OF THOSE GROUPINGS WHICH ARE REQUIRED. Though simple in concept, the general rule above is often particularly difficult to apply. However, there are two basic rules for making state assignments that at least in part serve the minimal criteria concept stated above.

Rule 1: *States having the same NEXT STATES for a given input condition should have assignments which can be grouped into logically adjacent cells in a map.*

An example of Rule 1 is shown in Figure 6-26. Note the significance of the phrase "given input condition." If the input branching conditions had *not all* been identical, the advantage gained by logical adjacent assignments would have been somewhat impaired. In any case, strive to unit distance those states that all have the same next state.

Fig. 6-26.   Example of using Rule 1.

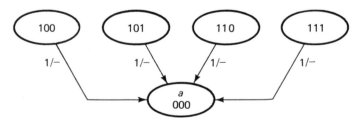

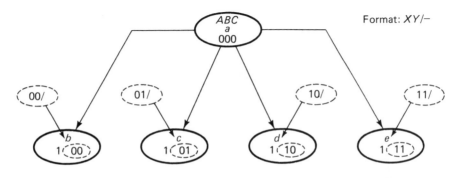

Fig. 6-27. Example of the corollary to Rule 2.

Rule 2: *States that are the NEXT STATES of a single state should have assignments which can be grouped into logically adjacent cells in a map. See Figure 6-27.*

Corollary to Rule 2: The assignments made to the NEXT STATES of a single state should be *assigned logically adjacent assignments* that correspond to the branching variable or variables. That is, select one bit or group of bits if a multi-way branch is called for, and make these bits match the code called for by the input condition on each branch. For example, see Figure 6-27. This is commonly referred to as a "reduced input dependency" assignment.

[handwritten margin note: Likewise, if output is 1 bit use least significant bit]

Note that the two least significant bits of the state assignments for states *b*, *c*, *d*, and *e* match branch input codes.

As mentioned above, many have proposed state assignment techniques and algorithms for selecting optimal or near optimal state assignments. In particular, some have developed procedures that give near optimal assignments for a particular type of Flip-Flop (D, JK, T, etc.), bringing up an interesting point. If a good state assignment is selected for a D Flip-Flop implementation, is it good for a JK Flip-Flop? In general, it has been proven that assignments that are optimal for one type are not necessarily optimal for another. Therefore, a state assignment should be influenced by the choice of Flip-Flop. In fact, this author has found that in some cases optimum results can be achieved by mixing the type of the Flip-Flops used. However, generally speaking, the JK Flip-Flop, because of flexible operational characteristics brought about by the extra decoding logic internal to the device, has the edge over the other Flip-Flops; but this is *not* a hard fact. At times, a D implementation for a particular assignment results in the simplest network.

6-9 DESIGN STEPS LEADING TO NEXT STATE DECODERS

The following steps are given to establish a procedure for developing the hardware for the NEXT STATE DECODER.

(1) Determine the number of Flip-Flops required for the memory element section.

(2) Using whatever criteria you choose, make a state assignment, making certain that each state is assigned a unique code. This is generally done on the state diagram and documented in a STATE MAP.

(3) Make a PRESENT/NEXT STATE TABLE from the state diagram. This table will form a multi-output TRUTH-TABLE for the NEXT STATE DECODER having the PRESENT STATE and the OUTSIDE WORLD VARIABLES as its inputs and the NEXT STATE specification as its outputs.

(4) Keeping in mind that the outputs of the NEXT STATE DECODER direct the control inputs of the Flip-Flops, plot the NEXT STATE maps for each Flip-Flop. This plotting is done *only* with the knowledge of the operational characteristics of the Flip-Flops used.

(5) Reduce the maps and formulate the NEXT STATE DECODER one output at a time.

An example of this procedure will be shown shortly, but before that examine how the Flip-Flop operational characteristics influence the design of the NEXT STATE DECODER as outlined in Step 4.

The *combination* of the NEXT STATE DECODER logic and special logic added to a basic cell determines what the NEXT STATE is to be for each Flip-Flop. Therefore, you must go through the mental exercise of examining the inputs of the NEXT STATE DECODER and the EXCITATION TABLE for Flip-Flops, and from this, cause the Flip-Flops to SET or RESET on the clock pulse.

For example, to cause a state variable to change from 0 to 1 at the output of a D Flip-Flop, a 1 must be present on the D input previous to the clock pulse edge. Thus the output code for the NEXT STATE DECODER for a D Flip-Flop implementation is identical to the NEXT STATE CODE. For a JK, two outputs from the NEXT STATE DECODER are required for each Flip-Flop. Here you might tend, quite justifiably, to assume that JK implementations could lead to a more complex NEXT STATE DECODER. This is not necessarily the case. Further, once the NEXT STATE maps for a D Flip-Flop implementation are plotted, a simple procedure can be used to automatically convert them to the other NEXT STATE maps for a JK and T implementation. This makes it easy to examine very quickly the logic required for each type of Flip-Flop implementation and to make a minimal selection.

DATA SAMPLE DESIGN EXAMPLE
CONTINUED:

A random state assignment is made for the example data sampling problem used throughout this chapter (see Figure 6-28).

Using the PRESENT/NEXT STATE TABLE shown in Figure 6-29, which has a multi-output TRUTH-TABLE form, the NEXT STATE maps are plotted for each output just as they would normally be done for any combinational design. *In doing this the NEXT STATE DECODER logic for a D Flip-Flop implementation is derived as an added bonus.* This is a result of the operational characteristics of the D Flip-Flop: that the TRUE NEXT CODE must be present at the output after the clock edge. Thus the NEXT STATE maps are as shown in Figure 6-30.

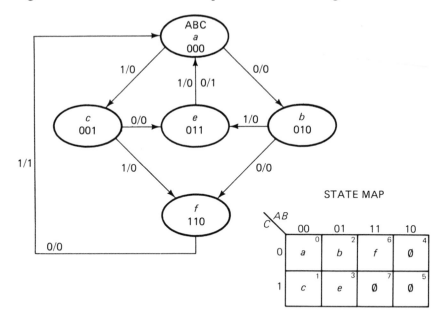

Fig. 6-28. A random state assignment for the odd number of 1 sequence detector example.

PRESENT STATE		INPUT	NEXT STATE			OUTPUT
$A_n B_n C_n$		X	A_{n+1}	B_{n+1}	C_{n+1}	OSS
0	a 000	0	0	1	0	0
1	000	1	0	0	1	0
2	c 001	0	0	1	1	0
3	001	1	1	1	0	0
4	b 010	0	1	1	0	0
5	010	1	0	1	1	0
6	e 011	0	0	0	0	1
7	011	1	0	0	0	0
8	Ø 100	0	Ø	Ø	Ø	Ø
9	100	1	Ø	Ø	Ø	Ø
10	Ø 101	0	Ø	Ø	Ø	Ø
11	101	1	Ø	Ø	Ø	Ø
12	f 110	0	0	0	0	0
13	110	1	0	0	0	1
14	Ø 111	0	Ø	Ø	Ø	Ø
15	111	1	Ø	Ø	Ø	Ø

Fig. 6-29. The PRESENT/NEXT STATE TABLE with state assignments taken from Figure 6-28.

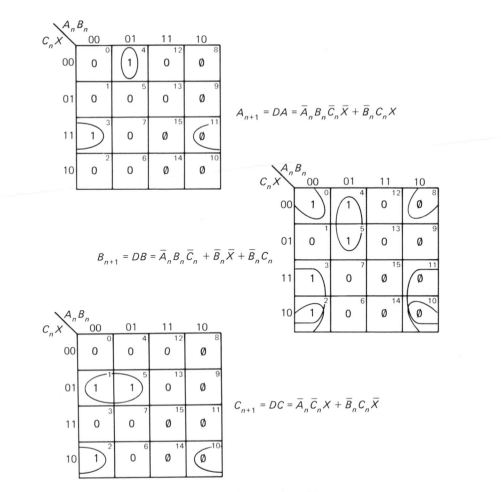

$$A_{n+1} = DA = \bar{A}_n B_n \bar{C}_n X + \bar{B}_n C_n X$$

$$B_{n+1} = DB = \bar{A}_n B_n \bar{C}_n + \bar{B}_n X + \bar{B}_n C_n$$

$$C_{n+1} = DC = \bar{A}_n \bar{C}_n X + \bar{B}_n C_n \bar{X}$$

Fig. 6-30. The NEXT STATE maps for the example problem.

It is important to keep in mind as you are plotting these maps that the NEXT STATE VARIABLES (A_{n+1}, B_{n+1}, and C_{n+1}) are functions of the input (X) and the PRESENT STATE VARIABLES (A_n, B_n, and C_n). Also, note that the unused states are filled in with $\emptyset$'s because these states never occur if the machine is functioning properly.

From the current example, this particular state assignment would need a NEXT STATE DECODER, which requires:

1	four-input AND function
4	three-input AND function
2	two-input AND function
1	three-input OR function
2	two-input OR function
10	gates with 27 inputs

Now applying the rules set forth earlier, make a state assignment and compare the results.

By studying Rules 1 and 2 and relating them to the example problem state diagram, the state assignment shown in Figure 6-31 is made. This state assignment is derived by applying the rules and developing the following arguments. Use Table 6-2 to aid you in your decision.

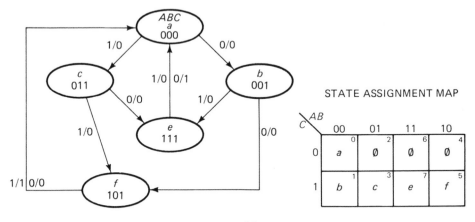

(a)

	PRESENT STATE	INPUT	NEXT STATE			OUTPUT
	$A_n\ B_n\ C_n$	X	A_{n+1}	B_{n+1}	C_{n+1}	OSS 1
0	a 000	0	0	0	1	0
1	000	1	0	1	1	0
2	b 001	0	·1	0	1	0
3	001	1	1	1	1	0
4	Ø 010	0	Ø	Ø	Ø	Ø
5	010	1	Ø	Ø	Ø	Ø
6	c 011	0	1	1	1	0
7	011	1	1	0	1	0
8	Ø 100	0	Ø	Ø	Ø	Ø
9	100	1	Ø	Ø	Ø	Ø
10	f 101	0	0	0	0	0
11	101	1	0	0	0	1
12	Ø 110	0	Ø	Ø	Ø	Ø
13	110	1	Ø	Ø	Ø	Ø
14	e 111	0	0	0	0	1
15	111	1	0	0	0	0

(b)

Fig. 6-31(a). A state assignment arrived at by applying Rules 1 and 2. (b) The PRESENT/NEXT STATE TABLE.

Rule 1: *States b and c both have e and f for next states*
and
States e and f both have a for a next state.

Further:

Rule 2: *States b and c both are the next states of a*
and
States e and f both are the next states of both b and c states.

Special note: These rules will not always be nonconflicting, so Rule 1 should take precedence over Rule 2 if a conflict arises. However, a special requirement introduced in Chapter 7 regarding asynchronous inputs alters this precedence.

TABLE 6-2

	Previous State(s)	State in Question	Next State(s)	
Rule 1 applies	e,f	a	c,b	Rule 2 applies
	a	b	e,f	
	a	c	e,f	
	b,c	e	a	
	b,c	f	a	

Observe from Figure 6-32 that the new state assignment results in a considerable savings, that is:

2	three-input AND functions
1	two-input AND function
1	two-input OR function
4	gates with 10 inputs

Thus by simply applying Rules 1 and 2 good results have been achieved. Whether or not it is optimum for a D Flip-Flop implementation is hard to say for certain, because there are 138 other assignments left to try. At this point criterion 4 comes into the picture. In short, is it really necessary to carry out an exhaustive search trying to save one or two more gates? This is a judgment you will have to make for yourself. If you are building only a small number of systems, then it is recommended that you not spend expensive engineering time worrying about how to save a gate or two.

However, there are a couple of other quick checks that you can make when reducing the NEXT STATE DECODER logic, to see if a JK or a T Flip-Flop might help in the reduction process. This is the subject of the next section.

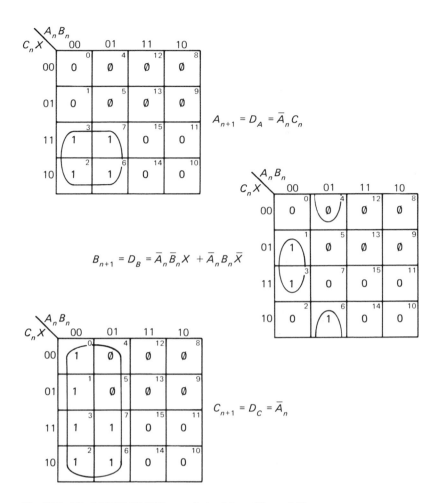

$$A_{n+1} = D_A = \bar{A}_n C_n$$

$$B_{n+1} = D_B = \bar{A}_n \bar{B}_n X + \bar{A}_n B_n \bar{X}$$

$$C_{n+1} = D_C = \bar{A}_n$$

Fig. 6-32. The NEXT STATE map derived from Figure 6-31.

6-10 TRYING A JK OR T FLIP-FLOP

It was just mentioned that once the NEXT STATE MAPS are plotted for a D Flip-Flop implementation, it is a simple process to convert these maps to the equivalent map for a JK or T Flip-Flop implementation. This becomes obvious once you remember the conversion of a JK or T Flip-Flop to a D Flip-Flop and remember just what the entries in the NEXT STATE map represent. In beginning the conversion process, quickly review the EXCITATION TABLE for each Flip-Flop and the hardware conversion of each to a D Flip-Flop as shown in Figures 6-33 and 6-34, and consider how this information leads the way to a direct JK or T Flip-Flop implementation.

Given a D Flip-Flop:

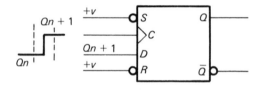

PRESENT STATE Q_n	NEXT STATE $\rightarrow Q_n + 1$	D
0	0	0
0	1	1
1	0	0
1	1	1

EXCITATION TABLE

(a)

Note: The NEXT STATE ($Q_n + 1$) of a
D Flip-Flop is identical to D.
Given a JK Flip-Flop

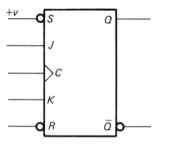

PRESENT STATE Q_n	NEXT STATE $\rightarrow Q_n + 1$	J	K
0	0	0	Ø
0	1	1	Ø
1	0	Ø	1
1	1	Ø	0

EXCITATION TABLE

(b)

Given a T Flip Flop:

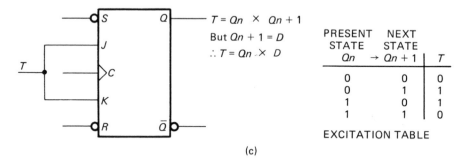

$T = Q_n \times Q_n + 1$
But $Q_n + 1 = D$
$\therefore T = Q_n \times D$

PRESENT STATE Q_n	NEXT STATE $\rightarrow Q_n + 1$	T
0	0	0
0	1	1
1	0	1
1	1	0

EXCITATION TABLE

(c)

Fig. 6-33. A quick review of the excitation tables for the D, JK and T Flip-Flops.

It should be noted in Figure 6-33(b) that any time the PRESENT STATE (Q_n) is 0, the K input is specified as a don't care condition, that is, Ø. Also, any time the PRESENT STATE is a 1, the J input is specified as a don't care condition, that is, Ø. You are probably saying, "so what?" Well, it turns out that if you make this observation, one-half of each map for a JK implementation can be plotted automatically with $\emptyset$'s and the rest can be filled in automatically from the NEXT STATE MAP plotted for a D implementation. How this works will be illustrated shortly. The table of hardware Flip-Flop conversions is shown in Figure 6-34.

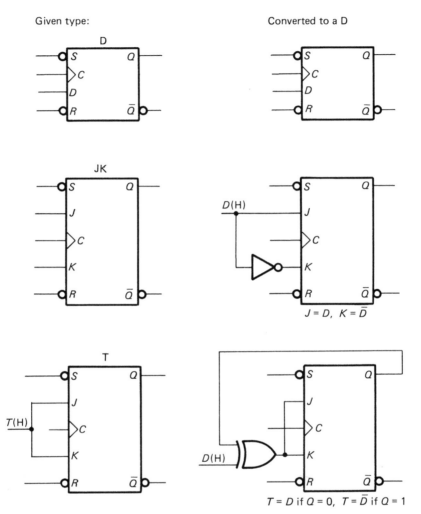

Fig. 6-34. Hardware conversion from T and JK Flip-Flops to a D Flip-Flop. Remember, if $Q=1$, $T=\bar{D}$ and if $Q=0$, $T=D$ because the exclusive OR gate can be used as a controlled inverter.

In Figures 6-33 and 6-34 observe that the conversion from a D implementation to a JK implementation is one of first entering $\emptyset$'s in the J map wherever *the state variable is* 1, then making a direct transfer for the rest of the cells because $J_A = D_A$ as can be seen in the conversion table.

To plot the K map from the D map, place $\emptyset$'s in all the cells where the present state of *that* state variable is equal to 0 and then fill the rest of the cells with the *complement* of the corresponding cell of the D map. This is done because $K_A = \bar{D}_A$. See Figure 6-35.

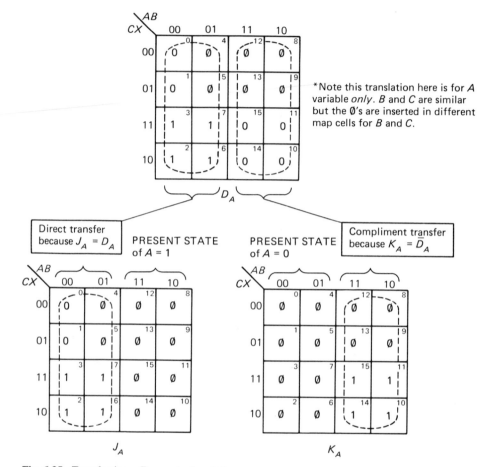

*Note this translation here is for *A* variable *only*. *B* and *C* are similar but the $\emptyset$'s are inserted in different map cells for *B* and *C*.

Direct transfer because $J_A = D_A$ PRESENT STATE of A = 1

PRESENT STATE of A = 0   Compliment transfer because $K_A = \bar{D}_A$

Fig. 6-35. Transferring a D map to J and K maps.

When transferring a D map to a T map, cells 0–7 in both maps are identical. This is because when the state variable, which in this case is $Q_A = A = 0$, $T_A = D_A$. Further, the cells 8–15 in the T map are the complements of the entries for the corresponding cells in the D map. This is because when $Q_A = A = 1$, $T_A = \bar{D}_A$. See Figure 6-36. Again, this can be verified by examining the hardware conversions shown in Figure 6-34.

Thus plotting a D NEXT STATE map is very simple and the conversion of that map to the JK maps or T is equally simple.

This is done in order to examine and compare the hardware required for each Flip-Flop type and make an optimal choice of Flip-Flops. The T Flip-Flop is discussed here because it is a simple process to convert a JK that is readily available to the T by connecting the J and K inputs together.

Another interesting point about the JK Flip-Flop that arises from the J and K maps being half filled with $\emptyset$'s is that the Boolean expressions for any given J_i or K_i are completely independent of Q_i. Because this is the case, both the J and K maps can be plotted from the NEXT STATE map into a single map with J entries plotted in the $Q_i = 1$ sector and the K entries in the $\overline{Q}_i = 0$ sector. When reading the map for J_i, assume all entries in the $Q_i = 0$ sector to be $\emptyset$'s and, likewise, when reading the map for K_i, assume all entries in the $Q_i = 1$ sector to be $\emptyset$'s. This is an interesting and map-saving technique that you may or may not want to employ.

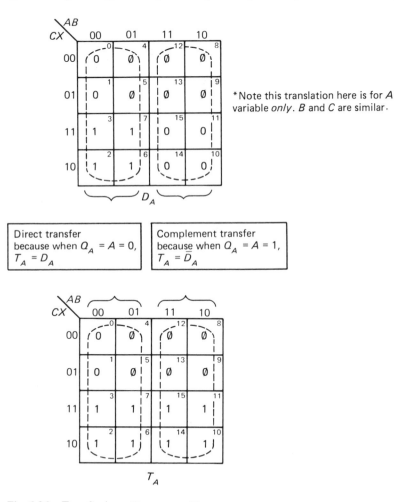

*Note this translation here is for A variable *only*. B and C are similar.

Direct transfer because when $Q_A = A = 0$, $T_A = D_A$

Complement transfer because when $Q_A = A = 1$, $T_A = \overline{D}_A$

Fig. 6-36. Transferring a D map to a T map.

Figures 6-37 and 6-38 show the JK and T maps for the example problem. On the final analysis, the JK implementation is the optimal solution with two gates and four inputs! This is a considerable savings over 10 gates and 27 inputs. Therefore, it can be concluded that the small amount of time dedicated to making this last assignment was worth it, because even if it were for nothing else, it is just plain pleasing to tighten things up. Note that the $\emptyset$ entries for J_B and J_C are different from J_A. Likewise, the $\emptyset$ entries for K_B and K_C are different from K_A.

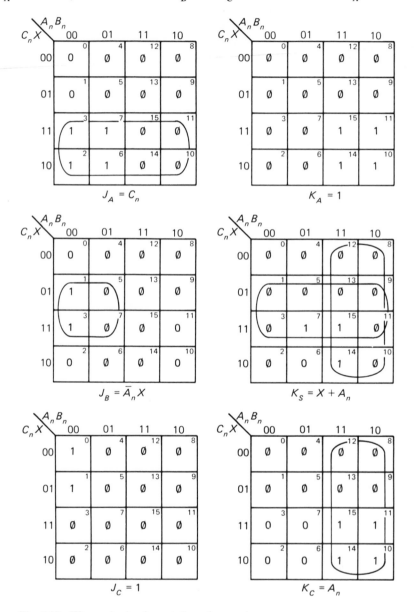

Fig. 6-37. JK map for implementation of example.

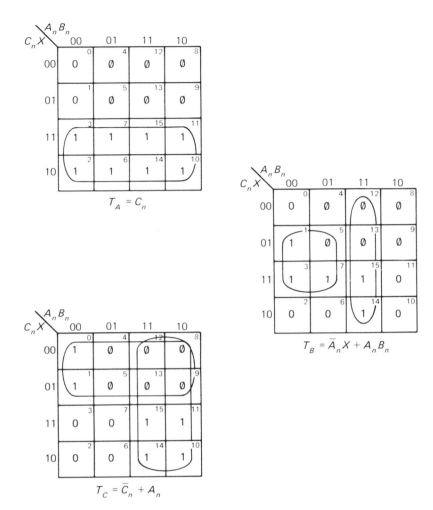

Fig. 6-38. The T maps for implementation of the example problem.

6-11 OUTPUT DECODER DESIGN

As mentioned earlier, a state assignment can be made that minimizes the logic hardware required to implement the OUTPUT DECODER. Generally speaking, the same criteria for minimal combinational hardware still holds: minimize the number of required 1's in the map and maximize the grouping for the ones that are required. However, the design of the OUTPUT DECODER is further complicated by the fact that OUTSIDE WORLD INPUT and OUTPUT conditions are specified by the problem itself. The following rule, if it can be applied, gives good results:

Rule 3: *States which have identical output specifications should be given assignments which can be grouped into adjacent cells in a map.*

Examine the example problem for the purpose of selecting a state assignment that minimizes the hardware needed to implement the OUTPUT DECODER. States a, b, and c should be given adjacent assignment according to Rule 3. Upon examining the state assignment used in Figure 6-31, you find that it fulfills Rule 3 also. Therefore, the OUTPUT MAP can be plotted directly from the table shown in Figure 6-31. See Figure 6-39.

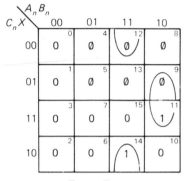

Fig. 6-39. The OUTPUT MAP for the state assignment found in Figure 6-31.

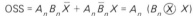

$$OSS = A_n B_n \bar{X} + A_n \bar{B}_n X = A_n (B_n \otimes X)$$

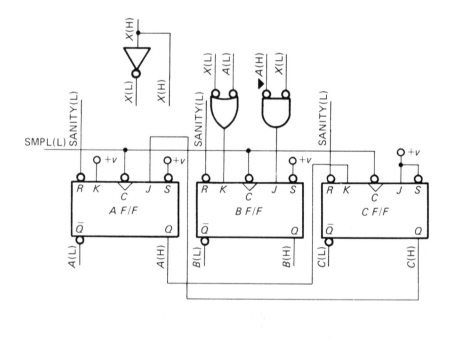

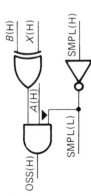

Fig. 6-40. The completed schematic of the example data sampling system.

The design is almost completed now, except for determining exactly during what time frame the conditional output (OSS) is to be issued as well as actually drawing the final schematics.

If the input X is truly an asynchronous input, it can change at any time with respect to the system clock; if this is the case, irregular width output (OSS) pulses are generated. Therefore, it is necessary to assume that it is "synched" in Step 4 when the output signal was chosen to be gated with the low voltage phase of SMPL. Therefore:

$$\text{OSS} = A \ \overline{(\text{SMPL})} \ (B \otimes X)$$

The completed schematic is shown in Figure 6-40.

Another example problem should reinforce your understanding of the mechanics of sequential design.

EXAMPLE 6-8:   Design a circuit that will function as prescribed by the state diagram in Figure 6-3. Since the state diagram is given, assume that it has been simplified. This design process is carried out in Figure 6-41(a).

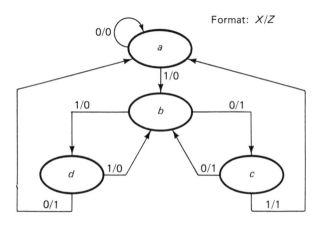

Fig. 6-41 (a). An illustration of the design step for Example 6-8.

The next step is to make a state assignment trying to optimize the NEXT STATE DECODER.

	Previous State(s)	State in Question	Next State(s)	
Rule 1	a,c,d a,c,d b b	a b c d	a,b c,d b,a a,b	Rule 2

States c and d have the same next states; therefore, c and d should have adjacent assignments according to Rule 1.

States *c* and *d* have the same previous state *b*; therefore, according to Rule 2 they should be adjacent.

States *a* and *b* are the NEXT STATE of a single state, that is, state *a*, therefore, *a* and *b* should be adjacent.

To optimize the OUTPUT DECODER, states *b* and *d* should be adjacent according to Rule 3. Thus the state assignment shown in Figure 6-41(b) is made.

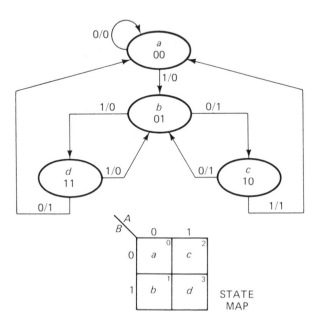

Fig. 6-41(b).

Now make the PRESENT/NEXT STATE table and plot NEXT STATE and OUTPUT maps, as shown in Figure 6-41(c). Note that for the OUTPUT map the choice is to use JK Flip-Flops.

Fig. 6-41(c).

PRESENT STATE $A_n B_n$	INPUT X	NEXT STATE A_{n+1} B_{n+1}	OUTPUT Z
a 00	0	0　0	0
00	1	0　1	0
b 01	0	1　0	1
01	1	1　1	0
c 10	0	0　1	1
10	1	0　0	1
d 11	0	0　0	1
11	1	0　1	0

The NEXT STATE maps

D Flip-Flops:

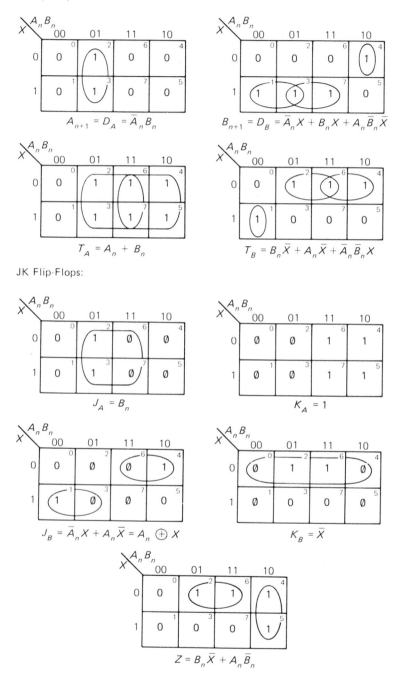

$A_{n+1} = D_A = \bar{A}_n B_n$

$B_{n+1} = D_B = \bar{A}_n X + B_n X + A_n \bar{B}_n \bar{X}$

$T_A = A_n + B_n$

$T_B = B_n \bar{X} + A_n \bar{X} + \bar{A}_n \bar{B}_n X$

JK Flip-Flops:

$J_A = B_n$

$K_A = 1$

$J_B = \bar{A}_n X + A_n \bar{X} = A_n \oplus X$

$K_B = \bar{X}$

$Z = B_n \bar{X} + A_n \bar{B}_n$

Fig. 6-41(c). (Cont.)

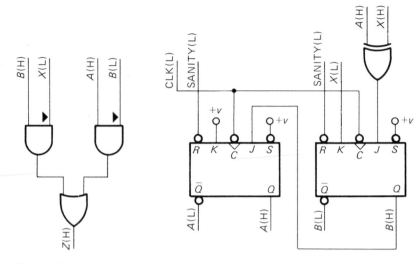

Fig. 6-41(d).

6-12 COUNTERS

The three examples of the sequence detector class of sequential circuits just covered demonstrate the major steps leading up to a completed design. This section covers the *counter* and its sequential behavior and applications, along with design of some special purpose counters that are not available in integrated circuit form. Counters are widely used for the following functions:

(1) Converting the *number* of input pulses into some prescribed code and storing this code.
(2) Generating special sequential codes.
(3) Time delay elements.

Counters are generally classed or specified by the following five definitive characteristics:

(1) Single- or multi-mode operation.
(2) Number of output bits.
(3) The number of unique states it can be caused to reside in, generally referred to as its *modulo number*.
(4) The code sequence it sequentially generates.
(5) Synchronous or asynchronous.

Single-mode counters are the simplest types of counters and can generally be modeled as shown in Figure 6-42. This model illustrates that the single-mode counter is a special sequential device with NO OUTSIDE WORLD INPUTS (save the clock) and NO OUTPUT DECODER. Thus, in a sense, it is a degenerate case of all sequential machines. Since these counters are specified as single mode, they basically sequence through a fixed number of pre-assigned states. Based on this definition and the characteristics stated above, the following specifications can be interpreted clearly. Given a counter specified as a single-mode, three-bit, modulo 6, binary-code counter with an asynchronous clear, you should immediately visualize the information given, as illustrated in Figure 6-43.

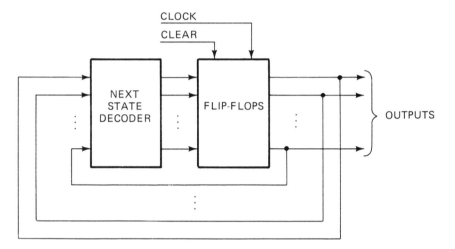

Fig. 6-42. Model for a single-mode counter.

It has been the author's experience that counters are often misunderstood when they are used for modulo counting purposes. Some people seem confused by the multiple outputs when they are expecting to see a device with a single output that issues a pulse once each modulo number. This confusion can be dispelled by recognizing that *one output* of an *n*-bit counter will go through a *complete change of events* in the modulo sequence (see Q_A in Figure 6-43(c)). Thus, if a problem requires counting the input pulses and signifying that six input pulses are received, Q_A is used as the single output, and each time it cycles through a complete change of events (up, then down), six input pulses have been received.

Along this same line, if an output pulse equal in duration to the CLOCK pulse is desired, then an OUTPUT DECODER SECTION could be added to decode the following conditions:

$$\text{MOD6 (H)} = \left(\overline{Q}_A \, \overline{Q}_B \, \overline{Q}_C \cdot \overline{\text{CLOCK}} \right)(\text{H})$$

There are many counters available in integrated circuit form; however, they are mostly multi-mode hexadecimal or decimal counters outputting a straight binary sequence. See Figure 6-44 for several examples of some important single-mode counters that are available in integrated circuit form. Counters are still designed when specialized counters are wanted. For example, suppose you need a three-bit, modulo 6, unit distance code counter with an asynchronous clear for a special sequence generator like the one specified in Figure 6-45.

Fig. 6-43. Pertinent information related to a single-mode, three-bit, modulo 6, binary counter. (a) Block diagram. (b) State diagram. (c) Timing diagram.

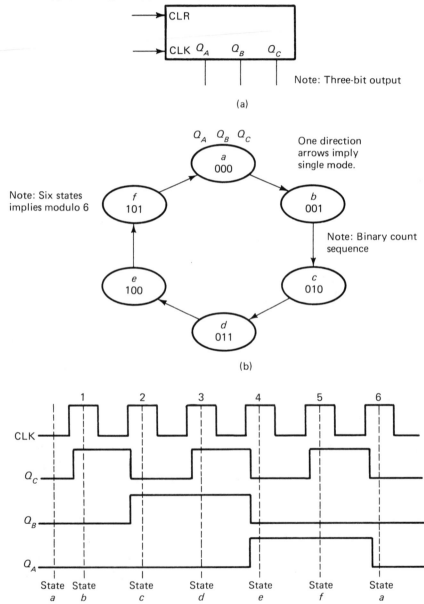

SN54160, SN74160 SYNCHRONOUS DECADE COUNTERS

SN54162, SN74162 synchronous decade counters are similar; however the clear is synchronous as shown for the SN54163, SN74163 binary counters at right.

SN54163, SN74163 SYNCHRONOUS BINARY COUNTERS

SN54161, SN74161 synchronous binary counters are similar; however, the clear is asynchronous as shown for the SN54160, SN74160 decade counters at left.

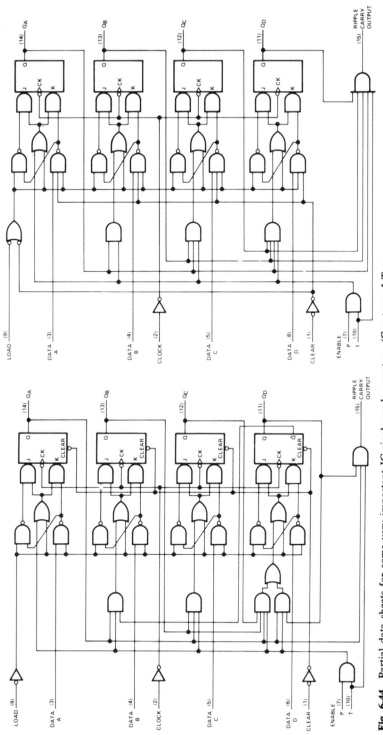

Fig. 6-44. Partial data sheets for some very important IC single-mode counters. (Courtesy of Texas Instruments, Inc.)

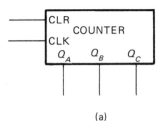

(a)

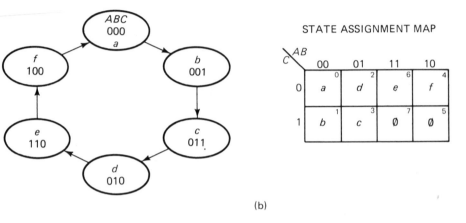

(b)

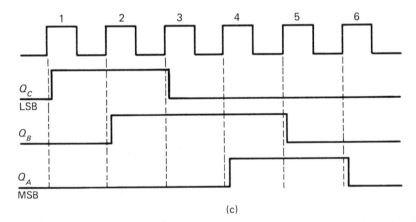

(c)

Fig. 6-45. The specification of a specialized counter. (a) A three-bit modulo 6 single-mode unit distance code counter defined by the state diagram in (b). (b) The state diagram for the three-bit modulo 6 single-mode counter. (c) Timing diagram.

Unit distance counters have some definite advantages over the conventional binary and decimal counters in that there is only *one* bit change per input change. Thus it is possible to directly decode the states without fear of suffering multi-bit change "flashing" which is a problem with all non-unit distance coded counters.

6-13 DESIGN OF SINGLE-MODE COUNTERS

The design of counter circuits is much easier than the design of circuits previously discussed because the exact number of states is given (i.e., no redundancy state check is needed) and the specifications prescribe the state assignment. Therefore, all there is left to do is to plot and to read the maps and draw up the schematics.

EXAMPLE 6-9: Complete the design of the counter specified in Figure 6-45 and add an ASYNCHRONOUS CLEAR feature. This design is carried out in Figure 6-46.

   The schematic for the three-bit modulo 6 counter is shown in Figure 6-45 using JK Flip-Flops.

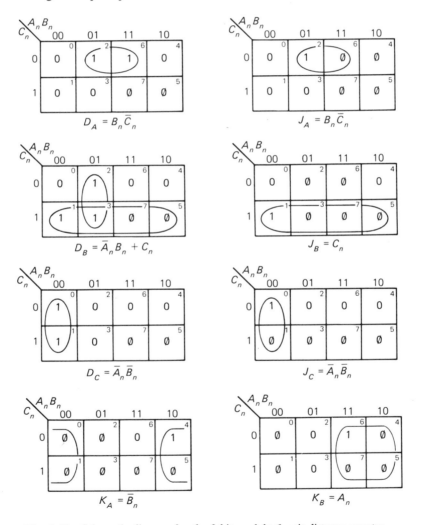

Fig. 6-46. Schematic diagram for the 3-bit modulo 6 unit distance counter specified in Figure 6-44.

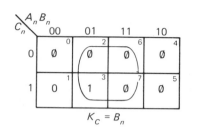

$$K_C = B_n$$

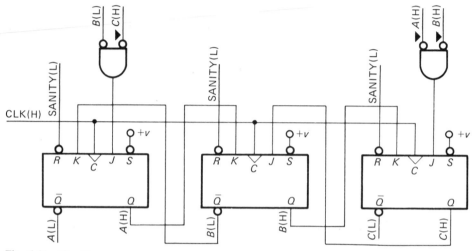

Fig. 6-46. (Cont.)

6-14 MULTI-MODE COUNTERS

Multi-mode counters are basically single-mode counters with some added outside world control. For example, an UP/DOWN counter, sometimes called a reversible counter, is a multi-mode counter capable of reversing its count sequence under external control. Figures 6-47 and 6-48 illustrate some typical specifications for multi-mode counters that are available as integrated circuits. Thus the multi-mode counter can be generalized as a *synchronous sequential circuit whose counting sequence can be altered by external control.*

Frankly speaking, since there is a wide array of multi-mode binary and decimal counters available that are cascadable, there seems little need for exhaustive design procedures in this area. *However, a word of special warning to those using integrated multi-mode counters*: Examine circuit specifications and circuit diagrams. If JK Flip-Flops are used in these devices, the "old 1's catching problem" is more than likely there; unless the specifications state explicitly that it is not there, then you must assume that it is. The basic problem with multi-mode counters designed with JK Flip-Flops without DATA LOCKOUT or edge-triggering occurs when the mode is changed. If the CLOCK input is not at the proper level, erroneous operation will result from a mode change. Thus, be cautious of such specifications as: "The UP CONTROL INPUT can be changed *only* when the CLOCK INPUT is HIGH." Review the specifications for the devices shown in Figures 6-44 and 6-47 for words like these. Because of limitations such as the 1's catching and other limiting sequential specifications, there will be times when the off-the-shelf counters will not do your job, and you will have to do your own design. Techniques for designing multi-mode counters are fairly standard and are outlined in the next section.

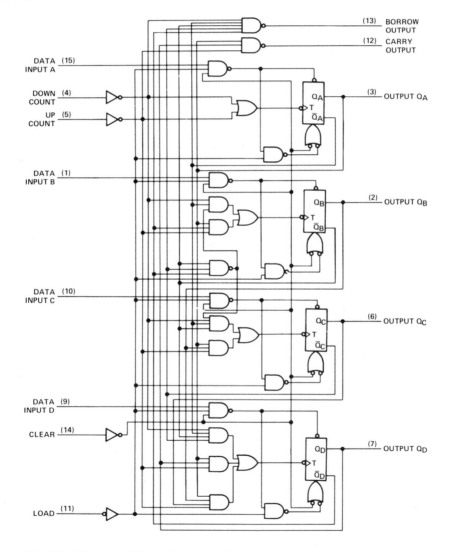

Fig. 6-47. (Courtesy of Texas Instruments, Inc.)

SYNCHRONOUS COUNTERS—POSITIVE-EDGE TRIGGERED

DESCRIPTION	COUNT FREQ	PARALLEL LOAD	CLEAR	TYP TOTAL POWER DISSIPATION	DEVICE TYPE AND PACKAGE				PAGE NO.
					−55°C to 125°C		0°C to 70°C		
DECADE	40 MHz	Sync	Sync-L	475 mW	SN54S162	J, W	SN74S162	J, N	
	25 MHz	Sync	Sync-L	93 mW	SN54LS162A	J, W	SN74LS162A	J, N	
	25 MHz	Sync	Async-L	93 mW	SN54LS160A	J, W	SN74LS160A	J, N	7-190
	25 MHz	Sync	Sync-L	305 mW	SN54162	J, W	SN74162	J, N	
	25 MHz	Sync	Async-L	305 mW	SN54160	J, W	SN74160	J, N	
DECADE UP/DOWN	40 MHz	Sync	None	500 mW	SN54S168	J, W	SN74S168	J, N	7-226
	25 MHz	Sync	None	100 mW	SN54LS168A	J, W	SN74LS168A	J, N	7-226
	25 MHz	Async	Async-H	85 mW	SN54LS192	J, W	SN74LS192	J, N	7-306
	25 MHz	Async	Async-H	325 mW	SN54192	J, W	SN74192	J, N	7-306
	20 MHz	Async	None	100 mW	SN54LS190	J, W	SN74LS190	J, N	7-296
	20 MHz	Async	None	325 mW	SN54190	J, W	SN74190	J, N	7-296
	3 MHz	Async	Async-H	42 mW	SN54L192	J	SN74L192	J, N	7-306
DECADE RATE MULTIPLIER, $\frac{1}{N_{10}}$	25 MHz	Set-to-9	Async-H	270 mW	SN54167	J, W	SN74167	J, N	7-222
4-BIT BINARY	40 MHz	Sync	Sync-L	475 mW	SN54S163	J, W	SN74S163	J, N	
	25 MHz	Sync	Sync-L	93 mW	SN54LS163A	J, W	SN74LS163A	J, N	
	25 MHz	Sync	Async-L	93 mW	SN54LS161A	J, W	SN74LS161A	J, N	7-190
	25 MHz	Sync	Sync-L	305 mW	SN54163	J, W	SN74163	J, N	
	25 MHz	Sync	Async-L	305 mW	SN54161	J, W	SN74161	J, N	
4-BIT BINARY UP/DOWN	40 MHz	Sync	None	500 mW	SN54S169	J, W	SN74S169	J, N	7-226
	25 MHz	Sync	None	100 mW	SN54LS169A	J, W	SN74LS169A	J, N	7-226
	25 MHz	Async	Async-H	85 mW	SN54LS193	J, W	SN74LS193	J, N	7-306
	25 MHz	Async	Async-H	325 mW	SN54193	J, W	SN74193	J, N	7-306
	20 MHz	Async	None	90 mW	SN54LS191	J, W	SN74LS191	J, N	7-296
	20 MHz	Async	None	325 mW	SN54191	J, W	SN74191	J, N	7-296
	3 MHz	Async	Async-H	42 mW	SN54L193	J	SN74L193	J, N	7-306
6-BIT BINARY RATE MULTIPLIER, $\frac{1}{N_2}$	25 MHz		Async-H	345 mW	SN5497	J, W	SN7497	J, N	7-102

Fig. 6-48. A listing of available synchronous integrated circuit counters (standard TTL, LSTTL, Schotky TTL, and CMOS). (Courtesy of Texas Instruments, Inc.)

6-15 DESIGN OF SPECIALIZED MULTI-MODE COUNTERS

The design techniques for multi-mode counters are illustrated nicely by the odd number of 1's design example. However, to reinforce the concepts learned in the previous example, another design is demonstrated.

EXAMPLE 6-10: Design a three-bit, modulo 6, unit-distance code, *up-down* counter with a synchronous CLEAR, one which has the same sequential code as Example 6-9. This design process is illustrated in Figure 6-49.

It is interesting to note that this is a case where the D Flip-Flop implementation is decisively the simplest to implement from a total gate count point of view, thus refuting such sweeping statements as: "JK implementations are always more optimal than D implementations."

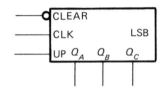

(a)

Format: UP/−

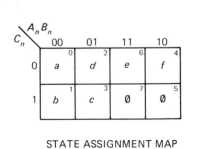

STATE ASSIGNMENT MAP

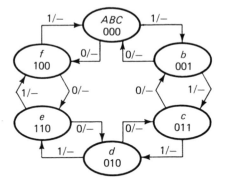

(b)

	PRESENT STATE	INPUT	NEXT STATE		
	$A_n\ B_n\ C_n$	UP	A_{n+1}	B_{n+1}	C_{n+1}
0	a 000	0	1	0	0
1	000	1	0	0	1
2	b 001	0	0	0	0
3	001	1	0	1	1
4	d 010	0	0	1	1
5	010	1	1	1	0
6	c 011	0	0	0	1
7	011	1	0	1	0
8	f 100	0	1	1	0
9	100	1	0	0	0
10	Ø 101	0	Ø	Ø	Ø
11	101	1	Ø	Ø	Ø
12	e 110	0	0	1	0
13	110	1	1	0	0
14	Ø 111	0	Ø	Ø	Ø
15	111	1	Ø	Ø	Ø

(c)

Fig. 6-49. The design steps leading to a three-bit, modulo 6 unit-distance counter. (a) Block diagram. (b) State diagram. (c) PRESENT/NEXT STATE assignment table. (d) The NEXT STATE maps. (e) JK maps. (f) Schematic diagram.

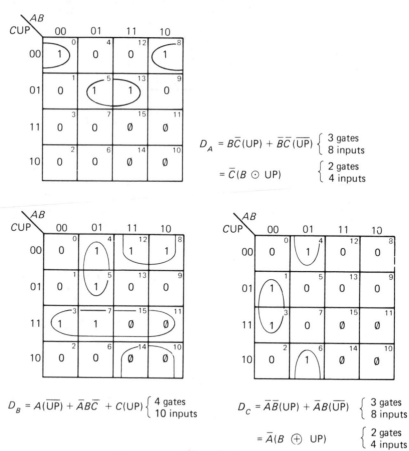

$$D_A = B\overline{C}(\text{UP}) + \overline{B}C\,(\overline{\text{UP}}) \quad \left\{ \begin{array}{l} 3 \text{ gates} \\ 8 \text{ inputs} \end{array} \right.$$

$$= \overline{C}(B \odot \text{UP}) \quad \left\{ \begin{array}{l} 2 \text{ gates} \\ 4 \text{ inputs} \end{array} \right.$$

$$D_B = A(\overline{\text{UP}}) + \overline{A}B\overline{C} + C(\text{UP}) \quad \left\{ \begin{array}{l} 4 \text{ gates} \\ 10 \text{ inputs} \end{array} \right.$$

$$D_C = \overline{A}\,\overline{B}(\text{UP}) + \overline{A}B(\overline{\text{UP}}) \quad \left\{ \begin{array}{l} 3 \text{ gates} \\ 8 \text{ inputs} \end{array} \right.$$

$$= \overline{A}(B \oplus \text{UP}) \quad \left\{ \begin{array}{l} 2 \text{ gates} \\ 4 \text{ inputs} \end{array} \right.$$

Fig. 6-49 (d).

Trying a JK implementation:

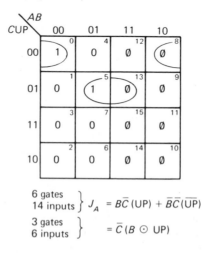

$$\left. \begin{array}{l} 6 \text{ gates} \\ 14 \text{ inputs} \end{array} \right\} \ J_A = B\overline{C}\,(\text{UP}) + \overline{B}C(\overline{\text{UP}})$$

$$\left. \begin{array}{l} 3 \text{ gates} \\ 6 \text{ inputs} \end{array} \right\} \qquad = \overline{C}\,(B \odot \text{UP})$$

Fig. 6-49 (e).

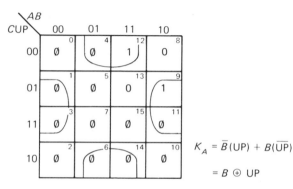

$$K_A = \overline{B}(\text{UP}) + B(\overline{\text{UP}})$$

$$= B \oplus \text{UP}$$

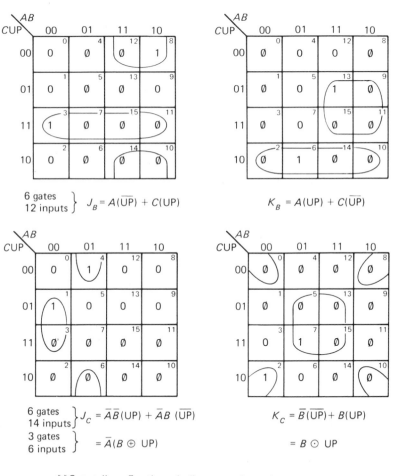

6 gates
12 inputs $\Bigg\}$ $J_B = A(\overline{\text{UP}}) + C(\text{UP})$

$$K_B = A(\text{UP}) + C(\overline{\text{UP}})$$

6 gates
14 inputs $\Bigg\}$ $J_C = \overline{A}\,\overline{B}(\text{UP}) + \overline{A}B\,(\overline{\text{UP}})$

3 gates
6 inputs $\Bigg\}$ $= \overline{A}(B \oplus \text{UP})$

$$K_C = \overline{B}(\overline{\text{UP}}) + B(\text{UP})$$

$$= B \odot \text{UP}$$

Gate tally: For the unit distance code up-down counter

D implementation — 10 gates and 26 inputs
JK implementation — 18 gates and 40 inputs

Fig. 6-49 (e). (Cont.)

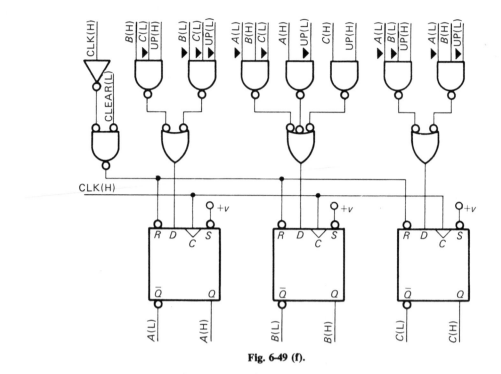

Fig. 6-49 (f).

Another interesting point is that using an edge-triggered Flip-Flop virtually eliminates the mode change fault caused by using Flip-Flops without the edge-triggering or data-lockout-type features.

All in all, a good design engineer should be able to design special multi-mode counters if the need arises. However, your first attempt in any given situation is to determine whether you could possibly use an integrated circuit for your application (see Figure 6-48). If not, you should attempt to design counters that are expandable, similar to the 7416X or 7419X series of counters. Several design exercises will be given to help you develop knowledge in this area.

The next two sections cover some other types of special counters: some found in integrated circuit form, others requiring design effort.

6-16 RIPPLE COUNTERS

Ripple counters such as the one in Figure 6-50 are asynchronous counters that differ distinctly from the full synchronous counters studied thus far. This distinction stems from the fact that the clock inputs of the Flip-Flops in the counting chain of a ripple counter are *not* tied together. In fact, the clock inputs are cascaded from output to input. Further, note that each Flip-Flop is fed back on itself, making it a modulo 2 counter. Therefore, a ripple counter is a cascade of modulo 2 counters, each triggered by the output of the preceding stage. Hence, its counting up-date process is one closely related to the ripple sent up a piece of taut rope by applying a quick jerk to one end.

Ripple counters such as the one shown in Figure 6-50 have the advantage of simplicity over synchronous counters, but are at a disadvantage in two aspects:

(1) speed;
(2) a forced straight binary-code sequence.

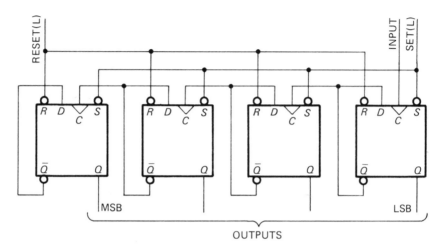

Fig. 6-50. A four-bit binary ripple counter.

Though the code sequence restriction is not a serious handicap, the rippling nature of the output update is. This rippling operation reduces the maximum counting frequency and aggravates the "glitching" problem related to using direct combinational decoding techniques for decoding the output code. This nasty problem is discussed further in Chapter 7.

The maximum frequency constraint of the ripple counter is established by the sum of the maximum transition time of the Flip-Flops in the counting chain. This constraint is established at the maximum count to the all zero "roll over" point.

> EXAMPLE 6-11: If an eight-stage ripple counter is to be designed using Flip-Flops with worst case transition times = 25 nsec, what is the maximum input frequency at which this counter will operate   Let:
>
> $T_{rp} \triangleq$ the worst case ripple through period. This is the max time it takes a 1 or 0 to completely ripple from the LSB to the MSB.
>
> $T_{Pd} \triangleq$ the worst case propagation delay for the individual Flip-Flops used.
>
> $$T_{rp} = \sum_{i=1}^{n} t_{Ti}$$
>
> or $T_{rp} = n_{t_T}$ if all t_T's are assumed equal.

For this problem:

$$T_{rp} \triangleq (8)(25) \text{ nsec} = 200 \text{ nsec}$$

$$\therefore f_{max} = \frac{1}{T_{rp}} = 5 \text{ MHz}$$

So in fact the same counter could be designed using the same Flip-Flops and synchronous techniques and made to operate at frequencies in excess of 25 MHz. However, this counter could be used at a significantly higher count rate if a count decoder circuit is not needed.

Thus ripple counters, particularly the large modulo number counters, have a significant frequency handicap if their outputs are to be decoded.

The alteration of the modulo number of a ripple counter, in theory, is as simple as decoding the max count number designed and asynchronously re-setting or setting the Flip-Flop back to an initial state. This is illustrated in Figure 6-51, where the same circuit shown in Figure 6-50 is altered to develop a decade (modulo 10) ripple counter.

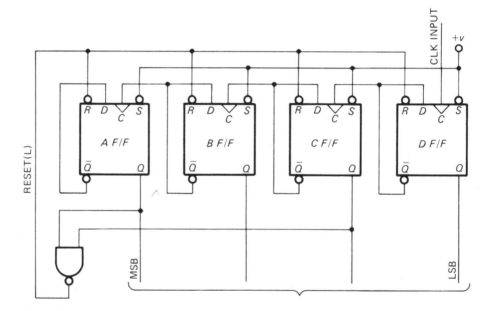

Fig. 6-51. A modulo 10 ripple counter.

The timing diagram shown in Figure 6-52 illustrates both the guaranteed transient conditions that prevail with *any* (synchronous or asynchronous) binary sequence counters as well as the transient reset states created by the asynchronous reset. These transient reset states further illustrate the finite possibility of only one of the Flip-Flops (*A* or *C*) being reset without the other being reset, and this situation can lead to some serious problems.

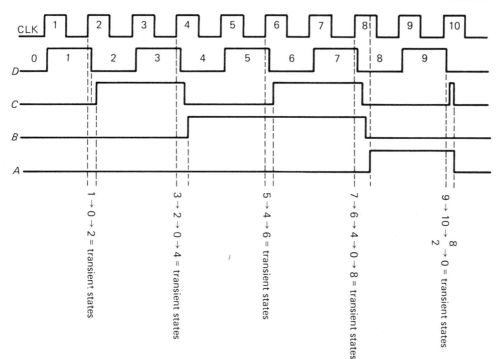

Fig. 6-52. The timing diagram for the modulo 10 ripple counter that illustrates the transient states guaranteed by a ripple counter.

ASYNCHRONOUS COUNTERS (RIPPLE CLOCK)—NEGATIVE-EDGE TRIGGERED

Description	Count Freq.	Parallel Load	Clear	Typ. Total Power Dissipation	Device Type And Package			
					−55°C to 125°C		0°C to 70°C	
	50 MHz	Yes	Low	240 mW	Sn54196	J, W	SN74196	J, N
	35 MHz	Yes	Low	150 mW	SN54176	J, W	SN74176	J, N
	32 MHz	Set-to-9	High	40 mW	SN54LS90	J, W	SN74LS90	J, N
	32 MHz	Set-to-9	High	40 mW	SN54LS290	J, W	SN74LS290	J, N
Decade	32 MHz	Set-to-9	High	160 mW	SN5490A	J, W	SN7490A	J, N
	32 MHz	Set-to-9	High	160 mW	SN54290	J, W	SN74290	J, N
	30 MHz	Yes	Low	60 mW	SN54LS196	J, W	SN74LS196	J, N
	3 MHz	Set-to-9	High	20 mW	SN54L90	J, N, T	SN74L90	J, N, T
	50 MHz	Yes	Low	240 mW	SN54197	J, W	SN74197	J, N
	35 MHz	Yes	Low	150 mW	SN54177	J, W	SN74177	J, N
	32 MHz	None	High	39 mW	SN54LS93	J, W	SN74LS93	J, N
	32 MHz	None	High	39 mW	SN54LS293	J, W	SN74LS293	J, N
4 bit binary	32 MHz	None	High	160 mW	SN5493A	J, W	SN7493A	J, N
	32 MHz	None	High	160 mW	SN54293	J, W	SN74293	J, N
	30 MHz	Yes	Low	60 mW	SN54LS197	J, W	SN74LS197	J, N
	3 MHZ	None	High	20 mW	SN54L93	J, N, T	SN74L93	J, N, T
Divide-by-12	32 MHz	None	High	39 mW	SN54LS92	J, W	SN74LS92	J, N
	32 MHz	None	High	160 mW	SN5492A	J, W	SN7492A	J, N
Dual decade	25 MHz	None	High	210 mW	SN54390	J, W	SN74390	J, N
	25 MHz	Set-to-9	High	225 mW	SN54490	J, W	SN74490	J, N
Dual 4-bit binary	25 MHz	None	High	190 mW	SN54393	J, W	SN74393	J, N

Fig. 6-53. A list of available integrated circuit ripple counters. (Courtesy of Texas Instruments, Inc.)

Because of the disadvantages of ripple counters they should be used with a certain degree of caution and with a knowledge of their limitations. See Figure 6-53 for a list of available asynchronous ripple-type counters. The next section introduces a synchronous counter that exhibits several advantages over the ripple and synchronous binary sequence counters.

6-17 RING COUNTERS

Ring counters (see Figure 6-57) are special purpose synchronous counters that are sometimes referred to as *Johnson* or *Moebius* counters. These sequential counters have special applications in cases where code sequences with symmetry are desired. There are basically two types of ring counters:

(1) Standard-ring
(2) Twisted-ring

The standard-ring counter requires n Flip-Flops to derive a modulo (n + 1) counter. The twisted-ring counter requires n/2 Flip-Flops for a modulo n counter. In most applications the ring counter is not really used for a counting function, but rather as a special sequence generator as mentioned above.

First consider the four-bit standard-ring counter sequences shown in Figure 6-54. Here a sort of diagonal symmetry is generated when a 1 is shifted or rotated through the four output bits.

A B C D		A B C D
0 0 0 0	or	0 0 0 0
1 0 0 0		0 0 0 1
0 1 0 0		0 0 1 0
0 0 1 0		0 1 0 0
0 0 0 1		1 0 0 0
0 0 0 0		0 0 0 0

Fig. 6-54. Two possible sequences for a four-bit standard-ring counter.

Consider the three-bit twisted-ring counter sequences shown in Figure 6-55. This figure shows that twisted-ring sequences are apparently generated by inverting one of the end bits (MSB or LSB) and shifting it into the other end bit on each clock pulse.

A B C		A B C
0 0 0	or	0 0 0
1 0 0		0 0 1
1 1 0		0 1 1
1 1 1		1 1 1
0 1 1		1 1 0
0 0 1		1 0 0
0 0 0		0 0 0

Fig. 6-55. Two possible three-bit twisted-ring counter sequences.

As previously discussed in the analysis section, ring counters can "hang" if they are not properly designed. Noise or power-up conditions can cause the counter to be jammed to one of the unused states from which it *will not* return to the main counting sequence. Therefore, it is necessary to design ring counters that are self-correcting (will not hang). We will do this using the traditional design method illustrating a general design technique that will avoid the anomaly.

EXAMPLE 6-12: Design a self-correcting 3-bit twisted-ring counter with the indicated counting sequence. This design is illustrated in Figure 6-56.

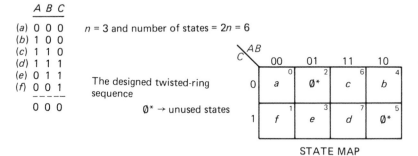

	A B C
(a)	0 0 0
(b)	1 0 0
(c)	1 1 0
(d)	1 1 1
(e)	0 1 1
(f)	0 0 1
	0 0 0

$n = 3$ and number of states $= 2n = 6$

The designed twisted-ring sequence

$\emptyset^* \rightarrow$ unused states

STATE MAP

(a)

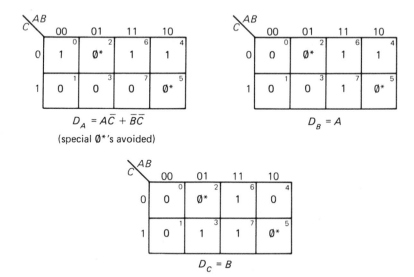

$D_A = A\overline{C} + \overline{B}\,\overline{C}$

(special $\emptyset^*$'s avoided)

$D_B = A$

$D_C = B$

(b)

Fig. 6-56. The design steps leading to a 3-bit self-correcting twisted-ring counter. (a) The sequence table and state map. (b) The maps.

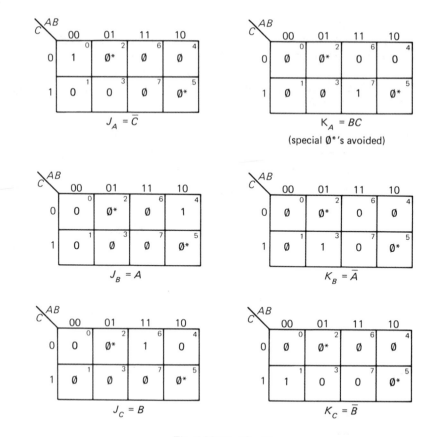

Fig. 6-56 (b). (Cont.)

The key to designing self-correcting ring counters is in the way the $\emptyset^*$ (unused state) entries are grouped in *one* of the NEXT STATE MAPS. Generally, the MSB or A map is grouped so that the $\emptyset^*$ entries are completely avoided; therefore, their value is forced to 0. As a result of this, if by chance one of the $\emptyset^*$ states is induced by noise, the next state for the counter will always be $A = 0$, $B = \emptyset$, and $C = \emptyset$ (see the D_A map in Figure 6-56). For the D implementation, observe that the mapping described above forces the $\emptyset^*$ in the next state of cell 2 to be 001 or state f; and the next state of the $\emptyset^*$ in cell 5 to be 010 cell 2. Thus if either $\emptyset^*$ state is induced, the counter will always recover. It may take two clock cycles, but it will recover. For the JK implementation, *one* of the six maps (J or K) must be grouped avoiding all the $\emptyset^*$ entries. Doing so results in the same self-correcting operation. This is generally done by grouping one of the maps, which will result in simpler implementation. For example, grouping K_A results in a simpler implementation than grouping J_A. Both the D and JK implementations of the three-bit self-correcting twisted-ring counter are shown in Figure 6-57.

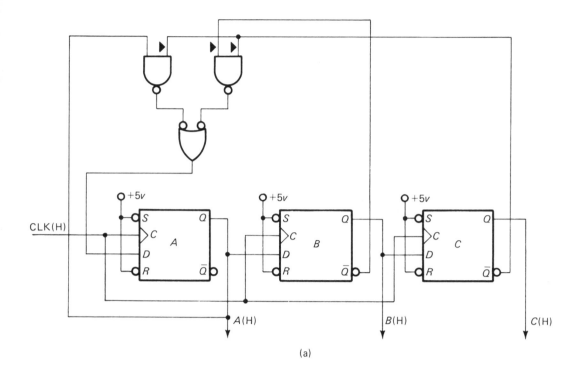

(a)

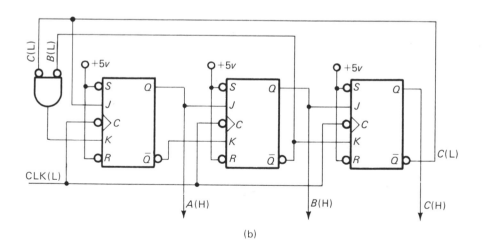

(b)

Fig. 6-57. (a) The D implementation of a self-correcting, three-bit (six-state) twisted-ring counter. (b) The JK implementation of a self-correcting, three-bit (six-state) twisted-ring counter.

6-18 APPLICATIONS OF RING COUNTERS

The output sequences of the ring counters present an interesting and useful pattern when viewed in a timing diagram (see Figure 6-58). In these timing diagrams observe that the twisted-ring counter yields both a unit-distance sequence and square-wave outputs. This makes time-state pulse generation a simple task. Six distinct time-state pulses can be generated by using a single 3-to-8 decoder, and since the output sequence is unit-distance, transient outputs from this decoder are no problem.

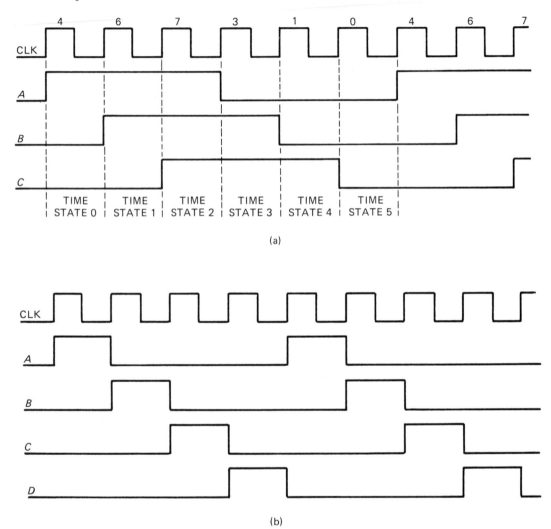

Fig. 6-58. (a) Timing diagram for a three-bit twisted-ring counter. (b) Timing diagram for a four-bit standard-ring counter.

The output of the four-bit standard-ring counter, by itself, generates four distinct and separate timing pulses. Further, it should be pointed out that self-correcting standard-ring counters can be designed by the same process used for the twisted-ring counter.

This analysis reveals at least one very important application for the ring counter, the time-state-pulse generation, which is widely used in computer design for timing control of the central processor unit (CPU). However, this is only one of many applications. Others are discussed later, so keep these interesting and important sequential circuits in mind when you are involved in system level design. The next section covers shift registers, which also can be adapted nicely to ring counters.

6-19 SHIFT REGISTERS

The *shift register* is another special synchronous circuit used widely as a fundamental building block in digital computers and other digital systems. The primary uses for shift registers are temporary data storage and bit manipulation. Shift registers, similar to counters, are classified by the following specifications:

(1) Number of bits
(2) Operation—single-mode or multi-mode

The classifications of operation modes are:

(1) PARALLEL IN–PARALLEL OUT: PIPO (sometimes referred to as BROADSIDE LOAD)
(2) PARALLEL IN–SERIAL OUT: PISO
(3) SERIAL IN–PARALLEL OUT: SIPO
(4) SERIAL IN–SERIAL OUT: SISO (bi-directional, shifts left and right)
(5) UNIVERSAL (a single device that is all of the above)

6-19.1 PARALLEL IN–PARALLEL OUT REGISTERS

The simplest of all registers is the PIPO-type register. A typical four-bit PIPO is shown in Figure 6-59. Also, shown in Figure 6-60, is the schematic of a commercial six-bit PIPO, the TTL SN74174. The PIPO operation is one of presenting data at the inputs and clocking the Flip-Flop to load in the data.

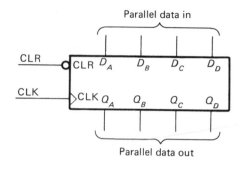

(a)

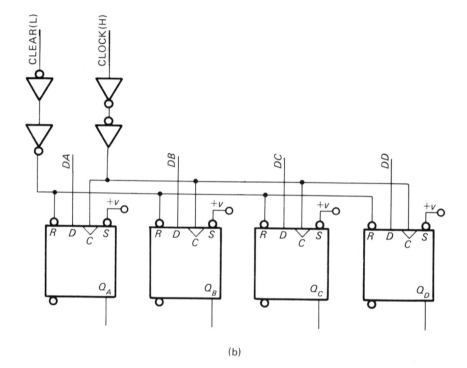

(b)

Fig. 6-59. A typical PIPO register. (a) Block diagram. (b) Schematic diagram.

Fig. 6-60. (facing page) A typical commercial six-bit PIPO register. (Courtesy of Texas Instruments, Inc.)

Functional block diagrams

'174, 'LS174, 'S174

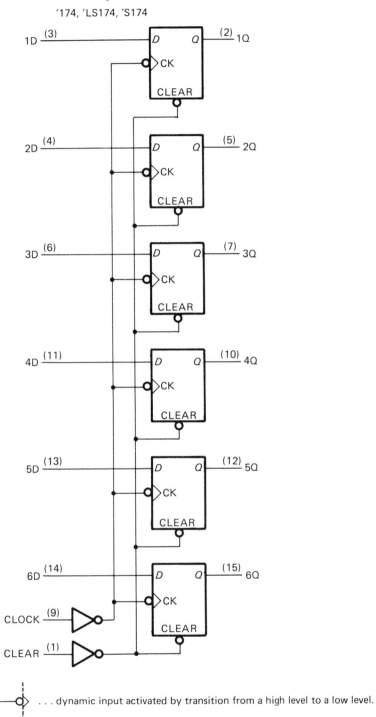

... dynamic input activated by transition from a high level to a low level.

6-19.2   SERIAL IN–SERIAL OUT REGISTERS

The SISO register is another single-mode-type register, sometimes referred to as the "bit bucket brigade" circuit. In short, the function of a SISO register is to present the input data to the single data input line, and then clock the internal Flip-Flops to sequentially move the bits right or left across these storage elements.

A typical four-bit SISO register is shown in Figure 6-61. Note further that by virtue of the design, this register can function also as a serial-in-parallel-out (SIPO) register.

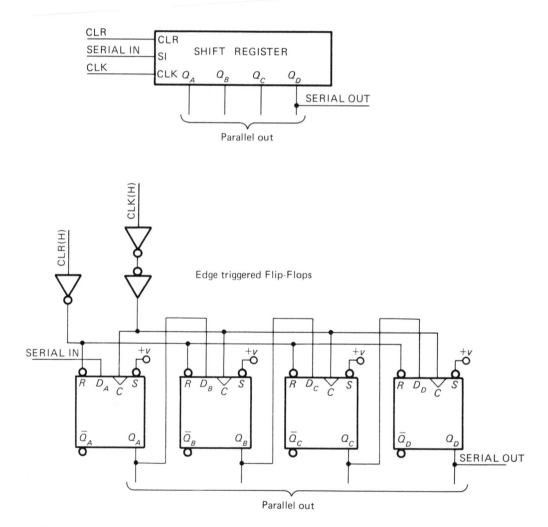

Fig. 6-61. A typical example of a combined SISO-SIPO shift-right register.

Studying the schematic in Figure 6-61, you see that the output Q_A is connected to the input D_B and Q_B to D_C, and so on. Thus, when the rising edge of the clock arrives, Q_A replaces Q_B and Q_B replaces Q_C, and so forth. Because of this, it is named the "shift-right SISO/SIPO." To make a shift-left SISO/PISO, the connections are reversed.

A modular approach to designing shift registers is starting to emerge. This modular approach to sequential design is illustrated in the next section.

6-19.3 MULTI-MODE AND UNIVERSAL SHIFT REGISTERS

Multi-mode shift registers are defined as those that have control inputs which allow the operation mode to be selectable. For example, SN74198 is by definition a multi-mode shift register (see Figure 6-62). In this figure the shift register is an eight-bit device having the feature that any of the three modes of operation or a no-operation can be selected. Also, note the 1's catching problem is pointed out.

The approach taken in designing shift registers such as the SN74198, as well as other array-type sequential circuits, is similar to the cellular approach taken earlier when designing n-bit full-adders. Once one cell of a full-adder modular system is designed in a general manner, all that remains is to interconnect the cells until the array is of desired length. The way this is done in sequential circuits is illustrated by using the Jth Flip-Flop cell in a register of arbitrary length, as shown in Figure 6-63.

Now all that remains is to determine what the next state of this Jth Flip-Flop is to be. Shift register operation dictates that the NEXT STATE (Q_{Jn+1}) is a function of the following:

(1) Q_J (its own present state)
(2) Q_{J+1} (for shifting left)
(3) Q_{J-1} (for shifting right)
(4) P_J (for parallel loading)
(5) Mode control inputs

Using this information a PRESENT/NEXT STATE TABLE is plotted with the state assignments, as shown in Figure 6-64.

Note that the state assignment entries for this example are quite different from those treated previously in that binary variables (Q_{J-1}, Q_{J+1}, and P_J) are used rather than standard 1's and 0's. However, by using map-entered variables as discussed in Chapter 3, the problem works out nicely. See Figure 6-65 for the NEXT STATE maps for both the D and JK implementation.

description

These 8-bit shift registers are compatible with most other TTL, DTL, and MSI logic families. All inputs are buffered to lower the drive requirements to one normalized Series 54/74 load, and input clamping diodes minimize switching transients to simplify system design. Maximum input clock frequency is typically 35 megahertz and power dissipation is typically 360 mW.

Series 54 devices are characterized for operation over the full military temperature range of -55°C to 125°C; Series 74 devices are characterized for operation from 0°C to 70°C.

SN54198 and SN74198

These bidirectional registers are designed to incorporate virtually all of the features a system designer may want in a shift register. These circuits contain 87 equivalent gates and feature parallel inputs, parallel outputs, right-shift and left-shift serial inputs, operating-mode-control inputs, and a direct overriding clear line. The register has four distinct modes of operation, namely:

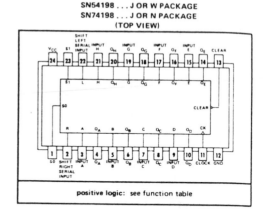

SN54198 . . . J OR W PACKAGE
SN74198 . . . J OR N PACKAGE
(TOP VIEW)

positive logic: see function table

Parallel (Broadside) Load
Shift Right (In the direction Q_A toward Q_H)
Shift Left (In the direction Q_H toward Q_A)
Inhibit Clock (Do nothing)

Synchronous parallel loading is accomplished by applying the eight bits of data and taking both mode control inputs, S0 and S1, high. The data is loaded into the associated flip-flop and appears at the outputs after the positive transition of the clock input. During loading, serial data flow is inhibited.

Shift right is accomplished synchronously with the rising edge of the clock pulse when S0 is high and S1 is low. Serial data for this mode is entered at the shift-right data input. When S0 is low and S1 is high, data shifts left synchronously and new data is entered at the shift-left serial input.

Clocking of the flip-flop is inhibited when both mode cont   inputs are low. The mode controls should be changed only while the clock input is high.

'198
FUNCTION TABLE

CLEAR	MODE		CLOCK	SERIAL		PARALLEL	OUTPUTS			
	S_1	S_0		LEFT	RIGHT	A . . . H	Q_A	$Q_B \ldots$	Q_G	Q_H
L	X	X	X	X	X	X	L	L	L	L
H	X	X	L	X	X	X	Q_{A0}	Q_{B0}	Q_{G0}	Q_{H0}
H	H	H	↑	X	X	a . . . h	a	b	g	h
H	L	H	↑	X	H	X	H	Q_{An}	Q_{Fn}	Q_{Gn}
H	L	H	↑	X	L	X	L	Q_{An}	Q_{Fn}	Q_{Gn}
H	H	L	↑	H	X	X	Q_{Bn}	Q_{Cn}	Q_{Hn}	H
H	H	L	↑	L	X	X	Q_{Bn}	Q_{Cn}	Q_{Hn}	L
H	L	L	X	X	X	X	Q_{A0}	Q_{B0}	Q_{G0}	Q_{H0}

H = high level (steady state), L = low level (steady state)
X = irrelevant (any input, including transitions)
↑ = transition from low to high level
a . . . h = the level of steady-state input at inputs A thru H, respectively.
Q_{A0}, Q_{B0}, Q_{G0}, Q_{H0} = the level of Q_A, Q_B, Q_G, or Q_H, respectively, before the indicated steady-state input conditions were established.
Q_{An}, Q_{Bn}, etc. = the level of Q_A, Q_B, etc., respectively, before the most-recent ↑ transition of the clock.

Fig. 6-62. A partial data sheet for the 74198 shift register. (Courtesy of Texas Instruments, Inc.)

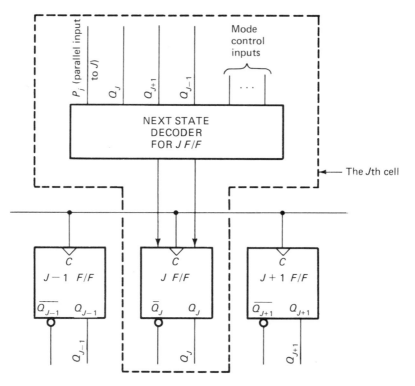

Fig. 6-63. The Jth cell of a multi-mode shift register.

	PRESENT STATE Q_{Jn}	INPUTS S_1 S_0	NEXT STATE Q_{Jn+1}
0	0	0 0	0
1	0	0 1	Q_{J-1}
2	0	1 0	Q_{J+1}
3	0	1 1	P_J
4	1	0 0	1
5	1	0 1	Q_{J-1}
6	1	1 0	Q_{J+1}
7	1	1 1	P_J

S_1 S_0	OPERATION
0 0	HOLD
0 1	SR
1 0	SL
1 1	LOAD

Fig. 6-64. The PRESENT/NEXT STATE TABLE for Q_J with state assignment based on the operation table shown.

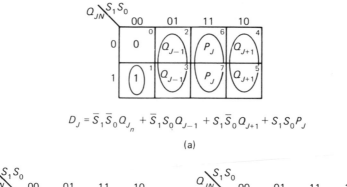

$$D_J = \bar{S}_1 \bar{S}_0 Q_{J_n} + \bar{S}_1 S_0 Q_{J-1} + S_1 \bar{S}_0 Q_{J+1} + S_1 S_0 P_J$$

(a)

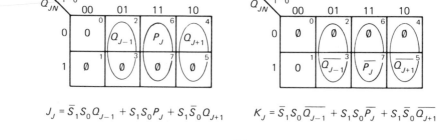

$$J_J = \bar{S}_1 S_0 Q_{J-1} + S_1 S_0 P_J + S_1 \bar{S}_0 Q_{J+1} \qquad K_J = \bar{S}_1 S_0 \overline{Q_{J-1}} + S_1 S_0 \overline{P_J} + S_1 \bar{S}_0 \overline{Q_{J+1}}$$

(b)

Fig. 6-65. (a) The NEXT STATE maps for the Jth cell of the multi-mode shift register. (b) The J and K map for a JK implementation of a multi-mode shift register.

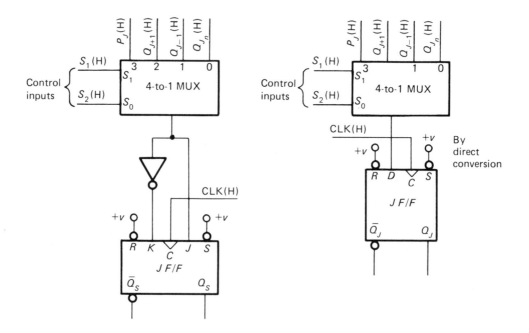

Fig. 6-66. Using multiplexors to implement the Jth cell of a multi-mode shift register.

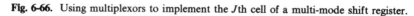

Because of the input-select feature of the operation of the general multi-mode shift register, a multiplexer is a natural for implementing the NEXT STATE DECODER for the Jth Flip-Flop. Thus the complete cell design for both D and JK Flip-Flops is shown in Figure 6-66.

6-20 SHIFT REGISTER SEQUENCES

The shift register which can be controlled to shift a 1 or 0 both left and right and has the parallel outputs available can become a very powerful, controlled sequence generator. As a result of this, shift register sequences are used extensively in the following fields:

(1) Secure and limited-access code generations
(2) Privacy encoding
(3) Multiple address coding
(4) Error correcting generators
(5) Prescribed period and sequence generators
(6) Random bit generators

To understand how a shift register can be used for all these varied functions, consider the system shown in Figure 6-67.

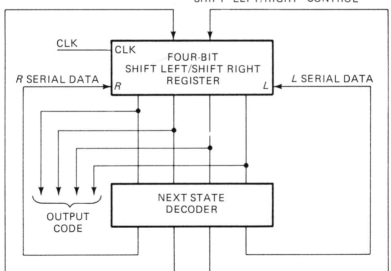

Fig. 6-67. The model for a sequence generator using a simple four-bit register.

The functions of the next state decoder are listed as follows:

(1) Control SHIFT LEFT and SHIFT RIGHT control inputs.
(2) Set up a 1 or 0 to the appropriate LEFT or RIGHT input.

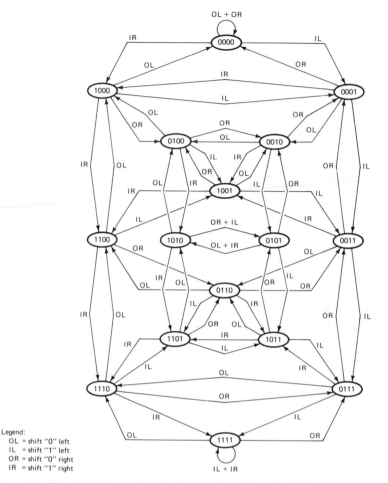

Fig. 6-68. The "kaleidoscope" state diagram describing the different sequences which can be derived from a 4-bit shift register.

The state diagram shown in Figure 6-68 is an illustration of the 256 possible sequences that can be derived from the simple model shown in Figure 6-67. From this "kaleidoscope" state diagram it is easy to spot both the twisted-ring counter sequences and the standard-ring counter sequences, as well as a whole host of other sequences, all of which are generated simply by controlling the shifting of a 1 or 0 left or right. For those interested in a further study of shift register sequences, you are referred to *Shift Register Sequences* by Solomon W. Golomb.

Now consider how a shift register can be used to derive the twisted- and standard-ring counters.

6-21 RING COUNTERS USING SHIFT REGISTER

Examine the following example to develop an understanding of shift register counters.

EXAMPLE 6-13: Design a self-correcting four-bit standard-ring counter using a 74194. Given:

(a)	0	0	0	0
(b)	1	0	0	0
(c)	0	1	0	0
(d)	0	0	1	0
(e)	0	0	0	1
	0	0	0	0

Now referring to Examples 6-11 and 6-12, note that the shift register should be locked into the SHIFT RIGHT mode and that controlling only the SERIAL RIGHT input or the control equation for D_A in the shift register insures self-correcting operation. Thus the map shown in Figure E6-1 is plotted.

$$D_A = \bar{A}\bar{B}\bar{C}\bar{D}$$

Fig. E6-1.

Avoiding all of the $\emptyset$ states guarantees self-correcting operation. The implementation of the four-bit self-correcting standard-ring counter is shown in Figure 6-69.

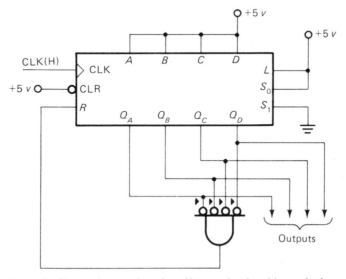

Fig. 6-69. The implementation of a self-correcting four-bit standard-ring counter using a 74194.

Of course, the same technique can be used to derive twisted ring counters of arbitrary length. This is left as an exercise.

Notice that the reason for selecting the MSB or LSB for the special map grouping is that these are the only accessible Flip-Flops. Note also that the ring counter in Figure 6-69 fits the general model set forth in Figure 6-67.

The next section introduces similar concepts related to the control of arrays of registers that makes up RANDOM-ACCESS MEMORIES or simply RAM's.

6-22 SHIFT REGISTERS AND MEMORY

As mentioned previously, shift registers are only one of the primary building blocks of digital computers. In fact, a digital computer can be thought of as an ordered array of registers, with a control unit that directs the flow of data through this array of registers. The ordered array of registers mentioned is generally considered to be classified as MEMORY. Memory, as mentioned in Chapter 5, comes in various types such as RAM's SAM's and CAM's. This section touches upon some of these devices, their relation to shift registers, and their operation.

6-22.1 REGISTERS AND SAM'S

A collection of multi-mode shift left-shift right SISO registers can be tipped up on end, as shown in Figure 6-70 to form what is called a memory "stack." By shifting right we "push" the stack down; by shifting left we "pop" the stack. Stacks are very handy sequential addressed memories (SAM's) and are used extensively in modern computing machines. Stacks such as the one shown in Figure 6-70 are commonly called a LIFO memory, which stands for LAST IN/FIRST OUT memory. There are also FIFO's (FIRST IN/FIRST OUT), which can be fabricated from shift registers. However, FIFO's can be implemented more easily with tristate output random-access memories (RAM's). FIFO memories, such as the one shown in Figure 6-71, are widely used STACK MEMORIES.

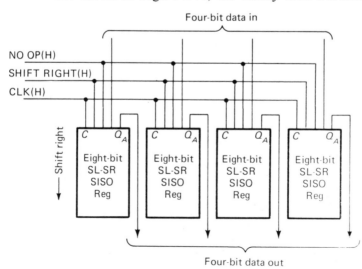

Fig. 6-70. An example of how SISO registers can be configured for a LIFO memory stack.

Distinctive Characteristics

- Plug-In replacement for Fairchild 3341
- Asynchronous buffer for up to 64 four-bit words
- Easily expandable to larger buffers

- Am2841 has 1 MHz guaranteed data rate
- Am2841A has 1.2MHz guaranteed data rate
- 100% reliability assurance testing in compliance with MIL-STD-883
- Special input circuit provides true TTL compatibility

FUNCTIONAL DESCRIPTION

The Am3341/Am2841/Am2841A is an asynchronous first-in first-out memory stack, organized as 64 four-bit words. The device accepts a four-bit parallel word D_0-D_3 under control of the shift in (SI) input. Data entered into the FIFO immediately ripples through the device to the outputs Q_0-Q_3. Up to 64 words may be entered before any words are read from the memory. The stored words line up at the output end in the order in which they were written. A read command on the shift out input (SO) causes the next to the last word of data to move to the output and all data shifts one place down the stack. Input ready (IR) and output ready (OR) signals act as memory full and memory empty flags and also provide the necessary pulses for interconnecting FIFOs to obtain deeper stacks.

Parallel expansion to wider words only requires that rows of FIFOs be placed side by side.

Reading and writing operations are completely independent, so the device can be used as a buffer between two digital machines operating asynchronously and at widely differing clock rates. Special input circuits are provided on all inputs to pull the input signals up to an MOS V_{IH} when a TTL V_{OH} is reached, providing true TTL compatibility without the inconvenience and extra power drain of external pull-up resistors. A detailed description of the operation is on pages 4 and 5 of this data sheet. The Am2841 and Am2841A are functionally identical to the Am3341, but are higher performance devices.

LOGIC BLOCK DIAGRAM

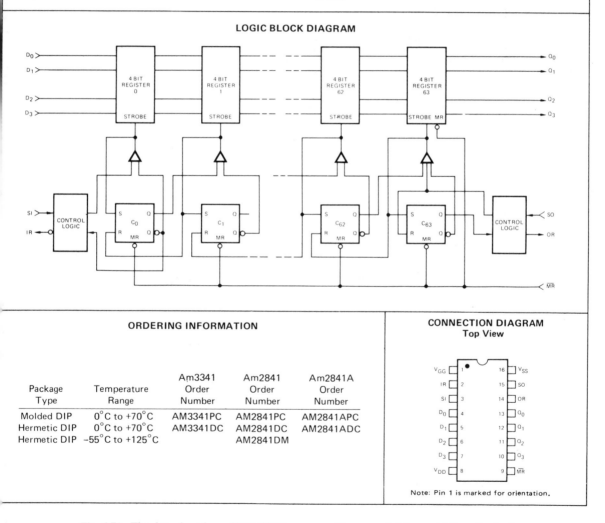

ORDERING INFORMATION

Package Type	Temperature Range	Am3341 Order Number	Am2841 Order Number	Am2841A Order Number
Molded DIP	0°C to +70°C	AM3341PC	AM2841PC	AM2841APC
Hermetic DIP	0°C to +70°C	AM3341DC	AM2841DC	AM2841ADC
Hermetic DIP	−55°C to +125°C		AM2841DM	

CONNECTION DIAGRAM
Top View

V_{GG}	1		16	V_{SS}
IR	2		15	SO
SI	3		14	OR
D_0	4		13	Q_0
D_1	5		12	Q_1
D_2	6		11	Q_2
D_3	7		10	Q_3
V_{DD}	8		9	$\overline{MR}$

Note: Pin 1 is marked for orientation.

Fig. 6-71. The data sheet for a 64×4 FIFO memory. (Courtesy of Advanced Micro Devices)

DESCRIPTION OF THE Am3341 FIFO OPERATION

The Am3341 FIFO consists internally of 64 four-bit data registers and one 64-bit control register, as shown in the logic block diagram. A "1" in a bit of the control register indicates that a four-bit data word is stored in the corresponding data register. A "0" in a bit of the control register indicates that the corresponding data register does not contain valid data. The control register directs the movement of data through the data registers. Whenever the nth bit of the control register contains a "1" and the $(n+1)$th bit contains a "0", then a strobe is generated causing the $(n+1)$th data register to read the contents of the nth data register, simultaneously setting the $(n+1)$th control register bit and clearing the nth control register bit, so that the control flag moves with the data. In this fashion data in the data register moves down the stack of data registers toward the output as long as there are "empty" locations ahead of it. The fall through operation stops when the data reaches a register n with a "1" in the $(n+1)$th control register bit, or the end of the register.

Data is initially loaded from the four data inputs D_0-D_3 by applying a LOW-to-HIGH transition on the shift in (SI) input. A "1" is placed in the first control register bit simultaneously. The first control register bit is returned, buffered, to the input ready (IR) output, and this pin goes LOW indicating that data has been entered into the first data register and the input is now "busy", unable to accept more data. When SI next goes LOW, the fall-through process begins (assuming that at least the second location is empty). The data in the first register is copied into the second, and the first control register bit is cleared. This causes IR to go HIGH, indicating the inputs are available for another data word.

The data falling through the register stacks up at the output end. At the output the last control register bit is buffered and brought out as Output Ready (OR). A HIGH on OR indicates there is a "1" in the last control register bit and therefore there is valid data on the four data outputs Q_0-Q_3. An input signal, shift out (SO), is used to shift the data out of the FIFO. A LOW-to-HIGH transition on SO clears the last register bit, causing OR to go LOW, indicating that the data on the outputs may no longer be valid. When SO goes LOW, the "0" which is now present at the last control register bit allows the data in the next to the last register to move into the last register position and on to the outputs. The "0" in the control register then "bubbles" back toward the input as the data shifts toward the output.

If the memory is emptied by reading out all the data, then when the last word is being read out and SO goes HIGH, OR will go LOW as before, but when SO next goes LOW, there is no data to move into the last location, so OR remains LOW until more data arrives at the output. Similarly, when the memory is full data written into the first location will not shift into the second when SI goes LOW, and IR will remain LOW instead of returning to a HIGH state.

The pairs of input and output control signals are designed so that the SO input of one FIFO can be driven by the IR output of another, and the OR output of the first FIFO can drive the SI input of the second, allowing simple expansion of the FIFO to any depth. Wider buffers are formed by allowing parallel rows of FIFOs to operate together, as shown in the application on the last page.

An over-riding master reset ($\overline{MR}$) is used to reset all control register bits and remove the data from the output (i.e. reset the outputs to all LOW).

1

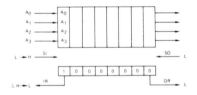

INITIAL CONDITION
FIFO empty, SI LOW IR HIGH, word "A" on inputs.

2

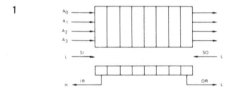

Write input into first stage by raising SI. (Δ = delay) IR goes LOW indicating data has been entered.

3

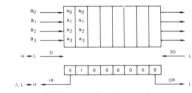

Release data into FIFO by lowering SI. After delay, data moves to second location, and IR goes HIGH indicating input available for new data word.

4

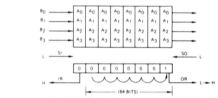

Data spontaneously ripple through registers to end of FIFO, causing OR to go HIGH. The time required for data to fall completely through the FIFO is the "Ripple-through Time".

5

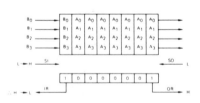

Word "B" written into FIFO

6

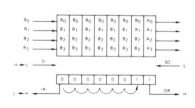

SI goes LOW allowing word "B" to fall through.

Fig. 6-72. (Courtesy of Advanced Micro Devices.)

7

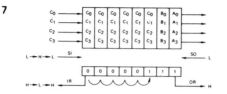

Word "C" written in same manner, and so on. When buffer is full, all control bits are 1's and IR stays LOW.

8

FIRST READ OPERATION

SO goes HIGH, indicating "Ready to Read". OR then goes LOW indicating "Data Read".

9

When SO goes LOW, the "0" in the last control bit bubbles toward the memory input. OR goes HIGH as the new word arrives at the output. IR goes HIGH when "0" reaches input.

10

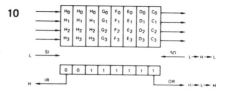

Read word "B" out, word "C" moves to output, and so on.

11

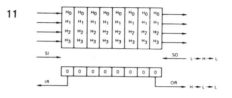

Read word "H". OR stays LOW because FIFO is empty. Word "H" remains in output until new word falls through.

Fig. 6-72. (Cont.)

The operation of the AM3341 FIFO is covered by the following description (see Figure 6-72) taken directly from AMD MOS/LSI data book.

6-22.2 REGISTERS AND RAM'S

The semiconductor Random-Access Memory commonly referred to as a RAM has wide applications; however, the major usage is related to computer systems. A RAM is a general multi-register memory system with both READ (accessing data internal to the RAM) and WRITE (loading data from the RAM into a predefined location) capabilities. Thus RAM's are often referred to as READ/WRITE MEMORIES. A RAM is functionally described in Figure 6-73.

Figure 6-73 shows that the address code is presented to the address decoder and the input and output data move in and out of the memory on the same set of I/O lines; and the read/write operation is controlled by a single WRITE(L)/READ(H) control line. Granted, this description is simplified somewhat from the actual devices available; however, it does depict the fundamental operations of a RAM.

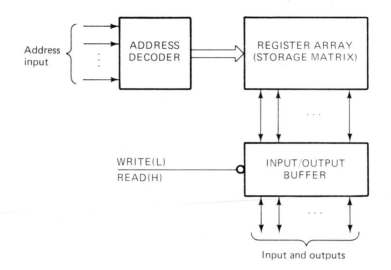

Fig. 6-73. A functional partition of a simple RAM.

Type	No. Of Bits	Description	Organization	Electrical Characteristics Over Temperature				
				Access Time Max.	Cycle Time Max.	Power Dissipation Max.[1] Operating/Standby	Supplies [V]	Page No.
1101A	256	Static Fully Decoded	256 x 1	1500ns	1500ns	685mW/340mW	+5,-9	2-4
1101A1	256	Hi-Speed Static Fully Decoded	256 x 1	1000ns	1000ns	685mW/340mW	+5,-9	2-4
1103	1024	Dynamic Fully Decoded	1024 x 1	300ns	580ns	400mW/67mW	+16,+19	2-8
1103-1	1024	Dynamic Fully Decoded	1024 x 1	150ns	340ns	400mW/76mW	+19,+22	2-13
1103A	1024	Dynamic Fully Decoded	1024 x 1	205ns	580ns	400mW/64mW	+16,+19	2-16
1103A-1	1024	Dynamic Fully Decoded	1024 x 1	145ns	340ns	625mW/10mW	+19,+22	2-21
1103A-2	1024	Dynamic Fully Decoded	1024 x 1	145ns	400ns	570mW/10mW	+19,+22	2-26
2101A	1024	Static, Separate I/O	256 x 4	350ns	350ns	300mW	+5	2-30
2101A-2	1024	Static, Separate I/O	256 x 4	250ns	250ns	350mW	+5	2-30
2101A-4	1024	Static, Separate I/O	256 x 4	450ns	450ns	300mW	+5	2-30
2101	1024	Static, Separate I/O	256 x 4	1000ns	1000ns	350mW	+5	2-34
2101-1	1024	Static, Separate I/O	256 x 4	500ns	500ns	350mW	+5	2-34
2101-2	1024	Static, Separate I/O	256 x 4	650ns	650ns	350mW	+5	2-34
2102A	1024	High Speed Static	1024 x 1	350ns	350ns	275mW	+5	2-38
2102A-2	1024	High Speed Static	1024 x 1	250ns	250ns	325mW	+5	2-38
2102A-4	1024	High Speed Static	1024 x 1	450ns	450ns	275mW	+5	2-38
2102A-6	1024	High Speed Static	1024 x 1	650ns	650ns	275mW	+5	2-38
2102AL	1024	Low Standby Power Static	1024 x 1	350ns	350ns	165mW/35mW	+5	2-38
2102AL-2	1024	Low Standby Power Static	1024 x 1	250ns	250ns	325mW/42mW	+5	2-38
2102AL-4	1024	Low Standby Power Static	1024 x 1	450ns	450ns	165mW/35mW	+5	2-38
M2102A-4	1024	Static, TA = -55°C to +125C	1024 x 1	450ns	450ns	350mW	+5	2-42
M2102A-6	1024	Static, TA = -55°C to +125C	1024 x 1	650ns	650ns	350mW	+5	2-42
2104	4096	16 Pin Dynamic	4096 x 1	350ns	500ns	744mW/37mW	+12,+5,-5	2-44
2104-2	4096	16 Pin Dynamic	4096 x 1	250ns	375ns	744mW/37mW	+12,+5,-5	2-44
2104-4	4096	16 Pin Dynamic	4096 x 1	300ns	425ns	756mW/36mW	+12,+5,-5	2-44
2107A	4096	22 Pin Dynamic	4096 x 1	300ns	700ns	458mW/10mW	+12,+5,-5	2-52
2107A-1	4096	22 Pin Dynamic	4096 x 1	280ns	550ns	516mW/16mW	+12,+5,-5	2-52
2107A-4	4096	22 Pin Dynamic	4096 x 1	350ns	840ns	405mW/10mW	+12,+5,-5	2-52
2107A-5	4096	22 Pin Dynamic	4096 x 1	420ns	970ns	376mW/11mW	+12,+5,-5	2-52
2107B	4096	22 Pin Dynamic	4096 x 1	200ns	400ns	648mW/12mW	+12,+5,-5	2-58
2107B-4	4096	22 Pin Dynamic	4096 x 1	270ns	470ns	648mW/13mW	+12,+5,-5	2-58
2107B-6	4096	22 Pin Dynamic	4096 x 1	350ns	800ns	840mW/25mW	+12,+5,-5	2-58

(SILICON GATE MOS)

Note 1: Power Dissipation calculated with maximum power supply current and nominal supply voltages

Fig. 6-74. A typical and representative listing of RAM's. (Courtesy of Intel Corporation)

	Type	No. Of Bits	Description	Organization	Electrical Characteristics Over Temperature					
					Access Time Max.	Cycle Time Max.	Power Dissipation Max.[1] Operating/Standby	Supplies [V]	Page No.	
SILICON GATE MOS	2111A	1024	Static, Common I/O with Output Deselect	256 x 4	350ns	350ns	300mW	+5	2-64	
	2111A-2	1024	Static, Common I/O with Output Deselect	256 x 4	250ns	250ns	350mW	+5	2-64	
	2111A-4	1024	Static, Common I/O with Output Deselect	256 x 4	450ns	450ns	300mW	+5	2-64	
	2111	1024	Static, Common I/O with Output Deselect	256 x 4	1000ns	1000ns	350mW	+5	2-68	
	2111-1	1024	Static, Common I/O with Output Deselect	256 x 4	500ns	500ns	350mW	+5	2-68	
	2111-2	1024	Static, Common I/O with Output Deselect	256 x 4	650ns	650ns	350mW	+5	2-68	
	2112A	1024	Static, Common I/O without Output Deselect	256 x 4	350ns	350ns	300mW	+5	2-72	
	2112A-2	1024	Static, Common I/O without Output Deselect	256 x 4	250ns	250ns	350mW	+5	2-72	
	2112A-4	1024	Static, Common I/O without Output Deselect	256 x 4	450ns	450ns	300mW	+5	2-72	
	2112	1024	Static, Common I/O without Output Deselect	256 x 4	1000ns	1000ns	350mW	+5	2-77	
	2112-2	1024	Static, Common I/O without Output Deselect	256 x 4	650ns	650ns	350mW	+5	2-77	
	2115	1024	Open Collector Static	1024 x 1	95ns	95ns	525mW	+5	2-81	
	2115-2	1024	Open Collector Static	1024 x 1	70ns	70ns	625mW	+5	2-81	
	2115L	1024	Low Power Static	1024 x 1	95ns	95ns	325mW	+5	2-81	
	2116	16384	16K Dynamic	16K x 1	250ns	375ns	900mW/24mW	+12,+5,	2-86	
	2125	1024	Three-State Static	1024 x 1	95ns	95ns	525mW	+5	2-81	
	2125-2	1024	Three-State Static	1024 x 1	70ns	70ns	625mW	+5	2-81	
	2125L	1024	Low Power Static	1024 x 1	95ns	95ns	325mW	+5	2-81	
SCHOTTKY BIPOLAR	3101	64	Fully Decoded	16 x 4	60ns	60ns	525mW	+5	2-87	
	3101A	64	High Speed Fully Decoded	16 x 4	35ns	35ns	525mW	+5	2-87	
	M3101	64	Fully Decoded (-55°C to +125°C)	16 x 4	75ns	75ns	546mW	+5	2-91	
	M3101A	64	High Speed Fully Decoded (-55°C to +125°C)	16 x 4	45ns	45ns	546mW	+5	2-91	
	3104	16	Content Addressable Memory	4 x 4	30ns	40ns	625mW	+5	2-93	
	3106	256	High Speed Fully Decoded (With Three-State Output)	256 x 1	80ns	80ns	650mW	+5	2-97	
	3106A	256	High Speed Fully Decoded (With Three-State Output)	256 x 1	60ns	70ns	650mW	+5	2-97	
	3106-8	256	High Speed Fully Decoded (With Three-State Output)	256 x 1	80ns	80ns	650mW	+5	2-97	
	3107	256	High Speed Fully Decoded (With Open Collector Output)	256 x 1	80ns	80ns	650mW	+5	2-97	
	3107A	256	High Speed Fuly Decoded (With Open Collector Output)	256 x 1	60ns	70ns	650mW	+5	2-97	
	3107-8	256	High Speed Fully Decoded (With Open Collector Output)	256 x 1	60ns	70ns	650mW	+5	2-97	
SIICON GATE CMOS	5101	1024	Static CMOS RAM	256 x 4	650ns	650ns	135mW/75uW	+5	2-101	
	5101-1	1024	Static CMOS RAM	256 x 4	450ns	450ns	135mW/75uW	+5	2-101	
	5101-3	1024	Static CMOS RAM	256 x 4	650ns	650ns	135mW/1mW	+5	2-101	
	5101-8	1024	Static CMOS RAM	256 x 4	800ns	800ns	150mW/2.5mW	+5	2-101	
	5101L	1024	Static CMOS RAM	256 x 4	650ns	650ns	135mW/30uW	+5	2-101	
	5101L-1	1024	Static CMOS RAM	256 x 4	450ns	450ns	135mW/30uW	+5	2-101	
	5101L-3	1024	Static CMOS RAM	256 x 4	650ns	650ns	135mW/400uW	+5	2-101	

Note 1 Power Dissipation calculated with maximum power supply current and nominal supply voltages

Fig. 6-74. (Cont.)

Most RAM's are classed as dynamic or static. Dynamic RAM's require "refreshing," making their use complicated. Static RAM's require no refreshing. The size of a RAM is specified by the number of addressable locations it has and its width. In other words, the number of addressable registers internal by the register length is specified. For example, a

$$1024 \times 4 \text{ RAM}$$

has 1024 four-bit addressable registers that can be read or written. When using RAM's pay particular attention to the ACCESS and CYCLE times specified. These times are defined in Figure 6-75. RAM's come in all shapes and sizes, both static and dynamic, MOS and bipolar, as the representative listing in Figure 6-74 illustrates.

6-23 FINAL NOTES

Semiconductor RAM's are generally designed to be used as modular units in a memory system. Thus they are generally equipped with ENABLE inputs so that they can be connected into a larger memory array.

A typical RAM, since it is a sequential machine in its own right, runs asynchronously to its controlling system; therefore timing considerations are critical. The RAM specified in Figure 6-75 is different than most in that it has a memory status signal available to indicate when the MEMORY is ready to do the next operation.

All in all, the register is an extremely important sequential device used in a variety of higher order sequential systems. Therefore, it is important that you understand register operation explicitly.

6-24 SUMMARY

In covering the analysis and design of what is referred to as the traditional sequential machine or the finite-state machine, the studies have moved through sequence detectors, sequence generators, counters, and shift register circuits with a strong emphasis on the traditional design methods used for developing small scale sequential circuits using standard Flip-Flops for the memory element. Further, it is intended that a good deal of insight and understanding was gained during this study because this material is expanded and applied to higher level sequential systems in the next four chapters.

Fig. 6-75. (*facing page*)Data Sheet for static RAM. (Courtesy of Advanced Micro Devices)

DISTINCTIVE CHARACTERISTICS

- 4k x 1 organization
- Fully static data storage – no refreshing
- Single +5V power supply
- High-speed – access times down to 200ns max.
- Low-power – 710mW max. – 350mW typ.
- Interface logic levels identical to TTL
- High noise immunity – 400mV worst case
- High output drive – two standard TTL loads
- DC standby mode – reduces power by > 80%
- Uniform switching characteristics
- Dual output controls – flexible output operations
- Address and data registers on-chip
- Constant power drain – no large surges
- Unique Memory Status signal
  - improves performance
  - simplifies timing
- MIL temperature range available
- 100% MIL-STD-883 reliability assurance testing

FUNCTIONAL DESCRIPTION

The Am9140 products are high performance, low-power, 4k-bit, static, read/write random access memories. They are implemented as 4096 words by 1 bit per word. The data input and output signals use separate pins for maximum flexibility.

All interface signal levels are identical to TTL specifications, providing good noise immunity and simplified system design. The three-state output will drive two full TTL loads or eight low-power Schottky loads for increased fan-out, better capacitive drive and improved bus interface capability.

Operational cycles are initiated when the Chip Enable signal goes HIGH. When the read or write is complete, Chip Enable goes LOW to prepare the memory for the next cycle. Address and Chip Select signals are latched on-chip to help simplify system timing. Output data is also latched and is available until into the next operating cycle.

The $\overline{WE}$ signal is HIGH for all read operations and is pulsed LOW during the Chip Enable time to perform a write. Memory Status is an output signal that indicates when data is valid and simplifies generation of CE.

These memories may be operated in a DC standby mode for significant reductions in power dissipation. Data are retained on a deselected chip with V_{CC} as low as 1.5V.

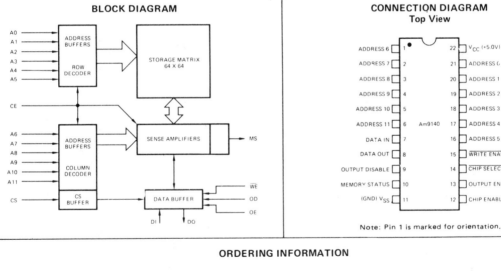

BLOCK DIAGRAM

CONNECTION DIAGRAM
Top View

Note: Pin 1 is marked for orientation.

ORDERING INFORMATION

Package Type	Ambient Temperature Specification	Access Time				
		500ns	400ns	300ns	250ns	200ns
Hermetic DIP	0°C to +70°C	AM9140ADC	AM9140BDC	AM9140CDC	AM9140DDC	AM9140EDC
	−55°C to +125°C	AM9140ADM	AM9140BDM	AM9140CDM		

Am9140

MAXIMUM RATINGS above which the useful life may be impaired

Storage Temperature	−65°C to +150°C
Ambient Temperature Under Bias	−55°C to +125°C
V_{CC} with Respect to V_{SS}	−0.5V to +7.0V
All Signal Voltages with Respect to V_{SS}	−0.5V to +7.0V
Power Dissipation	1.25W

The products described by this specification include internal circuitry designed to protect input devices from damaging accumulations of static charge. It is suggested, nevertheless, that conventional precautions be observed during storage, handling and use in order to avoid exposure to excessive voltages.

OPERATING RANGE

Part Number	Ambient Temperature	V_{CC}	V_{SS}
Am9140XDC	0°C ≤ T_A ≤ +70°C	+5.0V ·5%	0V
Am9140XDM	−55°C ≤ T_A ≤ +125°C	+5.0V · 10%	0V

ELECTRICAL CHARACTERISTICS over operating range (note 1)

Parameters	Description	Test Conditions	Am9140XDC Min	Typ	Max	Am9140XDM Min	Typ	Max	Units
V_{OH}	Output HIGH Voltage	$I_{OH} = -200\mu A$, $V_{CC} = 4.75V$ / $V_{CC} = 4.5V$	2.4			2.4 / 2.2			Volts
V_{OL}	Output LOW Voltage	$I_{OL} = 3.2mA$			0.4			0.4	Volts
V_{IH}	Input HIGH Voltage		2.0		V_{CC}	2.0		V_{CC}	Volts
V_{IL}	Input LOW Voltage		−0.5		0.8	−0.5		0.8	Volts
I_{LI}	Input Load Current	$V_{SS} \le V_{IN} \le V_{CC}$			10			10	µA
I_{LO}	Output Leakage Current	$V_{SS} \le V_{OUT} \le V_{CC}$, Output disabled			10			10	µA
I_{CC}	V_{CC} Supply Current	Max. V_{CC} Output disabled, $T_A = 25°C$		60	120		60	120	mA
		$T_A = 0°C$			135			135	
		$T_A = -55°C$						150	
C_{IA}	Input Capacitance (Address)	Test frequency = 1 MHz		3.0	6.0		3.0	6.0	pF
C_{OUT}	Output Capacitance	$T_A = 25°C$		4.0	7.0		4.0	7.0	pF
C_{IC}	Input Capacitance (Control)	All pins at 0V		6.0	9.0		6.0	9.0	pF

Notes: 1. Typical values are for $T_A = 25°C$, nominal supply voltage and nominal processing parameters.
2. The output buffer can be ON and output ACTIVE only as long as Output Enable is HIGH and Output Disable is LOW. If either condition is changed, the output buffer will turn OFF.
3. The timing diagram specifies the input data set-up and hold times with respect to the rising edge of $\overline{WE}$. If that edge occurs during CE LOW, the data set-up is referenced to the 2.0V level of the falling edge of CE and the data hold is referenced to the 0.8V level of the falling edge of CE.
4. The minimum write pulse width specification assumes that the falling edge of $\overline{WE}$ occurs more than 50ns after the rising edge of Chip Enable. $\overline{WE}$ may fall earlier, but the minimum write pulse width requirements should be extended to compensate.
5. CS, OE and OD may be operated at constant levels where appropriate.

Fig. 6-75 (Cont.)

SWITCHING CHARACTERISTICS over operating range

Parameters	Description	Test Conditions	Am9140A Min.	Am9140A Max.	Am9140B Min.	Am9140B Max.	Am9140C Min.	Am9140C Max.	Am9140E Min.	Am9140E Max.	Units
tC	Cycle Time		840		690		530		370		ns
tA	Access Time (CE to Output Valid Delay)		30	500	30	400	30	300	30	200	ns
tAS	Address to Chip Enable Set-up Time		0		0		0		0		ns
tAH	Chip Enable to Address Hold Time		200		170		130		100		ns
tCS	Chip Select to Chip Enable Set-up Time		0		0		0		0		ns
tCH	Chip Enable to Chip Select Hold Time		200		170		130		100		ns
tRS	Read to Chip Enable Set-up Time	Transition times ≤ 20ns	0		0		0		0		ns
tRH	Chip Enable to Read Hold Time	Output load = 1 TTL gate plus 50pF	0		0		0		0		ns
tOH	Chip Enable to Output OFF Delay	Input and output timing reference levels are 0.8V and 2.0V	0		0		0		0		ns
tDS	Data Input Set-up Time (Note 3)		300		250		200		150		ns
tDH	Data Input Hold Time (Note 3)		0		0		0		0		ns
tWS	Write to Chip Enable Set-up Time		300		250		200		150		ns
tWW	Write Pulse Width (Note 4)		300		250		200		150		ns
tCF	OE or OD to Output OFF Delay			210		175		135		100	ns
tCO	OE or OD to Output ON Delay			250		200		150		110	ns
tEH	Chip Enable HIGH Time		500		400		300		200		ns
tEL	Chip Enable LOW Time		300		250		200		150		ns

SWITCHING WAVEFORMS

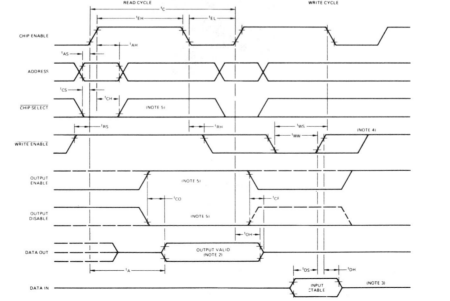

Fig. 6-75 (Cont.)

MEMORY STATUS SPECIFICATION FOR Am9140

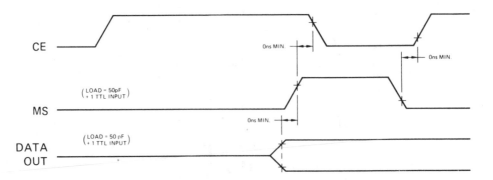

Memory Status is an output signal from the memory indicating the real access time of the part for the operating conditions then present. It will always indicate a data access time better than the worst-case specification for the part. The exact position of MS relative to CE will change from part to part and with changing temperature and supply voltage. It will always maintain its relationship to valid output data as shown above. Nominal delay from data to MS is 15ns.

The rising edge of MS also indicates that CE may go LOW. The falling edge of MS indicates that CE may go HIGH. Thus, the MS output fully specifies the CE requirement for any part under any set of operating conditions. In fact, CE = $\overline{MS}$; the MS output may be inverted and used as the CE input. See application note for more information about the use and operation of the Memory Status signal.

Metallization and Pad Layout

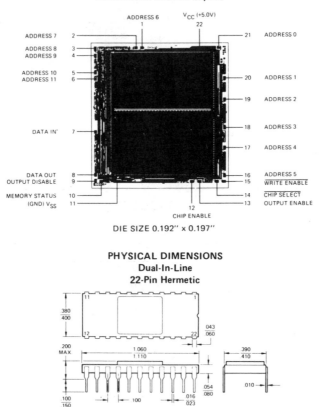

DIE SIZE 0.192″ x 0.197″

PHYSICAL DIMENSIONS
Dual-In-Line
22-Pin Hermetic

Fig. 6-75 (Cont.)

BIBLIOGRAPHY

1. *1977 Data Catalog, Intel*. Intel Corporation, Santa Clara, Calif., 1977.

2. ARMSTRONG, D. B. A Programmed Algorithm for Assigning Internal Codes to Sequential Machines. *IRE Trans. Electronic Computers*, EC-11, No. 4 (1962), 466–472.

3. BERARU, J. Map Entry Method for Sequential Counter Logic. *Electro-Technology* (1968), 51–52.

4. COPI, I. M. *Symbolic Logic*. New York: Macmillan, 1954.

5. GINSBURG, S. *Introduction to Mathematical Machine Theory*. Reading, Mass.: Addison-Wesley, 1962.

6. GOLUMB, S. (ed.) *Digital Communication with Space Applications*. Englewood Cliffs, N.J.: Prentice-Hall, 1964.

7. GRASSELLI, A., and LUCCIO, F. A Method of Minimizing the Number of Internal States in Incompletely Specified Sequential Networks. *IEEE Trans. Electronic Computers*, EC-14:3 (1965), 330–359.

8. HARTMANIS, J. On the State Assignment Problem for Sequential Machines, I. *IRE Trans. Electronic Computers*, EC-10:2 (1961), 157–165.

9. HARTMANIS, J., and STEARNS, R. E. *Algebraic Structure Theory of Sequential Machines*. Englewood Cliffs, N.J.: Prentice-Hall, 1966.

10. HILL, FREDRICK J., and PETERSEN, GERALD R. *Introduction to Switching Theory and Logical Design*, New York: Wiley, 1974.

11. HUFFMAN, D. A. The Synthesis of Sequential Switching Circuits. *J. Franklin Inst.*, **257**, No. 3 (1954), 161–190; No. 4 (1954), 275–303.

12. KOHAVI, Z. *Switching and Finite Automata Theory*. New York: McGraw-Hill, 1970.

13. MANO, M. MORRIS. *Computer Logic Design*. Englewood Cliffs, N. J.: Prentice-Hall, 1972.

14. MEALY, G. H. A Method for Synthesizing Sequential Circuits. *Bell System Tech. J.*, 34:5 (1955), 1045–1080.

15. MOORE, E. F. *Sequential Machines: Selected Papers*. Reading, Mass.: Addison-Wesley, 1964.

16. PAULL, M. C., and UNGER, S. H. Minimizing the Number of States in Incompletely Specified Sequential Switching Functions. *IRE Trans. Electronic Computers*, EC-8:3 (1959), 356–357.

17. *Schottky and Low-power Schottky Data Book Including Digital Signal Processing Handbook*, 2nd ed. Sunnyvale, Calif.: Advanced Micro Devices, 1977.

18. STEARNS, R. E., and HARTMANIS, J. On the State Assignment Problems for Sequential Machines, II. *IRE Trans. Electronic Computers*, EC-10:4 (1961), 593–603.

19. *The TTL Data Book for Design Engineers*, 2nd ed. Dallas: Texas Instruments, Inc., 1976.

20. TIEN, PAUL S. Sequential Counter Design Techniques. *Computer Design*, **10**, No. 2 (1971), 49–56.

21. TORNG, H. C. *Introduction to the Logical Design of Switching Systems*. Reading, Mass.: Addison-Wesley, 1964.

22. WICKES, WILLIAM E. *Logic Design with Integrated Circuits.* New York: Wiley, 1968.

23. WILLIAMS, GERALD E. *Digital Technology.* Chicago: Science Research Associates, 1977.

PROBLEMS AND EXERCISES

6-1. In your own words, compare the definition of "the STATE of a machine" set forth in Section 5-8 to the pictorial information shown in Figure 6-1.

6-2. Using your own words, give a clear and precise verbal description of the sequential circuit defined by the STATE DIAGRAM shown in Figure 6-3(b). In short, you are to make a clear and precise word specification. (*Hint:* Start with, "This system is to be designed such that an input line (X) is sampled on each rising-edge of the clock and ....")

6-3. Design a state diagram for a synchronous sequential machine that will perform according to the following specification: Starting from an initial state $A = 00$, this machine will sample an input line (START) and remain in this state until the START signal becomes ASSERTED. Upon the first rising edge which senses the START condition, this machine is to cycle from $A = 00$ to $B = 01$, to $C = 11$ on successive rising edges of the clock. Once in state C the START line is again sampled. If the START signal remains ASSERTED, the machine is to remain in state C generating an output (CONT) until the NOT-ASSERTED condition of START is sensed by the machine at which time it is to move to state $D = 10$, generate another output (DONE), then move back to state A.

6-4. Using the analysis concept and technique set forth in Sections 6-3 and 6-4, carry out a detailed (six-step) analysis through and including a complete state diagram on the following circuit (Figure P6-1). Make note of any particular operational properties that you believe to be questionable.

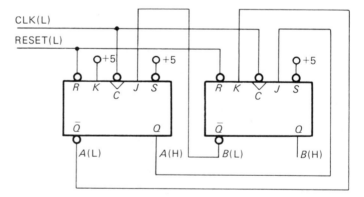

Fig. P6-1.

6-5. Repeat Problem 6-4 for the following circuit (Figure P6-2).

6-6. Repeat Problem 6-4 for the following circuit (Figure P6-3).

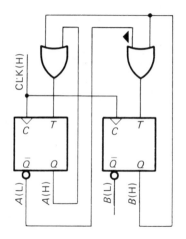

Fig. P6-2.

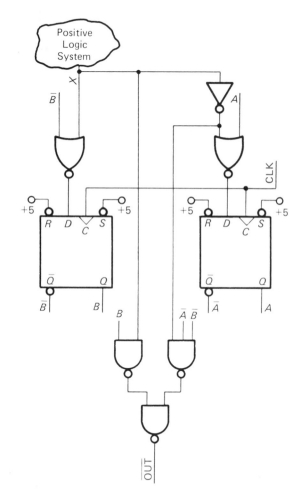

Fig. P6-3.

6-7. Repeat Problem 6-4 for the following circuit (Figure P6-4).

6-8. Repeat Problem 6-4 for the following circuit (Figure P6-5).

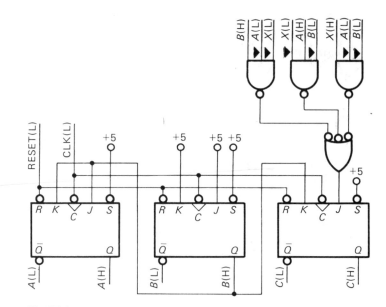

Fig. P6-4.

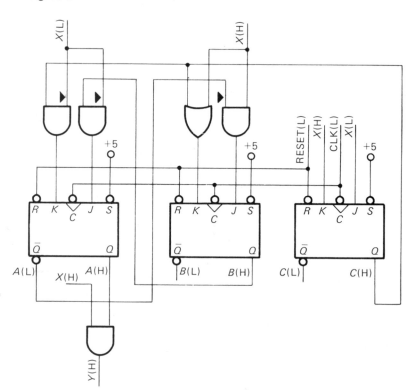

Fig. P6-5.

6-9. The following circuit (Figure P6-6) was taken from the schematic drawings of a commercial system. The circuit was titled as a modulo 7 (count by 7, which implies seven unique states in sequence) counter. However, it was found to have some operational anomalies. You are to analyze this circuit and identify its problems.

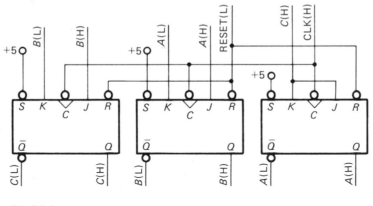

Fig. P6-6.

Note: Problems 6-10 to 6-15 require a knowledge of the information related to synchronous design up to and including step 5 of the design steps outlined in Section 6-6. (These problems relate to code sequence detectors).

6-10. Design a block diagram and a tight state diagram for a circuit which samples an input line $[x = 1(H)]$ on each rising-edge of the system clock (SYSCLK). This system is to take four samples before returning to its initial state. Further, this system is only to initiate an output if the 0111 sequence is detected. Make certain your system returns to the initial state on the rising-edge of the fourth clock pulse. Note further the data on the input line is changed only on the falling-edge of system clock. Make a primitive state table and examine it for redundancies.

6-11. Design a block diagram and a tight state diagram for a circuit which samples (with system CLK) an input line $[x = 1(L)]$. This system is to give an indication (SEQ DET(H)) each time the three-bit sequence 110 is detected in a *continuous data stream*. Note that the continuous data stream constraint allows for the three-bit sequences to overlap. The data line is updated on the rising-edge of the clock. Make certain your state diagram has no redundant states.

6-12. Design a block diagram and a tight state diagram for a circuit which monitors two (2) synchronized (updated together) data lines $X(H)$ and $Y(H)$. Your circuit is to give an indication [output OP(H)] if either the 10 or 01 sample was received once and only once in a four-sample sequence. Assume the data inputs are updated on the falling-edge of your system clock. Make certain your state diagram contains no redundant states.

6-13. Design a block diagram and a tight state diagram which monitors an input data line $[DAT = 1(H)]$ four consecutive times and displays a three-bit output $B_2 B_1 B_0$ after the fourth sample. This output is to be the binary equivalent of the number of 1 samples taken in the four-sample sequence. Assume the data line is updated on each rising-edge of your system clock.

6-14. Repeat Problem 6-10, but this time search for the 1101 sequence.

6-15. Using the rules set forth in Section 6-8, make a state assignment for the following state diagram (Figure P6-7).

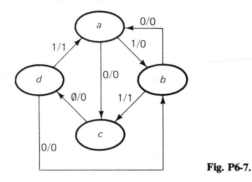

Fig. P6-7.

6-16. Using the state assignment rules set forth in Section 6-8, complete the state assignment for the portion of the following state diagram (Figure P6-8).

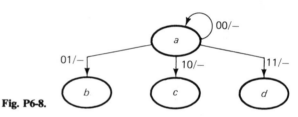

Fig. P6-8.

6-17. Make a state assignment for the following state diagram (Figure P6-9). (Use the rules set forth in Section 6-8.)

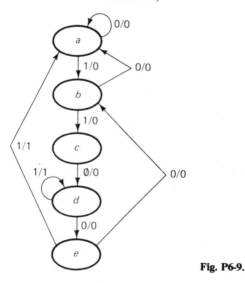

Fig. P6-9.

6-18. Make a state assignment for the state diagram designed for Problem 6-3. (Use the rules set forth in Section 6-8.)

6-19. Make a state assignment for the state diagram designed for Problem 6-10. (Use the rules set forth in Section 6-8.)

6-20. Make a state assignment for the state diagram designed for Problem 6-11. (Use the rules set forth in Section 6-8.)

6-21. Make a state assignment for the state diagram designed for Problem 6-12. (Use the rules set forth in Section 6-8.)

6-22. Make a state assignment for the state diagram designed for Problem 6-13. (Use the rules set forth in Section 6-8.)

6-23. Make a state assignment for the state diagram designed for Problem 6-14. (Use the rules set forth in Section 6-8.)

6-24. (a) Make another state assignment for the state diagram shown in Figure 6-31. Make certain your assignment violates the rules as much as possible.
(b) Derive the next state map for your state assignment.
(c) Simplify the next state maps and compare your results with the results shown in Figure 6-32.

6-25. (a) Convert the next states maps to J and K maps for Problem 6-23. (Use the idea set for Problem 6-10.)
(b) Make a comparison between the JK and the D implementation.
(c) Repeat part (a) and (b) but this time convert the next state maps to T maps.

6-26. (a) Derive the next state maps for the state assignment made for Problem 6-15.
(b) Derive the JK and T maps from the next state maps.
(c) Compare results, and draw the schematic diagram for the simplest implementation.

6-27. (a) Derive the next state maps for the state assignment made for Problem 6-17.
(b) Derive the JK and T maps from the next state maps and output map.
(c) Compare results and draw the schematic diagram for the simplest implementation (next state and output decoder).

6-28. Repeat parts (a), (b), and (c) of Problem 6-27 for the state assignment made for Problem 6-18.

6-29. Repeat parts (a), (b), and (c) of Problem 6-27 for the state assignment made for Problem 6-19.

6-30. Repeat parts (a), (b), and (c) of Problem 6-27 for the state assignment made for Problem 6-20.

6-31. Repeat parts (a), (b), and (c) of Problem 6-27 for the state assignment made for Problem 6-21.

6-32 Repeat parts (a), (b), and (c) of Problem 6-27 for the state assignment made for Problem 6-22.

6-33. Repeat parts (a), (b), and (c) of Problem 6-27 for the state assignment made for Problem 6-23.

6-34. (a) Carry out the complete design steps leading to a *Moore machine implementation* of Problem 6-11, including schematic diagrams.
(b) Compare your results with a Mealy machine.

6-35. Design a serial parity (odd) generation which defines the parity bit for a serial four-bit word. This parity bit is to be inserted into a blank time frame following the fourth data bit shifted out in accordance to the following timing diagram (Figure P6-10). Carry out the complete design including schematic diagrams using RET D Flip-Flops.

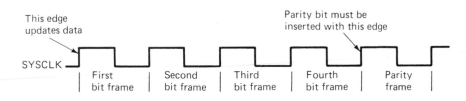

Fig. P6-10.

6-36. Use a state machine (state diagram) to convert an edge-triggered D Flip-Flop to an edge-triggered JK Flip-Flop.

6-37. Design a synchronous finite state machine which will sequence from state $a=00$ to state $b=11$ to state $c=10$ to state $d=01$, then reverse itself at state a and state d if the input COSQ(H) is ASSERTED. Any time the COSQ input is NOT-ASSERTED, the circuit is to revert to state a and hold. Carry out all steps for the design. Make your choice of Flip-Flops based on the minimal cost next state decoder implementation (use edge-triggered devices).

6-38. Carry out all steps necessary to complete the design of a modulo 6 pure Gray Code counter. Make your code reflective with respect to the second most significant bit. Make the optimal choice for your Flip-Flops.

6-39. Design a modulo 8 Gray Code up/down counter. Make your code reflective with respect to the most significant bit.

6-40. Carry out all steps to design a special sequential system that has two outputs defined by the following timing diagram (Figure P6-11).

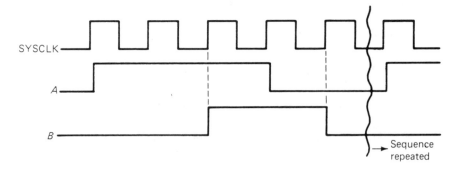

Fig. P6-11.

6-41. Design a modulo 10 Gray Code decade counter which can be cascaded with other identical counters to form a modulo n pure synchronous counter. This counter is to be designed to function identical to the 74160 series of counters (use only edge-triggered Flip-Flops).

(Sequence ⌐→0→1→3→2→6→14→10→11→9→8⌐)

6-42. Design a cascadable modulo 10 unit distance up/down counter which can be cascaded as described in Problem 6-40. Use only edge-triggered Flip-Flops. (*Hint*: use 74192 data sheet for reference.) See Figure 6-47.

6-43. Design an experiment to investigate the 1's catching problem with one of the 74160 series of counters. In reading the specifications in the data book, pay special attention to the limits given for use of the LOAD input. Explain the problem and its cause. Make a suggestion for using the device which will prevent any problem in this regard; verify that your method is a good one.

6-44. Design a counter whose operation is that of a decade counter but whose output will directly drive a seven-segment LED display. Your counter is to have as inputs clock and carry-in. As outputs, it is to have a carry-out which will be used to cascade modules of these decade counters and seven lines labeled A through G which directly drive an LED display. The machine will have no output forming logic. This means that there will be seven state variables. Use whatever techniques you can think of to minimize the size of tables and maps to be used in your design. Problem 3-46 illustrates connections for an LED display device. Presently, there is no commercial device available on a chip which performs this function, which is too bad, because it would be very useful. At the present time, in order to perform this operation, it is necessary to have a BCD counter chip and a BCD-to-seven segment decoder/driver chip. Some manufacturers make an LED display which has mounted on the case in a hybrid manner the BCD counter and the BCD-to-seven decoder/driver.

6-45. See Problem 6-40. Design a twisted-ring counter which will provide an identical output wave form. Make certain your counter is self-correcting.

6-46. Design the following odd length ring counters. (Make certain your counters are self-correcting.)
(a) Modulo 3
(b) Modulo 7
(c) Modulo 9
Hint: Odd length ring counters are not totally unit distance counters. They have one non-unit-distance transition. This generally follows the pivotal state. For example, modulo 5 ring counter sequence is:

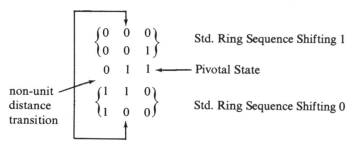

6-47. Design an odd (modulo 7) length ring counter which is initialized or reset to state 7 (111). Make certain that your counter is self-correcting.

6-48. Using a four-bit universal shift register (74194) and Figures 6-67 and 6-68, design a sequence generator which cycles through the following sequence:

```
                          1111
                          0111
                          1110
                  0000    1101
                  1000    1011
                  1100    0110
                  0110    0011
                  1101    0001
                  1011    0010
                  0111    1001
                  0011    1100
                  0001    0110
                          1101
                          1110
```

6-49. Using a universal shift register such as the 74194 (four-bit multi-mode) and Figure 6-67 as reference, design a self-correcting modulo 7 ring counter.

6-50. A stepper-motor drive circuit requires the following wave forms (four signal lines) as inputs (Figure P6-12):

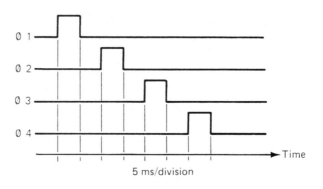

5 ms/division

Fig. P6-12.

Your task is to design a special sequence generator which will provide the necessary signals for this stepper-motor drive. Carry out all steps for your design including well-documented schematic diagrams. Also include the CLOCK circuit (see Chapter 5).

6-51. Review the operational characteristics of the AM2841 FIFO memory unit for the purpose of gaining an insight into the general operation of a FIFO memory.

Exercise: Design a small four-bit four-level FIFO memory using four four-bit PIPO registers, some tri-state buffers, and a sequential controller circuit which controls the operation of your FIFO memory. (*Hint*: Design your unit to work on a dual tri-state bus arrangement (Input Bus and an Output Bus).)

INTRODUCTION TO MULTI-INPUT

SYSTEM CONTROLLER DESIGN

7-1 INTRODUCTION

The studies preceding this chapter are mainly devoted to learning the basic tricks-of-the-trade for designing combinational and sequential circuits. These studies are concerned with the sub-functions or the bits and pieces that make up a digital system. The next step is directed toward SYSTEM LEVEL DESIGN. Here the processes of bringing a collection of sub-functions together into a "working" digital system is examined and put into action. It makes little or no difference how ingenious the sub-function designs are if they are not properly pulled together in the system design; the system will never fly.

In this chapter you are introduced to some very powerful systematic and practical approaches to sequential machine design. These approaches are general enough that they can be applied to designs using a variety of different hardware elements, be they designs centered around simple SSI or the more sophisticated MSI and LSI digital devices, or even the microprocessor. Further, this chapter deals with a structured approach to designing a special and important digital system, the MULTI-INPUT SYSTEM CONTROLLER. Along with this design approach, the fine details of designing reliable systems are presented. These techniques are fundamental in nature and provide further design insight as well as a variety of useful alternatives for system level designs. Also, documentation and the maintenance of that documentation are heavily stressed.

7-2 SYSTEM CONTROLLERS

As alluded to above, a great deal of digital system design time is spent with SYSTEM CONTROLLER specification and synthesis. But first, what is a SYSTEM CONTROLLER? As the introduction has indicated:

> The SYSTEM CONTROLLER, in general terms, is a special sequential machine (usually synchronous) designed to interpret system level control input sequences and in turn to generate system level output sequences.

Be certain that you are able to draw the proper distinction between the system controller and the system.

Using this definition as a basis, consider the block diagram (functional-partition) of a data logger *SYSTEM* shown in Figure 7-1. Here you see a block labeled *SYSTEM CONTROLLER* and surrounding this system controller is an array of various sub-systems including counters, registers, A/D's, multiplexers, and so forth. From this figure you can visualize the system controller receiving inputs from each of these sub-system devices as well as from the outside world, and in turn interpreting these inputs into controlling output sequences. Thus the system controller can be thought of as the NERVE CENTER of the total *SYSTEM* designed to orchestrate the behavior of the surrounding sub-systems. This concept is extremely important for it lends itself to many applications, and the use of this system controller idea leads to systematic and structured approaches to digital system design as shown throughout the next several chapters.

The basic physical distinction between a system controller, which is a sequential machine, and other sequential machines such as sequential code detectors, counters, and registers is the number of *control inputs*. For example, the system controller shown in Figure 7-1 has 13 controlling inputs. Further, this controller has four state variables; thus a traditional approach to the design would result in a PRESENT/NEXT STATE table with 17 variables resulting in a table with 131,072 rows! Further, as system controllers go, this one is small. This author has developed one large high-speed system controller with 82 controlling inputs and 7 state variables, and you don't need a calculator to know that 2^{89} is a very large number. Thus a new approach is needed for developing sequential machines that facilitate a large number of controlling inputs in a straightforward and simple manner. This chapter deals with the introductory concepts and design phases for what is called "small multi-input multi-branch controllers." Chapters 8 and 9 deal with the larger controllers designed around special devices. However, both of these chapters rely heavily on the material introduced in the following sections.

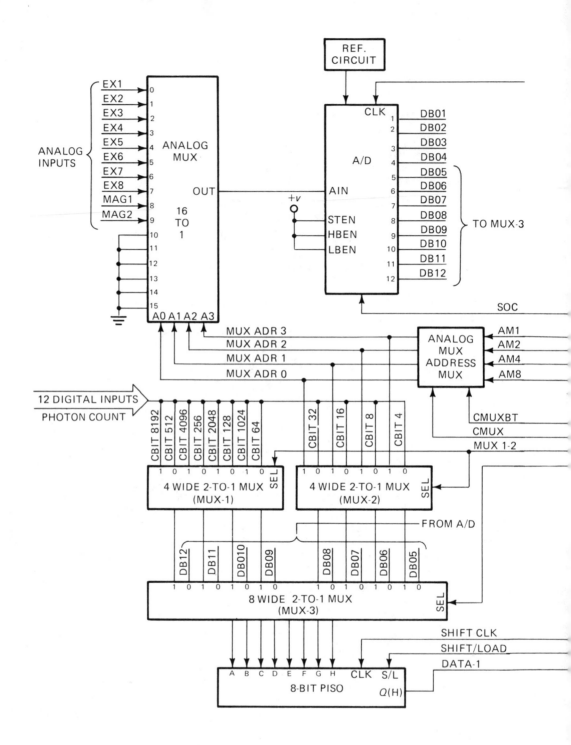

Fig. 7-1. The functional partition of a "data-logging" system.

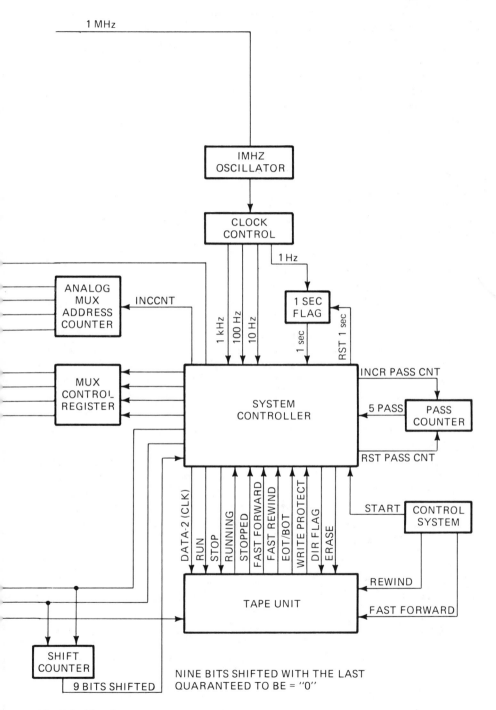

Fig. 7-1. (Cont.)

For those interested in where the application of a microprocessor fits into this system controller design, it can be said, generally, anywhere speed, power, and cost are not prohibitive. More specifically, the concepts set forth here are general and certainly appropriate for microprocessor applications; however, it is felt that their use for the typical application outlined in this chapter would be a wasteful overkill. In fact, this chapter is meant to provide the designer with a viable alternative to microprocessor-centered system controllers. On the other hand, the structured design concept stressed here is absolutely *necessary* when microprocessor-centered systems are used.

7-3 CONTROLLER DESIGN PHASES AND SYSTEM DOCUMENTATION

Considering what is said in Sections 7-1 and 7-2, along with viewing the functional partition of the system shown in Figure 7-1, it should be apparent that a structured design approach is called for. This structured approach needs to provide the designer with a system of checks and balances for evaluation, a road map if you will, to a completed design and most importantly a procedure that makes *design documentation* a necessary but natural outcome. It will be stressed: *Know what you are going to do and how you are going to do it and then document your work so you and others can understand it.* You will be given, or at least you should be given, design problems and asked to provide a complete documented design package. Your instructor may have specific ideas concerning documentation and will direct your activities; if not, the drafting standards in Appendix A, the following design phases, and example documentation provided will serve as guidelines for your designs.

The following phases are highly recommended as an algorithm for designing a working system, each of which is considered as a necessary segment of a documented package. It is agreed that some are very general, but nonetheless required; and if you find yourself skipping over some of them with the intent of total neglect, tell yourself that "you are about to foul out." Phases 1 through 4 will be the most difficult to conquer, but without a sound understanding of the information acquired in these steps, phase 5 will be an exercise in futility. The phases of design are listed as follows:

(1) Define the purpose and role of the system.
(2) Define the basic operations and limitations of the system or systems that the systems controller is to control. This can be aided by designing a first-cut flow diagram and basic block diagram.
(3) Using timing diagrams, define the timing and frequency of the system level input and output control signals. Also, make note of any particular timing constraints.
(4) Detail the sequential behavior of the system controller and, at the same time, determine register, temporary storage, special circuit, and other

sub-function requirements for both the system controller and the overall system. Along with this, develop detailed timing diagrams defining the system level and subfunction control, making notes related for any timing constraints.

(5) Develop an MDS diagram for system controller operation using Steps 1, 2, 3, and 4 as reference.

DO EARLIER ←—(6) Choose a system controller architecture and synchronizers from one of the basic variations suggested.

(7) Use suggested rules and constraints to make state assignments.

The following phases are regarded as particular steps related to SSI design.

(8) Design NEXT STATE DECODER logic for the Flip-Flop of your choice.

(9) Define controlling output requirements and design output decoder logic for "flash-free" operation (glitch free).

(10) A point of particular interest, particularly in large systems, is designing in manual "control-and-display" features as well as other special techniques for fault isolation.

7-4 DEFINING THE PURPOSE AND ROLE OF THE SYSTEM

At this juncture the designer must first come to grips with just what the total system, including the system controller, is to do. Systems generally are never stand-alone systems, but are sub-functions of yet a larger system. Therefore, it is up to the designer to sort through the specifications and system requirements and organize a conceptual control picture of the system and how it interacts with its surroundings. It might be found that the system as a whole is best broken down into several linked systems, each having a separate system controller. If specifications are given, they must be examined closely for gross incompatibilities; or if specifications must be generated, they too must be given the closest developmental scrutiny possible. All in all, this design phase is dedicated to familiarization with system requirements and getting the big picture of how the system relates to the rest of the world.

As an example of the thought processes you should go through during this phase, consider the following problem. *You are to design a data-logger system.* These specs are fairly vague, but by asking and obtaining the answers to the following questions, you can formulate a pictorial concept of what is required.

(1) What is a data-logger and what does it do? How does it do it?

(2) Why do you want a data-logger?

(3) What kind of medium is this logger to log on, and how big are the logs to be?

(4) What controls this data-logger?

(5) What are the operational characteristics of this controlling device?

(6) Where do you want this data-logger?

(7) When do you want this data-logger?

It can be seen that a great deal of information can be obtained from the correct answers to these questions—enough to formulate a bare-bones block diagram of the central system and its surroundings.

The following example is a set of specifications for a special data-logger. From these specifications, you should be able to answer the questions above.

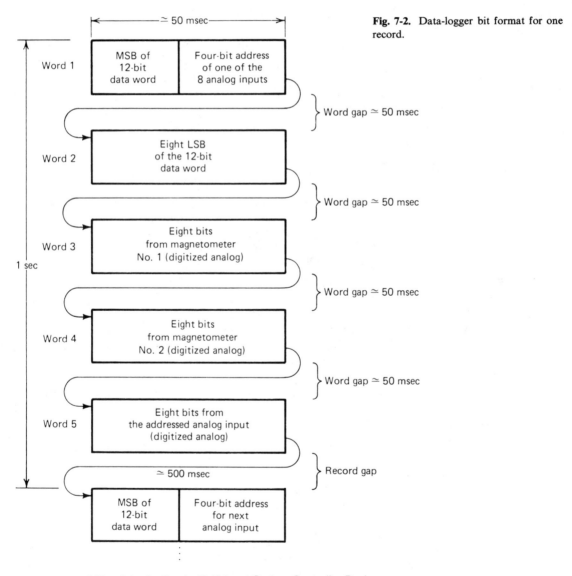

Fig. 7-2. Data-logger bit format for one record.

EXAMPLE 7-1:   Specs for a balloon flight data-logger.

You are to design a data-logger (real-time data recording system) flight-worthy for a high altitude balloon flight (up to 130,000 feet). This data-logger is to receive 12 parallel lines of digital data from a special digital system on board called a photon counter. Also, this logger is to receive 10 lines of analog data from special atmospheric monitoring transducers. This analog data must be digitized and recorded on a single track of a cassette tape, along with the 12 bits of digital data from the photon counter. Do all this and *conserve power*! By the way, the system is needed in two weeks.

A complete data record is to be made once each second and recorded in eight-bit serial words on the tape. The bit formatting for this system is shown in Figure 7-2.

Five eight-bit serial words (40 bits) make up a record and each record includes the data for just *one* of the eight out of ten analog inputs that must be digitized. Thus it will take eight records to make up a complete file of all eight multiplexed analog inputs. Note the timing indicated on the bit format chart. Each serial word takes approximately 50 msec to record, then a 50 msec space (word gap) is generated, then the next word is recorded and so forth until five words are recorded. Then a 500 msec space is generated indicating a record gap before the next sampling sequence is started. Words three and four are fixed and are always to be the digitized word from two special magnetometer analog inputs.

The system is to fire up on the START command that comes from the master balloon controller system, and synch itself to an internal one second clock and continue recording data formatted as prescribed above until commanded to stop ($\overline{START}$). Upon receiving a $\overline{START}$ signal, which is generated asynchronously, the system is to finish the current record and then proceed to an idle condition, stopping the tape.

7-5   DEFINING THE BASIC OPERATIONAL CHARACTERISTICS OF THE SYSTEM, THE CONTROLLING SYSTEMS, AND THE CONTROLLED SYSTEMS

It is at this juncture that you, as the designer, must define the system level control functions and start a bare-bones block diagram for the complete system. Equally important are the data path definitions and bus structure requirements. With these, the system documentation begins to develop and is augmented with first-cut flow diagrams and timing diagrams developed to define control sequences and data transfers. The timing should be developed in a general manner with considerable concern for the actual timing constraints in order to define the required sequence of events which produces the desired operation. It is important that you study the controlling sequences coming into, and emerging from, the system to assure that no timing or sequential incompatibilities exist. At this point the role of the system controller begins to emerge. If it lends clarity to the operational sequence picture, define mnemonics for control and data buses and use these in the first-cut flow and timing diagrams. Remember, mnemonics should be defined such that they suggest the actual operations to be performed.

For those who have had no flow diagram design experience, the symbols shown in Figure 7-3(a) are defined as follows. The "ellipse" is used as a terminal symbol, usually to denote an initial or start-up state. The "diamond" is used to make two-way or yes/no decisions. The "block" is used to symbolize "ACTION" states, that is, "do something." An introduction to the use of these symbols is illustrated in the following simple example.

EXAMPLE 7-2: Design a flow diagram that describes the sequential behavior of the system which will load a register and then will sequentially replace the contents of that register with its 2's complement. You are given the bare-bones block diagram shown in Figure 7-3(b) and the first-cut flow diagram shown in Figure 7-3(c).

From the information illustrated in Figure 7-3, observe that the bare-bones block diagram describes the control relationship of the system controller to the register, and the first-cut flow diagram describes at least *one* sequential process (algorithm) which yields the 2's complement of an eight-bit word.

The development of the first-cut flow diagram and bare-bones block diagram for the data-logger is shown in Figure 7-4. Again the bare-bones block diagram defines the control relationship of the system, and the first-cut flow diagram defines the basic sequential behavior. Finally, it must be stressed once more that the designer should have a firm understanding of these operational sequences before moving into the following phases and should have a reasonable confidence in the first-cut flow diagram's authenticity once it is completed.

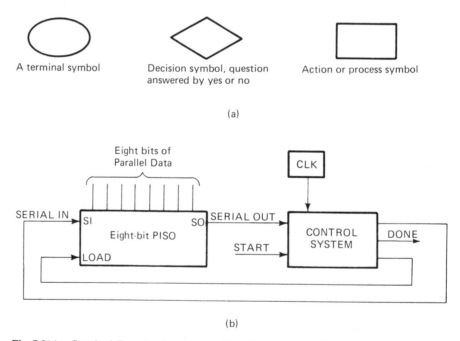

A terminal symbol

Decision symbol, question answered by yes or no

Action or process symbol

(a)

Eight bits of
Parallel Data

CLK

SERIAL IN

SI   SO SERIAL OUT

Eight-bit PISO

START

CONTROL
SYSTEM

DONE

LOAD

(b)

Fig. 7-3(a). Standard flow charting symbols. **(b).** The bare-bones block diagram for the 2's complement system.

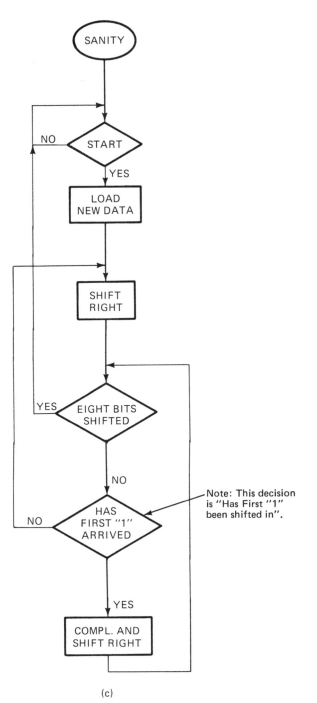

(c)

Fig. 7-3(c). First-cut flow diagram for the 2's complement system.

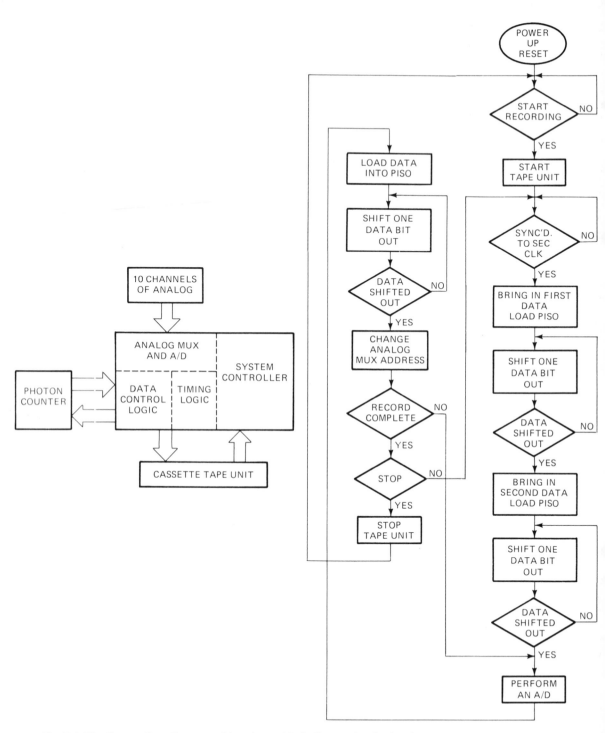

Fig. 7-4 The first-cut flow diagram and bare-bones block diagram for the data logger.

7-6 TIMING AND FREQUENCY CONSIDERATIONS

A good deal of time is required to study Section 7-5 and to become familiar with the system level sequences of the control and data. Section 7-6 is dedicated to working out the systems input and output timing relationships, or in other words, working out the causes and effects that inherently exist at the system level. The questions that must be answered are:

(1) At what point in time can a controlling input be expected? Will it be synchronous or asynchronous?
(2) How long will it remain asserted?
(3) How much time can elapse after this input is received until a control output response is required?
(4) At what point or within what time frame must the control signal be issued?
(5) How long must the output control signal remain asserted?

The answers to these questions are extremely important because they will determine to a large extent the system clock rate and the type of logic implementation that will be required for the system controller. Further, it will be shown later that asynchronous inputs pose real problems if not handled properly. Therefore, be as diligent as possible in defining the system level timing relationships including

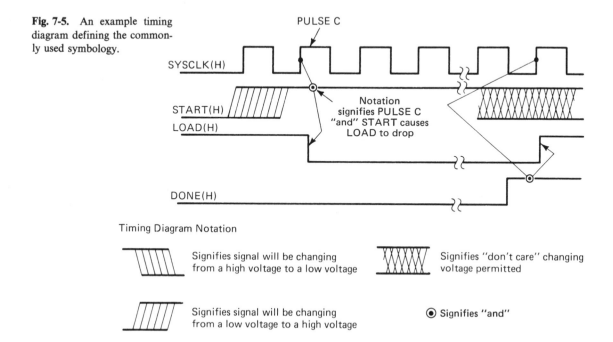

Fig. 7-5. An example timing diagram defining the commonly used symbology.

SYSCLK(H)

PULSE C

Notation signifies PULSE C "and" START causes LOAD to drop

START(H)

LOAD(H)

DONE(H)

Timing Diagram Notation

Signifies signal will be changing from a high voltage to a low voltage

Signifies signal will be changing from a low voltage to a high voltage

Signifies "don't care" changing voltage permitted

⊙ Signifies "and"

propagation delay—mistakes can and will be costly. See Figure 7-5 for the 2's complement system timing diagram. Pay particular attention to the special documentation.

7-7 FUNCTIONAL PARTITION AND DETAILED FLOW DIAGRAM DEVELOPMENT

It is now time to turn your attention inward to the system controller. With the information from Section 7-4, 7-5, and 7-6 at hand, the next step is to determine the system controller requirements of the central system. In short, the requirements for sub-functions such as registers, temporary storage, counters, line drivers, multiplexers, decoders, and other peripheral sub-systems as well as the controlling and controlled system should be identified and specified.

This identification and specification requirement is accomplished by designing a DETAILED FLOW DIAGRAM in conjuction with what is called a FUNCTIONAL PARTITION. Along with these, a detailed timing diagram should be developed (see Figure 7-6(b)). The detailed flow diagram is similar to the first-cut flow diagrams shown in Figures 7-3(c) and 7-4. However, it is much more *detailed* and the information it contains relates directly to the hardware illustrated in the functional partition. The functional partition is often referred to as a BLOCK DIAGRAM, but a well-prepared functional partition is much more than a simple block diagram (see Figure 7-1). The functional partition is meant to be a detailed illustration of the sub-system breakdown of a complete system. *It is designed and drawn to bring to light the control relationships between the system controller and its peripheral sub-systems (registers, counters, MUX's, etc.).* Also, it illustrates where the input and output controls of the system controller are to be directed to and from the *controlled* and *controlling* systems. Generally speaking, *controlled systems* are considered to be devices like A/D's, tape units, CRT's, and the like, whereas *controlling systems* are considered to be higher order systems like master control panels, computers, or other systems that have control over another system.

The design of the detailed flow diagram and functional partition are *processes carried out in unison requiring a certain degree of insight, judgment, and the ability to compromise and make trade-offs.* The design process is generally started by using the first-cut flow diagram as the framework of the detailed flow diagram. Starting from the beginning, this first-cut diagram is expanded using special symbology to meet the timing detail called for in Section 7-6. A special set of flow diagram constructs along with five basic concepts are developed for detailed flow diagram design in Section 7-8.2. As the detailed flow diagram is being developed, need for *special functions* will arise (counting, storing, data routing, data shifting, etc.). This is when you as the designer must exercise some degree of conservatism mixed with creativity in answering the basic question: "Can this required function be best incorporated within the framework of the system controller itself, or is it best to implement this function outside the system controller, treating it as a sub-function?" In either case, the system's documentation is to reflect the decision made. If it is decided that a counter module, a Flip-Flop flag, or a register is to be used as a sub-system, then it is added to the bare-bones block diagram generated in Section 7-5. At this time the designer should properly document the bare-bones block diagram, thus upgrading it toward a functional partition. This includes adding the appropriate control signals for this newly added sub-system. Also, a detailed timing diagram needs to be started. This process is continued in the same manner until the system's operational behavior is completely documented to the finest detail practical in three illustrations: (1) a DETAILED FLOW DIAGRAM (DFD) (see Figure 7-6(a)), (2) the system's FUNCTIONAL PARTITION (FP) (see Figure 7-1), and (3) the DETAILED TIMING DIAGRAM (DTD) (see Figure 7-6(b)).

Now, this all sounds cut and dried; however, you will find that it is really a process of converging on a solution and the probability of going through several iterations before the completed picture is derived is rather high. Keep in mind that it is important to keep the DFD, FP, and DTD in step with each other, and constantly keep updating the documentation. Then when you arrive at what you feel is what you want, your documentation package is up to date and you are ready to start the next phase.

Now refer again to Figure 7-1. It was decided that the required functions of the eight-bit PISO register, shift counter, pass counter, MUX address register, and clock control were best implemented outside the system controller. This was done because these functions could be implemented with existing integrated circuits. Now hopefully, as you read the specifications for the data-logger and relate these to the DFD, FP, and DTD, you can gain a fairly detailed understanding of how the system is to work and *about how much hardware is going to be required.*

These three documents serve as excellent design-review aids for other designers and supervisors who can quickly get the picture of what you are about to do and offer criticisms and make requests for modifications. The properly prepared functional partition, detailed flow diagrams, and timing diagrams serve other purposes also. For example, the functional partition can be used as a running scorecard for system fabrication with each sub-function being checked off the partition as it is completed. Along the same line, the partition provides you, the designer, with a composite picture of what needs to be done and potential roadblocks can be spotted, allowing you to schedule work allocations to these trouble spots early before they become a scheduling bottleneck. Another useful purpose of the functional partition is that it serves as a guide to system packaging —it aids you, the designer, in deciding how to physically partition the system and assign printed circuit layout, wire-wrap, and connector assignments. Further, the DFD and DTD provide an excellent framework from which software simulation can be developed. Before any commitment to hardware is made, the complete system can be simulated by software and design errors spotted early in the process. This is particularly important to those involved in integrated circuit development where design blunders can be extremely costly.

Thus it can be said without qualification that the DFD, FP, and DTD are essential to any documentation package.

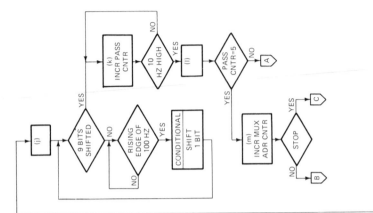
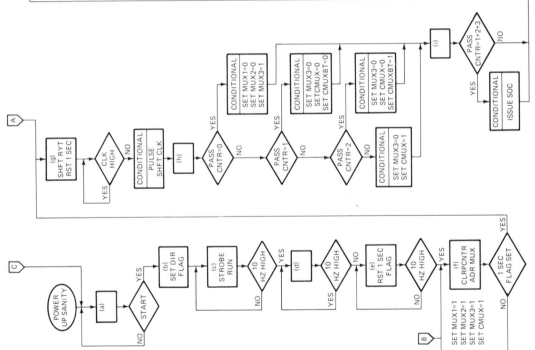

Fig. 7-6(a). Detailed flow diagram for data logger.

454

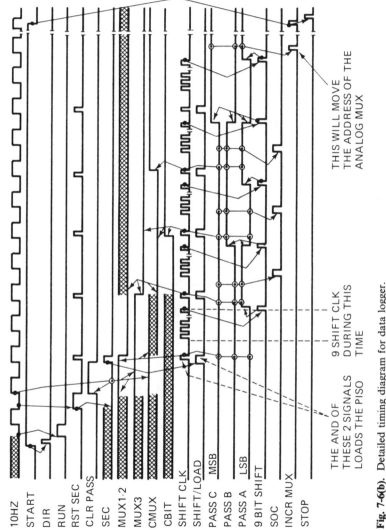

THIS WILL MOVE
THE ADDRESS OF THE
ANALOG MUX

9 SHIFT CLK
DURING THIS
TIME

THE AND OF
THESE 2 SIGNALS
LOADS THE PISO

10HZ
START
DIR
RUN
RST SEC
CLR PASS
SEC
MUX1-2
MUX3
CMUX
CBIT
SHIFT CLK
SHIFT/LOAD
PASS C   MSB
PASS B
PASS A   LSB
9 BIT SHIFT
SOC
INCR MUX
STOP

Fig. 7-6(b). Detailed timing diagram for data logger.

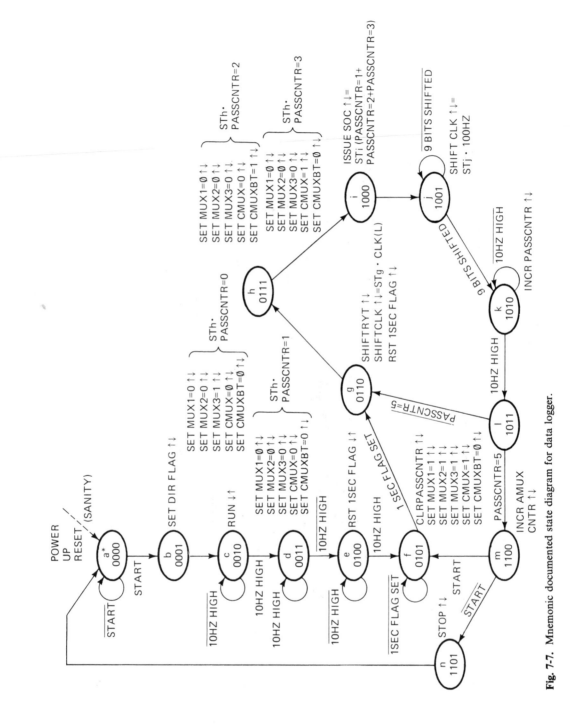

Fig. 7-7. Mnemonic documented state diagram for data logger.

7-8 SYSTEM CONTROLLER STATE SPECIFICATION (MDS DIAGRAM GENERATION)

Once you are confident of your functional partition and detailed flow diagram, the next step toward a hardware implementation is taken. In short, steps must be taken to move the design from the definition phase into the initial hardware phase. A special methodology allows the actual hardware required by the system controller itself to be closely specified. There are various methodologies from which to choose; one was introduced by Chris Clare in his book entitled *Designing Logic Systems using State Machines*. In this book Clare uses what he calls the Algorithmic State Machine Chart (ASM chart) to define and document the sequential behavior of a state machine. Clare uses a software flow charting type of symbol similar to that we used for the first-cut and detailed flow diagrams. Another medium used (see Figure 7-7), which this author calls Mnemonic Documented State diagrams (MDS diagrams), is employed in this text for the following important reasons:

(1) MDS diagrams are a mere extension of the traditional state diagrams treated in Chapter 6.
(2) MDS diagrams tend to be less voluminous than ASM charts.
(3) MDS diagrams as introduced here are documented in a manner identical to the process introduced for combinational design in Chapter 2 in that absolutely no reference is made to voltage *ASSERTION levels until hardware devices are actually being selected.*

This says that the Mnemonic Documented State diagram is a state diagram documented with mnemonics without polarizing elements that are intended only to symbolize ASSERTED and NOT-ASSERTED conditions. This is mentioned because it has been found that the introduction of voltage levels during a MDS diagram design is closely akin to the introduction of voltage levels in a TRUTH-TABLE. It just plain creates confusion. However, once the hardware is developed, the polarizing elements can be added to mnemonics of a MDS diagram, if you choose. By doing so, some claim they have found system debug to be somewhat easier.

7-8.1 MDSD SYMBOLOGY

Once you become familiar with the mnemonic symbology added to the traditional state diagram, this methodology is quite conceptual and MDS diagrams can be interpreted easily. This is illustrated by the following examples.

Consider an example MDS diagram shown in Figures 7-8(a) and 7-8(b). Observe from Figure 7-8(a) that the branching vectors for a MDS diagram are adorned with logic expressions rather than the 1's and 0's in the familiar

INPUT/OUTPUT

symbology introduced in Chapter 6. Figure 7-8(a) is an example of the typical

MDS diagram documentation for a multi-branch state (four in this case), *and the logic expressions associated with each branch define the INPUT branching conditions for that branch.* Thus a

$$\overline{START} \cdot \overline{READY}$$

input condition will hold the controller in state 0, where a

$$\overline{START} \cdot \overline{READY}$$

input condition will cause the controller to branch to state *X on the next CLK edge.*

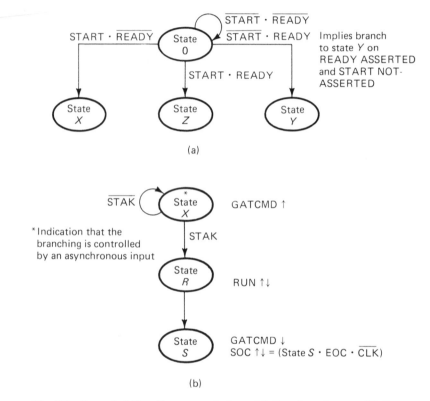

(a)

(b)

Fig. 7-8. Example MDS diagram symbology. (a) Four-branch state. (b) Output control generation.

Therefore, these logic expressions are pertinent to the description of the sequential behavior of a system controller. They also serve as the map-entered variables for the NEXT STATE DECODER reduction process. Thus it is important that these logic expressions be accurate before they are attached to the branching vectors. This illustrates the reason that a state diagram documented with this mnemonic symbology is called a mnemonic documented state diagram and there is very little new added to the traditional state diagram studied in Chapter 6. However, let it be said again: DON'T TRY TO PULL LOGIC VOLTAGE LEVELS INTO THESE BRANCHING EXPRESSIONS! Why? It was just stated that these expressions would be treated as MEV's and a map is a special TRUTH-TABLE, and voltage levels should never be entered in TRUTH-TABLES.

Before going on to Figure 7-8(b), consider the definitions of the following special notation descriptors:

↑: is defined as ASSERT with no voltage level implied.
↓: is defined as DE-ASSERT (negate) with no voltage level implied.
*: is defined as a special descriptor denoting that "branching from this state is controlled by an asynchronous variable."

Now consider Figure 7-8(b). Here again the notation deviates from

INPUT/OUTPUT

notation used in Chapter 6. This time it is the output specification notation that is varied. Rather than cramping the output notation under the input branching condition, it is located near its related *state*.

Consider Figure 7-8(b) and notice the asterisk (*) in state X.

As defined before, this * is a special descriptor signifying that the branching from state X is controlled by a variable which is implicitly or explicitly not synched to the system clock. Thus it is defined as an asynchronous variable; and special state assignments must be considered for the next state of states whose branching is controlled by an asynchronous input.

Now note from Figure 7-8(b) the following notation:

GATCMD ↑

associated with state X. This signifies that the output GATCMD is ASSERTED *upon the entrance into state X*. Now once an output is ASSERTED by the entrance into a state signified by the (↑) descriptor, it should be DE-ASSERTED (↓) also, either as the controller leaves the state or elsewhere. In this case GATCMD is DE-ASSERTED (↓) upon the entrance into state S. Thus you can really interpret (↑) and (↓) as logic ACTIONS and remember that they have *NO VOLTAGE LEVEL IMPLICATIONS*.

Now direct your attention to state R and the notation:

RUN ↑↓

This symbolizes that the output RUN is ASSERTED (↑) as the controller moves into state R and DE-ASSERTED (↓) as the controller moves out of state R. Thus the (↑↓) notation symbolizes a direct *decode* of state R, or it may be thought of as a state pulse or an immediate output of width equal to the time duration spent in the state.

Next note the notation associated with state S in Figure 7-8(b):

$$\text{SOC} \uparrow\downarrow = (\text{State } S \cdot \text{EOC} \cdot \overline{\text{CLK}})$$

This type of symbology is used for *conditional outputs*. Note that the output SOC is ASSERTED conditionally in state S; conditions in this case are that the input EOC must be ASSERTED and the inactive (NOT ASSERTED) period of the CLK must be present. Thus conditional outputs are easily depicted and are documented conceptually.

7-8.2 ADAPTATION

The previous section introduces the concepts and symbology related to MDS diagram documentation and interpretation as an extension of those introduced in Chapter 6. Now examine Figure 7-7, which is the fully documented MDS diagram for the data-logger example. This MDS diagram is derived by some methodology from the detailed flow diagram. But before considering this adaptation, step back for a second look at the concepts related to the development of flow diagrams and then relate these to the MDS diagram. Keep in mind that a properly developed detailed flow diagram is an invaluable documentation aid. Systematically developing a flow diagram that can be easily adapted to MDS diagrams, as well as several other developmental media including software flow charts, goes a long way in the direction of developing a *general design tool*. In order to build your insight into sequential machine specification, some concepts related to flow diagram development are covered and then these developments are related to a MDS diagram translation or adaptation. After this, adaptation of the detailed flow diagram in Figure 7-6(a) to the MDS diagram in Figure 7-7 should be obvious.

The adaptation or translation of the DECISION/ACTION concept of a flow diagram to the BRANCH/OUTPUT philosophy of the MDS diagram is straightforward because the two are closely related. However, the five concepts and illutrations set forth in the following section are aids to understanding both flow diagrams and MDS diagrams. Study them closely.

7-8.3 FLOW AND MDS DIAGRAM
CONSTRUCT CONCEPTS
AND ILLUSTRATIONS

Concept 1: An action block in a flow diagram defines a state in a MDS diagram as in Figures 7-9(a) and 7-9(b).

Therefore, we can say the definition of a MDS diagram state *begins* with an action block and ends with the next action block, following any decision path which is illustrated.

Concept 2. The branching conditions (branching expressions) for a state in a MDS diagram are derived by tracing the decision paths from the state definition action block to all other action blocks. This is illustrated in Figures 7-9(c)–7-9(e).

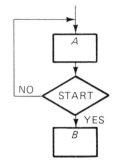

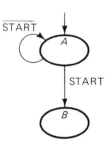

(a)

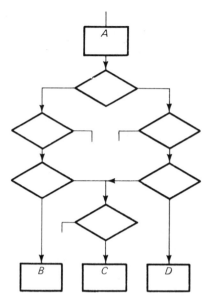

(b)

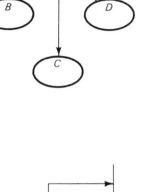

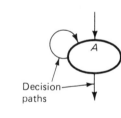

(c)

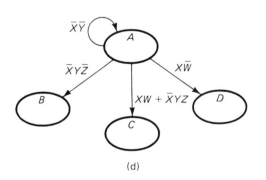

(d)

Fig. 7-9. Adaptation of flow diagram to MDS diagram. (a) Action block to states in MDS diagram. (b) Multi-state branching. (c) Branching conditions. (d) MDS diagram for flow diagram shown in (e).

System Controller State Specification (MDS Diagram Generation) **461**

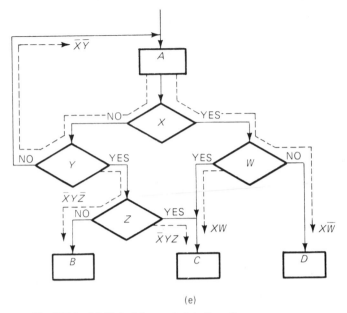

(e)

Fig. 7-9(e). Multi-decision and state flow diagram.

Concept 3. Avoid making branching decisions on more than one purely asynchronous decision variable. For example, in the following flow diagram (Figure 7-9(f)) and MDS diagram there are two variables that are independent of each other as well as independent of our control (asynchronous). The proper method is to define a new state as shown in Figure 7-9(g).

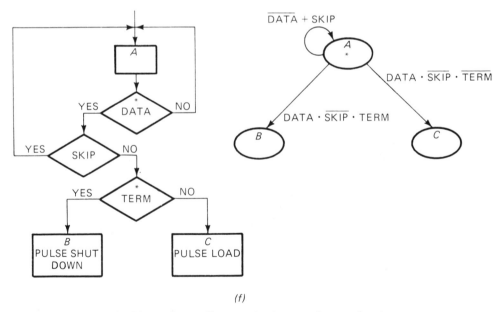

(f)

Fig. 7-9(f). Flow and state diagram using two asynchronous inputs.

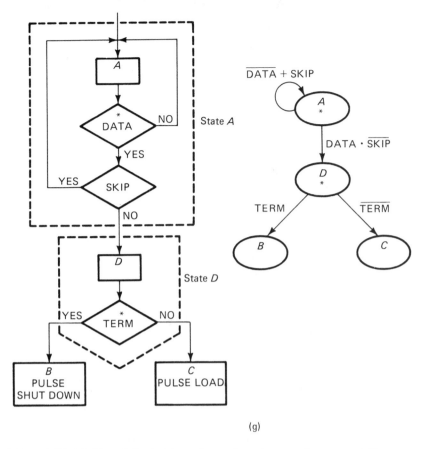

(g)

Fig. 7-9(g). Valid definition of the decision to be made on two asynchronous variables.

Concept 4. Generated outputs are to be symbolized by action notations in the action blocks. Outputs are to be defined as:

(1) Unconditional (immediate)
(2) Conditional (input dependent)

This is illustrated in Figures 7-9(h) and 7-9(i).

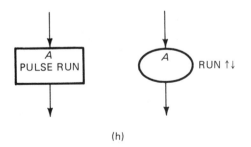

(h)

Fig. 7-9(h). Unconditional output specification.

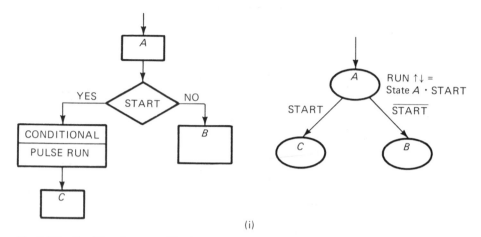

(i)

Fig. 7-9(i). Conditional out specification.

Warning: Never attempt to generate a conditional output on an asynchronous variable which can be changing during the generation of the output.

Concept 5. Unconditional and conditional outputs can be specified with duration time dependent on a decision variable, that is *ASSERT* and *wait* for response (see Figures 7-9(j) and 7-9(k)).

With these five basic relations well understood, you should be well-equipped to tackle the definition of any sequential finite-state machine. Also, the consistent use of these five concepts and illustrations becomes intuitive with a little practice, *but do be consistent with their use.* Avoid defining other relations unless it is absolutely necessary. Further, the detailed flow diagrams tend to become voluminous in relation to the equivalent MDS diagrams, making them a little unhandy during hardware development and checkout, but nonetheless they are important. On the other hand, once you become proficient in detailed flow diagram development, it will be tempting to modify the structure by adding extra design symbology to by-pass the MDS diagram development or to by-pass the flow diagram going straight to the MDS diagram. Thus merged the development of the detailed flow diagram and state diagram, both of which are really quite logical once one has other documentation, supporting the exact methodology and approach taken to develop the detailed flow diagram and the MDS diagram. But keep in mind that when the detailed flow diagram is in the development process, the system architecture is still in its formative stages; and there is still no real commitment to the *system controllers* hardware. Further, it is felt that the detailed flow diagram is a prime segment of conceptual documentation; therefore, it is best left uncluttered. Once a detailed flow diagram is developed as mentioned above and as shown later, a variety of techniques are available for deriving the system controller hardware and they need not be SYNCHRONOUS. Therefore, both the flow diagram and the MDS diagrams have their functions and it is felt that *both* are *necessary!*

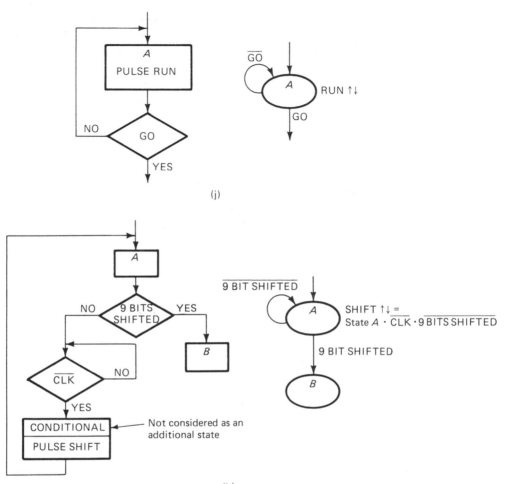

Fig. 7-9(j). Unconditional output with an input time duration dependency. (k) Conditional output with an input time duration dependency.

7-9 SYNCHRONIZING TWO SYSTEMS AND CHOOSING CONTROLLER ARCHITECTURE

Reflecting on the design phases covered thus far, a strong and consistent emphasis is placed on the marriage of independent systems. This so-called marriage requires the synchronization of the (1) sub-systems, (2) controlled systems, and (3) the controlling systems with the system controller. This all sounds complex, and it can be. However, there must be a beginning, and a simple definition of the synch problem is a way to begin.

The synchronization problem is simply one of the *system controller* knowing when or within what time frame it can expect *input changes* from its controlled and controlling systems.

Note that this definition does not mention the SYSCLK; however, the operation of the SYSCLK is implied in synchronization problems.

If the system controller is to do an effective control job, it must respond to input changes with the proper dispatch, and this calls for some means of synchronization.

The results of improper synchronization will lead to improper operation, which will be manifested by one or both of the following faults:

Fault 1: Input control changes can be "missed" and therefore ignored by the system controller.

Fault 2: The introduction of undefined state transitions.

Consider Fault 1 for a moment and visualize what can happen if an input condition is ASSERTED for a short period of time relative to the sample period of the system clock (see Figure 7-10). A little study shows that Fault 1 can be introduced. Keep in mind that "short" in this case implies that the duration of t_p *does not* satisfy the following relation:

$$f_c > \frac{1}{t_p}$$

where f_c = the frequency of system controller clock.

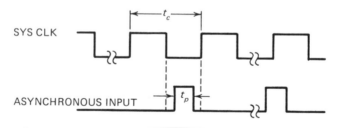

Fig. 7-10. An illustration of a missed short asynchronous input and its relation to the system clock which leads to Fault 1.

Though the problem previously referred to as the short input was an asynchronous input, the same problem prevails with short synchronous inputs also.

This figure shows that if the system controller is to see the short input pulse, the following relation must hold.

$$t_p > t_c$$

$$\text{Since} \quad f_c \triangleq \frac{1}{t_c}$$

$$\text{then} \quad f_c > \frac{1}{t_p}$$

There may be cases when it is impractical to increase the frequency of the system clock to meet this criterion, and so a scheme is needed to catch this input pulse and hold it until the system controller can service the control need. (If this can be done then the input is synchronized.) There are several techniques that can be used, all of which provide this catching action; but they are predicated on the following criterion:

$$f_p < f_c$$

Two such schemes are shown in Figure 7-11.

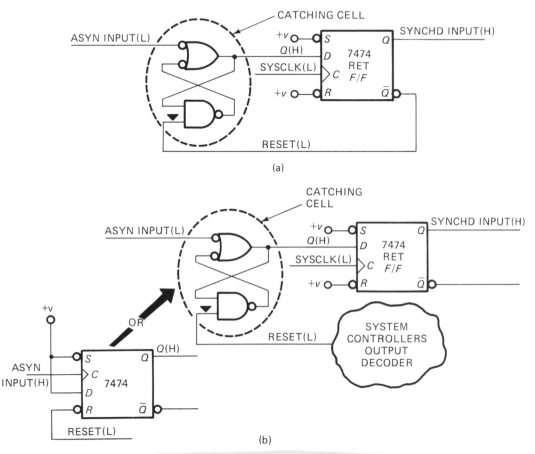

(a)

(b)

Fig. 7-11. Two illustrations of how a short synchronous input can be captured and held until the system controller can service the control need.

Figure 7-11(a) shows a special network made up from a binary cell and RET D Flip-Flop designed to catch the short pulse and hold it until the falling-edge of SYSCLK, at which time it is transferred to the output of the RET D Flip-Flop and held there for *one more complete system clock cycle*. Note also that the setting of the D Flip-Flop resets the cell. The circuit shown in Figure 7-11(b) has the advantage of a *controlled* reset of the catching cell. This circuit operates much the same as the one in Figure 7-11(a) in that the cell catches the input, then the D is loaded on the falling-edge of the system clock and thus it synchs the input to the system clock. Now the input is *held* until the system controller services the control or branching need of the input, at which time the cell can be reset by the controller and readied for the next input to be received. Keep in mind both techniques are based on the following assumptions:

(1) $t_p < t_c$ implying that t_p is short and infrequent in relation to the system clock (SYSCLK).
(2) State changes in the system controller are made on the *rising-edge* of the SYSCLK.
(3) The time period between the falling- and rising-edge of the clock (low period of SYSCLK) is greater than the *system's setting time*.

The operation of the two circuits in Figure 7-11 is illustrated with a timing diagram shown in Figure 7-12.

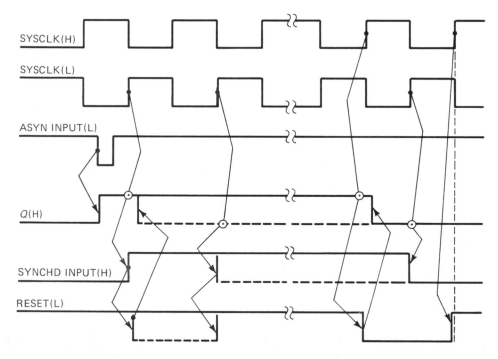

Fig. 7-12. The timing diagram illustrating the synching operation of the pulse-catching circuits shown in Figures 7-11(a) and 7-11(b).

It should be noted that in the discussion of the "short pulse catching" circuits, another technique of synchronization was touched upon. This is sometimes referred to as "level synchronization" and is characterized by the condition

$$t_p \gg t_c$$

Thus the input is defined as a "catching level," but the transitions take place asynchronously with respect to the system clock. In cases such as these, the same circuits described in Figures 7-11(a) and 7-11(b) are used, but this time the catching cell is omitted. By doing this, an asynchronous input is *locked in with the falling-edge of the system clock* in order to assure a *stable synchronized input on the next rising-edge* of the system clock.

The requirement of a stable input at the rising-edge of the system clock leads us into the discussion of Fault 2. Though an in-depth and practical discussion concerning this fault is discussed in Section 7-11, suffice it to say:

> Input changes that can cause the outputs of the NEXT STATE DECODER to change during the set-up and hold time period of the Flip-Flops making up the present state register will cause erratic behavior.

Thus, all asynchronous inputs must receive special treatment. However, it will be shown that this process is one of trade-off and is closely related to the state diagram design and will be treated later. Also, this is why the (*) is used to signify the branching conditions from a state controlled by an asynchronous variable.

7-9.1 THE HANDSHAKE

From the previous discussions asynchronous inputs seem to be inevitable and, along with that, they require special attention. Thus to partly eliminate the potential problems related to asynchronous inputs, the HANDSHAKE interface technique has been developed. A handshake implementation is a technique whereby some action is taken by one party (system) that serves to stimulate some action by the other party (other system). This second party action is to signal the first party that the initial action was acknowledged and that the next transmission can now proceed. This handshake concept is symbolized by a sample block diagram and a section of a MDS diagram shown in Figure 7-13.

This figure shows that the controlling system moves into a state and issues TAKE DATA and waits for the controlled system to return with DATA TAKEN. The controlled system is slaved to the controlling system and responds accordingly.

Thus the handshake is a sort of mutual agreement to synchronize, but nonetheless the two systems still must treat the other's input as an asynchronous input. By using this scheme and by making a proper state assignment, as illustrated later, the erratic behavior listed as Fault 2 *can be avoided.*

In summary, the interaction of systems operating independently from one another is one worthy of detailed study. Even though the synchronization schemes outlined above cover a wide application, there are interface situations that have not been covered. These are cases where input changes internal to one of the systems cause transient noise on its output control lines. That sounds like a design problem in the controlling system and it probably is, but it is one you might not have control over, and you might have to live with it by designing special circuits which sense the noise transient condition and delay any action until the noise has gone away. Another case: What do you do when the inputs are coming at a faster frequency than your master clock, or when you have several asynchronous inputs which can come in within the same time frame but must be resolved as to which came first? Another very important problem is discussed in Sections 7-11.1 and 7-11.2 related to the state assignment and MDS diagram design.

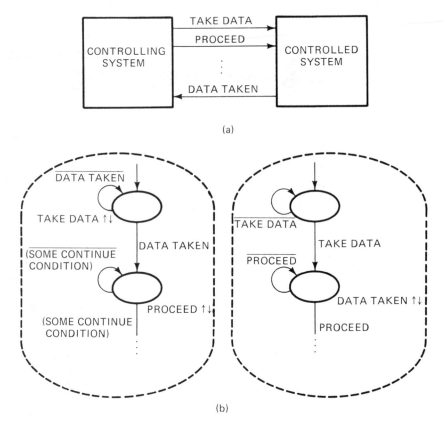

(a)

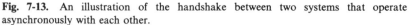

(b)

Fig. 7-13. An illustration of the handshake between two systems that operate asynchronously with each other.

7-9.2 CHOOSING THE CONTROLLER ARCHITECTURE

Once the preceding phases have been completed, you need to select the model for the system controller. Though the general model of sequential machines is inherent, it might be necessary to augment this model to enhance its operational characteristics. Thus the addition of several holding registers can improve the practical performance of the fundamental or classic sequential circuit. These models are shown in Figures 7-14(a), 7-14(b), and 7-14(c).

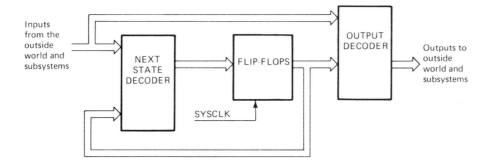

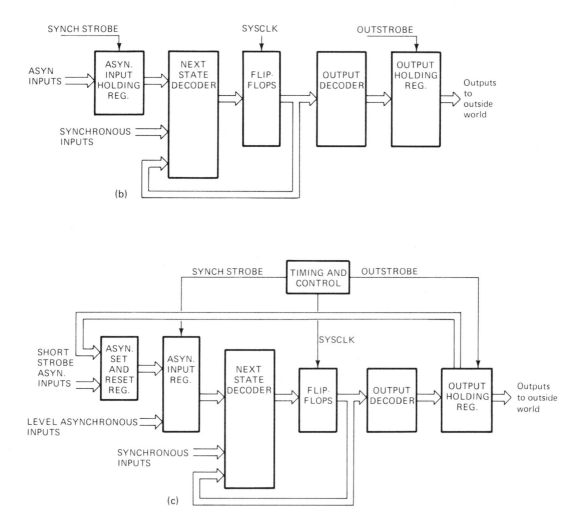

Fig. 7-14. (a) The classic sequential machine. (b) A sequential machine with an output holding register and asynchronous input holding register. (c) A sequential machine with an asynchronour SET/RESET register.

Notice that Figure 7-14(a) is the "functional partition" of the traditional and classic synchronous sequential machine. The functional partition in Figure 7-14(b) illustrates the machine with an ASYNCHRONOUS INPUT HOLDING REGISTER and an OUTPUT HOLDING REGISTER added. Figure 7-14(c) shows the same partition with an ASYNCHRONOUS SET/RESET REGISTER added. As mentioned above, these special registers are added to enhance the practical performance of the machine. First, the ASYNCHRONOUS INPUT HOLDING REGISTER is classified as the collection of all the D-type Flip-Flops used to synch-in the *changing level asynchronous inputs* discussed in Section 7-9.1. The signal SYNCH STROBE is used rather than a phase of the SYSCLK to indicate that any *properly* chosen pulse train can be used to synchronize the level asynchronous inputs. It has been found that the edge-triggered devices such as the 74174 and 74175 D PIPO's or equivalent serve nicely as ASYNCHRONOUS HOLDING REGISTERS.

Figure 7-14(c) shows the ASYNCHRONOUS SET/RESET REGISTER. This block symbolizes the collection of basic cells used for catching the short input discussed in Section 7-9.1. It has been found that devices such as Flip-Flops with ASYNCHRONOUS SET and CLEAR features (SN7474, etc.) or the $\overline{SR}$ quad latch (SN 74279) work nicely for this application. However, other operational characteristics must be considered before selecting the use of these special registers. These are covered in Section 7-11.2.

7-9.3 GLITCH-FREE OUTPUT GENERATION

It is noticed in Figures 7-14(b) and 7-14(c) that an OUTPUT HOLDING REGISTER is prescribed for the expressed purpose of "de-glitching" the output controls signal emerging from the OUTPUT DECODER. The "glitch" is that unwanted "spike" or transient output that increments some counter, clears some register, or starts some unwanted process at precisely the most *undesirable* time. This transient and undesirable spike is generally issued from any DECODER that is addressed with a sequence of NON-UNIT-DISTANCE-CODED inputs. This is an almost unavoidable situation. It is exemplified in Figure 7-15(a), which shows the six transient conditions possible on the transition from 111→000. Figure 7-15(b) is an actual photograph of the transient glitch taken from an actual circuit.

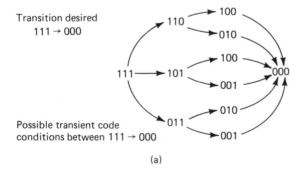

Transition desired
111 → 000

Possible transient code
conditions between 111 → 000

Fig. 7-15. (a) An illustration of the six possible transient conditions existing in the transition from 111 to 000.

(a)

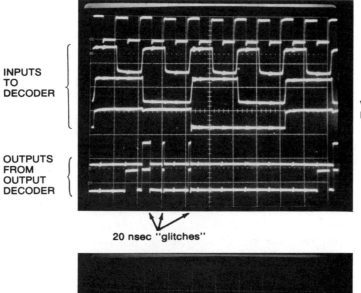

INPUTS
TO
DECODER

OUTPUTS
FROM
OUTPUT
DECODER

Vertical: 5v/div
Horizontal: 100 ns/div

20 nsec "glitches"

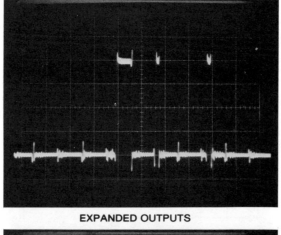

EXPANDED OUTPUTS

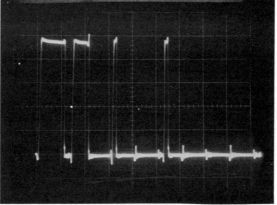

EXPANDED OUTPUTS

(b)

Fig. 7-15(b). Actual photographs of the glitching problem.

The transient codes indicated are generated by the simple fact that no two actions happen simultaneously as noted by an extension of the Heisenberg Uncertainty Principle, which says that even though a bank of Flip-Flops are all triggered from the same clock, *they will not all change state simultaneously* but in fact will change one by one. Granted one might have to measure the time interval between these changes in ever-increasing smaller increments as set forth by the Heisenberg Uncertainty Principle, but rest assured that no two actions happen exactly in coincidence.

Thus decoding the present state variables (outputs of Flip-Flops) using a combinational decoder can cause transient outputs unless the decoder is specifically designed to suppress the glitch. One glitch suppression method used *disables* the complete OUTPUT DECODER just prior to a state change and maintains this disabled condition for some prescribed period of time after the state change, allowing the transient conditions to settle out. Though effective, this disabling method has one basic drawback: Outputs that must remain ASSERTED through several states or through several CLK cycles are not allowed. This is because each ASSERTED output must be DE-ASSERTED prior to a state change (CLK edge) in order to avoid the glitch.

The D-type OUTPUT HOLDING REGISTER as indicated in Figures 7-14(b) and 7-14(c) eliminates the glitch by loading and holding the outputs of the OUTPUT DECODER *after* the state change transients have "died away." Further, by making use of the holding capability of the D-type register, those outputs that must remain ASSERTED for multi-state or CLOCK transitions also remain glitch-free. It should be noted that when using the OUTPUT HOLDING REGISTER the register must be updated after each state change. The timing diagram in Figure 7-16 illustrates the typical timing considerations related to the use of an OUTPUT HOLDING REGISTER.

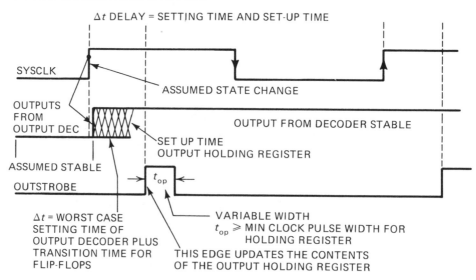

Fig. 7-16. A timing diagram illustration of how an OUTPUT HOLDING REGISTER can guarantee "glitch-free" outputs.

Here it is shown how the properly timed OUTSTROBE signal will load the OUTPUT HOLDING REGISTER and guarantee glitch-free outputs. Granted, more hardware is required and the output changes are delayed by Δt, but in most cases this is a small price to pay for guaranteed operation. In summary, de-glitching the control outputs of a system controller is not always necessary, for there are cases when an output might only drive a light or a LED or some similar combinational function. However, if an output signal from the system controller is intended to "start a process" or can be traced to the SET, CLEAR, LOAD, or CLOCK input of a sub-system device, de-glitching of one means or another is a necessary evil. Several exercises are given illustrating the identification and alternate solutions for output glitch.

7-10 THE STATE ASSIGNMENT

As mentioned in Chapter 6, a good deal of research has been put into finding optimal ways to make state assignments with the general results stated:

> "This technique gives good results; however, it doesn't guarantee optimal results."

The complexity of finding the optimal state assignment has been further compounded by the introduction of the multi-input system controller, and the increased number of inputs and state diagram complexity dampens the most ardent state assignment theorist. However, times have changed from the days when much of the state assignment and reduction criteria were developed. That was when electronic components were very expensive, especially Flip-Flops. Now other motivations are making themselves felt. As a result, the application of classic state reduction and assignment methods, economically speaking, is not always a good idea. Both should be considered as *possible* design processes, but not as absolutely necessary ones. In some situations state reduction does not reduce the overall cost, and it is true that the cost of the devices is often a minor part of the overall cost of a digital system, and saving cost at the expense of functional clarity, ease of maintenance, and design time is rarely justifiable. In fact, the major goal in controller design should always be the development of a system with desirable operation, done in a logical, reliable, and straightforward manner, in the shortest time possible, rather than attempting to cut every corner on parts costs. Presently, "it is he who is in the marketplace *first* with the 'good' product who is carrying away the big marbles." Thus it should be said that unless there is a real motivation to carry out detailed state reduction and state assignment studies, simply follow the rules and concepts set forth in Chapter 6.

(1) Spend time designing tight flow and MDS diagrams. Think! Then develop alternative sequential methods, evaluate and make a choice, but make them all tight.
(2) Use the "minimal locus" and "reduced input dependency" state assignment rules to your advantage.

Keep in mind two classic clichés: (1) the second law of thermodynamics plainly states, "There is no such thing as a free lunch" and (2) robbing Peter to pay Paul results in no savings at all.

7-10.1 THE STATE ASSIGNMENT AND THE ASYNCHRONOUS INPUT

Though it is stated clearly in most literature that "any unique state assignment will work; it may not be optimal, but it will work," it can be shown that this is not necessarily true. *In short, it will be shown that the following criteria must be adhered to in order to design reliable and well-behaved sequential machines.*

The NEXT STATES from a single state whose branching is controlled by an asynchronous variable MUST be given unit-distance state assignments.

This is Rule 2 from Chapter 6. Further, recognize that the rule applies to the cases where the *NEXT STATE is to be that same state*, that is, states that loop back on themselves. From this rule two design corollaries can also be stated.

(1) The branching conditions for any state should NEVER be controlled by more than one asynchronous variable.
(2) The NEXT STATES should be given unit-distance assignments, that is only *one* (1) *state variable should be affected*, implying that only one Flip-Flop in the present state register should be scheduled to change on a conditional asynchronous input variable.

Why must these rules be adhered to? *If the NEXT STATES of a single state whose branching is controlled by an asynchronous variable are not unit-distance coded, there exists a finite possibility that a transition to an undefined state can be induced, and this problem is recognized as Fault 2 defined in Section* 7-9. The finite possibility of an asynchronous input inducing the anomaly outlined above is illustrated by Example 7-3.

EXAMPLE 7-3: To illustrate the possible fault created by the improper state assignment to the next states of a state whose branching is controlled by an asynchronous input, the state assignment and resulting circuit shown in Figure 7-17 are used.

Figure 7-17 shows an extra level of delay through the INVERTER for $D_A(H)$. Thus the delay (Δt_2) added to the D_A input can cause an erroneous transition to state D rather than state B if the input change is timed just right. This anomaly is catastrophic and one that is totally unacceptable. This is particularly true because of its intermittent occurrence. Now, had the states B and C been given the following adjacent assignment:

$$b = 01$$

and

$$c = 11$$

then

$$d = 10$$

things would have turned out differently.

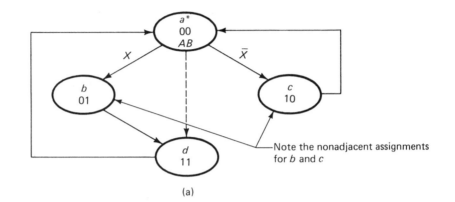

(a)

$$D_A = \overbrace{(\overline{A}\overline{X})} + \overline{A}B \quad D_B = \overbrace{(\overline{A}X)} + \overline{A}B$$
Note the inversion in X in these two terms.

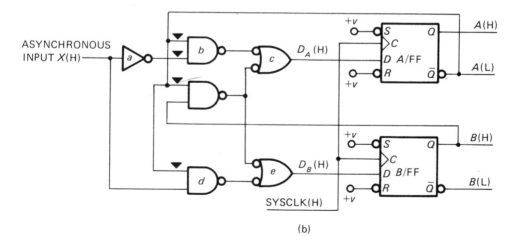

(b)

Fig. 7-17. (a) State diagram with an improper state assignment for processing an asynchronous input. (b) The circuit implement from the state diagram in (a).

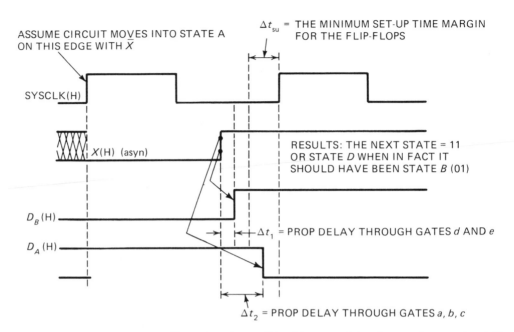

Δt_{su} = THE MINIMUM SET-UP TIME MARGIN FOR THE FLIP-FLOPS

ASSUME CIRCUIT MOVES INTO STATE A ON THIS EDGE WITH $\bar{X}$

SYSCLK(H)

X(H) (asyn)

RESULTS: THE NEXT STATE = 11 OR STATE D WHEN IN FACT IT SHOULD HAVE BEEN STATE B (01)

D_B (H)

Δt_1 = PROP DELAY THROUGH GATES d AND e

D_A (H)

Δt_2 = PROP DELAY THROUGH GATES a, b, c

Fig. 7-18. A timing diagram illustrating the possible effect caused by the asynchronous input X changing just to the minimum set-up time limits of the D Flip-Flop.

The circuit could be implemented as shown in Figure 7-19. Because of the composite delay through devices a, b, and c, there is still what can be termed as a troublesome transition. This is because the transition was made to state C rather than state B, but at least it didn't jump to a state whose transition was not defined. Situations such as this one must be viewed, for all practical purposes, as if X was plainly missed, so the $\bar{X}$ branch was the proper transition to make. A very important design consideration is that the two-way branch must be used cautiously if a transition like the one just illustrated can result in an *unrecoverable error*.

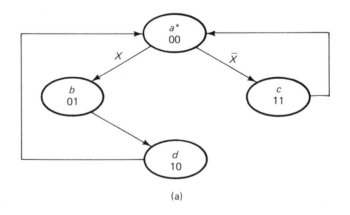

(a)

Fig. 7-19(a). Example of transition for adjacent assignments for states B and C.

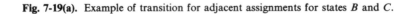

$$D_A = \overline{A}\,\overline{X} + \overline{A}B$$
$$D_B = \overline{A}\,\overline{B}$$

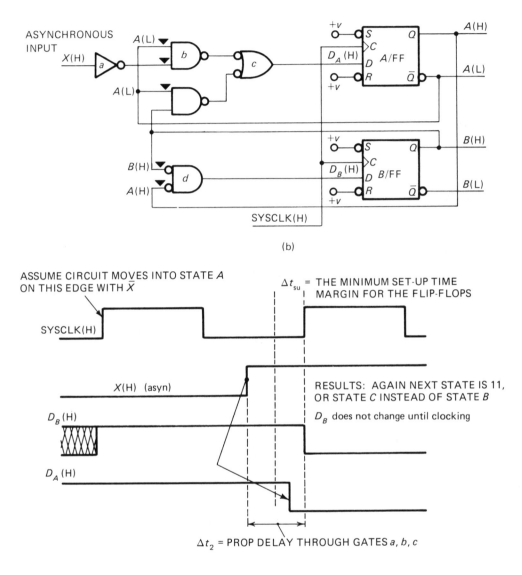

(b)

(c)

Fig. 7-19(b). Circuit for state diagram in (a). (c) The timing diagram showing state changes for the circuit (b).

Now the question is, how can these problems be prevented? One answer is to design your state diagram such that decisions made on asynchronous variables never fall into the form shown in Figures 7-17 or 7-19 by using state diagram constructs that have the structure shown in Figure 7-20.

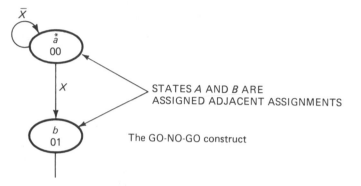

Fig. 7-20. The only acceptable state diagram construction that will not result in an anomalous transition.

In Figure 7-20 the machine is designed to remain in state *A* until the asynchronous input is *definitely* found ASSERTED. *Then and only then will the transition to state B be effected. You should recognize this MDS diagram construct as the handshake construct whereby the pitfalls of the asynchronous two-way branch can be avoided.*

7-10.2 THE UNRESOLVED SYNCHRONIZING PROBLEM

Up to this point the concepts related to the treatment of asynchronous inputs have been discussed. These concepts are related to using an edge-triggered D Flip-Flop that is clocked with a signal phase synchronized with the system clock. The sampling concept set forth here has been: "clock the 'D'—it will find the input high or low and the output will respond accordingly." In other words, if one edge of the synch clock missed the transition of the asynchronous input, the next edge will catch it, and everything will work out fine because there is no such thing as a *half a bit*—it has to be a 1 or 0. It is true that the high and low levels are the only *stable* levels, but the existence of a finite possibility of an unstable level (metastable level) poses a problem. This possible metastable level is related to the corollary stated earlier:

> The branching from a state cannot be controlled by more than *one* asynchronous variable.

The constraints set forth by this corollary are quite general and are equally applicable to the design of purely asynchronous circuits. For example, the application of the corollary is apparent in the SET/RESET constraints for the basic cells. It basically states that because of the finite bandwidth or frequency response limitations of logic devices, there are times when the anti-coincidence of two or more logic actions can no longer be resolved. This can be illustrated by relating the problem to a simple D Flip-Flop and the generalizing of the problem to all sequential machines. First consider the model of the D Flip-Flop shown in Figure 7-21.

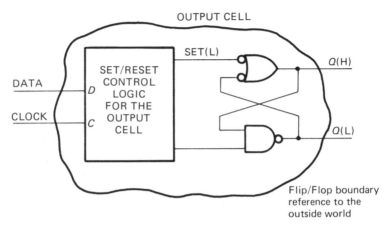

Fig. 7-21. The model of the edge-triggered "D" flip-flop drawn to illustrate its view of the outside world.

If the D Flip-Flop is used as a "stand alone" sequential system, it receives two asynchronous inputs (data and clock) which can come at unpredictable times, that is, as far as the Flip-Flop itself is concerned. Now examine what can happen at the SET output of the SET/RESET control logic if the setup and hold times are not met by you, the designer. First consider the gate providing the SET(L) signal which is modeled as an AND function ASSERTED LOW. This is shown in Figure 7-22.

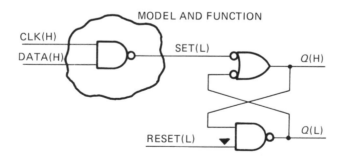

Fig. 7-22. An abbreviated model of the SET logic for "D" flip-flop.

Now turn your attention to Figure 7-23, which illustrates the practical responses of the SET(L) output when the data changes in close proximity to the clock edge. When the real effects of the finite bandwidth of the gate (rise and fall times) are taken into account, there exists the finite possibility of a "runt pulse" of varying amplitude being generated. Now if the amplitude of the runt pulse is *exactly the threshold level of the SET input of the output cell*, the cell will be driven to its metastable state.* The metastable state is the condition that is roughly defined as "half SET and half RESET." In other words, both outputs are at the threshold voltage level, as shown in Figure 7-24.

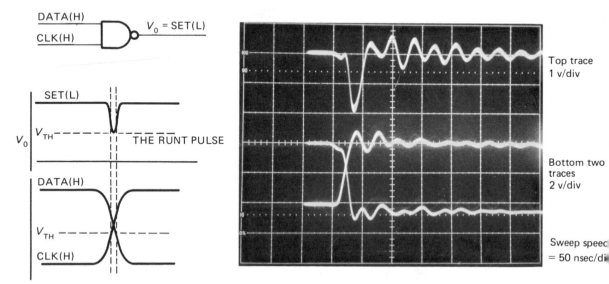

Fig. 7-23. An illustration of the real effect of the data input changing in close proximity to the triggering edge of the CLK.

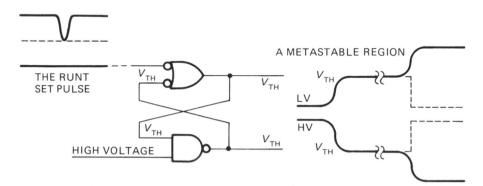

Fig. 7-24. An illustration of the output cell in its metastable condition induced by a "runt" pulse.

---

*This metastable condition has been modeled by Chaney, Ornstein, and Littlefield in their paper "Beware of the Synchronizer" and is shown in Figure 7-25.

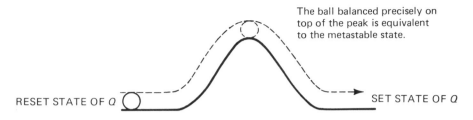

The ball balanced precisely on top of the peak is equivalent to the metastable state.

RESET STATE OF Q SET STATE OF Q

Fig. 7-25. An illustration of metastable condition of a Flip-Flop.

Figure 7-25 demonstrates that if the runt pulse possesses *exactly* enough energy to roll the ball just to the top, the ball will remain in this conditionally stable position until noise eventually moves it one way or the other. The unresolved question is "how long does this condition persist?" Personal interviews with practicing engineers have zeroed in the figure of 1 μsec as the maximum time limit for this metastable state in TTL, longer for CMOS. However, this time is definitely a function of the logic family used and is tied to both physical construction and the bandwidth (frequency response) of the gates. This illustrates the problem that can occur when a sequential circuit must resolve a state change based on *two totally asynchronous inputs*. Further, this same sort of anomalous symptom can be extended to higher order sequential systems, like system controllers, when the next state decisions are to be made on more than one asynchronous variable. In fact, as far as the Flip-Flops in the PRESENT STATE register are concerned, the metastable condition is always a possibility if the asynchronous input *is not* locked in and stable prior to the state-changing-edge of the SYSCLK. Since this is the case, some criteria must be established to avoid faulty operation. To this end the following three-part criterion is presented to guarantee the operation of a GO or NO-GO branch:

(1) Never try to resolve a next state decision on more than *one* asynchronous variable.
(2) Avoid the use of any MDS diagram construct other than the GO or NO-GO construct shown in Figure 7-20. This includes following the unit distance rules also.
(3) Never try to resolve a next state decision on an asynchronous variable whose frequency is greater than the system clock or one whose ASSERTED period is shorter than two complete periods of the synchronizing clock.

This criterion is based on the fact that a metastable condition is only precipitated by the rising-edge of the clock finding only a sliver of an input to work with. However, it will quickly be resolved on the succeeding rising-edge. Therefore, if the *metastable* voltage condition of a Flip-Flop, be it in the synchronizer section or present state register, is interpreted by the decoding logic *as a signal* to change state, everything is OK. However, if the logic interprets the metastable input as a NO-GO condition, then the next edge would resolve the branch condition. In review, a metastable condition can only be precipitated by a GO input condition that was just missed. Therefore, if it is interpreted as GO, it is OK; and if it is interpreted as a NO-GO first, it will be picked up on the next clock edge if the asynchronous variable meets the criteria set forth by criteria 3.

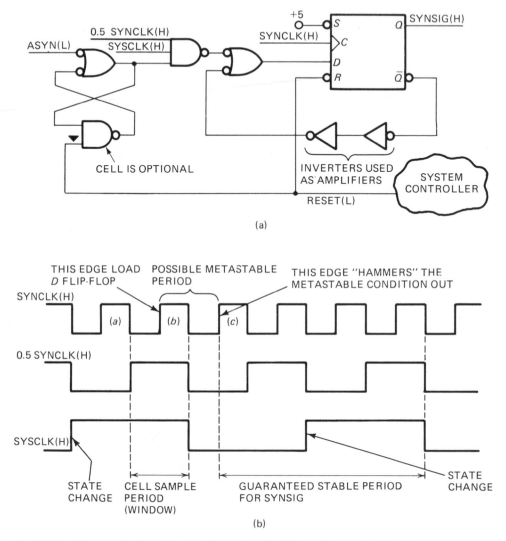

(a)

(b)

Fig. 7-26(a). The one-clock cycle metastable resolver. (b) Timing diagram for circuit in (a).

The rather novel circuit shown in Figure 7-26 with its associated timing diagram is a one-cycle metastable condition resolver. Observe that the D Flip-Flop output is coupled back around through two inverters into an OR operator and then into the D input. The timing diagram shows that the first edge of the SYSCLK calls for a state change. A short time later a "window" is opened by the falling-edge of pulse a which in turn is closed by the rising-edge of pulse c. In the center of this window the output of the catching cell, or a raw asynchronous input, is sampled by the rising-edge of pulse b. If this sampling precipitates a metastable condition in the D Flip-Flop (Q and $\overline{Q}$ sitting at V threshold), the output of $\overline{Q}$ is then amplified by the cascade of two INVERTERS which, by the way, will be held in or close to their linear region by the metastable voltage at the Flip-Flop's output. This amplification will assure a hard saturation level (low or high) at the output of the second inverter indicating a definite hit or definite miss such that when the rising-edge of pulse c arrives, the metastable condition will be quickly resolved. If the asynchronous input is sampled and found stable at the rising-edge of pulse b, the ASSERTED condition is locked into the D Flip-Flop and can be removed only by strobing the RESET line. Thus this circuit guarantees a stable high (hit) or low (miss) at the SYNSIG(H) output at each edge of the SYSCLK and the system controller is never faced with interpreting a metastable logic level. However, this system does require a multi-phase clock system and extra circuitry.

In summary, additional important facets are notched in the steps leading to reliable system controller design. If these particular facets are not properly treated, all sorts of intermittent failures can result because of the "can come at any time" nature of asynchronous inputs.

7-11 THE NEXT STATE DECODER

This phase can best be illustrated by an example, as will be done a little later. However, there are some general considerations to be made in choosing the type of Flip-Flop to be used for the present state register. It can be said with a reasonable certainly that the JK Flip-Flop results in a simple implementation. However, there can be times when a D type of implementation or even a mixed implementation would do the job cheaper. This all depends on the state assignment made; but generally the JK results in the most economical implementation. An example will be worked with all three types of Flip-Flops to illustrate the techniques that are to be used.

The most important point of this phase is learning the technique of plotting the next state maps directly from the MDS diagram; thus saving all the time-consuming details of generating a next state table as is done with classic or traditional synthesis processes.

7-11.1 OUTPUT DECODER

During this phase of the design, the state diagram output specification symbology given earlier aids in the development of the output functions. If properly done, the state diagram associates the output functions with the appropriate states. It is a simple matter to decode these states for each output for unconditional outputs or to develop the prescribed logic function described for CONDITIONAL OUT-PUTS. However, care must be exercised in making certain that no glitching is generated.

7-11.2 WORKED EXAMPLES

Next consider the applications of the suggested design phases by working through several examples. The first problem is to complete the serial 2's complement system.

> EXAMPLE 7-4: In the 2's complement system, you are given the assignment to finish the controller design which will start up and load a 74198 (broadside) on the command (START), then successively shift these bits out and serially replace the original word with its 2's complement. When the process is completed, the DONE signal is to be ASSERTED and held ASSERTED until the next START is received and recognized, at which time it is to be DE-ASSERTED. See Figure 7-27 for the updated bare-bones block diagram. See Figure 7-3(c) for the first-cut flow diagram.

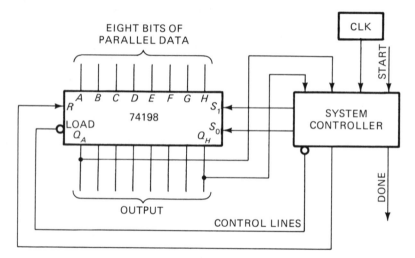

Fig. 7-27. Bare-bones block diagram for the 2's complement system. Note that the mode control on 74198 can only be changed when the CLK input is high, the old 1 and 0 catching problem.

Now, given the bare-bones block diagram and the first-cut flow diagram, complete the functional partition and the detailed flow diagram as shown in Figures 7-28 and 7-29. Note that the most important timing constraint is assuring that the clock is high before a mode change is issued to the 74198. It can be seen from the functional partition in Figure 7-28 that for this particular design the counter, the bit flag Flip-Flop (Q_A of the 74198), the inverter, and the EXOR gate were selected as subfunctions of the system controller. Thus in this particular implementation it was decided that the functions of these devices should be provided outside the system controller. However, as an exercise it is left for the reader to design an alternate controller that incorporates these functions into the controller itself. The timing diagram for the 2's complement system is shown in Figure 7-30. This was developed *during the same time interval as the detailed flow diagram and functional partition.* Note S_1 and S_0 changed only when SYSCLK is high.

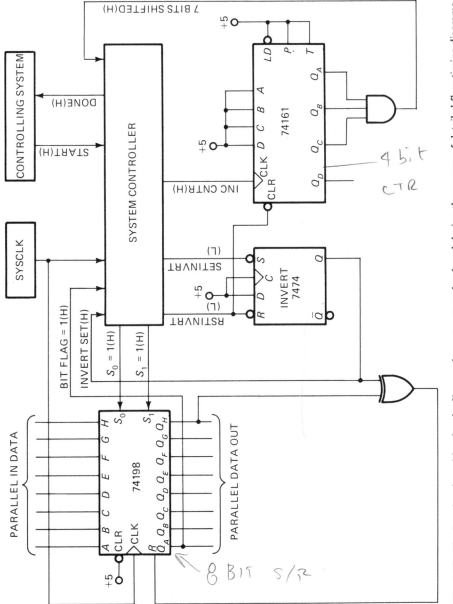

Fig. 7-28. The functional partition for the 2's complement system developed during the process of detailed flow timing diagrams shown in Figures 7-29 and 7-30.

487

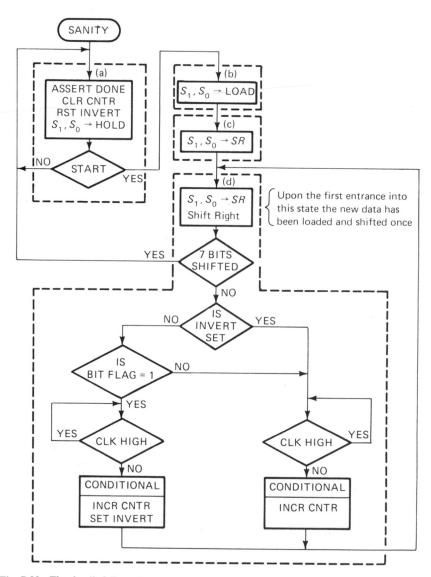

Fig. 7-29. The detailed flow diagram for the 2's complement system.

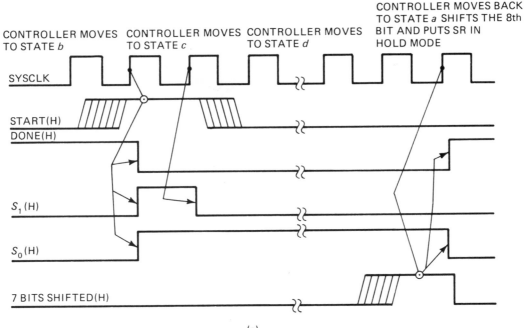

(a)

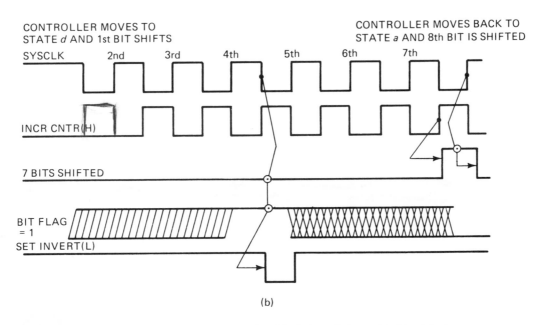

(b)

Fig. 7-30. (a) Overall timing relations. (b) Specific timing relations related to state *d*.

Now consider the MDS diagram shown in Figure 7-31 illustrating the adaptation of the detailed flow diagram to a state diagram structure. The flow diagram state constructs enclosed by dotted lines map directly to the states in the MDS diagram; and the action blocks serve as the root of each state, all in accordance with the concepts and illustrations set forth in Section 7-8.3. Note further the use of "conditional-outputs," all of which are conditional on the low period of the SYSCLK. This is a fairly standard technique used to minimize the number of states.

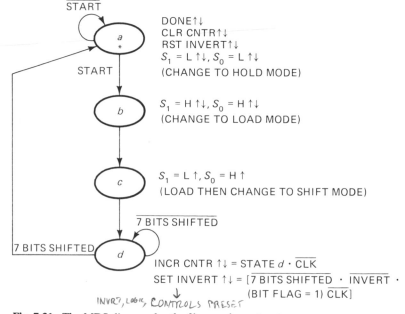

Fig. 7-31. The MDS diagram for the 2's complement system.

In summary, this is one systematic and well-defined implementation for the 2's complement system. Granted there are others, some not so general, but they will perform the function. However, the approach presented here is a structured design philosophy exemplifying the role of the system controller and its relation to the other devices of the system. Once again it is important that you note the identification of each MDS diagram state in the flow diagram. Here each state starts with an ACTION BLOCK and its definition ends with the entry into another ACTION BLOCK. The branching conditions are determined for each branch in the MDS diagram by tracing out the decision paths leading from the ACTION BLOCK, which defines that state, to all other ACTION BLOCKS including itself. This same procedure determines the *conditional output* specifications. For example, see the specification for SET IN-VERT which is a conditional output specified for state *d*. Here SET INVERT is ASSERTED conditionally with $\overline{7\ \text{BITS SHIFTED}}$ and $\overline{\text{INVERT SET}}$ and BIT

FLAG = 1 and $\overline{\text{CLK}}$, all of which can be traced through the detailed flow diagram.

Now consider one more design problem illustrating the use of the design phases (1–9). This problem requires you to interpret a set of detailed specifications and further illustrate the functionality of the system controller concept. Special thanks to Prof. Richard Ohran of Brigham Young University for suggesting a problem such as this back in 1971.

EXAMPLE 7-5:   The Pop Machine Controller

Introduction and specifications. The El-Rip-O Vending Machine Company wishes to update its Model 1909 mechanical vending machine. It is desired that a first generation digital controlled prototype system be developed for test and evaluation; nothing really fancy, just an evaluation prototype. The El-Rip-O Company has entered into an OEM (Original Equipment Manufacturers) agreement with the Futzel–Boopsdink Pipe and Die Company to provide the coin receiver, coin changer, and pop dropping systems for the new El-Rip-O Model 1971 system when it is fully developed.

Preliminary specifications. The initial digital control system should be developed such that it will direct the control of the coin receiver, coin changer, and pop drop mechanics and provide the El-Rip-O Company with a system capable of automatically dispensing soda pop at 30¢ per can and making the proper change retrieval for the following coin sequences of nickels, dimes quarters, and half-dollars.

Prescribed operation.   Upon the insertion of each coin, the controller is to record the coin value and issue the proper change, if required, in nickels only, then drop a can of soda pop. At this time a solenoid is to be activated that lets the coins collected in the coin sequence drop into a common collector box. This system is to have a coin release feature for the manual release of jammed coins and coins collected in "short" sequences, and the coin release feature is also intended to reset the system to an initial condition.

Coin receiver specification.   The Futzel–Boopsdink Pipe and Die Model CR-1971 coin receiver is described by the following features:

(1) single slot coin entry;
(2) electronic coin detection;
(3) guaranteed coin detection for U.S. half dollars, quarters, dimes, and nickels;
(4) automatic nonvalid and bent coin rejection;
(5) all control inputs and outputs are standard TTL compatible;
(6) coin-catching mechanism and manual coin release feature;
(7) a special mechanical mechanism that prevents coin over-run.

Electrical specifications. See Figure 7-32.

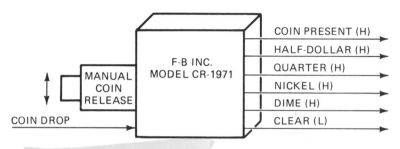

Fig. 7-32. Block diagram of CR-1971.

Signal description.

> COIN DROP—an input that commands the CR-1971 to drop collected coins into the common collection box.
>
> CLEAR—an output that will go to a 5 volt ±0.5 level for the duration of the depression of the coin release.
>
> COIN PRESENT—an output signifying that a coin is present in the coin receiver and denomination has been determined.
>
> HALF DOLLAR,—outputs signifying the denomination of coin present.
> QUARTER, DIME
> and NICKEL

The timing relationship between COIN PRESENT, HALF-DOLLAR, QUARTER, DIME, and NICKEL is described by the timing diagram shown in Figure 7-33.

Coin changer. The Futzel–Boopsdink Pipe and Die Model CC-1971 coin changer (see Figure 7-34), developed by the Stuck–Muzzey subsidiary, features:

(1) fast, reliable, electro-mechanical nickel-ejecting system (100 msec per nickel maximum);
(2) special READY status output which indicates when another coin ejection sequence can be started;
(3) automatic load of 50 nickels reserve.

> EJECT NICKEL— TTL compatible input, pulse triggered with minimum width of 10 msec restriction.
>
> CHANGER READY—an output status line indicating the changer will respond to EJECT NICKEL.

Timing relations. See Figure 7-35.

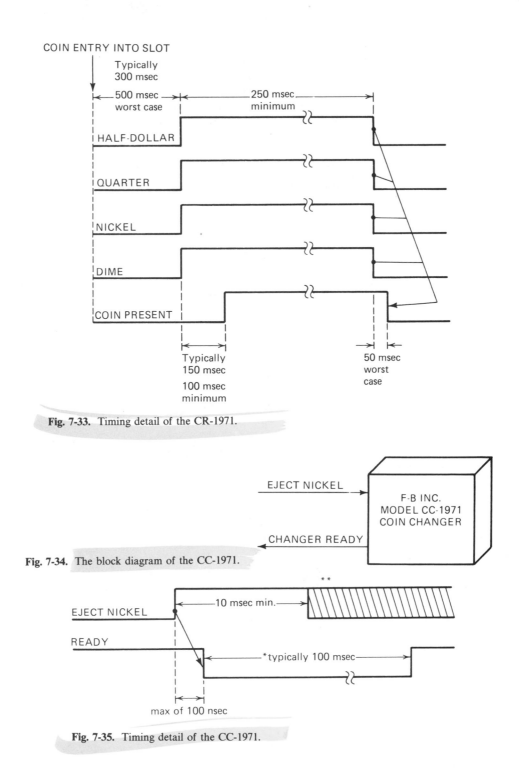

COIN ENTRY INTO SLOT

Typically
300 msec

|←— 500 msec —→|←——— 250 msec ———→|
     worst case   minimum

HALF-DOLLAR

QUARTER

NICKEL

DIME

COIN PRESENT

Typically
150 msec

100 msec
minimum

50 msec
worst
case

Fig. 7-33. Timing detail of the CR-1971.

EJECT NICKEL

F-B INC.
MODEL CC-1971
COIN CHANGER

CHANGER READY

Fig. 7-34. The block diagram of the CC-1971.

**

EJECT NICKEL |←—— 10 msec min. ——→|

READY

|←—— *typically 100 msec ——→|

|←→| max of 100 nsec

Fig. 7-35. Timing detail of the CC-1971.

Pop-drop mechanism The Futzel-Boopsdink Model PD-1971 pop-drop mechanism developed by Bend-A-Can Division (see Figure 7-36) is a fast solenoid operated device featuring:

(1) single TTL compatible drop command input;
(2) pulse operated with 10 msec minimum pulse width;
(3) status READY line

Timing and operation is identical to that of the coin changer.

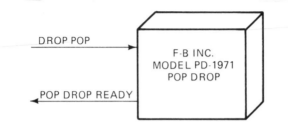

DROP POP

F-B INC.
MODEL PD-1971
POP DROP

POP DROP READY

Fig. 7-36. The block diagram of the PD-1971. Note that POP DROP READY will not return to the READY status if the mechanism is jammed.

7-11.3 SYSTEM DEVELOPMENT

First let it be noted that the system to be designed has certain frailties related to its cheating the customer as well as the customer cheating it. However, since this development is only an evaluation prototype, these frailties can be temporarily overlooked. The specifications for a foolproof system are given as a design exercise and left for you to work out the fine details.

Phase I. Because of your intimate knowledge of vending machines derived from the everyday encounters with these beasts (see Figure 7-37), along with the specifications given, Phase I is pretty well covered.

Fig. 7-37. Man and the vending machine.

Phase II. From the knowledge accounted for in Phase I, the bare-bones block diagram as shown in Figure 7-38 can be readily developed. This bare-bones block diagram is supported by the first-cut flow diagram shown in Figure 7-39. Note that this flow diagram clearly defines the proposed big picture sequential behavior of the controller operation. Now keep in mind that this proposed operation is but one of several possible alternatives. However, it was selected on the basis of the following criteria:

(1) It provides a practical and effective system.
(2) The author feels that it nicely demonstrates the logical sequence of events.
(3) It also demonstrates how properly designed "hard wired" systems can have a reasonable degree of flexibility.

Though these criteria are somewhat biased, the concept of making a selection from several possible alternatives should not be considered as such. It is very important that you derive several alternatives and then select one of these based on some criteria. Now these criteria can vary depending on the design requirements, but the major cornerstones should be:

(1) Practicality
(2) Effectiveness
(3) Efficiency
(4) Degree of flexibility

The flexibility facet should be treated in the light of possible future applications and modifications. This is in keeping with the invariable fact that somebody will want something changed at the most inopportune time. However, don't let these anticipations completely override your preliminary preparations; just keep them in mind. For example, though there is no mention of price changes or multi-pop selection requirements in the specifications for the pop machine, these features are included with no real extra effort or cost. They are simply a natural fallout of the proposed system.

VENDING MACHINE SYSTEM

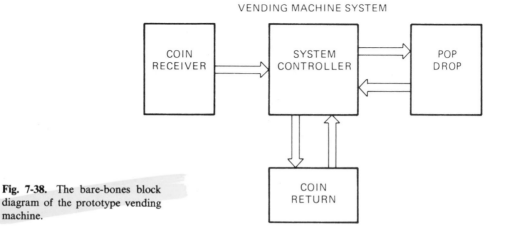

Fig. 7-38. The bare-bones block diagram of the prototype vending machine.

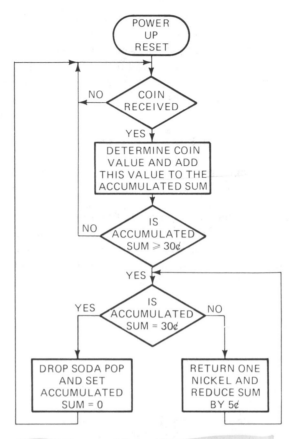

Fig. 7-39. A proposed first-cut flow diagram defining the vending machine's basic operation.

7-11.4 THE DETAILED FLOW DIAGRAM, FUNCTIONAL PARTITION AND MDS DIAGRAM DESCRIPTION

The detailed flow diagram shown in Figure 7-40 defines the exact sequential behavior of the functional partition shown in Figure 7-41. It should be clear that this flow diagram is an extension to the first-cut diagram. Along with this it also defines the timing relations of the control signal to and from the subsystems. The functional partition typifies the system controller in its presiding role. It should be noted that the arithmetic operations called for are carried out by the interconnection of the ADDER, PIPO REGISTER, DOWN COUNTER, and COMPARATOR. The PIPO REGISTER was added to insure the edge-triggered loading of the COUNTER. This register/counter complex is referred to as the ACCUMULA-

TOR (ACC) in this example. Further, it should be noted that a "strappable" compare word allows for easy price changing up to 75¢. The value of each coin is then encoded to the binary value of the number of nickels it represents in accordance with the indicated encoding (w_4, w_3, w_2, w_1) specification table. This encoded value is then added to the present value of the accumulator on the rising-edge of COIN PRESENT. Thus the basic functions called for by the first-cut and detailed flow diagram are brought to light with a hardware description. Note further that the IC package count is up to six packages, all with 16 pins or less.

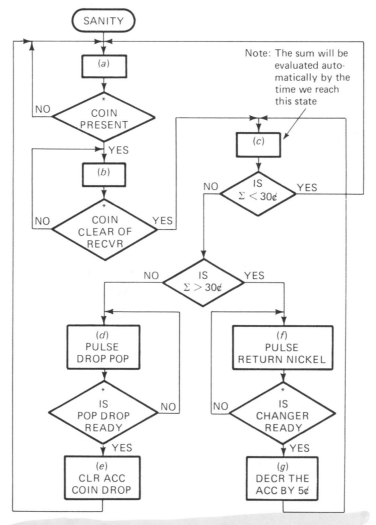

Fig. 7-40. The detailed flow diagram for the prototype pop machine system controller.

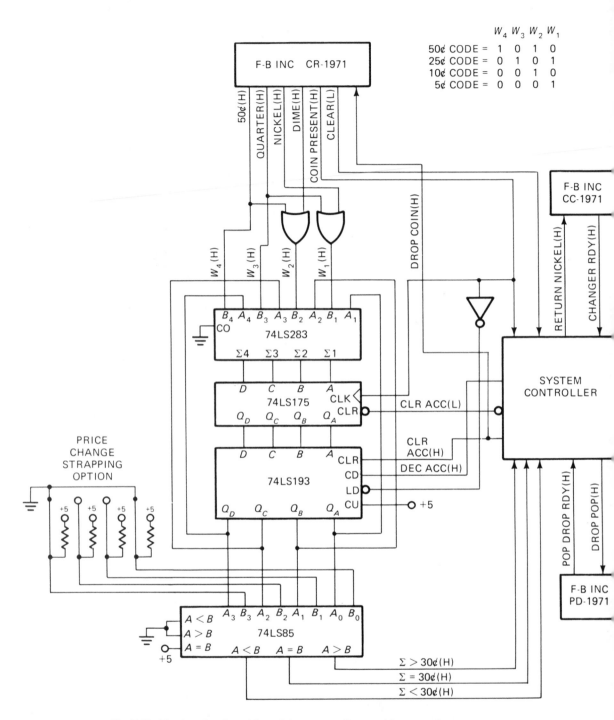

Fig. 7-41. The functional partition of the pop vending machine control system.

The seven-state MDS diagram for the system controller is shown in Figure 7-42. All branching conditions and outputs are clearly specified in close accordance with the specification set forth in the detailed flow diagram. The branching decisions based on asynchronous inputs are properly identified and are defined by the GO, NO-GO decision construct discussed in Section 7-10.1

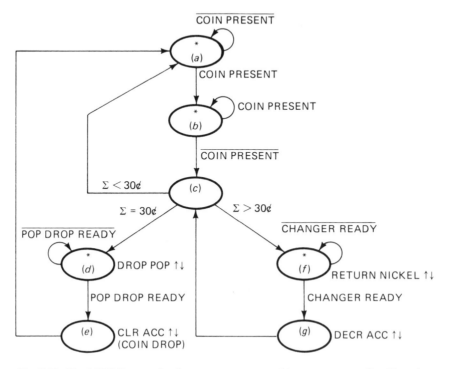

Fig. 7-42. The MDS diagram for the prototype pop machine system controller. Note that it is assumed CLR ACC ↑↓ causes the coins to drop.

7-11.5 THE HARDWARE IMPLEMENTATION OF THE NEXT STATE AND OUTPUT DECODER

Up to this point the major effort has been directed toward the system's three D's: Definition, Description, and Documentation. Now some of the practical aspects of an actual hardware development process are presented. The first step in this development process is to make a state assignment in accordance with the rules set forth earlier, paying strict attention to asynchronous branching (see Figure 7-43). A state map (regular K-map) is used to aid the state assignment process. Here the rules related to asynchronous branching variables are given the highest priority.

This priority calls for the following state assignment constraints:

a adjacent to *b*
b adjacent to *c*
d adjacent to *e*
f adjacent to *g*

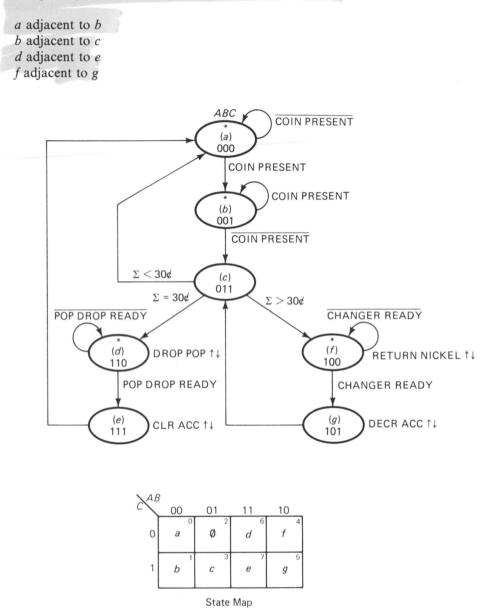

Fig. 7-43. The system controller MDS diagram for the prototype pop machine complete with a state assignment and state map.

The rest of the states are assigned with some reference to the simple rules set forth in Chapter 6 and the list in Table 7-1. However, no exhaustive attempt is made to optimize the state assignment.

TABLE 7-1   State assignment listing

Previous States	State in Question	Next State	Assignment Suggestions
$a, c\,e$	a^*	b	$a\,\mathrm{ADJ}\,b^*;\ a, c, e\,\mathrm{ADJ}$
a, b^*	b^*	b, c	$b\,\mathrm{ADJ}\,c^*;\ a\,\mathrm{ADJ}\,b^*$
b	c	a, d, f	$a, d, f\,\mathrm{ADJ};\ b\,\mathrm{ADJ}\,c^*$
c, d	d^*	e	$d\,\mathrm{ADJ}\,e^*;\ c\,\mathrm{ADJ}\,d$
d	e	a	$\mathrm{NR};\ d\,\mathrm{ADJ}\,e^*$
c, f	f^*	g	$f\,\mathrm{ADJ}\,g^*;\ c\,\mathrm{ADJ}\,f$
f	g	c	$\mathrm{NR};\ f\,\mathrm{ADJ}\,g^*$

*→a must assignment; NR→NO Requirement

7-12   NEXT STATE DECODER MAPS

Once a state assignment is made, the next design step determines the first real commitment to any specific type of hardware. This example demonstrates the ease with which small sequential machines can be implemented at the SSI gate and Flip-Flop level, knowing well that other alternatives do exist. This ease is brought about in part by taking advantage of the inherent application of the VARIABLE-ENTERED MAP. Using VEM's bypasses the tedious detail of filling out a PRESENT/NEXT STATE TABLE by going *directly from the MDS diagram to the NEXT STATE maps*. The plotting of the VEM's is a simple process. However, it does require a *properly documented MDS diagram* and some ability to recognize, by inspection, the CONDITIONAL SET OPERATIONS called for in this MDS diagram. This process is described in the following paragraph.

Next State Map Plotting Process

Using a MDS diagram with a state assignment, select a state, then examine the branching mnemonics to *all* NEXT STATES of the selected state; and enter into the STATE CELL of the NEXT STATE MAP the Boolean expression that defines all of the SET CONDITIONS $(0 \rightarrow 1, 1 \rightarrow 1)$ that are required for the chosen state variable in that state. Thus these CONDITIONAL SET EXPRESSIONS become MAP ENTERED VARIABLES in the NEXT STATE MAPS.

This process is repeated for each STATE VARIABLE of each STATE until the NEXT STATE maps are completed. Remember, the NEXT STATE maps are the D-maps from which JK and T maps can be readily obtained. The described processes are clearly demonstrated in Figures 7-44 and 7-45. Pay particular attention to the entry in state cell c in the D_A map. Here you see:

$$(= + >)$$

which indicates that the A Flip-Flop is set by the next clock edge if the machine is in: STATE c AND (=) OR (>) are ASSERTED. The rest of the MEV ENTRIES are obvious. However, it is recommended that a map be generated for each Flip-Flop and these maps be plotted in parallel, one state at a time, using the state map as a reference for the state cell location.

From Figures 7-44 and 7-45 notice that the JK does yield a circuit implementation requiring fewer gates (11 gates or four IC packages). Thus the new grand total for the system equals nine IC packages, some with spare gates, which really isn't too bad considering the capabilities of the overall system. However, the design for the OUTPUT DECODER must be completed.

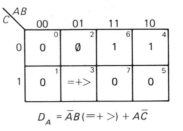

$$D_A = \bar{A}B(=+>) + A\bar{C}$$

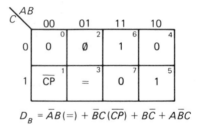

$$D_B = \bar{A}B(=) + \bar{B}C(\overline{CP}) + B\bar{C} + A\bar{B}C$$

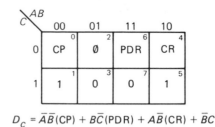

$$D_C = \bar{A}\bar{B}(CP) + B\bar{C}(PDR) + A\bar{B}(CR) + \bar{B}C$$

Legend: CP = COIN PRESENT
=+> = (Σ = 30¢) + (Σ > 30¢)
CR = CHANGER READY
PDR = POP DROP READY

Fig. 7-44. The NEXT STATE or D maps for the proto-type pop machine system controller.

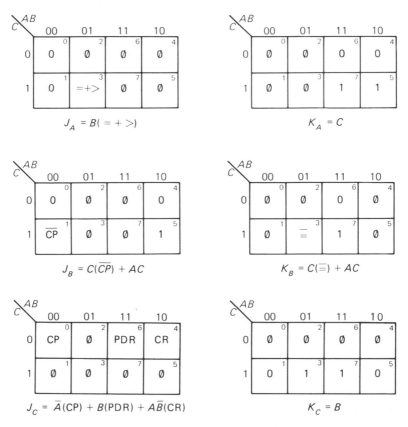

$$J_A = B(= + >)$$

$$K_A = C$$

$$J_B = C(\overline{CP}) + AC$$

$$K_B = C(\equiv) + AC$$

$$J_C = \overline{A}(CP) + B(PDR) + A\overline{B}(CR)$$

$$K_C = B$$

Requires 11 gates, or four IC packages with spare gates.

Fig. 7-45. The NEXT STATE DECODER maps for a JK implementation.

7-13 THE OUTPUT DECODER

The design of the OUTPUT DECODER is like any other combination decoder design problem that can be summed up quickly by the following process:

Make up a map for *each* output. Plot the map using MEV for the conditional variables, then simplify and implement.

However, many times maps serve no useful purpose. For example, in the present system controller there is no output that is a function of more than one (1) state. This information can be quickly gleaned from inspecting the MDS diagram. Therefore, in cases such as these, it is recommended that you make up a simple output list. This output list is nothing more than a list of every required output and the states and conditions related to the generation of these outputs. For example, the MDS diagram in Figure 7-43 would have the following list:

$$\text{RETURN NICKEL} = A\overline{B}\,\overline{C}$$

$$\text{DECR ACC} = A\overline{B}C$$

$$\text{DROP POP} = AB\overline{C}$$

$$\text{CLR ACC} = ABC$$

From this expression list observe that none can be further simplified. Therefore, each requires a simple three-input gate (AND function) with the inputs connected to the PRESENT STATE VARIABLES (ABC). However, the ever present glitch problem exists because of our state assignment. The transition from 111→000 introduces the possibility of a glitch in three states. But the real question is which three states. Previous studies indicate that all six of the remaining states are vulnerable when the 111→000 transition is made. Therefore, some sort of glitch prevention must be introduced. In cases with a smaller number of bits changing (two in this case), the possible transitions can be traced in a state map for easy identification of possible glitch problems. However, the 111→000 transition overrides the need for any further glitch studies.

Since there are no outputs which must remain ASSERTED over several states, an OUTPUT HOLDING REGISTER would appear to be an overkill. However, DROP POP and RETURN NICKEL generated in states D and F must be held stable all during these states. Therefore, a holding register is probably called for. Therefore, four three-input NAND gates (74LS10) are chosen for the output decoder and a 74LS175 is chosen as the OUTPUT HOLDING REGISTER. For the completed schematic of the total system controller including the OUTPUT DECODER, see Figure 7-46. From this figure observe that the grand total IC package count is 14, all of which are standard or established 14 or 16 pin IC's (see parts list in Table 7-2).

TABLE 7-2   Parts List

Quantity	Number	Description
1	74LS283	Four-bit adder
1	74LS193	Hex up/down counter
2	74LS175	Quad D PIPO
2	74LS112	Dual edge-triggered JK Flip-Flop
1	74LS85	Four-bit comparator
2	74LS32	Quad of two-input OR
2	74LS10	Triple three-input NAND
1	74LS08	Quad of two-input AND
*1	7404	Hex of inverters
$\frac{1}{14}$	74LS00	Quad of two-input NAND

*The standard 7404 was chosen because of the high drive requirement of the clock input on the 74LS112 (four std LS loads per input)

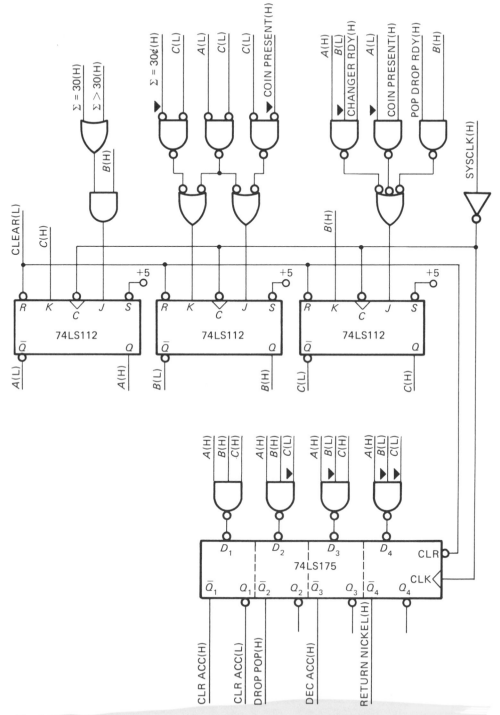

Fig. 7-46. The complete JK implementation of the system controller for the pop vending machine system.

7-14 CLOCK FREQUENCY DETERMINATION

One concept not touched upon for the design is the SYSCLK frequency. Generally speaking, this consideration is selected on the following criteria:

(1) System cycle speed requirements.
(2) Minimum output durations for immediate outputs generated from a straight state decode.
(3) Frequency stability.

For this design and specifications, a high speed controller is not needed. However, the system clock should be at least two times faster than the fastest changing asynchronous input transition period. Doing this further simplifies the design. This forces the electromechanical devices to set system speed limits. Thus a clock frequency of

$$1\text{kHz}$$

would do nicely (many times over) in this respect.

Criterion 2 plays no practical part in our clock frequency decision. All outputs to the electro-mechanical devices are self-timed by a handshake and therefore require no lower boundary timing constraint. All the internal systems function with pulse widths from dc to 50 nsec; therefore, they too contribute no practical constraints. Criterion 3 is of no real concern either. Therefore, the choice is a simple RC timed system clock such as:

$$\text{SYSCLK} = 1\text{ kHz} \pm 20\% \text{ square waves}$$

7-15 POWER SUPPLY REQUIREMENTS

It has been the author's experience that cutting corners on the system power supply is not advisable. Those with troubleshooting experience testify if a system is *down*, check the power supply *first*. Therefore, overspecify your power supply a little bit, maybe 30 to 50%. By doing this you can possibly avoid the problems associated with driving a power supply to its limits. The author's philosophy is: "Let the power supply 'loaf' and it will perform better." Now obviously a 300% loaf factor is probably out of reason; however, a 30% loaf margin is felt to be adequate.

Based on this, the power supply requirements can be determined. The current requirement data taken from a manufacturer's data book is listed in Table 7-3.

Considering the values in Table 7-3 are the absolute worst case values, it is felt that a power supply with the following specification is adequate:

$$5\text{v} \pm 0.2\text{v}, 200 \text{ ma power supply}$$

TABLE 7-3 The worst case power requirement for the system IC's

Device	$I_{CC}(ma)@5v$
(1) 74LS283	15.0
(2) 74LS175	30.0
(1) 74LS193	15.0
(2) 74LS112	16.0
(1) 74LS85	8.0
(2) 74LS32	19.6
(2) 74LS10	6.6
(1) 74LS08	8.8
(1) 7404 (Std)	33.0
(1) 74LS00	4.4
TOTAL	159 ma worst case
or $\simeq 0.75$ watts	

with an OVER-VOLTAGE-PROTECT (OVP) feature to protect the system devices in the event of a power supply regulator failure.

7-16 CONTROL AND DISPLAY

One more important concept related to any digital system is to build in some way to debug the initial system. The bare essentials of a built-in debugging system should include:

(1) The ability to "single-step" the clock.
(2) A visual display of the PRESENT STATE and the NEXT STATE variables.
(3) Manual control over the inputs.
(4) A visual display of the outputs.

With these control and display (C and D) features you can completely single-step check your systems and detect and correct logic errors and faulty circuits. Having control over the inputs and PRESENT and NEXT STATES presented in a visual display allows you to select a PRESENT STATE and set up the branching conditions for this state, and then immediately check to see if the proper NEXT STATE is displayed. If not, the "bits in error" (the incorrect outputs of the NEXT STATE DECODER) can be traced back to the source of the problem and fixed without finding out after the clock pulse that you had an error. During this phase of checkout a colored pencil should be used to trace out *all* possible paths of the

MDS diagram. A special decoder like the one shown in Figure 7-47 is required for displaying the NEXT STATE of a JK Flip-Flop. These features can be built up on a pluggable module that can be removed after checkout.

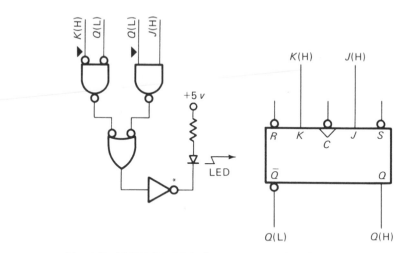

Fig. 7-47. NEXT STATE indicator for a JK Flip-Flop.

Next the "at speed tests" or "on the fly checkout" should be carried out. It is during this phase of system debug that timing tolerances are checked and documented, the outputs are checked for glitches, and the system's ground system is checked. Recovery from power transients and noise tolerance is documented. Then the system should be "heat-cycled" within the specified limits of the devices used. Before doing this, carefully consider the manufacturer's specifications regarding the temperature range limits to avoid "baking in" failures from exceeding the temperature limitations. Power cycle your system while heat cycling. It is a proven fact that most IC failures occur during the initial phases of operation; and heat and power cycling greatly increase the precipitation rate of these hidden frailties. By doing so, field debugging can be reduced. There are several good books written on reliability and the Mean Time–Between Failure (MTBF); those interested should consult these for further study.

Further, several equipment manufacturers do provide highly developed STATE ANALYZERS for enhancing your dynamic debug capabilities. Several of these important tools are shown in Figure 7-48. These analyzers are designed specifically to log and document the sequential behavior of a synchronous sequential machine while it is running at speed. Each has interesting "trapping" and delayed starting features, all added to make your system debug easier.

One final note: Even though the system debug concepts have been delayed until last, this in no way should be construed as the order of their importance. For

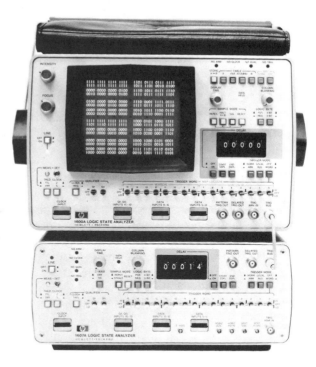

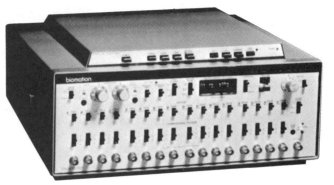

Fig. 7-48. Several commercial sequential logic analyzers.

in fact, one of your first considerations should be: "How am I going to check this system, and more importantly, how can I design the system such that check-out can be carried out easily?"

7-17 CONCEPTS RELATED TO THE USE OF CONDITIONAL OUTPUTS

Up to this point little has been said regarding the application and use of CONDITIONAL OUTPUTS. However, it has been mentioned that conditional outputs are those generated with an input dependency. Further, it was pointed out that this dependency *should not* be related to any asynchronous variable, but nothing has been said related to the advantages or disadvantages of conditional outputs. Thus an illustrative example, given shortly, utilizes the conditional output to an apparent advantage. The apparent advantage stems from the fact that using conditional outputs allows the designer to implement this example design using a seven state machine. On the other hand, had a strict Moore machine been used utilizing "immediate outputs," 13 states would have been required to implement the *same algorithm*. The crux of the question is: "Did the six states saved really constitute a significant savings in the overall hardware costs? Or was a trade-off made beween NEXT STATE DECODER hardware and OUTPUT DECODER hardware?" Instinctively a state reduction seems to result in an overall hardware reduction in NEXT STATE DECODER hardware, and this is reasonably true, but not absolutely true in every case. There are cases when the addition of an extra state variable allows for a more optimal state assignment that ultimately results in a more minimal NEXT STATE DECODER, even though an extra Flip-Flop is used. However, adding an extra state variable generally increases the complexity of the OUTPUT DECODER hardware because of the extra bit added. This same sort of increased complexity is prevalent when CONDITIONAL OUTPUTS are defined because each requires extra decoding. Thus it is difficult to make a completely general statement as to which is best. Therefore, the philosophy adopted is that CONDITIONAL OUTPUTS are used when their use points to one of the following advantages or conditions:

(1) When an output is most definitely dependent on a *synchronous* input;
(2) If states can be saved without significantly increasing logic complexity;
(3) If the system's clarity, speed, or power is enhanced.

Otherwise, use IMMEDIATE OUTPUTS. Thus you have a mixed system and, if done properly, the best of both worlds. The following example is offered to help you further your understanding of the application of CONDITIONAL OUTPUT and you will be asked to carry out some detailed studies related to this problem. STUDY IT CAREFULLY.

EXAMPLE 7-6: The Pop Machine Revisited

After the initial evaluation of the prototype pop machine control systems, it was felt that some modifications should be made in the COIN RECEIVER, CHANGER, and POP DROP as well as the sequential behavior of the system controller. These modifications would enhance the customer relations and system acceptability.

The prevailing philosophy is to develop a system that is to give the pop-buying customer the best possible treatment under system failure conditions (jammed pop or coin mechanisms), yet protect the interest of the vending machine company. In short, this system has the following specifications:

(1) The system should return the customer's money if the pop drop becomes jammed during a transaction, then proceed to an OUT OF ORDER condition.

(2) The system should allow no coins to enter the machine if the machine is out of pop or in process of a transaction.

(3) If the coin changer jams or runs low on returnable coins, the system is to go into a USE CORRECT CHANGE ONLY mode of operation but remain operational until the system restores itself or an attendant brings the system back.

(4) If the customer has more money in the machine than necessary and the coin changer jams, the system should revert to the USE CORRECT CHANGE ONLY mode and attempt to give the customer a pop. If the pop drop jams under this condition, the system is to revert to an OUT OF ORDER mode, at which time the customer is obliged to contact the vending machine owner for a refund. Under this condition the system should "load" and hold all registers constant so the attendant can determine exactly what he owes the customer.

These modifications require only a slight change in the functional partition. These are:

(1) A means of clamping and storing compare value (0) ($CV=0$) such that the csutomer's money can be returned if the pop drop is jammed. (Use a Flip-Flop driving open collector gate to clamp the compare value. Maybe a cleaner approach would be to use a four-wide 2-to-1 MUX (74LS157).)

(2) A means of storing the USE CORRECT CHANGE MODE. Another Flip-Flop that can be RESET by the coin changer and SET by the system controller.

(3) A means of driving the OUT OF ORDER light and USE CORRECT CHANGE ONLY light.

The following modifications are to be made on the COIN RECEIVER updating it to the FP Model 1971-A:

(1) The manual coin release lever is to be removed from customer access and made available only to the attendant.

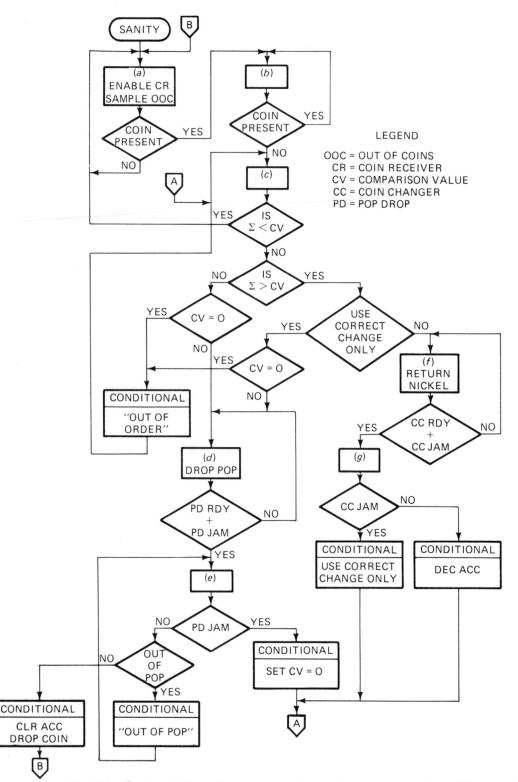

Fig. 7-49. The detailed flow diagram for the minimal cheat system controller utilizing conditional outputs.

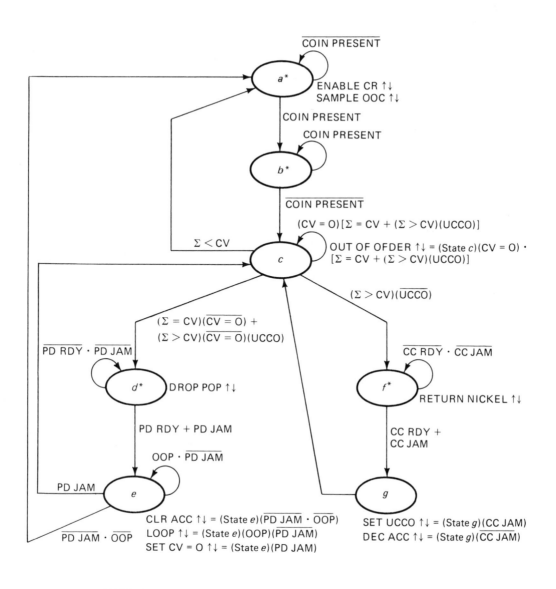

COIN PRESENT ——

a^*

ENABLE CR ↑↓
SAMPLE OOC ↑↓

COIN PRESENT

COIN PRESENT

b^*

——COIN PRESENT

$(CV = O)[\Sigma = CV + (\Sigma > CV)(UCCO)]$

OUT OF ORDER ↑↓ = (State c)(CV = O) ·
$[\Sigma = CV + (\Sigma > CV)(UCCO)]$

$\Sigma < CV$

c

$(\Sigma > CV)(\overline{UCCO})$

$(\Sigma = CV)(\overline{CV = O}) +$
$(\Sigma > CV)(\overline{CV = O})(UCCO)$

$\overline{PD\ RDY} \cdot \overline{PD\ JAM}$

d^* DROP POP ↑↓

$\overline{CC\ RDY} \cdot \overline{CC\ JAM}$

f^*

RETURN NICKEL ↑↓

PD RDY + PD JAM

OOP · $\overline{PD\ JAM}$

CC RDY +
CC JAM

PD JAM

e

g

$\overline{PD\ JAM} \cdot \overline{OOP}$

CLR ACC ↑↓ = (State e)($\overline{PD\ JAM} \cdot \overline{OOP}$)
LOOP ↑↓ = (State e)(OOP)($\overline{PD\ JAM}$)
SET CV = O ↑↓ = (State e)(PD JAM)

SET UCCO ↑↓ = (State g)(CC JAM)
DEC ACC ↑↓ = (State g)($\overline{CC\ JAM}$)

LEGEND

```
 OOC = OUT OF COINS
  CR = COIN RECEIVER
  CV = COMPARISION VALUE
UCCO = USE CORRECT CHANGE ONLY
  CC = COIN CHANGER
  PD = POP DROP
 OOP = OUT OF POP
LOOP = LIGHT OUT OF POP
```

Fig. 7-50. The minimal cheat system controller MDS diagram utilizing conditional outputs.

(2) A special input ENABLE *CR*(L) is to be added that will ENABLE or DISABLE the coin receiver. If disabled, the coin receiver will reject all coins to the coin return slot.

Both the Model CC-1971 coin change and the Model PD-1971 pop drop have been updated to the *A* models. The update on the CC-1971-A provides the system controller with three signals (CC READY(H), CC JAM(H), and OUT OF COINS(L)). These internal modes now allow the system controller to ascertain the status of the changer. CC READY and CC JAM are mutually exclusive, meaning that the changer will return with *one or the other* after being stimulated. If the number of nickels left is ≤ 15, the OUT OF COINS(L) signal will become ASSERTED until more nickels are received. This OUT OF COINS signal will be valid at the time CC READY or CC JAM becomes ASSERTED. The model PD-1971-A pop drop system operates identical to the coin changer and has the following signals defined: PD READY(H), PD JAM(H), and OUT OF POP(L) (valid at time of PD READY or PD JAM).

Figures 7-49 and 7-50 illustrate how the new updated "minimal cheat" system is to work. These figures also illustrate the application of CONDITIONAL OUTPUT. The completion of this system is left as an exercise. Study it closely for it is intended that you are to find a better way of providing the same functions.

7-18 SUMMARY

It is interesting to note that the pop machine type of problems just covered illustrate many typical design considerations related to digital control problems. Further, it is interesting to note that the method of attack presented rendered solutions which are deceptively simple, considering the relative complexity of the control problem. Along with this simplicity, the solution methods illustrate the "system controller" concept, asynchronous input handling, state assignment concepts, and gate/Flip-Flop level implementation using VEM's, presenting a fairly well-rounded illustration.

Normally the pop machine type of control problem is thought of as one best solved by a microprocessor-based controller. However, in view of the solutions presented here, it is not totally clear at this time that a microprocessor could do the job better and cheaper, even over a simple SSI implementation. Considering some of the methods of implementations using standard off-the-shelf MSI devices, which are presented in the next two chapters, it becomes even more unclear.

Because of this it is important that you think through your design requirements thoroughly. It may or may not be a microprocessor that will provide the best solution at the lowest cost. Therefore, develop several alternative solutions, then make a value judgment as to which of these alternatives is best and be able to defend your choice and proceed from this point of strength. Unless future applications and cost considerations warrant it, avoid "driving a carpet tack with a twenty pound sledge hammer" type of design.

It was mentioned above that you should develop alternative solutions and this requires extra time, which undoubtedly will be in short supply. Therefore, it is advisable that you have a reasonably pat attack to solving problems in order that you can minimize this time. Hopefully, that is what you have developed during your studies in this chapter. *However, whatever your attack, keep your documentation package clean, neat, and up-to-date. It will pay off in the long run.*

BIBLIOGRAPHY

1. BENTLEY, JAMES H. "The Foolproof Way to Sequencer Design. *Electronic Design*, **10** (1973).

2. BERARU, J. Map Entry Method for Sequential Counter Logic. *Electro-Technology*, 51–52 (1968).

3. BERNDT, HELMUT. Functional Microprogramming as a Logic Design Aid. *IEEE Trans. Computers*, C-19, No. 10 (1970), 902–907.

4. BLAKESLEE, THOMAS R. *Digital Design with Standard MSI and LSI*. New York: Wiley, 1975.

5. BOND, JOHN. Interfacing Peripheral Devices with Minicomputers. *EDN*, December 5, 1973.

6. BOOTH, TAYLOR L. *Digital Networks and Computer Systems*. New York: Wiley, 1971.

7. CHANEY, T. J., LITTLEFIELD, W. M., and ORNSTEIN, S. M. "Beware the Synchronizer," in Digest of Papers of the Six Annual IEEE Computer Society International Conference, San Francisco, California, September, 1972, 317–319.

8. CLARE, CHRISTOPER R. *Designing Logic Systems Using State Machines*. New York: McGraw-Hill, 1973.

9. CRISCIMAGNA, TONY N. Start Logic Design with Flow Diagram. *Electronic Design*, **25** (1971), 56–59.

10. GOODMAN, S. E., and HEDETNIEMI, S. T. *Introduction to the Design and Analysis of Algorithms*. New York: McGraw-Hill, 1977.

11. HILL, FREDRICK J., and PETERSEN, GERALD R. *Introduction to Switching Theory and Logical Design*. New York: Wiley, 1974.

12. KNUTH, DONALD E. *The Art of Computer Programming*. Menlo Park, Calif.: Addison-Wesley, 1968.

13. KOHAVI, Z. *Switching and Finite Automata Theory*. New York: McGraw-Hill, 1970.

14. LANGDON, GLEN G., JR. *Logic Design: A Review of Theory and Practice*. New York: Academic, 1974.

15. RHYNE, V. THOMAS. *Fundamentals of Digital Systems Design*. Englewood Cliffs, N.J.: Prentice-Hall, 1973.

16. RICHARDS, CHARLES L. An Easy Way to Design Complex Program Controllers. *Electronics*, Feb. 1 (1973), 107–113.

17. TIEN, PAUL S. Sequential Counter Design Techniques. *Computer Design*, **10**, No. 2 (1971), 49–56.

18. VANDLING, G. C., and WALDECKER, D. E. The Microprogram Technique for Digital Logic Design. *Computer Design*, **8**, No. 8 (1969), 44–51.

PROBLEMS AND EXERCISES

Note to Instructor and Students

In order to fully utilize the material presented in this chapter, considerable system level design should be carried out. However, system design requires a good deal of close communication between those who prepare systems specifications and those who are trying to implement these same specifications. Because of the obvious gap between you and myself (author), something else must be done. Therefore, the author has provided an outlined list of system level design projects with broad specifications rather than a voluminous list of operation criteria. By doing this you and your instructor are allowed to work out and negotiate the actual operation specifications as it is done in a real-life engineering atmosphere. Keep in mind that it is important that all your work, specifications included, be well documented and done in a neat and well-ordered fashion.

Note: The reader should be familiar with the information in Sections 7-1 through 7-7 before starting the following exercises.

7-1. Suppose you were asked to design a reaction timer that is to be designed to generate an output (GO) (light an LED) at some random period of time after a START button is pressed. Then measure (and display) the time interval between the issuance of the signal GO and the actuation of the human reaction switch RACT.

    Exercise: From this sketchy information, develop a basic block diagram and first-cut flow diagram defining the basic operation of this system as you see it. Assume ± 0.1 msec to be the timing accuracy desired. (Watch the bouncing switches.)

7-2. Taking the information developed in Problem 7-1, develop a bare-bones block diagram and first-cut flow diagram defining a digital tug-of-war. The system is to work similar to the reaction time, but in this case the contestant who responds first to the random GO light moves an LED indicator one place in his direction. A possible display could be a line of eleven LED's with the center LED lit by RESET. Then as a player wins, he moves the lit LED one place in his direction. Play is to continue until one player moves the lit LED all the way to his end. At this time "winner" signal is generated.

    Exercise: Be as ingenious as you like but be practical in defining the bare-bones block and first-cut flow diagrams.

7-3. Carry out all steps necessary to design a first-cut flow diagram (algorithm) and bare-bones block diagram for controlled sequence generator. This sequence generator is to reset itself upon the power-up condition. It is then to wait until it receives the START SEQUENCE input STRTS(L) (asynchronous). It is then to cause the three-bit output to sequence from $000 \rightarrow 001 \rightarrow 011 \rightarrow 010$ at a 1 KHz rate, then stop and wait for the EXECUTE input to be ASSERTED (EX(H)) at which time it will reset to 011 and sequence at a 100 Hz rate from $011 \rightarrow 100 \rightarrow 101$ and stop and wait for the FIN(L) input at which time it will sequence from $101 \rightarrow 111 \rightarrow 110 \rightarrow 000$ at a 10 Hz rate and stop, waiting to START the next round of sequence.

7-4. Design a square wave duty cycle discriminator system controlled by a system controller. This system is to measure the time difference between the alternate low and high portions of a low frequency quasi square wave signal (0.1 to 100 Hz). You are to carry out all steps for this design, including documentation. You can expect a variation in duty cycle of up to ±90%. In other words, the ratio of Hightime/Low-time can vary from 9/1 to 1/9. Your system is to be controlled by four signals generated by switches START(L), X(H), Y(H), RESET(L). The operation is to be as follows:

RESET(L): initializes the system
START(L): system is to remain in the initial state until START is received.

X	Y	Operation Time difference measurements should be accurate to ±0.1 msec
0	0	Take one difference latch display and return to initial state and wait for START.
0	1	Measure only high portion of waveform Latch Display and return to initial state and wait for START.
1	0	Measure only low portion of waveform latch display and return to initial state and wait for START.
1	1	Continuously update display with difference measure.

Hint: Develop a stable oscillator (crystal controlled), and have your system controller control the cascade of pre-setable modulo 10 up/down counters that directly drive seven segment (displays) (TIL 308) for direct readout of the time difference. See Texas Instruments optoelectronics data book for data related to the TIL 308 display. *Watch 1's and 0's catching problem when using up/down counters.*

7-5. Carry out all design steps necessary to design a first-cut flow diagram and bare-bones block diagram for an interface between an eight-bit microcomputer system and a twelve-bit A/D as shown in Figure P7-1.

7.6. Carry out the necessary steps to design a first-cut flow diagram (fundamental algorithm) and bare-bones block diagram for a controller and system that will ADD two four-bit unsigned binary numbers ($B_3B_2B_1B_0$ and $A_3A_2A_1A_0$) which are stored in two separate *four-bit PIPO's*. You are given *one* single-bit full-adder (see Figure 4-6) and the results of the addition are to be stored in a five-bit SIPO. Your system should RESET itself upon power-up and is to initiate its operation when it receives the START(L) signal (asynchronous input) which indicates both four-bit PIPO's are loaded. Upon completion of the serial addition your system is to issue ANSRDY(L) and hold this condition until the next START(L) command.

7-7. Carry out the necessary design steps to design a first-cut flow diagram and bare-bones block diagram for a system that will perform a *binary to NBCD* conversion using the Shift and ADD six (0110) if the present four binary bits comprise a number greater than 1001 (9). Your system should be designed such that it will facilitate a twelve-bit binary to NBCD conversion initiating its operation with START(H) (asynchronous) and signal its completion with BCDRDY(L). Assume the binary number to be converted is stored in PISO register. Assume that you can control the serial shift operation of this register. (*Hint:* Start by shifting in four-bits. Examine these to determine if value > 1001. If it is, add 0110 (use an SN74283) and store and pass the carry, and repeat until the BCD equivalent is stored in four-bit PIPO's.)

7-8. Refer back to Problem 7-1. Then carry out the design steps necessary to design the functional partition and detailed flow diagram. Include timing diagrams if necessary.

7-9. Refer back to Problem 7-2. Then carry out the design steps necessary to design the functional partition and detailed flow diagram. Include timing diagrams if necessary.

7-10. Refer back to Problem 7-3. Then carry out the design steps necessary to design the functional partition and detailed flow diagram. Include timing diagrams if necessary.

7-11. Refer back to Problem 7-4. Then carry out the design steps necessary to design the functional partition and detailed flow diagram. Include timing diagrams if necessary.

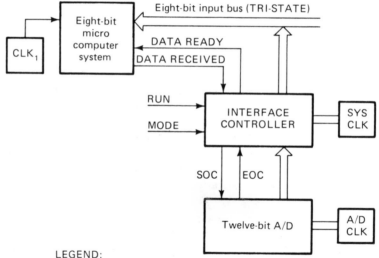

LEGEND:

Run: An input from a panel switch that controls the start and stop of data transfers.

Mode: An input from a panel switch that controls the input word format. If mode is high only the eirght least significant bits are sent in. If mode is low, the four most significant bits are sent in first, followed by the eight least significant bits.

SOC: Is the command to start a conversion.

EOC: Is the signal back from the A/D indicating a conversion is complete.

DATAREADY: Is the signal that notifies the micro computer system that data is *READY to be put* on the input bus (TRI-STATE).

DATARECEIVED: Is the signal from the micro computer indicating that data has been read in (proceed).

Note: All systems operate on different CLOCKS.

Fig. P7-1.

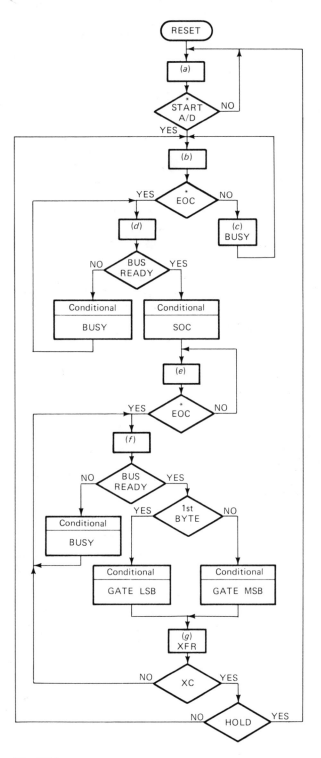

Fig. P7-2.

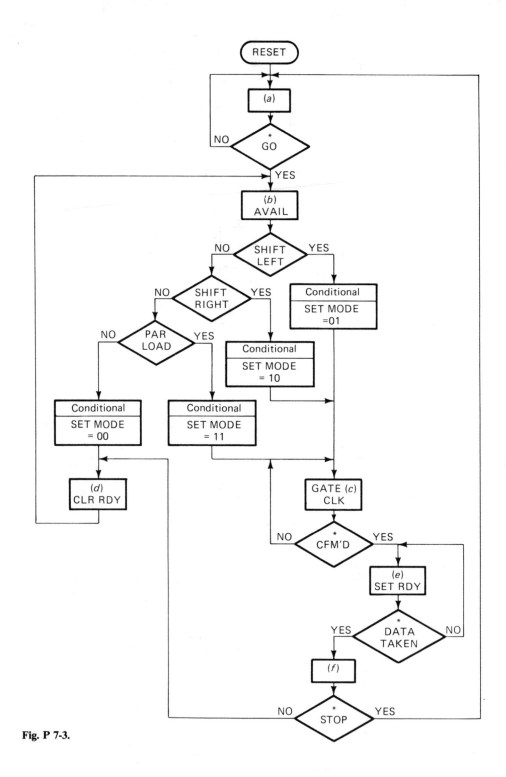

Fig. P 7-3.

7-12. Refer back to Problem 7-5. Then carry out the design steps necessary to design the functional partition and detailed flow diagram. Include timing diagrams if necessary.

7-13. Refer back to Problem 7-6. Then carry out the design steps necessary to design the functional partition and detailed flow diagram. Include timing diagrams if necessary.

7-14. Refer back to Problem 7-7. Then carry out the design steps necessary to design the functional partition and detailed flow diagram. Include timing diagrams if necessary.

7-15. Given the detailed flow diagram shown in Figure P7-2, develop the MDS diagram. Make certain that the MDS diagram is fully documented.

7-16. Repeat Problem 7-15 for the flow diagram shown in Figure P7-3.

7-17. Refer back to Problem 7-8, then carry out the conversion of the detailed flow diagram to the MDS diagram.

7-18. Refer back to Problem 7-9, then carry out the conversion of the detailed flow diagram to the MDS diagram.

7-19. Refer back to Problem 7-10, then carry out the conversion of the detailed flow diagram to the MDS diagram.

7-20. Refer back to Problem 7-11, then carry out the conversion of the detailed flow diagram to the MDS diagram.

7-21. Refer back to Problem 7-12, then carry out the conversion of the detailed flow diagram to the MDS diagram.

7-22. Refer back to Problem 7-13, then carry out the conversion of the detailed flow diagram to the MDS diagram.

7-23. Refer back to Problem 7-14, then carry out the conversion of the detailed flow diagram to the MDS diagram.

7-24. (a) Make a state assignment for the state diagram shown in Figure 7-31.
(b) Plot and reduce the next state maps using MEV's, thus deriving the next state decoder logic for a D Flip-Flop implementation.
(c) Convert the next state map to JK maps. Reduce and compare with results obtained in (b).
(d) Complete the system shown in Figure 7-28.

7-25. *The following problem does not necessarily illustrate the system controller concept which is presently being stressed. However, it is inserted here to illustrate the use of flow and MDS diagrams for conventional sequential designs: It is intended that this problem will give you a sufficient start in using MEV technique for sequential circuit design when the circuit has more than one input variable. Further, it is intended that you be familiar with the information related to MEV's and sequential design set forth in Section 7-12.*
(a) Design the flow and MDS diagram for the sequential system defined as:

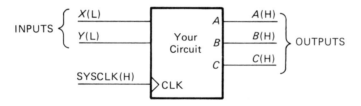

Inputs X and Y are asynchronous inputs that control the output sequence on outputs A, B, and C according to the following table:

Seq Control		ABC Sequence*
X	Y	
0	0	Stays in state 0
0	1	↱0→1→2→3→4→5 ↴
1	0	↱0←1←3←5←7↴
1	1	↱0←2←4←6↴

*The decimal digits represent the minterm number represented by the outputs.

Note: That the only time the circuit is to check for SEQ control changes is in state 0.
(b) Make an appropriate state assignment for your state diagram and develop the next state maps using MEV technique. Then develop the JK maps.

7-26. Figures P7-4 through P7-10 are typical MDS diagrams derived for a variety of controller applications.

Exercise: For each of these MDS diagrams, make a state assignment and plot and reduce the next state maps. Convert these maps to JK maps, then plot and reduce the output maps for each of the MDS diagrams.
(a) Figure P7-4.
(b) Figure P7-5.
(c) Figure P7-6.
(d) Figure P7-7.
(e) Figure P7-8.
(f) Figure P7-9.
(g) Figure P7-10.

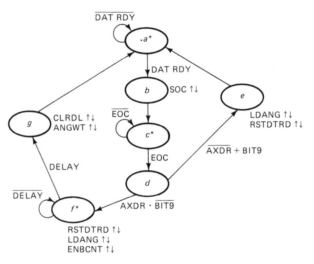

Fig. P 7-4.

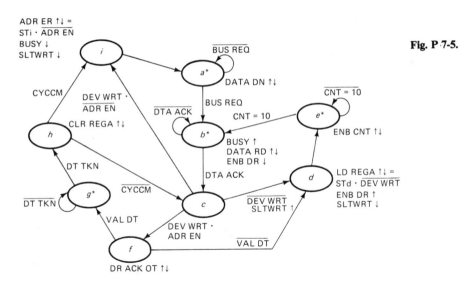

Fig. P 7-5.

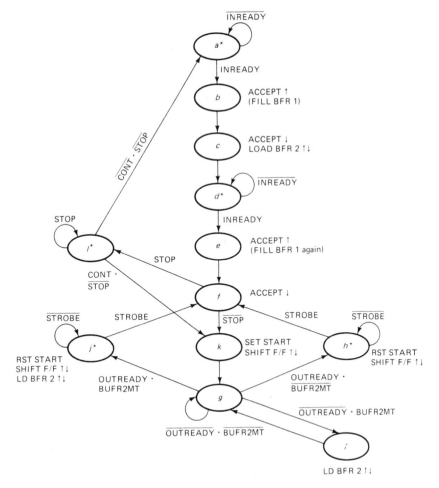

Fig. P 7-6.

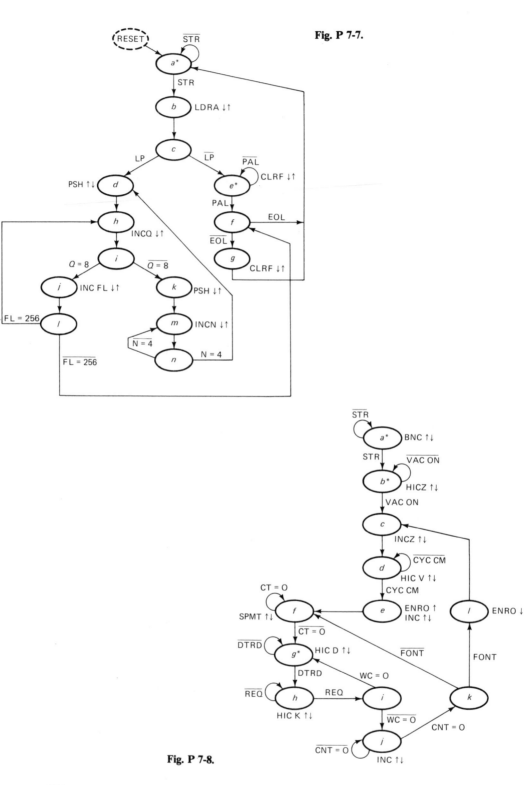

Fig. P 7-7.

Fig. P 7-8.

Fig. P 7-9.

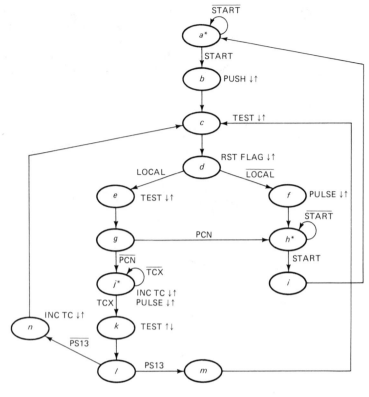

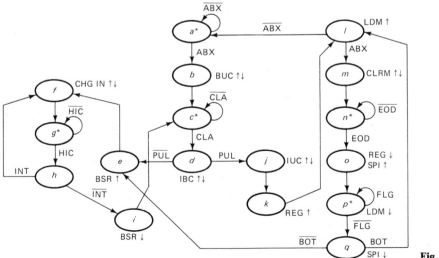

Fig. P 7-10.

7-27. Refer to Problem 6-44, then consider the two state diagrams shown in Figure P7-11. Notice that the input for one machine is defined as the output of the other machine and vice versa, which we have defined as a "Handshake." Further, note that the state variables of these two machines are to drive the seven segment display. Explain the operation of these "linked" machines as a seven segment drive.

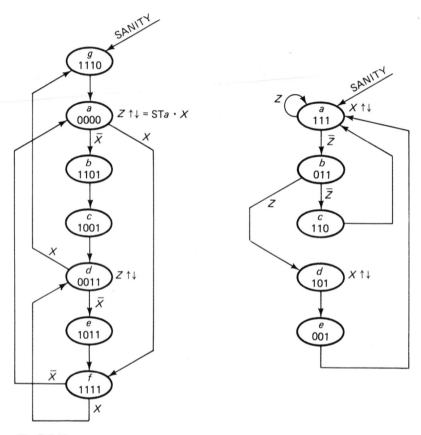

Fig. P 7-11.

Note: The following "idea" problems are system level design problems—the ones requiring the aforementioned negotiation. Endeavor to make your designs as complete as possible and at the same time keep your documentation neat and up to date.

7-28. Carry out the steps necessary to design a four-way traffic light controller, one that will handle traffic flow at high rates in any of four directions. Associate a left turn with all four directions as well as a pedestrian crosswalk switch.

7-29. Carry out the steps necessary to design a system controller that controls the elevator for a seven-story building. Be as sophisticated as you like, but keep your system .clean and straightforward. Basically what your controller is to do is respond to floor call switches and in-car floor select switches and determining where to go next.

7-30. You are to design a special purpose sub-system to a larger system. The purpose of your system is to accept two binary numbers and deliver their product. Number A is delivered to your system parallel form, four bits wide. Number B is delivered to your system in serial form, LSB first; the length of number B (number of bits) is variable. Your system is to produce the product in serial form.

The major system delivers to your system the signal PARLDA(H), which states that the four-bit number A is available on a four-bit bus. Four to ten clock periods later, the major system delivers the signal SERLDB(H), which states that the serial data B will be available on the next clock period. Simultaneously with the final serial data bit, the major system delivers the signal SEREND(H), which states that the final serial data bit is now being transmitted. If the sequence of these signals is in error, your system should reset. The signals from the major controller have exactly the same period as the clock for your system. However, their phase relationship to the clock is unknown and variable. Thus, all signals from the major controller must be assumed asynchronous. The parallel data A will be valid on the bus from the time PARLDA is asserted until after SERLDB is deasserted.

7-31. Carry out the necessary steps to design a special controller and system that is to control the drive circuit for a stepping motor. This controller is to receive a 16-bit word from a computer bus when it sees SDSEL(L) and RDS(L) ASSERTED. The 16-bit word is to be broken into two segments as shown in Figure P7-12.

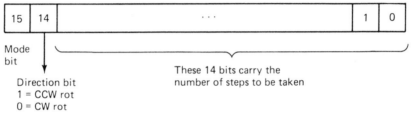

Fig. P 7-12.

If the mode bit = 1, the system controller is to step (at 100 step/sec) the stepping motor continuously in the CCW direction until a mechanical limit switch is activated then stop for 0.1 sec, then start stepping the motor at a 100 step/sec rate in the CW direction until the exact number of steps specified by the least significant 14 bits. If the mode bit = 0, the system controller is to step the stepping motor from its present position in the direction specified by the direction bit until either limit switch has been reached or the step number is completed, then stop.

7-32. Carry out the necessary steps for the design of the controller and system for a high speed UART (Universal Asynchronous Receiver and Transmitter). This system should have operation similar to the slow speed integrated circuit UART but it must be able to send and receive serial data at a 1 MHz rate. Carry out all design steps.

7-33. Figures P7-13 and P7-14 illustrate a partial functional partition and control flow diagram of a system that will perform a multiplication of two eight-bit binary numbers. Your task is to complete the design, including the system controller. Then graphically illustrate how the system functions, using several examples. Make certain your design is neatly drawn and documented. Note that this is an excellent laboratory exercise. Try for high speed operation.

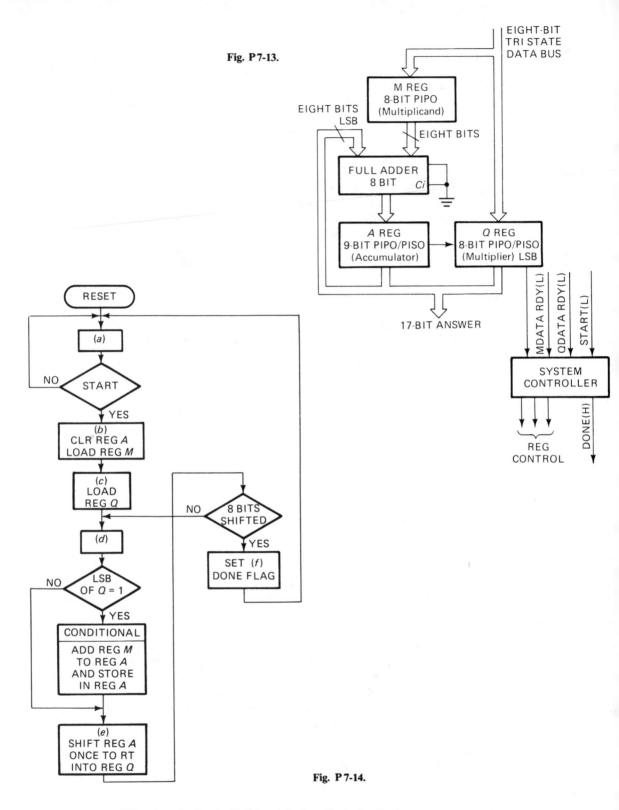

Fig. P 7-13.

EIGHT-BIT
TRI STATE
DATA BUS

M REG
8-BIT PIPO
(Multiplicand)

EIGHT BITS
LSB

EIGHT BITS

FULL ADDER
8 BIT C_i

A REG
9-BIT PIPO/PISO
(Accumulator)

Q REG
8-BIT PIPO/PISO
(Multiplier) LSB

17-BIT ANSWER

MDATA RDY(L)
QDATA RDY(L)
START(L)

SYSTEM
CONTROLLER

REG
CONTROL

DONE(H)

RESET

(a)

START
NO
YES

(b)
CLR REG A
LOAD REG M

(c)
LOAD
REG Q

(d)

LSB
OF Q = 1
NO
YES

CONDITIONAL
ADD REG M
TO REG A
AND STORE
IN REG A

(e)
SHIFT REG A
ONCE TO RT
INTO REG Q

8 BITS
SHIFTED
NO
YES

SET (f)
DONE FLAG

Fig. P 7-14.

7-34. The Teletypewriter (TTY)* (or the electronic equivalent thereof) is the most commonly used computer terminal. It consists of a keyboard and a typing element. It differs from a normal typewriter in that when a key is depressed, an electronic digital code is generated as output, and the typing element can be controlled remotely by similar digital input. Some of these devices are built such that a key depression automatically (by an internal mechanism or circuit) results in the *typing* of the corresponding character. These are sometimes termed as being "half duplex" in operation. Others are built with the keyboard and typing element as logically separate devices. In them a key stroke only generates the corresponding digital output. They are considered "full duplex" devices. Still others are switchable between half and full duplex. (Note that in a half duplex teletypewriter, the typing element has two input sources; the keyboard and the externally generated digital codes.)

TTY input and output lines each consist of a single signal line that carries the digital character codes in a serial fashion. The character coding most commonly used in computer terminals is called ASCII (American Standard Code for Information Interchange) wherein each character is encoded as seven information bits plus one parity bit, for a total of eight bits per character.

A list of the codes and their corresponding meanings is given in Chapter 1. Notice that there are a number of codes besides those used for letters, numbers, and other common symbols. These are nonprinting and have been assigned meanings not germane to the use of teletypewriters with computers. Many teletypewriters do not even accommodate all of the printable characters due to reasons of economy, but the full ASCII coding scheme is still employed.

In order to facilitate recognition of the serially encoded ASCII characters, it is necessary to be able to determine the proper time at which to sample the signal line. As the use of a single line precludes the possibility of clocking the data on an independent line, there are only two remaining possible methods. (1) A self clocked signal encoding could be utilized, or (2) a fixed data rate could be imposed with a special "start" signal for synchronization of the receiver. The latter is used for teletypewriters, and has the conventions as described in the following:

When the signal line is idle, it will remain in the high state. Preceding the transmission of an ASCII character code, the line is dropped to LOW for a period of 1/110 of a second. Immediately following in time will appear the eight-bits of ASCII code, 1/110 of second for each bit, high for a 1 value and low for a 0. (The parity bit is the last to appear.) Then the line will return to high for at least 1/110 of a second periods. The next character can then be initiated at any following instant, repeating a similar cycle.

Figure P-7-15 shows the format for both signals coming *from* the TTY keyboard and going *to* the typing element. The transmission of an ASCII character is asynchronous in that it may begin at any instant during the time when the line is idle. However, once begun, as announced by the dropping of the line to low, the information bits appear at fixed intervals of time. This presupposes the requirement that the receiving device must be able to keep time or generate its own clock that can be initialized at the proper instant and then measure out current 1/110 of a second intervals during the time when the character bits are present.

It would be very difficult to assure that the "receiver" clock has identically the same frequency as the "sender" clock. However, since characters are short (only eight bits) and

---

*This exercise will possibly require special help from your instructor.

the receiver is resynchronized (its clock is initialized) for each character, there could be somewhat greater than 5% disparity in clock frequencies before recognition would be impaired. Receiver circuits must be "smart" enough to account for this possible (and probable) disparity, and be designed so as to sample or interpret the information being transmittedd at the most efficacious instants.

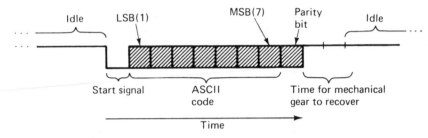

Fig. P 7-15. The TTY signal format.

There are several points which might be noted at this time: (1) Teletypewriters of the breed described can transmit or receive up to ten characters per second (one start bit, eight information bits including parity, and two end bits or a total of 11 bits per character, sent serially at a rate of 110 bits per second). (2) On a full duplex device the output line could be tied to the input line, making it virtually half duplex in operation. (3) Since the two high's following each character are chiefly for mechanical "recovery" time, on *electronic* TTY equivalents they need not both be present. However, for compatability sake, these electronic TTY's use the same scheme when running at normal TTY rates. There is no inherent reason why these electronic terminals could not run at faster rates than mechanical TTY's (especially when transmission is originated by a computer), and most are switchable to higher data rates. (Up to about 4800 bits per second is common.) When running at these rates most devices use conventions identical to those described earlier except that only one termination bit is used and the clocking is set to a faster (mutually agreed upon) rate.

Exercise: Your assignment is to design a TTY receiver. That is, (1) you are to design and build a circuit that can receive the serial representation for ASCII characters as generated by a teletypewriter keyboard; (2) display the ASCII code on a light panel; and (3) then at the push of a button transmit that character back to the printing element of the TTY.

7-35. You are to design a data-logging system given a 12-bit analog to digital (A/D) converter and small four-track digital magnetic tape recorder. The A/D generates a 12-bit parallel word whose binary weight is equivalent to the value of the analog voltage at its input when a START-OF-CONVERSION (SOC) pulse (≥ 1 μsec) is applied to it. When the conversion is through (approximately 100 μsec after SOC), the A/D will issue a 1 μsec $\pm 10\%$ pulse called END-OF-CONVERSION (EOC). The 12-bit data word will be stable at the same time as the rising-edge of EOC.

The small four-track tape unit is an incremental transport that must be commanded to write with a positive going pulse $\geq$ 50 μsec in length (WRT). The input data to be recorded must be held stable for 10 μsec before the rising-edge of WRT. When the data has been recorded and the tape has moved to the next position, the tape unit will ASSERT an output named RDY. RDY will be dropped by the tape unit on the rising-edge of WRT. A special input (IRG) provided to the tape unit when a pulse ≥ 50 μsec in length is applied to this input. The tape unit will generate an *inter-record gap* that is 3/8 in. of blank tape. A *file gap* is 3/4 in. = 2 (3/8 in.) of blank tape. RDY will also go down at the rising-edge of IRG. The incremental tape speed is effectively 75 in./sec. Also, the tape unit provides two other output signals EOT (END OF TAPE) and BOT (BEGINNING OF TAPE). The BOT signal is an indication that the tape is in its starting position; the EOT signal is a signal that indicates there is approximately 3 in. of tape left and to stop recording as soon as possible. The packing density is 800 bpi (bits per inch).

You are to configure a system that will do a conversion once each 25 msec and record the data on the tape in the following format. After *initiation* (power up reset) and after a START COMMAND and with tape in position (BOT), a file gap with a file number starting with 0000 should be recorded, then another file gap. The data is to be recorded from here four bits at a time until 3000 four-bit words (RECORD) have been recorded. At this time an inter-record gap is to be generated, and then the word 1111 (EOR) character is to be recorded, and then another inter-record gap. After ten RECORDS have been recorded, a file gap is to be generated, then the file count word is recorded, then another file gap. This says in the center of each file gap sequence the next file number is to be recorded. This process is to continue until ten files have been recorded or the END OF TAPE (EOT) signal from the tape unit is received. Also, an outside world HALT signal can stop the recording process. Under all of these three termination conditions, a file gap is to be generated with the 1110 (EOF) character recorded and the tape is stopped. There is to be no restart feature.

Exercise: You are to carry out all steps of design through the generation of the MDS diagram.

SYSTEM CONTROLLERS UTILIZING
COMBINATIONAL MSI/LSI CIRCUITS

8-1 INTRODUCTION

Chapter 7 introduces the fundamentals of a structured approach to digital systems design. Further, the chapter covers the concepts of reducing the drudgery of table-making by introducing the MDS diagram and the map-entered-variable method for plotting the NEXT STATE MAPS. This is a quick and immediate transfer from the MDS diagrams to the NEXT STATE MAP, then to logic expressions to a SSI implementation. This chapter covers the concepts related to the use of combinational MSI and LSI circuits for both the NEXT STATE and OUTPUT DECODERS of a system controller. A study of the applicability of MSI decoders and multiplexers to system controller design is presented, followed by a study of the applicability of Read Only Memories (ROM's) and Programmable Logic Arrays (PLA's) to large scale system controllers.

Large scale system controllers are generally classified by the number of states in the state diagram. It is shown in Chapter 7 that system controllers with 16 or fewer states can be implemented in a straightforward manner with three or four variable maps and SSI logic. However, when the number of states exceeds 16, the mapping problem begins to become very tedious. Also, when the number of input variables increases, the design problem becomes more complex.

The design phases introduced in Chapter 7 are equally valid for the design concept stressed here. The major differences between using SSI and MSI or LSI devices is in the implementation methods used. However, in any implementation the following should be stressed:

(1) Keeping the design, implementation, and operation as conceptual and straightforward as possible.
(2) Minimizing the actual package (IC) count, thereby reducing the production cost and long-term maintenance to a minimum as well as lending redesign flexibility to the system.

Because of the devices used, the fundamental architectures appear to differ from the classic architectures discussed in Chapter 7. However, this is merely an illusion, for the input and output logic blocks still exist; but different circuits are used to implement these functional blocks. Because of this, the different hardware implementations that are allowed are referred to as system configurations rather than architectures.

For the purpose of illustrating the implementation differences of the various configurations to be studied, the pop vending machine problem is used as the source of reference for some of the configurations. It is true that this diagram does not meet large system qualifications, but its use illustrates the techniques that are used on more complex systems.

8-2 USING MSI DECODERS IN SYSTEM CONTROLLERS

The definition of the NEXT STATE and OUTPUT DECODER suggests the use of a MSI decoder for these functions. Consider some of the techniques that allow the use of these devices for the functions described above, with the idea of enhancing the controller cost and flexibility.

EXAMPLE 8-1: Consider the applicability of a 3-to-8 MSI integrated circuit decoder to the decoding functions called for by the seven-state prototype pop machine system controller shown in Figure 7-43.

First, it is necessary to develop a general system configuration for a system controller utilizing a MSI decoder as shown in Figure 8-1. As you view this figure, you should see that the MSI decoder can reduce the SSI logic required to implement both the NEXT STATE and OUTPUT DECODER. This savings is brought about by virtue of the fact that the MSI decoder has a single output that identifies each state of the machine. This *single* output can then be used to reduce the STATE VARIABLE dependency of the NEXT STATE and OUTPUT DECODER logic. This reduced dependency is recognized by remembering first that the NEXT STATE code is a function of both the *n*-STATE VARIABLES and the OUTSIDE WORLD INPUTS. Thus, if the *n*-NEXT STATE VARIABLES can be reduced to one variable, a sizable savings in hardware should be realized.

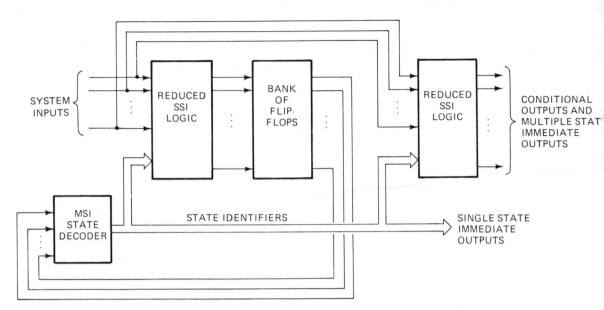

Fig. 8-1. A general system configuration for a system controller utilizing a MSI decoder.

Now, the same MDS diagram and state assignment that are used in Chapter 7 are used for this example (see Figure 8-2).

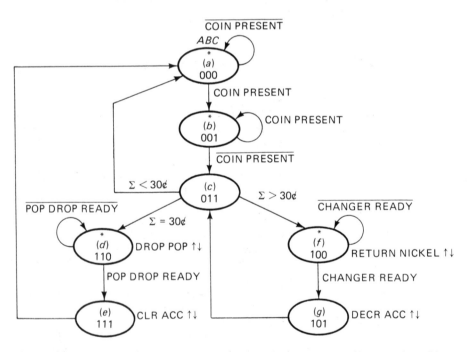

Fig. 8-2. The system controller MDS diagram for the prototype pop machine complete with a state assignment.

Step 1: Now use the NEXT STATE MAP for the JK implementation as shown in Figure 8-3.

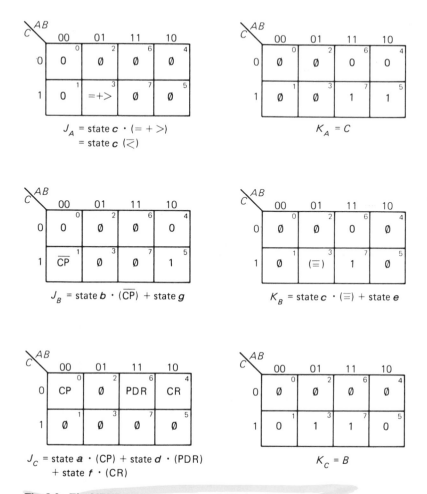

Fig. 8-3. The NEXT STATE maps for a MSI decoder and JK Flip-Flop implementation.

Figure 8-3 shows that rather than carrying out the map-reading process, which generally reduces the state variable dependency, you simply read out the MEV "anded" with the STATE IDENTIFIER (output of the decoder). Note further that all maps that can be reduced down to a single NEXT STATE VARIABLE are reduced and implemented directly (see K_A and K_C in Figure 8-3). For the completed implementation of the prototype system controller utilizing a 74LS138 decoder and a 74LS175 output holding register, see Figure 8-4.

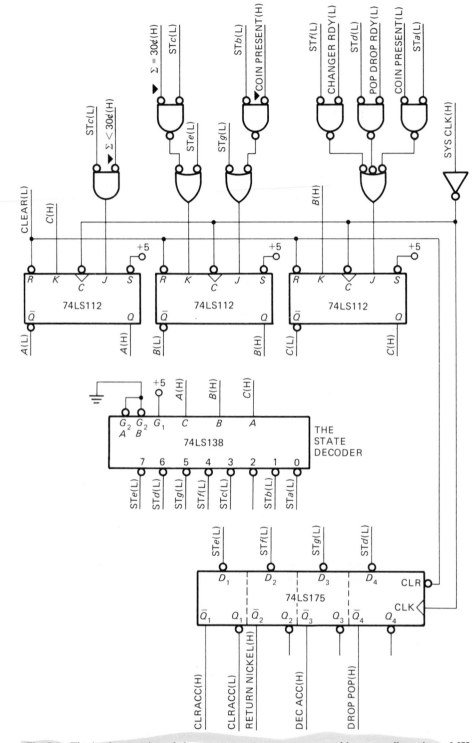

Fig. 8-4. The implementation of the seven-state prototype pop machine controller using a MSI Decoder.

8-3 USING MSI MULTIPLEXERS IN SYSTEM CONTROLLERS

In keeping with the philosophy set forth in Section 8-2, a set of multiplexers could be used in system controller implementations. Again a general system configuration similar to that for the decoder implementation must be established. This is referred to as the DIRECT-ADDRESSED-MULTIPLEXER-CONFIGURATION and is shown in Figure 8-5. A study of this configuration reveals that the next state variables are a function of both the present state of the machine and the outside world input conditions. Thus, the multiplexers are directly used to decode the present state of the machine and select the appropriate conditional branching variables (inputs) which determine the next state of the machine.

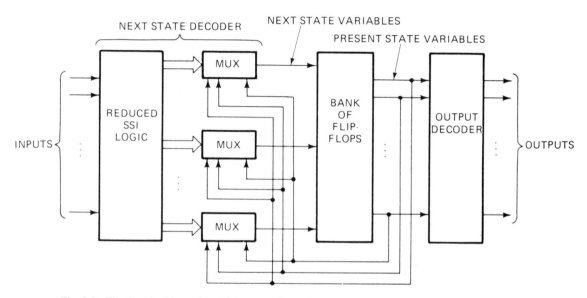

Fig. 8-5. The direct addressed multiplexer configuration.

As will be shown using the combinational logic power of multiplexers, a large number of outside world inputs can be facilitated without a great deal of book-work, tabulation, and complex map reading. *Generally speaking, when a system controller is subjected to a large number of outside world inputs, not all of these inputs are conditional inputs for each state of the machine.* In fact, more than four inputs are rarely implicated in the next state decision for any given state. Only one of these is allowed to be an asynchronous input. This is where the role of the multiplexer really shines. Again, in direct terms, the multiplexer's role is to decode the present state of the machine and address the appropriate input lines to form the next state as its outputs. By doing this the input-forming logic design is held to a minimum. It should be pointed out that a multiplexer is required for *each* state variable and thus a five-variable problem would require five multiplexers. However, the redesign or the modification of this configuration is done very easily. In the following discussion the main attention is directed toward the design of the input-forming logic. The output decoder is implemented in the same manner as was the decoder implementation in Figure 8-4.

The implementation of a direct addressed multiplexer system controller is straightforward in that the exact same approach is taken here as was taken for the decoder implementation. Starting with the VEM's as before, the appropriate multiplexer connections called for are made. The identical process outlined in Chapter 4 is used for the implementation of Boolean expressions (see Example 8-2).

EXAMPLE 8-2: Derive the direct addressed multiplexer configuration using D Flip-Flops for the seven-state system controller for the prototype pop machine. See the maps in Figure 8-6.

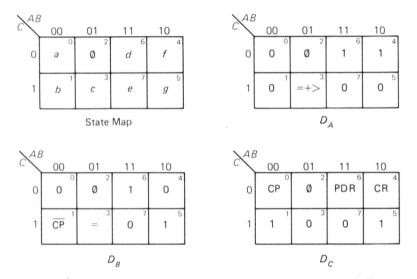

Fig. 8-6. The NEXT STATE MAPS for a multiplexer implementation.

The multiplexer can be implemented directly from these maps, as shown in Figure 8-7.

From this figure and the functional partition shown in Figure 7-41, observe that the system controller can almost totally be implemented with MSI devices. Granted, this is not the most efficient use of the multiplexers. However, a reasonable degree of flexibility is built into the system. This flexibility stems from two facts:

(1) the use of MSI multiplexers for the NEXT STATE decoder;
(2) the use of the MSI decoder for the output decoder.

It can be seen that by using these two devices design changes that require different branching conditions can be quickly implemented by simply rearranging the data inputs to the multiplexers. Output generation changes that are required can be carried out by simply changing the inputs to the OUTPUT HOLDING REGISTER.

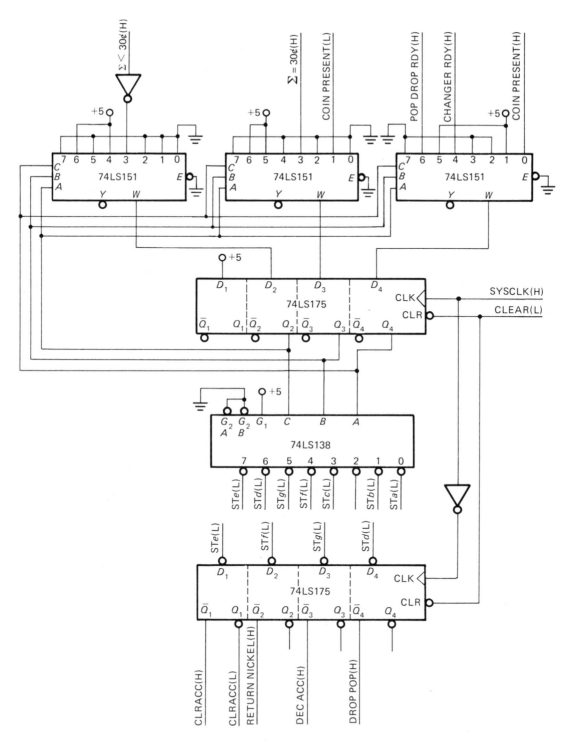

Fig. 8-7. The direct addressed multiplexer implementation of the seven-state pop machine controller.

It should be noted that if JK Flip-Flops were specified, the NEXT STATE DECODER can be implemented using 4-to-1 MUX's. This problem is left as an exercise. The next section introduces a more complex MDS diagram and a slightly different implementation using JK Flip-Flops.

8-4 SYSTEM CONTROLLERS WITH MORE COMPLEXITY

This section introduces a MDS diagram that is considerably more complex than the seven-state MDS diagram for the pop machine (see Figure 8-8). The actual operational description for the system that this MDS diagram relates to is not introduced, since it serves no useful purpose at this time. This MDS diagram is merely used to further the study into implementation methods of system controllers using MSI and LSI devices.

As an introduction to this new MDS diagram, consider the first segment of a direct addressed multiplexer implementation utilizing JK Flip-Flops and 8-to-1 multiplexers. Note that since there are four present state variables, something must be done in order to entertain these four signals with a device that has only three address inputs. Consider Example 8-3.

EXAMPLE 8-3: Utilizing the MDS diagram shown in Figure 8-8, develop an implementation procedure for developing system controllers with the direct-addressed-multiplexer configuration with JK Flip-Flops and multiplexers that have $(n-1)$ address inputs when there are n present state variables.

Again, the first step is to plot the NEXT STATE maps directly from the state diagram (see Figure 8-9). Now, remember that the major motivation for using JK Flip-Flops is to hopefully reduce the input forming logic. You ask: "If you are using multiplexers and, in a sense, disregarding the logic reduction problem, then why would you want to use JK Flip-Flops?" The answer to this question is quite simple. It has been found that using JK Flip-Flops requires the use of two multiplexers for each state variable. However, these MUX's are one-half the physical size of the MUX's required when using D Flip-Flops. The savings can be very real when one 24-pin IC can be traded for two 16-pin IC's, particularly when printed circuit board real estate is at a premium.

Now consider the D map (D_A) from Figure 8-9 as shown again in Figure 8-10 and develop the J_A and K_A maps that are also shown in Figure 8-10.

Now note that the expression read from the J_A map has only the states from 0 to 7 involved—those states where $A = 0$. On the other hand, the expression for the K_A map is only involved with the states where $A = 1$. Therefore, the A present state variable can be connected back to the enable inputs on the MUX, as shown in Figure 8-11. What this implies is that the MUX controlling the J_A input is only enabled when $A = 0$ (the states from 0 to 7); and the MUX controlling the K_A input is only enabled when $A = 1$ (the states from 8 to 15). The upshot of this is that the multiplexer size is reduced by one-half by the $\emptyset$ entries $= 0$ in the J and K maps. Keep in mind that a MUX/JK implementation can be of real use when MUX size is a critical factor. The completion of this design is left as an exercise. The next section develops an alternative and more efficient use of the multiplexers.

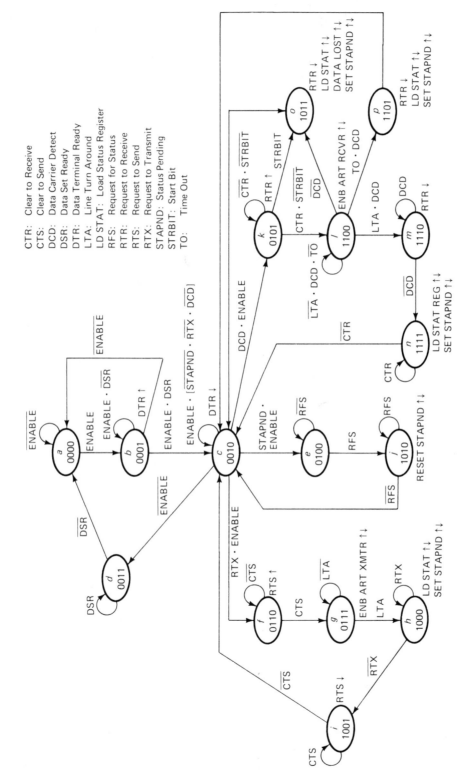

CTR: Clear to Receive
CTS: Clear to Send
DCD: Data Carrier Detect
DSR: Data Set Ready
DTR: Data Terminal Ready
LTA: Line Turn Around
LD STAT: Load Status Register
RFS: Request for Status
RTR: Request to Receive
RTS: Request to Send
RTX: Request to Transmit
STAPND: Status Pending
STRBIT: Start Bit
TO: Time Out

Fig. 8-8. A more complex MDS diagram.

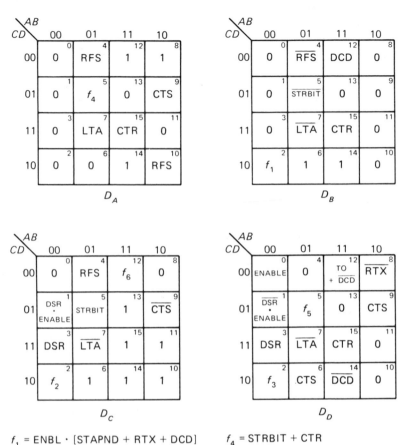

$$f_1 = \text{ENBL} \cdot [\text{STAPND} + \text{RTX} + \text{DCD}] \qquad f_4 = \text{STRBIT} + \text{CTR}$$
$$f_2 = \overline{\text{ENBL}} + \text{RTX} + (\overline{\text{STAPND}} \cdot \text{DCD}) \qquad f_5 = \overline{\text{CTR}} + \text{STRBIT}$$
$$f_3 = \overline{\text{ENBL}} + \text{DCD} \qquad f_6 = \overline{\text{DCD}} + \text{LTA}$$

Fig. 8-9. The NEXT STATE maps for the MDS diagram shown in Figure 8-8.

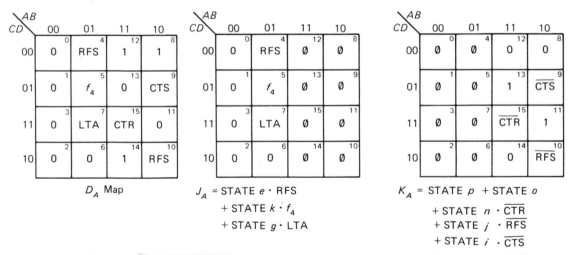

$$J_A = \text{STATE } e \cdot \text{RFS}$$
$$+ \text{STATE } k \cdot f_4$$
$$+ \text{STATE } g \cdot \text{LTA}$$

$$K_A = \text{STATE } p + \text{STATE } o$$
$$+ \text{STATE } n \cdot \overline{\text{CTR}}$$
$$+ \text{STATE } j \cdot \overline{\text{RFS}}$$
$$+ \text{STATE } i \cdot \overline{\text{CTS}}$$

Fig. 8-10. The D_A and J_A and K_A maps for implementation of the MDS diagram shown in Figure 8-8.

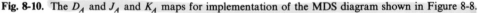

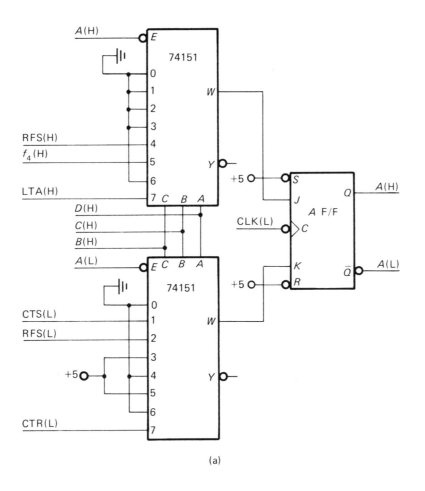

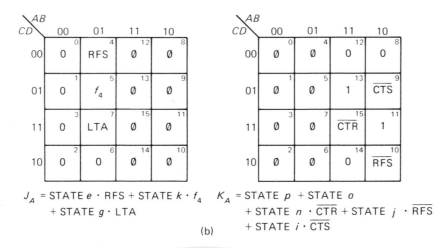

J_A = STATE e · RFS + STATE k · f_4
$\quad$ + STATE g · LTA

K_A = STATE p + STATE o
$\quad$ + STATE n · $\overline{\text{CTR}}$ + STATE j · $\overline{\text{RFS}}$
$\quad$ + STATE i · $\overline{\text{CTS}}$

(b)

Fig. 8-11. (a) The multiplexer implementation. (b) The J_A and K_A maps.

8-5 INDIRECT-ADDRESSED MULTIPLEXER CONFIGURATION

The direct addressed configuration just introduced has many advantages, such as cycle speed and ease of implementation. It also has one basic disadvantage, the inefficient use of the multiplexers. This disadvantage can be seen by examining the repeated assignment of 1's and 0's to the multiplexer inputs shown in Figures 8-7 and 8-11. This inefficient use of the multiplexer can be eliminated by the use of the indirect addressed configuration shown in Figure 8-12. Here, again, the next state variables are a function of the present state of the machine as well as the present input conditions. Therefore, it is still a classic architecture; however, the present-state-to-MUX address decoder eliminates the multiple assignment of a single input variable to the multiplexers by addressing the MUX at the same input location each time that input variable is required. This special decoder can be implemented with a Read-Only-Memory or a Read-Only-Memory-type circuit, thus making it a relatively simple but very effective addition. *In direct terms, this special decoder decodes the present state of the machine and in turn addresses the multiplexers in such a way that the appropriate input variables form the next state of the machine.* It should be noted that the addition of this circuitry reduces the multiplexer size (number of inputs), but not the number of multiplexers. This configuration still requires one multiplexer for each state variable.

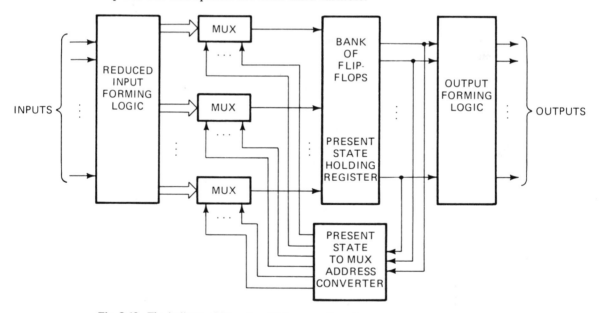

Fig. 8-12. The indirect addressed multiplexer configuration.

The design techniques utilized for this configuration are almost identical to those of the direct address configuration with one exception: the actual use of the maps vary somewhat. A special table is made up from the maps for the decoder requirements and is filled in state by state until all states have been covered. An example will now be worked illustrating this technique. The same MDS diagram in Figure 8-8 is utilized for evaluation purposes. The technique is to first make up a multiplexer address and logic assignment table as shown in Table 8-1. This is done directly from the NEXT STATE maps. Note that the entries are made in order moving down the table. Ground is assigned to the 0th multiplexer inputs and V_{CC} is assigned to all number 1 inputs. Only the decimal number is assigned to the multiplexer addresses as you work down the table. Each time a new input variable is called for, it is assigned the next higher address. This process is repeated until each state is covered. Then the largest address number in each MUX column indicates the width (number of inputs) of the multiplexer required as well as the address bit pattern for the multiplexer. The next step is to use the multiplexer address and logic assignment table to specify the decoder specification table as shown in Table 8-2. This decoder specification table can be used to specify the input/output requirement of a ROM or PROM, should you choose to use one of these devices. Also, the multiplexer-address and logic assignment table is used to design the pre-input-forming logic as well as to denote the input specifications for each multiplexer. When this is done, the design is complete except for the output decoder specification that is discussed later. Note again the importance of the state diagram and the next state maps and how the tables relate directly to these two fundamental pieces of documentation. The schematic for this implementation is not drawn. However, you need only relate the results to the block diagram shown in Figure 8-12 to visualize the implementation.

TABLE 8-1 Multiplexer addressing and logic for indirect multiplexer addressing

	MUX No. 4		MUX No. 3		MUX No. 2		MUX No. 1	
State	ADR	Logic	ADR	Logic	ADR	Logic	ADR	Logic
0000	0	GND	0	GND	0	GND	2	ENBL
0001	0	GND	0	GND	2	DSR·ENABLE	3	$\overline{\text{DSR}\cdot\text{ENABLE}}$
0010	0	GND	2	$f_1{}^*$	3	$f_2{}^*$	4	$f_3{}^*$
0011	0	GND	0	GND	4	DSR	5	DSR
0100	2	RFS	3	$\overline{\text{RFS}}$	5	RFS	0	GND
0101	3	STRBIT+CTR	4	$\overline{\text{STRBIT}}$	6	STRBIT	6	$\overline{\text{CTR}}$ +STRBIT
0110	0	GND	1	V_{CC}	1	V_{CC}	7	CTS
0111	4	LTA	5	$\overline{\text{LTA}}$	7	$\overline{\text{LTA}}$	8	$\overline{\text{LTA}}$
1000	1	V_{CC}	0	GND	0	GND	9	$\overline{\text{RTX}}$
1001	5	CTS	0	GND	8	$\overline{\text{CTS}}$	7	CTS
1010	2	RFS	0	GND	1	V_{CC}	0	GND
1011	0	GND	0	GND	1	V_{CC}	0	GND
1100	1	V_{CC}	6	DCD	9	LTA + $\overline{\text{DCD}}$	10	$\overline{\text{DCD}}$ +TO
1101	0	GND	0	GND	1	V_{CC}	0	GND
1110	1	V_{CC}	1	V_{CC}	1	V_{CC}	11	$\overline{\text{DCD}}$
1111	6	CTR	7	CTR	1	V_{CC}	12	CTR
		7 Input MUX		8 Input MUX		9 Input MUX		13 Input MUX

TABLE 8-2 MUX address decoder specification

Present State	MUX No. 4 ADR	MUX No. 3 ADR	MUX No. 2 ADR	MUX No. 1 ADR
0000	000	000	0000	0010
0000	000	000	0010	0011
0010	000	010	0011	0100
0011	000	000	0100	0101
0100	010	011	0101	0000
0101	011	100	0110	0110
0110	000	001	0001	0111
0111	100	101	0111	1000
1000	001	000	0000	1001
1001	101	000	1000	0111
1010	010	000	0001	0000
1011	000	000	0001	0000
1100	001	110	1001	1010
1101	000	000	0001	0000
1110	001	001	0001	1011
1111	110	111	0001	1100

8-6 READ ONLY MEMORIES (ROM'S)

The rise in READ-ONLY-MEMORY applications has been exponential in nature. Presently, there is hardly a new digital system that doesn't boast of a specification such as "microprogram controlled," "new ROM or PLA has made this product reliable and economical," "microprocessor controlled," and so forth. The ROM, though simple in concept, had to wait until the semiconductor industry could produce these devices economically; since then they have become one of the most widely used components ever produced.

What is a ROM? That question can best be answered by the following statement: A ROM is a "digital dictionary," a memory device whose output code is dependent on an input code. The ROM is sometimes referred to as READ-ONLY-STORAGE, fixed memory, permanent storage, or dead memory, but basically it is an array-type multiple-output combinational circuit having basically the model shown in Figure 8-13.

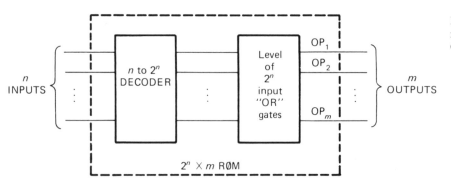

Fig. 8-13. A functional model of $2^n \times m$ READ ONLY MEMORY.

Figure 8-14 illustrates an example of a homemade ROM showing how the various outputs of the decoder section are connected into the "OR" level section, and making these connections is called ROM PROGRAMMING. From this figure notice that it would be relatively easy to connect any or all of the decoder outputs to the inputs of each output OR function.

ROM's are characterized or specified by their "size." This size or bit number is determined by the following expression:

$$\text{ROM size} = 2^n \times m$$
$$\text{"}x\text{" is read as "by"}$$

where n = number of inputs
m = number of outputs

For example, a ROM with ten inputs and eight outputs would be specified as an

$$8k \text{ ROM}$$
or
$$1024 \times 8 \text{ ROM}$$

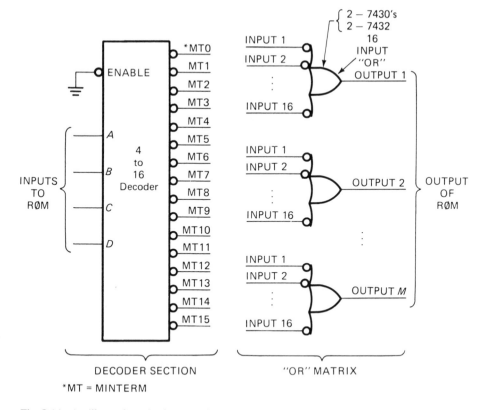

Fig. 8-14. An illustration of a homemade ROM using standard devices.

8-7 ROM'S, PROM'S, AND APPLICATIONS

Some examples of ROM or PROM applications are:

(1) Code converters
(2) Arithmetic look-up tables
(3) Random logic
(4) Waveform generators
(5) Master scan character generators
(6) Microprogramming

The INPUT/OUTPUT specification for a ROM is done basically with a TRUTH-TABLE. The following example illustrates the use of a ROM for a code conversion application.

EXAMPLE 8-4: Use a small (4×4) ROM to convert four-bit BCD to an Excess-3 code (see Figure 8-15).

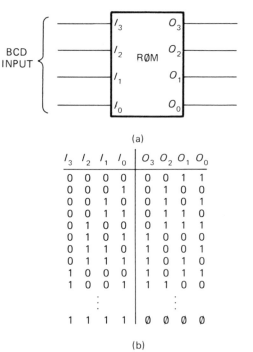

(a)

I_3	I_2	I_1	I_0	O_3	O_2	O_1	O_0
0	0	0	0	0	0	1	1
0	0	0	1	0	1	0	0
0	0	1	0	0	1	0	1
0	0	1	1	0	1	1	0
0	1	0	0	0	1	1	1
0	1	0	1	1	0	0	0
0	1	1	0	1	0	0	1
0	1	1	1	1	0	1	0
1	0	0	0	1	0	1	1
1	0	0	1	1	1	0	0
$\vdots$				$\vdots$			
1	1	1	1	0	0	0	0

(b)

Fig. 8-15. The INPUT/OUTPUT specification for a 4×4 ROM designed to convert BCD to Excess-3.

The actual process of getting the 1's and 0's in the output column varies. Some ROM's are programmed at the factory using a semiconductor process called "masking." Other ROM's are field-programmable (called PROM's) and are permanently programmed (burned-in) by "burning out" selected "fusible links" inside the package by applying current pulse to specific terminals. Others can be programmed by other nondestructible means, and then erased with ultraviolet light. These are called EPROM's (Eraseable PROM) or sometimes READ-MOSTLY-MEMORIES (RMM's).

The PROM, like its predecessor the READ-ONLY-MEMORY (ROM), is a single-chip large scale integrated solid state device embodying the equivalence of thousands of gates and is used mainly for providing an addressable selection of multi-bit words. Figure 8-16 illustrates the logic of a typical PROM. Unlike the ROM, the PROM can be programmed by the user in-house by burning out the fusible links shown, thus saving the manufacturer's masking charges. This simple and inexpensive programming feature not only allows the user to design normal memory functions, but also to select an almost unlimited number of Boolean expressions to be used for combinational and sequential logic design. The following device listing shown in Table 8-3 indicates that there is a wide variety of ROM and PROM devices to choose from. Figure 8-17 is a selection of shortened specification sheets for a generic PROM family. Generic implies a family of devices with a high degree of commonality.

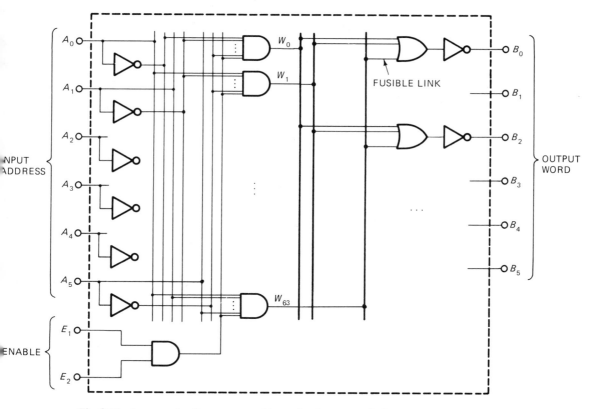

Fig. 8-16. An example of a programmable read only memory logic.

HM-76XX

GENERIC PROM FAMILY

ORGANIZATIONS

PART NUMBER	*OUTPUT	TOTAL BITS	WORDS X BITS/WORD
HM-7602	OC	256	32 X 8
HM-7603	TS		
HM-7610	OC	1024	256 X 4
HM-7611	TS		
HM-7620	OC	2048	512 X 4
HM-7621	TS		
HM-7640	OC	4096	512 X 8
HM-7641	TS		
HM-7642	OC	4096	1024 X 4
HM-7643	TS		
HM-7644	APU		

*OC – Open-Collector
*TS – Three-State
*APU – Active Pull-Up

FEATURES

- Common D. C. Electrical Characteristics and Programming Procedure

- Simple, High Speed Programming Procedure (1 Second per 1024 Bits, Typical)

- Expandable – "Open-Collector" or "Three-State" Outputs and Chip Enable Inputs

- Inputs and Outputs TTL Compatible
  - ▶ Low Input Current - 400µA Logic "0", 40µA Logic "1"
  - ▶ Full Output Drive - 16mA Sink, 2mA Source

- Fast Access Time - Guaranteed for Worst Case N^2 Sequencing, Over Commercial and Military Temperature and Voltage Ranges

- Pin Compatible with Industry Standard PROM's and ROM's

DESCRIPTION

The HM-76XX Generic PROM's comprise a completely compatible family having common D.C. electrical characteristics and identical programming requirements. They are fully decoded, high speed, field programmable ROM's and are available in all commonly used organizations, with both open-collector and three-state outputs. All bits are manufactured storing a logical "1" (outputs high), and can be selectively programmed for a logical "0" (outputs low.)

The nichrome fuse technology is the same as is used in the JAN approved MIL 38510/201 PROM and in all other Harris PROM's.

The field programmable PROM can be custom programmed to any pattern using a simple programming procedure. Schottky Bipolar circuitry provides fast access time, and features temperature and voltage compensation to minimize access time variations.

All pinouts are compatible to industry standard PROM's and ROM's.

In addition to the conventional storage array, extra test rows and columns are included to assure high programmability, and guarantee parametric and A.C. performance. Fuses in these test rows and columns are blown prior to shipment.

PACKAGES

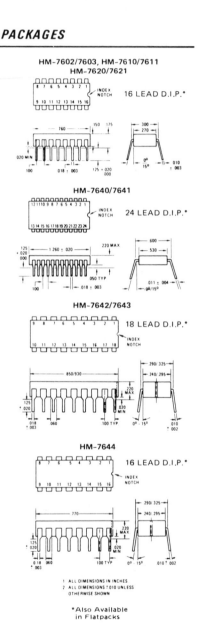

Fig. 8-17. Specifications for a generic family of ROM's. (Courtesy of Harris Semiconductor)

HM-7602/03
32 x 8

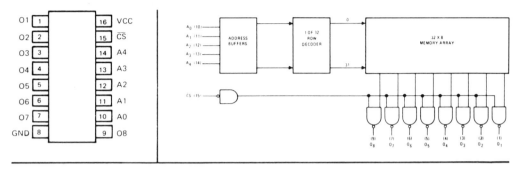

HM-7610/11
256 x 4

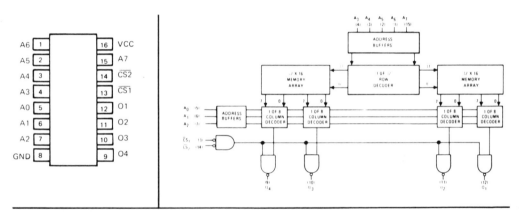

HM-7620/21
512 x 4

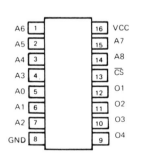
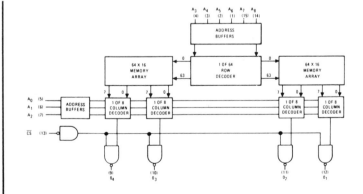

Fig. 8-17. (Cont.)

HM-7640/41
512 x 8

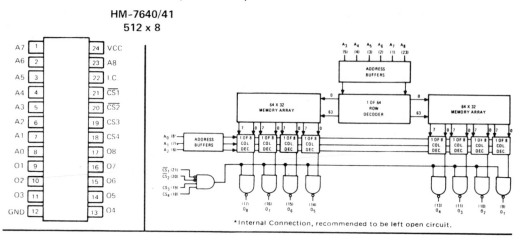

*Internal Connection, recommended to be left open circuit.

HM-7642/43
1024 x 4

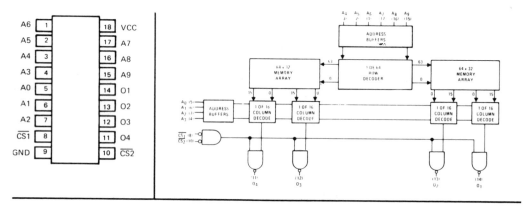

HM-7644
1024 x 4

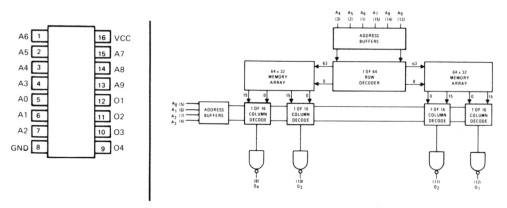

Fig. 8-17. (Cont.)

BIPOLAR ROM AND PROM FAMILY

	Type	No. Of Bits	Organization	Output [1]	Maximum Access (ns)	Maximum Power Dissipation [2] (mW)	Operating Temperature Range (°C)	Power Supply (V)	Page No.
SCHOTTKY BIPOLAR ROMs	3301A	1024	256 x4	O.C.	45	657	0 to 75	5V ± 5%	3-26
	M3301A	1024	256 x4	O.C.	60	657	-55 to 125	5V ± 5%	3-29
	3302A	2048	512 x 4	O.C.	70	735	0 to 75	5V ± 5%	3-31
	3302A-4	2048	512 x 4	O.C.	90	735	0 to 75	5V ± 5%	3-31
	3302AL6	2048	512 x 4	O.C.	90	580/240	0 to 75	5V ± 5%	3-31
	3322A	2048	512 x 4	T.S.	70	735	0 to 75	5V ± 5%	3-31
	3322A-4	2048	512 x 4	T.S.	90	735	0 to 75	5V ± 5%	3-31
	3322AL6	2048	512 x 4	T.S.	90	580/240	0 to 75	5V ± 5%	3-31
	3304A	4096	512 x 8	O.C.	70	998	0 to 75	5V ± 5%	3-34
	3304A-4	4096	512 x 8	O.C.	90	998	0 to 75	5V ± 5%	3-34
	3304AL6	4096	512 x 8	O.C.	90	735/240	0 to 75	5V ± 5%	3-34
	3324A	4096	512 x 8	T.S.	70	998	0 to 75	5V ± 5%	3-34
	3324A-4	4096	512 x 8	T.S.	90	998	0 to 75	5V ± 5%	3-34
SCHOTTKY BIPOLAR PROMs	3601	1024	256 x4	O.C.	70	685	0 to 75	5V ± 5%	3-37
	3601-1	1024	256 x4	O.C.	50	685	0 to 75	5V ± 5%	3-37
	M3601	1024	256 x4	O.C.	90	685	-55 to 125	5V ± 5%	3-41
	3621	1024	256 x4	T.S.	70	685	0 to 75	5V ± 5%	3-37
	3621-1	1024	256 x4	T.S.	50	685	0 to 75	5V ± 5%	3-37
	3602	2048	512 x 4	O.C.	70	735	0 to 75	5V ± 5%	3-43
	3602-4	2048	512 x 4	O.C.	90	735	0 to 75	5V ± 5%	3-43
	3602L-6	2048	512 x 4	O.C.	90	580/240	0 to 75	5V ± 5%	3-43
	3622	2048	512 x 4	T.S.	70	735	0 to 75	5V ± 5%	3-43
	3622-4	2048	512 x 4	T.S.	90	735	0 to 75	5V ± 5%	3-43
	3622L-6	2048	512 x 4	T.S.	90	580/240	0 to 75	5V ± 5%	3-43
	3604	4096	512 x 8	O.C.	70	998	0 to 75	5V ± 5%	3-46
	3604-4	4096	512 x 8	O.C.	90	998	0 to 75	5V ± 5%	3-46
	3604L-6	4096	512 x 8	O.C.	30	735/240	0 to 75	5V ± 5%	3-46
	3624	4096	512 x 8	T.S.	70	998	0 to 75	5V ± 5%	3-46
	3624-4	4096	512 x 8	T.S.	90	998	0 to 75	5V ± 5%	3-46
	M3604	4096	512 x 8	O.C.	90	1045	-55 to 125	5V ± 10%	3-49
	M3604-6	4096	512 x 8	O.C.	120	770/250	-30 to 125	5V ± 5%	3-49
	3605	4096	1024 x 4	O.C.	50	787	0 to 75	5V ± 5%	3-52
	3605-1	4096	1024 x 4	O.C.	70	787	0 to 75	5V ±5%	3-52
	M3624	4096	512 x 8	T.S.	90	1045	-55 to 125	5V ± 10%	3-49
	3625	4096	1024 x 4	T.S.	70	787	0 to 75	5V ± 5%	3-52
	3625-1	4096	1024 x 4	T.S.	50	787	0 to 75	5V ± 5%	3-52

Note 1: O.C. and T.S. are open collector and three-state output respectively.
Note 2: The "L" series devices have a low power dissipation option.

ROM and PROM Programming Instructions	3-55

Table 8-3. (Courtesy of Intel)

MOS ROM AND PROM FAMILY

	Type	No Of Bits	Organization	Output[1]	Maximum Access (ns)	Maximum Power Dissipation (mW)	Operating Temperature Range (°C)	Power Supply (V)	Page No.
SILICON GATE MOS ROM	1302	2048	256 x8	T.S.	1 us	885	0 to 70	5V ± 5% -9V ± 5%	3-5
	2308	8192	1024 x 8	T.S.	450	775	0 to 70	5V ± 5% 12V ± 5% -5V ± 5%	3-16
	2316A	16384	2048 x8	T.S.	850	515	0 to 70	5V ± 5%	3-20
SILICON GATE MOS PROM	1702A	2048	256 x8	T.S.	1 us	885	0 to 70	5V ± 5% -9V ± 5%	3-9
	1702AL	2048	256 x8	T.S.	1 us	221	0 to 70	5V ± 5% -9V ± 5%	3-13
	1702A-2	2048	256 x8	T.S.	650	959	0 to 70	5V ± 5% -9V ± 5%	3-9
	1702AL-2	2048	256 x8	T.S.	650	221	0 to 70	5V ± 5% -9V ± 5%	3-13
	1702A-6	2048	256 x8	T.S.	1.5 us	885	0 to 70	5V ± 5% -9V ± 5%	3-9
	2704	4096	512 x 8	T.S.	450	800	0 to 70	5V ± 5% 12V ± 5% -5V ± 5%	3-23
	2708	8192	1024 x 8	T.S.	450	800	0 to 70	5V ± 5% 12V ± 5% -5V ± 5%	3-23

Note 1: O.C. and T.S. are open collector and three-state output respectively.

ROM and PROM Programming Instructions	3-55

Table 8-3. (Cont.)

Figure 8-18 is a selection of a shortened specification sheet for an EPROM. Thus it is easy to see that with a wide variety of programmable ROM's there is opportunity to enhance the field of programmable logic design.

This programmable logic design capability is most interesting because it can lead to extensive savings in small production runs. This feature can also lead to complex designs with a minimal logic package count, physical space requirements, and circuit board complexity.

Methods are presented illustrating the implementation of the PROM in combinational and, in particular, sequential circuit design.

Fig. 8-18(a). (*facing page*)
Data sheet for 1702 PROM.
(Courtesy of Intel)

intel®

1702A

2K (256 x 8) UV ERASABLE PROM

1702A-2	0.65 us Max.
1702A	1.0 us Max.
1702A-6	1.5 us Max.

- **Fast Access Time: Max. 650 ns (1702A–2)**
- **Fast Programming: 2 Minutes for all 2048 Bits**
- **All 2048 Bits Guaranteed* Programmable: 100% Factory Tested**

- **Static MOS: No Clocks Required**
- **Inputs and Outputs DTL and TTL Compatible**
- **Three-State Output: OR-tie Capability**

The 1702A is a 256 word by 8-bit electrically programmable ROM ideally suited for uses where fast turn-around and pattern experimentation are important. The 1702A undergoes complete programming and functional testing prior to shipment, thus insuring 100% programmability.

Initially all 2048 bits of the 1702A are in the "0" state (output low). Information is introduced by selectively programming "1"s (output high) in the proper bit location. The 1702A is packaged in a 24 pin dual in-line package with a transparent lid. The transparent lid allows the user to expose the 1702A to ultraviolet light to erase the bit pattern. A new pattern can then be written into the device.

The circuitry of the 1702A is completely static. No clocks are required. Access times from 650ns to 1.5μs are available. A 1702AL family is available (see 1702AL data sheets for specifications) for those systems requiring lower power dissipation than the 1702A.

A pin-for-pin metal mask programmed ROM, the Intel 1302, is also available for large volume production runs of systems initially using the 1702A.

The 1702A is fabricated with silicon gate technology. This low threshold technology allows the design and production of higher performance MOS circuits and provides a higher functional density on a monolithic chip than conventional MOS technologies.

*Intel's liability shall be limited to replacing any unit which fails to program as desired.

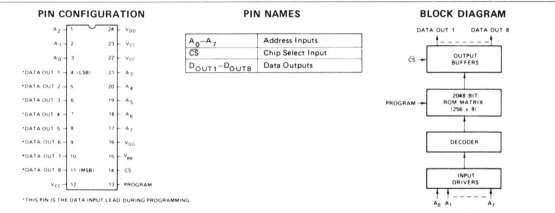

PIN CONFIGURATION

*THIS PIN IS THE DATA INPUT LEAD DURING PROGRAMMING

PIN NAMES

A_0–A_7	Address Inputs
$\overline{CS}$	Chip Select Input
D_{OUT1}–D_{OUT8}	Data Outputs

BLOCK DIAGRAM

NOTE: In the read mode a logic 1 at the address inputs and data outputs is a high and logic 0 is a low.

U.S. Patent No. 3660819

intel®

2708, 2704

8K AND 4K UV ERASABLE PROM

- **2708 1024x8 Organization**
- **2704 512x8 Organization**

- ■ **Fast Programming —**
  Typ. 100 sec. For All 8K Bits
- ■ **Low Power During Programming**
- ■ **Access Time — 450 ns Max.**
- ■ **Standard Power Supplies —**
  +12V, +5V, -5V

- ■ **Static — No Clocks Required**
- ■ **Inputs and Outputs TTL**
  Compatible During Both Read
  and Program Modes
- ■ **Three-State Output — OR-Tie**
  Capability

The Intel 2708/2704 are high speed 8192/4096 bit erasable and electrically reprogrammable ROM's (EPROM) ideally suited where fast turn around and pattern experimentation are important requirements.

The 2708/2704 are packaged in a 24 pin dual-in-line package with transparent lid. The transparent lid allows the user to expose the chip to ultraviolet light to erase the bit pattern. A new pattern can then be written into the devices.

A pin for pin mask programmed ROM, the Intel 2308, is available for large volume production runs of systems initially using the 2708.

The 2708/2704 is fabricated with the time proven N-channel silicon gate technology.

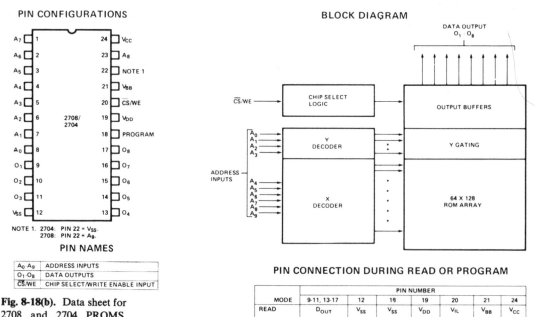

PIN CONFIGURATIONS

NOTE 1. 2704: PIN 22 = V_{SS}.
2708: PIN 22 = A_9.

PIN NAMES

A_0-A_9	ADDRESS INPUTS
O_1-O_8	DATA OUTPUTS
$\overline{CS}$/WE	CHIP SELECT/WRITE ENABLE INPUT

Fig. 8-18(b). Data sheet for 2708 and 2704 PROMS. (Courtesy of Intel)

BLOCK DIAGRAM

PIN CONNECTION DURING READ OR PROGRAM

MODE	PIN NUMBER						
	9-11, 13-17	12	18	19	20	21	24
READ	D_{OUT}	V_{SS}	V_{SS}	V_{DD}	V_{IL}	V_{BB}	V_{CC}
PROGRAM	D_{IN}	V_{SS}	Pulsed V_{IHP}	V_{DD}	V_{IHW}	V_{BB}	V_{CC}

8-8 USING A PROM FOR RANDOM LOGIC

EXAMPLE 8-5: Suppose it is desired to implement the following unsimplified Boolean expressions using a ROM or PROM.

$$F_1 = BC\overline{D} + A\overline{C}\,\overline{D} + AB\overline{C}D + A\overline{B}CD$$

$$F_2 = \overline{A}\,\overline{B}CD + \overline{A}\,C\overline{D} + ABC\overline{D} + A\overline{C}D$$

$$F_3 = AB + AC + BC$$

$$F_4 = \overline{A}\,B\overline{C}D + \overline{A}\,BC\overline{D} + \overline{A}\,C\overline{D} + \overline{B}C$$

When simplified, these combinational expressions require 17 gates with 50 inputs or approximately ten 14-pin DIP packages for implementation.

The first step in PROM implementation might be to plot the combinational expressions in a Karnaugh map to expand them into their canonical sum-of-product form as shown in Figure 8-19. Programming the PROM is the next step in the design. This step requires the multi-function TRUTH-TABLE shown in Figure 8-20. This TRUTH-TABLE is plotted directly from the Karnaugh maps in Figure 8-19 and becomes a specification of the memory contents.

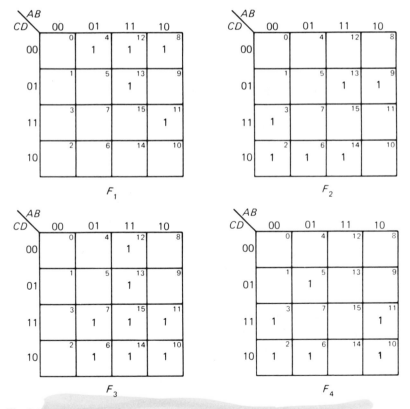

Fig. 8-19. The Karnaugh map expansion of the expressions F_1, F_2, F_3, and F_4.

Address	Contents
$A\ B\ C\ D$	$F_1\ F_2\ F_3\ F_4$
0 0 0 0 0	0 0 0 0
1 0 0 0 1	0 0 0 0
2 0 0 1 0	0 1 0 1
3 0 0 1 1	0 1 0 1
4 0 1 0 0	1 0 0 0
5 0 1 0 1	0 0 0 1
6 0 1 1 0	0 1 1 1
7 0 1 1 1	0 0 1 0
8 1 0 0 0	1 0 0 0
9 1 0 0 1	0 1 0 0
10 1 0 1 0	0 0 1 1
11 1 0 1 1	1 0 1 1
12 1 1 0 0	1 0 1 0
13 1 1 0 1	1 1 1 0
14 1 1 1 0	0 1 1 0
15 1 1 1 1	0 0 1 0

Fig. 8-20. The multi-function TRUTH-TABLE (ROM Table) used to program the PROM.

The symbolic representation of the solution to this combination logic problem is shown in Figure 8-21.

$$F_1 = \bar{A}BC\bar{D} + AB\bar{C}\bar{D} + A\bar{B}C\bar{D} + AB\bar{C}D + A\bar{B}CD$$

$$F_2 = AB\bar{C}D + A\bar{B}\bar{C}D + \bar{A}\bar{B}CD + \bar{A}\bar{B}C\bar{D} + \bar{A}BC\bar{D} + ABC\bar{D}$$

$$F_3 = AB\bar{C}\bar{D} + AB\bar{C}D + \bar{A}BCD + ABCD + \bar{A}BC\bar{D} + \bar{A}\bar{B}CD + ABC\bar{D} + \bar{A}\bar{B}C\bar{D}$$

$$F_4 = \bar{A}BC\bar{D} + \bar{A}\bar{B}CD + A\bar{B}CD + \bar{A}\bar{B}C\bar{D} + \bar{A}BCD + A\bar{B}C\bar{D}$$

Fig. 8-21. The completed PROM implementation of the combinational problem.

Another example is an interesting one taken from a research project undertaken by the author. Most are familiar with the work of Dr. Ray Dolby in tape recording for high fidelity reproduction. Dr. Dolby's systems are known worldwide for both quality and price. However, they all have the basic problems of distortion introduced by channel separation and compression problems between recording and playback. The following block diagram (Figure 8-22) is an eight-channel digital Dolby system designed to minimize this distortion by adding more channels and using ROM's for the compression and decompression compensation curves. The advantage of using ROM's and digital filters is that they don't drift with time and temperature. It should also be noted that a random logic system controller using a ROM was used in this system.

Another very important application of the ROM is microprogramming. A simple dual bus computer is shown in Figure 8-23. It should be noted that a computer in a broad generality is nothing more than a collection of registers and a control unit. The control unit by definition is the system controller of the machine and it usually performs its control functions based on a fixed set of predetermined instructions (input codes). This hardwired concept leaves the machine virtually inflexible as far as changes go. This is where microprogramming has made its in-roads. Microprogramming has three basic advantages:

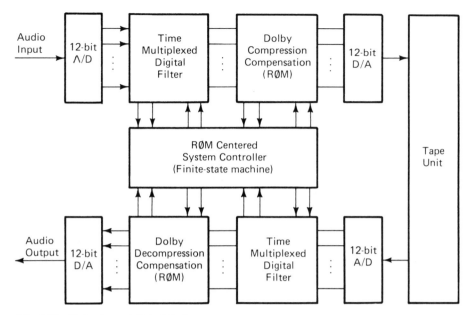

Fig. 8-22. Eight-channel digital Dolby system.

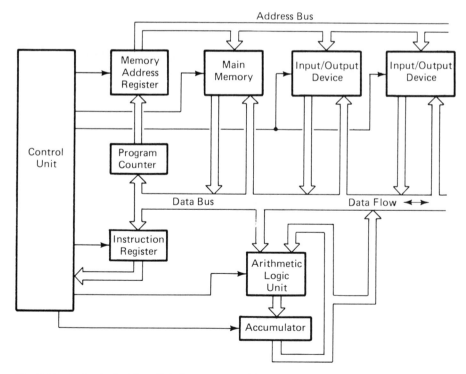

Fig. 8-23. A simple dual-bus digital computer architecture.

(1) increasing the speed of a machine;

(2) making the machine adaptable to software written for other machines;

(3) upward and downward compatibility over a wide range of computer models within a series.

Consider for a moment how microprogramming can accomplish these advantages. As shown in Figure 8-24, the control unit is usually a hardwired unit that interprets input information and translates it into output control sequences on a *fixed* number of control lines. Rather than the fixed or hardwired finite-state machine, a microprogram machine has a programmable controller within the control unit that generates the control sequences based on a stored program of micro-instruction as shown in Figure 8-25. Thus observe that a basic machine instruction like LOAD ACCUMULATOR from memory location X can be and is broken down into a sequence of micro-instructions generated by the programmable system controller.

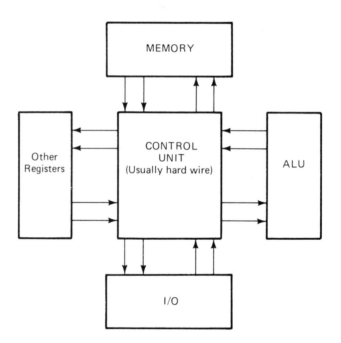

Fig. 8-24. A simple block diagram of a general computer.

This very simple architecture allows for the easy change of control sequences by merely changing the ROM or microprogram. The main advantages are generally categorized into speed and flexibility. The speed advantage is gained because the "fetch" instructions take typically one-fifth the time taken by the main memory. Flexibility is obvious; for any time a machine's instruction set can be changed by simply changing a ROM or by reading a new program into a "writeable control-store memory" (RAM), the advantages should be obvious.

As mentioned earlier, ROM's, PROM's, or EPROM's are used widely in microprocessor systems. Thus they are useful system components and more will be said about PROM's and their application in relation to sequential machines later.

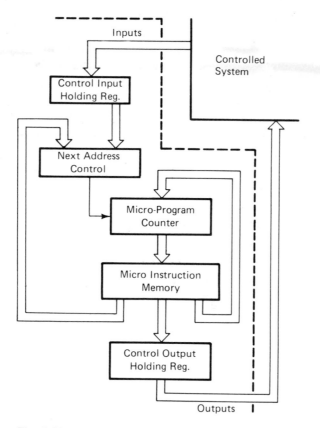

Fig. 8-25. An architecture for a microprogrammed control unit.

8-9 PROGRAMMED LOGIC ARRAYS (PLA'S)

This section discusses the basics of the LSI circuit known as the PLA and its field programmable version called the FPLA. Further, the difference in PLA's and ROM's is discussed, and some examples of PLA applications are given.

As its name suggests, the PLA is an array logic device designed to implement random logic expressions in sum-of-product form in a way similar to that of the ROM. However, the PLA differs considerably in structure from the ROM, as is shown in Figure 8-26.

One outstanding difference in these two structures is in the input decoding units. The ROM has an exhaustive input decoder and the PLA has a programmable AND matrix decoder. This difference eliminates the inefficient storage of unwanted MINTERMS that is required of a ROM because of its exhaustive n to 2^n input decoder. A PLA allows you to program simplified logic expressions rather than the canonical forms required when using ROM's. Because of this, PLA's

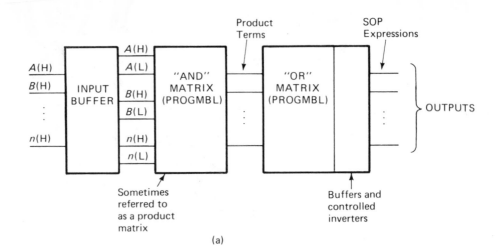

(a)

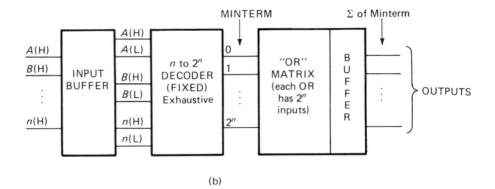

(b)

Fig. 8-26. Structure comparison between a PLA and a ROM. (a) PLA structure. (b) ROM structure.

typically can accommodate many more inputs than ROM's without stressing the boundary conditions imposed by the practical limits set by the semiconductor process used. What this says is that you can only put so much on a chip. Therefore, for random logic generation, the PLA is more efficient than the ROM. To illustrate the implementation of a simple random logic expression, using a PLA and a ROM consider the following example.

EXAMPLE 8-6: It is desired to implement the logic expression set forth in the following map:

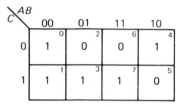

$$F = \Sigma 0, 1, 3, 4, 7$$

$$F_{PLA} = \overline{A}\,\overline{B} + BC + \overline{B}\,\overline{C} \quad \text{(logic expression for a PLA)}$$

$$F_{ROM} = \overline{A}\,\overline{B}\,\overline{C} + \overline{A}\,\overline{B}\,C + \overline{A}\,B\,C + A\,\overline{B}\,\overline{C} + A\,B\,C \quad \text{(logic expression for a ROM)}$$

The implementation of F is shown in Figures 8-27(a) and 8-27(b) using an elementary ROM and PLA.

PLA's are sized or specified by the following description:

$$A \times B \times C$$

where

A = number of inputs

B = total number of unique product terms capable
     (number of inputs each OR gate has)

C = number of outputs (different logic expression available)

Therefore the specifications for PLA such as the Signetics FPLA 82S100 mean that:

$$16 \times 48 \times 8$$

implies that this PLA is capable of generating eight different logic outputs each with a maximum of 48 unique product terms made up of any combination of 16 input variables.

The 82S100 serves as an excellent example for illustrating the actual internal structure of a FPLA. The structure of this device is shown in Figure 8-28.

The circuit shown in Figure 8-29 illustrates the equivalent logic path and TRUTH-TABLE for the 82S100 FPLA.

The title of the specification for the 82S100/101 is shown in Figure 8-30.

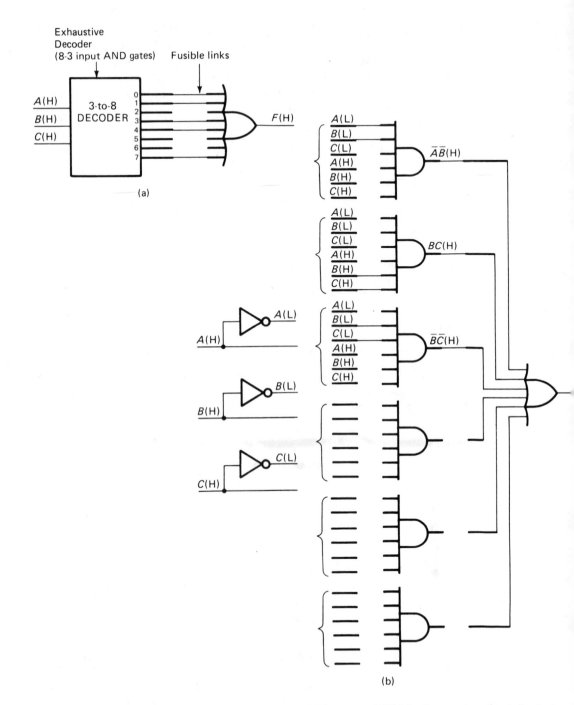

Fig. 8-27. Implementations of Example 8-6. (a) Elementary ROM implementation. (b) A $3 \times 6 \times 1$ elementary PLA implementation.

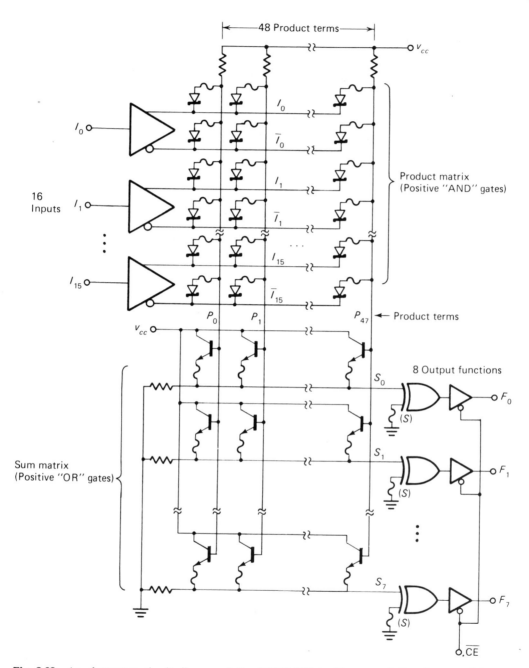

Fig. 8-28. An elementary circuit diagram of the 82S100 FPLA. (Courtesy of Signetics, copyright February 1977, Sunnyvale, California, Signetics Field Programmable Logic Arrays, pp. 1–4.)

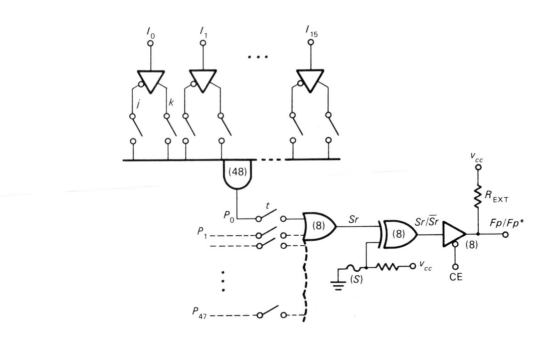

Note:
For each of the 8 outputs either the function Fp (active high)
or Fp^* (active low) is available. But not both. The required
function polarity is user programmable via fuse (S).

(a)

LET:

$P_n = \Pi_0^{15}(k_m I_m + j_m \overline{I_m})$; $k = 0, 1, X$ (Don't Care)

$n = 0, 1, 2, \ldots, 47$

$S_r = f(\Sigma_0^{47} t_n P_n)$; $r \equiv p = 0, 1, 2, \ldots, 7$

where:

Unprogrammed state : $j_m = k_m = 0$; $t_n = 1$

Programmed state : $j_m = \overline{k_m}$; $t_n = 0$

MODE	P_n	$\overline{CE}$	$\overset{?}{S_r} = f(P_n)$	F_p	F_p^*
Disabled (82S101)	X	1	X	1	1
Disabled (82S100)				Hi-Z	Hi-Z
Read	1	0	YES	1	0
	0	0		0	1
	X	0	NO	0	1

(b)

Fig. 8-29. (a) The equivalent logic path of the 82S100/101. (b) The TRUTH-TABLE from the 82S100/101. (Courtesy of Signetics, Field Programmable Logic Arrays.)

BIPOLAR FIELD-PROGRAMMABLE LOGIC ARRAY (16X48X8 FPLA) 82S101 (OPEN COLLECTOR) 82S100 (TRI-STATE)

82S100
82S101

FEBRUARY 1976
DIGITAL 8000 SERIES TTL/MEMORY

DESCRIPTION

The 82S100 (Tri-State Outputs) and the 82S101 (Open Collector Outputs) are Bipolar Programmable Logic Arrays, containing 48 Product terms (AND terms), and 8 Sum terms (OR terms). Each OR term controls an output function which can be programmed either true active-High (Fp), or true active-Low (Fp*). The true state of each output function is activated by any logical combination of 16 input variables, or their complements, up to 48 terms. Both devices are field-programmable, which means that custom patterns are immediately available by following the fusing procedure outlined in this data sheet.

The 82S100 and 82S101 are fully TTL compatible, and include chip-enable control for expansion of input variables, and output inhibit. They feature either Open Collector or Tri-State outputs for ease of expansion of product terms and application in bus-organized systems.

FEATURES

- **FIELD PROGRAMMABLE (Ni-Cr LINK)**
- **INPUT VARIABLES—16**
- **OUTPUT FUNCTIONS—8**
- **PRODUCT TERMS—48**
- **ADDRESS ACCESS TIME—50 ns, MAXIMUM**
- **POWER DISSIPATION—600mW, TYPICAL**
- **INPUT LOADING—(−100μA), MAXIMUM**
- **OUTPUT OPTION:**
    TRI-STATE OUTPUTS—82S100
    OPEN COLLECTOR OUTPUTS—82S101
- **OUTPUT DISABLE FUNCTION:**
    TRI-STATE—Hi-Z
    OPEN COLLECTOR—Hi
- **CERAMIC DIP**

APPLICATIONS

**LARGE READ ONLY MEMORY
RANDOM LOGIC
CODE CONVERSION
PERIPHERAL CONTROLLERS
LOOK-UP AND DECISION TABLES
MICROPROGRAMMING
ADDRESS MAPPING
CHARACTER GENERATORS
SEQUENTIAL CONTROLLERS**

PIN CONFIGURATION

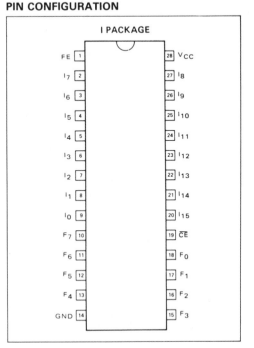

FPLA EQUIVALENT LOGIC PATH

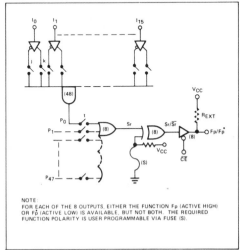

NOTE:
FOR EACH OF THE 8 OUTPUTS, EITHER THE FUNCTION Fp (ACTIVE HIGH) OR Fp (ACTIVE LOW) IS AVAILABLE, BUT NOT BOTH. THE REQUIRED FUNCTION POLARITY IS USER PROGRAMMABLE VIA FUSE (S).

Fig. 8-30. (Courtesy of Signetics, Field Programmable Logic Arrays.)

8-10 APPLICATIONS OF PLA'S AND FPLA'S

The application of PLA's and in particular FPLA's is practically unbounded. In fact, these devices pose a viable alternative to all types of combinational logic design, and when coupled with sequential devices (counters, Flip-Flops) their application is even more far-reaching. The following quote from Napoleone Cavlan, Manager of Advanced Products Marketing for Signetics Corporation, sums up the application and future of the PLA.

> Since the practical introduction of microprogramming in the last decade or so, microcode has progressively displaced random logic in step with the growing availability of user Programmable Read-Only-Memories (PROM's). However, even with PROM's, designers soon realized that their rigid addressing structure made them unsuitable in a wide variety of applications which could greatly benefit from a structured logic approach.
>
> Recently, microprocessors have provided a quantum jump in design flexibility in applications requiring about 30 IC packages, and beyond. When fewer packages are required, the inherent speed limitation, software requirements, and support circuitry of microprocessors place them out of range of a broad spectrum of applications.
>
> These in general involve algorithms which require a high speed logic decision based on a large number of controlling variables. It is here that we step into the basic domain of Field Programmable Logic Arrays, encompassing applications in microprogramming, code conversion, random logic, look-up and decision tables, high speed character generators, etc. Moreover, when combined with a few storage elements (Flip-Flops), FPLA's can implement powerful logic machines of the Mealy/Moore form for the realization of finite state sequential controllers for traffic, process, peripheral devices, and other similar applications.

Some practical applications of FPLA's will be illustrated shortly.

8-11 SYSTEM CONTROLLER DESIGNS CENTERED AROUND ROM'S AND PROM'S

We have just illustrated several examples of ROM and PROM usage as combinational logic substitution devices. From this point of view, consider an obvious application for a ROM or PROM, that being a direct replacement for the NEXT STATE and OUTPUT DECODER logic of a system controller. Consider Example 8-7.

EXAMPLE 8-7: Using the direct addressed ROM or PLA configuration shown in Figure 8-31, develop the ROM PROGRAM TABLE for the control logic of the seven state prototype pop machine controller that is shown in Figure 8-32. Pay particular attention to the actual connections made to the ROM, because this information is pertinent to the format of the PROGRAM TABLE shown in Table 8-4.

TABLE 8-4 The Partial ROM program specification for the seven state pop machine controller

	Present State				System Inputs				Next State				System Outputs			
	A	B	C	PDR	>	=	CR	CP	A	B	C		DP	RN	DA	CA
	I_7	I_6	I_5	I_4	I_3	I_2	I_1	I_0	O_7	O_6	O_5	O_4	O_3	O_2	O_1	O_0
State A	0	0	0	0	0	0	0	0	0	0	0	Ø	0	0	0	0
	0	0	0	0	0	0	0	1	0	0	1	Ø	0	0	0	0
	0	0	0	0	0	0	1	0	0	0	0	Ø	0	0	0	0
	0	0	0	0	0	0	1	1	0	0	1	Ø	0	0	0	0
	:	:	:		:	:	:		:	:	:		:	:		
	0	0	0	1	1	1	1	1	0	0	1	Ø	0	0	0	0
State B	0	0	1	0	0	0	0	0	0	1	1	Ø	0	0	0	0
	0	0	1	0	0	0	0	1	0	0	1	Ø	0	0	0	0
	:	:	:		:	:	:		:	:	:		:	:		
	0	0	1	1	1	1	1	0	0	1	1	Ø	0	0	0	0
	0	0	1	1	1	1	1	1	0	0	1	Ø	0	0	0	0
State Ø	0	1	0	Ø	0	Ø	Ø	Ø	Ø	Ø	Ø	Ø	Ø	Ø	Ø	Ø
	:	:	:		:	:	:		:	:	:		:	:		
	0	1	0	Ø	Ø	Ø	Ø	Ø	Ø	Ø	0	Ø	Ø	Ø	Ø	Ø
State C	0	1	1	0	0	0	0	0	0	0	0	Ø	0	0	0	0
	:	:	:		:	:	:		:	:	:		:	:		
	0	1	1	0	0	1	0	0	1	1	0	Ø	0	0	0	0
	:	:	:		:	:	:		:	:	:		:	:		
	0	1	1	0	1	0	0	0	1	0	0	Ø	0	0	0	0
State F	1	0	0	0	0	0	0	0	1	0	0	Ø	0	1	0	0
	:	:	:		:	:	:		:	:	:		:	:		
	1	0	0	0	0	0	1	0	1	0	1	Ø	0	1	0	0
State G	1	0	1	0	0	0	0	0	0	1	1	Ø	0	0	1	0
	:	:	:		:	:	:		:	:	:		:	:		
	1	0	1	1	1	1	1	1	0	1	1	Ø	0	0	1	0
State D	1	1	0	0	0	0	0	0	1	1	0	Ø	1	0	0	0
	:	:	:		:	:	:		:	:	:		:	:		
	1	1	0	1	0	0	0	0	1	1	1	Ø	1	0	0	0
State E	1	1	1	0	0	0	0	0	0	0	0	Ø	0	0	0	1
	:	:	:		:	:	:		:	:	:		:	:		
	1	1	1	0	0	0	0	0	0	0	0	Ø	0	0	0	1

We see from Table 8-4 that this particular configuration is wasteful from the point of view of efficient ROM storage usage. However, in a different situation the seemingly wasted branching address ($\emptyset$ words) can be used for special diagnostic purposes. The next section introduces another ROM-centered configuration that more efficiently uses the ROM storage for limited branching MDS diagrams.

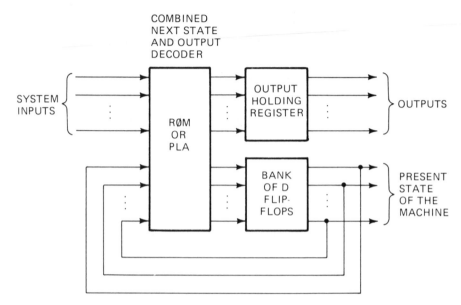

Fig. 8-31. The direct-addressed ROM or PLA configuration.

8-12 INDIRECT-ADDRESSED MULTIPLEXER/ROM CONFIGURATION

The last section illustrates a flexible application of a ROM used as both a NEXT STATE and OUTPUT DECODER. However, this flexibility is paid for in wasted ROM. This section introduces a configuration that utilizes the ROM more efficiently by restricting the NEXT STATE BRANCHING possibilities from each state (see Figure 8-33). Basically this configuration trades ROM width for ROM length, by restricting the branching words assigned to each state by using extra ROM outputs to address the multiplexers. The outputs of these multiplexers are referred to as "branching flags," and the required number of these branching flags is determined by the maximum number of branches required for any state. In short, if the worst case number of branches is four, then two branching flags are required. To illustrate the application of this configuration, consider Example 8-8.

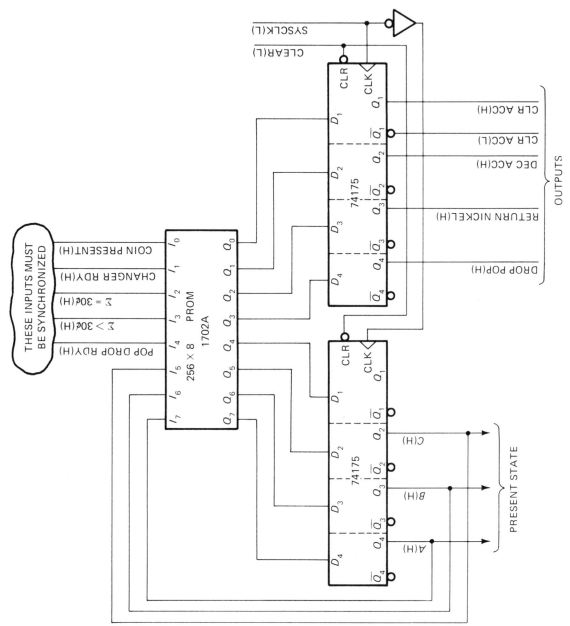

Fig. 8-32. The ROM centered system controller for the seven-state pop machine controller.

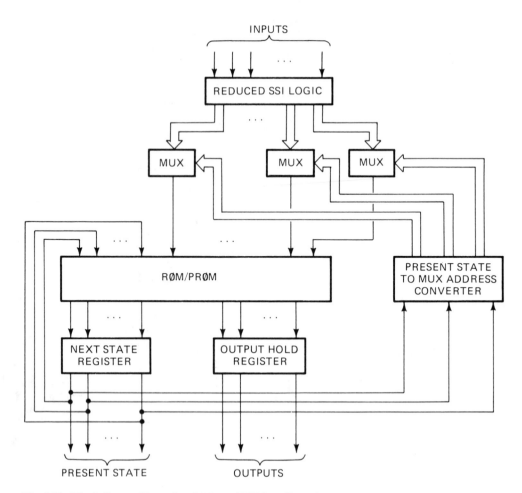

INPUTS

PRESENT STATE

OUTPUTS

Fig. 8-33. The indirect-addressed multiplexer/ROM configuration.

EXAMPLE 8-8: Consider the implementation of the seven-state pop machine controller implemented with INDIRECT-ADDRESSED MULTIPLEXER/ ROM configuration shown in Figure 8-34. It has been found by experience that when large designs are implemented with the configuration, an additional table should be kept to document the MUX address section of the ROM. By doing so, the confusion related to what input goes where is avoided. It should be noted that for complete flexibility each MUX should have its own address bus. However, this was not done with the pop controller for obvious reasons. See the ROM program specification in Table 8-5, which is filled out directly from the MDS diagram in Figure 8-2. Granted, the seven-state pop machine controller does not fully illustrate the applicability of this configuration. However, it is revisited in Chapter 9 in order to demonstrate its relationship to a bit-slice controller.

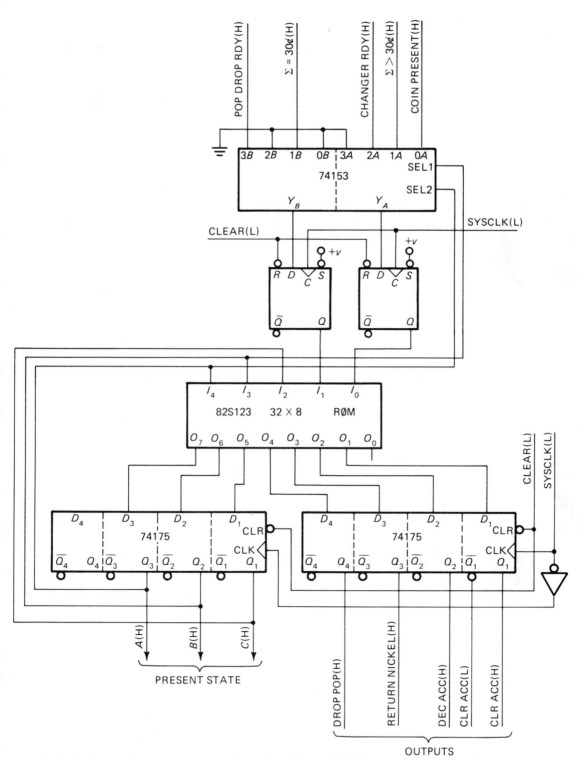

Fig. 8-34. The four-way branch indirect-addressed multiplexer/ROM implementation of the seven-state pop machine controller.

TABLE 8-5 ROM Program Specification for the Seven-state Pop Machine Controller

		A	B	C			D_A	D_B	D_C	PD	RN	DA	CA	Present state to MUX ADR converter specifications	
		I_4	I_3	I_2	I_1	I_0	O_7	O_6	O_5	O_4	O_3	O_2	O_1	SEL_2	SEL_1
State		0	0	0	0	0	0	0	0	0	0	0	0	0	0
A		0	0	0	0	1	0	0	1	0	0	0	0	0	0
		0	0	0	1	0	0	0	0	0	0	0	0	0	0
		0	0	0	1	1	0	0	1	0	0	0	0	0	0
State		0	0	1	0	0	0	1	1	0	0	0	0	0	0
B		0	0	1	0	1	0	0	1	0	0	0	0	0	0
		0	0	1	1	0	0	1	1	0	0	0	0	0	0
		0	0	1	1	1	0	0	1	0	0	0	0	0	0
State		0	1	0	0	0	Ø	Ø	Ø	Ø	Ø	Ø	Ø	Ø	Ø
Ø		0	1	0	0	1	Ø	Ø	Ø	Ø	Ø	Ø	Ø	Ø	Ø
		0	1	0	1	0	Ø	Ø	Ø	Ø	Ø	Ø	Ø	Ø	Ø
		0	1	0	1	1	Ø	Ø	Ø	Ø	Ø	Ø	Ø	Ø	Ø
State		0	1	1	0	0	0	0	0	0	0	0	0	0	1
C		0	1	1	0	1	1	0	0	0	0	0	0	0	1
		0	1	1	1	0	1	1	0	0	0	0	0	0	1
		0	1	1	1	1	Ø	Ø	Ø	0	0	0	0	0	1
State		1	0	0	0	0	1	0	0	0	1	0	0	1	0
F		1	0	0	0	1	1	0	1	0	1	0	0	1	0
		1	0	0	1	0	1	0	0	0	1	0	0	1	0
		1	0	0	1	1	1	0	1	0	1	0	0	1	0
State		1	0	1	0	0	0	1	1	0	0	1	0	Ø	Ø
G		1	0	1	0	1	0	1	1	0	0	1	0	Ø	Ø
		1	0	1	1	0	0	1	1	0	0	1	0	Ø	Ø
		1	0	1	1	1	0	1	1	0	0	1	0	Ø	Ø
State		1	1	0	0	0	1	1	0	1	0	0	0	1	1
D		1	1	0	0	1	1	1	0	1	0	0	0	1	1
		1	1	0	1	0	1	1	1	1	0	0	0	1	1
		1	1	0	1	1	1	1	1	1	0	0	0	1	1
State		1	1	1	0	0	0	0	0	0	0	0	1	Ø	Ø
E		1	1	1	0	1	0	0	0	0	0	0	1	Ø	Ø
		1	1	1	1	0	0	0	0	0	0	0	1	Ø	Ø
		1	1	1	1	1	0	0	0	0	0	0	1	Ø	Ø

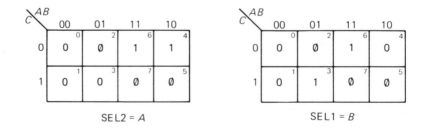

SEL2 = A

SEL1 = B

8-13 SYSTEM CONTROLLER DESIGN CENTERED AROUND AN FPLA

As it has been pointed out, the FPLA differs from PROM in several aspects. The major aspect is the way the information is coded for the device. However, the end result is basically the same when each is used as a random logic generator. Figure 8-31 illustrates the basic configuration of a FPLA or PROM centered controller. The practical aspects of the application of a FPLA in this system controller is considered in Example 8-9.

> EXAMPLE 8-9: To illustrate the application of the 82S100/110 FPLA, consider its application to the seven-state prototype pop machine controller.
>
> *Special note:* It is strongly advised that you read the data sheet thoroughly in order to fully inform yourself about programming this device. Along with this, the following worked example helps to illustrate how this device can be used.
>
> **Step 1:** Start with the desired logic expressions, which for our example are:
>
> $$D_A = \overline{A}B(=) + \overline{A}B(>) + A\overline{C}$$
> $$D_B = \overline{A}B(=) + \overline{B}C(\overline{CP}) + B\overline{C} + A\overline{B}C$$
> $$D_C = \overline{A}\,\overline{B}(CP) + B\overline{C}(PDR) + A\overline{B}(CR) + \overline{B}C$$
> $$\text{DECR ACC} = A\overline{B}C$$
> $$\text{CLR ACC} = ABC$$
> $$\text{DROP POP} = AB\overline{C}$$
> $$\text{RETURN NICKEL} = A\overline{B}\,\overline{C}$$
>
> If the specifications for the 82S100 are examined, you find that a total of *48 unique product terms* are available, each made up from 16 possible input variables.
>
> **Step 2:** Now simply give *each* of the different product terms a P_n number and proceed:

$$P_0 = \overline{A}B(=) \qquad P_9 = \overline{B}C$$
$$P_1 = \overline{A}B(>) \qquad P_{10} = ABC$$
$$P_2 = A\overline{C} \qquad P_{11} = AB\overline{C}$$
$$P_3 = \overline{B}C(\overline{CP}) \qquad P_{12} = A\overline{B}\,\overline{C}$$
$$P_4 = B\overline{C}$$
$$P_5 = A\overline{B}C$$
$$P_6 = \overline{A}\,\overline{B}(CP)$$
$$P_7 = B\overline{C}(PDR)$$
$$P_8 = A\overline{B}(CR)$$

From this listing and Figure 8-33 observe:

$$F_0 = D_A = P_0 + P_1 + P_2 \qquad F_4 = \text{DECR ACC} = P_5$$
$$F_1 = D_B = P_0 + P_3 + P_4 + P_5 \qquad F_5 = \text{CLR ACC} = P_{10}$$
$$F_2 = D_C = P_6 + P_7 + P_8 + P_9 \qquad F_6 = \text{DROP POP} = P_{11}$$
$$F_3 = \text{Not defined} \qquad F_7 = \text{RETURN NICKEL} = P_{12}$$

This list is then transferred to the approved program table as shown in Table 8-6.

Special note: It has been found that program writing is made easier by starting your programming process using a schematic with the "pin" assignments like Figure 8-35.

Fig. 8-35. The seven-state pop machine system controller implemented with an FPLA.

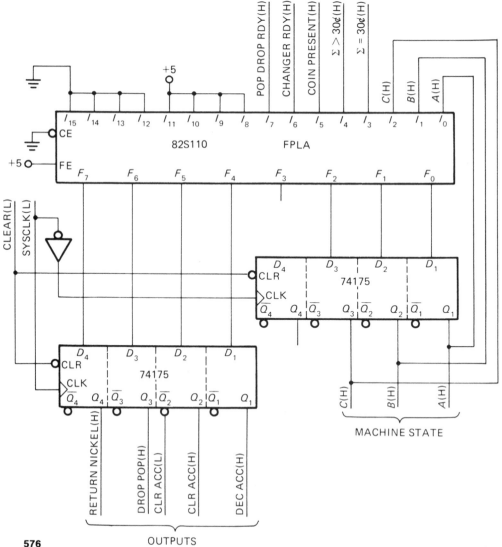

OUTPUTS

16 X 48 X 8 FPLA PROGRAM TABLE

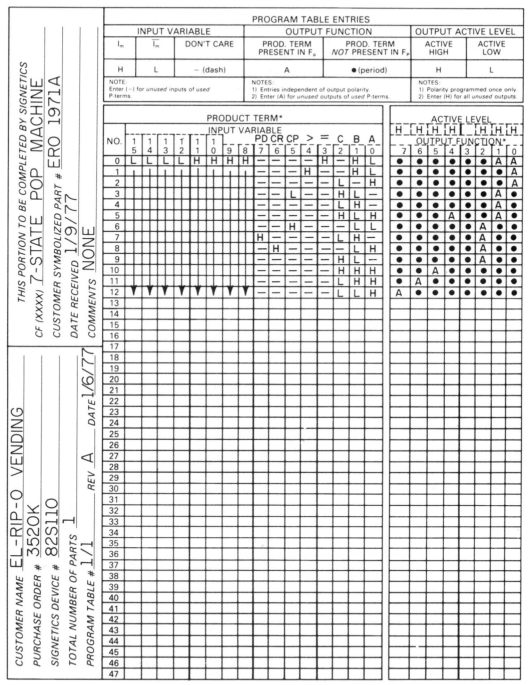

	PROGRAM TABLE ENTRIES						
	INPUT VARIABLE			OUTPUT FUNCTION		OUTPUT ACTIVE LEVEL	
	I_m	$\overline{I_m}$	DON'T CARE	PROD. TERM PRESENT IN F_p	PROD. TERM *NOT* PRESENT IN F_p	ACTIVE HIGH	ACTIVE LOW
	H	L	– (dash)	A	● (period)	H	L

NOTE: Enter (–) for *unused* inputs of *used* P-terms.

NOTES: 1) Entries independent of output polarity. 2) Enter (A) for *unused* outputs of *used* P-terms.

NOTES: 1) Polarity programmed once only. 2) Enter (H) for all *unused* outputs.

Left panel (vertical text):

THIS PORTION TO BE COMPLETED BY SIGNETICS
CF (XXXX) 7-STATE POP MACHINE   ERO 1971A
CUSTOMER SYMBOLIZED PART #
DATE RECEIVED 1/9/77
COMMENTS NONE

CUSTOMER NAME EL-RIP-O VENDING
PURCHASE ORDER # 3520K
SIGNETICS DEVICE # 82S110
TOTAL NUMBER OF PARTS 1
PROGRAM TABLE # 1/1   REV A   DATE 1/6/77

Main program table:

ACTIVE LEVEL (output polarity, all): H H H H H H H H

NO.	15	14	13	12	11	10	9	8	PD(7)	CR(6)	CP(5)	>(4)	=(3)	C(2)	B(1)	A(0)	7	6	5	4	3	2	1	0
0	L	L	L	L	H	H	H	H	−	−	−	−	H	−	H	L	●	●	●	●	●	●	A	A
1									−	−	−	H	−	−	H	L	●	●	●	●	●	●	●	A
2									−	−	−	−	L	−	L	H	●	●	●	●	●	●	●	A
3									−	−	L	−	−	H	L	−	●	●	●	●	●	●	A	●
4									−	−	−	−	L	H	−		●	●	●	●	●	●	A	●
5									−	−	−	−	H	L	H		●	●	●	A	●	●	A	●
6									−	−	H	−	−	L	L		●	●	●	●	●	A	●	●
7									H	−	−	−	−	L	H	−	●	●	●	●	●	A	●	●
8									−	H	−	−	−	L	H		●	●	●	●	●	A	●	●
9									−	−	−	−	H	L	−		●	●	●	●	●	A	●	●
10									−	−	−	−	H	H	H		●	●	A	●	●	●	●	●
11									−	−	−	−	L	H	H		●	A	●	●	●	●	●	●
12	∨	∨	∨	∨	∨	∨	∨	∨	−	−	−	−	L	L	H		A	●	●	●	●	●	●	●
13																								
14																								
15																								
16																								
17																								
18																								
19																								
20																								
21																								
22																								
23																								
24																								
25																								
26																								
27																								
28																								
29																								
30																								
31																								
32																								
33																								
34																								
35																								
36																								
37																								
38																								
39																								
40																								
41																								
42																								
43																								
44																								
45																								
46																								
47																								

*Input and Output fields of *unused* P-terms can be left blank.

11

Table 8-6. 16×48×8 FPLA table. (Courtesy of Signetics)

8-14 SUMMARY

Chapter 8 introduces a whole host of implementation techniques, all of which have certain features that make them attractive to certain applications. More than this, these configurations provide you, as the designer, with viable alternatives in all types of applications. The next chapter introduces the concepts related to using MSI and LSI *sequential devices* in a manner similar to that used in introducing MSI and LSI combinational devices in this chapter.

BIBLIOGRAPHY

1. 1977 *Data Catalog, Intel,* Intel Corporation, 1977.

2. BENTLEY, JAMES H. The Foolproof Way to Sequencer Design. *Electronic Design,* **10** (1973).

3. BERNDT, HELMUT. Functional Microprogramming as a Logic Design Aid. *IEEE Trans. Computers,* **C-19,** No. 10 (1970), 902–907.

4. BLAKESLEE, THOMAS R. *Digital Design with Standard MSI and LSI.* New York: Wiley, 1975.

5. CARR, W. N., and MIZE, J. P. *MOS/LSI Design and Applications.* New York: McGraw-Hill, 1972.

6. MILES, GENE, and NICHOL, JOHN. For Sequential Control, FPLA's. *Electronic Design,* **22** (1976), 164–169.

7. MRAZEK, DALE, and MORRIS, MELVIN. PLA's Replace ROM's for Logic Designs. *Electronic Design,* **22** (1973), 66–70.

8. National Semiconductor. *How to Design with Programmable Logic Arrays,* Application Note No. AN-89. Santa Clara, Calif: National Semiconductor Corp., 1973.

9. RICHARDS, CHARLES L. An Easy Way to Design Complex Program Controllers. *Electronics,* (1973), 107–113.

10. *Signetics Digital Linear MOS Data Book.* Sunnyvale, Calif.: Signetics Corporation, 1974.

11. Texas Instruments. *Designing with TTL PROMS and ROMS,* Bulletin No. CB-162. Dallas, Texas: Texas Instruments, 1974.

12. UIMARI, DAVID. PROM's—A Practical Alternative to Random Logic. *Electronic Products,* Jan. 21 (1974), 75–91.

13. VANDLING, G. C., and WALDECKER, D. E. The Microprogram Technique for Digital Logic Design. *Computer Design,* **8,** No. 8 (1969), 44–51.

PROBLEMS AND EXERCISES

Since the major emphasis of the material presented in this chapter is placed on the comparative utilization of the higher order combinational devices in sequential machines, the implementation problems from Chapter 7 will serve as the best possible source of exercises. In short, it is intended that each implementation technique introduced here be tried on at least two selected problems from Chapter 7. By doing this, a comparison can be made as to the relative advantages (disadvantages) of each implementation scheme. This is particularly true in the cases of the ROM and PLA implementation where the combinational as well as the sequential applications of these devices is treated.

Therefore, the general problem for Chapter 8 should read as follows: Select a controller implementation from Chapter 7 or any other source and carry out the complete implementation of this problem using:

> the model shown in Figure 8-1
> or the direct-addressed multiplexer configuration
> or the indirect-addressed multiplexer configuration
> or direct-addressed RØM or PLA configuration
> or the indirect-addressed ROM configuration
> or the indirect-addressed FPLA configuration
> or the indirect-addressed multiplexer/ROM configuration

Then evaluate your design relative to its complexity by comparing your results to other implementations tried. Be certain to include maximum clocking frequency and general flexibility. In short, develop a feeling for what type controller configuration should be used for a given requirement. Finally, can you develop an alternate general configuration that you feel has better flexibility and simplicity?

INTRODUCTION TO PROGRAMMABLE

SYSTEM CONTROLLERS

9-1   INTRODUCTION

Chapters 7 and 8 demonstrate different ways to design system controllers using a variety of different combinational logic devices. All of these techniques use either a parallel in–parallel out D-type register or JK Flip-Flop register for the basic memory element. This chapter demonstrates the use of other sequential MSI and LSI devices for the memory element, namely, multi-mode shift registers, cascadable counters, and bit-slice sequencers. In keeping with the spirit of standard approaches, *no specialized configurations that serve a limited scope of problems using nonstandard and unavailable devices are employed,* and while keeping the design general an attempt is made to minimize part count and cost and to increase flexibility.

One of the main reasons for considering standard MSI shift registers and counters for the memory elements in system controller sequencers is that each of these devices is a sequential machine in its own right. The *internal* combinational logic and Flip-Flops, coupled with some external control inputs, provide the designer with a device that has some basic sequencing functions (counting or shifting). Since the counting and shifting operations are closely allied to the process of state-to-state transition, and since the state-to-state transition process must be synthesized for every system sequence using plain Flip-Flops, why not use some device that has this feature already built in? It will be shown that these devices, because of their functions, can be utilized efficiently providing the proper design procedures are taken. The proper design procedure, of course, includes selecting the right device for the "job." The other reason for this study is that it provides an introduction to the concepts of *programmable sequential machines.*

The general sequential model that is used throughout the discussion is shown in Figure 9-1. As you examine this figure, it should be apparent that the sequential operation of this machine is determined by the combinational NEXT STATE CONTROL logic, and this is basically done by forming the NEXT STATE of the machine while controlling the parallel and serial inputs and the provided external mode control inputs. These external control inputs include operations such as: shift-left, shift-right, parallel load, hold count enable, and load.

During the design process which closely parallels that of Chapters 7 and 8, you will be asking questions such as: "In this state do I want to SHIFT LEFT with a 1 or 0, or do I want a PARALLEL LOAD, conditionally or unconditionally, to generate the next state?"; rather than "Do I want to SET or RESET a Flip-Flop, conditionally or unconditionally, as in Chapters 7 and 8?" The word "conditionally," if you remember, refers to a *state change depending on an outside world input being ASSERTED or NOT-ASSERTED* and implies that a MEV is used, whereas "unconditionally" refers to a *state change independent of any outside world input.*

With these concepts in mind, let's get right into some applications to illustrate the design process using a shift register.

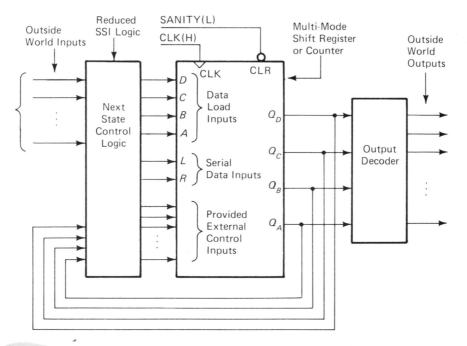

Fig. 9-1. The general model of the system controller sequential circuit utilizing shift registers and counters as the memory element.

9-2 SYSTEM CONTROLLERS CENTERED AROUND A MSI SHIFT REGISTER

If you select the proper and available shift register and follow some design and state assignment constraints, this device can and will produce some very effective results in terms of design flexibility and hardware savings. To illustrate the techniques involved, consider the AM74LS194 or AM74S194 device, which is a fully synchronous SIPO, PIPO, PISO, and SISO four-bit shift register. The specification sheet for this device is shown in Figure 9-2. This device was selected because of its edge-triggered synchronous LOAD/SHIFT operations and asynchronous CLEAR features that are deemed desirable for the applications described in the introduction.*

As mentioned in the introduction, using a device such as the AM74LS194 imposes some design constraints. However, these design constraints are not formidable; they are simply in keeping with the statement: "Know your devices, the functional features and operational limitations, and use good sense."

The first such constraint to be addressed when using a shift register such as the AM74LS194 is the *state assignment problem*. Keep in mind what decisions are to be made in any given state:

(1) Do I shift a 0 left?
(2) Do I shift a 1 left?
(3) Do I shift a 0 right?
(4) Do I shift a 1 right?
(5) Do I do a parallel load?

Therefore, in making a state assignment, philosophically you should try to do as many simple "shifting" operations as possible. In short, if you could complete a state assignment by simply shifting a 1 to the left without having to perform any other operation, then do it! Understanding increases as you see the actual design process unfold. However, let it be said again: *The basic device-imposed considerations governing your NEXT STATE ASSIGNMENT are*:

(1) Do I call for shift right or left with a 1 or 0? Conditionally or unconditionally?
(2) Do I call for a parallel load? Conditionally or unconditionally?

Now consider that you were given the MDS diagram shown in Figure 9-3 and you were asked to design the next state control logic and memory element section of a system controller with the AM74LS194 shift register. Of course the first step would be to make a state assignment. As mentioned earlier, this is done by mixing an assortment of shifting 1's and 0's right and left or parallel loading the device.

---

*The AM74LS194 series is not plagued with the 1's and 0's catching problem (see data sheet).

Am54LS/74LS194A · Am54LS/74LS195A
Four-Bit High-Speed Shift Registers

Distinctive Characteristics

- Parallel load or shift right with $J\overline{K}$ inputs on Am54LS/74LS195A
- Shift left, right, parallel load or do nothing on Am54LS/74LS194A
- Fully synchronous shifting and parallel loading
- Buffered common clock
- Buffered common active-LOW clear
- 100% reliability assurance testing in compliance with MIL-STD-883

FUNCTIONAL DESCRIPTION

The Am54LS/74LS194A and Am54LS/74LS195A are 4-bit registers that exhibit fully synchronous operation in all operating modes. The Am54LS/74LS195A can either parallel load all four register bits via the parallel inputs (A, B, C, D) or shift each of the four register bits right one place. The shifting or parallel loading is under control of the shift/load input (S/L). When the shift/load input is LOW, data is loaded from the parallel data inputs; when the shift/load input is HIGH, data is loaded from the register bits on the left. The first bit, Q_A, is loaded via the J and $\overline{K}$ inputs in the shift mode.

The Am54LS/74LS194A operates in four modes under control of the two select inputs, S_0 and S_1. The four modes are parallel load (data comes from the parallel inputs), shift right (data comes from the flip-flop to the left, with the Q_A bit input from R), shift left (data comes from the flip-flop to the right, with the Q_D input from L), and hold or do nothing (each flip-flop receives data from its own output).

For both devices the outputs change state synchronously following a LOW-to-HIGH transition on the clock input, CP. Both devices have an active-LOW synchronous clear (CLR) which forces all outputs to the LOW state ($\overline{Q}_D$ HIGH) independent of any other inputs.

Because all the flip-flops are D-type they do not catch 0's or 1's, and the only requirements on any inputs is that they meet the short set-up and hold time intervals with respect to the clock LOW-to-HIGH transition.

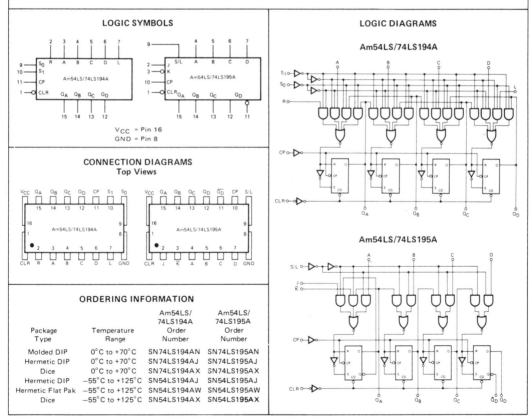

LOGIC SYMBOLS

V_{CC} = Pin 16
GND = Pin 8

CONNECTION DIAGRAMS
Top Views

LOGIC DIAGRAMS

Am54LS/74LS194A

Am54LS/74LS195A

ORDERING INFORMATION

Package Type	Temperature Range	Am54LS/ 74LS194A Order Number	Am54LS/ 74LS195A Order Number
Molded DIP	0°C to +70°C	SN74LS194AN	SN74LS195AN
Hermetic DIP	0°C to +70°C	SN74LS194AJ	SN74LS195AJ
Dice	0°C to +70°C	SN74LS194AX	SN74LS195AX
Hermetic DIP	−55°C to +125°C	SN54LS194AJ	SN54LS195AJ
Hermetic Flat Pak	−55°C to +125°C	SN54LS194AW	SN54LS195AW
Dice	−55°C to +125°C	SN54LS194AX	SN54LS195AX

Fig. 9-2(a). Data sheet for the AM74LS194 shift register. (Courtesy of Advanced Micro Devices)

Am25LS194A·Am25LS195A
Four-Bit High-Speed Shift Registers

Distinctive Characteristics

- Parallel load or shift right with JK inputs on Am25LS195A.
- Shift left, right, parallel load or do nothing on Am25LS194A
- 35 MHz guaranteed clock frequency
- 8mA sink current over full military temperature range

- 50mV improved V_{OL} compared to Am74LS
- 440μA source current
- Fully synchronous shifting and parallel loading
- Buffered common active-LOW clear
- 100% reliability assurance testing in compliance with MIL-STD-883

FUNCTIONAL DESCRIPTION

The Am25LS194A and Am25LS195A are 4-bit registers that exhibit fully synchronous operation in all operating modes. The Am25LS195A can either parallel load all four register bits via the parallel inputs (A, B, C, D) or shift each of the four register bits right one place. The shifting or parallel loading is under control of the shift/load input (S/L). When the shift/load input is LOW, data is loaded from the parallel data inputs; when the shift/load input is HIGH, data is loaded from the register bits on the left. The first bit, Q_A, is loaded via the J and $\overline{K}$ inputs in the shift mode.

The Am25LS194A operates in four modes under control of the two select inputs, S_0 and S_1. The four modes are parallel load (data comes from the parallel inputs), shift right

(data comes from the flip-flop to the left, with the Q_A bit input from R), shift left (data comes from the flip-flop to the right, with the Q_D input from L), and hold or do nothing (each flip-flop receives data from its own output).

For both devices the outputs change state synchronously following a LOW-to-HIGH transition on the clock input, CP. Both devices have an active-LOW synchronous clear (CLR) which forces all outputs to the LOW state ($\overline{Q}_D$ HIGH) independent of any other inputs.

Because all the flip-flops are D-type they do not catch 0's or 1's, and the only requirements on any inputs is that they meet the short set-up and hold time intervals with respect to the clock LOW-to-HIGH transition.

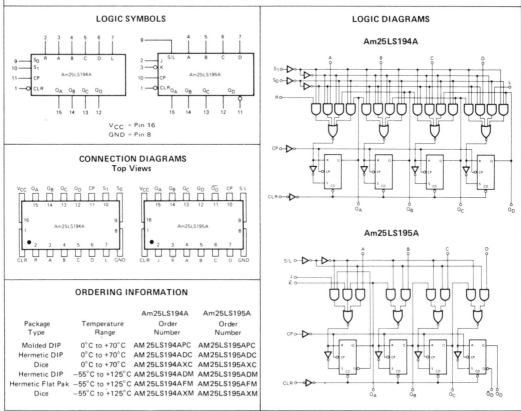

LOGIC SYMBOLS

V_{CC} = Pin 16
GND = Pin 8

CONNECTION DIAGRAMS
Top Views

LOGIC DIAGRAMS

Am25LS194A

Am25LS195A

ORDERING INFORMATION

Package Type	Temperature Range	Am25LS194A Order Number	Am25LS195A Order Number
Molded DIP	0°C to +70°C	AM25LS194APC	AM25LS195APC
Hermetic DIP	0°C to +70°C	AM25LS194ADC	AM25LS195ADC
Dice	0°C to +70°C	AM25LS194AXC	AM25LS195AXC
Hermetic DIP	−55°C to +125°C	AM25LS194ADM	AM25LS195ADM
Hermetic Flat Pak	−55°C to +125°C	AM25LS194AFM	AM25LS195AFM
Dice	−55°C to +125°C	AM25LS194AXM	AM25LS195AXM

Fig. 9-2(b). Data sheet for the AM25LS194 shift register. (Courtesy of Advanced Micro Devices)

Though this sounds simple, the actual optimal state assignment is quite subtle. *This is particularly true if you are faced with handling ASYNCHRONOUS inputs and at the same time you are trying to avoid parallel loading operations.* Also, the state assignment process is confounded somewhat by the fact that many times (as in the example) the number of states (seven) requires only three state variables, but the AM74LS194 has four state variables hardwired. If this extra state variable is used unnecessarily, it tends (but not always) to complicate the next state control logic. Therefore, strive to use only the correct number of state variables unless you can avoid making more than one parallel load by doing so. These concepts are illustrated by example.

EXAMPLE 9-1: Consider the thought processes involved in making a state assignment to the MDS diagram shown in Figure 9-3 (see Figure 9-4). Here

Fig. 9-3. A proposed state diagram for some system control function.

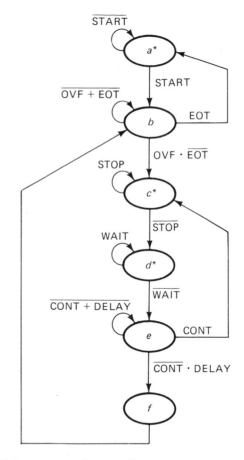

simple hold-to-shift operations are called for to meet the unit-distance constraints induced by the ASYNCHRONOUS inputs. A little study indicates that it is impossible to meet these constraints and at the same time to avoid more than one parallel load operation. Therefore, the state assignment illustrated is based on the state variables Q_B, Q_C, and Q_D. This implies that Q_A is to be treated as a Ø if a unique three-bit code assignment centered around Q_B, Q_C, and Q_D can be devised. Thus state a is given the 0000 assignment for RESET reasons. Once in state a you "hold" or shift a 1 left conditional on START, moving to state b. In state b you hold or shift a 1 left conditionally on OVF·$\overline{\text{EOT}}$ or shift a 0 right conditionally on EOT. The rest of the state assignment is made based on this same sort of thinking. However, there are two observations that should be pointed out:

Fig. 9-4. The state diagram with a shift left and right assignment.

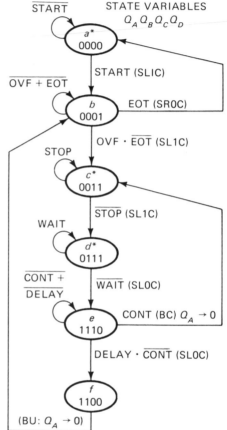

(1) Note that the Johnson or ring counter sequence down through state f allows simple shift operations for each state change except the ones from e to c and f to b. It should also be noted that the $Q_B Q_C Q_D$ were kept unique; therefore Q_A could be ignored to some extent.
(2) It is interesting to make the following contrast: Now the problem (state assignment) is being adapted to the device operational characteristics, where as in earlier chapters the devices were adapted to the state assignment. *This contrast points to the first concept of programmable controllers, that being that the problem is adapted to the hardware rather than the hardware being adapted to the problem.*

9-3 DESIGN AND IMPLEMENTATION PRACTICES USING THE AM74LS194

To assure a standard approach to implementation, several new maps are introduced, namely: The ACTION MAP, MODE CONTROL MAPS, and DATA INPUT MAPS (both parallel and serial). The function of these maps is discussed as each is used. However, philosophically the entries in these maps are made on the three important "ACTION questions":

(1) Do I shift left? If so, do I shift a 1 or 0? Is the shift conditional or unconditional?
(2) Do I shift right? If so, do I shift a 1 or 0? Is the shift conditional or unconditional?
(3) Do I do a parallel load? If so, what is the data input code? Is the parallel load conditional or unconditional?

Because you must ask yourself these questions for each state, you need an ACTION MAP and some shortened mnemonics for the "actions" to be taken. These mnemonics are:

SL1C = Shift left 1 conditional
SL0C = Shift left 0 conditional
SL1U = Shift left 1 unconditional
SL0U = Shift left 0 unconditional

SR1C = Shift right 1 conditional
SR0C = Shift right 0 conditional
SR1U = Shift right 1 unconditional
SR0U = Shift right 0 unconditional

BC = Branch conditional
BU = Branch unconditional

These newly defined maps and action mnemonics are treated through a familiar example. For obvious comparative reasons, we go back to the seven-state pop machine controller.

EXAMPLE 9-2:   Illustrate the design processes leading to an implementation of the seven-state prototype pop machine system controller utilizing the AM74LS194 multi-mode shift register in a step-by-step manner.

Step 1:   Given the MDS diagram in Figure 9-5, consider the shift register sequence state assignment process based on the constraint imposed by the asynchronous inputs. Observe that four hold-to-shift sequences and five parallel load operations are called for by this state assignment. The asynchronous inputs seriously limit flexibility. In short, there is a problem with states c and f. See Exercise 9-3 in the problem set. However, the example continues.

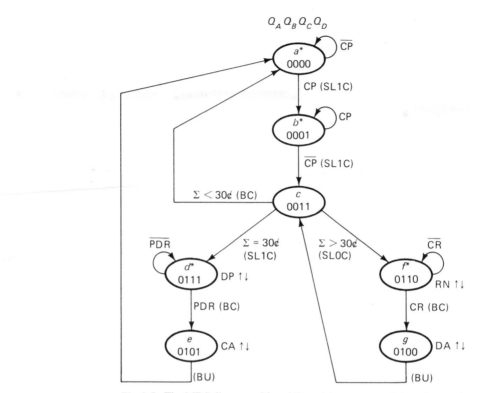

Fig. 9-5. The MDS diagram with a shift register sequence state assignment for the seven-state pop machine controller.

Step 2: Plot the STATE MAP and ACTION MAP. The ACTION MAP is a map plotted with the ACTION MNEMONICS, providing a visual display of what action or actions are called for in each state in order for the next state to be generated (see Figure 9-6).

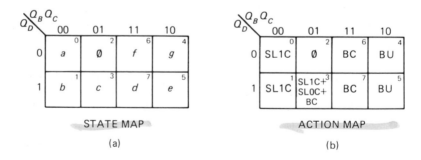

Fig. 9-6. The STATE MAP and ACTION MAP for the 7-state MDS diagram in Figure 9-5.

Step 3: Plot the MODE CONTROL MAPS. In this step the designer must enter into S_0 and S_1 maps the proper code in order that the proper operation is specified for each state. This is when the action map and the mode control TRUTH-TABLE for the AM74LS194 are used. The specification sheet in Figure 9-2 shows that:

S_1	S_0	ACTION
0	0	Hold (no action)
0	1	SR (shift right)
1	0	SL (shift left)
1	1	Branch (load)

See Figure 9-7.

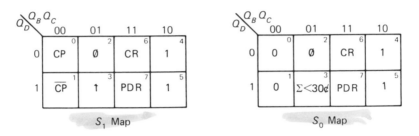

Fig. 9-7. The MODE CONTROL MAPS for the 7-state MDS diagram.

These MODE CONTROL MAPS are plotted directly from the MDS diagram; however, care must be exercised to make the proper entry for the more complex conditional shift and load entries. For example, in state c, SL1C + SL0C + BC operations are called for, and the actual entry for the S_1 and S_0 maps must be resolved. This can be done using a simple TRUTH-TABLE as shown in Figure 9-8.

Fig. 9-8. A simple TRUTH-TABLE which aids in the resolution of the $S_1 S_0$ map entries for states that are specified as SHIFT and BRANCH states.

$\Sigma < 30$ ¢	S_1	S_0	
0	1	0	(shift left operation)
1	1	1	(load operation)

$$\therefore S_1 = 1 \text{ and } S_0 = \Sigma < 30 \text{ ¢}$$

Keep in mind that the $S_1 S_0$ maps merely set up the mode control. Thus it is assumed that the SERIAL and PARALLEL DATA INPUTS are set-up to load the appropriate bit or bits independently from these maps. Setting up the data input is the subject of the next step.

Step 4: Plot the INPUT DATA MAPS. This step refers to the AC-TION MAP to determine the entries for the SERIAL DATA INPUTS when shifting operations are called for and to the entries for the PARALLEL DATA INPUTS when a branch is called for. See Figure 9-9 for the SERIAL DATA INPUT MAPS and Figure 9-10 for the PARALLEL INPUT DATA MAPS.

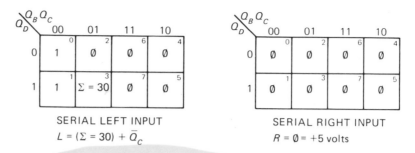

SERIAL LEFT INPUT
$L = (\Sigma = 30) + \bar{Q}_C$

SERIAL RIGHT INPUT
$R = \emptyset = +5$ volts

Fig. 9-9. The SERIAL DATA INPUT MAPS for the AM74LS194 implementation of the 7-state MDS diagram in Figure 9-5.

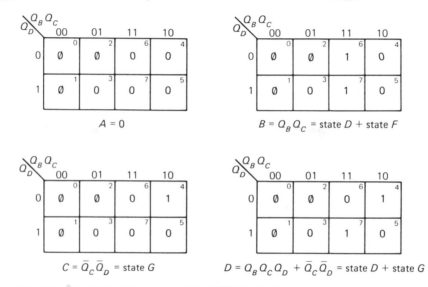

$A = 0$

$B = Q_B Q_C$ = state D + state F

$C = \bar{Q}_C \bar{Q}_D$ = state G

$D = Q_B Q_C Q_D + \bar{Q}_C \bar{Q}_D$ = state D + state G

Fig. 9-10. The PARALLEL INPUT DATA MAPS for the AM74LS194 implementation of the 7-state MDS diagram in Figure 9-5.

Step 5: Choose combinational logic and draw up the schematic. Since the S_1 and S_0 maps are reasonably complex, there is a choice of using MUX's or SSI or any other devices to develop the appropriate expression for S_1(H) and S_0(H). Let us use multiplexers for S_1 and S_0 and SSI for the rest.

Remember that when the maps are plotted and the multiplexer is addressed by the state of the machine, the map entries in each cell are the logic variables connected to the MUX input with the same input number as the map cell. See Figure 9-11 for the circuit realization centered around the AM74LS194.

From all this you see that when the logic is designed straight from the maps, and the maps are plotted straight from the MDS diagram, a straightforward, logical, and standard design process emerges.

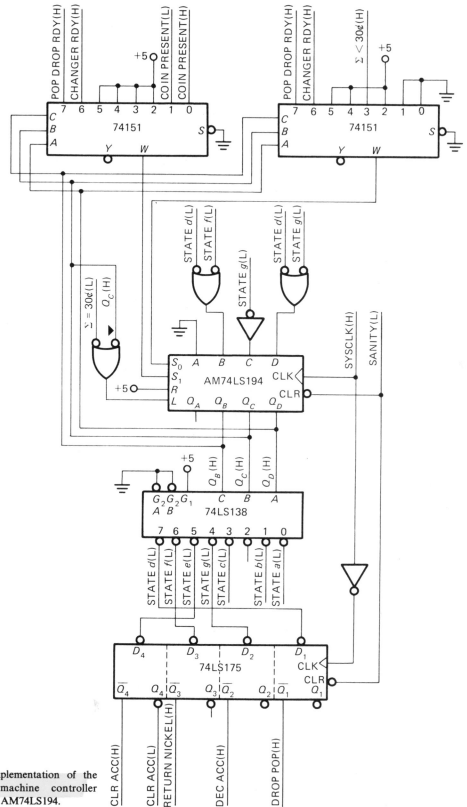

Fig. 9-11. The implementation of the seven-state pop machine controller centered around an AM74LS194.

The experienced observer should be noticing that filling out an ACTION MAP is a form of microprogramming. Some interesting things are starting to unfold, as you will see in the next section. From Figure 9-11 this particular system configuration does lead to an interesting implementation, one probably considered not quite optimal for this particular problem. But it is one worthy of consideration for other problems where strictly shifting operations can be called out. In summary, consider the possibility of putting the AM74LS194 under FPLA or PROM control, or better yet, RAM control, and you have a configuration worth considering for general application. These considerations are left as exercises and should be studied in depth.

In the next section we consider using a cascadable counter as the present state register in hopes of uncovering a better system configuration yet.

9-4 SYSTEM CONTROLLERS CENTERED AROUND A MSI COUNTER

In the same line of thought that was used in the last section for the MSI shift register, a parallel development can be made for a MSI multi-mode counter. Therefore, if you select the proper and available counter and follow some design and state assignment contraints, favorable results can be achieved. The AM7416X series of counters have some operational features that make them attractive when considering their use as the memory element in a system controller. In particular, the SN74LS161 or AM25LS161 counter is selected to illustrate the design steps and general approaches. See Figure 9-12 for the data sheet description of the AM74LS161 counter. It is noted that the AM25LS161 is functionally equivalent to the AM74LS161.

The basic operation features that make this counter attractive are:

(1) Four-bit binary synchronous and cascadable
(2) Asynchronous clear (sanity)
(3) Edge-triggered (no 1's and 0's catching problems)
(4) Synchronous load (branching)
(5) A count enable control (conditional branch and count)

It should be kept in mind that the general shift register model shown in Figure 9-1 can be used for the applications of this series of counters. The only difference you will find is that the state assignment problem differs somewhat and the shift register configuration has a slight edge over the counter configuration in terms of flexibility. However, philosophically the two configurations are almost identical.

As mentioned, when a counter such as the AM74LS161 (AM25LS161) is used, the ACTIONS that must be considered to change a state are:

(1) Do I continue the count sequence? or
(2) Do I branch by parallel loading the counter?
    These questions can be broken down further:

Am54LS/74LS160·Am54LS/74LS161
Am54LS/74LS162·Am54LS/74LS163
Synchronous Four-Bit Counters

Distinctive Characteristics

- 4-bit synchronous counters
- Synchronously programmable
- Internal look-ahead counting
- Carry output for n-bit cascading

- Synchronous or asynchronous clear
- Advanced low-power Schottky technology
- 100% reliability assurance testing in compliance with MIL-STD-883

FUNCTIONAL DESCRIPTION

The Am54LS/74LS160, Am54LS/74LS161, Am54LS/74LS162 and Am54LS/74LS163 synchronous, presettable counters have internal look-ahead carry and ripple carry output for high-speed counting applications. The Am54LS/74LS160 and Am54LS/74LS162 are decade counters and the Am54LS/74LS161 and Am54LS/74LS163 are 4-bit binary counters. Counting or loading occurs on the positive transition of the clock pulse. A LOW level on the load input causes the data on the A, B, C and D inputs to be shifted to the appropriate Q outputs on the next positive clock transition

The Am54LS/74LS160 and Am54LS/74LS161 feature an asynchronous clear. A LOW level at the clear input sets the Q outputs LOW regardless of the other inputs. The Am54LS/74LS162 and Am54LS/74LS163 have a synchronous clear. A LOW level at the clear input sets the Q outputs LOW after the next positive clock transition regardless of the enable inputs.

Both count-enable inputs P and T must be HIGH to count. Count enable T is included in the ripple carry output gate for cascading connection.

LOGIC DIAGRAMS

Am54LS/74LS160 Synchronous Decade Counter

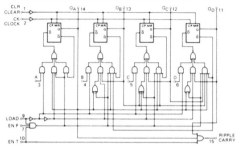

Am54LS/74LS162 synchronous decade counters are similar; however, the clear is synchronous as shown for the Am54LS/74LS163 binary counters.

Am54LS/74LS163 Synchronous Binary Counter

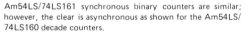
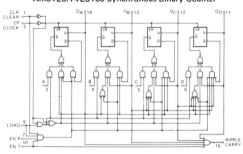

Am54LS/74LS161 synchronous binary counters are similar; however, the clear is asynchronous as shown for the Am54LS/74LS160 decade counters.

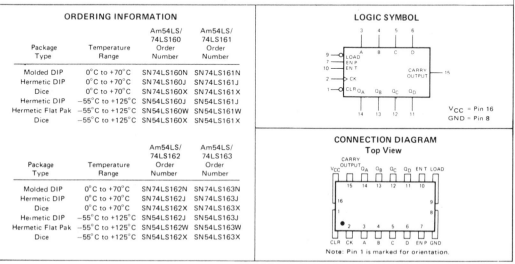

ORDERING INFORMATION

Package Type	Temperature Range	Am54LS/74LS160 Order Number	Am54LS/74LS161 Order Number
Molded DIP	0°C to +70°C	SN74LS160N	SN74LS161N
Hermetic DIP	0°C to +70°C	SN74LS160J	SN74LS161J
Dice	0°C to +70°C	SN74LS160X	SN74LS161X
Hermetic DIP	−55°C to +125°C	SN54LS160J	SN54LS161J
Hermetic Flat Pak	−55°C to +125°C	SN54LS160W	SN54LS161W
Dice	−55°C to +125°C	SN54LS160X	SN54LS161X

Package Type	Temperature Range	Am54LS/74LS162 Order Number	Am54LS/74LS163 Order Number
Molded DIP	0°C to +70°C	SN74LS162N	SN74LS163N
Hermetic DIP	0°C to +70°C	SN74LS162J	SN74LS163J
Dice	0°C to +70°C	SN74LS162X	SN74LS163X
Hermetic DIP	−55°C to +125°C	SN54LS162J	SN54LS163J
Hermetic Flat Pak	−55°C to +125°C	SN54LS162W	SN54LS163W
Dice	−55°C to +125°C	SN54LS162X	SN54LS163X

LOGIC SYMBOL

V_{CC} = Pin 16
GND = Pin 8

CONNECTION DIAGRAM
Top View

Note: Pin 1 is marked for orientation.

Fig. 9-12(a). Data sheet for the AM74LS161 counter. (Courtesy of Advanced Micro Devices)

Am25LS160·Am25LS161
Am25LS162·Am25LS163
Synchronous Four-Bit Counters

Distinctive Characteristics

- 4-bit synchronous counters, synchronously programmable
- 35 MHz guaranteed clock frequency
- 8mA sink current over full military temperature range
- 50mV improved V_{OL} compared to Am74LS
- 440μA source current
- 3ns hold time
- Synchronous or asynchronous clear
- 100% reliability assurance testing in compliance with MIL-STD-883

FUNCTIONAL DESCRIPTION

The Am25LS160, Am25LS161, Am25LS162 and Am25LS163 synchronous, presettable counters have internal look-ahead carry and ripple carry output for high-speed counting applications. The Am25LS160 and Am25LS162 are decade counters and the Am25LS161 and Am25LS 163 are 4-bit binary counters. Counting or loading occurs on the positive transition of the clock pulse. A LOW level on the load input causes the data on the A, B, C and D inputs to be shifted to the appropriate Q outputs on the next positive clock transition. The load need meet only the set-up and hold time requirements with respect to the clock.

The Am25LS160 and Am25LS161 feature an asynchronous clear. A LOW level at the clear input sets the Q outputs LOW regardless of the other inputs. The Am25LS162 and Am25LS163 have a synchronous clear. A LOW level at the clear input sets the Q outputs LOW after the next positive clock transition regardless of the enable inputs.

Both count-enable inputs P and T must be HIGH to count. Count enable T is included in the ripple carry output gate for cascading connection. The enable P or T inputs need meet only the set-up and hold time requirements with respect to the clock.

LOGIC DIAGRAMS

Am25LS160 Synchronous Decade Counter

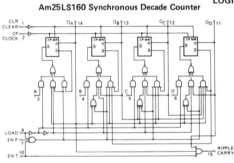

Am25LS162 synchronous decade counters are similar; however, the clear is synchronous as shown for the Am25LS163 binary counters.

Am25LS163 Synchronous Binary Counter

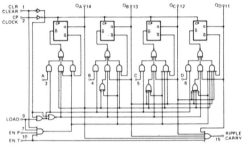

Am25LS161 synchronous binary counters are similar; however, the clear is asynchronous as shown for the Am25LS160 decade counters.

ORDERING INFORMATION

Package Type	Temperature Range	Am25 LS160 Order Number	Am25 LS161 Order Number
Molded DIP	0°C to +70°C	AM25LS160PC	AM25LS161PC
Hermetic DIP	0°C to +70°C	AM25LS160DC	AM25LS161DC
Dice	0°C to +70°C	AM25LS160XC	AM25LS161XC
Hermetic DIP	−55°C to +125°C	AM25LS160DM	AM25LS161DM
Hermetic Flat Pak	−55°C to +125°C	AM25LS160FM	AM25LS161FM
Dice	−55°C to +125°C	AM25LS160XM	AM25LS161XM

Package Type	Temperature Range	Am25 LS162 Order Number	Am25 LS163 Order Number
Molded DIP	0°C to +70°C	AM25LS162PC	AM25LS163PC
Hermetic DIP	0°C to +70°C	AM25LS162DC	AM25LS163DC
Dice	0°C to +70°C	AM25LS162XC	AM25LS163XC
Hermetic DIP	−55°C to +125°C	AM25LS162DM	AM25LS163DM
Hermetic Flat Pak	−55°C to +125°C	AM25LS162FM	AM25LS163FM
Dice	−55°C to +125°C	AM25LS162XM	AM25LS163XM

LOGIC SYMBOL

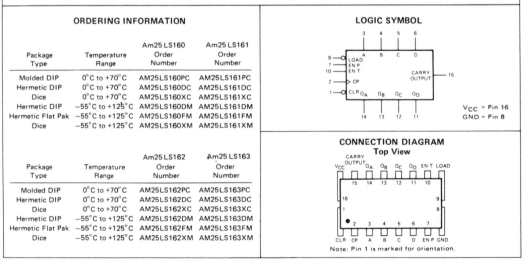

V_{CC} = Pin 16
GND = Pin 8

CONNECTION DIAGRAM
Top View

Note: Pin 1 is marked for orientation.

Fig. 9-12(b). Data sheet for the AM25LS161 counter. (Courtesy of Advanced Micro Devices)

(1) Do I continue to count conditionally?
(2) Do I continue to count unconditionally?
(3) Do I branch conditionally?
(4) Do I branch unconditionally?

The shorter mnemonics for these actions are:

(1) CC
(2) CU
(3) BC
(4) BU

Remember, "conditionally" means depending on an input condition.

EXAMPLE 9-3:   Consider the same basic state diagram found in Figure 9-3 and
devise a state assignment based on the AM74LS161. See Figure 9-13.

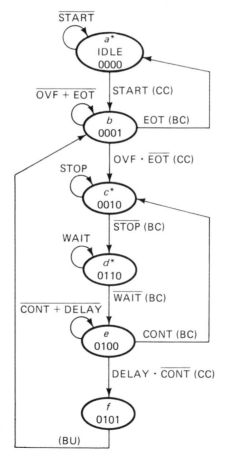

Fig. 9-13. A count-branch state assignment.

As we view the state assignment for the MDS diagram in Figure 9-13, we see again the asynchronous input places constraints on a natural counter sequence. This brings up the point: Wouldn't it be nice if we had a four-bit Gray code counter with specifications similar to those of the AM74LS161 (AM25LS161)? However, the next section shows that even having a Gray code counter will not completely solve the asynchronous state assignment constraint.

Now again, for obvious reasons, let's consider implementing the seven-state pop machine system controller with a counter-centered implementation.

EXAMPLE 9-4:   Illustrate the design processes leading to an implementation of the seven-state prototype pop machine system controller utilizing the AM74LS161 (AM25LS161) counter.

Step 1:   When using the AM74LS161 (AM25LS161) counter, we see that rather than shifting left or right with a 1 or 0, we are constrained to continue in a "binary count sequence" or "branch" by performing a synchronous load operation. Based on this criterion, a count-branch state assignment is illustrated in Figure 9-14. The STATE and ACTION maps for that diagram are in Figure 9-15.

Note that the assignment is identical to that used in both Chapters 7 and 8.

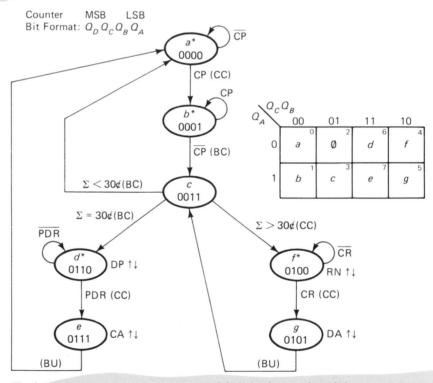

Fig. 9-14. A state assignment for an AM74LS161 implementation of the seven-state pop machine system controller.

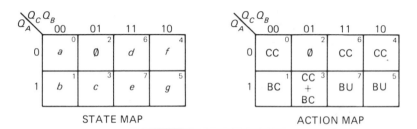

STATE MAP   ACTION MAP

Fig. 9-15. The STATE MAP and ACTION MAP for the 7-state MDS diagram shown in Figure 9-14.

Step 2: Plot the MODE CONTROL MAPS. In this step the design must enter into two maps, the LOAD MAP and the COUNT ENABLE MAP, the appropriate code that will cause the counter to continue counting or branch conditionally or unconditionally. To aid in this effort use the MODE CONTROL TABLE shown in Figure 9-16. Therefore, from the ACTION MAP and the MDS DIAGRAM we can plot the MODE CONTROL MAPS (Figure 9-17).

Fig. 9-16. The MODE CONTROL TABLE for AM74LS161 counter.

COUNT ENABLE	LOAD	ACTION
0	0	Hold count
1	0	Cont. count
0	1	Load—implies load
1	1	Load—overrides count

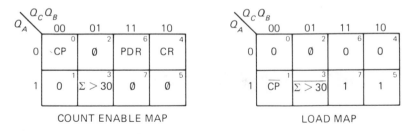

COUNT ENABLE MAP   LOAD MAP

Fig. 9-17. The MODE CONTROL MAPS.

It should be noted that when plotting these control maps, a CC entry in the ACTION MAP results in the entry of a MEV in the COUNT ENABLE MAP. This MEV is the variable that must be ASSERTED to enable the "continue count" action. Also, note that since the "load" action overrides the "count" action (see TRUTH-TABLE), the corresponding entry in the BRANCH MAP must be a 0. This overriding feature allows Ø's to be plotted in the COUNT ENABLE MAP when the ACTION is BU *but not BC*. Further, we see that if the ACTION IS CC+BC, THE ENTRY IN THE COUNT ENABLE MAP is the conditional count variable, or 1, and the entry in the LOAD MAP is the branch variable. However, if the COUNT variable (say X) is the complement of the BRANCH variable ($\bar{X}$), the entry in the COUNT ENABLE MAP equals 1.

As we plot these mode control maps we find few problems until we come to a state like state *C*. Here a multi-branch (>2 way) causes us some difficulty as illustrated in the next step.

Step 3: Plot the PARALLEL DATA MAPS. During this step the next state assignment code is plotted into the PARALLEL DATA MAP at the cells in the ACTION MAP that have anything to do with a branch action, namely, states *b*, *c*, *e*, and *g*. ∅'s are entered at CC entries because they represent "don't care" branch states. This is because the next state is generated by a count increment.

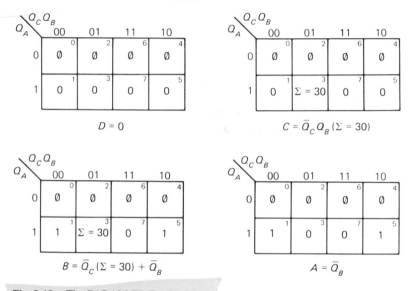

Fig. 9-18. The PARALLEL DATA MAPS.

Step 4: (See Figure 9-18.) Design and implement the logic called for by *all the maps* and connect to the appropriate inputs of the AM74LS161 (AM25LS161) as follows. Let's use MUX's again for the relatively complex expression and maps and a 3-to-8 decoder and SSI logic for the rest. The completed circuit is found in Figure 9-19.

Observe that the circuit realization shown in Figure 9-19 requires an amount of hardware similar to that for the shift register realization shown in Figure 9-11. Again, we should be able to trace the design straight from the MDS diagram to a map for each input to the counter if we keep Figure 9-1 in mind. All this leads to some logical and standard design steps that can be applied to a wide number of problems. Several design exercises will be assigned using this approach.

The next section illustrates how this configuration can be extended into a *programmable* type of system controller.

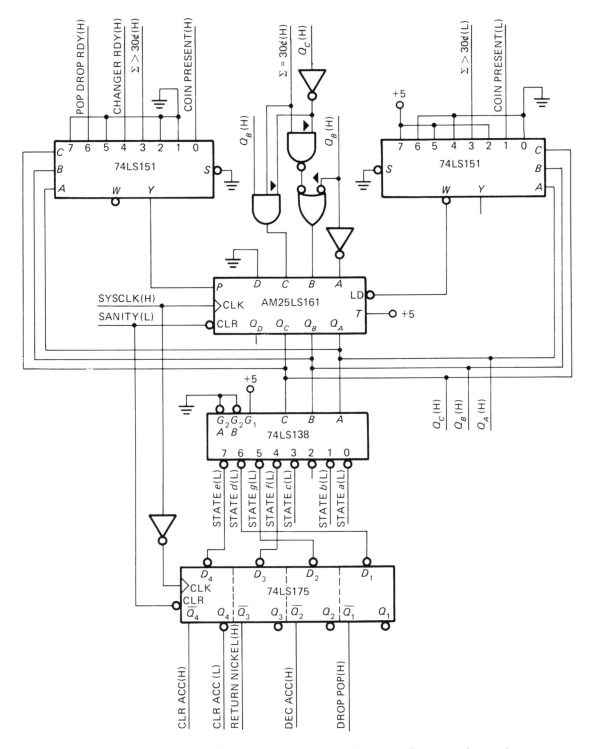

Fig. 9-19. The implementation of the seven-state pop machine controller centered around an AM25LS161.

9-5 THE CONCEPTS OF A PROGRAMMABLE SYSTEM CONTROLLER

The utmost in the eyes of most digital system designers is the completely programmable, fast, and simple-to-use device, one that matches the impact that the high-quality integrated circuit op-amp has made on the analog world. This microprocessor device should provide a simple, straightforward approach to the implementation of a circuit whose operation is completely specified by a detailed MDS diagram, and should be able to react (generate outputs) to input conditions in nanoseconds. Further, it would be desirable to have this "controller" direct the activities of an Arithmetic-Logic-Unit (ALU), some collection of registers, and some main memory in order that data processing operations can be done likewise. Though we don't presently have this special device, the following developments have very special operational features.

Let us delay the discussion of these control features required for the data processing features and concentrate on what fundamental control features are desired to optimally implement a system controller whose operation can be specified by an MDS diagram. If we concentrate our effort here, the data processing control features will follow automatically. This is based on the fact that the data processing activity in a well-designed digital computer can be directed by a programmable system controller. Another name for a machine with the features just described is a microprogrammable machine or computer.

9-6 SOME BASIC DESIRABLE FEATURES OF A PROGRAMMABLE CONTROLLER

By studying a state diagram like the ones discussed in this text, we can itemize some basic features that would be desirable to have incorporated in a programmable controller. A programmable controller is one in which a designer can program the device's operation by filling out a ROM table or maybe, better yet, one that allows programing in a higher level assembly-type language straight from an MDS diagram. Further, this controller should be modular so it can be expanded to an n-state machine.

9-7 GENERAL REQUIREMENTS

Assuming that the programmable device (see Figure 9-20) has an array type memory, one in which basic internal operation instructions and output codes can be stored, and a controllable *counter* (program counter) or *register* (memory address register) used to select or address the stored instructions, the following features are desirable.

(1) It should be able to start processing a stored instruction program starting from an arbitrary location in memory.

(2) It should process instructions conditionally or unconditionally stepping in sequence through the memory (counting operation).

(3) It should have the inherent capability of processing the next instruction or "branching" to another location in a stored instruction list conditionally or unconditionally.

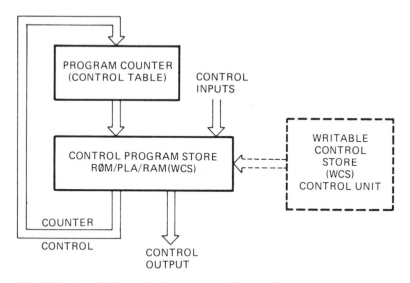

Fig. 9-20. A model for a simple programmable controller.

The word "processing" in this list of features is meant to represent the operation of generating an output to the outside word and making a decision as to what the next output code is to be, based on the present input conditions and the present state or memory location it is presently addressing.

Then, more specifically, a programmable system controller should possess the following basic operational or action-taking features:

(1) Increment the program counter (PC←PC+1) to the next instruction conditionally, that is, step to the next step in the sequence based on an *input* condition or conditions.

(2) Increment the program counter (PC←PC+1) to the next instruction unconditionally, that is, step to the next step in the sequence independent of *any* input condition or conditions.

(3) Branch or vector the program counter to some other location (not PC←PC+1) in memory conditional, that is, jump to a new state which is not in the direct count sequence based on an input condition or conditions.

(4) Branch or vector the program counter to some location other than (PC+1) independent of an input condition or conditions.

(5) Be able to *increment* or *branch* the program counter conditionally based on an input condition or conditions, that is, be able to make the decision to continue counting or branch from any given state.

These basic features form the minimal set of instructions from which a designer can actually program logic by transforming these features into *five basic micro-instructions*.

To illustrate this very interesting capability, consider the "four-bit slice" architecture shown in Figure 9-21.* For the most part, the system's sequential operation is revealed by the familiar circuits used. However, basically it is the format or the encoding of the "internal control word" which explicitly defines the machine's operation. There are several ways to encode the internal control word or micro-instructions, one of which is shown in Figure 9-22 using 12 bits.

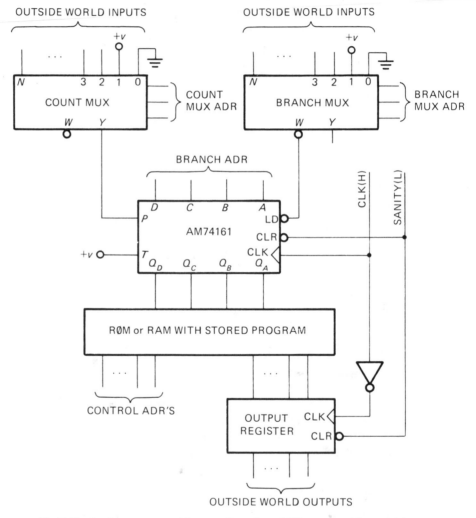

Fig. 9-21. A microprogrammable controller using a MSI counter with special features.

---

*Bit-slice is a term used to indicate the device can be cascaded to make up an *n*-bit composite machine.

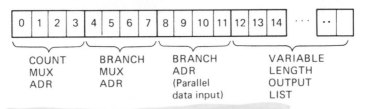

Fig. 9-22. The bit format of the micro-instructions for the system shown in Figure 9-21.

The first four bits (0, 1, 2, and 3) are encoded to select the CONDITIONAL CONTINUE-COUNTING INPUT VARIABLE that will cause the program to "hold its count" until a particular input condition is met, then increment to the next instruction location. Bits 4, 5, 6, and 7 are to be encoded to select the CONDITIONAL BRANCHING INPUT VARIABLE that will cause the program counter to hold until a particular branching input condition is met and then branch or "jam" this program counter to the instruction address specified by the BRANCH ADDRESS. Note the difference between COUNT and BRANCH. Count implies increment the code in the program counter by 1, whereas BRANCH implies load the counter with some code that is typically *not* the next-count code; however, it could be.

Since bits 8, 9, 10, and 11 are to be encoded to select the BRANCH ADDRESS *if a BRANCH is called for*, these bits carry the next state code when a BRANCH or a BRANCH/COUNT instruction is to be processed.

Bits 12, 13, ... are optional bits assigned for outputs called the OUTPUT LIST.

With the internal control micro-instruction word formulated as indicated in Figure 9-22, the five basic micro-instructions are made available. These instructions are as follows:

(1) COUNT CONDITIONAL (VARIABLE): CC(VARIABLE)–(OUTPUT LIST)
Example: CC(START)–(LOAD) would read as count conditional on the input variable START, or hold present count on $\overline{\text{START}}$ and ASSERT LOAD.

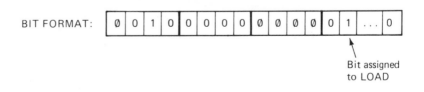

Note: This format indicates START is connected to Count MUX input number 2. The Branch MUX is addressed to MUX input number 0 to inhibit Branch and the ∅'s in bits 8, 9, 10, and 11 are there because no branch action is called for.

(2) COUNT UNCONDITIONAL: CU–(OUTPUT LIST)

This reads as count unconditional, which implies step to the next state automatically.

BIT FORMAT:

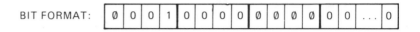

Note: This format indicates the Count MUX is addressed to input number 1 which will always be tied to a logic "1" and the Branch MUX to logic "0," thereby always causing an increment of the PC.

(3) BRANCH UNCONDITIONAL: BU(X)–(OUTPUT LIST)

Example: BU(6)–(0) reads as BRANCH to state 6 unconditionally and says that the next state is (0110) independent of any input condition, and ASSERT *NO* output.

BIT FORMAT:

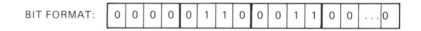

Note: This format indicates that the Branch MUX is addressed to input number 1, which will always invoke a BRANCH ACTION, and 8, 9, 10, and 11 are set to state 6.

(4) BRANCH CONDITIONAL: BC(VARIABLE)(X)–(OUTPUT LIST)

Example: BC(STOP)(B)–(0) would read branch to state *B* on the variable STOP and ASSERT *NO* output when state *B* is assigned the 0011 code.

BIT FORMAT:

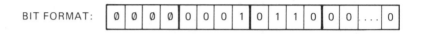

Note: This format indicates that STOP is connected to the Branch MUX input number 6. Zero's must be inserted for COUNT MUX address to avoid a program increment while waiting for the Branch variable.

(5) COUNT/BRANCH CONDITIONAL: CBC(VARIABLE), (VARIABLE)(X)–(OUTPUT LIST)

Example: BCC(OVF·$\overline{EOT}$), (EOT)(A)–(LOAD, RN) reads as continue the count on OVF·$\overline{EOT}$ conditional, or branch on EOT to state *A* (state *A* = 0000). Also, ASSERT both LOAD and RN.

BIT FORMAT:

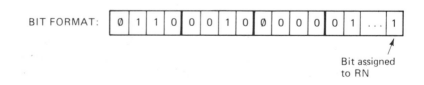

Bit assigned to RN

Note: This format indicates that the Count MUX is addressed to input number 6, to which OVF · $\overline{\text{EOT}}$ is connected, and EOT is connected to Branch MUX input number 2. Bits 8, 9, 10, and 11 are set to 0000, which is the branch address.

9-8 NOTES RELATED TO THE MICRO-INSTRUCTIONS

It is noted that there are some options related to the NEXT STATE CODE specifications in a micro-instruction.

For example:

(1) If you already have a state assignment, then BU(6) – (0) is a valid instruction when (0110) is to be the next state.
(2) If you do not have a state assignment, then BU(D) – (0) is also a valid instruction for the case where state d is to be the next state.

This is mentioned because it is possible (as in the author's case) that you will have an automatic assembler program that will make the state assignment and assign the variables to the MUX inputs. In this case, you need not worry about giving a numeric value to the BRANCH ADDRESS; it will be taken care of automatically.

Further, it should be noted that the outputs are *all* IMMEDIATE TYPE. CONDITIONAL OUTPUTS require extra program steps or extra hardware between the ROM and output holding register.

Now, before considering an actual application of this microprogrammed controller, let us briefly outline one major constraint induced by the instruction code and architecture. This constraint is: *Only two-way MDS diagram branches are allowed*. Thus we will have to modify our flow and MDS diagram development such that this constraint can be accommodated. However, this is not serious, particularly in view of another configuration that will be introduced later.

Now consider an example problem illustrating how the simple programmable architecture can be utilized, as well as how a control program can be written in a higher level language.

EXAMPLE 9-5: Illustrate the implementation of the adapted eight-state MDS diagram for the pop machine system controller shown in Figure 9-23. It should be noted that this MDS diagram has been devised in order to conform to the two-way branch constraint.

We can now write a control program listing using the five basic micro-instructions, which describe the system operation. First, we will write the program assuming that no state assignment has been made (see Table 9-1). Then we will write a program based on the state assignment illustrated in Figure 9-23 (see Table 9-2).

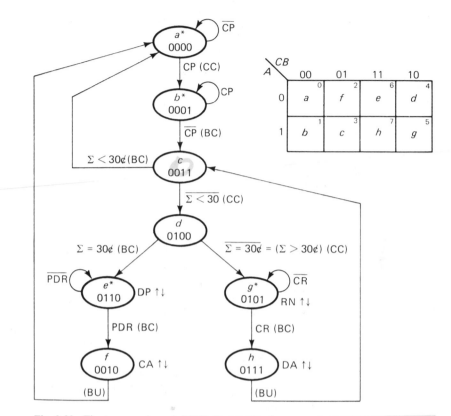

Fig. 9-23. The two-way branch MDS diagram for the prototype system controller.

TABLE 9-1 **The micro-program listing of MDS diagram in Figure 9-23**

Memory Location	Control Instruction
A	CC(CP)–(0)
B	BC($\overline{\text{CP}}$)(C)–(0)
C	CBC($\overline{\Sigma < 30¢}$),($\Sigma < 30¢$)(A)–(0)
D	CBC($\overline{\Sigma = 30¢}$),($\Sigma = 30¢$)(E)–(0)
E	BC(PDR)(F)–(DP)
F	BU(A)–(CA)
G	BC(CR)(H)–(RN)
H	BU(C)–(DA)

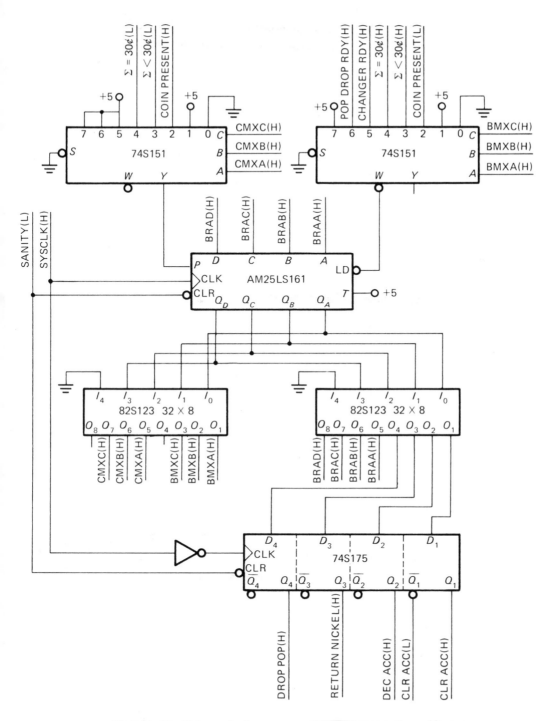

Fig. 9-24. The high speed microprogrammable system controller architecture.

TABLE 9-2 **The micro-program listing based on the state assignment shown in Figure 9-23**

Memory Location		Control Instruction
A	0000	CC(CP)–(0)
B	0001	BC($\overline{CP}$)(3)–(0)
C	0011	CBC($\overline{\Sigma<30\varepsilon}$),($\Sigma<30\varepsilon$)(0)–(0)
D	0100	CBC($\overline{\Sigma=30\varepsilon}$),($\Sigma=30\varepsilon$)(6)–(0)
E	0110	BC(PDR)(2)–(DP)
F	0010	BU(0)–(CA)
G	0101	BC(CR)(7)–(RN)
H	0111	BU(3)–(DA)

Now, from Table 9-2 we can quickly list the micro-code listing to be stored in the control memory. This is shown in Table 9-3.

TABLE 9-3 **The micro-code for the control program in table 9-2**

State Identifier	Memory Location	C MUX ADR	B MUX ADR	Branch ADR	CA	Output Branch List RN	DA	DP
A	0 0 0 0	Ø 0 1 0	0 0 0 0	Ø Ø Ø Ø	0	0	0	0
B	0 0 0 1	Ø0 Ø0 Ø0 Ø0	0 0 1 0	0 0 1 1	0	0	0	0
F	0 0 1 0	Ø Ø Ø Ø	0 0 0 1	0 0 0 0	1	0	0	0
C	0 0 1 1	Ø 0 1 1	0 0 1 1	0 0 0 0	0	0	0	0
D	0 1 0 0	Ø 1 0 0	0 1 0 0	0 1 1 0	0	0	0	0
G	0 1 0 1	Ø Ø Ø Ø	0 1 0 1	0 1 1 1	0	1	0	0
E	0 1 1 0	Ø Ø Ø Ø	0 1 1 0	0 0 1 0	0	0	0	1
H	0 1 1 1	Ø Ø Ø Ø	0 0 0 1	0 0 1 1	0	0	1	0

See the implementation shown in Figure 9-24. This illustrates an expandable four-bit slice type of machine, one that is certainly an overkill for the pop machine controller in terms of input capability and speed. However, the point being made is the following: *With a small selection of standard devices you can develop a high speed programmable controller that is expandable to n bits*.

9-9 PROGRAM CONTROLLERS WITH FIXED INSTRUCTION SET

The last section demonstrates the concept of microprogramming as applied to a programmable sequence controller. This section introduces the concept of a programmable controller with a "FIXED INSTRUCTION SET." By fixed it is implied that each operation carried out by the controller is selectable by a *fixed code* input. This fixed code input is commonly referred to as the OPERATION

CODE or simply the OPCODE. Let us introduce the concept of fixed instruction sequence controllers by considering the development carried out in Example 9-6.

EXAMPLE 9-6: It is desired to convert a standard AM74LS161 counter into a fixed instruction sequence controller by developing a special opcode decoder for the LOAD and COUNT ENABLE inputs. The fixed instruction set and op-code listing are given in Table 9-4.

TABLE 9-4 The INSTRUCTION, LISTING and definition for the AM74LS161 fixed instruction sequence controller shown in Figure 9-24.

Mnemonic	$OPCODE = OC_{2-0}$	Instruction Function
HIC	000	Hold then increment on Condition. Test Flag input: If Flag is NOT ASSERTED, hold present state, i.e., NEXT STATE = PRESENT STATE. If Flag is ASSERTED, NEXT STATE = PRESENT STATE + 1, i.e., NS = PS + 1.
HBC	001	Hold then branch on Condition. Test Flag input: If Flag is NOT ASSERTED, hold present state, i.e., NS = PS. If Flag is ASSERTED, NS = LOAD INPUTS, i.e., do parallel load.
IUC	010	Increment unconditionally. NS = PS + 1, i.e., increment the counter by 1.
BUC	011	BRANCH unconditionally. NS = LOAD INPUTS, i.e., do parallel load.
IBC	100	Increment on $\overline{\text{CONDITION}}$. BRANCH on CONDITION. Test Flag: If NOT ASSERTED INCREMENT, NS = PS + 1. If ASSERTED, NS = LOAD INPUTS.

From the information in Table 9-4 and the mode control definition for the AM74LS161 counter, we can derive the TRUTH-TABLE, MAPS, and circuit for the instruction decoder. See Figure 9-25. Once established, the circuit shown in the figure can be integrated into a general bit-slice system controller configuration, such as the one shown in Figure 9-26. This controlled counter will be referred to as MYCA-I, an acronym for MY Control Architecture version One.

Example 9-7 illustrates the use of MYCA-I and its instruction set in solving the pop machine problem.

EXAMPLE 9-7: This example illustrates the use of the MYCA-1 utilizing the instruction word format shown in Figure 9-27.

The MDS diagram shown in Figure 9-23 and the circuit shown in Figure 9-28 support the program listing shown in Table 9-5.

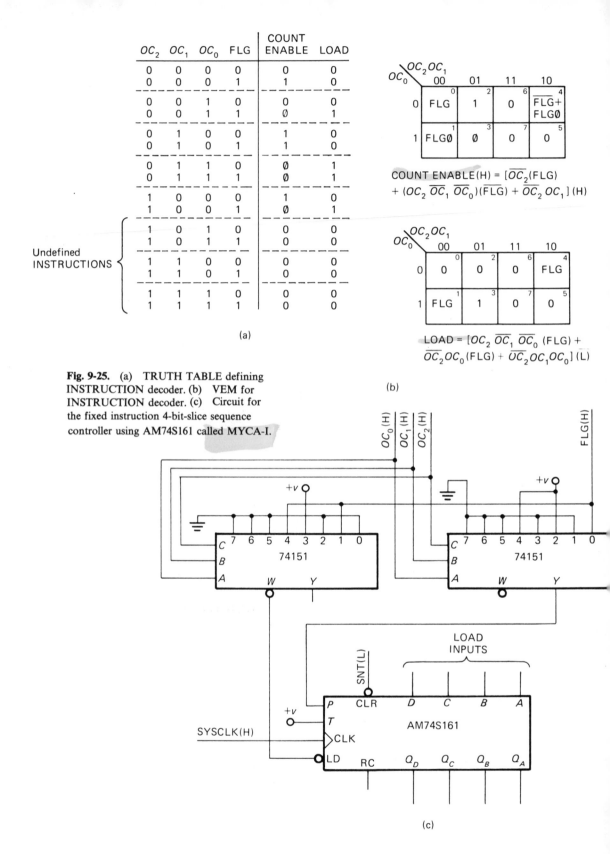

OC_2	OC_1	OC_0	FLG	COUNT ENABLE	LOAD
0	0	0	0	0	0
0	0	0	1	1	0
0	0	1	0	0	0
0	0	1	1	Ø	1
0	1	0	0	1	0
0	1	0	1	1	0
0	1	1	0	Ø	1
0	1	1	1	Ø	1
1	0	0	0	1	0
1	0	0	1	Ø	1
1	0	1	0	0	0
1	0	1	1	0	0
1	1	0	0	0	0
1	1	0	1	0	0
1	1	1	0	0	0
1	1	1	1	0	0

Undefined INSTRUCTIONS (rows $OC_2 OC_1 OC_0$ = 101, 110, 111)

(a)

OC_0 \ $OC_2 OC_1$

	00	01	11	10
0	FLG	1	0	FLG + FLG0
1	FLG0	Ø	0	0

COUNT ENABLE(H) = $[\overline{OC_2}(FLG) + (OC_2\, \overline{OC_1}\, \overline{OC_0})(\overline{FLG}) + \overline{OC_2}\, OC_1\,](H)$

OC_0 \ $OC_2 OC_1$

	00	01	11	10
0	0	0	0	FLG
1	FLG	1	0	0

LOAD = $[OC_2\, \overline{OC_1}\, \overline{OC_0}\, (FLG) + \overline{OC_2} OC_0 (FLG) + \overline{OC_2} OC_1 OC_0\,](L)$

(b)

Fig. 9-25. (a) TRUTH TABLE defining INSTRUCTION decoder. (b) VEM for INSTRUCTION decoder. (c) Circuit for the fixed instruction 4-bit-slice sequence controller using AM74S161 called MYCA-I.

(c)

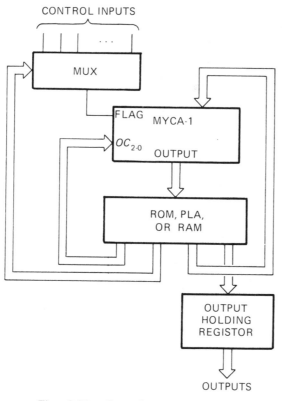

Fig. 9-26. General system controller centered around MYCA-I.

Fig. 9-27. The bit format for the MYCA-1 centered pop machine controller.

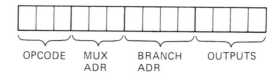

OPCODE | MUX ADR | BRANCH ADR | OUTPUTS

TABLE 9-5 The sequence control program for the MYCA-I implementation of the prototype pop machine controller

State	MEM LOC	Function	OPCODE	MUX ADR	Branch ADR	Outputs CA RN DA DP
A	0000	HIC(*CP*)	000	000	~~0000~~	0000
B	0001	HBC(CP)	001	101	0011	0000
F	0010	BUC	011	~~000~~	0000	1000
C	0011	IBC($\Sigma < 30$c)	100	001	0000	0000
D	0100	IBC($\Sigma = 30$c)	100	010	0110	0000
G	0101	HBC(CR)	001	100	0111	0100
E	0110	HBC(PDR)	001	011	0010	0001
H	0111	BUC	011	~~000~~	0011	0010

Thus our first introduction to high speed fixed-instruction controllers is easy and straightforward. Further, this introduction serves as a valuable aid to our understanding of MYCA-II and the three other bit-slice controllers to be introduced in this chapter as well as microprocessors in general.

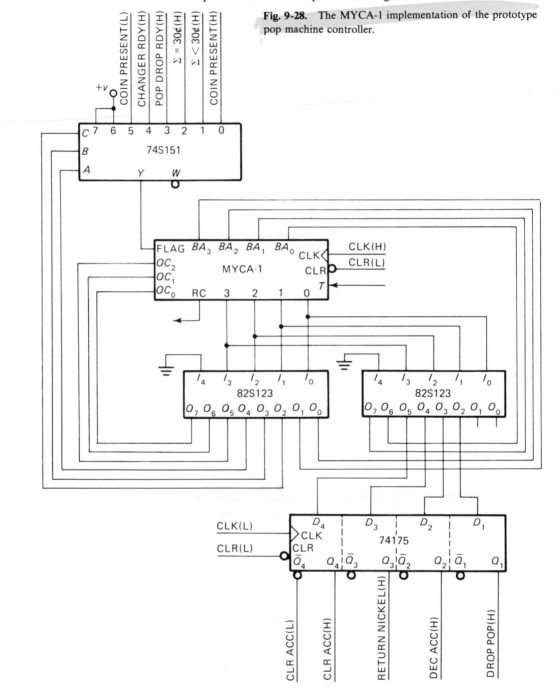

Fig. 9-28. The MYCA-1 implementation of the prototype pop machine controller.

9-10 PROGRAMMABLE SEQUENCE CONTROLLERS WITH SUB-ROUTINE CAPABILITY

The author has found in several cases that having a system controller with the ability to test a condition in some state X and then branch on this condition to a separate sequence of states, then return to the state following state X, would be a distinct advantage. In software developments this type of operation is classified as *Jumping to a Sub-Routine.* By sub-routine handling it is meant that there are tasks related to control problems that must be repeated over and over under various conditions as well as various time periods during the life-cycle of a control sequence. For example, data retrieval systems call for specific code preambles to be attached to various data sequences. High speed data formatters require the interjection of specific data routing sequences. There are many other sequential requirements for which it would be desirable to have a system controller capable of jumping to a sub-routine and then returning to the original main control sequence. Also, having sub-routine capability makes it possible to divide-and-conquer large control problems into sub-routine tasks.

Developing a sequence controller with sub-routine execution power requires several additional features: (1) the introduction of a *Branch to Sub-Routine on FLAG Condition* (BSR) instruction, (2) some conditional Return from Sub-Routine (RSR) instructions, and (3) some additional hardware to facilitate these instructions. Further, it requires developing main control sequence definitions (flow diagrams) that facilitate the efficient use of sub-routines and assure that a return from a sub-routines operation returns the controller to the proper state. Typically the return from a sub-routine places the controller at state $= X + 1$ if the BSR instruction is issued at state $= X$. Figure 9-29 illustrates the prototype pop machine MDS diagram constructed in such a way that the RETURN-NICKEL sequence is treated as a SUB-ROUTINE. From this figure notice that the added luxury of having a conditional return-from-sub-routine instruction costs very little (one extra state). This is considered a price worth paying in other instances when the control algorithm is very complex or when this sub-routine function is to be exercised several times at different points in the control sequence.

Examining the "in-line memory" locations (state assignment) for the control sequences shown in Figure 9-29, we see a basic problem. This problem arises from the fact that even though our proposed machine is programmable, *it is not immune* to the asynchronous input constraint for the state assignment. Therefore we must latch the FLAG input early in the instruction cycle in order to be able to use any state assignment like the one proposed in Figure 9-29. This point is addressed later in an actual application.

To this point we have established a desire to include the BSR and RSR instructions with the five basic instructions designed into MYCA-1. Also we will see later that it is nice to have the LOAD JAM ADDRESS (LJA) instruction. The BSR, RSR, and LJA instructions are defined in Table 9-6.

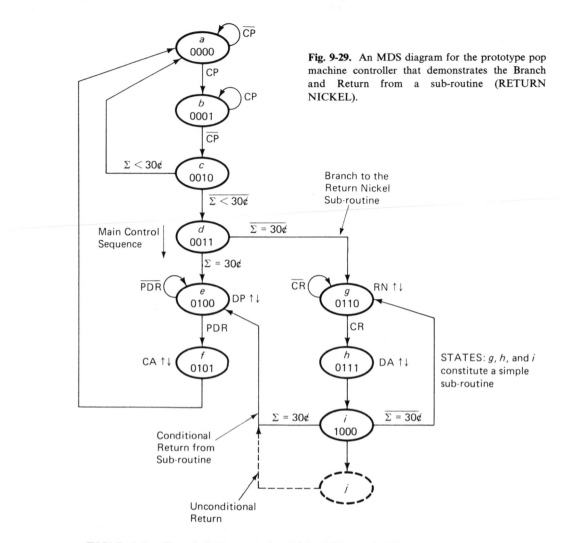

Fig. 9-29. An MDS diagram for the prototype pop machine controller that demonstrates the Branch and Return from a sub-routine (RETURN NICKEL).

TABLE 9-6. The definition of the BSR, RSR, and LJA Instructions

Mnemonic	OPCODE = OC_{2-0}	Instruction function
BSR	101	BRANCH to SUB-ROUTINE and save code of the next state. Test Flag input: If Flag is NOT ASSERTED, NS = PS + 1. If Flag is ASSERTED, NS = LOAD INPUT *and* PS + 1 is stored on top of stack
RSR	110	RETURN conditionally from sub-routine. Test Flag input: If Flag is NOT ASSERTED, NS = LOAD INPUTS. If Flag is ASSERTED, NS = TOP OF STACK (TOS).
LJA	111	TEST FLAG: If Flag is NOT ASSERTED: NS = PS + 1. If Flag is ASSERTED, NS = JAM INPUTS and PS + 1 is stored on top of stack.

Up to now we have used the word STACK in reference to some special memory element. The next section defines a stack and its operation in relation to the newly added instructions.

9-11 MYCA-I PLUS AN ADDER AND STACK

Consider Figure 9-30. Here we see MYCA-I with three fundamental blocks (STACK, ADDER, and MUX) added to it. This configuration we call MYCA-II for "My control architecture version number two." Basically these additions expand the power of MYCA-I significantly, allowing for sub-routine execution as well as future *INTERRUPT* handling.

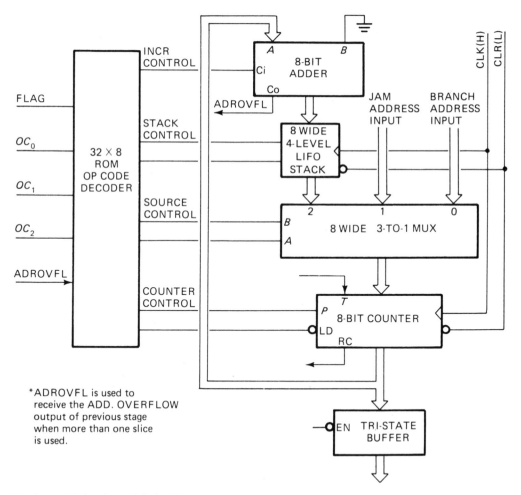

Fig. 9-30. MYCA-II, an eight bit-slice programmable sequence controller.

First observe that the addition of the eight wide 3-to-1 MUX has expanded MYCA-II's next state source over MYCA-I. This addition now makes it possible to SELECT the next state from three sources: (1) JAM ADDRESS inputs for the LJA instruction, (2) BRANCH ADDRESS inputs, and (3) top level of the LIFO STACK. The ADDER provides for the INCREMENT function required in the BSR instruction. The STACK is the special sequential accessed memory unit used to store the return address mentioned earlier. The configuration and operation of this STACK is illustrated in Figure 9-31. This illustration shows that four levels of nested sub-routines are possible.

Thus the additions to MYCA-I have certainly increased its flexibility and control power. Note also that the bit-slice concept is provided such that two or more MYCA-II's can be simply cascaded. It is interesting to note that *two* MYCA-II's expand the system to 65 K states!

The instruction decoder ROM program for MYCA-II is summarized in Table 9-7.

TABLE 9-7   MYCA-II Instruction Decoder Program

Mne.	Undefined	OC_2	OC_1	OC_0	FLAG	P(H)	LD(L)	B(H)	A(H)	SI(H)	SO(H)	Carry(H)	Function
HIC	0	0	0	0	0	0	0	0	0	0	0	0	NS=PS
	0	0	0	0	1	1	0	0	0	0	0	0	NS=PS+1
HBC	0	0	0	1	0	0	0	0	0	0	0	0	NS=PS
	0	0	0	1	1	0	1	0	0	0	0	0	NS=BA
IUC	0	0	1	0	0	1	0	0	0	0	0	0	NS=PS+1
	0	0	1	0	1	1	0	0	0	0	0		
BUC	0	0	1	1	0	0	1	0	0	0	0	0	NS=BA
	0	0	1	1	1	0	1	0	0	0	0		
IBC	0	1	0	0	0	1	0	0	0	0	0	0	NS=PS+1
	0	1	0	0	1	0	1	0	0	0	0	0	NS=BA
BSR	0	1	0	1	0	1	0	0	0	0	0	0	NS=PS+1
	0	1	0	1	1	0	1	0	0	0	1	1	NS=Sub-routine Address TOS←PS+1
RSR	0	1	1	0	0	0	1	0	0	0	0	0	NS=BA
	0	1	1	0	1	0	1	1	0	1	0	0	NS=TOS; THEN STACK IS POPPED
LJA	0	1	1	1	0	1	0	0	0	0	0	0	NS=PS+1
	0	1	1	1	1	0	1	0	1	0	1	1	NS=JA; TOS←PS+1
			⋮ Undefined		⋮			⋮					

Notes: NS = NEXT STATE   JA = JAM ADDRESS
PS = PRESENT STATE   TOS = TOP OF STACK
BA = BRANCH ADDRESS   ← = replaced by

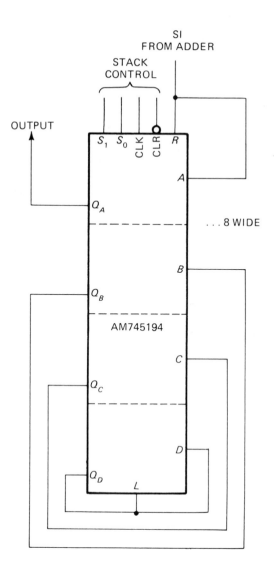

SI
FROM ADDER

STACK
CONTROL

OUTPUT

S_1 S_0 CLK CLR R

A

Q_A

... 8 WIDE

B

Q_B

AM745194

C

Q_C

D

Q_D L

OPERATION	S_1	S_0	STACK OPERATION
HOLD	L	L	$Q_i \leftarrow Q_i$
(SR) PUSH	L	H	$Q_A \leftarrow S_I$, $Q_B \leftarrow Q_A$, $Q_C \leftarrow Q_B$, $Q_D \leftarrow Q_C$
(SL) POP	H	L	$Q_A \leftarrow Q_B$, $Q_B \leftarrow Q_C$, $Q_C \leftarrow Q_D$, $Q_D \leftarrow Q_D$
(P or LD) LOAD Q_A	H	H	$Q_A \leftarrow S_I$, $Q_B \leftarrow Q_B$, $Q_C \leftarrow Q_C$, $Q_D \leftarrow Q_D$

Fig. 9-31. The general configuration and operation of MYCA-II's LIFO stack.

Figure 9-32 illustrates the basic model for the use of MYCA-II as a *system controller*.

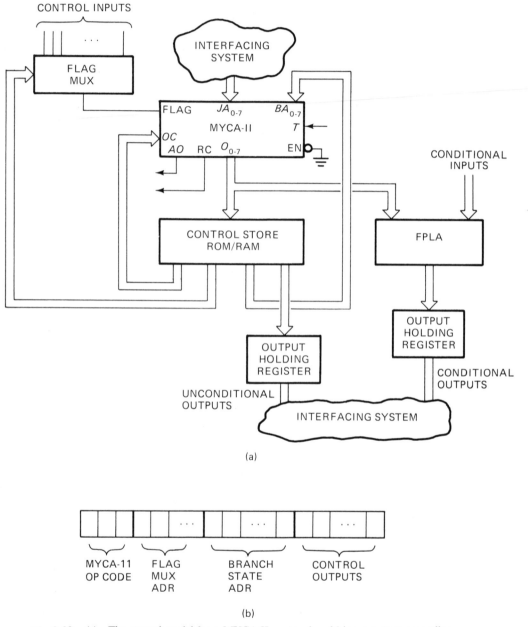

(a)

(b)

Fig. 9-32. (a) The general model for a MYCA-II centered multi-input system controller. (b) The proposed bit-format for the instruction word.

9-12 THE 8X02 CONTROL STORE SEQUENCER

The device data for the 8X02 control store sequencer is shown in Figure 9-33. Observe that the 8X02 is similar to MYCA-II in many respects. See Table 9-8 for a listing of the 8X02's instructions, and notice that the important HIC and HBC instructions are *not* available directly. However, you will see that they can be generated by combining several instructions. Likewise MYCA-II does not have the PLP and BLT instructions but they too can be generated with the basic instruction set. Other contrasts include: the 8X02 has (1) no direct LJA instruction, (2) no direct asynchronous CLEAR, and (3) no bit-slice expansion capabilities as the MYCA-II does. However, it fits into a 28-pin package and is a ten-bit machine.

TABLE 9-8   The Instruction set for 8X02

Mnemonic	Description	Function AC2 1 0	Test	Next address	Stack	Stack pointer
TSK	Test and skip	000	False	Current + 1	N.C.	N.C.
			True	Current + 2	N.C.	N.C.
INC	Increment	001	X	Current + 1	N.C.	N.C.
BLT	Branch to loop if test input true	010	False	Current + 1	X	Decr
			True	Stack reg file	POP (read)	Decr
POP	POP stack	011	X	Stack reg file	POP (read)	Decr
BSR	Branch to subroutine if test input true	100	False	Current + 1	N.C.	N.C.
			True	Branch address	PUSH (Current + 1)	Incr
PLP	Push for looping	101	X	Current + 1	PUSH (Current Addr)	Incr
BRT	Branch if test input true	110	False	Current + 1	N.C.	N.C.
			True	Branch address	N.C.	N.C.
RST	Set micro-program address output to zero	111	X	All 0's	N.C.	N.C.

Figure 9-34 shows the 8X02 modelled as a finite-state machine capable of transversing 1024 unique states. Further, it can be seen that the next state code is program selectable via ten wide 5-to-1 mux from one of five different sources: (1) BRANCH ADDRESS inputs, (2) PRESENT STATE (ADR) + 1, (3) PRESENT STATE + 2, (4) TOP OF STACK (TOS), and (5) the zero-state for programmed RESET. The 8X02 has a ten-bit edge-triggered present state register, a four-level LIFO stack, a controlled ADDER, and a tri-state output buffer. Like MYCA-II the 8X02 has an instruction decoder that controls the execution of the eight basic instructions.

OBJECTIVE SPECIFICATION   8X02-XL,I

DESCRIPTION

The Signetics 8X02 is a Low-Power Schottky LSI device intended for use in high performance microprogrammed systems to control the fetch sequence of microinstructions. When combined with standard ROM or PROM, the 8X02 forms a powerful microprogrammed control section for computers, controllers, or sequenced logic.

FEATURES

- Low power Schottky process
- 77ns cycle time (typ)
- 1024 microinstruction addressability
- N-way branch
- 4-level stack register file (LIFO type)
- Automatic push/pop stack operation
- "Test & skip" operation on test input line
- 3-bit command code
- Tri-state buffered outputs
- Auto-reset to address 0 during power-up
- Conditional branching, pop stack, & push stack

PIN CONFIGURATION

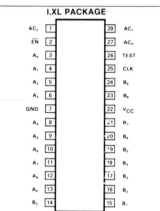

BLOCK DIAGRAM

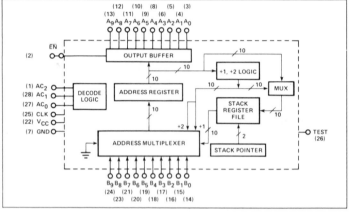

PIN DESCRIPTION

PIN	SYMBOL	NAME AND FUNCTION	TYPE
5-6 8-13	A_0-A_9	Microprogram Address outputs	Three-state Active high
1,28,27	AC_0-AC_2	Next Address Control Function inputs All addressing control functions are selected by these command lines.	Active high
14-21 23-24	B_0-B_9	Branch Address inputs Determines the next address of an N-way branch when used with the BRANCH TO SUBROUTINE (BSR) or BRANCH ON TEST (BRT) command.	Active high
2	$\overline{EN}$	Enable input When in the low state, the Microprogram Address outputs are enabled.	Active low
25	CLK	Clock input All registers are triggered on the low-to-high transition of the clock.	
26	TEST	Test input Used in conjunction with four NEXT ADDRESS CONTROL FUNCTION commands to effect conditional skips, branches, and stack operations.	Active high
7	GND	Ground	
22	V_{CC}	+5 Volt supply	

Fig. 9-33. Technical data sheet for the 8X02. (Courtesy of Signetics)

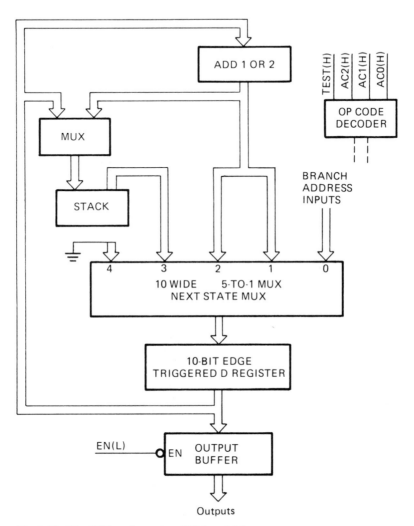

Fig. 9-34. The 8X02 re-drawn in a FSM model form.

Figure 9-35 illustrates the general model of a 8X02 centered multi-input system controller along with a proposed bit format for the microcoded instruction word.

The functional description of the 8X02 instruction set is shown in Table 9-9.

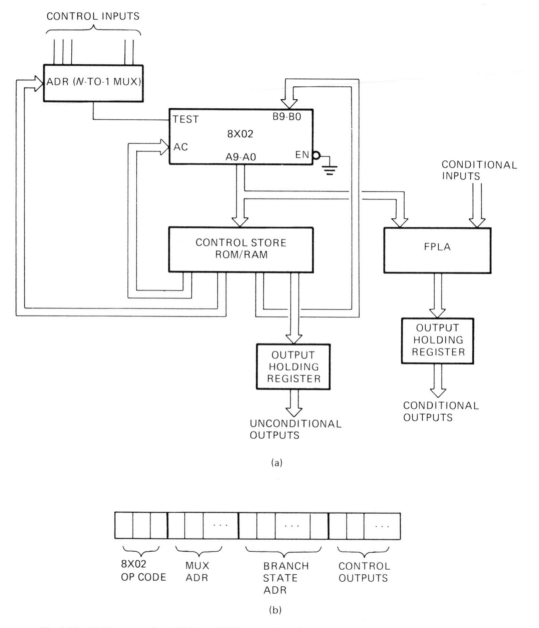

(a)

(b)

Fig. 9-35. (a) The general model for a 8X02 centered multi-input controller along with (b) The proposed bit-format for the control INSTRUCTION WORD.

TABLE 9-9 The functional description of the 8X02 instruction set

Mnemonic	Function description
TSK	$AC_{2-0} = 000$: TEST & SKIP Perform test on TEST INPUT LINE.
	If test is FALSE(LOW): Next Address = Current Address + 1, Stack Pointer unchanged
	If test is TRUE(HIGH): Next Address = Current Address + 2 (i.e. Skip next microinstruction), Stack Pointer unchanged
INC	$AC_{2-0} = 001$: INCREMENT Next Address = Current Address + 1 Stack Pointer unchanged
BLT	$AC_{2-0} = 010$: BRANCH TO LOOP IF TEST CONDITION TRUE. Perform test on TEST INPUT LINE.
	If test is FALSE(LOW): Next Address = Current Address + 1, Stack Pointer decremented by 1
	If test is TRUE(HIGH): Next Address = Address from Stack Register File (POP), Stack Pointer decremented by 1
POP	$AC_{2-0} = 011$: POP STACK Next Address = Address from Stack Register File (POP) Stack Pointer decremented by 1
BSR	$AC_{2-0} = 100$: BRANCH TO SUBROUTINE IF TEST CONDITION TRUE. Perform test on TEST INPUT LINE.
	If test is FALSE(LOW): Next Address = Current Address + 1, Stack Pointer unchanged
	If test is TRUE(HIGH): Next Address = Branch Address Input (B_{0-9}), Stack Pointer incremented by 1 PUSH (write) Current Address + 1 → Stack Register File
PLP	$AC_{2-0} = 101$: PUSH FOR LOOPING Next Address = Current Address + 1 Stack Pointer incremented by 1 PUSH (write) Current Address → Stack Register File
BRT	$AC_{2-0} = 110$: BRANCH ON TEST CONDITION TRUE Perform test on TEST INPUT LINE.
	If test is FALSE(LOW): Next Address = Current Address + 1, Stack Pointer unchanged
	If test is TRUE(HIGH): Next Address = Branch Address Input (B_{0-9}), Stack Pointer unchanged
RST	$AC_{2-0} = 111$: RESET TO ZERO Next Address = 0 Stack Pointer unchanged

(Courtesy of Signetics, Technology Leadership, Bipolar Microprocessor).

These instructions can be related to the five basic sequence functions outlined earlier in the following manner.

1. *Count Conditional:* can be implemented with BRT with the complement of the conditional input multiplexed to the TEST input and BRANCH ADR = *X*

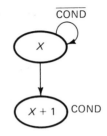

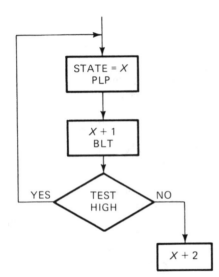

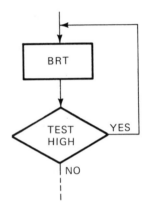

2. *Count Unconditional:* can be implemented directly with the INC instruction.

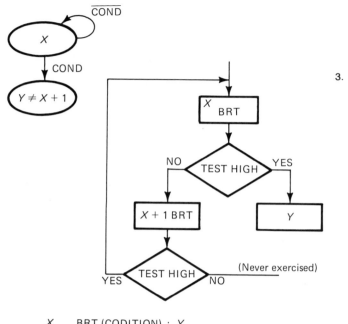

3. *Branch Conditional:* can be implemented by the following set of INSTRUC- TIONS

X   BRT (CODITION) : Y
X + 1 BRT (TEST HIGH): X

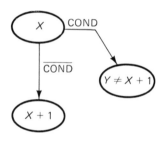

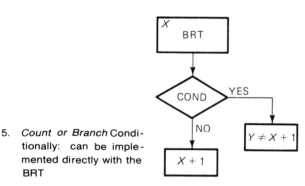

4. *Branch Unconditional:* can be implemented directly with BRT (TEST HIGH) w/ BRCH ADR = Y and TEST input multiplexed to a HIGH VOLT- AGE

5. *Count or Branch* Condi- tionally: can be imple- mented directly with the BRT

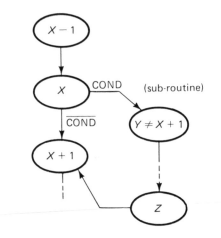

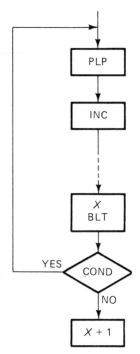

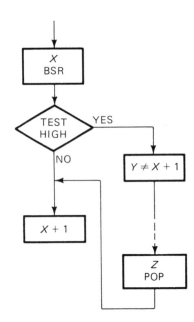

6. (optional) Branch to Sub-routine: can be implemented using both BSR and POP

7. The PLP and BLT instructions: can be used for hardware "DO LOOPS" for example counters and delay Functions.

9-13   THE APPLICATION OF THE 8X02 TO SYSTEM CONTROL FUNCTIONS

The previous development illustrates how the 8X02 instruction sequences can be related to the five basic sequential functions of a programmable FSM. Next consider the direct application of these ideas to solving a control problem specified by a flow diagram and MDS diagram.

EXAMPLE 9-8:   Consider the application of the 8X02 for the implementation of the prototype version of the pop machine controller defined in Figure 9-36. We consider first the sequence-control-program related to the system configuration shown in Figure 9-35, then come back to specify the required outputs.

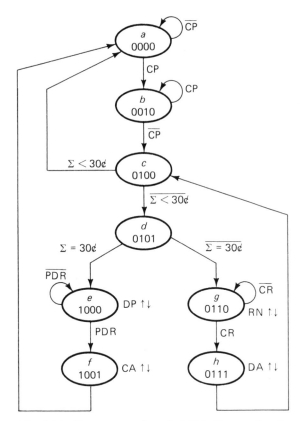

Fig. 9-36. The two-way branch MDS diagram for the 8X02 implementation of the prototype pop machine controller.

Table 9-10 illustrates the instruction mnemonic and microcode listing for the 8X02 implementation shown in Figure 9-37.

TABLE 9-10   The sequence control program for the 8X02 implementation of the prototype system controller

State	MEM LOC	Function	OPCODE	MUX ADR	Branch ADR	CA RN DA DP
State A	{0000	BRT($\overline{\text{CP}}$)	110	000	0000	0000
State B	{0001	BRT($\overline{\text{CP}}$)	110	000	0011	0000
	{0010	BRT(1)	110	110	0001	0000
State C	{0011	TSK($\overline{\Sigma<30}$)	000	001	0000	0000
	{0100	RST	111	0000	0000	0000
State D	{0101	BRT($\Sigma=30$)	110	010	1000	0000
State G	{0110	BRT($\overline{\text{CR}}$)	110	101	0110	0100
State H	{0111	BRT(1)	110	110	0011	0010
State E	{1000	BRT($\overline{\text{PDR}}$)	110	100	1000	0001
State F	{1001	RST	111	0000	0000	1000

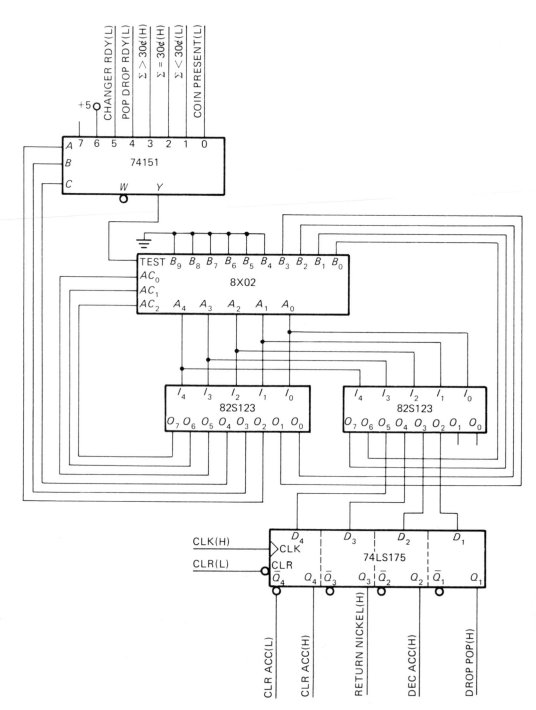

Fig. 9-37. 8X02 system configuration for the implementation of the prototype pop machine controller.

We see that using the 8X02 provided another viable avenue to the implementation of high speed programmable sequence controller.

Figure 9-38 illustrates the technical information related to the SN74S482, a four-bit-slice expandable control element. It should be noted that the 74S482 is similar in architecture to MYCA-II and the 8X02. This device is quite versatile in that it can be used to control a sequence in two different ways: (1) It can be configured as illustrated in Figure 9-39 and used as a microprogrammed controller using the suggested internal control word, or (2) It can be a separate instruction decoder for the S_1, S_2, S_3, S_4, S_5, S_6, and C_i inputs can be added, thus making the 74S482 a fixed instruction controller similar in operation to MYCA-II and 8X02. This conversion is left as an exercise; however, we will illustrate how the five basic instructions can be derived via a microprogramming approach. First consider how the *count unconditional* operation can be specified using the system and internal control word specified in Figure 9-39.

COUNT UNCONDITIONAL:

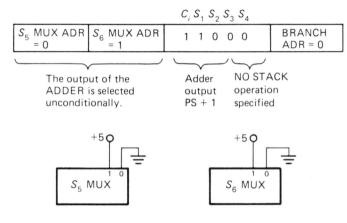

COUNT CONDITIONALLY:

Assume the conditional variable (CV) is connected to S_5 MUX input number X and this variable is *ASSERTED LOW*.

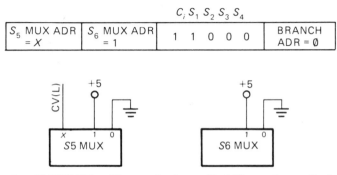

Notice that the SN74S482 will remain in a "hold" mode until the conditional variable becomes ASSERTED. At this time the output of the ADDER is selected and the $NS = PS + 1$.

- 4-Bit Slice is Cascadable to N-Bits
- Designed Specifically for Microcontroller/ Next-Address Generator Functions
- Increment/Decrement by One (Immediate or Direct Symbolic Addressing Modes)
- Offset, Vector, or Branch (Indexed or Relative Addressing Modes)
- Store Up to Four Returns or Links (Program Return Address from Subroutine)
- Program Start or Initialize (Return to Zero or Clear Mode)
- On-Chip Edge-Triggered Output Register (Provides Steady-State Micro-Address/ Instruction)
- High-Density 20-Pin Dual-in-Line Package with 300-Mil Row Pin Spacing

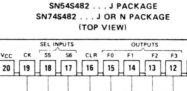

SN54S482 . . . J PACKAGE
SN74S482 . . . J OR N PACKAGE
(TOP VIEW)

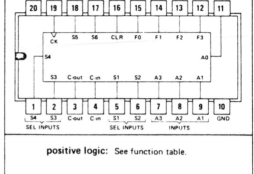

positive logic: See function table.

description

The 'S482 is a high-performance Schottky TTL 4-bit-slice control element for use in any computer/control application requiring the coupling of high-performance bipolar speeds with the flexibility of microprogram control and bit-slice expandability. When used as a next-address generator, two 'S482 elements can address up to 256 words of microprogram; three elements can addresss up to 4096 words of microprogram; or a number of 'S482 elements can generate N words in multiples of four lines.

Comprised of an output register, push-pop stack, and a full adder, the 'S482 provides the capability to implement multiway testing needed to generate or to determine and select the source of the next function of microprogram address.

functional block diagram

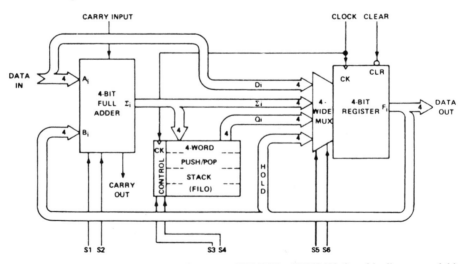

Fig. 9-38. Technical data sheets for types SN54S482, SN74S482 four-bit-slice expandable control elements. (Courtesy of Texas Instrument)

TYPES SN54S482, SN74S482
4-BIT-SLICE EXPANDABLE CONTROL ELEMENTS

output register and source functions

The 4-bit edge-triggered register provides a steady-state output throughout each system clock cycle. An asynchronous clear extends the multiway testing to directly implement system initialization at ROM address zero.

Two source-select lines (S5, S6) provide the output register with access to either the current instruction (no change), an operand or address stored in the push-pop stack, the output of a four-function full adder, or a direct data-in address port. The sources and functions are summarized in Tables I and II.

TABLE I. REGISTER-SOURCE FUNCTIONS

SELECT		REGISTER INPUT SOURCE
S5	S6	
L	L	DATA-IN PORT (Di)
L	H	FULL ADDER OUTPUTS (Σi)
H	L	PUSH-POP STACK OUTPUTS (Qi)
H	H	REGISTER OUTPUTS (HOLD)

H $\equiv$ high level, L $\equiv$ low level

TABLE II. PUSH-POP STACK CONTROL AND REGISTER-SOURCE FUNCTIONS

		INPUTS				INTERNAL	OUTPUTS
	S3	S4	S5	S6	CLOCK	CLEAR	QiA	Fi
HOLD	X	X	X	X	L	H	QiA0	Fi0
CLEAR	X	X	X	X	X	L	QiA0	L
PUSH-POP STACK "HOLD"	L	L	L	L	↑	H	QiA0*	Di
	L	L	L	H	↑	H	QiA0*	Σi
	L	L	H	L	↑	H	QiA0*	QiA0
	L	L	H	H	↑	H	QiA0*	Fi0
PUSH-POP STACK "LOAD"	L	H	L	L	↑	H	Σi*	Di
	L	H	L	H	↑	H	Σi*	Σi
	L	H	H	L	↑	H	Σi*	QiA0
	L	H	H	H	↑	H	Σi*	Fi0
PUSH-POP STACK "POP"	H	L	L	L	↑	H	QiB0†	Di
	H	L	L	H	↑	H	QiB0†	Σi
	H	L	H	L	↑	H	QiB0†	QiA0
	H	L	H	H	↑	H	QiB0†	Fi0
PUSH-POP STACK "PUSH"	H	H	L	L	↑	H	Σi‡	Di
	H	H	L	H	↑	H	Σi‡	Σi
	H	H	H	L	↑	H	Σi‡	QiA0
	H	H	H	H	↑	H	Σi‡	Fi0

MSB   LSB
i $\equiv$ 3, 2, 1, 0
Ai $\equiv$ Data inputs
QiA $\equiv$ Push-pop stack word A output (internal)
QiA0 $\equiv$ the level of Qi before the indicated inputs conditions were established.

Fi $\equiv$ Device outputs
Fi0 $\equiv$ the level of Fi before the indicated input conditions were established.
Σi $\equiv$ Adder outputs (internal)
*QiB, QiC, QiD do not change
†QiD0 → QiD, QiD0 → QiC, QiC0 → QiB, QiB0 → QiA
‡QiA0 → QiB, QiB0 → QiC, QiC0 → QiD

Fig. 9-38. (Cont.)

The SN74S482 and MC2909 Integrated Circuit Sequence Controllers **631**

push-pop stack control

The 4-word push-pop stack can be used for nesting up to four levels of program or return (link) addresses. In the load mode, the first (top) word is filled with new data from the output of the full adder, and no push occurs meaning that previous data at that location is lost. However, all other word locations in the push-pop stack remain unchanged. In the push mode, the new word is again entered in the first (top) location; however, previous data residing in the top three words are pushed down one word location and retained at their new locations. The bottom word is written over and lost.

In the pop mode, words in the push-pop stack move up one location on each clock transition. A unique function is provided by the bottom (fourth) register as its content is retained during the pop mode, and after 3 clock transitions, all words in the stack are filled with the operand/address that occupied the bottom register.

The operand/address will remain available indefinitely if stack functions are limited to the pop or hold modes.

The push-pop stack functions are shown in Tables II and III.

TABLE III. PUSH-POP STACK FUNCTIONS

	FUNCTION	SEL.		REG. D	REG. C	REG. B	REG. A	INPUT/ OUTPUT
		S3	S4					
BIT 0	LOAD	L	H	Q_iD0	Q_iC0	Q_iB0	← Σ_i	Σ_i IN
BIT 1	PUSH	H	H	← Q_iC0	← Q_iB0	← Q_iA0	← Σ_i	Σ_i IN
BIT 2	POP	H	L	↶ → Q_iD0	→ Q_iD0	→ Q_iC0	→ Q_iB0	Q_iA OUT
BIT 3	HOLD	L	L	Q_iD0	Q_iC0	Q_iB0	Q_iA0	Q_iA OUT

µlink operations show previous data location after clock transition.

full adder

The four-function full adder is controllable from select inputs S1 and S2 to perform:

A or B incrementation, or decrementation of B

Unconditional jumps or relative offsets

No change

Return to zero or one

Incrementation can be implemented by forcing a carry (high) into the ALU. In this mode either of the following options are possible:

1. Increment (A plus zero plus carry)

2. Increment B (zero plus B plus carry), or decrement B (all highs at A then A plus B with carry input low and disregard, don't use, carry out)

3. Increment the jump or offset (A plus B plus carry)

Fig. 9-38. (Cont.)

full adder (continued)

4. Start at zero or one and increment on each clock (select zero plus zero plus carry, then select zero plus B plus carry), or set register to N and decrement B (see 2 above).

5. No change (carry input is always active and removal of carry combined with either the ALU or register hold mode will retain the current address).

Unconditional jumps can be implemented by applying and selecting the jump directly from the data inputs to the output register. Offset can be accomplished by summing the output register with the offset magnitude (A plus B) with carry low.

The ALU functions are shown in Table IV.

TABLE IV. ADDRESS CONTROL FUNCTIONS

INPUTS		INTERNAL
S1	S2	Σi
H	H	0 PLUS 0 PLUS C-in
H	L	0 PLUS Bi PLUS C-in
L	H	Ai PLUS 0 PLUS C-in
L	L	Ai PLUS Bi PLUS C-in

compound generator functions

As the function-select lines of the register sources, push-pop stack, and adder are independent, compound functions can be selected to occur on the next clock transition.

Subroutine branches and returns can be simplified by saving the return or link addresses in the push-pop stack. This branch-and-save function can be accomplished on the same clock time as follows:

DATA-IN	ADDER	PUSH-POP STACK	REGISTER SOURCE
Branch address	Zero plus B plus one	Push	Data-in
	(S1 = H, S2 = L)	(S3 = S4 = H)	(S5 = S6 = L)

Up to four branches can be made with the return stored in the 4-word push-pop stack.

absolute maximum ratings over operating free-air temperature (unless otherwise noted)

Supply voltage, V_{CC} (see Note 1) . . . . 7 V
Input voltage . . . . 5.5 V
Off-state output voltage . . . . 5.5 V
Operating free-air temperature range: SN54S482 . . . . −55°C to 125°C
SN74S482 . . . . 0°C to 70°C
Storage temperature range . . . . −65°C to 150°C

NOTE 1. All voltage values are with respect to network ground terminal.

Fig. 9-38. (Cont.)

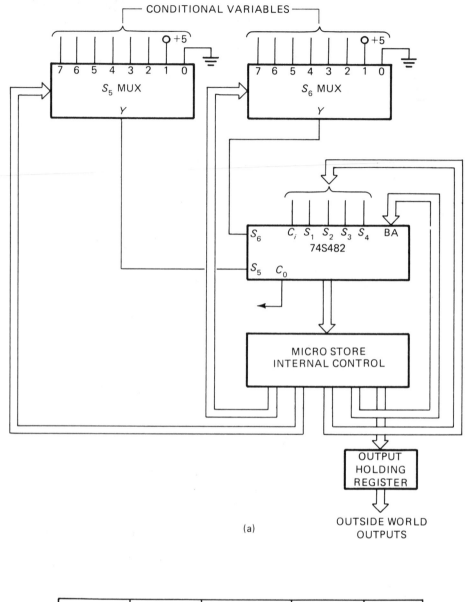

CONDITIONAL VARIABLES

7 6 5 4 3 2 1 0 S_5 MUX   Y

7 6 5 4 3 2 1 0 S_6 MUX   Y

S_6 C_i S_1 S_2 S_3 S_4 BA
74S482
S_5 C_0

MICRO STORE
INTERNAL CONTROL

OUTPUT
HOLDING
REGISTER

(a)

OUTSIDE WORLD
OUTPUTS

S_5 MUX ADR Field	S_6 MUX ADR Field	STACK/ADDER CONTROL	BRANCH ADDRESS	OUTPUT

(b)

Fig. 9-39. (a) A typical microprogrammed configuration centered around the 74S482. (b) The internal control word bit format for the indicated configuration.

BRANCH UNCONDITIONAL: TO STATE Z

The branch unconditional operation is specified as follows:

S_5 MUX ADR = 0	S_6 MUX ADR = 0	Ø Ø Ø 0 0	BRANCH ADR = Z

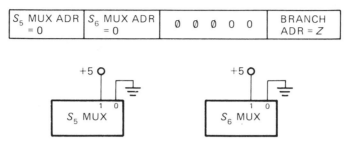

Here the next state select MUX is unconditionally directed to the D or branch address inputs and the branch is implemented.

BRANCH CONDITIONALLY: TO STATE Z

The branch conditionally operation is specified as follows: Assume the conditional variable is *ASSERTED LOW* and connected to S_5 MUX at input X and the S_6 MUX at input Y.

S_5 MUX ADR = X	S_6 MUX ADR = Y	Ø Ø Ø 0 0	BRANCH ADR = Z

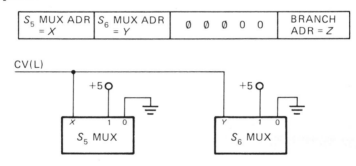

Thus the SN74S482 is held in the "hold" mode until the conditional variable becomes ASSERTED. At this time the branch address inputs are selected and the branch takes place.

COUNT OR BRANCH CONDITIONALLY TO STATE Z

The count on NOT-ASSERTED branch on ASSERTED operation is specified as follows assuming the conditional variable (CV) is *ASSERTED LOW* and is connected to the S_6 MUX input X.

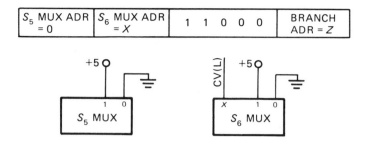

S_5 MUX ADR = 0	S_6 MUX ADR = X	1	1	0	0	0	BRANCH ADR = Z

Thus the count or branch instruction can be implemented quite easily. It should be noted that various other operations can be specified by varying the ADDER and STACK control bit in the internal control word. These are left as exercises. However, you are warned that PUSH and POP stack operations must be carefully specified when used in computers with conditional count or branch instructions in order to avoid unwanted multiple push and pop operations of the stack.

Figure 9-40 illustrates the technical information related to the MC2909 (AM2909) microprogram sequencer. The 2909, since its introduction, has become the industry standard high speed sequencer intended for sequencing through a series of microinstructions contained in a ROM or PROM. It is most widely used for the control of AM2901, which is a four-bit bipolar microprocessor slice; however, it can be configured in other ways also. The restructured architecture of the 2909 shown in Figure 9-41 differs structurally from MYCA-II, 8X02, and the SN74S482. Because of its architecture the use of the 2909 as a programmable sequence controller is somewhat different in comparison to the devices studied thus far. This is demonstrated in Figure 9-42, which illustrates a microprogrammed system and the proposed internal control word.

Using the configuration shown in Figure 9-42, it is possible to derive the following instruction formats for the five basic operations.

COUNT UNCONDITIONAL: WITH NO STACK OPERATION IMPLIED

		C_i	R_E	Z_E	F_E	PUP	
S_1 MUX ADR = 0	S_0 MUX ADR = 0	1	0	0	0	0	BRANCH ADR = 0

COUNT CONDITIONAL: WITH NO STACK OPERATION IMPLIED

Assume the conditional variable (CV) is connected to S_0 MUX input and this variable is ASSERTED HIGH:

S_1 MUX ADR = 0	S_0 MUX ADR = X	1	1	0	0	0	BRANCH ADR = 0

MC2909
MICROPROGRAM SEQUENCER

DISTINCTIVE CHARACTERISTICS

4-bit slice cascadable to any number of microwords

Internal address register

Branch input for N-way branches

Cascadable 4-bit microprogram counter

4 x 4 file with stack pointer and push pop control for nesting microsubroutines.

Zero input for returning to the zero microcode word

Individual OR input for each bit for branching to higher microinstructions

Three-state outputs

All internal registers change state on the LOW-to-HIGH transition of the clock

GENERAL DESCRIPTION

The MC2909 is a four-bit wide address controller intended for sequencing through a series of microinstructions contained in a ROM or PROM. Two MC2901's may be interconnected to generate an eight-bit address (256 words), and three may be used to generate a twelve-bit address (4K words).

The MC2909 can select an address from any of four sources. They are: 1) a set of external direct inputs (D); 2) external data from the R inputs, stored in an internal register; 3) a four-word deep push/pop stack; or 4) a program counter register (which usually contains the last address plus one). The push/pop stack includes certain control lines so that it can efficiently execute nested subroutine linkages. Each of the four outputs can be OR'ed with an external input for conditional skip or branch instructions, and a separate line forces the outputs to all zeroes. The outputs are three-state.

MICROPROGRAM SEQUENCER BLOCK DIAGRAM

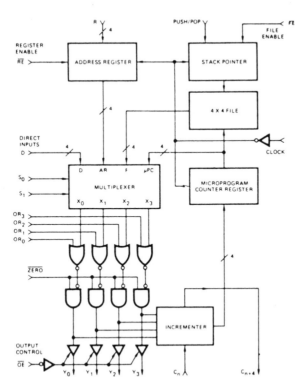

Fig. 9-40. Technical data sheets for the MC2909 microprogram sequencer. (Courtesy of Advanced Micro Devices)

The MC2909 is a bipolar microprogram sequencer intended for use in high-speed microprocessor applications. The device is a cascadable 4-bit slice such that two devices allow addressing of up to 256-words of microprogram and three devices allow addressing of up to 4K words of microprogram. A detailed logic diagram is shown in Figure 2.

The device contains a four-input multiplexer that is used to select either the address register, direct inputs, microprogram counter, or file as the source of the next microinstruction address. This multiplexer is controlled by the S_0 and S_1 inputs.

The address register consists of four D-type, edge-triggered flip-flops with a common clock enable. When the address register enable is LOW, new data is entered into the register on the clock LOW-to-HIGH transition. The address register is available at the multiplexer as a source for the next microinstruction address. The direct input is a four-bit field of inputs to the multiplexer and can be selected as the next microinstruction address. This allows an N-way branch where N is any word in the microcode.

The MC2909 contains a microprogram counter (μPC) that is composed of a 4-bit incrementer followed by a 4-bit register. The incrementer has carry-in (C_n) and carry-out (C_{n+4}) such that cascading to larger word lengths is straight-forward. The μPC can be used in either of two ways. When the least significant carry-in to the incrementer is HIGH, the microprogram register is loaded on the next clock cycle with the current Y output word plus one (Y+1 → μPC.) Thus sequential microinstructions can be executed. If this least significant C_n is LOW, the incrementer passes the Y output word unmodified and the microprogram register is loaded with the same Y word on the next clock cycle (Y → μPC). Thus, the same microinstruction can be executed any number of times by using the least significant C_n as the control.

The last source available at the multiplexer input is the 4 x 4 file (stack). The file is used to provide return address linkage

stack pointer (SP) which always points to the last file word written. This allows stack reference operations (looping) to be performed without a push or pop.

The stack pointer operates as an up/down counter with separate push/pop and file enable inputs. When the file enable input is LOW and the push/pop input is HIGH, the PUSH operation is enabled. This causes the stack pointer to increment and the file to be written with the required return linkage — the next microinstruction address following the subroutine jump which initiated the PUSH.

If the file enable input is LOW and the push/pop control is LOW, a POP operation occurs. This implies the usage of the return linkage during this cycle and thus a return from subroutine. The next LOW-to-HIGH clock transition causes the stack pointer to decrement. If the file enable is HIGH, no action is taken by the stack pointer regardless of any other input.

The stack pointer linkage is such that any combination of pushes, pops or stack references can be achieved. One microinstruction subroutines can be performed. Since the stack is 4 words deep, up to four microsubroutines can be nested.

The ZERO input is used to force the four outputs to the binary zero state. When the ZERO input is LOW, all Y outputs are LOW regardless of any other inputs (except $\overline{OE}$). Each Y output bit also has a separate OR input such that a conditional logic one can be forced at each Y output. This allows jumping to different microinstructions on programmed conditions.

The MC2909 features three-state Y outputs. These can be particularly useful in military designs requiring external Ground Support Equipment (GSE) to provide automatic checkout of the microprocessor. The internal control can be placed in the high-impedance state, and preprogrammed sequences of microinstructions can be executed via external access to the control ROM/PROM.

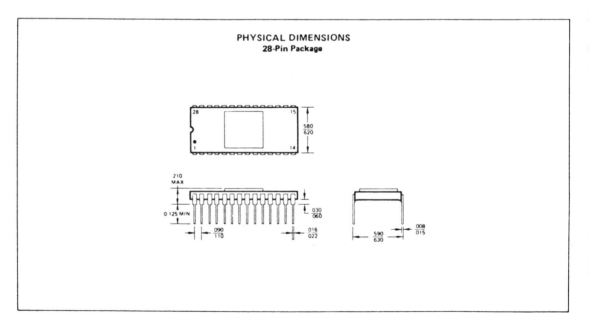

PHYSICAL DIMENSIONS
28-Pin Package

Fig. 9-40. (Cont'd)

DEFINITION OF TERMS

A set of symbols is used in this data sheet to represent various internal and external registers and signals used with the MC2909. Since its principle application is as a controller for a microprogram store, it is necessary to define some signals associated with the microcode itself. Figure 3 illustrates the basic interconnection of MC2909, memory, and microinstruction register. The definitions here apply to this architecture.

Inputs to MC2909

S_1, S_0	Control lines for address source selection
$\overline{FE}$, PUP	Control lines for push/pop stack
$\overline{RE}$	Enable line for internal address register
OR_i	Logic OR inputs on each address output line
$\overline{ZERO}$	Logic AND input on the output lines
$\overline{OE}$	Output Enable. When $\overline{OE}$ is HIGH, the Y outputs are OFF (high impedance)
C_n	Carry-in to the incrementer
R_i	Inputs to the internal address register
D_i	Direct inputs to the multiplexer
CP	Clock input to the AR and μPC register and Push-Pop stack

Outputs from the MC2909

Y_i	Address outputs from MC2909. (Address inputs to control memory.)

C_{n+4} Carry out from the incrementer

Internal Signals

μPC	Contents of the microprogram counter
AR	Contents of the address register
STK0-STK3	Contents of the push/pop stack. By definition, the word in the four-by-four file, addressed by the stack pointer is STK0. Conceptually data is pushed into the stack at STK0; a subsequent push moves STK0 to STK1; a pop implies STK3 → STK2 → STK1 → STK0. Physically, only the stack pointer changes when a push or pop is performed. The data does not move. I/O occurs at STK0.
SP	Contents of the stack pointer

External to the MC2909

A	Address to the control memory
I(A)	Instruction in control memory at address A
μWR	Contents of the microword register (at output of control memory). The microword register contains the instruction currently being executed.
T_n	Time period (cycle) n

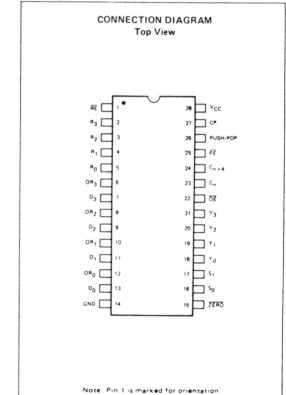

CONNECTION DIAGRAM
Top View

Note: Pin 1 is marked for orientation

Figure 3. Microprogram Sequencer Control.

Fig. 9-40. (Cont.)

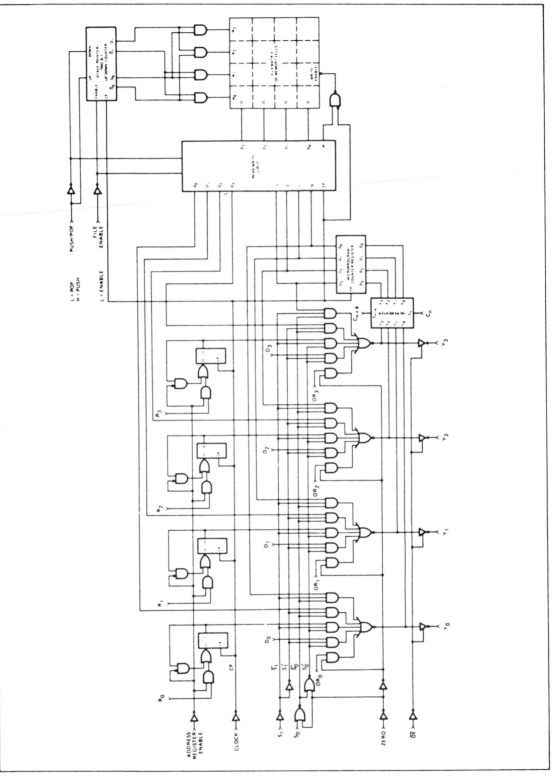

Fig. 9-40. (Cont.)

OPERATION OF THE MC2909

Figure 5 lists the select codes for the multiplexer. The two bits applied from the microword register (and additional combinational logic for branching) determine which data source contains the address for the next microinstruction. The contents of the selected source will appear on the Y outputs. Figure 5 also shows the truth table for the output control and for the control of the push/pop stack. Figure 6 shows in detail the effect of S_0, S_1, $\overline{FE}$ and PUP on the MC2909. These four signals define what address appears on the Y outputs and what the state of all the internal registers will be following the clock LOW-to-HIGH edge. In this illustration, the microprogram counter is assumed to contain initially some word J, the address register some word K, and the four words in the push/pop stack contain R_a through R_d.

Address Selection

OCTAL	S_1	S_0	SOURCE FOR Y OUTPUTS	SYMBOL
0	L	L	Microprogram Counter	μPC
1	L	H	Address register	AR
2	H	L	Push-Pop stack	STK0
3	H	H	Direct inputs	D_i

Output Control

OR_i	$\overline{ZERO}$	$\overline{OE}$	Y_i
X	X	H	Z
X	L	L	L
H	H	L	H
L	H	L	Source selected by S_0 S_1

Z = High Impedance

Synchronous Stack Control

$\overline{FE}$	PUP	PUSH-POP STACK CHANGE
H	X	No change
L	H	Increment stack pointer, then push current PC onto STK0
L	L	Pop stack (decrement stack pointer)

CYCLE	S_1, S_0, $\overline{FE}$, PUP	μPC	AR	STK0	STK1	STK2	STK3	Y_{OUT}	COMMENT	PRINCIPLE USE
N	0 0 0 0	J	K	Ra	Rb	Rc	Rd	J	Pop Stack	End
N+1	—	J+1	K	Rb	Rc	Rd	Ra	—		Loop
N	0 0 0 1	J	K	Ra	Rb	Rc	Rd	J	Push μPC	Set-up
N+1	—	J+1	K	J	Ra	Rb	Rc	—		Loop
N	0 0 1 X	J	K	Ra	Rb	Rc	Rd	J	Continue	Continue
N+1	—	J+1	K	Ra	Rb	Rc	Rd	—		
N	0 1 0 0	J	K	Ra	Rb	Rc	Rd	K	Pop Stack;	End
N+1	—	K+1	K	Rb	Rc	Rd	Ra	—	Use AR for Address	Loop
N	0 1 0 1	J	K	Ra	Rb	Rc	Rd	K	Push μPC;	JSR AR
N+1	—	K+1	K	J	Ra	Rb	Rc	—	Jump to Address in AR	
N	0 1 1 X	J	K	Ra	Rb	Rc	Rd	K	Jump to Address in AR	JMP AR
N+1	—	K+1	K	Ra	Rb	Rc	Rd	—		
N	1 0 0 0	J	K	Ra	Rb	Rc	Rd	Ra	Jump to Address in STK0;	RTS
N+1	—	Ra+1	K	Rb	Rc	Rd	Ra	—	Pop Stack	
N	1 0 0 1	J	K	Ra	Rb	Rc	Rd	Ra	Jump to Address in STK0;	
N+1	—	Ra+1	K	J	Ra	Rb	Rc	—	Push μPC	
N	1 0 1 X	J	K	Ra	Rb	Rc	Rd	Ra	Jump to Address in STK0	Stack Ref (Loop)
N+1	—	Ra+1	K	Ra	Rb	Rc	Rd	—		
N	1 1 0 0	J	K	Ra	Rb	Rc	Rd	D	Pop Stack;	End
N+1	—	D+1	K	Rb	Rc	Rd	Ra	—	Jump to Address on D	Loop
N	1 1 0 1	J	K	Ra	Rb	Rc	Rd	D	Jump to Address on D;	JSR D
N+1	—	D+1	K	J	Ra	Rb	Rc	—	Push μPC	
N	1 1 1 X	J	K	Ra	Rb	Rc	Rd	D	Jump to Address on D	JMP D
N+1	—	D+1	K	Ra	Rb	Rc	Rd	—		

X = Don't Care, 0 = LOW, 1 = HIGH, Assume C_n = HIGH

Figure 6. Output and Internal Next-Cycle Register States for MC2909.

Fig. 9-40. (Cont.)

The SN74S482 and MC2909 Integrated Circuit Sequence Controllers **641**

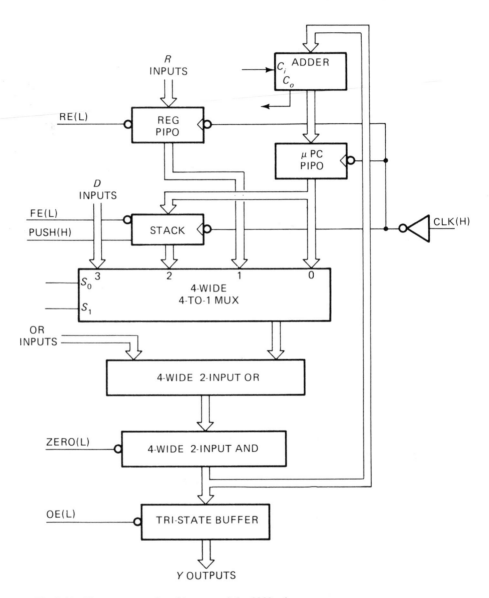

Fig. 9-41. The restructured architecture of the 2909 microprogram sequencer.

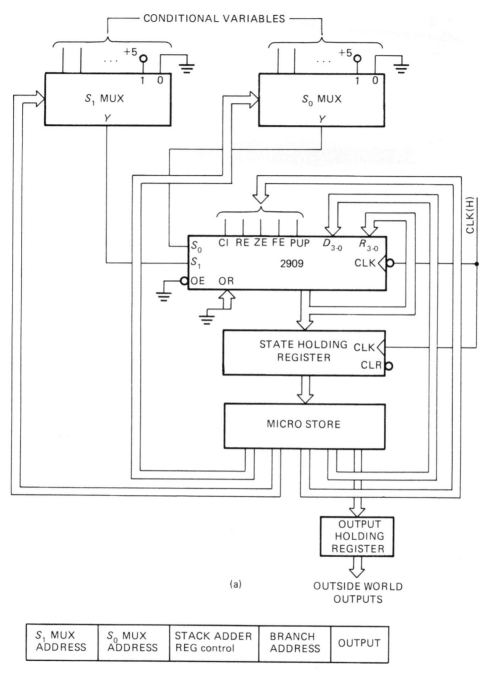

CONDITIONAL VARIABLES

S_1 MUX

+5

1 0

Y

S_0 MUX

+5

1 0

Y

CLK(H)

S_0
S_1
OE OR

CI RE ZE FE PUP $D_{3\text{-}0}$ $R_{3\text{-}0}$

2909

CLK

STATE HOLDING
REGISTER

CLK
CLR

MICRO STORE

(a)

OUTPUT
HOLDING
REGISTER

OUTSIDE WORLD
OUTPUTS

S_1 MUX ADDRESS	S_0 MUX ADDRESS	STACK ADDER REG control	BRANCH ADDRESS	OUTPUT

(b)

Fig. 9-42. (a) A microprogrammable configuration centered around the 2909. (b) The internal control word bit format for the indicated configuration.

BRANCH UNCONDITIONAL TO STATE *Z:*
WITH NO STACK OPERATION
IMPLIED

S_1 MUX ADR = 1	S_0 MUX ADR = 1	Ø	Ø	0	0	Ø	BRANCH ADR = Z

BRANCH CONDITIONALLY TO STATE Z:
WITH NO STACK OPERATION IMPLIED

Assume the conditional variable is connected to S_1 MUX input number X and is *ASSERTED HIGH*:

S_1 MUX ADR = X	S_0 MUX ADR = Y	1	Ø	0	0	Ø	BRANCH ADR = Z

Thus the five basic operations can be implemented with a 2909 centered controller. Further it should be obvious that other operations can be specified also. These are left as an exercise.

9-15 SUMMARY

We have introduced the basic concept of utilizing an existing sequential device with fixed sequential behavior and adapting the design requirements to fit the constraints of the device. This we loosely refer to as *programming the device to solve the problem.* Based on this point of view we have covered both microprogramming and fixed instruction methods for solving sequence control functions using a variety of devices. It is intended that this introduction serve a twofold purpose: (1) to provide a viable alternative to control problems when speed and flexibility are of importance, and (2) to provide an introduction to microprocessors in general.

BIBLIOGRAPHY

1. BERNDT, HELMUT. Functional Microprogramming as a Logic Design Aid. *IEEE Trans. Computers*, **C-19**, No. 10 (1970), 902–907.

2. BOULAYE, GUY G. *Microprogramming*. New York: Wiley, 1971.

3. BROCK. *Designing with MSI: Counters and Shift Registers* (Vol. I). Sunnyvale, Calif.: Signetics, 1970.

4. GOLD, JIM. Bipolar Controllers—They're Fast, Cheap and Easy to Use. *Electronic Design*, **22** (1976), 106–110.

5. HUSSON, SAMIR S. *Microprogramming Principles and Practices*. Englewood Cliffs, N.J.: Prentice-Hall, 1968.

6. KATZAN, HARRY, JR. *Microprogramming Primer*. New York: McGraw-Hill, 1977.

7. New Products. 4-bit Bipolar/LSI Processor Slice Cuts Microcycle Time to 100 nsec. *Electronic Design*, **15**, (1975), 77–78.

8. *Schottky and Low-power Schottky Data Book Including Digital Signal Processing Handbook*, 2nd ed. Sunnyvale, Calif.: Advanced Micro Devices, 1977.

9. Signetics. *How to Design with the Control Store Sequencer 8X02...3*. Application Note No. 3, Signetics, Sunnyvale, California, 1977.

10. *Signetics Digital Linear MOS Data Book*. Sunnyvale Calif.: Signetics Corporation, 1974.

11. *The TTL Data Book for Design Engineers*, 2nd ed.: Dallas, Texas: Texas Instruments, 1976.

12. VANDLING, G. C., and WALDECKER, D. E. The Microprogram Technique for Digital Logic Design. *Computer Design*, **8**, No. 8 (1969), 44–51.

PROBLEMS AND EXERCISES

9-1. Discuss any advantages or disadvantages of the model shown in Figure 9-1.

9-2. Discuss the relative merits of obtaining a state assignment that is based on shifting operations only when a shift register like the AM74LS194 is being used for the memory element in a FSM.

9-3. Analyze the operation of the AM74LS194 and draw a conclusion as to why the state assignment constraint for states controlled by asynchronous inputs must be unit distance.

9-4. Using the following timing data, determine the worst case timing constraint placed on a FSM by using an AM74LS194 shift register in a system controller that incorporates a random selection of shifts and parallel loads operation, i.e., what is the worst case delay constraint created by the 74LS194 itself?

Switching Characteristics (T_A = +25°C)

Parameters	Description	Test Conditions	Am54LS/74LS194A Min.	Typ.	Max.
t_{PLH}	Clock to Output			14	22
t_{PHL}	Clock to Output			17	22
t_{PHL}	Clear to Output			19	30
t_{pw}	Clock Pulse Width		20		
t_{pw}	Clear Pulse Width		20		
t_s	Mode Control Set-up Time	V_{CC} = 5V	30		
t_s	Data Input Set-up Time	C_L = 15pF	20		
t_s	Clear Recovery to Clock	R_L = 2kΩ	25		
t_h	Data Hold Time		0		
t_R	Shift/Load Release Time Am54LS/74LS195A Only				—
$f_{MAX.}$	Maximum Clock Frequency		25	36	

9-5. Carry out the AM74LS194 implementation for the controller problem specified by the MDS diagram in Figure 9-4.

9-6. Make an alternate state assignment and repeat the design called for in Problem 9-5.

9-7. Select an implementation problem from Chapter 7 and carry out the controller implementation centered around an AM74LS194. Once complete, compare results with previous implementations and determine the maximum clock rate for your circuit.

9-8. Develop a general sequential configuration for a sequence controller which is centered around the AM74LS194 using a ROM as the next state control logic. Using this configuration, implement the MDS diagram in Figure 9-5 and compare your results with that of Figure 9-11.

9-9. Repeat Problem 9-8, but this time utilize the 82S110 FPLA (see Chapter 8).

9-10. Repeat Problem 9-3, but this time use the AM74LS161 counter for your analysis.

9-11. Repeat Problem 9-4, but this time use the AM74LS161 counter and the following timing data for your analysis.

Switching Characteristics (T_A = +25°C)

Parameters	Description		Test Conditions	Min.	Typ.	Max.	Units
t_{PLH}	Clock to Carry Output				20		ns
t_{PHL}					18		
t_{PLH}	Clock to Q Output with Load Input HIGH				10	18	ns
t_{PHL}					12	20	
t_{PLH}	Enable T to Carry Output				8	14	ns
t_{PHL}					8	14	
t_{PLH}	Clock to Q Output with Load Input LOW				10	18	ns
t_{PHL}					12	20	
t_{PHL}	Clear to Q Output (Note 1)		V_{CC} = 5.0V, C_L = 5.0pF, R_L = 2kΩ		18	28	ns
t_{pw}	Pulse Width	Clock		25			ns
		Clear		20			
t_s	Set-up Time	Data – A, B, C, D		20			ns
		Enable P		20			
		Load, Enable T		20			
		Clear (Note 2)		20			
t_h	Hold Time – Any Input			3			ns
$f_{MAX.}$	Maximum Clock Frequency			35	50		MHz

9-12. Carry out the AM74LS161 implementation for the controller problem specified by the MDS diagram in Figure 9-13.

9-13. Make an alternate state assignment for the MDS diagram in Figure 9-13 and repeat the design called for in Problem 9-12.

9-14. In Section 9-4 it is mentioned that shift register implementation holds a slight edge over counter implementation. What in your estimation is this edge?

9-15. Select an implementation problem from Chapter 7 or any other source and carry out the controller implementation centered around an AM74LS161. Once complete, compare results with previous implementations. Also determine the maximum clock rate for your circuit.

9-16. Develop the micro-control program (see Table 9-3) using the microprogrammable controller configuration shown in Figure 9-21 and a state assignment of your choice for Figure 9-13.

9-17. Repeat Problem 9-16 for an alternate state assignment for the MDS diagram shown in Figure 9-23. List any ideas you may have developed in relation to better ways to make a state assignment.

9-18. Select an implementation problem from Chapter 7 or any other source (re-configure the MDS diagram if necessary) and carry out a complete design using the microprogrammable controller configuration shown in Figure 9-24. Be certain to document your design completely. Once complete, compare results with previous implementations.

9-19. Using your own words, discuss the concept of utilizing a microprogrammable fixed instruction set control sequence (i.e., based on your experience in controller design, evaluate the functionality of MYCA-I and MYCA-II).

9-20. Select at least two implementation problems from Chapter 7 or any other source, then implement these problems with MYCA-I and MYCA-II. Try to select one problem that can be restructured such that it illustrates the use for one or more SUBROUTINES. Make a comparative evaluation between the two implementations.

9-21. Implement the same selected problems used in Problem 9-20, but restructured with the 8X02 control store sequencer. Make a comparative evaluation between these results and those obtained in Problem 9-20.

9-22. Select at least two implementation problems from Chapter 7 or any other source, then implement them using the 74S482 configuration shown in Figure 9-39. Be certain to utilize the same microinstruction bit format.

9-23. Using a method similar to that used to develop MYCA-II convert the 74S482 into an expandable bit-slice fixed instruction set control sequencer. (Develop the IN-STRUCTION DECODER using a BIPOLAR ROM.) Start with MYCA-II's instruction set, then expand it to facilitate any other instruction you may feel is appropriate. Be certain to maintain the same instruction bit format as shown in Figure 9-27.

9-24. Repeat Problem 9-22, but this time use the MC2909 device and the configuration illustrated in Figure 9-42.

9-25. Repeat Problem 9-23, but this time use the MC2909 device.

Note: The following problems are special exercises which will require some outside research and extra effort.

9-26. Consider the following list of device numbers and manufacturers:
  AM2910—Advanced Micro Devices, Inc.
  AM2930—Advanced Micro Devices, Inc.
  AM2931/32—Advanced Micro Devices, Inc.
  MMI 67110—Monolithic Memories, Inc.
  Fairchild—9408—Fairchild, Inc.
Each of these devices can be utilized in the same manner as MYCA-II, the 8X02, 74S482, and AM/MC2909. *Exercise:* Obtain data sheets for these devices and develop fixed instruction controller configurations for each, then make a comparative evaluation.

9-27. Figure P9-1 is an illustration of how a fixed instruction controller can be configured into a bus-oriented control system where devices requiring control information are treated as addressable output ports (destination ports) and those devices inputting control information are treated as addressable input ports (source ports). Using a modified MYCA-II, work out the details related to the actual hardware requirements. Also work up an instruction-bit format. In general, bring this block diagram up to a working system.

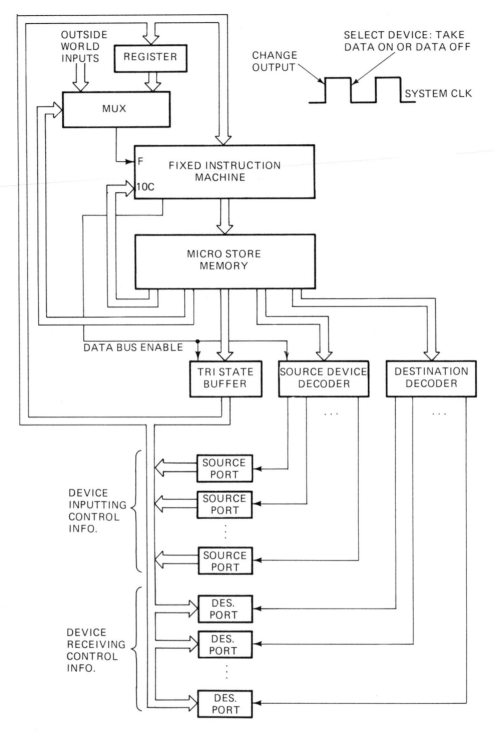

Fig. P 9-1. The general model of the system controller sequential circuit utilizing shift registers and counters as the memory element.

CHAPTER 10

ASYNCHRONOUS FINITE-STATE
MACHINES

10-1 INTRODUCTION

The previous four chapters present some practical and applied aspects related to designing *synchronous* sequential machines. This chapter treats some of the practical aspects of designing *clockless* sequential machines, more often referred to as *asynchronous finite-state machines*. For example, consider the classical asynchronous circuit shown in Figure 10-1. This figure shows that asynchronous sequential machines are characterized by two features:

   (1) The absence of the familiar Flip-Flop.
   (2) They appear to be *combinational circuits with feedback*.

Further, Figure 10-1 demonstrates that if the logic gates are considered to be ideal (those with propagation delay equal 0), and the delay is lumped at the feedback point and this delay is treated as memory, the sequential models shown in Figures 10-2(a) and 10-2(b) can be derived.

As mentioned in Chapter 5, the *asynchronous machine* should be considered as the fundamental sequential machine because the concepts related to asynchronous machines underpin the operational characteristics of synchronous machines. This is borne out by the fact that the clocked Flip-Flop, which is the heart of a synchronous machine, is within itself an *asynchronous machine*. However, there are two important reasons why the study of asynchronous circuits has been delayed until now:

   (1) Presently, the major emphasis in sequential machine design is directed towards synchronous machines and their application.

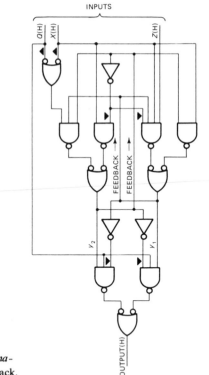

Fig. 10-1. A typical example of an *asynchronous finite-state ma-chine* characterized to be a combinational circuit with feedback.

(2) A certain level of insight into sequential machine behavior and design maturity is a desirable prerequisite for a study of asynchronous finite-state machines.

Fig. 10-2. (a) The block diagram model of a general asynchronous finite-state machine.

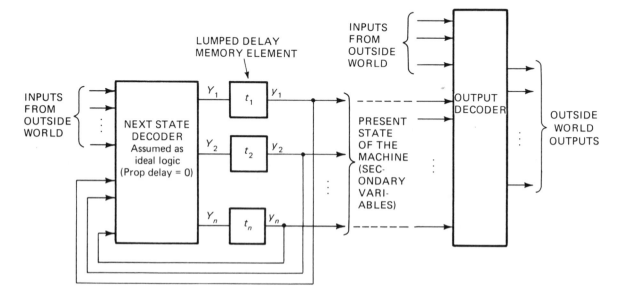

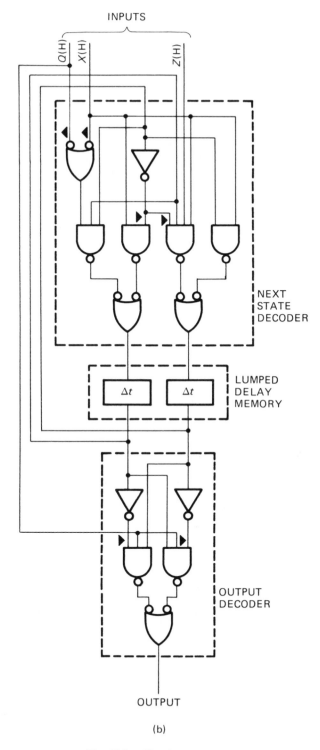

(b)

Fig. 10-2. (Cont.)

10-2 WHY ASYNCHRONOUS CIRCUITS?

Aside from the fact that a study of asynchronous machines is interesting and intellectually challenging, they can and do have practical applications. Undoubtedly the reader who is familiar with contemporary design practices will ask: "If asynchronous circuits are so important, why don't we see asynchronous circuits in John Doe's digital design?" The author's answer to this question is basically this: "Asynchronous circuits are not widely understood, and because of this the ominous sounding words and phrases such as CRITICAL RACES, STATIC HAZARDS, DYNAMIC HAZARDS, ESSENTIAL HAZARDS, and OSCILLA-TIONS tend to cause designers to steer away from asynchronous practices." In short, designers do not want anything to do with a machine that could have such obviously undesirable operational features. However, those who steer away from asynchronous machines for the reasons mentioned above and take complete solace in the belief that synchronous circuits avoid all these nasty characteristics *don't understand synchronous circuits either*. In fact, unless a synchronous machine is a purely synchronous machine (having no asynchronous inputs), it, too, is subject to the same sort of erratic behavior. The roots of the understanding of the "why's" of erratic behavior lie in the understanding of asynchronous theory. For example, the understanding of the faulty behavior caused by an improper state assignment for states controlled by an asynchronous input comes from a knowledge of asynchronous circuit behavior.

Thus any state with a transition based on an asynchronous variable must be associated with a *unit-distance* state assignment, be it a state in a synchronous or asynchronous machine. A close comparison indicates that the only real difference in the two machines is that the next state of an asynchronous machine is almost always determined by an asynchronous input. This comparison can be validated by taking a close look at a synchronous machine that entertains asynchronous inputs and utilizes D Flip-Flops for its memory element. This scrutiny reveals that if any of the D Flip-Flops are viewed as a separate entity, it by itself must be classified as an asynchronous circuit. And this circuit is required to resolve its next state based on two asynchronous inputs: (1) the *CLOCK* and (2) the DATA input. From Chapter 7, remember that this situation should receive special attention in order to avoid operational errors.

All of this demonstrates that the problems that plague the synchronous designer are not all that different from those of the asynchronous designer and that a good understanding of asynchronous practices sheds light and understanding on synchronous practices.

Another reason for studying asynchronous circuits is that they do have application in instances when sequential action is required but a synchronous circuit is not applicable for the following reasons:

(1) Clock is not available or practical, or
(2) speed requirements exceed synchronous capability.

The next section presents the scope, direction, and philosophy of the rest of the chapter.

10-3 SCOPE

It is not the purpose of this chapter to delve into *all* the facets of asynchronous machine design, but it is intended that the practical and conceptual points related to the design of asynchronous circuits be covered. Further, it will be shown that practical and reliable small scale asynchronous machines can be designed and implemented in a straightforward manner by avoiding the step-by-step recipe approach that is so often taken. Hopefully this will be done by first treating analysis methods for the purpose of developing a mapping concept that relates input changes to state transitions and in turn leads the way into the traditional design approach. Then, once the traditional design approach has been developed, it will be extended to using a map-entered-variable approach, which can be applied to larger multi-input asynchronous machine design.

10-4 ASYNCHRONOUS ANALYSIS

As mentioned, the concepts set forth in analysis will greatly enhance your understanding of the traditional design approach. To this end let's introduce a method of analysis by considering the following example.

> *EXAMPLE 10-1:* Consider the asynchronous circuit shown in Figure 10-3. It is our purpose to determine the sequential behavior of this machine in two ways: (1) develop an EXCITATION MAP, and (2) develop a STATE DIAGRAM. In short, we are to develop some graphical pictures that describe the circuit's behavior under varying input stimuli.

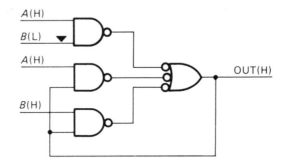

Fig. 10-3. An asynchronous circuit to analyze.

The first step in the analysis process is to model the circuit in a manner such that the three major blocks of any sequential circuit can be identified. We do this by putting the circuit into what is called its "fundamental mode model" as shown in Figure 10-4. Once we have the circuit model as shown, we see that one of two conditions exists:

$$\text{either} \quad Y(t) = y(t + \Delta t)$$
$$\text{or} \quad Y(t) \neq y(t + \Delta t)$$

These two conditions are the bases for the following statements:

If $Y(t) = y(t + \Delta t)$ the circuit is STABLE or *not* in transition, and
if $Y(t) \neq y(t + \Delta t)$ the circuit is UNSTABLE or in transition from one stable
state to the next.

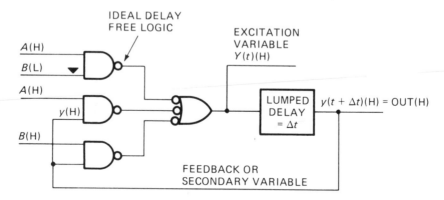

Fig. 10-4. The asynchronous machine shown in Figure 10-3 transformed into its fundamental mode model.

Further, it can be seen from Figure 10-4 that in general

$$Y(t) = f(\text{inputs}, \text{feedback})$$

More specifically, for our problem

$$Y(t) = f[A, B, y(t + \Delta t)]$$

more simply stated as:

$$Y = A\bar{B} + Ay + By$$

which is reinforced by the observation that an asynchronous circuit is a combinational circuit with feedback. Based on this combinational nature, we can plot a special map for Y as shown in Figure 10-5. This special map is called the EXCITATION MAP.

Fig. 10-5. The excitation map for the circuit shown in Figure 10-4.

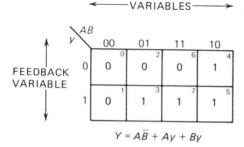

Now once the excitation map is plotted, we have a graphical or pictorial means of making the comparison between Y and y for the express purpose of determining if the circuit is *stable* or *unstable* under all input and feedback conditions. This is done by remembering for each map entry:

If $Y = y$ the circuit is not changing state nor will it change state until an input change causes it to do so.

If $Y \neq y$ the circuit is in a transition mode caused by an input change.

Now for each map entry for which $Y = y$, we will circle the entry in the cell to indicate the circuit is stable and leave the rest of the cells unmarked (see Figure 10-6).

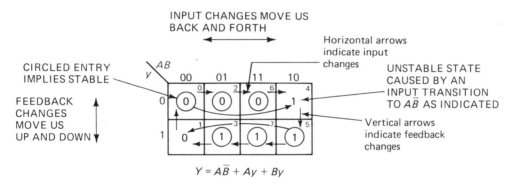

$$Y = A\bar{B} + Ay + By$$

Fig. 10-6. The excitation map with stable and unstable states of Y indicated.

The map in Figure 10-6 indicates that the circuit has six stable input/feedback conditions and two unstable input/feedback conditions. In each unstable state (cell), there is a code for the row to which the (Y) variable will be transferring. Herein lies an important point: *The code in the unstable cell is the code for the next row to which the feedback variable will move after the appropriate propagation delay has elapsed. Likewise, it is important to remember that if the Y entry in the cell matches the y or row code for that cell, then the input and feedback conditions for that cell define a stable state.* Thus we picture the sequential operation as follows: *Input changes moving us back and forth horizontally in the rows of the map and feedback variable changes moving us vertically up and down in the columns of the map.* Once this is understood we have a conceptual aid that allows us to plot the sequential behavior of an asynchronous machine.

The state diagram for the circuit can also be extracted from the excitation map by recognizing that both the input conditions and feedback condition define what we will call a **PRIMITIVE STATE** of an asynchronous machine. See Figure 10-7 for the complete step-by-step analysis documentation including the primitive state diagram for the circuit shown in Figure 10-7(a).

It should be pointed out that the primitive state diagram differs somewhat from the traditional state diagrams in that there are typically many more so-called *primitive states* than the number of feedback variables would allow. Thus we will see later how several of these primitive states can be merged together to define one finite state in terms of the feedback variable code. For example, in Example 10-1 shown in Figure 10-7 we see six primitive states that merge three at a time to form the two finite feedback states $y=0$ and $y=1$.

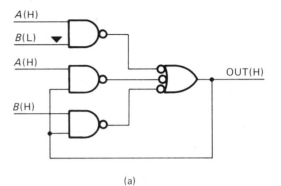

(a)

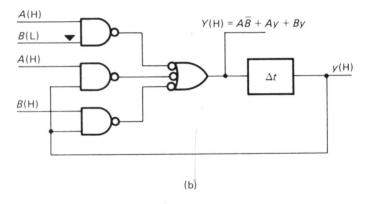

(b)

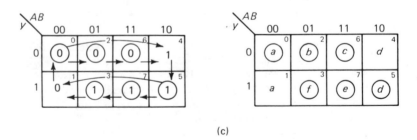

(c)

Fig. 10-7. The complete step-by-step analysis documentation for the circuit shown in (a). (a) Circuit to analyze. (b) Circuit put into its fundamental mode model. (c) The excitation maps. (d) The primitive state diagram.

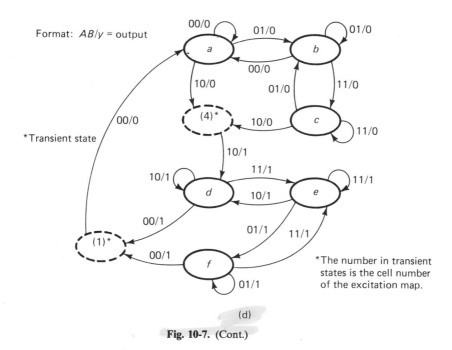

Format: *AB/y* = output

*Transient state

*The number in transient
states is the cell number
of the excitation map.

(d)

Fig. 10-7. (Cont.)

By way of review, we see that the process of analysis is one of first putting the circuit to be analyzed into a recognizable model and identifying the EXCITATION VARIABLES (Y's) and FEEDBACK VARIABLES (y's), then writing the Boolean expression for:

$$Y(t) = f(\text{inputs}, y\text{'s})$$

The next step is plotting the EXCITATION MAP from this expression in order to identify all of the primitive stable states and transient states from which we can derive the definitive primitive state diagram.

In the past example, the feedback variable served also as the output, as is the case many times. However, there are cases when an output decoder is also included. In cases such as these it is necessary to plot an OUTPUT MAP and include the output sequence code on the primitive state diagram. This is illustrated in the next example.

EXAMPLE 10-2: The circuit shown in Figure 10-8 is the schematic diagram for the SN74120 pulse synchronizer. Let us consider the analysis of the machine treating the output of the cross-coupled NAND cell in the upper left as X(H).

From the fundamental mode model of the 74120 shown in Figure 10-9 we see the following:

Inputs: X(H), C(L), and M(H)
Feedback variables: y(L), y_1(H), and y_2(H)

- Generates Either a Single Pulse or Train of Pulses Synchronized with Control Functions

- Ideal for Implementing Sync-Control Circuits Similar to those Used in Oscilloscopes

- Latched Operation Ensures that Output Pulses Are Not Clipped

- High-Fan-Out Complementary Outputs Drive System Clock Lines Directly

- Internal Input Pull-Up Resistors Eliminate Need for External Components

- Diode-Clamped Inputs Simplify System Design

- Typical Propagation Delays:

    9 Nanoseconds through One Level
    16 Nanoseconds through Two Levels

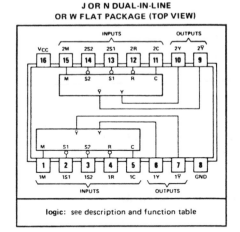

J OR N DUAL-IN-LINE OR W FLAT PACKAGE (TOP VIEW)

logic: see description and function table

functional block diagram

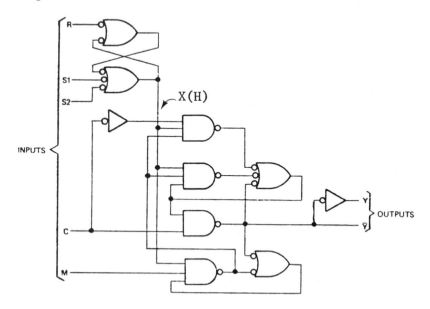

Fig. 10-8. The schematic diagram for the SN74120 pulse synchronizer (Courtesy of Texas Instrument)

Let's continue our analysis assuming the mode control $M(H)$ is always ASSERTED. Figure 10-9 shows the 74120 put in its fundamental mode model.

$$Y = y_1 \overline{C}$$

$$Y_1 = y + y_1 X(\overline{X} + \overline{M} + \overline{y}_2) + CX(\overline{X} + \overline{M} + \overline{y}_2)$$

$$Y_2 = y + XMy_2$$

And if we assume M is ASSERTED then:

$$Y = \overline{C}y_1 = \text{output}$$

$$Y_1 = y + Xy_1\overline{y}_2 + CX\overline{y}_2$$

$$Y_2 = y + Xy_2$$

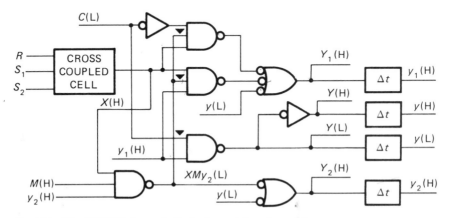

Fig. 10-9. The SN74120 drawn in its fundamental mode model.

Before plotting the EXCITATION MAP for the 74120, let us introduce some special notation related to asynchronous analysis. First, the EXCITATION MAP is plotted as a *composite map* made up of the superimposed set of maps for Y, Y_1, and Y_2. This is done to simplify the comparison between the feedback code (row code) and the plotted value for Y, Y_1, and Y_2 for the purpose of determining stability or instability. Further, the transition states sometimes called CYCLE states are shown in both the EXCITATION MAPS as well as the primitive state diagram. The transition states are shown as dotted symbols, with the map cell number enclosed for identification. This clarifies the delay processes in the sequential behavior of the machine under analysis.

Now the excitation map is plotted from the expressions for Y, Y_1, and Y_2 as shown in Figure 10-10. Note that the transition paths have been traced with arrows. It should be noted also that the designer of the 74120 utilized "cycle states" in several instances to move in a unit distance manner from one state to the next. See the transitions from ⓕ to ⓖ, ⓖ to ⓓ, and ⓗ to ⓔ. These cycle states are also shown in the primitive state diagram in Figure 10-11. Thus we have completed a rather complex analysis with considerable ease.

From our study we see the SN74120 is a circuit that issues one and only one *clean* clock pulse each time the X input is *cycled*. Also, the primitive state diagram illustrates the problems that can be created if an input is changed when the circuit is in transition mode. For example, the inputs should be held constant during the cycle from ⓗ to ⓔ, otherwise an unpredictable state transition is likely to occur. This operational constraint is specified in the data sheet for the 74120 in terms of setup and hold times for the control inputs in the same manner as was done for the Flip-Flops studied in Chapter 5.

This example concludes our study of the analysis of asynchronous machines; however, it is important to note that most of the salient points of design have been touched upon. These basic points are:

(1) States in an asynchronous machine must be given unit distance assignments.
(2) Cycling transitions are apparently used to carry out the unit distance requirements.
(3) Reliable branching decisions can be made only on a single input change.
(4) Primitive states are identified by both the input conditions and the state of the feedback variables.
(5) There must be some method for merging primitive states that under similar input changes require no specified feedback code change.
(6) It should be obvious that if a design process can lead us to an excitation map the implementation is but a short step away, this step being reading the map rather than plotting it.

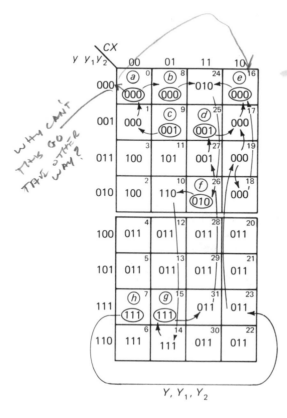

Fig. 10-10. The superimposed excitation maps for Y, Y_1, and Y_2 of the 74120 with the M input tied high.

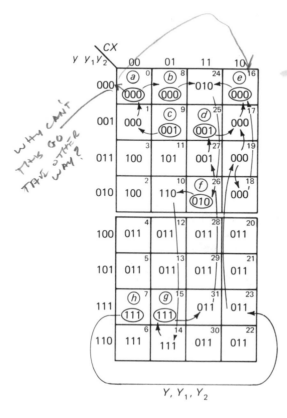

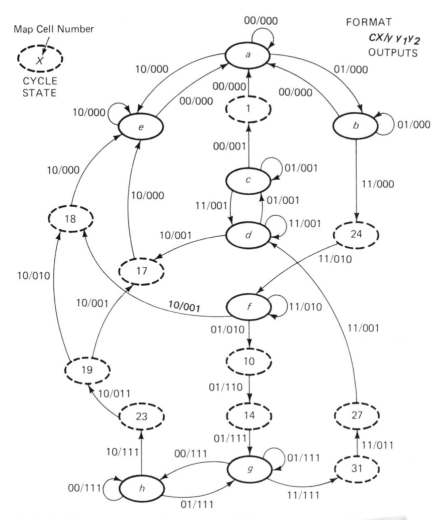

Fig. 10-11. The primitive state diagram for the 74120 with the M input tied high.

The next section introduces the traditional approach to the design of asynchronous circuit and from time to time relates back to these basic points.

10-5 THE DESIGN OF ASYNCHRONOUS MACHINES

As mentioned in the previous section, the design of asynchronous circuits is closely related to the analysis process, and the information learned in analysis can readily be applied to a design process. It was further mentioned that it would be advantageous to gain a conceptual understanding of asynchronous operation in order to avoid the "plug in and turn the crank" methodology for design. Hence you, the reader, are advised to study the following steps for understanding rather than mechanics.

The following design steps are offered as a logical design process for developing asynchronous circuits by reversing the steps to analysis as much as possible:

(1) Receive specifications and formulate precisely what the machine is to do.

(2) Develop a primitive state diagram that defines the desired *output sequences* for the prescribed input sequences.

Related notes:

    (a) Keep in mind that input events must be thought of as a *sequence of events*. This is mentioned because often two states that have identical input and output specifications cannot be classed as equivalent since their occurrence in the total sequence are completely independent.

    (b) Keep your primitive state diagram tight to avoid the introduction of redundant states.

    (c) Obviously the primitive state diagram derived for design will not specify cycles and state assignments; they come later.

(3) Make up a primitive state table from your primitive state diagram.

Related notes:

    (a) This is done as the first step towards the development of the excitation map. In short, the primitive state table will evolve into the excitation map.

    (b) It is assumed that each input change requires a separate and unique primitive state. Thus the table is made with one stable state per row. Input change specifications are to be placed along the top of the table.

(4) Merge the primitive state table.

Related notes:

    (a) This is the second step in the evolution of the primitive state table toward the final excitation map.

    (b) This is a process of identifying those primitive states that can be compressed into *one* stable state based on the concept that *no feedback state change is required* for two or more input conditions. In short, the merge process is one of identifying those primitive states that *are related by input sequences* and can be lumped together into a single stable state, that is, finding the states that can be put together in the same row of the excitation map. This can be done independent or dependent of the actual circuit *outputs*. Thus there can be a *mixed output merge* or a *nonmixed output merge*.

(5) Find a state assignment for the rows of the merged primitive state table.

Related notes:

    (a) This is the third step in the evolution of the primitive state table toward the excitation map.

    (b) For this step, a knowledge of the implications of $Y(t)=y(t+\Delta t)$ and $Y(t)\neq y(t+\Delta t)$ is imperative.

(c) In this step a state code is assigned to the feedback variables (y's), which are then related to the transitions in the merged table to assure unit-distance transitions from state to state. Once this is completed the excitation map is close at hand.

(6) Transform the merged table into the excitation map.

Related notes:

(a) This is the final step in the evolution of the primitive state table into the excitation map.

(b) In this step the alphabetic notations for the stable states in the merged table are replaced with the *codes* of the rows in which they reside.

(c) The alphabetic notation for the unstable or transition states are given the codes of the *next row* to which the machine is to transfer. Here notice how cycles can be prescribed to assure unit distance state changes (row codes) are guaranteed.

(7) Derive the expressions for the excitation variables (Y's) by reading the excitation map.

Related notes:

(a) Once the excitation map is at hand, the actual circuit can be implemented from the expressions read from the map in a process exactly opposite to that of analysis.

(b) For multiple feedback systems (those with more than one y), it is advisable to plot a single excitation map for each of the Y's specified to avoid the confusion of trying to read the composite map. This will be illustrated later. It is at this point that hazards are to be removed by overlapping adjacent groupings.

(8) Make an output decoder map.

Related notes:

(a) Based on the knowledge that an output (Z) is in general a function of both the inputs and the state of the machine, the function notation is:

$$Z = f(\text{inputs, feedback})$$

(b) Therefore, make up a map similar to the excitation map to specify under what input and feedback condition there is to be an output generated. This is done easily for the *stable states* by simply inserting the derived output codes into the output map at the location of the stable states in the excitation map. However, considerable care must be exercised to prevent transient outputs *during a transition*. In short, if the output condition specified in the beginning state is the same as the ending state, it must be specified the same also through all of the intervening transition states; otherwise transient glitches will be generated.

(9) Draw up schematics to the specifications of the excitation and output maps. Make certain you have properly documented your design.

(10) Perform a quick independent analysis of your design to make certain it performs as specified. At this time specify the set-up and hold times and

analyze the circuit's behavior if input changes do happen during a transition.

Consider the very simple design problem outlined in Example 10-3.

EXAMPLE 10-3: To illustrate the design process just outlined, let us design a circuit that will duplicate the sequential operation of the BASIC CELL.

Step 1: We should visualize the circuit in block diagram form to help conceptualize its physical characteristics as shown in Figure 10-12.

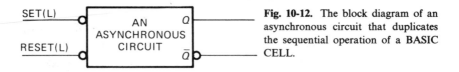

Fig. 10-12. The block diagram of an asynchronous circuit that duplicates the sequential operation of a BASIC CELL.

Step 2: Based on our familiarity with the prescribed sequential behavior of the circuit, we define its operation with a primitive state diagram (see Figure 10-13).

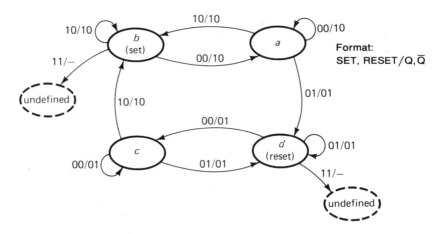

Fig. 10-13. The primitive state diagram of the circuit that duplicates the action of a BASIC CELL.

Step 3: Develop a primitive flow table from the primitive state diagram. Keep input change notation along the top edge of the table (see Figure 10-14).

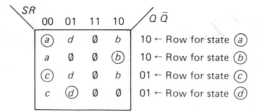

Fig. 10-14. The primitive flow table derived from the primitive state diagram for the circuit that duplicates the sequential operation of the basic cell.

Again it is important to note that the structure of the primitive flow table is developed with the idea that it will eventually evolve into the excitation map. Therefore, it might be better to think of it as a primitive excitation map. Thus we use the flow table to set up the form of the final excitation map and to define the transition from one stable state to the next stable state, assuming only *one transition state* is needed between the two. For example, see Figure 10-15.

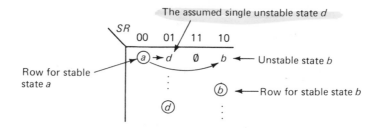

Fig. 10-15. An illustration of the assumed single transition state between two stable states.

From Figure 10-15 we conclude that the uncircled letters in a column are merely indicators *of the stable state* in that same column in which the circuit will eventually reside.

Step 4: The next step is taken to examine the possibility of grouping more than one stable state in each row of the primitive flow table. This process is called *merging*. The results of merging generally lead to a more simple realization of a circuit. Let us back up for a moment to examine the structure of the primitive flow table. We see that if we were to develop our circuit directly from an excitation map that was developed *directly* from the primitive flow table, all transitions between stable states would be associated with *both a change in input and a change in the feedback variables*, and the double association would be wasteful because many transitions between stable states require *no* feedback variable change. Thus the merging process is one of finding those primitive states that can be grouped together under a single feedback variable code, that is, grouped together in the same row of the primitive flow table. The result of a merge is called the MERGED FLOW TABLE, but it is nothing more than the excitation map *without a code* assigned to the rows.

The following merge rules are offered for the beginner; however, after a little practice the merging process can be done at the state diagram level.

Merging Rules:

(1) Two or more rows can merge, within the rows, if there are no conflicting state numbers in any column. For example, two rows can merge if each column contains either two like state identifying letters, one state number, and a Ø, or two Ø's.

(2) All state letters in the merging rows are written in the respective columns of the merged row. If a state letter is circled in one of the merging rows, it is circled in the merged row, retaining the stable state designations.

Note that the *output specifications* (*Q*'s) for each stable state recorded in the primitive flow table *in no way affect merging processes* and are not usually repeated in the merged flow table. However, the primitive flow table with this specification will be referred to later when the output decoder is designed.

Generally there is more than one way of merging the rows of a flow table and the choice of mergers can affect circuit economy. To aid in the merging process a merge diagram is recommended (see Figure 10-16(a)). To construct a merge diagram the *stable state letters* are arranged in basically a circular array with output code listed above each state, and the letters are used here only to identify the rows of the primitive flow table. See Figure 10-16. If, in the flow table, two rows can be merged according to the rules, the corresponding stable state numbers in the merger diagram are connected by a line. All pairs of rows are examined for a possible merger, and after all connecting lines have been drawn, the merger diagram is inspected for an optimal way of merging. The aim, in general, is to merge in order to obtain the minimum number of rows in the merged flow table, and it is desirable to carry out the merge such that a nonmixed merge is defined if possible. Nonmixed refers to merge states with identical outputs.

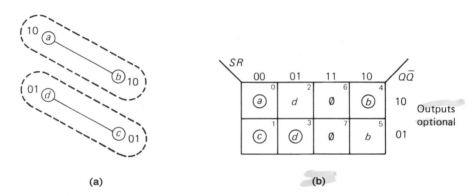

(a)   (b)

Fig. 10-16. (a) Merge diagram. (b) Merged flow table for the circuit that duplicates the sequential operation of the basic cell.

When designing a sequential circuit, it is felt that both types of merges, mixed and nonmixed, should be considered and the choice of which is best should be based on engineering judgment. Things that affect this judgment should be speed and gate count. It should be obvious that if an output can be taken from a secondary with relatively fewer gates, the circuit will be faster. The concept here is one of making the circuit more parallel in nature and thus reducing the costly delay of multi-level machines.

From Figure 10-16 we see that we have derived a nonmixed merge and reduced the number of rows from four to two.

Step 5. Making a state assignment or row code assignment to assure a unit distance transition between states is no problem for a *two*-row or single feedback excitation map. To illustrate the process, first let us complete Step 5 for our example problem and then go back and treat the feedback assignment more specifically (see Figure 10-17).

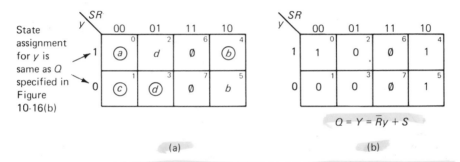

State assignment for y is same as Q specified in Figure 10-16(b)

	SR			
y	00	01	11	10
1	(a)	d	$\emptyset$	(b)
0	(c)	(d)	$\emptyset$	b

	SR			
y	00	01	11	10
1	1	0	$\emptyset$	1
0	0	0	$\emptyset$	1

$$Q = Y = \bar{R}y + S$$

(a)   (b)

Fig. 10-17. The excitation maps for the circuit that duplicates the sequential operation of the basic cell.

Figure 10-17(b) shows that we have replaced the stable alphabetic symbol with the 1, 0 code for Y using the criteria:

$$Y(t) = y(t)$$
$$Y(t) = y(t + Gdt) \rightarrow \text{stable}$$
$$Y(t) \neq y(t + \Delta t) \rightarrow \text{unstable}$$

and in turn we have developed the excitation map, the same excitation map we used during our analysis studies. Since our example is quite simple, let us finish it and then consider some of the more subtle aspects of the state assignment process. From the excitation map in Figure 10-17(b) we see that the circuit shown in Figure 10-18(a) can be derived and can be redrawn as in Figure 10-18(b) in the more familiar form.

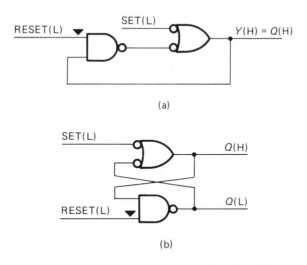

Fig. 10-18. The schematic of the basic cell designed in a step-by-step manner.

The row assignment process is not generally as simple as the one for this example. *The state assignment process is simply a process of selecting a row code assignment for the merge flow table that will provide for unit-distance feedback code transitions from one stable state to the next.* At times this process might require a cycle through several transition states *in a column*, as demonstrated in the analysis section. Since cycles seem to be a definite possibility, let us take a closer look at cycles and other phenomena called RACES.

10-6 CYCLES AND RACES

As mentioned in the last section, once the merged flow table has been obtained, the next step is the assignment of feedback codes to the rows of the merged flow table. Following this, an excitation map or Y map is obtained from this merged flow table. Then the Boolean expressions for the excitation variables (Y's) are read directly from the Y-map. Before these steps are more closely examined, the concepts of cycles, noncritical races, and critical races should be understood.

It is felt that these terms are best defined when illustrated by example. Remember that when an input change (column to column jump) induces a transition, *the code in the transition cells are indicators of where (row) the circuit is heading*. This is mentioned again because it is an important concept.

EXAMPLE 10-4: The case considered now is that of an input change inducing a feedback transition through *more than one unstable state*. Such a succession of two or more feedback changes is called a *cycle* (see Figure 10-19).

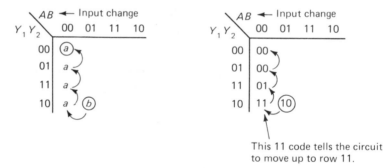

Fig. 10-19. An example illustration of a "cycle".

With the cycle and single feedback variable changes discussed thus far, each feedback code differed from the present state in only one bit; therefore, only one feedback variable was unstable at any time. If *more than one feedback variable* is in transition at any time, a RACE condition is said to exist. See Figure 10-20.

Here we see that if the inputs shift from 01 to 00, this causes both feedback variables to start to change from 11 toward a 00. However, the state 01 or 10 might be reached first because of unequal delays in the two feedback paths of the circuit. In this problem, it does not matter which one it goes to (00, 01, or 10) because ultimately it will cycle into state ⓐ. *This type of race is called a noncritical race.* However, if there exist *two nonequivalent stable states in the same column* and a race is introduced in that column by exciting more than one feedback variable, there could be trouble. *Such a race is termed a critical race.*

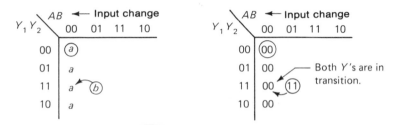

Fig. 10-20. An example of a RACE; in particular, a noncritical race.

See Figure 10-21. A race in a column can only be critical if more than one stable state exists in the column.

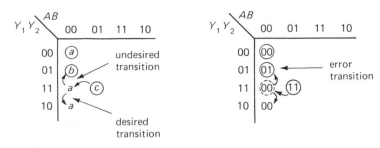

Fig. 10-21. An example of a critical race.

Here we see that if AB changes from $01 \rightarrow 00$, both feedback variables are excited. If they both change somehow to 00 or to 10, operation is carried out as specified. However, if it so happens that the change is to 01, then the circuit will drift into the unwanted stable state ⓑ. From this we see that the behavior of a circuit with a critical race is not predictable; therefore, critical races represent improper design and must be avoided. However, *noncritical races* and cycles are not only permissible, but many times are required. Cycles are used to avoid critical races or to introduce desired additional time delays in secondary transitions; and noncritical races are useful in obtaining a more minimal circuit realization.

With a knowledge of cycles and races, we are now prepared to undertake an in-depth look at the state assignment process. By way of review, a two-row flow table presents no secondary assignment problems. One secondary is required with the assignment $y = 0$ for the first row and $y = 1$ for the second row. However, when making secondary assignments for flow tables of three or more rows, we cannot assign secondary states arbitrarily because of the possibility of critical races. For these flow tables a *transition* map or state map is helpful in deriving error-free assignments with the minimum number of required feedback variables (see Figure 10-22). The transition map is nothing more than the state map, similar to those used in synchronous design. Note the feedback variables are the map variables.

The assignment of a feedback state to a row in the flow table is associated with the entry of the row reference or state identification letter in the corresponding square of the transition map in a manner identical to that treated in Chapters 6 and 7. In keeping with the unit distance criteria, all possible row-to-row transitions must be examined. If there is a transition between two particular rows, the feedback states for the two rows should be given a unit distance assignment. If it is *impossible* to locate the rows in an adjacent manner, an attempt to derive a cycle or a noncritical race should be made. Keep in mind that an assignment free of critical races may not always be possible as a result of the initial number of feedback variables. In cases such as these, additional feedback variables are required to allow for the extra needed dimension. These concepts are illustrated later in several complete examples.

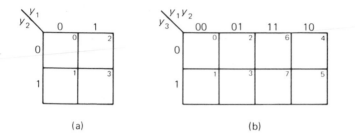

<table>
<tr><td>(a)</td><td>(b)</td><td></td></tr>
</table>

Fig. 10-22. Example transition or state maps. (a) Two-variable transition map. (b) Three-variable transition map.

10-7 PLOTTING AND READING THE EXCITATION MAP

Once the merged flow table has been given the row assignment, it becomes the excitation map with alphabetic characters representing the state value for the excitation variables (Y's). The plotting of the excitation map is the simple process of replacing each of the circled (stable) states in the map with their appropriate row code, then completing the map by filling in the row codes for the transition states.

Once the excitation map is plotted, the reading process for the Y expression can begin. The state assignment and excitation map-reading processes are demonstrated in Example 10-5.

> EXAMPLE 10-5: Example 10-3 covers the design of a basic cell and illustrates the basic design methodology. Now let us design another basic memory element similar to the cell, but one that will help resolve the indeterminate resultant state after the cell has had *both* the SET and RESET input ASSERTED simultaneously. This memory cell is to be designed in such a way that any time the SET and RESET are both ASSERTED, it is to go to a SET state ($Q=1$, $\overline{Q}=0$) and remain there until the following sequence is carried out:
>
> > First, both inputs have been brought to the NOT-ASSERTED condition, then the RESET input alone is RE-ASSERTED.
> >
> > Now the cell will move to a RESET condition ($Q=0$, $\overline{Q}=1$).
>
> This particular example has been chosen because it demonstrates how cycles and noncritical races can be used not only to insure reliable operation, but also to minimize the hardware required. This is demonstrated by the three different transition options illustrated in Figure 10-23. The complete design process for our special memory cell is documented in Figure 10-23. It is advised that this example be followed through carefully.

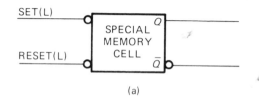

(a)

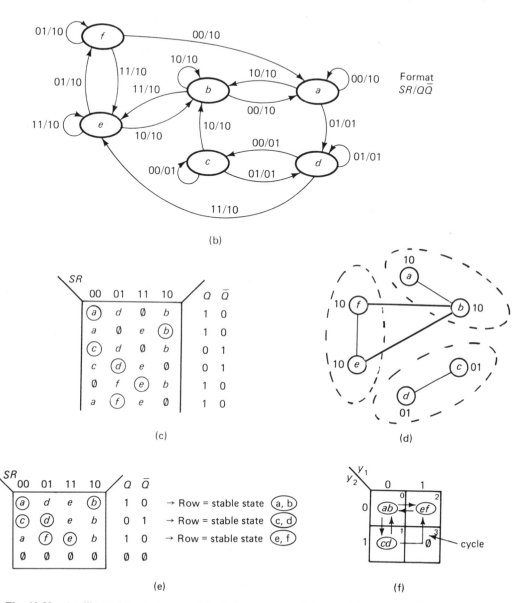

(b)

(c)

(d)

(e)

(f)

Fig. 10-23. An illustration of the complete design process of the special memory cell specified in Example 10-5. (a) The block diagram of the special memory cell specified by Example 10-5. (b) Primitive state diagram specifying the SET dominant feature. (c) Primitive state table. (d) Non mixed merge diagram. (e) Merged table: three rows require two feedback variables. (f) Transition map or state map.

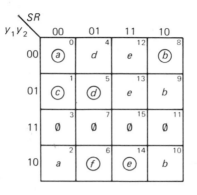
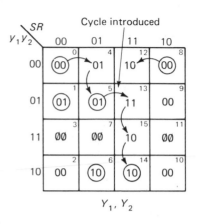

(g)

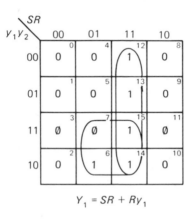

$$Y_1 = SR + Ry_1$$

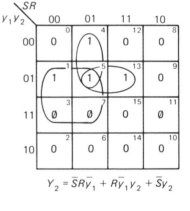

$$Y_2 = \overline{SR}\overline{y}_1 + R\overline{y}_1y_2 + \overline{S}y_2$$

(h)

Noncritical race introduced that could result in an oscillation between 12 and 13

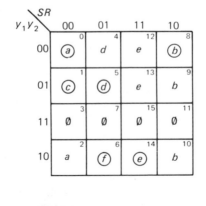
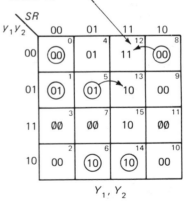

(i)

Fig. 10-23 g-h-i (Cont.). (g) Excitation maps with cycle. (h) Y maps. (i) Excitation maps with noncritical race between cell 12 and 8 and cell 5 and 13.

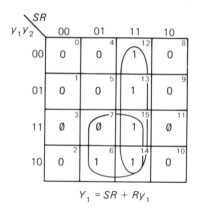

$$Y_1 = SR + R\bar{y}_1$$

(j)

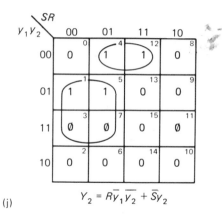

$$Y_2 = R\bar{y}_1\bar{y}_2 + \bar{S}y_2$$

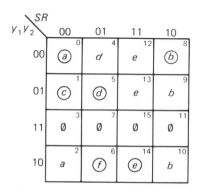

(k)

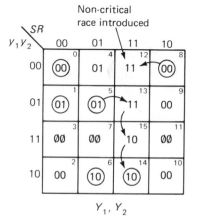

Non-critical
race introduced

$$Y_1, Y_2$$

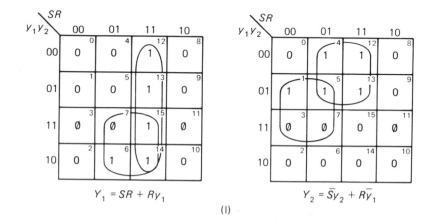

$$Y_1 = SR + R\bar{y}_1$$

$$Y_2 = \bar{S}y_2 + R\bar{y}_1$$

(l)

Fig. 10-23 j-k-l. (Cont.) (j) Y maps. (k) Excitation maps with noncritical race and cycle. (l) Y maps.

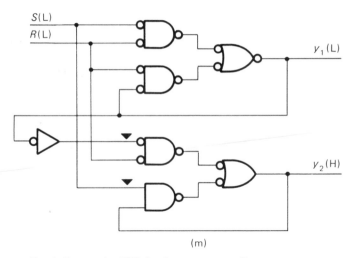

(m)

Fig. 10.23. (m) Circuit diagram for SET dominant memory cell.

10-8 HAZARDS

Example 10-5 covers the concepts of making state assignments and plotting and reading the excitation maps. However, in general the reading of the maps must be carried one step further to avoid HAZARDS. A hazard is an unwanted transient (spike or glitch) precipitated by unequal path delays through a combinational network. In short, an input change can cause momentary unwanted outputs to occur. The occurrence of these hazards is demonstrated in Example 10-6.

> *EXAMPLE 10-6:* The circuit shown in Figure 10-24 illustrates the generation of a hazard. Also, it illustrates the use of a map for identifying hazard situations.

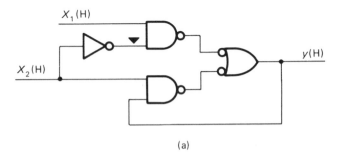

(a)

Fig. 10-24. (a) An example sequential circuit that will generate a hazard.

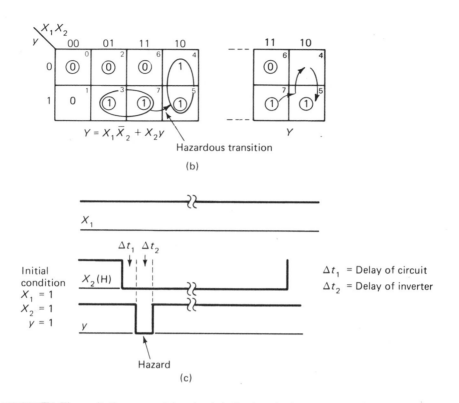

Fig. 10-24. (b) The excitation map of the circuit indicating the hazardous transition. (c) The timing diagram illustrating the hazard.

The timing diagram in Figure 10-24(c) is supported by the following discussion:

Assume at	$t = 0^-, X_1 X_2 y = 111$; cell 7 in the map
Therefore,	$Y = X_1 \bar{X}_2 + X_2 y = 1 \cdot 0 + 1 \cdot 1 = 1$
Then at	$t = 0, X_2$ makes the transition from $1 \to 0$; a move to cell 5
Then at	$t = \Delta t_1 Y = 1 \cdot 0 + 0 \cdot 1 = 0$ (hazard)
then at	$t = \Delta t_1 + \Delta t_2, Y = 1 \cdot 1 + 0 \cdot 1 = 1$

It is interesting to note that the hazard is *not* present when the reverse transition is carried out as shown.

Assume at	$t = 0^-, X_1 X_2 y = 101$
Therefore,	$y = X_1 \bar{X}_2 + X_2 y = 1 \cdot 1 + 0 \cdot 1 = 1$
Then at	$t = 0, X_2$ makes the transition from $0 \to 1$
Then at	$t = \Delta t_1, Y = 1 \cdot 1 + 1 \cdot 1 = 1$
Then at	$t = \Delta t_1 + \Delta t_2, Y = 1 \cdot 0 + 1 \cdot 1 = 1$

Circuits that exhibit hazard generation have map patterns which forewarn the designer of the pending problem. *This map pattern is characterized by groupings that are adjacent and not overlapped* (see Figure 10-24(b)). Note that the two map groupings independently cover two cells (5 and 7), but the two groupings do not overlap. This shows that the 1→0 transition of the changing variable will generate a hazard. *Further, it can be shown that generally in cases like this it is the 1→0 transition that generates the hazard.* The solution to the hazard problem is to cover the adjacent cells with a redundant grouping that overlaps both groupings. See Figures 10-25(a) and 10-25(b) to see how a "cover term" can be added that eliminates a hazard.

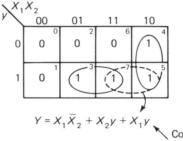

$$Y = X_1 \bar{X}_2 + X_2 y + X_1 y$$

Cover term added to eliminate the hazard

(a)

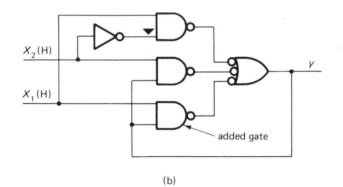

(b)

Fig. 10-25. (a) The excitation map showing the hazard cover term addition. (b) The circuit with the added gate for hazard suppression.

See Figure 10-26 for further examples of potential hazards and the mapping covers for their elimination.

There are basically three types of hazards: static, such as the one just illustrated, dynamic, and essential.

(1) Static hazard—a single momentary transient in an output signal that should have remained static in response to an input change.

(2) Dynamic hazard—a multiple momentary transient in an output signal that should have changed only once in response to an input change.

(3) Essential hazard—an operational error causing a transition to an improper state in response to an input change, generally caused by an excessive delay to a feedback variable in response to an input change.

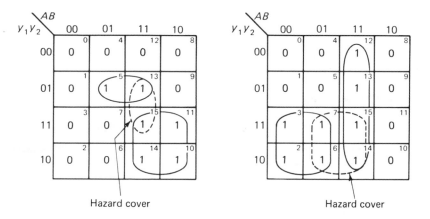

Hazard cover   Hazard cover

Fig. 10-26. Further examples of potential hazards and map covers for their elimination.

See Figure 10-27 for example of static and dynamic hazards.

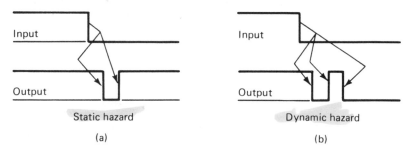

Static hazard   Dynamic hazard

(a)   (b)

Fig. 10-27. Examples of static and dynamic hazards.

It can be shown that both static and dynamic hazards can be eliminated by the same mapping cover method. However, an essential hazard is something different from a transient output and will be covered later in an example.

In summary, transient outputs (hazards) for feedback variables are certainly classed as undesirable because they too can cause operational problems in two ways:

(1) They can, in special cases, cause faulty state transitions.

(2) They present an undesirable glitch to any decoding device to which it is connected.

However, they are relatively easy to remove and should pose no real problem if they are covered properly. It was pointed out above that it is the 1→0 transition that generates a hazard, and this is mentioned again because there are many times when this transition is *not* prescribed in an excitation map or output map. Therefore, adding hardware to cover a hazard that can never occur is wasteful.

10-9 ESSENTIAL HAZARDS

Essential hazards, like static and dynamic hazards, are caused by delay. However, they differ in two ways:

(1) They exist only in sequential circuits with two or more feedbacks.
(2) If they exist, they result from a combination of both delay and the design specifications.

This means that certain sequential requirements give rise to sequential circuits which *possess the possibility* of having an essential hazard. In particular, "toggling"-type circuits exhibit the potential of having an essential hazard. It is potential because there are circuits that are prone to built-in essential hazards, yet they do not exhibit the malady. To illustrate this, consider Example 10-7.

EXAMPLE 10-7: Design a binary toggle circuit that changes state with each rising-edge of the clock input. See Figure 10-28 for the design development.

Fig. 10-28. The design development for the binary toggle circuit called for in Example 10-7. (a) Block and timing diagrams. (b) The primitive state diagram.

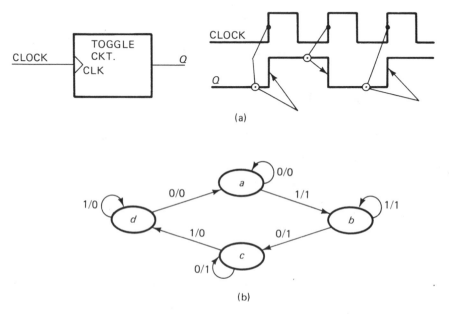

(a)

(b)

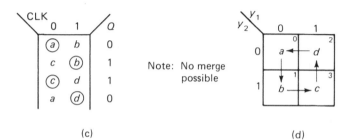

(c)   (d)

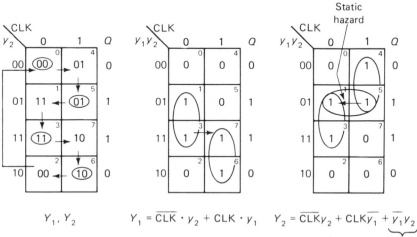

Y_1, Y_2 $Y_1 = \overline{CLK} \cdot y_2 + CLK \cdot y_1$ $Y_2 = \overline{CLK}y_2 + CLK\overline{y_1} + \overline{y_1}y_2$

(e)

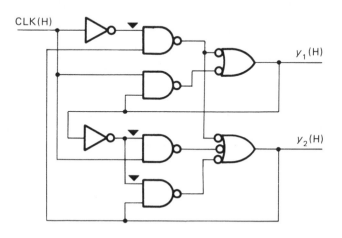

(f)

Fig. 10-28 (c) Primitive state table. (d) State map. (e) Excitation map and Y maps. (f) Circuit diagram.

Take a moment to examine the schematic for the binary toggle circuit shown in Figure 10-29. In this figure the static hazard cover is deliberately removed and delay notation is added to augment the analysis. Keep in mind that the removal of the static hazard cover *in no way* affects the analysis of the *potential essential hazard* which this circuit has.

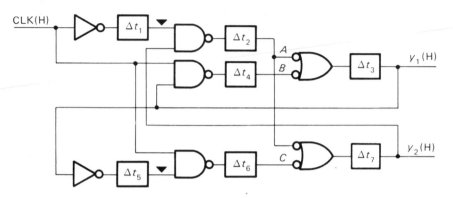

Fig. 10-29. The binary toggle circuit re-drawn with delay notation.

The timing diagram shown in Figure 10-30 demonstrates the sequential behavior of the toggle circuit defined under the assumption that all Δt's are equal. Also, this timing diagram identifies the static hazard that was predicted. Further, based on the stated assumptions for the Δt's, no sequential anomaly exists. To support this assumption, the circuit was built up with TTL devices and found to function as predicted. See Figure 10-31(a), which is an actual photograph of the circuit's input and output. Note the static hazard in $y_2(Q)$. Figure 10-31(b) shows the same outputs with the hazard cover.

Now see Figure 10-32. Here the Δt_1 has been increased to $7\Delta t$ (seven inverters) and the effects of an essential hazard can be seen. This figure shows that y_1's response to the rising-edge of CLK is delayed by seven delay units, and because of this added delay the circuit is cycled from $\textcircled{a} \rightarrow b \rightarrow \textcircled{b} \rightarrow d \rightarrow \textcircled{a}$ without stopping at state $\textcircled{b}$. Thus the effect of an essential hazard caused by delaying the response of a feedback to an input change has been demonstrated.

Figure 10-32(b) shows an actual photograph of the binary toggle's input and outputs when delay units (inverters) were introduced for Δt_1. This figure substantiates the predicted behavior. It was interesting and encouraging to note that with $\Delta t_1 \leq 5\Delta t$ the circuit continued to operate normally at room temperatures.

This suggests that circuits which are prone to misbehavior due to essential hazards need not always be cast aside as bad. You need only use worst case delay analysis to determine if an essential hazard is going to be a problem. Also, not all asynchronous machines are subject to essential hazard problems. Unger in his work introduced a rather simple analysis method to determine whether a circuit is prone to essential hazards. This method allows you to examine the structure of the excitation map and quickly spot the possibility of an essential hazard. This is shown in Figure 10-33.

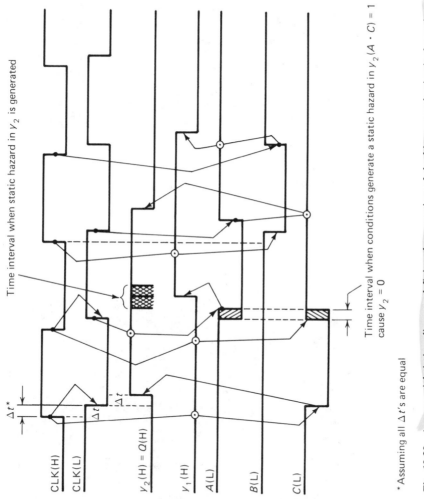

Time interval when static hazard in y_2 is generated

Time interval when conditions generate a static hazard in $y_2(A \cdot C) = 1$ cause $y_2 = 0$

CLK(H)

CLK(L)

$y_2(H) = Q(H)$

$y_1(H)$

$A(L)$

$B(L)$

$C(L)$

Δt^*

Δt

Δt

*Assuming all Δt's are equal

Fig. 10-30. A sequential timing diagram defining the operation of the binary toggle circuit shown in Figure 10-29.

681

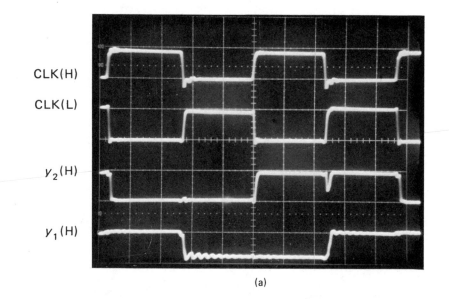

(a)

Fig. 10-31. Actual photographs of the input and outputs of the binary toggle circuit fabricated with TTL logic. (a) Note the hazard in y_2, whereas in (b) the hazard has been removed.

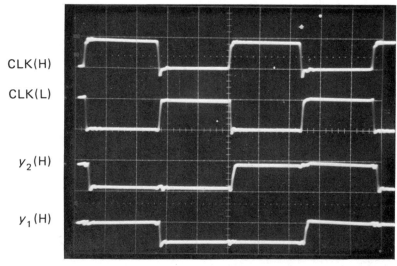

(b)

Fig. 10-31(b) (Cont.)

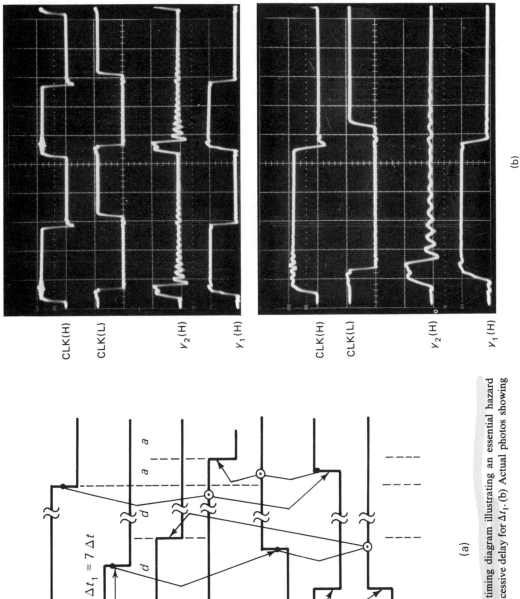

Fig. 10-32. (a) A sequential timing diagram illustrating an essential hazard precipitated by introducing excessive delay for Δt_1. (b) Actual photos showing the essential hazard.

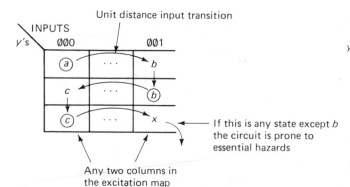

Unit distance input transition

INPUTS
y's   000   001

If this is any state except *b* the circuit is prone to essential hazards

Any two columns in the excitation map

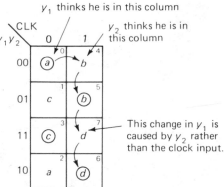

y_1 thinks he is in this column

CLK
$y_1 y_2$ 0   1

y_2 thinks he is in this column

This change in y_1 is caused by y_2 rather than the clock input.

Fig. 10-33. An example structure of an excitation map that defines the operation of a circuit which is prone to essential hazards.

Fig. 10-34. An illustration of how the behavior of a circuit that is prone to an essential hazard can be traced in the excitation map.

Reexamining the excitation map for the binary toggle shown in Figure 10-28(c) or 10-28(e) you see that if the circuit is initially in state ⓐ and the clock makes the transition from 0→1, and if y_1's response to this CLK transition is delayed until y_2's response to the clock edge has a chance to come back around and change y_1 before CLK(L), the circuit will jump to *b* then to ⓑ, but here it finds that the input and feedback conditions for *d* to be the next state. Therefore, it moves on to *d*, then to state ⓓ. This is shown in Figure 10-34.

Figure 10-34 indicates that if the unstable state directly under ⓑ had been *b*, the circuit would *not* have jumped to ⓓ, but rather back to ⓑ, resulting in correct sequential behavior with a static hazard in y_1.

This concludes the study of hazards and it is hoped that your study of these realities has broadened your understanding to the point where *fear will not* be your motivation for not using asynchronous circuits.

The next section includes several more examples that further demonstrate the design methodology on more complicated problems.

10-10   MORE WORKED EXAMPLES

Let us now consider a design problem that is somewhat more complicated than the last three and is one that will be used to demonstrate some other design methodologies later.

EXAMPLE 10-8:   In most large *synchronous* machines it is desirable to have a special asynchronous circuit that allows the operator to "meter" out one clean system clock pulse by simply depressing a switch. This single clock pulse is then used to "step" the synchronous machine through its sequence one step at a time. Hence we call this machine our SINGLE STEP PULSE CIRCUIT.

We are to design a special asynchronous circuit that receives two inputs: (1) SYS CLK and (2) Single Step. This circuit is to issue one and only one clean positive going clock pulse each time the single step input is cycled. See Figure 10-35 for the design development for the single-step pulse circuit. Here the circuit development is the same as that for the previous examples down to and including step h. In steps i and j the maps related to the output decoder are shown. Here the output expressions specified by the definition of the problem are read from what is commonly called a Z or OUTPUT map. Any output in general is expressed as:

$$OUTPUT = f(\text{inputs, feedback})$$

The output map is plotted in the same manner as in synchronous design. Again, decoder glitches must be designed out by a careful mapping procedure. This procedure is as follows:

(1) Develop a blank map identical to that of the excitation map.
(2) For each stable state in the excitation map, plot the desired output code in the corresponding cell (see Figure 10-35(h)).

After all the outputs for the stable state have been plotted, the *next step is to assign codes to the transition states to be assured that no transient outputs are generated during transition*. This is done according to the following procedure.

(1) If, during a transition, the output for the initial and final stable states are the *same*, then the same output MUST be assigned for all unstable states involved in the transition between the two. See Figure 10-35(j) and study the transitions from cell 12 to cell 9, 5 to 15, 9 to 0, and 14 to 4.
(2) The output assignment for all unstable states not covered by rule 1 may be optional except that in all transitions *involving a change in the output*, the output must change only once. An exception must be noted only when there are two or more unstable states involved in a transition; oscillatory changes of output states are thus prevented. See Figure 10-35(j) and study the transitions from cell 15 to cell 10 and 5 to 1.

Once the output map is plotted according to these procedures, it is to be read in the standard manner including hazard cover when necessary (see Figure 10-35(j)).

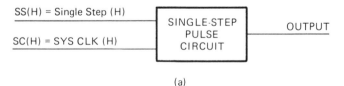

SS(H) = Single Step (H)

SC(H) = SYS CLK (H)

SINGLE-STEP PULSE CIRCUIT

OUTPUT

(a)

Fig. 10-35. The design development for the single-step pulse circuit specified in Example 10-8. Again it is recommended that you follow through the design to assure your understanding. (a) Block diagram.

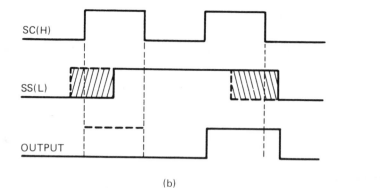

(b)

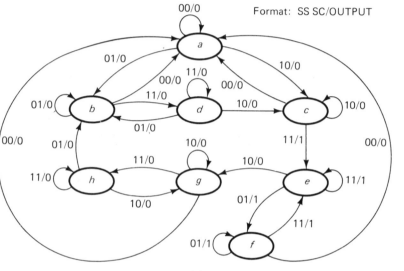

Format: SS SC/OUTPUT

(c)

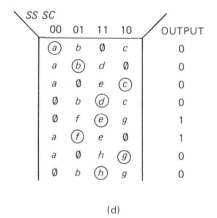

SS SC				OUTPUT
00	**01**	**11**	**10**	
ⓐ	b	Ø	c	0
a	ⓑ	d	Ø	0
a	Ø	e	ⓒ	0
Ø	b	ⓓ	c	0
Ø	f	ⓔ	g	1
a	ⓕ	e	Ø	1
a	Ø	h	ⓖ	0
Ø	b	ⓗ	g	0

(d)

Fig. 10-35. (Cont.) (b) Timing diagram. (c) Primitive state diagram. (d) Primitive state table.

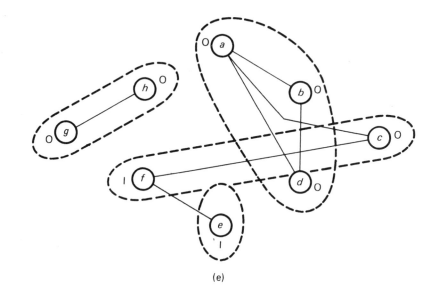

(e)

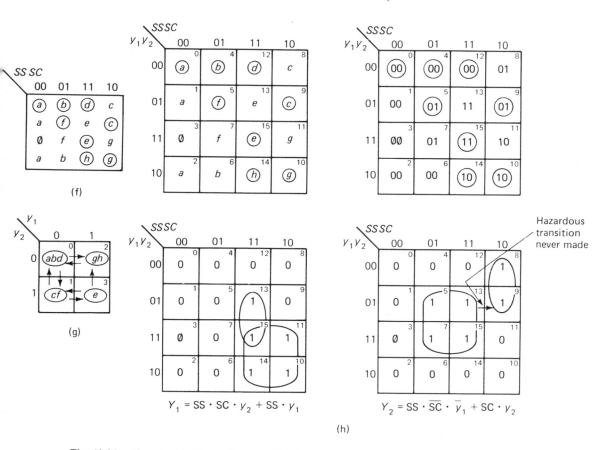

$$Y_1 = SS \cdot SC \cdot y_2 + SS \cdot y_1$$

$$Y_2 = SS \cdot \overline{SC} \cdot \overline{y}_1 + SC \cdot y_2$$

(h)

Fig. 10-35. (Cont.) (e) Merge diagram. (f) Merge table. (g) State map. (h) Excitation map and Y maps.

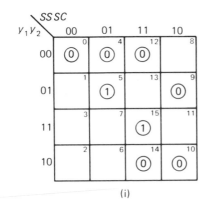

(i)

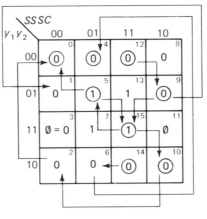

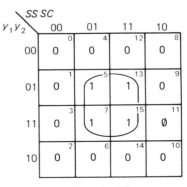

Output = SC · y_2

(j)

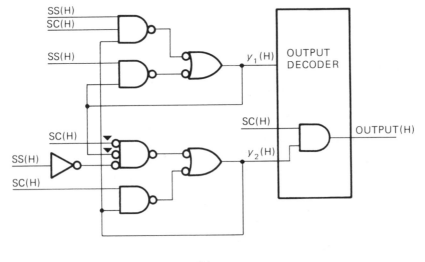

(k)

Fig. 10-35. (Cont.) (i) Primitive output or Z map. (j) Output maps. (k) Circuit diagram for single step pulse.

688 Asynchronous Finite-State Machines

The past several examples have covered the basics of traditional asynchronous machine design. The following examples illustrate some different ideas related to the design of a synchronous finite state machine. For example, it has been found that the use of a basic cell for an output buffer of an asynchronous circuit can, in many cases, reduce both the required hardware *as well as the design time required* to develop various types of circuits, particularly Flip-Flop action types of machines. The architecture of this type of machine is illustrated in Figure 10-36.

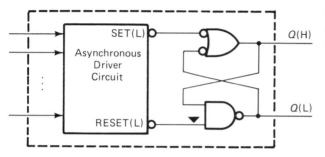

Fig. 10-36. The model of an asynchronous circuit that utilizes a basic cell for an output buffer.

The idea of designing with a model such as the one shown in Figure 10-36 is based on the concept of SETTING or RESETTING a cell with an asynchronous driver circuit based on specifications for the circuit's operation. This is demonstrated in Example 10-9.

EXAMPLE 10-9: Design an edge-triggered D Flip-Flop based on the model in Figure 10-36 and SET/RESET operation of a basic cell. The design method is developed in Figure 10-37.

A little study suggests that the circuit diagram in Figure 10-37(h) of the Flip-Flop has a strong similarity to the SN7474. Thus a method has been developed for utilizing the memory function of a basic cell to provide the following:

(1) output buffering;
(2) double rail outputs;
(3) reduced design complexity.

The next section extends these ideas to a design approach for asynchronous circuits that closely parallels the approach developed in Chapter 7 for synchronous machines.

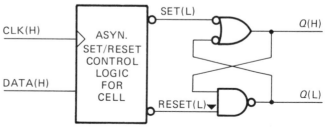

Fig. 10-37. (a) Block diagram.

(a)

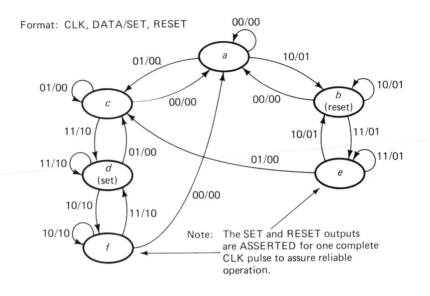

Format: CLK, DATA/SET, RESET

Note: The SET and RESET outputs are ASSERTED for one complete CLK pulse to assure reliable operation.

(b)

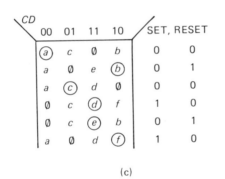

CD	00	01	11	10	SET, RESET	
a	*c*	Ø	*b*	0	0
a	Ø	*e*	*b*	0	1
a	*c*	*d*	Ø	0	0
Ø	*c*	*d*	*f*	1	0
Ø	*c*	*e*	*b*	0	1
a	Ø	*d*	*f*	1	0

(c)

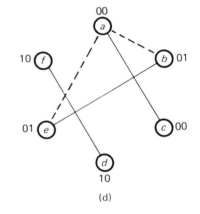

(d)

CD	00	01	11	10	SET, RESET	
a	*c*	*d*	*b*	0	0
a	*c*	*e*	*b*	0	1
a	*c*	*d*	*f*	1	0

(e)

(f)

Fig. 10-37. (Cont.) The design development for an edge-triggered "D" Flip-Flop centered around the model shown in Figure 10-36. (b) Primitive state diagram. (c) State table. (d) Merge diagram. (e) Merge table. (f) State map.

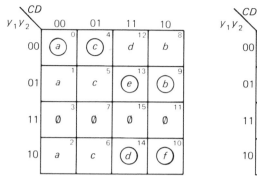 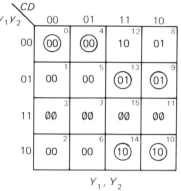

Y_1, Y_2

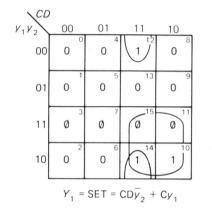

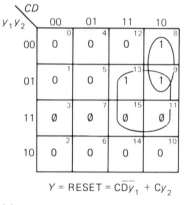

$Y_1 = \text{SET} = CD\bar{y}_2 + Cy_1$

$Y = \text{RESET} = C\bar{D}\bar{y}_1 + Cy_2$

(g)

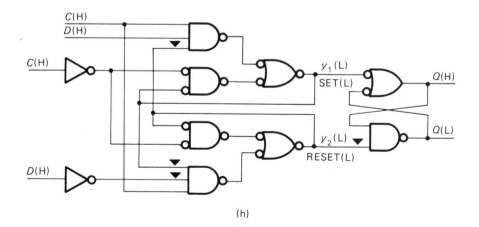

(h)

Fig. 10-37. (Cont.) (g) Excitation and Y maps. (h) Circuit diagram.

10-11 THE MAP-ENTERED-VARIABLE APPROACHES TO ASYNCHRONOUS DESIGN

There are design methods related to asynchronous circuits similar to those introduced in Chapter 7 for synchronous circuits. These methods are used to reduce the paperwork required to design multi-input asynchronous controllers. *However, care must be taken in the development of the flow and MDS diagrams defining the sequential behavior of an asynchronous controller.* Aside from this, the design phases including constraints are practically identical. Two MEV approaches are illustrated:

(1) The *cell-centered* design method
(2) A *contemporary approach* to asynchronous circuit design

Both are discussed in the following sections.

Cell-Centered Asynchronous Design. Many times when interface circuits are to be designed, the designer is confronted with the problems of bringing together two distinct systems operating totally asynchronously. Because the interface is complicated by a large number of interacting control lines, a multi-input asynchronous interface controller must be developed. Timing conditions and response times generally further complicate the design of system synchronizers. Fortunately, most systems have been designed in such a way that a "handshake" control can be implemented. It should be remembered from Chapter 7 that the handshake implies that system A will respond to some single stimulus from system B and in turn relay back to system B a single output, indicating that system A has received that stimulus. This action stimulates system B to move on in its sequence. Fortunately, this type of operation is quite common to interface design, but many times, as mentioned above, the response time for one or both of the systems is a critical factor. In this case the traditional synchronizers based on system clocks would not suffice, particularly if the frequency of the system clock is relatively slow in comparison to the required response time.

This section outlines a technique with which these problems can be solved for the most part using an asynchronous machine. In order to design an asynchronous *multi-input/output* controller which could satisfy the critical response time requirement, some approach other than the classical asynchronous approach is needed to prevent becoming bogged down with monstrous flow tables, merge diagrams, and general bookwork. As an introduction to this approach, consider the model shown in Figure 10-38. It is important to keep in mind that this handshake controller design method serves as an introduction to the next section. Therefore, it is to be treated as a useful and practical design method, but generally the circuits derived utilizing this method require a little more hardware than circuits derived from other methodologies, although they do work and they are easy to design.

The model in Figure 10-38 illustrates that this machine is basically designed to move through a sequence asynchronously, generating outputs based on a sequence of input conditions just like any other finite-state machine. What is different about this machine is the design process. This process is very similar to the one illustrated in Chapter 7, the main difference being that a basic cell is used rather than a clocked Flip-Flop. The block model shown in Figure 10-38 suggests that the major effort in the design process is the design of the SET/RESET control logic, which entails the design of a decoder for each cell by asking the following question: "Is this cell to be SET or RESET or left as is?" based on its present state, the present state of the other cells in the circuit, and present input conditions. Therefore, you need only examine the state diagram with state assignments defining the operation and then determine for each state the answer to the question asked above. Keep in mind that the constraints of this design approach are identical to those discussed earlier:

(1) Branching on more than one asynchronous input is not allowed.
(2) Unit distance state assignments must be made, except where noncritical races are used.
(3) Time must be allowed for the machine to "settle" into a stable state before the next input change is introduced.

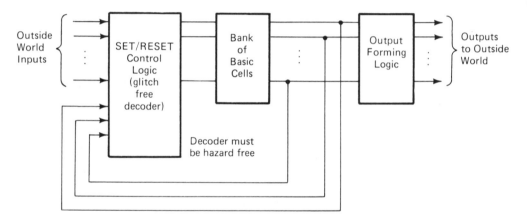

Fig. 10-38. Block model of a "cell-centered" asynchronous handshake controller.

Now let us cover the design method to be used in the development of the cell-centered asynchronous machines.

(1) Study specifications to make certain that you completely understand the requirements and that these requirements can be met by a cell-centered design.
(2) Develop a detailed flow diagram that accurately defines the circuit's behavior. Be certain that there is no overlooked input transition that will upset the operation. It is during this step that you ferret out redundant and unneeded states, and at the same time merge your flow diagram, keeping in mind the state assignment requirements.
(3) Transfer the flow diagram to an MDS diagram and make a state assignment.

(4) Plot the SET/RESET maps for the required basic cells directly from the MDS diagram using MEV techniques. *Keep in mind never to prescribe a simultaneous SET and RESET on the same cell.*

(5) Read SET/RESET maps, check for hazards, and draw up circuit diagrams for the SET/RESET control logic (see Section 10-13).

(6) Plot and read the output map and draw up the circuit diagram for the output decoder.

(7) Analyze your design.

These steps are demonstrated in Example 10-10.

EXAMPLE 10-10: Design an asynchronous handshake controller whose operation is defined by the following description and block diagram (see Figure 10-39).

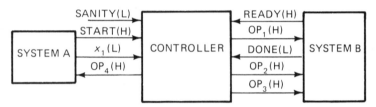

Fig. 10-39. Block diagram for system proposed in Example 10-10.

The function of the controller is: Upon a SANITY (RESET system) the controller is to move to an initial state and remain there until system A issues a START control. At this time the controller is to move to another state and raise OP_1 to system B. System B responds with READY. Now, depending on the level of x_1, set up earlier, the controller will move to one of two states and issue either OP_2 or OP_3 to system B and will then wait for system B to respond with DONE. Upon receipt of DONE the controller will move back to state a and issue OP_4 to system A indicating the process is complete.

Based on the functional description given, we can develop the detailed flow diagram shown in Figure 10-40. The next step is to transfer the flow diagram to an MDS diagram as shown in Figure 10-41.

After the MDS diagram has been developed, the next step is to design the SET/RESET control logic for cell A and cell B using the MEV approach and an understanding of the sequential behavior of the basic cell. This is done in Figure 10-42. Remember to avoid the possibility of a simultaneous SET and RESET operation. The excitation table for the basic cell shown in Figure 10-42 helps to avoid this problem. The circuit diagram for the completed circuit is shown in Figure 10-43.

The next step is to develop the output decoder logic using output maps as shown in Figure 10-44.

Figure 10-45 shows the complete circuit diagram for the handshake controller defined in Example 10-10.

You are again reminded that, as always with sequential circuits, sufficient time must be allotted for the set-up and hold times of an input condition. In other words, input changes during a state transition upset asynchronous and synchronous machines. This timing consideration is to be thought out thoroughly while the detailed flow diagram is being developed. Though it seems that the cell-centered method for designing asynchronous circuits is specifically related to a handshake interface type application, this is not the case.

Consider the design of the single-step pulse circuit using the handshake method, and then make a comparison based on design ease and circuit complexity. It will be seen that an edge-triggered or "lockout" type of design philosophy is used.

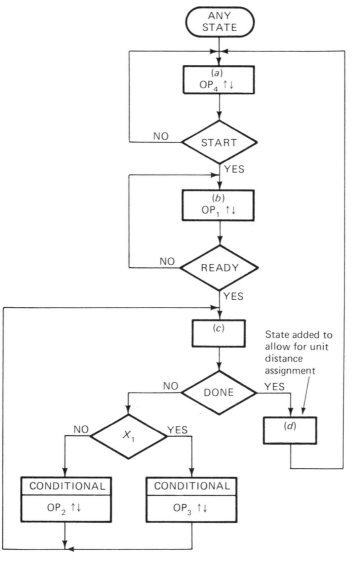

Fig. 10-40. Detailed flow diagram for Example 10-10.

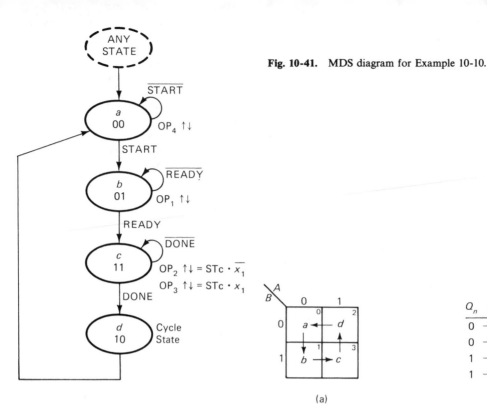

Fig. 10-41. MDS diagram for Example 10-10.

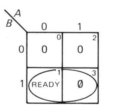

(a)

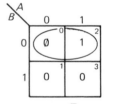

Q_n		Q_{n+1}	S	R
0	→	0	0	Ø
0	→	1	1	0
1	→	0	0	1
1	→	1	Ø	0

(b)

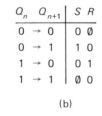

SET A(L) = [B(READY)] (L)

RESET A(L) = ($\bar{B}$)(L) = B(H)

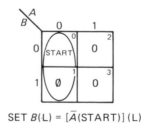

SET B(L) = [$\bar{A}$(START)] (L)

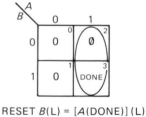

RESET B(L) = [A(DONE)] (L)

(c)

Fig. 10-42. (a) The state map for the MDS diagram shown in Figure 10-41. (b) The excitation table for the basic cell. (c) The SET/RE-SET control map for the circuit specified in Example 10-10.

Fig. 10-43. The circuit diagram for the SET/RESET control logic and the basic cells of the cell-centered specified controller in Example 10-10.

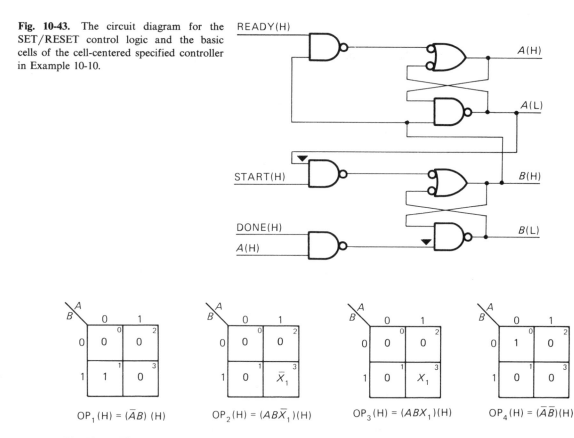

OP$_1$(H) = ($\overline{A}B$) (H)   OP$_2$(H) = ($AB\overline{X}_1$)(H)   OP$_3$(H) = (ABX_1)(H)   OP$_4$(H) = ($\overline{A}\,\overline{B}$)(H)

Fig. 10-44. The output map for the cell-centered controller specified in Example 10-10.

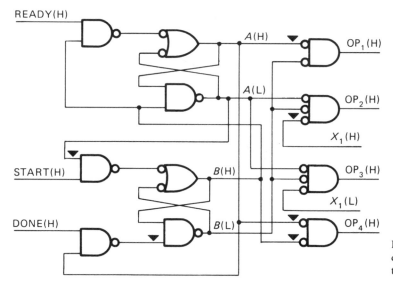

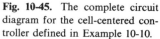

Fig. 10-45. The complete circuit diagram for the cell-centered controller defined in Example 10-10.

EXAMPLE 10-11: Design the single-step pulse circuit using the cell-centered design methodology. Figure 10-46(a) illustrates the familiar flow chart description of the single-step pulse circuit, which is then converted to the MDS diagram shown in Figure 10-46(b). Figure 10-46(c) shows the state map and the SET and RESET maps for the two required cells. Figure 10-46(d) illustrates the complete circuit diagram for the single-step machine.

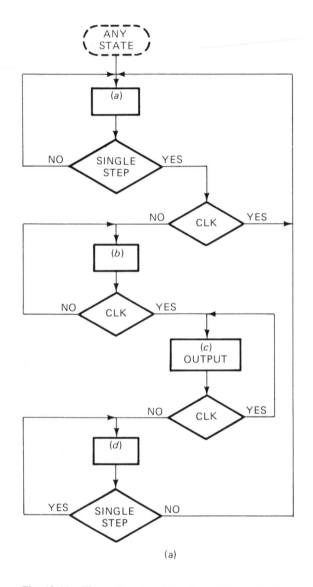

(a)

Fig. 10-46. The cell-centered implementation of the single-step pulse circuit of Example 10-11. (a) Flow diagram.

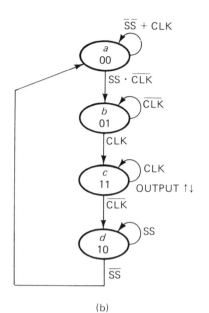

(b)

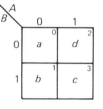

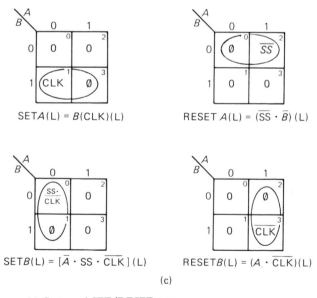

(c)

Fig. 10-46. (Cont.) (b) MDS diagram. (c) State and SET/RESET maps.

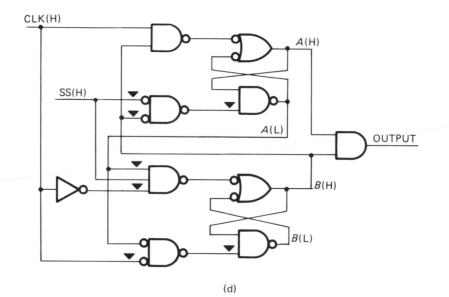

CLK(H)

SS(H)

A(H)

A(L)

OUTPUT

B(H)

B(L)

(d)

Fig. 10-46. (Cont.) (d) Circuit diagram for single step.

Compared with the circuit designed by the traditional method, this circuit does require several more gates. However, as stated previously, the design process is considerably less complex. The next section develops yet another MEV approach.

10-12 A CONTEMPORARY APPROACH TO ASYNCHRONOUS DESIGN

The last section demonstrates an asynchronous design method centered around the SET/RESET programming of a basic cell. Even though this design approach yields functional circuits, the implementation typically requires more gate hardware than the equivalent circuit designed by the traditional methods. This section introduces the MEV approach to asynchronous design that incorporates the advantages of both methods.

Just as Chapter 7 shows how the map-entered-variable concept opens the door to a practical method of designing multi-input synchronous machines, this section shows how the MEV approach can be applied to asynchronous machine design. In short, the same design phases outlined in Chapter 7 can be carried out for designing asynchronous machines with the major design emphasis placed on flow diagram and MDS diagram design based on the premise that all inputs are asynchronous. The following steps provide a design framework for developing multi-input asynchronous machines using a contemporary approach:

(1) Gain a complete understanding of the desired functional requirements of the circuit to be designed.

(2) Develop a complete and detailed flow diagram. Do an exhaustive study here, leaving no input condition to chance. Also, keep in mind that all states must have unit distance assignments. With this in mind, look for the possibility of building in cycles and noncritical races as you develop your flow diagram, and assure yourself that when a state assignment is made that all transitions can be assigned unit-distance codes.

(3) Transform your detailed flow diagram into a MDS diagram using the standard methodology.

(4) Once you feel that your circuit is completely specified, develop your state assignment with a state map with the y's as the map variables. This is in keeping with using the outputs of the Flip-Flops as the map variables in synchronous design.

(5) Once a state assignment is made and a unit distance transition is assured, you are ready to develop the excitation map using the y's and the *map variables and the inputs as the MEV's*. These maps are to be read in the standard way, eliminating hazards to arrive at the excitation expression:

$$Y's = f(y's, \text{inputs})$$

(6) Once the excitation maps are read, plot the output maps for each output specified, using MEV's also, and eliminate hazards.

(7) Draw up circuit diagrams for your circuit and perform a quick analysis on the circuit's functional performance.

This design approach is demonstrated in Example 10-12.

EXAMPLE 10-12: For comparison purposes, design the single-step pulse circuit using the MEV approach. This design is developed in Figures 10-47 and 10-48. It should be noted that the detailed flow and MDS diagrams shown in Figure 10-47 are identical to those for the handshake design in Figure 10-46. The state map and excitation maps along with the circuit diagram are shown in Figure 10-48.

The MEV approach has significantly reduced the bookwork effort in the design process to an applied and conceptual methodology. However, the real design effort has been spent in defining the operation of the machine in an unambiguous manner with the flow and the MDS diagram.

The traditional analysis of the circuit shown in Figure 10-48 is shown in Figure 10-49. Here we see that the circuit performs as specified by the flow diagram. It should be noted from the analysis that this circuit is designed in such a way that even short single-step inputs are recognized, and this sensitivity causes the circuit to generate an output even when the clock is very slow. This is something that the circuit for Example 10-8 in Figure 10-35(k) *does not do*.

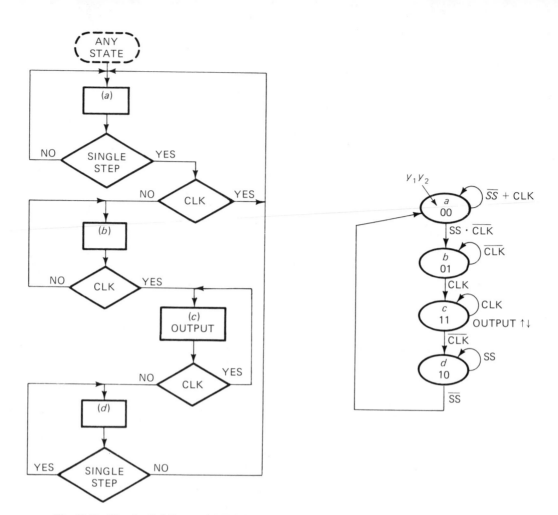

Fig. 10-47. The detailed flow and MDS diagrams for the single-step pulse circuit to be designed using the contemporary approach.

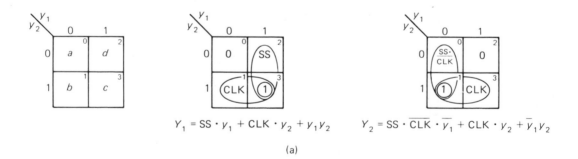

$$Y_1 = SS \cdot y_1 + CLK \cdot y_2 + y_1 y_2 \qquad Y_2 = SS \cdot \overline{CLK} \cdot \overline{y_1} + CLK \cdot y_2 + \overline{y_1} y_2$$

(a)

Fig. 10-48. (a) The state map and excitation maps for the MEV design approach for single-step pulse circuits.

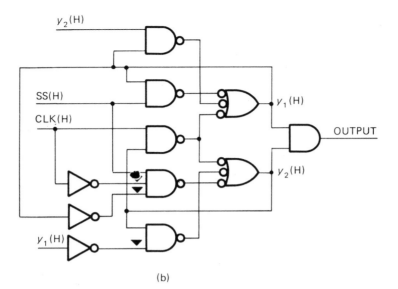

(b)

Fig. 10-48. (Cont.) (b) Circuit diagram for single step.

Fig. 10-49. The analysis excitation map for a single-step pulse circuit shown in Figure 10-48.

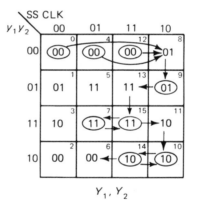

Y_1, Y_2

10-13 HAZARDS IN CIRCUITS DEVELOPED BY THE MEV METHOD

The question of how hazards can be identified and removed during the design process when the MEV method is used comes up consistently. This is because the identifying "adjacent groupings" are obscured by the mapping process. However, you will see that static hazards can be identified in VEM's in a manner similar to that introduced earlier. In short, four possible grouping arrangements in a VEM can be identified as potential static hazards. These are:

(1) adjacent groupings of 1's;
(2) adjacent groupings of *identical* MEV's;

(3) adjacent groupings between a 1's grouping and identical MEV groupings;
(4) MEV and $\overline{MEV}$ groupings that cover the same 1 entry.

The groupings that identify hazards are quite easily identified in the VEM. This is illustrated in Figure 10-50. Notice that all but one of the potential hazards are identifiable by the "adjacent grouping" technique. The one that is not identifiable (see Figure 10-50(d)) by this technique has its own identifiable feature. Thus hazards can be spotted easily and should cause no real concern. Also, a quick check for hazards can be made by examining the simplified expression. This is done by looking for two terms, one with a complemented variable, the other with the same variable uncomplemented. For example, see Figure 10-51.

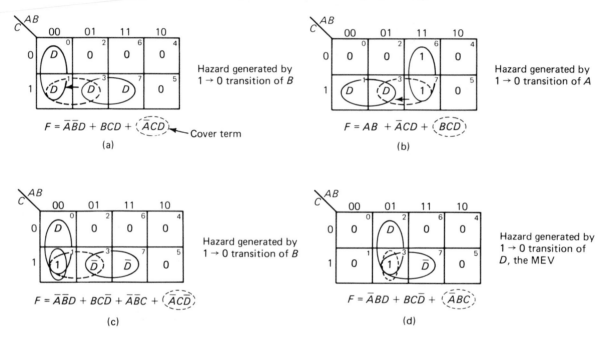

Fig. 10-50. Illustrations of potential hazards identified in VEM's. (a) An illustration of a potential hazard identified by adjacent grouping of identical MEV's. (b) An illustration of a potential hazard identified by adjacent groupings of 1's and MEV's. (c) An illustration of adjacent groupings of 1's, MEV's, and $\overline{MEV}$'s. (d) An illustration of a potential hazard identified by a grouping of the MEV and $\overline{MEV}$ covering the same 1.

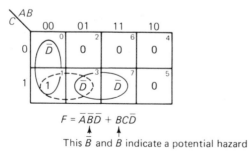

Fig. 10-51. An illustration of how hazards can be identified and covered by inspecting the simplified expression.

Observe that the cover is generated simply by ANDING the residue of the two terms, that is,

$$(\overline{A}\,\overline{D})(C\overline{D}) = \overline{A}\,C\overline{D}$$

Again you are reminded to make certain that the cover is really necessary before you add extra hardware.

As another illustration of the contemporary approach to asynchronous design, consider the following example. The specifications for this example call for a true multi-input asynchronous sequential machine.

EXAMPLE 10-13: The MDS diagram shown in Figure 10-52 was derived from a high speed radar processor/computer interface requirement. This requirement was so stringent that a synchronous controlled interface was considered impractical for several reasons. The actual specification of the interface requirement is left out at this time; however, the actual implementation of this multi-input asynchronous controller is felt to be important. The MDS diagram is used to develop the actual hardware assuming an existing flow diagram.

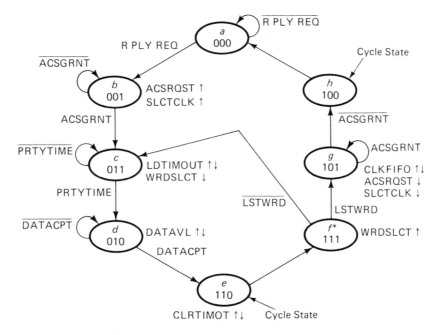

Fig. 10-52. The MDS diagram of an asynchronous controller for a radar processor/computer interface. Note that the LSTWRD input will be stable upon entry into state f.

The MDS diagram illustrates that the sequential behavior of this controller is based on *five inputs* and three feedback variables which, in a practical sense, virtually eliminate the use of the traditional approach. However, the actual design and implementation using the MEV approach produces results quickly. This is shown by the development in Figure 10-53. The output decoder logic that is not shown was derived by using a 3-to-8 decoder (74S138).

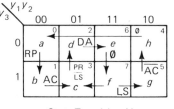

State Transition Map

Let: RP = RPLY REQ
AC = ACSGRNT
PR = PRTYTIME
DA = DATACPT
LS = LSTWRD

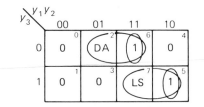

$$Y_1 = y_2\bar{y}_3(DA) + y_1 y_3(LS) + y_1 y_2\bar{y}_3 + y_1\bar{y}_2 y_3$$

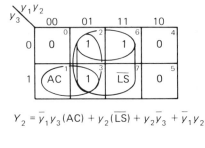

$$Y_2 = \bar{y}_1 y_3(AC) + y_2(\overline{LS}) + y_2\bar{y}_3 + \bar{y}_1 y_2$$

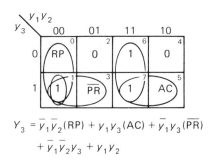

$$Y_3 = \bar{y}_1\bar{y}_2(RP) + y_1 y_3(AC) + \bar{y}_1 y_3(\overline{PR})$$
$$+ \bar{y}_1\bar{y}_2 y_3 + y_1 y_2$$

Fig. 10-53. The design development for the radar controller specified in Example 10-13.

As the last example, let us consider the possibility of using MSI/LSI devices for implementing asynchronous machines. See Example 10-14, which illustrates a technique for implementing a multi-input asynchronous machine with multiplexers and decoders. Before beginning this example, it should be pointed out that using multiplexers for the next state decoder *can lead to a static hazard problem.* This problem stems from the fact that the hazard cover process is bypassed because there is no map grouping process associated with a MUX implementation of combinational logic. This is basically true in cases where array-type logic is used and the hazard cover process is neglected. However, there are cases, such as the problem specified by Example 10-14, when static hazards pose no special problem, but speed and package count are of importance. In cases such as these, you should consider the design process outlined in Example 10-14.

EXAMPLE 10-14: It is required to develop a small switch-controlled asynchronous machine that will control the FREE RUN/SINGLE CYCLE/SINGLE INSTRUCTION execution mode of a certain microprocessor. The operation of the microprocessor is illustrated in the block diagram and flow diagram shown in Figure 10-54.

Fig. 10-54. (a) The block diagram illustrating the relation between the switch bank in the control panel and the microprocessor. (b) The flow diagram describing the control sequence of the RUN/ SINGLE CYCLE/SINGLE IN- STRUCTION feature for a microprocessor control panel.

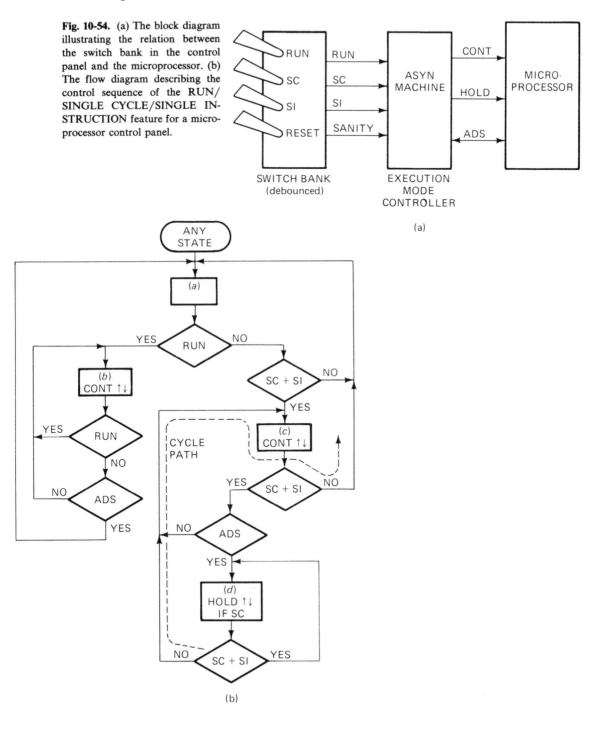

Figure 10-55(a) illustrates the MDS diagram description of the execution mode controller. Note that a cycle is used to avoid the requirement of an additional feedback variable. Once the operation is completely specified in an unambiguous manner, the Y_1 and Y_2 maps are plotted in a manner identical to that done earlier in this section. These are shown in Figure 10-55(b).

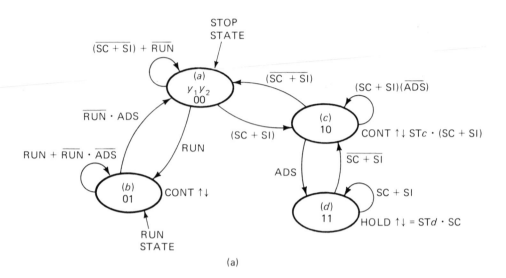

(a)

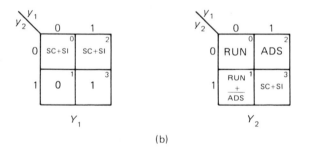

(b)

Fig. 10-55. (a) The MDS diagram for the asynchronous execution mode controller described in Example 10-14. (b) The excitation maps for Y_1 and Y_2.

Now once the excitation maps are plotted, it is a simple process to assign the multiplexer inputs the map-entered expressions found in the excitation maps and to use the address inputs for the feedback. See Figure 10-56 for the completed execution controller. Note that the complete circuit requires only four IC packages.

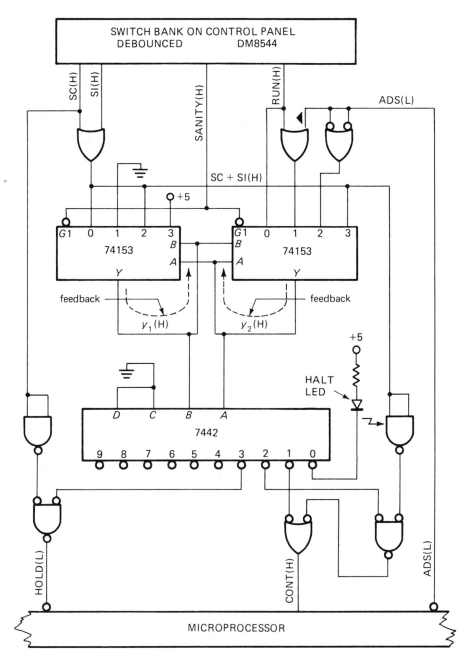

Fig. 10-56. The block diagram illustrating the relation between the switch bank in the control panel and the micro-processor.

This example shows that MSI devices can be used to an advantage providing the hazard problem is considered to be of no real consequence.

10-14 SUMMARY

In closing, it is thought fitting to present the last example which requires the application of logic design principles in conjunction with a microprocessor application to illustrate that there is still need for sound logic design principles, even though microprocessor utilization is expanding exponentially. Though the asynchronous studies have moved quickly, it is felt that enough information has been developed to allow you to further develop your design expertise through several design exercises outlined in the problem set. In short, it is hoped that this chapter has helped you to better understand asynchronous design and application practices and has opened the door for you to develop better methods for designing practical and reliable sequential machines.

BIBLIOGRAPHY

1. CALDWELL, S. H. *Switching Circuits and Logical Design*, New York: Wiley, 1958.

2. CRISCIMAGNA, TONY N. Start Logic Design with Flow Diagram. *Electronic Design*, **25** (1971), 56–59.

3. EICHELBERGER, E. B. Hazard Detection in Combinational and sequential Switching Circuit, *IBM J. Res. and Dev.*, **9:2** (1965).

4. HILL, FREDRICK J., and PETERSEN, GERALD R. *Introduction to Switching Theory and Logical Design*, New York: Wiley, 1974.

5. HUFFMAN, D. A. The Design and Use of Hazard-Free Switching Networks, *J. ACM*, **4** (1957), 47.

6. LANGDON, GLEN G., JR. *Logic Design: A Review of Theory and Practice*, New York: Academic, 1974.

7. MALEY, GERALD A. *Manual of Logic Circuits*, Englewood Cliffs, N. J.: Prentice-Hall, 1970.

8. MALEY, GERALD A. and EARLE, JOHN *The Logic Design of Transistor Digital Computers*, Englewood Cliffs, N.J.: Prentice-Hall, 1963.

9. MARCUS, MITCHELL P. *Switching Circuits for Engineers*, Englewood Cliffs, N.J.: Prentice-Hall, 1967.

10. McCLUSKEY, E. J. Fundamental Mode and Pulse Mode Sequential Circuits, *Proc. IFIP Congress 1962.* Amsterdam: North-Holland, 1962.

11. *The TTL Data Book for Design Engineers*, 2nd ed. Dallas: Texas Instruments, 1976.

12. UNGER, S. H. Hazards and Delays in Asynchronous Sequential Switching Circuits, *IRE Trans. Circuit Theory*, **CT-6** (1959), 12.

13. UNGER, STEPHEN H. *Asynchronous Sequential Switching Circuits*, New York: Wiley, 1969.

PROBLEMS AND EXERCISES

10-1. Given the circuit shown in Figure P10-1:
  (a) Convert the circuit into its fundamental mode model.
  (b) Derive the excitation variable expression.
  (c) Plot the excitation maps and identify the stable and unstable states (see Figure 10-7(c)).
  (d) Derive the primitive state diagram. Indicate all transient states (see Figure 10-7(d)).
  (e) Analyze the operational characteristics of the device.

10-2. Repeat the steps given in Problem 10-1 for Figure P10-2.

10-3. Repeat the steps given in Problem 10-1 for Figure P10-3.

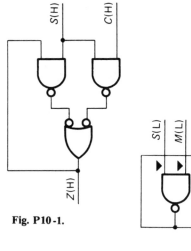

Fig. P10-1.

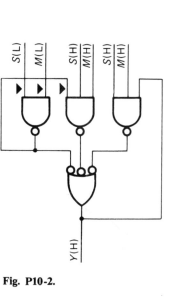

Fig. P10-2.

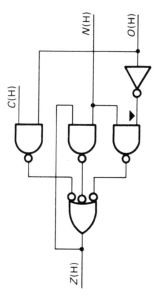

Fig. P10-3.

10-4.   Repeat the steps given in Problem 10-1 for Figure P10-4.

10-5.   Repeat the steps given in Problem 10-1 for Figure P10-5.

10-6.   Repeat the steps given in Problem 10-1 for Figure P10-6.

10-7.   Repeat steps given in Problem 10-1 for Figure P10-7.

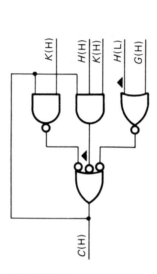

Fig. P10-4.

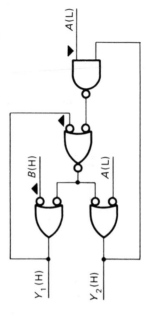

Fig. P10-5.

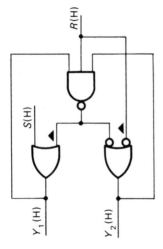

Fig. P10-6.

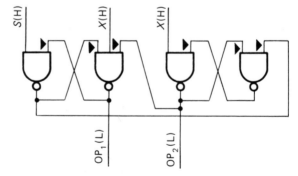

Fig. P10-7.

10-8. Repeat the steps given in Problem 10-1 for
(a) Figure 10-1 in the text.
(b) Figure 10-48(b) in the text.

10-9. Develop a primitive state diagram and state table for the following problem. (Keep state diagram tight.) A sequential circuit is required that has two inputs, A and B (ASSERTED LOW) and one output Z(H). The output Z is to be ASSERTED at the end of the input sequence $AB = 00 \rightarrow 01 \rightarrow 11$ and remain ASSERTED until the end of the input sequence $AB = 11 \rightarrow 10 \rightarrow 00$. Assume at this time that only one input will change at a time.

10-10. Develop a primitive state diagram and state table for the following problem. (Keep state diagram tight.) You are to design a sequential door lock using two widely separated debounced momentary switches (A and B). Your system is to open the door when A is pushed, then B is pushed and released twice, then A is pushed again. Once the lock is open, it can be relocked by pushing B at least once. (*Hint*: Remember that this is to be thought of as a continuous sequence problem A, B, B, A using *momentary switches, widely separated*.)

10-11. Design a primitive state diagram and state table for an asynchronous circuit that is defined as a sample gate. This circuit is to have two inputs, gate (D), and sample (S); and one output (LD) operates as follows. The output is to be deasserted (low) when the S input is deasserted (low). When the S input is asserted, the output (LD) moves to the level of the data (D) input and holds this level until S is deasserted. Assume initially that the two inputs never change simultaneously.

10-12. Design a primitive state diagram and state table for the following circuit. This circuit is to have two inputs and one output. The two inputs are oscillator (O) and gate (G) and the output mnemonic (OP). When the gate (G) is deasserted, the output is to remain at a low level. When the input is asserted (high), the output will gate the oscillator (O) to the output with no "shaved" initial or final pulses. Assume initially that the two inputs never change simultaneously.

10-13. Design a primitive state diagram and state table for a circuit with two asynchronous inputs (X and Y) and one output Z. This circuit is to be designed so that if *any* change takes place on X or Y, Z is to change states. Assume initially that the two inputs never change simultaneously.

10-14. Design a primitive state diagram and construct the primitive flow table for a special circuit that has two inputs (AB) and two outputs (LE). The two outputs (L and E) are to reflect an indication of which input changed last. Assume at this time that the inputs do not change simultaneously.

10-15. Design a primitive state diagram and construct the primitive flow table which defines the operation of a special circuit. This circuit has three inputs (A, B, and R) and one output (X). The R (RESET) is the input which drives X back to its NOT-ASSERTED state (LOW). The B input is a varying width pulse which lights an LED but is quasi random in its occurrence. The A input comes from a human actuated debounced switch. When B turns on the LED, the person is to react by pushing the A switch and releasing it. The idea is to have X light another LED if and only if the person under test is able to push and release the A switch while B is still ASSERTED. The X output will remain ASSERTED until R is depressed, at which time the test is to start over.

10-16. Define a primitive state diagram and construct the primitive flow table for a rising-edge triggered D Flip-Flop.

10-17. Figure P10-8 illustrates several primitive flow tables. First examine these tables for possible redundant states (see Section 6-7 for review of redundant state identification and removal). Then strive for a nonmixed merge for:
(a) Figure P10-8 (a).
(b) Figure P10-8 (b).
(c) Figure P10-8 (c).
(d) Figure P10-8 (d); merge the best possible way.

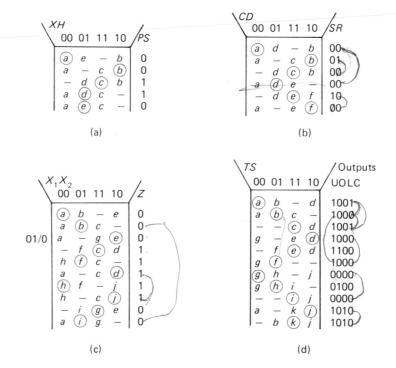

(a)

(b)

(c)

(d)

Fig. P10-8.

10-18. Problems 10-9 through 10-16 require the design of a primitive flow table. First examine the flow table for possible redundant states (see Section 6-7 for review of redundant state identification and removal). Then strive for the optimal merge for the primitive flow table defining:
(a) Problem 10-9.
(b) Problem 10-10.
(d) Problem 10-11.
(d) Problem 10-12.
(e) Problem 10-13.
(f) Problem 10-14.
(g) Problem 10-15.
(h) Problem 10-16.

10-19. (Refer to Problem 10-17.) Develop a *noncritical race* transition map and make the secondary assignment (row assignment) for the merged table for (i.e., develop the excitation maps):
(a) Problem 10-17(a).
(b) Problem 10-17(b).
(c) Problem 10-17(c).
(d) Problem 10-17(d).
Refer to Figure 10-23 for aid in this process.

10-20. Refer to Problem 10-19. Read the excitation map and plot output map eliminating all hazards, then draw the circuit diagrams for:
(a) Problem 10-19(a) (refer to Figure P-10-8(a)).
(b) Problem 10-19(b) (refer to Figure P-10-8(b)).
(c) Problem 10-19(c) (refer to Figure P-10-8(c)).
(d) Problem 10-19(d) (refer to Figure P-10-8(d)).

10-21. (Refer to Problem 10-18.) Develop a noncritical race transition map and make the secondary assignment (row assignment) for the merged table (develop the excitation maps) for:
(a) Problem 10-18(a) (refer to Problem 10-9).
(b) Problem 10-18(b) (refer to Problem 10-10).
(c) Problem 10-18(c) (refer to Problem 10-11).
(d) Problem 10-18(d) (refer to Problem 10-12).
(e) Problem 10-18(e) (refer to Problem 10-13).
(f) Problem 10-18(f) (refer to Problem 10-14).
(g) Problem 10-18(g) (refer to Problem 10-15).
(h) Problem 10-18(h) (refer to Problem 10-16).

10-22 (Refer to Problem 10-21.) *Perform an inspection analysis on your design. Be certain to determine what happens if simultaneous input changes do occur. Then determine how and where your circuit can be reset after power up. In short, do you know what stable state your circuit will be in after power is applied? Can you set the input conditions after power is applied and guarantee that your circuit will move to a known state? Next, examine your problem for essential hazards.* Read the excitation map, removing the hazards, and draw up schematic diagrams for:
(a) Problem 10-21(a).
(b) Problem 10-21(b).
(c) Problem 10-21(c).
(d) Problem 10-21(d).
(e) Problem 10-21(e).
(f) Problem 10-21(f).
(g) Problem 10-21(g).
(h) Problem 10-21(h).

10-23 Design a circuit of your choice that will exhibit a potential essential hazard, then carry out a timing diagram analysis illustrating how this hazard can be induced by adding delay. Then, once it has been induced, assume that this delay is invariable and attempt to eliminate the induced essential hazard by adding delay in a feedback. Then ask the question, "Has this 'curing' delay created other hazard problems elsewhere in the circuit?"

10-24. Refer to Figure 10-37(h).

(a) Could the propagation delay of this Flip-Flop be improved by using three-input NAND gates for the cell and feeding the outputs (2) of the AND functions for the SET/RESET decoder directly to the cell inputs?

(b) Would this wiring change impair the operation of the complete circuit?

10-25. Using the model shown in Figure 10-36 and Example 10-9 as references, design a rising edge triggered T Flip-Flop. If possible, make your Flip-Flop operate as fast as possible. Establish setup and hold times for your circuit.

10-26. Select one or more of the problem ranging from 10-9 to 10-15 and implement them using the technique demonstrated in Example 10-9. Completely analyze your circuits' operation.

10-27. The state diagram shown in Figure P10-9 defines the handshake control sequence for a high speed direct memory access interface control unit. Use the cell-centered approach treated in Section 10-11 to design the logic for this MDS diagram.

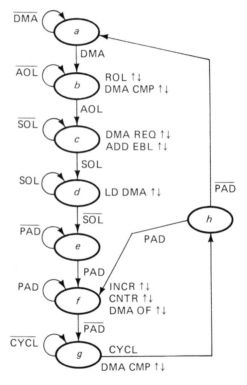

Fig. P10-9.

10-28. Design a rising-edge-triggered D Flip-Flop using the cell-centered approach treated in Section 10-11. Make certain all static hazards are removed from SET/RESET decoder. (Note that the state diagram definition must be well thought through.) Compare your results with Figure 10-37(h).

10-29. Select at least two problems from the set 10-9 through 10-15, then carry out the complete design process as outlined in Section 10-12.

Note: The following problems comprise a set of interesting and practical circuits to be designed by methods of your choice. It is felt that each circuit should be designed in at least two ways for comparison purposes.

10-30. The following two wave forms are produced by a certain shaft encoder.

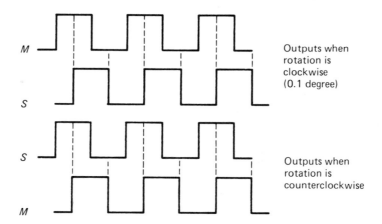

Outputs when rotation is clockwise (0.1 degree)

Outputs when rotation is counterclockwise

Design a special circuit that will light an LED when the shaft rotation is clockwise and turn the LED off when the shaft rotation is counterclockwise.

10-31. Suppose you have two dc motors that turn two separate precision shaft encoders such as the one shown in Problem 10-30. One of these motors is defined as the MASTER Unit and the other is defined as the SLAVE unit. When these motors are running, a course control system maintains the speed of the slave within ±10% of the MASTER. You are to design a sequential circuit that will output a pulse whose width will indicate the degree of phase error between the SLAVE and MASTER. Also, there should be an output indicating that the SLAVE is leading the MASTER(HIGH) and the SLAVE is lagging the MASTER(LOW). Assume MASTER speed 1 ±20%.

10-32. Refer to Problem 7-4. Design an asynchronous circuit that will perform the pulse width discrimination specified, only this time disregard the single sample switch functions. In short, your circuit is to continuously perform the task of controlling the up/down counter to provide the continuous measurements.

10-33. Using the single-step-pulse concept, a synchronous decade counter like the SN74160 and a BCD thumb-wheel switch, design a programmable pulse generator. In short, design a circuit that issues the number of clean clock pulses equal to the number specified by the thumb-wheel switch.

APPENDIX

DRAFTING AND DOCUMENTATION

STANDARDS MANUAL

PREFACE

This manual has been prepared in an attempt to standardize digital system schematic drafting and system documentation done under the auspices of the Digital Systems Group at Utah State University. The rules set forth have been tried and tested and deemed worthy of adoption by anyone doing digital system design, but in particular these rules *must* be followed strictly by anyone working within or for the Digital System Group. Any deviations must be approved before they can be adopted.

Further, this manual was prepared to complement the MIXED LOGIC DESIGN as set forth in the article "Polarized Mnemonics, Logic State Indicators, and Zonal Coordinates." It is therefore assumed that anyone using this standards manual is fully familiar with the concepts of MIXED LOGIC DESIGN.

The gates and circuits commonly used by the Digital System Group are shown in the appendix. The symbols shown for each circuit will be used for all schematics.

GENERAL DOCUMENTATION STANDARDS

(1) All logic drawings and stuff sheets are to be prepared on the same size sheet, using approved drafting techniques.
(2) All documentation is to be done in pencil and must be neat and legible.
(3) If practical, keep the number of sheets in each subseries below 20.

(4) Use blueprints of masters for debugging and wire listing.

(5) All wire lists, edge card assignment sheets, ECN's, and cable lists are to be placed in a system book.

(6) The master drawings and system book must contain a complete record of documentation for the system, which will include all engineering-change-notices (ECN's).

TECHNIQUES SUGGESTED FOR POLARIZED MNEMONICS IMPLEMENTATION AND DOCUMENTATIONS

SCHEMATIC

(1) Use paper with zonal coordinates, which is a special paper having addressable sectors for the purpose of identifying geographical locations (see p. 117).

(2) A title block, located in the lower right-hand corner, should include system identification, sheet number, board number, and can include a general function description. The sheet number must be unique to that system only, and the board number identifies the board where the hardware is located. The drawing number is used for filing; initial your design and date when completed.

EXAMPLE A-1:

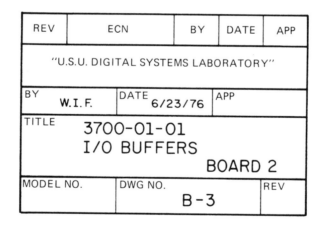

REV	ECN	BY	DATE	APP
"U.S.U. DIGITAL SYSTEMS LABORATORY"				

BY W.I.F.	DATE 6/23/76	APP

TITLE
3700-01-01
I/O BUFFERS
BOARD 2

MODEL NO.	DWG NO. B-3	REV

I/O Buffer—names the drawing on the sheet for quick reference

$$3700 - 01 - 01 = \underbrace{XXXX} - \underbrace{YY} - \underbrace{ZZ}$$

Product Identi-fication   Sub Unit No.   Series No.

$B - 3$ = drawing identification

The alphabetic character of the drawing identification is assigned by the following criteria:

A—index type of information
B—functional schematics
C—equipment layout (stuff sheets, PC board, component location)
D—state diagrams and flow charts
E—timing diagrams
F—cabling diagrams and layouts
G—block diagrams
H—sheet metal drawings
K—card cage assembly drawings and layout

(3) All drawings must be neat, clear, and done in pencil, allowing room for all labeling, cross-reference information, and possible engineering changes. Drawings must be dark enough for blue printing (use F lead).
(4) All logic drawings must flow from top to bottom of the sheets with inputs toward the top and outputs toward the bottom. Use only a MTL-STD-806C three-quarter size logic template.
(5) The recommended logic symbols for commonly used circuits are shown on pages 737–742.
(6) Any special purpose gates not shown in the appendix will be labeled with the circuit number.

Example A-2:

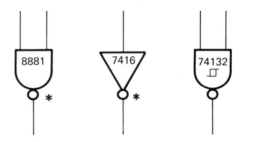

(7) Special circuits such as MSI and LSI devices will require special attention. If no standard drafting symbol is shown in the appendix for a device, one must be synthesized using a rectangle. Care must be taken to label all inputs and outputs inside the drafting symbol (rectangle). This labeling should be done in such a manner as to describe the actual circuit operation. Be sure to include the circuit family number. Keep inputs to the device on upper edge and sides; all outputs on the bottom. See the following example.

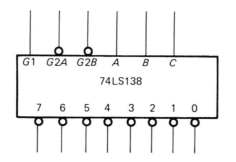

(8) Use the cross-reference technique to avoid massive and confusing line drawing. All nonconnected lines must be labeled and cross-referenced.

(9) All cross-referenced leads must have a mnemonic that is unique, that defines the logic function as closely as possible, and carries the correct polarizing element.

   (a) The polarizing element is placed in parenthesis: RDATA = 1(0) or RDATA = 1(L).

   (b) When fan-out demands require several leads that are logically the same, an alphabetic character is placed after the polarizing element.

EXAMPLE A-4:

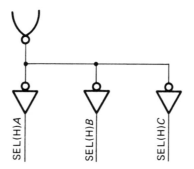

(10) Cross-referencing formats are to be used for any nonconnected logic line. This cross-reference information must detail the destination of this line, i.e., "where it is going." The cross-reference *format* must be general and unchanging.

The general format is XXXX, YY, Z, W:

$$XXXX \rightarrow \text{system series}$$
$$YY \rightarrow \text{schematic sheet number}$$
$$Z \rightarrow \text{alphabetic coordinate}$$
$$W \rightarrow \text{numeric coordinate}$$

   (a) Cross-references with only a letter and number indicate a location on the same sheet.

   (b) When a number precedes the letter and number, the location is on another sheet which has that number.

(c) If a lead goes to another schematic series, the schematic series must precede the sheet number and location.

EXAMPLE A-5: The information contained within the box is strictly used as example information indicating the location of the logic line WRT(L). Normally this information could be obtained from the title block and the zonal coordinates of the schematic sheet. Similar examples will be used throughout this paper.

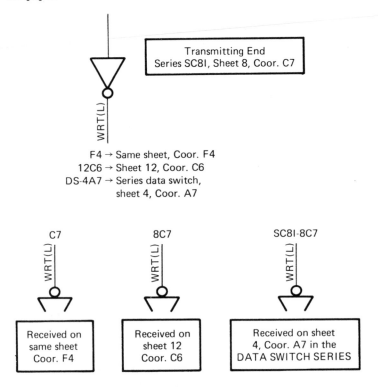

Offboard connections will need additional documentation requirements. Normally any offboard connections will go through one connector to another connector or into a cable. In any case a special format must be used to signify this operation. This will be added to the cross-reference information previously described. A definite ordering sequence must be followed. This is:

List first: all on same sheet coordinates
second: all same board coordinates
third: offboard connection information
fourth: same series connections
fifth: separate series connections

The offboard connection format for edge card and cable connection is as follows:

ECC YYY(ZZ)

ECC→Edge card connector will always precede the edge card pin assignment
YYY→Edge card pin number
(ZZ)→(Connector pin number)

CBL ZZZ-WW

     CBL→Cable
     ZZZ→Cable number
     WW→Live pin number

EXAMPLE A-6:

ECC YYY(ZZ)→Edge card connector, edge card pin assignment (connector pin number)
CBL ZZZ-WW→Cable, cable number, live pin number
XXXX   →System name, sheet number, zonal coordinate
- -
XXXX   →System name, sheet number, zonal coordinate
CBL ZZZ-WW→Cable number and live pin number
ECC YYY(ZZ)→Edge card assignments (connector pin number)

Special note: In regards to the orderly documentation requirements as set forth, it is a known fact that when schematics are being drawn, edge card and cable assignments information may not be known. It is therefore acceptable to use the following notation on prototype schematics. However, the master schematics must be updated to satisfy these rules before system documentation is complete.

COMPLETE EXAMPLE OF CROSS-REFERENCING:

Transmitting End
Sheet 12 Coor. D4
SC8I Series

A3→Same sheet, Coor. A3
6F0→Sheet 6, Coor. F0
7H4→Sheet 7, Coor. H4
ECC-JF2(12)→Edge card connector JF2 (connector pin 12)
CBL-4AA-13→Cable 4AA, live pin 13
DS-4F3→Data switch series, sheet 4, Coor. F3
$ Cable has Viking connector on receiving end

*The $ sign has been added to allow for special information that must be added

$ Cable has an AMP connector on transmitting end
SC8I-12D4→SC8I series, sheet 12, Coor. D4
CBL-4AA-C4→Cable 4AA, live pin C4
ECC-S12(13)→Edge card connector S12 (connector pin 13)
E1→Same sheet, Coor. E1
D8→Same sheet, Coor. D8

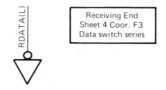

Receiving End
Sheet 4 Coor. F3
Data switch series

(11) All communication lines leaving or entering the boards should be ASSERTED at the low signal level for noise immunity.
(12) Fan-out shall never exceed logic family recommended maximum. When fan-out is greater than one, list all cross references at the output and reference all inputs to that output. When a signal goes to the same coordinates more than once, list the coordinate that number of times.

EXAMPLE A-7:

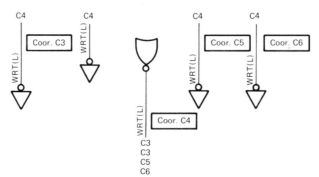

(13) When there is a direct connection between two devices and it is required to break out a cross-reference lead, do as follows:

EXAMPLE A-8:

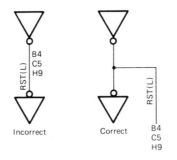

(14) Inputs should not be left floating because of noise problems. Outputs that are not used must be defined with a "No Connection" (NC) note (don't tie outputs, only inputs).

(15) Mnemonics will change only after the signal passes through some transforming logic. The polarizing element is the only thing that changes when an inverter is used.

EXAMPLE A-9:

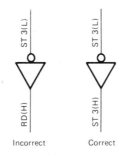

(15a) *Special Case*: There are times when using a single or unique mnemonic to describe several different logic operations becomes a handicap. In cases such as these, use a PAPER GATE as shown to FAN OUT different mnemonics from a single mnemonic.

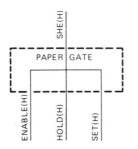

(16) All connections are shown with a dot. Cross connections are as follows.

EXAMPLE A-10:

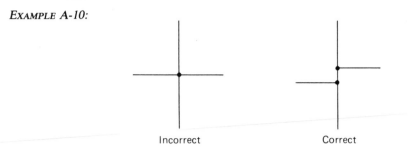

Incorrect   Correct

(17) All gates will be labeled with the IC pin assignment as well as the printed circuit board coordinate locating the chip.

EXAMPLE A-11:

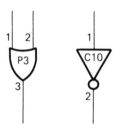

(18) Resistors and components are labeled with both the socket location and header pin assignments. A header is defined as an IC socket that allows discrete component mounting.

EXAMPLE A-12

This resistor is mounted on a header in socket C4.

(19) Make sure all incompatibilities are flagged.

EXAMPLE A-13:

▼ → Inhibit   ▲ → Enable

STUFF SHEET

(1) The stuff sheet is a block diagram of the board with socket locations indicated. Each socket location is referenced by a zonal coordinate on the board (see example).

(2) If more than one printed circuit board is required, then determine a feasible partition of the schematics by trial and error. Never share the same schematic with two or more separate boards. To aid in this process,

use edge card assignment sheets and total chip capability of the boards. When determining the chip number for each board, leave approximately 10% blank for debugging purposes. As each schematic sheet is assigned to a board, fill in the title block.

(3) Assign the larger IC's (greater than 18 pin) first. Then begin to locate connecting logic in sockets close by. Keep all wires as short as possible.

(4) As each chip location is assigned, first identify the chip by its family number in the top partition of the bug location block. Then identify each gate with the zonal coordinate and the schematic sheet number where it can be found. *Note*: Gate letters for each package are assigned as shown in the appendix.

At this same time the gate will also be labeled on schematics with the socket location and IC pin assignments on the inputs and outputs. Don't try to label inputs and outputs until gate letters have been assigned. The order of listing in the location block is important to the assignment of pin numbers of the gates.

EXAMPLE A-14:

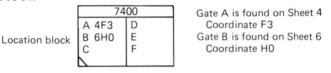

Location block

Gate A is found on Sheet 4
Coordinate F3
Gate B is found on Sheet 6
Coordinate H0

(5) The standard board has +v on pin 14, 16, 18, etc. and Ground on 7, 8, 9, etc. If an assigned chip has a different assignment, the board must be changed. Show this by blacking the corner of the location block, indicating foil is to be cut.

EXAMPLE A-15:

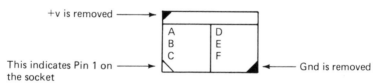

+v is removed

This indicates Pin 1 on the socket

Gnd is removed

(6) The number of gates can be as many as six and as few as one in each chip. Unused lines are crossed out and unassigned gates are left blank in the location block.

All larger circuits (MSI and LSI) are considered one gate circuits because they have only one location.

EXAMPLE A-16:

	7400	
A 3F4	D	
B 4H0	E ———	
C	F ———	

A 7400 has only four gates so the last two lines are crossed out and unused gates left blank

EXAMPLE A-17:

74150	
A 7D1	D ———
B ———	E ———
C ———	F ———

The MUX is located on
Sheet 7 Coordinate D1

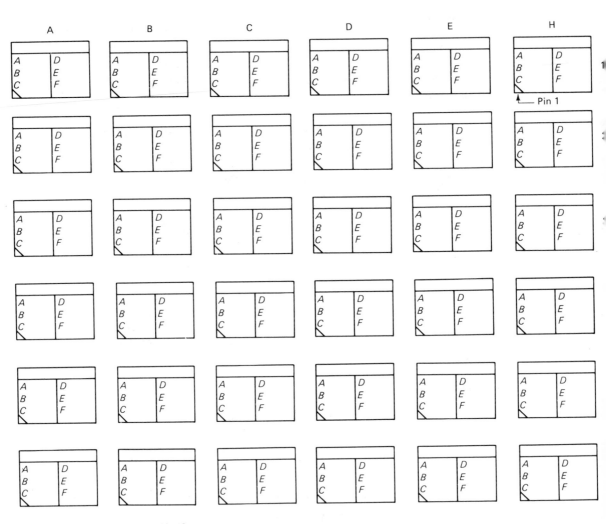

Each socket may be a 14, 16, 18,
20, 22, 24, 28, 40 pin

EXAMPLE OF STUFF SHEET

(7) The IC resistor package must have all assigned resistors listed with zonal
coordinates also.

EXAMPLE A-18:

34A10K	
A 6A3, 6A4	D 7A4, 7A3
B 6A5, 6A6	E 7B0, 8B9
C 6B0, 6B1	F 8C1, 8C3

(8) If any headers are used, a diagram of the header is placed on the schematic. The socket is labeled as a header with each component listed similar to the resistor packs. The locations are that of the components, not the diagram of the header.

EDGE CARD ASSIGNMENT

(1) Each board must have a list of all off-the-board connections called an *edge card assignment sheet*. This list must show the one-to-one correspondence between the pin on the board and the connector pin (see example). All edge card assignments will follow this format with all pins listed.

Example of Edge Card Assignment

UNIT NAME: *DATA SWITCH*   CIS 100-2   PAGE: *1/4*

BOARD NUMBER(S): 3   A END ASSIGNMENT

	LEAD NAME	LOCATION	DESTINATION
1	GND		
2	GND		
3	V_{CC}		
4	V_{CC}		
5	A1-10 *WRT (H)*	*6H4*	*Bd #1 A2-10 (21)*
6	A1-9 *RDO (L)*	*5A3*	*Bd #2 A2-12 (23)*
7	A1-12 *LLTAD (H)*	*6H3*	*Bd #1 A2-9 (22)*
8	A1-11 *LCRST (L)*	*5BO*	*CBL #4AA (C4)*
9	A1-14 *LCRWD (L)*	*5B1*	*CBL #4AA (C8)*
10	A1-13		
11	A1-16		
12	A1-15		
13	A1-2		
14	A1-1 *SEL (L)*	*7G5*	*Bd #3 A1-16 (11)*
15	A1-4		
16	A1-3		
17	A1-6		
18	A1-5 *SEC (L)*	*7B4*	*CBL #3A (7)*
19	A1-8		
20	A1-7		
21	A2-10		
22	A2-9		
23	A2-12		

(row 14 destination) Board—Edge Card—Connector
Number   Pin   Pin

(row 18 destination) Cable Number—Live Pin

Connector Edge Card
Pin   Pin

Location on
Schematic Sheets

(2) The title will include:
   (a) unit or series identification
   (b) board number
   (c) type of board
   (d) board connector name
   (e) page number   (The page number is made up of two parts: (1) page number and (2) number of page for that list.)

EXAMPLE A-19:   page 1 of 4 pages. Most boards will have more than one edge card connector, therefore each connector will be given a name, number, or letter to identify that connector.

(3) For each pin used the lead name, location, and destination will be filled in.
   (a) Lead name is the mnemonic used for that signal with the polarizing element.
   (b) Location is the geographic location of the signal on the schematic sheet.
   (c) Destination is where the signal originates or terminates.
(4) The edge card assignment sheet will follow the wire list for each board in the system book.

WIRE LISTING

(1) *All wire listing is done in pencil.* Each board must have a complete pin-to-pin wire list; divide into schematics.
(2) Each pin is defined by the socket location and the pin number.

EXAMPLE A-20: S3-2:   Socket S3 pin 2

(3) Sheets for wire listing will all follow the same format (see example).
(4) Title is made up of four parts:
   (a) unit name or series identification
   (b) schematic sheet number
   (c) board number
   (d) page number   (The page number is made up of two parts: (1) page number and (2) number of pages for the schematic.)

EXAMPLE A-21: 3/8-   page 3 of 8 pages
Each schematic has its own numbering system.

(5) Blueprint all master copies, never wire list from master copies.
(6) As each logic line is listed, trace over with a colored pencil on blueprint copy.
(7) When only two points are connected, list one pin in the FROM column and the other in the TO column (see example).
(8) When more than two pins are connected, a "daisy-chain" is formed, with the beginning pin in the FROM column and the others listed down

the TO column (see example). Make sure all lead names that are available are listed.

(9) Skip two lines between each individual entry.

(10) Keep all wires as short as possible. Do not backtrack across the board from pin to pin. THINK!!

EXAMPLE A-22:

	M1-4	N2-3		B6-8	C4-1
		C4-1			M3-4
	INCORRECT	M3-4		INCORRECT	M1-4
		B6-8			N2-3

(11) Keep all edge cards at the end of the runs.

EXAMPLE A-23:

P3-9   R4-7

   ECC S1-12

(12) Make GND and VCC pins the first pin in the daisy chains.

UNIT NAME: SC8I   BOARD: 1

SCHEMATIC SHEET: 4   PAGE: 2/12

WIRED	FROM	TO	CHECKED	LEAD NAME
	A6-4	F4-13		RB7 (H)
		H3-13		
	W1-3	Z1-1		
	W1-5	ECC-AK-1		MDO (L)
	W1-7	ECC-AM-1		MDI (L)
	Z1-7	W1-11		GND
		W1-9		
		W1-6		
		W1-4		
	S1-8	O1-4		GND
		O1-6		
		O1-9		
		O1-11		

(13) At the first of the wire list for each board, make up a board preparation sheet. These are to give a general description of the board with a list of pin sockets and their locations. This must include all cuts to be made on the board, and the wiring of +v and GND where it is needed.

(14) Lists are kept in system books divided by board numbers. Be neat!

CABLE LISTING

(1) All cable listing is done with the same format (see example).

(2) There must be a complete pin-to-pin list for each cable.

(3) The title is made up of:
    (a) cable number or name;
    (b) page number similar to that of the wire list;

EXAMPLE A-24:   4/10:   page 4 of 10 pages

Example of Cable Listing

CABLE NO: 7   CONNECTOR TYPE   END A _AMP_
PAGE: 2/3   END B _VIKING_

		PIN ASSIGNMENT	
SIGNAL	COLOR CODE	A END	B END
LLTAD (L)	RED	1	C4
	BLK	2	C5
LLWRT (L)	ORN	3	D4
	BLK	4	D5
LLRST (L)	YEL	5	B1
	BLK	6	B2

(c) connector type, the name of the connector.

EXAMPLE A-25:   END A is the transmitting end
END B is the receiving end

(4) Most cables will be twisted color coded pairs with a signal line and a GND line. Keep GND wire in bottom segment and signal wire in top segment of cable assignment sheet.
(5) Do not place two separate cables on one page.
(6) Cable lists are kept in the system book divided by internal and external cables. Be neat!

ENGINEERING CHANGE NOTICES

(1) All changes made on a system after hardware is started or completed are listed as an Engineering Change Notice (ECN). Each change must be completely documented before any hardware is changed.
(2) After wirewrap has been started on a board, no changes are made until the initial wirewrap is completed and checked.
(3) The changes are drawn on the original blueprints first, and must be drawn on these prints. An ECN is written up on ECN list sheets, with all *removes* listed first and *adds* listed second.
(4) Each ECN is numbered and the title is completely filled in.
   (a) Numbering of ECN's is for the complete system.
   (b) Page numbers are for that ECN only, with page number and number of pages.
   (c) Purpose is a general function description of the change and why the change.
(5) All *removes* are listed backwards from the wire list with the last pin wired listed first.
(6) An * is placed beside each assignment where:
   (a) a wrap will still remain on the pin after *removes* are made;
   (b) a wrap is already on that pin.
(7) After the change is *completely* documented, the hardware can be changed and all master drawings, wire lists, and other documentation must be updated.
(8) NEVER make any change in hardware until completely documented first. Never remove or add any hardware until documented. Make sure all changes are documented by an ECN.
(9) The ECN's must be a complete written record of all changes and placed in the system book; so be NEAT.
(10) After each ECN update of the master, schematics must be dated and documented in the revision columns above the title block.

ECN Cover Sheet

REQUEST COMPLETION BY _____   DATE _____

ENGINEERING CHANGE NOTICE

1. Unit Name:

2. Change Number:

3. Area Affected:
   a. Wire Wrap   _____
   b. Stuff Sheet   _____
   c. Mechanical   _____
   d. Other (specify)   _____

4. Apply Change to Following:

5. Change has been applied to following by Engineering:

6. Reason for Change:

7. Special Instructions:

ENGINEERING CHANGE NOTICE

UNIT NAME: SC8I   BOARD NO.: 1

DATE: APRIL 8, '74   PAGE NO.: 1/2

ORGINATE BY: W.I.F.   ECN NO: 3   SCHEMATIC SHEET NO.: 4

Purpose   TAKE SANITY SWITCH OUT

       NO LONGER NEEDED

WIRE LIST UPDATED   4/13/74

SCHEMATIC UPDATED   4/10/74

WIRED	FROM	TO	CHECKED	LEAD NAME
	REMOVE:			
	C1-5	M8-1		LRESET (H)
		S6-8		
	C1-6	M8-5		RRSET (H)
		S6-5		
	E4-9	E4-5		
		M8-6		
		M8-2		
	E4-3	E4-1		
		M8-3		
		M8-4		

UNIT NAME: SC8I

ECN NO. 3

BOARD NO: 1

PAGE NO: 2/2

SCHEMATIC SHEET NO.: 4

WIRED	FROM	TO	CHECKED	LEAD NAME
	ADD:			
	SG-5	C1-6		
		E4-1		
		E4-3		
	E4-11 *	E4-5		
		E4-9		

DRAFTING SYMBOLS
AND EXAMPLE DRAWINGS

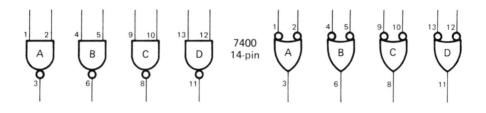

7400
14-pin

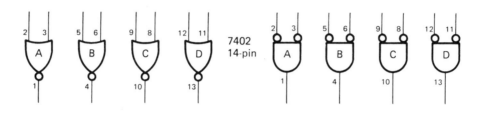

7402
14-pin

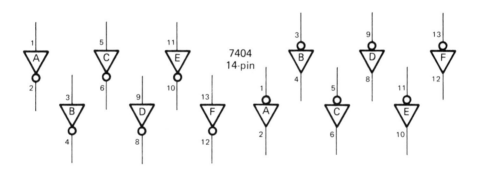

7404
14-pin

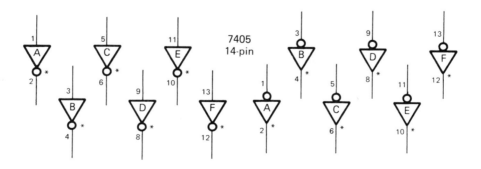

7405
14-pin

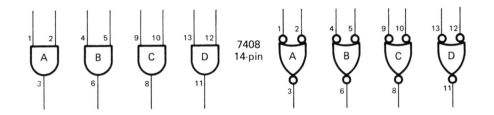

7408
14-pin

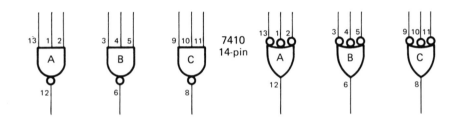

7410
14-pin

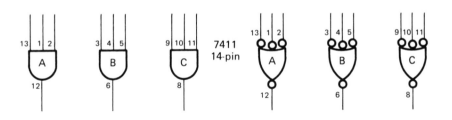

7411
14-pin

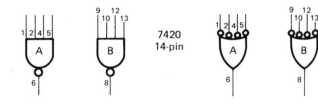

7420
14-pin

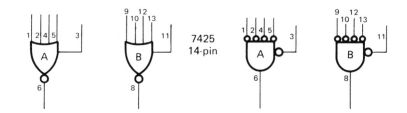

7425
14-pin

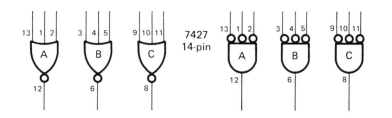

7427
14-pin

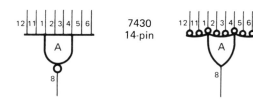

7430
14-pin

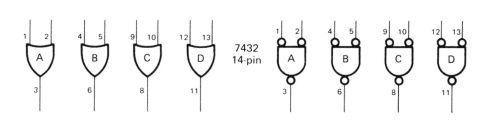

7432
14-pin

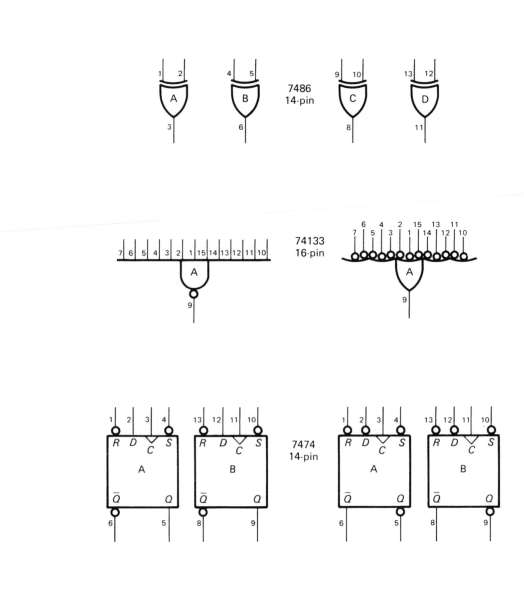

7486
14-pin

74133
16-pin

7474
14-pin

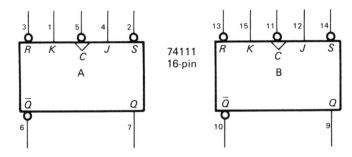

74111
16-pin

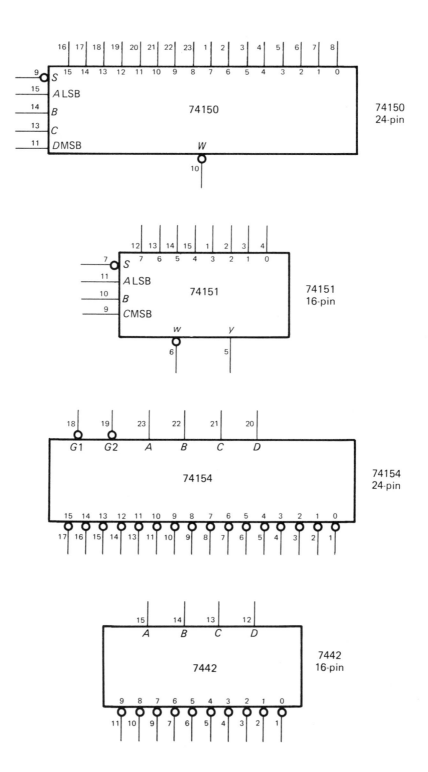

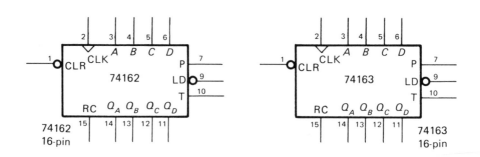

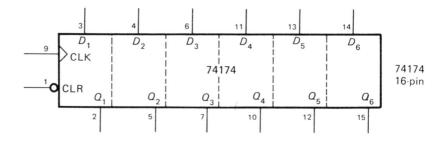

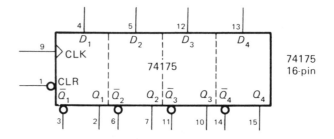

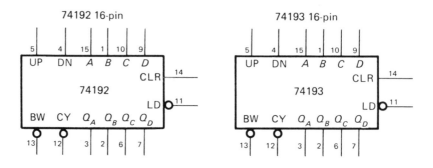

BOOZER PROGRAM

```
( 8 7 4 0 0 3 ) C A N D E / C O D E 2 1 0   O N   P A C K
= = = = = = = = = = = = = = = = = = = = = = = = = = = = =
```

```
%   THIS PROGRAM WAS PREPARED BY THE ELECTRICAL ENGINEERING DEPARTMENT
%   AT UTAH STATE UNIVERSITY SEPT, 1977.  IT WAS IMPLEMENTED ON A
%   BURROUGHS 6700 IN EXTENDED ALGOL 60.  THE AUTHOR ASSUMES NO
%   RESPONSIBILITY IN THE IMPLEMENTATION OR USE OF THIS PROGRAM.
%
%   THE PROGRAM FINDS A MINIMALLY REDUCED EXPRESSION OF A BOOLEAN
%   LOGIC PROBLEM.  THE PRIME IMPLICANTS ARE ALSO MADE AVAILABLE TO
%   THE USER.  THE PROGRAM WILL ACCEPT MAP ENTERED VARIABLES AS WELL
%   AS PARTIALLY REDUCED EXPRESSIONS.
%
%   THE PROGRAM IS A SELF EXPLANATORY TIMESHARE PROGRAM.  WHEN THE
%   MAP ENTERED VARIABLES ARE ASKED FOR THEY ARE LISTED ONE PER LINE
%   IN ANY SEQUENCE.  THE LIST IS TERMINATED BY A '#'.
%   THE TERMS ARE ARE INPUT IN THE FOLLOWING FORMAT:
%     STATE VARIABLE <DELIMITER> (EXPRESSION <DELIMITER> OPTIONAL)
%           VALUE.
%   DELIMITERS ARE ANY CHARACTERS OTHER THAN LETTERS, NUMBERS,
%   OPERATORS, OR THE END OF INPUT SYMBOL (#). THE OPERATORS ARE
%   AND (.), OR (+), UNARY MINUS ('), DASH (=), AND PARENTHESES ().
%   STATE VARIABLES ARE THE TERMS OR RANGE OF TERMS TO BE ASSIGNED THE
%   VALUE SPECIFIED.  EXPRESSIONS ARE EVALUATED FROM LEFT TO RIGHT,
%   NO PRECEDENCE IS ASSUMED.  ALL ORDERING MUST BE DONE WITH
%   PARENTHESES, ONLY ONE LEVEL IS ALLOWED.  ALL TERMS SPECIFIED
%   BY THE EXPRESSION ARE ASSIGNED AS SPECIFIED BY THE VALUE.
%   TERMS TO BE ASSERTED SPECIFIED BY '1', DON'T CARE TERMS '0',
%   AND ANY OTHER NUMBER IS NOT ASSERTED.
```

```
BEGIN

FILE
    OUTP(KIND=REMOTE,BUFFERS=1,MAXRECSIZE=12);

FILE
    INP(KIND=REMOTE,BUFFERS=1,MAXRECSIZE=12);

TRANSLATETABLE
    NUMBERTOEBCDIC(48"000102030405060708090A0B0C0D0E0F10111213141516171819"
        TO "ABCDEFGHIJKLMNOPQRSTUVWXYZ");

REAL
    BASENUMBER,              %START IN FIRST PARTITION
    BEGINRANGE,              %SIZE OF GROUP IN FIRST PARTITION
    CHECKUP,
    COLUMNSLEFT,             %COLUMNS LEFT ON INPUT IMAGE
    CON,                     %CONSTRAINT NUMBER LAST USED
    CNT,                     %TEMPORARY COUNTER USED AS NEEDED
    CNT1,                    %DITTO
    CNT2,                    %DITTO
    ENDRANGE,                %END OF GROUP IN FIRST PARTITION
    FSIZE,                   %FUNCTION SIZE 2**NUMBER OF VARIABLES
    INWHAT,                  %TELLS WHAT TOKEN IS
    LASTCHECK,               %SIZE OF GROUP LOOKING FOR
    LGROUP,                  %LARGEST GROUP POSSIBLE IN PROBLEM
    MEVTERMS,                %NUMBER OF MEV TERMS 2**MEV'S
    MINNUMBER,               %MINTERM WORKING WITH
    NOV,                     %NUMBER OF VARIABLES
    NOVM1,                   %NUMBER OF VARIABLES MINUS ONE
    NUMBEROFMEV,             %NUMBER OF MEV'S
    NUMMIN,                  %NUMBER OF MINTERMS ASSERTED
    PARENCOUNT,              %NUMBER OF PARENTHESES IN EXPRESSION
    PARTNO,                  %PARTITION NUMBER WORKING WITH
    STATETERMS,              %2** STATE VARIABLES
    STATEVAR,                %NUMBER OF STATE VARIABLES
    TEMP,                    %WHOEVER NEEDS IT USES IT
    TEMP1,                   %DITTO
    TEMP2,                   %DITTO
    TERMVALUE,               %VALUE OF SPECIFIC TERM AT INPUT
    TOKENVALUE,              %WHAT NEXT TOKEN IS
    TOPOFSTACK,              %TOP OF SYMBOL STACK
    TOPOFTERM,               %NUMBER OF TERMS
    TRYTERM,                 %TERM JUST FOUND
    TTERMASSERTED;           %ASSERTION LEVELS OF TERM JUST FOUND
BOOLEAN
    CHECKON,
    ENDINPUT,                %SIGNAL END OF INPUT LIST
    ENDOFCARD,               %INCOMPLETE INPUT EXPRESSION
    EQUAL,                   %ALL EQUAL SOLUTIONS DESIRED
    INEXPRESSION,            %PROCESSING TERM INPUT EXPRESSION
    NOTALLONES,              %MAP DOESN'T REDUCE TO '1'
    NOTALLZEROS,             %MAP DOESN'T REDUCE TO '0'
    NOTINPUTERROR,           %EXPRESSION OK SO FAR
    OPERATORLAST,            %TO INSURE PROPER SYNTAX
    PARENTH,                 %LEFT PARENTH HAS BEEN ENCOUNTERED
    PRIME,                   %PRIME IMPLICANTS WANTED
    RANGER,                  %USED IN INPUT OF TERMS
    THERE;                   %SYMBOL IN SYMBOL TABLE
ARRAY
    ATEMP[0:9],              %A TEMPORARY ARRAY FOR ANYONE
    EXPRESSION[0:9],         %CODE OF INPUT EXPRESSIONS
    EXPRESSION1[0:9],        %USED TO BUILD EXPRESSIONS
```

```
        INBUFF[0:11],                %INPUT BUFFER
        MEVLIST[0:20],               %SYMBOL TABLE OF MEV'S
        OPERATOR[0:0],               %STORES OPERATOR CODE TO BUILD EXPRESSIONS
        OPERATOR1[0:0],              %USED IF LEFT PARENTH FOUND
        OUTBUFF[0:11],               %OUTPUT BUFFER
        TOKENBUFFER[0:11],           %STORES TOKEN JUST FOUND
        TOKENVALA[0:0];              %CONTAINS TOKEN VALUE
BOOLEAN ARRAY EVALUATION[0:9];
POINTER                     %ALL POINTERS POINT TO ARRAYS AS SPECIFIED BY NAME
        PTOATEMP,
        PTOEXPRESSION,
        PTOEXPRESSION1,
        PTOINBUFF,
        PTOOPERATOR,
        PTOOPERATOR1,
        PTOOUTBUFF,
        PTOTOKEN,
        PTOTOKENVALA;
%   THE FOLLOWING ARE USED TO FIND POWERS OF TWO QUICKLY.
VALUE ARRAY TWOTO(2**0,2**1,2**2,2**3,2**4,2**5,2**6,2**7,2**8,2**9,2
        **10,2**11,2**12,2**13,2**14,2**15,2**16,2**17,2**18,2**19,2**20,
        2**21,2**22,2**23,2**24,2**25,2**26,2**27,2**28,2**29);

VALUE ARRAY OMTWOTO(2**0-1,2**1-1,2**2-1,2**3-1,2**4-1,2**5-1,2**6-1,
        2**7-1,2**8-1,2**9-1,2**10-1,2**11-1,2**12-1,2**13-1,2**14-1,
        2**15-1,2**16-1,2**17-1,2**18-1,2**19-1,2**20-1,2**21-1,2**22-1,
        2**23-1,2**24-1,2**25-1,2**26-1,2**27-1,2**28-1,2**29-1);

TRUTHSET
    DIGIT("0123456789");

TRUTHSET
    OPRATOR(".+'()-");

TRUTHSET
    ENDINP("#");

TRUTHSET
    ALPHABET(ALPHA AND NOT DIGIT);

TRUTHSET
    NOTNOISE(ALPHA OR OPRATOR OR ENDINP);

DEFINE
        BLANK            = " " #;
PICTURE

    ZEROIT(ZZ9);

VALUE ARRAY OPERATORLIST
    ("'        ","."        ,"+        ,"(        ,")        ,"-        ");

PROCEDURE GETTOKEN;
%   THIS PROCEDURE SCANS THE INPUT BUFFER FOR THE NEXT ITEM OF
%   THE INPUT STRING.  THE TYPE OF ITEM FOUND IS RETURNED IN THE
%   VARIABLE INWHAT:
%           0-VARIABLE
%           1-NUMBER
%           2-OPERATOR
%           3-END OF INPUT.
%   THE VALUE OF THE ITEM, OR ITS POSITION IN THE SYMBOL TABLE
%   IS RETURNED IN THE VARIABLE TOKENVALUE.  A FLAG (ENDOFCARD)
%   SIGNALS WHEN THE END OF INPUT STRING IS ENCOUNTERED.
```

```
BEGIN
REAL
    A I

    REPLACE PTOTOKEN BY BLANK FOR 18I
    SCAN PTOINBUFFIPTOINBUFF FOR COLUMNSLEFTICOLUMNSLEFT UNTIL IN
        NOTNOISEI
    IF COLUMNSLEFT=0 THEN
        ENDOFCARD I= TRUE
    ELSE
        BEGIN
        A I= COLUMNSLEFTI % TO GET RID OF DELTAI
        IF PTOINBUFF IN ALPHABET THEN
            INWHAT I= 0
        ELSE
            IF PTOINBUFF IN OPRATOR THEN
                INWHAT I= 2
            ELSE
                IF PTOINBUFF IN DIGIT THEN
                    INWHAT I= 1
                ELSE
                    INWHAT I= 3I
        CASE INWHAT OF
                BEGIN
                    BEGIN
                        REPLACE PTOTOKEN BY PTOINBUFFIPTOINBUFF FOR
                            COLUMNSLEFTICOLUMNSLEFT WHILE IN ALPHAI
                        TOKENVALUE I= MASKSEARCH(TOKENBUFFER[0],
                            48"FFFFFFFFFFFF",MEVLIST[NUMBEROFMEV+1])I
                        ENDI
                    BEGIN
                        REPLACE PTOTOKEN BY PTOINBUFFIPTOINBUFF FOR
                            COLUMNSLEFTICOLUMNSLEFT WHILE IN DIGITI
                        A I= A-COLUMNSLEFTI
                        TOKENVALUE I= INTEGER(PTOTOKEN,A)I
                        ENDI
                    BEGIN
                        REPLACE PTOTOKEN BY PTOINBUFFIPTOINBUFF FOR 1I
                        COLUMNSLEFT I= *-1I
                        TOKENVALUE I= MASKSEARCH
                            (TOKENBUFFER[0],48"FFFFFFFFFFFF",OPERATORLIST)I
                        ENDI
                    ENDINPUT I= TRUEI% # END INPUT SYMBOL
                    END OF CASEI
            ENDI
        END GETTOKENI

PROCEDURE OUTPUTTERM(X,Y)I
%   THIS PROCEDURE OUTPUTS A TERM.  TWO PARAMETERS ARE REQUIRED.
%   THE FIRST HAS THE VARIABLES PRESENT IN THE TERM. BIT 47
%   CORRESPONDS TO THE FIRST VARIABLE ETC.  THE SECOND
%   PARAMETER TELLS WHETHER OR NOT THAT VARIABLE IS ASSERTED.
%   THE SAME BIT CORRESPONDENCE IS USED.
    REAL
        X,
        Y I
                BEGIN
                    PTOOUTBUFF I= OUTBUFF[0]I
                    PTOATEMP I= ATEMP[0]+5I
                    REPLACE PTOOUTBUFF BY " " FOR 72I
                    FOR ATEMP[0]I=0 STEP 1 UNTIL NOVM1 DO
                        IF BOOLEAN(X.[47-ATEMP[0]I1]) THEN
                            BEGIN
                            REPLACE PTOOUTBUFFIPTOOUTBUFF BY "(")
```

```
                    IF ATEMP[0]<STATEVAR THEN
                        REPLACE PTOOUTBUFF;PTOOUTBUFF BY
                            PTOATEMP FOR 1 WITH NUMBERTOEBCDIC
                    ELSE
                        REPLACE PTOOUTBUFF;PTOOUTBUFF BY POINTER
                            (MEVLIST[NUMBEROFMEV-ATEMP[0]+STATEVAR])
                            FOR 6 WHILE IN ALPHA;
                    IF BOOLEAN(Y,[47-ATEMP[0]:1]) THEN
                    ELSE
                        REPLACE PTOOUTBUFF;PTOOUTBUFF BY 48"7D";
                    REPLACE PTOOUTBUFF;PTOOUTBUFF BY ")",
                        BLANK FOR 1;
                    END;
            WRITE(OUTP,12,OUTBUFF);
            END OUTPUTTERM;


%   START OF FIRST BLOCK
%   THIS BLOCK FIGURES THE SIZE FOR THE PROBLEM AND BUILDS THE
%   MAP ENTERED VARIABLE SYMBOL TABLE.
            NUMMIN := CON := -1;
            PTOTOKENVALA := POINTER(TOKENVALA)+5;
            PTOINBUFF := POINTER(INBUFF);
            PTOTOKEN := POINTER(TOKENBUFFER);
            PTOOUTBUFF := POINTER(INBUFF);
            REPLACE PTOOUTBUFF BY BLANK FOR 72;
            PTOINBUFF := POINTER(INBUFF);
            REPLACE INBUFF BY BLANK FOR 72;
            REPLACE PTOOUTBUFF BY "NUMBER OF STATE VARIABLES?   ",
                48"00",BLANK FOR 3;
            WRITE(OUTP[STOP],5,INBUFF);
            READ(INP,/,NOV);
            NUMBEROFMEV := -1;
            REPLACE PTOOUTBUFF BY
                "ARE YOU USING MAP ENTERED VARIABLES?   ",48"00",
                BLANK FOR 4;
            WRITE(OUTP[STOP],7,INBUFF);
            READ(INP,3,INBUFF);
            SCAN PTOINBUFF;PTOINBUFF UNTIL IN ALPHA;
            IF PTOINBUFF="Y" THEN

            BEGIN
            REPLACE PTOOUTBUFF BY "LIST MAP ENTERED VARIABLES.   ",
                BLANK FOR 5;
            WRITE(OUTP,5,INBUFF);
            REPLACE PTOOUTBUFF BY "TERMINATE LIST WITH '#'",
                BLANK FOR 5;
            WRITE(OUTP,4,INBUFF);
            WHILE NOT ENDINPUT DO
                BEGIN
                COLUMNSLEFT := 72;
                PTOINBUFF := POINTER(INBUFF);
                READ(INP,12,INBUFF);
                GETTOKEN;
                IF INWHAT=0 THEN
                    BEGIN
                    IF TOKENVALUE<0 THEN
                        MEVLIST[NUMBEROFMEV := *+1] := TOKENBUFFER[0]
                    ELSE
                        BEGIN
                        REPLACE PTOOUTBUFF BY PTOTOKEN FOR 6,
                            " ALREADY DEFINED",BLANK FOR 2;
                        WRITE(OUTP,3,INBUFF);
                        END;
                    END
                END
```

```
                        ELSE
                            IF INWHAT=3 THEN
                            ELSE
                                BEGIN
                                REPLACE PTOOUTBUFF BY
                                  "IMPROPER FORMAT, PLEASE REENTER",
                                  BLANK FOR 5;
                                WRITE(OUTP,6,INBUFF);
                                END;
                        END;
                      END;
                  REPLACE PTOOUTBUFF BY "THERE WERE",
                    (NUMBEROFMEV+1) FOR 3 DIGITS," MAP ENTERED VARIABLES",
                    (NUMBEROFMEV+NOV+1) FOR 3 DIGITS," VARIABLES TOTAL",
                    BLANK FOR 5;
                  REPLACE PTOOUTBUFF+10 BY PTOOUTBUFF+10 WITH ZEROIT;
                  REPLACE PTOOUTBUFF+35 BY PTOOUTBUFF+35 WITH ZEROIT;
                  WRITE(OUTP[SPACE 2],9,INBUFF);
                  MEVTERMS := OMTWOTO[NUMBEROFMEV+1];
                  STATETERMS := OMTWOTO[NOV];
                  STATEVAR := NOV;
                  NOV := *+NUMBEROFMEV+1;
                  NOVM1 := NOV-1;
                  FSIZE := (MEVTERMS+1)*(STATETERMS+1)-1;
                  BEGIN
%   SECOND BLOCK
%   THIS BLOCK ALLOCATES ARRAYS FOR THE FUNCTION AND FIRST PARTITION
%   AS WELL AS THE SUM VECTOR.  THE FUNCTION IS INPUT, AND SOME
%   PRELIMINARY CALCULATIONS DONE.  THESE CALCULATIONS ARE NECESSARY
%   FOR FUTURE ARRAY ALLOCATIONS AS WELL AS MINIMIZING THE PROBLEM.
ARRAY

    LOOK[0:NOV],
    CONST[0:FSIZE],
    WORKOUT[0:NOV],
    FUNCT[0:FSIZE];
DEFINE
      FUNCTION[X]   = FUNCT[X].[1:2] #,
      PARTITION[X,Y] =
                      FUNCT[Y].[47-X:1] #,
      SUM[X]        = FUNCT[X].[6:5] #;
                  PTOOUTBUFF := INBUFF[0];
                  REPLACE PTOOUTBUFF BY "ENTER TERMS   ";
                  WRITE(OUTP,2,INBUFF);
                  REPLACE PTOOUTBUFF BY "TERMINATE LIST WITH '#'",
                    BLANK FOR 5;
                  WRITE(OUTP[SPACE 2],4,INBUFF);
                  EVALUATION[0] := TRUE;
                  ENDINPUT := FALSE;
                  PTOOPERATOR := POINTER(OPERATOR);
                  PTOOPERATOR1 := POINTER(OPERATOR1);
                  WHILE NOT ENDINPUT DO
                      BEGIN
                      OPERATORLAST := NOTINPUTERROR := INEXPRESSION :=
                        TRUE;
                      TEMP := TEMP1 := -1;
                      RANGER := ENDOFCARD := PARENTH := FALSE;
                      READ(INP,12,INBUFF);
                      PTOINBUFF := POINTER(INBUFF);
                      COLUMNSLEFT := 72;
                      GETTOKEN;
                      REPLACE PTOOPERATOR BY BLANK FOR 1;
                      PTOEXPRESSION := POINTER(EXPRESSION);
                      IF INWHAT=1 THEN
                          IF TOKENVALUE<=STATETERMS THEN
                              BEGINRANGE := ENDRANGE := TOKENVALUE
```

748   Appendix B

```
        ELSE
            BEGIN
            NOTINPUTERROR := FALSE;
            REPLACE PTOOUTBUFF BY
              "INVALID MINTERM NUMBER",BLANK FOR 3;
            WRITE(OUTP,4,INBUFF);
            END
    ELSE
        IF INWHAT=3 THEN
        ELSE
            BEGIN
            NOTINPUTERROR := FALSE;
            REPLACE PTOOUTBUFF BY "IMPROPER TERM FORMAT",
              BLANK FOR 5;
            WRITE(OUTP,4,INBUFF);
            END;
WHILE INEXPRESSION AND NOTINPUTERROR AND NOT
  ENDOFCARD DO
    BEGIN
    GETTOKEN;
    IF ENDOFCARD THEN
        BEGIN
        NOTINPUTERROR := FALSE;
        REPLACE PTOOUTBUFF BY
          "INCOMPLETE INPUT FORMAT",BLANK FOR 2;
        WRITE(OUTP,4,INBUFF);
        END
    ELSE
        CASE INWHAT OF
            BEGIN
                BEGIN
                    IF TOKENVALUE=-1 THEN
                    BEGIN
                    NOTINPUTERROR := FALSE;
                    REPLACE PTOOUTBUFF BY
                      "UNKNOWN VARIABLE",BLANK FOR 3;
                    WRITE(OUTP,3,INBUFF);
                    END
                ELSE
                    IF OPERATORLAST THEN
                        BEGIN
                        RANGER := TRUE;
                        OPERATORLAST := FALSE;
                        TOKENVALA[0] := TOKENVALUE;
                        IF PARENTH THEN
                            BEGIN
                            PARENCOUNT := *+2;
                            REPLACE PTOEXPRESSION1:
                              PTOEXPRESSION1 BY 48"03",
                            PTOTOKENVALA FOR 1 END
                              ELSE REPLACE
                              PTOEXPRESSION:
                              PTOEXPRESSION BY 48"03",
                              PTOTOKENVALA FOR 1;

                        END
                    ELSE
                        BEGIN
                        NOTINPUTERROR := FALSE;
                        REPLACE PTOOUTBUFF BY
                          "IMPROPER TERM FORMAT",
                          BLANK FOR 5;
                        WRITE(OUTP,4,INBUFF);
                        END
            END;
```

```
            BEGIN
        %DIGIT
            INEXPRESSION := FALSE;
            IF PARENTH THEN
                BEGIN
                NOTINPUTERROR := FALSE;
                REPLACE PTOOUTBUFF BY
                    " ) EXPECTED ";
                WRITE(OUTP,2,INBUFF);
                END;
            IF TOKENVALUE=0 THEN
                TERMVALUE := 3
            ELSE
                IF TOKENVALUE=1 THEN
                    TERMVALUE := 1
                ELSE
                    TERMVALUE := 0;
            IF ENDOFCARD THEN
            ELSE
                GETTOKEN;
            IF ENDOFCARD THEN
            ELSE
                BEGIN
                NOTINPUTERROR := FALSE;
                REPLACE PTOOUTBUFF BY
                    "IMPROPER TERM FORMAT",
                    BLANK FOR 5;
                WRITE(OUTP,4,INBUFF);
                END;
            IF OPERATORLAST AND PTOEXPRESSION
                NEQ POINTER(EXPRESSION) THEN
                BEGIN
                NOTINPUTERROR := FALSE;
                REPLACE PTOOUTBUFF BY
                    "IMPROPER TERM FORMAT",
                    BLANK FOR 5;
                WRITE(OUTP,4,INBUFF);
                END;
            IF NOTINPUTERROR THEN
                IF PTOOPERATOR=BLANK THEN
                ELSE
                    REPLACE PTOEXPRESSION:
                        PTOEXPRESSION BY
                        PTOOPERATOR FOR 1;
            REPLACE PTOEXPRESSION:PTOEXPRESSION
                BY 48"04";
            END;
            IF OPERATORLAST AND TOKENVALUE NEQ 3
                AND TOKENVALUE NEQ 5 THEN
                BEGIN
                NOTINPUTERROR := FALSE;
                REPLACE PTOOUTBUFF BY
                    "IMPROPER TERM FORMAT",
                    BLANK FOR 5;
                WRITE(OUTP,4,INBUFF);
                END
            ELSE
                IF PARENTH THEN
                    CASE TOKENVALUE OF
                        BEGIN
                            0:BEGIN
                                PARENCOUNT := *+1;
                                REPLACE
                                    PTOEXPRESSION1:
                                    PTOEXPRESSION1 BY
                                    48"00";
                                END;
```

```
3:BEGIN
      NOTINPUTERROR :=
         FALSE;
      REPLACE PTOOUTBUFF BY

         ") EXPECTED "
         "SCANNING )",BLANK
         FOR 4;
      WRITE(OUTP,4,INBUFF);
      END;
4:IF PTOEXPRESSION1=
  POINTER(EXPRESSION1) THEN
  BEGIN
    REPLACE PTOOUTBUFF BY
      "MISSING VARIABLE",
      BLANK FOR 4;
    WRITE(OUTP,3,INBUFF);
    NOTINPUTERROR := FALSE;
    END ELSE BEGIN
      IF PTOOPERATOR1=BLANK
        THEN
        ELSE
          BEGIN
          REPLACE
            PTOEXPRESSION1:
            PTOEXPRESSION1
            BY PTOOPERATOR1
            FOR 1;
          PARENCOUNT := *+1;
          END;
      REPLACE PTOEXPRESSION
        :PTOEXPRESSION BY
        POINTER
        (EXPRESSION1)FOR
        PARENCOUNT;
      PARENTH := FALSE;
      END;
5:BEGIN
      NOTINPUTERROR := TRUE
        ;
      REPLACE PTOOUTBUFF BY

         "ILLEGAL AT THIS "
         "TIME =",BLANK FOR
         4;
      WRITE(OUTP,4,INBUFF);
      END;
BEGIN
    OPERATURLAST := TRUE;
    IF PTOOPERATOR1=BLANK
      THEN
      ELSE
        BEGIN
        REPLACE
          PTOEXPRESSION1:
          PTOEXPRESSION1 BY
          PTOOPERATOR1 FOR 1;
        PARENCOUNT := *+1;
        END;
    TOKENVALA[0] :=
      TOKENVALUE;
    REPLACE PTOOPERATOR1 BY
      PTOTOKENVALA FOR 1;
    END;
END OF CASE
```

```
        ELSE
          CASE TOKENVALUE OF
            BEGIN
              0:REPLACE PTOEXPRESSION:
                PTOEXPRESSION BY 48"00";
              3:BEGIN
                    PARENCOUNT := 0;
                    PARENTH := TRUE;
                    PTOEXPRESSION1 :=
                      POINTER
                      (EXPRESSION1);
                    REPLACE PTOOPERATOR1
                      BY BLANK;
                    END;
              4:BEGIN
                    NOTINPUTERROR :=
                      FALSE;
                    REPLACE PTOOUTBUFF BY
                      "( EXPECTED "
                      "SCANNING )",BLANK
                      FOR 5;
                    WRITE(OUTP,4,INBUFF);
                    END;
              5:IF RANGER THEN BEGIN
                    NOTINPUTERROR :=
                      FALSE;
                    REPLACE PTOOUTBUFF BY
                      "ILLEGAL AT THIS ",
                      "TIME",BLANK FOR 4;
                    WRITE(OUTP,4,INBUFF);
                    END ELSE BEGIN
                    RANGER := TRUE;
                    GETTOKEN;
                    IF INWHAT=1 THEN
                      IF (ENDRANGE :=
                        TOKENVALUE)<
                        BEGINRANGE OR
                        ENDRANGE>
                        STATETERMS THEN
                        BEGIN
                        NOTINPUTERROR
                          := FALSE;
                        REPLACE
                          PTOOUTBUFF BY

                          "ILLEGAL AT",
                          " THIS TIME",
                          BLANK FOR 4;
                        WRITE(OUTP,4,
                          INBUFF);
                        END;
                  END;
            BEGIN
              OPERATORLAST := TRUE;
              IF PTOOPERATOR=BLANK
                THEN
              ELSE
                REPLACE PTOEXPRESSION
                  :PTOEXPRESSION BY
                  PTOOPERATOR FOR 1;
              TOKENVALA[0] :=
                TOKENVALUE;
              REPLACE PTOOPERATOR BY
                PTOTOKENVALA FOR 1;
              END;
            END OF CASE;
```

```
        IF PTOEXPRESSION=POINTER(EXPRESSION)
          THEN
            INEXPRESSION := FALSE
        ELSE
            BEGIN
            REPLACE PTOOUTBUFF BY
              "IMPROPER TERM FORMAT",
              BLANK FOR 5;
            WRITE(OUTP,4,INBUFF);
            NOTINPUTERROR := FALSE;
            END;
        END OF CASE;
            IF INEXPRESSION AND NOT NOTINPUTERROR THEN
                BEGIN
                NOTINPUTERROR := FALSE;
                REPLACE PTOOUTBUFF BY "EXPRESSION TOO LONG",
                  BLANK FOR 6;
                WRITE(OUTP,4,INBUFF);
                END;
            END;
        IF ENDINPUT OR NOT NOTINPUTERROR THEN
        ELSE
            FOR BASENUMBER:=BEGINRANGE STEP 1 UNTIL ENDRANGE
                DO
                FOR TEMP:=0 STEP 1 UNTIL MEVTERMS DO
                    BEGIN
                    TOPOFSTACK := 0;
                    PTOEXPRESSION := POINTER(EXPRESSION);
                    WHILE(TEMP1:=REAL(PTOEXPRESSION,1)) NEQ 4
                        DO
                        BEGIN
                        PTOEXPRESSION := *+1;
                        CASE TEMP1 OF
                            BEGIN
                            EVALUATION[TOPOFSTACK] := NOT
                              EVALUATION[TOPOFSTACK];
                            EVALUATION[TOPOFSTACK := *-1] :=
                              EVALUATION[TOPOFSTACK] AND
                              EVALUATION[TOPOFSTACK+1];
                            EVALUATION[TOPOFSTACK := *-1] :=
                              EVALUATION[TOPOFSTACK] OR
                              EVALUATION[TOPOFSTACK+1];
                            BEGIN
                              EVALUATION[TOPOFSTACK := *+1]
                                := BOOLEAN(TEMP,
                                [REAL(PTOEXPRESSION,1):1]);
                              PTOEXPRESSION := *+1;
                              END;
                            END OF CASE;
                        END;
                    IF EVALUATION[TOPOFSTACK] THEN
                        FUNCTION[BASENUMBER*(MEVTERMS+1)+TEMP]
                            := TERMVALUE;
                    END;
            END;
    FOR CNT:=0 STEP 1 UNTIL FSIZE DO
        BEGIN
        CONST[CNT] := -1;
        IF FUNCTION[CNT]=0 THEN
            NOTALLONES := TRUE
        ELSE
            IF FUNCTION[CNT]=1 THEN
                BEGIN
                NOTALLZEROS := TRUE;
                NUMMIN := *+1;
                CONST[CNT] := CON := *+1;
                END;
        END;
```

```
                     BEGIN
%    THIRD BLOCK
%    THE MINIMIZATION IS DONE IN THIS BLOCK.  A PROCEDURE PERFORMS
%    THE FIRST PARTITION ON ALL VARIABLES.  THE PRIME IMPLICANTS ARE
%    FOUND IN THE PROCEDURE CHECKASIZE.  THE MINIMIZATION IS DONE USING
%    ZERO-ONE OPTIMIZATION.
ARRAY

    CONSTRAINT[0:NUMMIN, 0:2*NOV],
    WEIGHT[1:NUMMIN+2],
    TERM[1:NUMMIN+2],
    TERMASSERTED[1:NUMMIN+2];
PROCEDURE FIRSTPARTITION;
%    THIS PROCEDURE CALCULATES THE FIRST PARTITION ON ALL VARIABLES
%    AND STORES IT IN THE ARRAY CALLED PARTITION.
    BEGIN
    REAL
        GROUPSTART;

        FOR PARTNO:=0 STEP 1 UNTIL NOVM1 DO
            BEGIN
            TEMP := TWOTO[NOVM1-PARTNO];
            FOR GROUPSTART:=TEMP STEP 2*TEMP UNTIL FSIZE DO
                FOR MINNUMBER:=0 STEP 1 UNTIL TEMP-1 DO
                    BEGIN
                    TEMP1 := GROUPSTART+MINNUMBER;
                    TEMP2 := IF (FUNCTION[TEMP1]*FUNCTION[TEMP1-TEMP]>0)
                      THEN 1 ELSE 0;
                    PARTITION[PARTNO,TEMP1] := TEMP2;
                    PARTITION[PARTNO,TEMP1-TEMP] := TEMP2;
                    END;
            END;
        END FIRSTPARTITION;
PROCEDURE FINDISLANDS;
%    THIS PROCEDURE FIND ALL OF THE ISLANDS IN THE PROBLEM AND
%    OUTPUTS THE TERMS.
    BEGIN
    REAL
        MOSTSUM;

        FOR MINNUMBER:=0 STEP 1 UNTIL FSIZE DO
            IF FUNCTION[MINNUMBER]>0 THEN
                BEGIN
                FOR PARTNO:=0 STEP 1 UNTIL NOVM1 DO
                    SUM[MINNUMBER] := SUM[MINNUMBER]+
                    PARTITION[PARTNO,MINNUMBER];
                IF FUNCTION[MINNUMBER]=1 AND SUM[MINNUMBER]=0 THEN
                BEGIN
                TOPOFTERM := *+1;
                FOR CNT:=0 STEP 1 UNTIL NOVM1 DO
                    TERM[TOPOFTERM].[47-CNT:1] := 1;
                CONSTRAINT[CONST[MINNUMBER],0] := TOPOFTERM;
                WEIGHT[TOPOFTERM] := 1;
                TEMP := MINNUMBER;
                FOR CNT:=NOVM1 STEP-1 UNTIL 0 DO
                    IF TEMP<TWOTO[CNT] THEN
                    ELSE
                        BEGIN
                        TERMASSERTED[TOPOFTERM].[47-NOVM1+CNT:1] := 1;
                        TEMP := *-TWOTO[CNT];
                        END;
                    END;
                IF SUM[MINNUMBER]>MOSTSUM THEN
                    MOSTSUM := SUM[MINNUMBER];
                END;
                CNT1 := CNT := 0;
                IF MOSTSUM>0 THEN
```

```
                    BEGIN
                    FOR CNT:=MOSTSUM STEP-1 WHILE CNT1<TWOTO[CNT] DO
                        FOR CNT2:=0 STEP 1 UNTIL FSIZE DO
                            IF SUM[CNT2]=CNT THEN
                                CNT1 := *+1;
                    END;
                LGROUP := CNT+1;
                END FINDISLANDS;
                        IF CHECKON THEN
                            WRITE(OUTP,*//,NUMMIN);
                        IF NOTALLZEROS AND NOTALLONES THEN
                            BEGIN
                            FIRSTPARTITION;
                            FINDISLANDS;
                            END;
                        BEGIN
ARRAY

   SAVEMIN1[0:OMTWOTO[LGROUP]],
   SAVEMIN[0:OMTWOTO[LGROUP]];
BOOLEAN PROCEDURE CHECKASIZE;
%   THIS PROCEDURE GIVEN A MINTERM AND GROUPSIZE FINDS ALL OF THE
%   TERMS OF THAT SIZE, INVOLVING THAT MINTERM.
   BEGIN
   BOOLEAN
      FOUNDAGROUP;

   REAL
      NECESS;
      TEMP := -1;
      FOR CNT:=0 STEP 1 UNTIL NOVM1 DO
         IF PARTITION[CNT,MINNUMBER]=1 THEN
            LOOK[TEMP := *+1] := CNT;
      FOR CNT:=0 STEP 1 UNTIL LASTCHECK-1 DO
         WORKOUT[CNT] := CNT;
      WORKOUT[LASTCHECK] := TEMP+1;
      LOOK[TEMP+1] := NOV;
      WORKOUT[LASTCHECK-1] := *-1;
      DO BEGIN
            IF WORKOUT[LASTCHECK-1]=TEMP THEN
               FOR TEMP1:=LASTCHECK-1 STEP-1 WHILE TEMP1>1 AND
                  WORKOUT[TEMP1]=WORKOUT[TEMP1-1]+1 DO
            ELSE
               TEMP1 := LASTCHECK;
            WORKOUT[TEMP1-1] := *+1;
            FOR CNT:=TEMP1 STEP 1 UNTIL LASTCHECK-1 DO
               WORKOUT[CNT] := WORKOUT[CNT-1]+1;
            TEMP1 := MINNUMBER;
            CNT := 0;
         DO BEGIN
               SAVEMIN[CNT] := TEMP1;
               CNT := *+1;
               FOR CNT1:=0 STEP 1 WHILE NOT BOOLEAN(CNT,[CNT1:1])
                  DO
                  ;
               TEMP2 := NOVM1-LOOK[WORKOUT[CNT1]];
               END UNTIL FUNCTION[TEMP1 := TEMP1+(IF
                  BOOLEAN(TEMP1,[TEMP2:1])THEN-TWOTO[TEMP2]ELSE
                  TWOTO[TEMP2])]=0 OR CNT=OMTWOTO[LASTCHECK];
         SAVEMIN[CNT] := TEMP1;
         IF FUNCTION[TEMP1]=0 THEN
         ELSE
            BEGIN
            NECESS := *+1;
            TRYTERM := TTERMASSERTED := TEMP2 := 0;
```

```
                    TEMP1 := MINNUMBER;
                    FOR CNT:=NOVM1 STEP-1 UNTIL 0 DO
                        BEGIN
                            IF TEMP1<TWOTO[CNT] THEN
                ELSE
                    BEGIN
                    TTERMASSERTED.[47-NOVM1+CNT:1] := 1;
                    TEMP1 := *-TWOTO[CNT];
                    END;
                IF LOOK[WORKOUT[TEMP2]]=NOVM1-CNT THEN
                    TEMP2 := *+1
                ELSE
                    TRYTERM.[47-NOVM1+CNT:1] := 1;
                END;
            THERE := FALSE;
            CNT := TOPOFTERM;
            IF TOPOFTERM=0 THEN
            ELSE
                DO BEGIN
                    CNT :=
                      MASKSEARCH(TRYTERM,48"FFFFFFFFFFC0",TERM[CNT]);
                    IF CNT GEQ 0 THEN
                        IF REAL(BOOLEAN(TRYTERM)AND
                          BOOLEAN(TTERMASSERTED)) IS REAL(
                          BOOLEAN(TRYTERM)AND
                          BOOLEAN(TERMASSERTED[CNT+1])) THEN
                            THERE := TRUE;
                    END UNTIL CNT LEQ 0 OR THERE;
            IF NOT PRIME AND NECESS=1 THEN
                FOR CNT:=0 STEP 1 UNTIL OMTWOTO[LASTCHECK] DO
                    SAVEMIN1[CNT] := SAVEMIN[CNT];
            IF THERE THEN
            ELSE
                BEGIN
                TERM[TOPOFTERM := *+1] := TRYTERM;
                WEIGHT[TOPOFTERM] := NOV-LASTCHECK;
                TERMASSERTED[TOPOFTERM] := TTERMASSERTED;
                FOR CNT:=0 STEP 1 UNTIL OMTWOTO[LASTCHECK] DO
                    IF CONST[SAVEMIN[CNT]] GEQ 0 THEN
                        BEGIN
                        FOR CNT1:=0 STEP 1 WHILE
                          CONSTRAINT[CONST[SAVEMIN[CNT]],CNT1] NEQ 0
                          DO
                            ;
                        CONSTRAINT[CONST[SAVEMIN[CNT]],CNT1] :=
                          TOPOFTERM;
                        END;
                END;
            FOUNDAGROUP := TRUE;
            END;
        END UNTIL WORKOUT[0]=TEMP-LASTCHECK+1;
CHECKASIZE := FOUNDAGROUP;
IF NOT PRIME AND NECESS=1 THEN
    FOR CNT:=0 STEP 1 UNTIL OMTWOTO[LASTCHECK] DO
        FUNCTION[SAVEMIN1[CNT]] := 3;
END CHECKASIZE;

CHECKUP := 5;
IF NOTALLZEROS AND NOTALLONES THEN
    BEGIN
    WRITE(OUTP,//,"DO YOU WANT THE PRIME "
      "IMPLICANTS?");
    READ(INP,12,INBUFF);
    PTOINBUFF := INBUFF[0];
    SCAN PTOINBUFF:PTOINBUFF UNTIL IN ALPHA;
    PRIME := (PTOINBUFF="Y");
    FOR MINNUMBER:=0 STEP 1 UNTIL FSIZE DO
```

```
                          BEGIN
                          IF SUM(MINNUMBER)>0 AND
                             FUNCTION(MINNUMBER)<3 THEN
                               FOR LASTCHECK:=
                                  MIN(LGROUP,SUM(MINNUMBER)) STEP-1
                                  WHILE NOT CHECKASIZE DO
                                      ;
                          END;
                      IF PRIME THEN
                          FOR CNT:=1 STEP 1 UNTIL TOPOFTERM DO
                              OUTPUTTERM(TERM(CNT),TERMASSERTED(CNT))
                                  ;
                      BEGIN
ARRAY

    OUTPUTLIST(0:TOPOFTERM+2);
PROCEDURE ZERONEOPT;
%   THIS PROCEDURE PERFORMS A ZERO-ONE MINIMIZATION ON THE
%   GENERATED FUNCTION WITH ITS CONSTRAINT EQUATIONS.  THE
%   METHOD FOLLOWS THE ALGORITHM DEVELOPED BY EGON BALAS WITH
%   THE RESTRICTION ON THE PROBLEM THAT ALL CONSTRAINT EQUATIONS
%   ARE OF THE "EQUAL TO OR GREATER THAN ONE" TYPE AND ALL
%   COEFFICIENTS IN THE OBJECTIVE FUNCTION AND THE CONSTRAINT
%   EQUATIONS ARE POSITIVE.  THE VARIABLES ARE AS FOLLOWS;
%           ZBAR-THE BEST POSSIBLE SOLUTION BEING TRIED M
%           S   -THE VARIABLES IN THE PRESENT SOLUTION.
%           T   -THE FREE VARIABLES IN THE PROBLEM
%           Y   -THE CONSTRAINT EQUATIONS SPECIFIED BY NUMBER.
    BEGIN
    INTEGER
       I,

       J,
       K,
       NEWZ,
       ZBAR;
    BOOLEAN
       DONE,
       ITIN;
    INTEGER ARRAY IC(1:TOPOFTERM+2),
       S(1:TOPOFTERM+2),
       T(1:TOPOFTERM+2),
       Y(1:NUMMIN+2);
    BOOLEAN PROCEDURE CONSTRAINTEVAL;
%   THIS PROCEDURE EVALUATES EACH CONSTRAINT EQUATION SUBJECT
%   TO THE VALUES IN THE S-VECTOR AND T-VECTOR.
       BEGIN
       INTEGER
          NT,

          NYV,

          SUM,
          TEST;
       BOOLEAN
          CONSTRVAL;
          CONSTRAINTEVAL := FALSE;
          CONSTRVAL := FALSE;
          FOR I:=1 STEP 1 UNTIL TOPOFTERM+1 DO
              IC(I) := 0;
          I := 1;
          WHILE S(I) NEQ 0 AND I<TOPOFTERM+2 DO
             BEGIN
             IF S(I)>0 THEN
                 IC(S(I)) := 1
             ELSE
                 IC(-S(I)) := -1;
```

```
            I := *+1
        END;
    I := 1;
    IF ITIN THEN
        WHILE T[I]>0 AND I<TOPOFTERM+2 DO
            BEGIN
            IC[T[I]] := 1;
            I := *+1
            END;
    NYV := 0;
    NT := 0;
    NEWZ := 0;
    FOR I:=0 STEP 1 WHILE S[I+1] NEQ 0 DO
        IF S[I+1]>0 THEN
            NEWZ := *+WEIGHT[S[I+1]];
    IF NEWZ LEQ ZBAR THEN
        BEGIN
        FOR I:=0 STEP 1 WHILE I LEQ NUMMIN AND NOT
          (CONSTRVAL AND ITIN) DO
            BEGIN
            SUM := 0;
            K := 0;
            WHILE CONSTRAINT[I,K] NEQ 0 DO
                BEGIN
                IF IC[CONSTRAINT[I,K]]>0 THEN
                    SUM := *+1;
                K := *+1
                END;
            IF SUM<1 THEN
                BEGIN
                NYV := *+1;
                Y[NYV] := I+1;
                CONSTRAINTEVAL := TRUE;
                CONSTRVAL := TRUE;
                END;
            END;
        IF NOT ITIN AND CONSTRVAL THEN
            BEGIN
            I := 1;
            WHILE Y[I] NEQ 0 AND I<NUMMIN+2 DO
                BEGIN
                K := 0;
                WHILE CONSTRAINT[Y[I]-1,K] NEQ 0 DO
                    BEGIN
                    IF IC[CONSTRAINT[Y[I]-1,K]]=0 THEN
                        BEGIN
                        TEST := 0;
                        FOR J:=1 STEP 1 UNTIL NT DO
                            IF T[J]=CONSTRAINT[Y[I]-1,K] THEN
                                TEST := 1;
                        IF TEST NEQ 1 THEN
                            BEGIN
                            NT := *+1;
                            T[NT] := CONSTRAINT[Y[I]-1,K];
                            END;
                        END;
                    K := *+1
                    END;
                I := *+1;
                END;
            END;
        END;
    END;
END CONSTRAINTEVAL;
```

```
      PROCEDURE SANDTUPGRADE;
%     THIS PROCEDURE ADDS THE PROPER VARIABLE TO THE SOLUTION
%     VECTOR (S) FORM THE FREE VARIABLES IN T.
      BEGIN
      INTEGER
         ISVAL,

         SUM,
         SUM2;
      BOOLEAN
         LOOPEND;
         SUM := -10000;
         I := 1;
         WHILE T[I]>0 AND I<TOPOFTERM+2 DO
            BEGIN
            SUM2 := 0;
            J := 1;
            WHILE Y[J] NEQ 0 AND J<NUMMIN+2 DO
               BEGIN
               LOOPEND := FALSE;
               K := 0;
               WHILE(CONSTRAINT[Y[J]-1,K]>0 AND NOT LOOPEND) DO
                  BEGIN
                  IF CONSTRAINT[Y[J]-1,K]=T[I] THEN
                     BEGIN
                     SUM2 := *+1;
                     LOOPEND := TRUE
                     END;
                  K := *+1
                  END;
               J := *+1
               END;
            IF SUM2>SUM THEN
               BEGIN
               SUM := SUM2;
               ISVAL := T[I]
               END;
            I := *+1
            END;

         I := 1;
         WHILE S[I] NEQ 0 AND I<TOPOFTERM+2 DO
            I := *+1;
         S[I] := ISVAL;
         FOR I:=0 STEP 1 UNTIL TOPOFTERM DO
            T[I+1] := 0;
         FOR I:=0 STEP 1 UNTIL NUMMIN DO
            Y[I+1] := 0;
         END SANDTUPGRADE;

   DONE := FALSE;
   ZBAR := 1000000000;
   WHILE NOT DONE DO
      BEGIN
      ITIN := FALSE;
      IF NOT CONSTRAINTEVAL THEN
         BEGIN
         IF NEWZ<ZBAR THEN
            BEGIN
            ZBAR := NEWZ;
            FOR I:=0 STEP 1 UNTIL TOPOFTERM DO
               OUTPUTLIST[I] := 0;
            K := 0;
            FOR I:=0 STEP 1 UNTIL TOPOFTERM DO
               IF S[I+1]>0 THEN
                  BEGIN
                  OUTPUTLIST[K] := S[I+1];
                  K := *+1
                  END;
```

```
                    FOR I:=K STEP-1 WHILE S[I] LEQ 0 AND I>1 DO
                        ;
                    S[I] := -S[I];
                    FOR K:=I+1 STEP 1 UNTIL TOPOFTERM+1 DO
                        S[K] := 0;
                    END
                ELSE
                    BEGIN
                    IF S[1]<0 THEN
                        DONE := TRUE
                    ELSE
                        BEGIN
                        FOR I:=TOPOFTERM+1 STEP-1 WHILE S[I] LEQ 0 AND I>1
                            DO
                                ;
                        S[I] := -S[I];
                        FOR K:=I+1 STEP 1 UNTIL TOPOFTERM+1 DO
                            S[K] := 0;
                        END;
                    END
                END
            ELSE
            BEGIN
            ITIN := TRUE;
            IF CONSTRAINTEVAL THEN
                IF S[1]<0 THEN
                    DONE := TRUE
                ELSE
                    BEGIN
                    FOR I:=TOPOFTERM+1 STEP-1 WHILE S[I] LEQ 0 AND I>1
                        DO
                            ;
                    S[I] := -S[I];
                    FOR K:=I+1 STEP 1 UNTIL TOPOFTERM+1 DO
                        S[K] := 0;
                    END
            ELSE
                SANDTUPGRADE;
            END;
        END;
    END ZERONEOPT;
                    ZERONEOPT;
                    WRITE(OUTP[SPACE 2]);
                    WRITE(OUTP[SPACE 2],//,"THE MINIMIZED "
                        "EXPRESSION IS ");
                    FOR CNT:=0 STEP 1 WHILE OUTPUTLIST[CNT]>0
                        DO
                        OUTPUTTERM(TERM[OUTPUTLIST[CNT]],
                            TERMASSERTED[OUTPUTLIST[CNT]]);
                    END;

        END
    ELSE
        IF NOT NOTALLZEROS THEN
            WRITE(OUTP,//,"THE MINIMIZED EXPRESSION "
                "IS '0'")
        ELSE
            WRITE(OUTP,//,"THE MINIMIZED EXPRESSION "
                "IS '1'");
        END;

    END;

END;
```

INDEX